# THE CAMBRIDGE HANDBOOK ON CLIMATE LITIGATION

With over 2,500 climate-related cases filed worldwide, climate litigation is rapidly evolving but lacks a comprehensive resource for guiding judicial approaches. *The Cambridge Handbook on Climate Litigation* fills this void, offering an authoritative guide to climate litigation's complex landscape. Judges, lawyers, and scholars will find insights into how courts globally have addressed recurring issues, from causation to human rights impacts. Building on the rich transnational judicial dialogue already occurring within climate litigation, the Handbook distils emerging best practices with an eye towards the progressive development of the field. Its unique focus on replicable strategies in case law makes it a strategic resource for shaping the future of climate litigation. This title is also available as open access on Cambridge Core.

Margaretha Wewerinke-Singh is Associate Professor of Law at the University of Amsterdam, Adjunct Professor of Law at the University of Fiji, and Member of the Permanent Court of Arbitration. Her publications, including her book *State Responsibility, Climate Change and Human Rights under International Law* (2019), have been widely cited in scholarship and judicial decisions. She practices from Blue Ocean Law, a boutique international law firm based in Guam.

Sarah Mead is a New Zealand-trained lawyer who specialises in international environmental law and human rights law – with a focus on States' obligations in light of the climate crisis. Sarah has published widely on the topic of international climate change law and is co-editor of the collection *The Environment through the Lens of International Courts and Tribunals* (2022). She currently serves as the Co-Director of Climate Litigation Network.

# The Cambridge Handbook on Climate Litigation

Edited by

MARGARETHA WEWERINKE-SINGH

SARAH MEAD

Assistant Editor

JOE UDELL

CAMBRIDGE
UNIVERSITY PRESS

CAMBRIDGE
UNIVERSITY PRESS

Shaftesbury Road, Cambridge CB2 8EA, United Kingdom

One Liberty Plaza, 20th Floor, New York, NY 10006, USA

477 Williamstown Road, Port Melbourne, VIC 3207, Australia

314–321, 3rd Floor, Plot 3, Splendor Forum, Jasola District Centre, New Delhi – 110025, India

103 Penang Road, #05–06/07, Visioncrest Commercial, Singapore 238467

Cambridge University Press is part of Cambridge University Press & Assessment, a department of the University of Cambridge.

We share the University's mission to contribute to society through the pursuit of education, learning and research at the highest international levels of excellence.

www.cambridge.org
Information on this title: www.cambridge.org/9781009409179

DOI: 10.1017/9781009409155



First published 2025

*A catalogue record for this publication is available from the British Library*

*Library of Congress Cataloging-in-Publication Data*
NAMES: Wewerinke-Singh, Margaretha, editor. | Mead, Sarah, editor.
TITLE: The cambridge handbook on climate litigation /
edited by Margaretha Wewerinke-Singh; Sarah Mead.
DESCRIPTION: 1. | New York : Cambridge University Press, 2025. | Includes bibliographical references and index.
IDENTIFIERS: LCCN 2024061441 | ISBN 9781009409179 (hardback) | ISBN 9781009409155 (ebook)
SUBJECTS: LCSH: Climatic changes – Law and legislation. | Environmental law, International. | Climate change mitigation – International cooperation.
CLASSIFICATION: LCC K3585.5 .C365 2025 | DDC 344.04/6–dc23/eng/20250103
LC record available at https://lccn.loc.gov/2024061441

ISBN 978-1-009-40917-9 Hardback
ISBN 978-1-009-40918-6 Paperback

# Contents

# Figures and Tables

FIGURES

TABLES

# Contributors

**Randall S. Abate** The George Washington University Law School

**Juan Auz** Tilburg Law School

**Lisa Benjamin** Lewis & Clark Law School

**Michael C. Blumm** Lewis & Clark Law School

**Sam Bookman** Harvard Law School

**Susana Borràs-Pentinat** Rovira i Virgili University

**Sarah Connors** European Space Agency

**Meinhard Doelle** Dalhousie University

**Christina Eckes** University of Amsterdam

**Patricia Galvao Ferreira** Dalhousie University

**Mark Gibney** University of North Carolina-Asheville

**Lucy Maxwell** Climate Litigation Network

**Sarah Mead** Climate Litigation Network

**L. Delta Merner** Union of Concerned Scientists

**Petra Minnerop** Durham University

**Jasmina Nedevska** Uppsala University

**Friederike Otto** Imperial College London

**Minal Pathak** Ahmedabad University

**Rachel M. Pemberton** Lewis & Clark Law School

**Carly A. Phillips** Union of Concerned Scientists

**Elvira Poloczanska** Alfred Wegener Institute

**Joeri Rogelj** Imperial College London

**Annalisa Savaresi** University of Eastern Finland; University of Stirling

**Sara Seck** Dalhousie University

**Joana Setzer** London School of Economics

**Shreya Some** Technical University of Denmark

**Joe Udell** Climate Litigation Network

**Christina Voigt** University of Oslo

**Margaretha Wewerinke-Singh** University of Amsterdam; University of Fiji

**Marcela Zúñiga** Diego Portales University Law School

# Foreword

In recent years, climate change and its adverse effects have consistently been escalating. It is one of the most pressing crises that humans and nature are facing (if not the foremost). All over the world, individuals and groups are seeking recourse to courts in order to compel governments and corporations to take effective action. Recent waves in climate litigation have certainly 'rocked the boat' in the best sense of the expression, but everything indicates that we are yet to experience the highest tide. This momentum for climate litigation is not only the context in which this Handbook was conceived but also one of the reasons why it will hopefully be relevant to many involved in this global fight.

The book – at its core – investigates the role of the judiciary in addressing climate change. It analyses the central legal arguments that are being brought to courts and the judicial reasoning applied by them.

Although the courts are increasingly expected to play a seminal role in global efforts to combat dangerous climate change, there is currently no dedicated resource available to assist the judiciary in responding to the myriad of legal challenges that tend to arise in the expanding landscape of climate change litigation.

Recognising the courts' need for such a resource, *The Cambridge Handbook on Climate Litigation* aims to fill this gap. Drawing on emerging 'best practice' from around the world, it aims to provide a readily available, well-researched overview to help judges navigate the complex legal issues that frequently arise in this evolving field. It identifies those aspects of emerging 'best practice' that are most easily scalable across jurisdictions, drawing on landmark judgments as well as decisions that are less well-known but have the potential to inspire legal reasoning in future cases.

*The Cambridge Handbook on Climate Litigation* is ideally positioned to increase awareness and sensitivity among judges for climate change issues and to increase their legal climate change knowledge, capability, and expertise. It also aims at providing lawyers, scholars, negotiators, decision-makers, students, and environmental activists with one of the most thorough analyses of climate change litigation. The well-defined and comprehensive structure of the Handbook will guide readers through an extensive landscape of almost every aspect of the topic, including: climate change law in different jurisdictions, climate science, political doctrine, human rights, extraterritoriality, duty of care, the interlinkages with biodiversity and rights of nature, intergenerational equity, climate justice, and the future of climate litigation.

*The Cambridge Handbook on Climate Litigation* is a project of the International Union for Conservation of Nature (IUCN) World Commission on Environmental Law (WCEL) and was carried out by WCEL's Climate Change Law Specialist Group (CCLSG). WCEL is the largest global network worldwide of environmental lawyers, judges, scholars, and other legal professionals from cross-cutting disciplines. It aims to advance environmental law around the globe by providing specialised knowledge and assistance to strengthen the legal foundations of the conservation of nature and ecologically sustainable development through the conceptual advancement of environmental principles, norms, and laws, and by building the capacity of communities to benefit from the environmental rule of law.[1] The CCLSG is a specialist group of the WCEL which works on legal aspects of addressing climate change and its adverse impacts internationally and nationally.[2]

WCEL also functions as the principal source of legal advice to the IUCN. The most prominent example of this capacity is the preparation by WCEL of all written statements by the IUCN in the advisory proceedings on climate change at the International Tribunal on the Law of the Sea,[3] the Inter-American Court on Human Rights,[4] and the International Court of Justice.[5] IUCN was authorised by the respective courts to participate in all three proceedings, and WCEL members acted as the IUCN legal counsels and pleaded the cases before the courts.

It is with great pride that the IUCN WCEL sees this publication becoming a reality. It was through WCEL's CCLSG, which I chaired from 2016 to 2021, that work on this project started. Its conclusion was made possible thanks to the support of WCEL's CCLSG current chairs, Francesco Sindico and Fabiano de Andrade Correa.

Most importantly, our deepest thanks go to the two editors of the book – Margaretha Wewerinke-Singh and Sarah Mead – both members of the WCEL

1 For more information, see 'World Commission on Environmental Law' (*IUCN*) <www.iucn.org/commissions/world-commission-environmental-law> accessed 21 April 2024.

2 For more information, see 'IUCN WCEL Climate Change Law Specialist Group' (*IUCN*) <www.iucn.org/our-union/commissions/group/iucn-wcel-climate-change-law-specialist-group> accessed 21 April 2024.

3 For more information, see International Tribunal for the Law of the Sea, Request for an Advisory Opinion Submitted by the Commission of Small Island States on Climate Change and International Law, Written Statement of the International Union on the Conservation of Nature and Natural Resources – World Commission on Environmental Law, Ocean Law Specialist Group <www.itlos.org/fileadmin/itlos/documents/cases/31/written_statements/2/C31-WS-2-2-IUCN.pdf> accessed 21 April 2024.

4 For more information, see Inter-American Court of Human Rights, Observations on the Request for an Advisory Opinion <www.corteidh.or.cr/observaciones_oc_new.cfm?lang=en&lang_oc=en&nId_oc=2634> accessed 21 April 2024.

5 For more information, see International Court of Justice, Obligations of States in respect of Climate Change <www.icj-cij.org/case/187> accessed 21 April 2024.

CCLSG, for their unwavering dedication and the profound diligence with which they carried out this book project in times of constantly evolving jurisprudence. It has been a joy and honour working with both of them and seeing the book moving from an idea to a powerful result. Many thanks go also to all the chapter authors involved. They are the brightest minds in the field of climate law, governance, and science, and it is a true privilege and honour having them on board. We owe them our sincerest gratitude for having contributed their time, energy, and expertise to bring this project to fruition.

It has been a massive piece of work for the editors Margaretha Wewerinke-Singh and Sarah Mead, together with the chapter authors, but the result speaks for itself. Our hope is that this Handbook serves not only as a guide but also as an inspiration for every reader that would like to engage and contribute to reverting climate change with the urgency it demands.

**Prof Dr Christina Voigt, Chair, International Union for Conservation of Nature World Commission on Environmental Law**

# Acknowledgements

*The Cambridge Handbook on Climate Litigation* stands as a testament to the collaborative efforts and dedication of a diverse group of experts, institutions, and volunteers from all corners of the globe. The organic growth of this group throughout the lifespan of this project has now made it impossible to acknowledge every contributor by name. With apologies for omissions, we still wish to highlight some members of this extraordinary group whose contributions have been critical.

First, we are profoundly grateful to the IUCN-WCEL members and numerous other experts across the globe who have helped us to build a robust empirical base for this project. Their contributions range from identifying key decisions and providing detailed case reports to helping us keep our database up-to-date. We specifically wish to acknowledge Elena Aydos, Lisa Benjamin, Caio Borges, Sébastien Jodoin, David Boyd, Stuart Bruce, Javier Camarena, Christel Cournil, Mirjana Drenovak Ivanovic, Sandrine Dubois, Edgar Fernández Fernández, Paula Galbiatti Silveira, Justine Garrett, Sangeeta Roy, Arvind Jasrotia, Maša Kovič Dine, Katrina Kuh, Warren Gary Lavey, Bernard Namanya, Erick Pajares, Oliver Ruppel, Mercy Teko, Akhtar Uz Zaman, Gerd Winter, Hermann Ott, Lucy Edwards, Nicole Smith, Maud Sarliève, Hasminah Paudac, Amanda Misasi, Sonam Gordhan, Simon Milnes, Gabrielle Cornette, Gregor Schamschula, Alessandra Lehmen, André De Castro dos Santos, Ana Paula Chagas, Ana Flávia Trevizan, Morgan McGinnn, Daniel (Eduardo) Cortés Cortés, Elodie Fesquet, Anastasia Steinlein, Filippo Fantozzi, Hicham Kaddoum, Katharina Neumann, Marine Segura, Paul Mougeolle, Emer Slattery, Andrew Jackson, Tim Crosland, Joe Snape, Caterina Freytag, Iva Aurer, Jenny Sandvig, Peter Dawson, Marit Tjelmeland, Carole Billiet, Audrey Baeyens, Daniel Galpern, Stuart Bruce, Ruby Rorty, Mark Burrows, Douglas Sanders, Ilona Miller, and Guy Dwyer.

We also owe a debt of gratitude to Justice Antonio Benjamin and Christina Voigt for their insightful contributions and guidance, which have greatly shaped the direction of this Handbook. Moreover, we are thankful to Francesco Sindico and Fabiano de Andrade Correa, who provided priceless support in their capacity as co-chairs of the IUCN-WCEL CCLSG. Marjan Peeters deserves special credit for her invaluable contributions to the design of the project.

Special appreciation is also due to Susan Kath, Sam Bookman, and Nathalya Desterro at the Cyrus Vance Center for International Justice, Professor Nicholas Robinson at the International Council of Environmental Law, Joana Setzer of the Grantham Institute on Climate Change and the Environment, Maria-Antonia Tigre and Michael Burger at the Sabin Center for Climate Change Law, Catalina Pizarro Tapia at the United Nations Environment Programme, Dennis van Berkel from the Urgenda Foundation, and Briony Eales and Maria Cecilia Sicangco at the Asian Development Bank. We could not have built the comprehensive dataset that underpins this Handbook without their expert assistance in utilising and expanding existing databases and resources.

We should not fail to thank each of the experts who served as chapter authors for joining us in what at times appeared to be an arduous journey. Many of these authors not only provided text that now forms the 'flesh' of the Handbook but also played key roles in methodology development and project design. We are conscious that our ambitions for this Handbook resulted in significant demands on each of the authors' time, and we are grateful for their patience and perseverance in responding to streams of editorial feedback that may have seemed incessant.

Our gratitude extends further to the exceptionally talented interns and volunteers who have worked tirelessly on several aspects of the project, and to Rabya Khan and Chiara Montanari for facilitating their contributions through the University of Chicago's Metcalf Internship Programme. In particular, the assistance of Andrea Paolo Olivei, Lena Maghraoui, and Solange Reppas has been essential in overcoming numerous challenges and ensuring the project's success. We are also deeply grateful to Tejas Rao, who not only contributed case analysis but also provided excellent editorial assistance in the project's final stages.

A special note of thanks is due to our brilliant assistant editor, Joe Udell, whose dedication and meticulous efforts have been pivotal in bringing this Handbook to fruition. His ever-high spirits and sense of humour made working with him a real pleasure.

This Handbook ultimately reflects the collective wisdom and expertise of an ever-growing community of scientists, lawyers, scholars, experts, and others who share a commitment to just climate action. For this, we are most grateful.

Finally, during the completion of this Handbook, the international environmental law community lost a gifted and dedicated colleague with the passing of Meinhard Doelle (1964–2022). Meinhard made indispensable contributions to environmental law scholarship during his academic career spanning almost twenty years, and we are honoured to publish his co-authored chapter on international law posthumously, with the permission of his wife, Wendy. May his optimism and vision continue to inspire our field.

# Table of Cases

## AFRICAN COMMISSION ON HUMAN AND PEOPLES' RIGHTS



## ARBITRAL TRIBUNALS



## EUROPEAN COURT OF JUSTICE



## EUROPEAN COURT OF HUMAN RIGHTS

## EUROPEAN COMMITTEE OF SOCIAL RIGHTS



## INTERNATIONAL COURT OF JUSTICE/PERMANENT COURT OF INTERNATIONAL JUSTICE

## INTER-AMERICAN COMMISSION ON HUMAN RIGHTS



## INTER-AMERICAN COURT OF HUMAN RIGHTS

## INTERNATIONAL TRIBUNAL ON THE LAW OF THE SEA



## UN COMMITTEE ON THE RIGHTS OF THE CHILD



## UN HUMAN RIGHTS COMMITTEE



## ARGENTINA

## AUSTRIA



## AUSTRALIA



## BELGIUM



## BRAZIL

CANADA



COLOMBIA



CHILE



CZECHIA

ECUADOR



FRANCE



GERMANY



INDIA

INDONESIA



ITALY



IRELAND



KENYA



NEPAL

## NETHERLANDS



## NEW ZEALAND



## NORWAY

## PAKISTAN



## PHILIPPINES



## SOUTH AFRICA

## SRI LANKA



## SWEDEN



## SWITZERLAND



## UGANDA



## UNITED KINGDOM

UNITED STATES OF AMERICA

# Table of Treaties

# Abbreviations

| | |
|---|---|
| ACHPR | African Commission on Human and Peoples' Rights |
| ACHR | American Convention on Human Rights |
| ACODE | Advocates Coalition for Development and Environment |
| ADPF | Ação de Descumprimento de Preceito Fundamental (Brazil) |
| AIR | All India Reporter |
| AJIL | American Journal of International Law |
| ALR | Australian Law Reports |
| App | Application |
| AR6 SYR | IPCC Synthesis Report of the Sixth Assessment Report |
| ARPS | Annual Review of Political Science |
| Art | Article |
| Arts | Articles |
| BCLR | Boston College Law Review |
| CBDR-RC | Principle of common but differentiated responsibilities and respective capabilities |
| CCLR | Carbon & Climate Law Review |
| CDR | Carbon dioxide removal |
| CERD | Committee interpreting the International Convention on the Elimination of all forms of Racial Discrimination |
| CESCR | Committee on Economic, Social and Cultural Rights |
| Cf | Confer, meaning compare |
| CHRP | Commission on Human Rights of the Philippines |
| Cir | Circuit (United States) |
| CJ | Chief Justice |
| CJEL | Columbia Journal of Environmental Law |
| CJEU/ECJ | Court of Justice of the European Union |
| CJIL | Chinese Journal of International Law |
| CLJ | Cambridge Law Journal |
| CLR | Commonwealth Law Reports |

| | |
|---|---|
| CMA | Conference of the Parties serving as the Meeting of the Parties to the Paris Agreement |
| COP | Conference of the Parties |
| COSIS | Commission of Small Island States on Climate Change and International |
| CRC | United Nations Committee on the Rights of the Child |
| Doc | Document |
| EBP | Emerging Best Practice |
| ECHR | European Convention on Human Rights |
| ECJ/CJEU | Court of Justice of the European Union |
| ECR | European Court Reports |
| ECtHR | European Court of Human Rights |
| ed | Editor |
| eds | Editors |
| e.g. | For example |
| EIA | Environmental Impact Assessment |
| EJIL | European Journal of International Law |
| eKLR | Kenya Law Reports (electronic) |
| ELR | Environmental Law Review |
| ENSO | El Niño–Southern Oscillation |
| EPA | Environmental Protection Agency (United States) |
| ESIA | Environmental and social impacts assessment |
| et al | And others |
| EU | European Union |
| EWCA | England and Wales Court of Appeal |
| EWHC | England and Wales High Court of Justice |
| FCA | Federal Court of Australia |
| FCAFC | Full Court of the Federal Court of Appeal (Australia) |
| GEC | Global emissions per capita |
| GELR | Georgetown Environmental Law Review |
| GHG | Greenhouse gas |
| GMST | Global mean surface temperature |
| HRC | Human Rights Committee |
| IACHR | Inter-American Commission on Human Rights |
| IACtHR | Inter-American Court of Human Rights |
| IAHRS | Inter-American Human Rights System |
| IAM | Integrated Assessment Models |
| ibid | Ibidem |
| ICCPR | International Covenant on Civil and Political Rights |
| ICESCR | International Covenant on Economic, Social and Cultural Rights |
| ICJ | International Court of Justice |
| ICLQ | International and Comparative Law Quarterly |

| | |
|---|---|
| i.e. | That is |
| IEHC | Irish High Court |
| IEL | International Environmental Law |
| IJCL | International Journal of Constitutional Law |
| ILC | International Law Commission |
| ILM | International Legal Materials |
| IPCC | Intergovernmental Panel on Climate Change |
| ITLOS | International Tribunal for the Law of the Sea |
| IUCN | International Union for Conservation of Nature |
| J | Judge/Justice |
| JEL | Journal of Environmental Law |
| JHRE | Journal of Human Rights and the Environment |
| KLJ | Kings Law Journal |
| LDC | Least Developed Countries |
| LJIL | Leiden Journal of International Law |
| LSE | London School of Economics |
| Ltd | Limited |
| MEA | Multilateral Environmental Agreement |
| n | Note |
| NDC | Nationally Determined Contribution |
| NDCs | Nationally Determined Contributions |
| NGO | Non-Governmental Organisation |
| NHRI | National Human Rights Institutions |
| No | Number |
| NSWLEC | Land and Environment Court of New South Wales (Australia) |
| NZCA | New Zealand Court of Appeal |
| NZHC | New Zealand High Court |
| NZLR | New Zealand Law Reports |
| NZSC | New Zealand Supreme Court |
| OECD | Organisation for Economic Co-operation and Development |
| OHCHR | Office of the High Commissioner on Human Rights |
| OJLS | Oxford Journal of Legal Studies |
| ONSC | Ontario Superior Court of Justice (Canada) |
| Ors | Others |
| OxHRH | Oxford Human Rights Hub |
| PA | Paris Agreement |
| PCIJ | Permanent Court of International Justice |
| PELR | Pace Environmental Law Review |
| PIL | Public Interest Litigation |
| PLD | All Pakistan Legal Decisions |
| PPCDAm | Action Plan for the Prevention and Control of Deforestation in the Amazon |

| | |
|---|---|
| QIL | Questions of International Law |
| QLC | Queensland Land Court (Australia) |
| QMLJ | Queen Mary Law Journal |
| RDS | Royal Dutch Shell |
| RECIEL | Review of European, Comparative and International Environmental Law |
| Rep | Reports |
| RIAA | Reports of International Arbitral Awards |
| S | Section |
| SAFLII | Southern African Legal Information Institute |
| SC | Supreme Court |
| SCC | Supreme Court Cases (India) |
| SCR | Supreme Court Reports (India) |
| SCRA | Supreme Court Reports Annotated (Philippines) |
| SIDS | Small Island Developing States |
| SPM | Summary for Policymakers |
| SSP | Shared Socioeconomic Pathway |
| TEL | Transnational Environmental Law |
| TFEU | Treaty on the Functioning of the European Union |
| UKHL | United Kingdom House of Lords |
| UKSC | United Kingdom Supreme Court |
| UN | United Nations |
| UNCIO | United Nations Conference on International Organization |
| UNCLOS | United Nations Convention on the Law of the Sea |
| UNEP | United Nations Environment Programme |
| UNFCCC | United Nations Framework Convention on Climate Change |
| UNGA | United Nations General Assembly |
| UNGP | United Nations Guiding Principles on Business and Human Rights |
| UNHR | United Nations Human Rights |
| UNTC | United Nations Treaty Collection |
| UNTS | United Nations Treaty Series |
| US | United States |
| v | Versus |
| VCAT | Victorian Courts and Tribunals (Australia) |
| VCLT | Vienna Convention on the Law of Treaties |
| VJEL | Vermont Journal of Environmental Law |
| WG | Working Group (of the IPCC) |
| WJELP | Washington Journal of Environmental Law and Policy |
| YLJ | Yale Law Journal |
| ZAGPPHC | North Gauteng High Court (South Africa) |

# 1

# Introduction

## *Margaretha Wewerinke-Singh and Sarah Mead**

The second decade of the twenty-first century marked a turning point in the landscape of climate change law and governance, with the judiciary rising to prominence in climate action.[1] Born from profound dissatisfaction – if not outright frustration – with the sluggish pace at which the executive and legislative branches of governments are addressing climate change, this legal frontier has seen more than a thousand new filings since the adoption of the Paris Agreement.[2] This surge represents more than just a rise in litigation: it is a strategic movement, increasingly aiming for systemic, transformative changes rather than merely targeting specific instances of pollution.[3]

High-profile victories, such as the judgments in *State of the Netherlands v Urgenda Foundation*[4] and *Leghari v Pakistan*,[5] have lent momentum to this trend. These landmark judgments have inspired a multitude of similar initiatives across jurisdictions, shaping policy discussions and public debates outside the courtroom.[6] Researchers have found that successful 'framework cases' of this kind have significantly influenced government decision-making on climate change, leading to the development and implementation of more ambitious policies.[7] For instance, courts have ordered

* Margaretha Wewerinke-Singh is Associate Professor of Sustainability Law at the University of Amsterdam and an attorney at Blue Ocean Law. Sarah Mead is Co-Director of the Climate Litigation Network.

1 Joyeeta Gupta, *The History of Global Climate Governance* (Cambridge University Press 2014).

2 Jacqueline Peel and Hari M. Osofsky, 'Climate Change Litigation' (2020) 16(1) Annual Review of Law and Social Science 21.

3 Lucy Maxwell, Sarah Mead, and Dennis van Berkel, 'Standards for Adjudicating the Next Generation of Urgenda-Style Climate Cases' (2022) 13(1) JHRE 35.

4 *State of the Netherlands (Ministry of Economic Affairs and Climate Policy) v Stichting Urgenda* [2019] ECLI:NL:HR:2019:2007 (Supreme Court of the Netherlands).

5 *Asghar Leghari v Federation of Pakistan etc* PLD 2018 Lahore 364 [11].

6 Jacqueline Peel and Jolene Lin, 'Transnational Climate Litigation: The Contribution of the Global South' (2019) 113 AJIL 679.

7 Joana Setzer, Catherine Higham, and Emily Bradeen, 'Challenging Government Responses to Climate Change through Framework Litigation' (*LSE Grantham Research Institute on Climate Change and the Environment*, September 2022) <www.lse.ac.uk/granthaminstitute/wp-content/uploads/2022/09/Challenging-government-responses-to-climate-change-through-framework-litigation-final.pdf> accessed 10 March 2024.

governments to increase emissions reduction efforts,[8] to clarify climate plans,[9] and to implement existing targets.[10] Reflecting these developments, the International Panel on Climate Change has concluded that 'climate litigation can affect the stringency and ambitiousness of climate governance'.[11] This trend has continued to accelerate, with groundbreaking decisions from the European Court of Human Rights (ECtHR) in the cases of *KlimaSeniorinnen*, *Carême*, and *Duarte Agostinho* in April 2024,[12] and the Advisory Opinion of the International Tribunal for the Law of the Sea (ITLOS) on climate change and marine protection in May 2024.[13]

Amid this burgeoning landscape of climate litigation, an increasingly diverse set of cases is being brought to the courts. The range of litigation, in terms of both geography and legal substance, presents a complex area of law that requires specialised legal knowledge and guidance.

Recognising this need, *The Cambridge Handbook on Climate Litigation* was designed to guide judges, lawyers, scholars, and other actors in navigating the labyrinth of legal intricacies that define the climate change litigation landscape. The question at heart: in what ways could the judiciary play a constructive role in fighting the climate crisis and addressing its consequences? Drawing on a vast array of cases, the book delineates 'emerging best practice' from multiple jurisdictions worldwide. It not only identifies the scalable aspects of emerging best practice from various significant and lesser-known judgments but also explores how these practices might influence and inspire legal reasoning in future cases.

Acutely aware of the extensive cultural, socio-economic, and legal diversity across countries and jurisdictions, this book does not aim to prescribe one-size-fits-all solutions to the challenges that climate change litigation poses. Instead, it uncovers and analyses common themes and critical differences within this rapidly evolving field. By offering a comprehensive analysis, this book provides insights into the future of climate litigation worldwide and its potential to contribute to law, policy, and, ultimately, the survival of our planet and the well-being of its inhabitants.

## 1.1 METHODOLOGY

*The Cambridge Handbook on Climate Litigation* traces its roots to the International Union for the Conservation of Nature (IUCN) World Commission on Environmental

8 For example, in the Netherlands, Germany, and Belgium.

9 For example, in Ireland and the United Kingdom.

10 For example, in France.

11 Intergovernmental Panel on Climate Change, *AR6 Synthesis Report: Climate Change 2023* 13.4.2 <www.ipcc.ch/report/sixth-assessment-report-cycle/> accessed 10 March 2024.

12 *Verein KlimaSeniorinnen Schweiz and Others v Switzerland* App no 53600/20 (ECtHR); *Duarte Agostinho v Portugal and 32 other States* App no 39371/20 (ECtHR); *Carême v France* App no 7189/21 (ECtHR).

13 *Request for an Advisory Opinion Submitted by the Commission of Small Island States on Climate Change and International* Law *(Request for Advisory Opinion Submitted to the Tribunal)*, ITLOS Case No 31 (Advisory Opinion of 21 May 2024).

Law (WCEL) and, more specifically, its Climate Change Law Specialist Group (CCLSG). The need for a comprehensive guide to aid the judiciary in navigating the complex terrain of climate litigation was first identified by Justice Antonio Benjamin during his time as the Chair of the WCEL, an idea that was embraced by Christina Voigt when she assumed leadership of the CCLSG. Their shared commitment to this initiative has never wavered, with Christina Voigt contributing a chapter and nurturing its development during her tenure as the Chair of the WCEL. Their dedication and guidance have been instrumental in bringing this project to fruition. This collaborative spirit was carried forward by Francesco Sindico and Fabiano De Andrade Correa, who took up the leadership of the CCLSG and have provided ongoing support for the initiative.

The WCEL, an international network of professionals spanning lawyers, judges, and scholars across disciplines and geographies, offered the ideal platform for this project. The WCEL advances environmental law around the globe, contributing to its progressive development through expert knowledge and assistance, and building the capacity of communities to benefit from the environmental rule of law.[14] The CCLSG, as a specialist group of the WCEL, functions as the principal source of legal technical advice to the IUCN, its members, and the WCEL on legal aspects of addressing climate change and its adverse impacts.[15] Members of the WCEL and its specialist groups serve in a personal and voluntary capacity. The collective global expertise of these groups has proven to be instrumental in realising the ambitious vision of this project: to produce a resource that encapsulates climate jurisprudence from across the globe, catering to a global audience.

Building on Justice Benjamin's initial vision, the primary aim of the Handbook is to augment judicial understanding and proficiency in matters related to climate change law. Beyond the judiciary, it serves as a reservoir of knowledge for parties involved in climate lawsuits, aiding in the design and strategy of future cases, and providing a rich foundation for further legal scholarship and teaching in this rapidly evolving field.

The project unfolded in two interconnected stages. The first stage entailed the establishment of the empirical basis for the project, drawing on the vast global network of the WCEL and CCLSG to identify contributors who reported on climate change case law in their respective jurisdictions. In this process, we used a template to collect detailed information on how judges have navigated key issues that commonly arise in climate change litigation, such as: the political question doctrine; scientific uncertainty; human rights; extraterritoriality; causation; and attribution. The issues addressed in the template were purposefully broad-ranging, encouraging

14 For more information, see 'World Commission on Environmental Law' (*IUCN*) <www.iucn.org/commissions/world-commission-environmental-law> accessed 10 March 2024.

15 'IUCN WCEL Climate Change Law Specialist Group' (*IUCN*) <www.iucn.org/our-union/commissions/group/iucn-wcel-climate-change-law-specialist-group> accessed 10 March 2024.

members to identify any and all potentially scalable approaches that arise from the cases in question. Over 200 reports were completed, each reviewed by the project leads, with gaps in coverage and quality addressed with the support of the Cyrus R Vance Center for International Justice and various academic institutions.

The second stage commenced with the development of an analytical framework aimed at ensuring a consistent structure across chapters. A workshop was convened with all authors, each a leading expert in their respective field, to discuss and refine our methodology. One of the central themes of our discussion was the notion of 'best practice'. After scrutinising this term, we decided to adopt the more flexible and versatile term 'emerging best practice', reflecting the nascent and dynamic nature of the field. We defined 'emerging best practice' as legal reasoning that is not only rigorous but also contributes to the protection of the climate system or enhances resilience in the face of the climate crisis. Despite the potential limitations of this definition, its simplicity and flexibility allowed authors to delve into a nuanced exploration of the judicial decisions shaping the field of climate litigation across the world. Following the workshop, authors were tasked with discerning 'emerging best practice' on each issue from the data collected in the first stage.

The diverse cohort of authors, hailing from various disciplines, jurisdictions, and backgrounds, has added depth and breadth to this Handbook. Each author has interpreted 'emerging best practice' within their respective contexts, weaving their perspectives and deep-seated knowledge into the larger fabric of the Handbook. In cases where their understanding deviates from our general definition, the authors explicitly outline the reason for this deviation.

Ultimately, *The Cambridge Handbook on Climate Litigation* is an expedition that charts unexplored territories, unearths innovative pathways, and navigates potential roadblocks in climate litigation. Our hope is that this Handbook does more than merely document the current landscape. We aspire for it to inspire dialogue, spur innovative legal reasoning, and shape the future discourse and practice of climate litigation.

## 1.2 OVERVIEW

The book commences with two foundational chapters that bridge the science–law divide. Sarah Connors and others – in Chapter 2, 'A Scientific Overview of Climate Change' – provide a primer on climate science for legal practitioners and scholars, offering essential scientific background to understand the context of climate litigation. Carly A. Phillips, L. Delta Merner, and Friederike Otto, in Chapter 3 on 'Attribution Science', build upon this foundation and delve deeper into the scientific underpinnings of attributing climate change impacts to specific causes. They illustrate how these scientific developments are enhancing our ability to pinpoint the causes of climate impacts, an evolution crucial to a range of procedural and substantive issues that may arise in climate litigation.

Part I of the Handbook, 'Preliminary Issues', begins with a chapter by Randall S. Abate on 'Standing' (Chapter 4). Abate explores the intricacies of the legal principle of standing, its role in climate litigation, and how it impacts the ability of parties to bring climate change-related lawsuits. He discusses how different interpretations of standing across various jurisdictions can either impede or facilitate climate litigation. Abate distils emerging best practice from this analysis, providing an insightful guide for future climate lawsuits. He identifies emerging best practice in interpreting standing rules in a flexible manner, thus allowing a broader range of actors to bring climate-related lawsuits and enhancing access to justice.

Following this, Juan Auz, in the chapter on 'Admissibility' (Chapter 5), delves into the factors determining whether a climate case can be heard in court. He provides a clear understanding of the criteria for admissibility and their potential implications on the trajectory of climate litigation. He also delves into the interplay between domestic and international legal rules and norms and their influence on the criteria for admissibility. Auz's analysis reveals that a restrictive interpretation of admissibility criteria can present formidable barriers to access to justice, particularly for those who are most impacted by climate change. In light of these challenges, Auz's distillation of emerging best practice highlights instances where courts and quasi-judicial bodies have interpreted admissibility criteria to ensure access to justice. Specifically, he highlights cases where these bodies have considered human rights and justice imperatives in their decisions on admissibility. These decisions highlight the potential for an inclusive and equitable approach to climate litigation, one that aligns with the global nature of the climate crisis and the urgent need for climate justice.

Concluding the first part, Christina Eckes, Jasmina Nedevska, and Joana Setzer examine the 'Separation of Powers' (Chapter 6). Their chapter offers a comprehensive exploration of how the balance of power between the judiciary and other branches of government plays out in climate litigation. The authors critically analyse key cases where these doctrines have been invoked, shedding light on how these doctrines shape courts' approaches to climate cases. They underscore the significant variation in how this issue is dealt with across jurisdictions, acknowledging the diversity of constitutional and legal frameworks globally. Despite this diversity, they distil an emerging best practice where courts are increasingly recognising their crucial role in safeguarding fundamental rights and constitutional values in the context of climate change. This recognition, they note, is not a one-directional or universal trend but a nuanced evolution detectable across various jurisdictions and legal systems.

In Part II, titled 'Merits', the book shifts its focus to the substantive aspects of climate litigation. Margaretha Wewerinke-Singh and Lucy Maxwell initiate this part with Chapter 7 on 'Human Rights'. They dissect how human rights laws have been harnessed in climate cases, scrutinising key judgments that have applied human rights frameworks to climate change and the implications of these legal strategies for both claimants and defendants. Their analysis of emerging best practice reveals a growing acceptance of the notion that a State's failure to take adequate action to address climate change constitutes a breach of human rights obligations, and this recognition is shaping legal strategies in climate litigation at the national and international levels.

Subsequently, Mark Gibney, in his chapter on 'Extraterritoriality' (Chapter 8), discusses how the cross-border nature of climate impacts is addressed within climate litigation. He scrutinises the interpretation of 'jurisdiction' and related procedural and substantive issues, such as standing and the territorial scope of human rights obligations, in the context of these transboundary impacts. His thorough analysis showcases how these legal principles and procedural rules either facilitate or constrain courts and quasi-judicial bodies in grappling meaningfully with these impacts. In his exploration of key decisions, Gibney unravels their implications for the global governance of climate change and the challenges and opportunities they present for transboundary climate lawsuits. He distils emerging best practices that reveal how courts and quasi-judicial bodies, through judicious interpretation of legal principles, are grappling with the global dimensions of climate change.

Despite the complexities inherent in integrating extraterritorial considerations into climate litigation, Gibney posits an optimistic outlook. He highlights how visionary legal reasoning can tackle these complexities in a manner that is both legally sound and conducive to ensuring access to justice for those most affected by climate impacts. This optimism is further bolstered by recent developments in climate litigation, including advisory opinion proceedings pending before several international courts and tribunals. These developments hold significant promise for the future of climate litigation, with the potential emergence of novel jurisprudence transforming our approach to litigating and adjudicating climate change as a global problem.

Continuing in this part, 'Duty of Care' by Christina Voigt and Joe Udell (Chapter 9) examines the principle of the duty of care in the context of climate litigation. They explore how this principle has been invoked in a growing range of jurisdictions, in different ways, to hold governments and corporations accountable for their respective contributions to climate change. By analysing judicial decisions in prominent cases such as *Urgenda* in the Netherlands and *Neubauer* in Germany, they explore the potential of the principle to compel more ambitious climate action in pending and future cases. The emerging best practice they identify suggests a growing willingness of courts to recognise a duty of care for governments and corporations towards citizens in relation to climate change.

Following this, Rachel M. Pemberton and Michael C. Blumm's chapter on 'International Atmospheric Trust' (Chapter 10) delves into the application of the public trust doctrine in climate litigation. Historically, this doctrine has maintained that certain natural and cultural resources should be held in trust for the public, with the government acting as a trustee. Mary Wood's seminal work on atmospheric trust litigation has been pivotal in extending the public trust doctrine to the realm of climate change, by conceptualising the climate system as an atmospheric trust that governments are entrusted to preserve for present and future generations.[16] Building upon Wood's theoretical framework, Pemberton and Blumm delve into the practical application and interpretation of this doctrine in climate litigation, examining key cases across various jurisdictions, including the United States, Canada, India, Pakistan, and Uganda. Through their examination, the authors distil emerging best practices, revealing the successes and challenges encountered when invoking the public trust doctrine in climate litigation. They underscore the potential of this doctrine to shape future climate cases and inspire more robust climate action, reflecting a growing recognition among courts worldwide of their own role in safeguarding the atmospheric trust.

In Chapter 11, Susana Borràs-Pentinat delves into the 'Rights of Nature', an emerging legal paradigm that ascribes legal rights to natural entities. This approach, which marks a radical departure from anthropocentric legal frameworks, represents a pioneering stride towards acknowledging and safeguarding the inherent worth of the natural world. Borràs-Pentinat presents an in-depth exploration of how this innovative legal approach has been employed in climate litigation. Drawing on concrete examples from countries such as Ecuador and Colombia, she elucidates the transformative potential of this paradigm in the realm of climate litigation. One of the most compelling aspects of this approach, as Borràs-Pentinat underscores, is the shift it instigates in our legal and ethical relationship with the natural world. By conferring rights upon nature, it challenges the traditional conception of nature as mere property or resource, promoting a more holistic and respectful relationship with our environment. This shift, as Borràs-Pentinat argues, can play a critical role in achieving climate justice, by ensuring that the rights and interests of nature itself are upheld and protected in the face of climate change. The analysis of emerging best practice reveals that, while still in its early stages, the rights of nature approach is starting to gain traction in climate litigation around the world. The chapter also highlights the promising potential of this paradigm to spur further innovation in climate law and policy, and to deepen our understanding and respect for the natural world.

Part III, 'Regime Interaction and Interpretation', commences with a chapter by Sarah Mead and Meinhard Doelle on 'International Law' (Chapter 12). They examine how international law is interpreted and applied in climate litigation, discussing cases where international climate obligations have been invoked in domestic courts. They explore the interplay between international and domestic law, and how it can shape the outcomes of climate litigation. Mead and Doelle's exploration of emerging best practice reveals a progressive trend: domestic courts are increasingly incorporating international climate obligations into their rulings. This trend not

[16] Mary Christina Woods, 'Atmospheric Trust Litigation Across the World' in Ken Coghill and others (eds) *Fiduciary Duty and the Atmospheric Trust* (Ashgate Publishing 2012).

only underscores the significance of international law in shaping domestic legal responses to climate change but also amplifies the capacity of domestic legal systems to address the impacts of climate change more effectively. Moreover, they spotlight emerging best practices from regional and international bodies. They argue that these practices demonstrate the potency of international legal norms in influencing the trajectory of climate litigation, fostering a global legal landscape that is increasingly responsive to the climate crisis. Their analysis offers insights into how the synergetic relationship between international and domestic law can be harnessed to forge stronger and more effective legal responses to climate change.

Patricia Galvao Ferreira's discussion on 'Common but Differentiated Responsibilities and Respective Capabilities' (Chapter 13) provides a critical analysis of this cornerstone principle of international climate law and its implications for climate litigation. The principle recognises the differentiated responsibilities and capabilities of countries in addressing climate change, acknowledging the historical contribution of developed nations to global greenhouse gas emissions and the greater capacity these nations possess to mitigate climate change and adapt to its impacts.[17] Ferreira offers a comprehensive examination of how this principle has been invoked and interpreted in climate litigation. She critically analyses key cases where the principle has been raised, and assesses the legal reasoning employed by courts and tribunals who have given it a specific meaning. Ferreira identifies instances of emerging best practice where the principle has been interpreted and applied in ways that enhance climate justice outcomes. She notes that such instances do not yet constitute a uniform trend. Nonetheless, these instances illustrate the potential of this principle in shaping the delineation of responsibilities in climate lawsuits, considering fairness, equity, and historical responsibility. Through her analysis, Ferreira underscores the potential of the principle to contribute to the development of a more equitable and just climate jurisprudence. She highlights how the nuanced interpretation and application of this principle in legal judgments can significantly influence the outcomes of climate litigation.

The section concludes with Chapter 14 on 'Intergenerational Equity' by Sam Bookman and Margaretha Wewerinke-Singh. The chapter sheds light on how this principle, which posits a responsibility to ensure that future generations inherit a habitable planet, has been invoked in climate cases. The authors examine how this principle has been interpreted and applied across different jurisdictions, highlighting the notable contributions of jurisprudence from the Global South in shaping the development and understanding of the principle. Through an examination of leading cases from around the world, they highlight how courts in these jurisdictions have infused their decisions with a consideration for future generations, thereby advancing a more inclusive and long-term perspective on climate justice.

[17] Patricia Galvao Ferreira, '"Common but Differentiated Responsibilities" in the National Courts: Lessons from *Urgenda v The Netherlands*' (2022) 5(2) TEL 329–351.

The authors distil instances of emerging best practice where the principle of intergenerational equity has been invoked to guide legal reasoning and judicial decisions in climate cases. They underscore the potential of this principle to shape future climate litigation, particularly as the impacts of climate change increasingly span across generations. The analysis reveals how this principle can be operationalised to ensure a fairer distribution of climate-related burdens and benefits between current and future generations.

Part IV, 'Liability and Evidence', begins with a chapter by Annalisa Savaresi on 'State Responsibility' (Chapter 15). Savaresi provides an in-depth exploration of the circumstances under which States can be held responsible for climate change. Savaresi starts by outlining the fundamental principles and conditions for State responsibility under international law. She then extends this discussion to explore how these principles are translated and applied in domestic legal contexts. Her analysis bridges the gap between international and domestic law, shedding light on how each legal sphere influences the shape and contours of State responsibility in relation to climate change. Further, she explores the legal consequences that flow from the establishment of State responsibility. This includes obligations to cease wrongful conduct, provide guarantees of non-repetition, and repair the damage caused. Savaresi enriches her analysis with insights drawn from key climate cases that have tested the limits of State responsibility. These cases reveal how courts and quasi-judicial bodies are grappling with the challenges of attributing climate harms to State actions and omissions, and the implications of holding States accountable for these harms. In distilling emerging best practice, Savaresi identifies innovative judicial interpretations and legal strategies that have expanded the ambit of State responsibility in climate litigation. These include approaches that consider the cumulative contribution of a State's actions and policies to global greenhouse gas emissions, as well as those that take into account a State's capacity and responsibility to prevent foreseeable climate harms. Through her chapter, Savaresi provides readers with a deeper understanding of the evolving landscape of State responsibility in climate litigation, and its potential to drive more effective and equitable responses to climate change.

Following on from this exploration of State responsibility, Lisa Benjamin and Sara Seck discuss the intricate issue of 'Causation' in the context of climate litigation (Chapter 16). They explore the challenges of proving causation in a complex and interconnected system like the climate, where multiple actors contribute to the overall impacts. The authors highlight the significance of probabilistic approaches, recognising that establishing direct causation can be challenging due to the nature of climate change and the cumulative nature of greenhouse gas emissions. In their exploration of emerging best practices, Benjamin and Seck underscore the growing recognition among courts of the need for flexible and nuanced interpretations of causation requirements in climate litigation. They highlight innovative judicial strategies that utilise scientific evidence and expert testimony to assess the contribution of specific actors to climate impacts, even in the absence of direct causation. They emphasise the importance of interdisciplinary collaboration between legal and scientific experts to navigate the complexities of causation in climate cases. By incorporating and further developing these emerging best practices, courts can facilitate an accurate and fair distribution of responsibilities through the cases they adjudicate.

In her chapter on 'Climate Causality: From Causation to Attribution' (Chapter 17), Petra Minnerop delves into one of the most challenging aspects of climate litigation: attributing climate change impacts to specific actors or actions. This exploration builds on the insights provided in the earlier chapter on 'Attribution Science' (Chapter 3), which outlines the scientific process of attributing climate phenomena to human activities. Shifting focus to the legal realm, Minnerop explores how courts and quasi-judicial bodies grapple with the scientific complexities of attribution. In particular, she analyses how these legal bodies assess and weigh the scientific evidence, navigate the inherent uncertainties, and determine the legal relevance of attribution findings in climate cases. Through a detailed review of key climate cases from around the world, Minnerop uncovers a variety of approaches to the issue of attribution. These cases highlight the diverse legal strategies employed by litigants to establish the causal links necessary for liability and the evolving understanding of courts in grappling with scientific complexities. In distilling emerging best practice, Minnerop identifies instances where courts have acknowledged the collective and cumulative nature of climate harms, accepted partial attribution as a basis for liability, and applied innovative legal doctrines to overcome attribution-related challenges. Throughout her chapter, Minnerop underscores the critical role of attribution in climate litigation, noting its potential to hold both States and corporations accountable for their contributions to climate change.

Juan Auz and Marcela Zúñiga's chapter on 'Remedies' in climate litigation (Chapter 18) provides a critical analysis of the types of remedies sought and awarded in climate cases and reflect on the implications of current trends. Drawing on a comprehensive analysis of climate lawsuits from around the world, Auz and Zúñiga provide insights into the diverse range of remedies that have been sought to address the adverse impacts of climate change. They then shed light on the different considerations and approaches that courts have taken when determining appropriate remedies. In their exploration of emerging best practices, Auz and Zúñiga highlight instances where courts have adopted innovative and transformative approaches to remedies in climate litigation. They examine creative legal mechanisms that go beyond traditional compensatory measures and explore the potential of remedies such as injunctive relief, restitution, and declaratory judgments to address the multifaceted challenges posed by climate change.

The section concludes with a chapter by Margaretha Wewerinke-Singh and Joe Udell on 'Recent Landmark Decisions: Advancing Climate Litigation and State Obligations' (Chapter 19). This chapter provides an in-depth analysis of two groundbreaking decisions that were handed down after the completion of the main body of the Handbook: the ITLOS Advisory Opinion on climate change and marine protection, and the judgment of the ECtHR in *Verein KlimaSeniorinnen Schweiz and Others v Switzerland*. The authors situate these decisions within the broader context of climate litigation, examining their implications for future cases and drawing connections to the themes explored in other chapters. They demonstrate how these decisions both reflect and advance emerging best practice in climate jurisprudence, potentially inspiring further innovation based on science and rigorous legal reasoning.

In our concluding chapter, 'The Future of Climate Litigation' (Chapter 20), we reflect on the evolving landscape of climate litigation and speculate on its future trajectory. We begin by underscoring the remarkable progress that has been made in climate litigation, highlighting the significant role it has played in shaping legal responses to the climate crisis. We emphasise that the journey of climate litigation is far from over and that the field is poised for continued advancements and innovations.

One significant area that we identify as holding immense potential is loss and damage-related litigation. We explore the growing recognition of loss and damage as a critical aspect of climate impacts and discuss how legal actions seeking compensation for losses and damages could gain momentum in the future. We also highlight the importance of integrating principles of justice, equity, and human rights into the legal framework for addressing loss and damage. We then discuss the prospects of advancing cases against a wide range of private polluters for their contributions to climate change and the implications of these cases for driving systemic change – before turning to how litigation against governments will likely evolve. Furthermore, we explore the emerging intersection between climate impacts and biodiversity loss, highlighting the potential for cases that link these two critical global challenges. We discuss the evolving legal frameworks that recognise the interconnections between climate change and biodiversity, and the opportunities for litigation that seeks to protect and restore ecosystems as a means of addressing climate impacts. We underscore the importance of holistic approaches that integrate climate and biodiversity considerations in legal strategies and highlight the potential for novel legal arguments and precedents in this area. Finally, we touch upon the potential for inter-State litigation to play a significant role in addressing the global nature of the climate crisis. We explore the potential avenues for resolving disputes and the potential for litigation to shape international climate governance and cooperation. In wrapping up, we underscore the importance of continued innovation, collaboration, and strategic legal approaches to address the urgent challenges posed by the climate crisis.

Advancing from the specifics of each chapter, we hope that this Handbook will serve as an essential catalyst, stimulating scholarly dialogue and encouraging the continued growth and dynamism of this field. From the outset, our aim has been to scrutinise a range of substantive issues that traverse jurisdictions, offering a rich exploration of the intersections between climate litigation and other legal domains and capturing national, regional, and international case law. However, we are aware that our coverage of issues has not been exhaustive – for example, we have paid relatively little attention to corporate law and competition law. Moreover, as the breadth and complexity of climate case law and related legal scholarship continue to evolve, new issues will arise, all meriting further scrutiny. One example is legal issues emerging from the development and implementation of novel carbon-neutral or carbon capture technologies.[18] Scholarship focusing on specific jurisdictions or regions will also remain relevant and needed as climate litigation evolves. In the meantime, we envisage this Handbook will act as a pivotal milestone in scholarship and practice on climate change litigation.

Finally, as we reflect on the journey of creating this Handbook, we cannot help but note the profound personal significance it has held for us. During the course of this project, we each welcomed a new child into our lives – Margaretha's son Amaian in 2021, and Sarah's son Rafael in 2023. The presence of these new lives, alongside Margaretha's daughter Adira, has served as a constant reminder of the vital importance of caregiving in the struggle for climate justice. It has underscored the need for transformative action across all sectors of society, including the legal and academic spheres.

In this context, we offer this Handbook as a resource for all those engaged in caregiving through the power of the law. We hope that the legal strategies and insights compiled here will not only inform and inspire those engaged in climate litigation but also contribute to the broader struggle for climate justice. Ultimately, our aim is to help build a world that fully supports and values the work of caregivers in all their diverse roles.

[18] Ian Havercroft and others (eds), *Carbon Capture and Storage: Emerging Legal and Regulatory Issues* (Bloomsbury Publishing 2018).

# 2

# A Scientific Overview of Climate Change

*Sarah Connors, Elvira Poloczanska, Shreya Some, Minal Pathak, and Joeri Rogelj**

## KEY MESSAGES

This chapter provides an overview of the science behind, the impacts of, and the adaptation and mitigation actions available to limit further changes to the climatic system. All messages come from reports of the latest (sixth) assessment cycle of the Intergovernmental Panel on Climate Change (IPCC).

After more than thirty years of the IPCC conducting assessments, the evidence that human activities have changed the climate is undisputable. Each assessment has significantly enhanced the scientific understanding and certainty regarding the causes and impacts of climate change. The IPCC's most recent assessment stipulates that human activities since 1850–1900 have 'unequivocally' caused global warming, with global surface temperature reaching 1.1°C (2°F) in the decade 2011–2020 (1.09 [0.95 to 1.20]°C). Greenhouse gas emissions over this period, predominantly from fossil fuel burning followed by land-use change, would have warmed the Earth *even more* than what has been observed but their total warming effect has been partly counteracted by air pollutant emissions, which have an overall cooling effect. Carbon dioxide is the greenhouse gas that contributes the most to the warming (~0.8°C), followed by methane (~0.5°C), nitrous oxide (~0.1°C), and fluorinated gases (~0.1°C). Natural climate variability, such as solar or volcanic activity, has had a negligible effect on global warming over this period.

The IPCC's assessments also provide increasingly detailed insight into the consequences of anthropogenic climate change. These consequences have propelled the

* Sarah Connors is a Climate Applications Scientist at the European Space Agency, formerly at IPCC Working Group 1 Technical Support Unit, Université Paris Saclay. Elvira Poloczanska is a Visiting Fellow, Plymouth Marine Laboratory, formerly at IPCC Working Group 2 Technical Support Unit, Alfred Wegener Institute. Shreya Some is a Postdoctoral Researcher at the Technical University of Denmark, formerly at IPCC Working Group 3 Technical Support Unit, Ahmedabad. Minal Pathak is an Associate Professor at Ahmedabad University, formerly at IPCC Working Group 3 Technical Support Unit, Ahmedabad, India. Joeri Rogelj is a Professor of Climate Science and Policy at Imperial College London and a (coordinating) lead author on the IPCC Special Report on Global Warming of 1.5°C and the IPCC Sixth Assessment Report.

Earth's climate into uncharted territory. Many of the climatic changes being felt across the globe are unprecedented in over hundreds, thousands, and even millions of years. Atmospheric carbon dioxide concentrations are at their highest in over two million years, for example. Anthropogenic or human-induced climate change, including more frequent and intense extreme events, has already caused widespread adverse impacts and related losses and damages to nature and people, beyond natural climate variability. The adverse effects of human-induced climate change are already felt in every region of the world. Risks of adverse impacts and related losses and damages escalate as global warming continues to rise, the risks being higher than present for global warming of 1.5°C, and even higher at 2°C.

The regional contributions of greenhouse gas emissions have been, and still are, vastly unequal. Countries that have contributed the least greenhouse gas emissions are disproportionately affected by these changes, as they are often more vulnerable and more at risk to these changes. They also have the least capacity to adapt to the adverse climate impacts. As of 2019, North America contributed the highest share of historical cumulative carbon dioxide emissions (23%) followed by Europe (16%) and East Asia (12%). Per capita emissions in 2019 show that Least Developed Countries (LDCs) and Small Island Developing States (SIDS) have much lower emissions than the global average. Globally, the top 10 per cent of households with the highest per capita emissions account for up to 45 per cent of global greenhouse gas emissions,[1] whereas the bottom 50 per cent of households only contribute up to 15 per cent of emissions.

Despite an overall slower growth between 2010–2019, global greenhouse gas emissions over this decade were higher than any other previous decade. Greenhouse gas emissions need to be reduced immediately and drastically in order to meet the long-term temperature goal of the Paris Agreement. To prevent further increases in temperatures, we need to either stop all carbon dioxide emissions from human activities or reach a point where any remaining emissions of carbon dioxide are balanced by activities that remove carbon dioxide from the atmosphere permanently – or at least for many centuries. We need to achieve net-zero carbon dioxide emissions by around 2050 to have *about a 50 per cent chance* that global temperatures will be limited to 1.5°C global warming. Near-term $CO_2$ emissions reductions over the coming years and until 2030 are critical to achieve a transformation in line with limiting warming to 1.5°C. Strong, rapid, and sustained reductions in other greenhouse gas emissions such as methane are also needed, which would also improve air quality. However, stabilising temperatures does not mean that global warming would go back down to previous levels, unless global net-negative carbon dioxide emissions can be achieved through which carbon dioxide is actively removed from the atmosphere. Many changes that are already observed cannot be reversed – only stopped, slowed, or stabilised.

[1] Consumption-based emissions, emissions released to the atmosphere in order to generate the goods and services consumed by a certain entity (e.g. a person, firm, country, or region).

Many climate changes and associated impacts respond roughly linearly to rising carbon emissions. This means that every increment of emissions leads to noticeable and discernible climate changes and impacts on nature and society. Adding further urgency to the call for action is that global temperatures will continue to increase until at least mid century under all emissions scenarios considered, even under strong mitigation scenarios. In addition, because some aspects of the climate respond very slowly to temperature changes, they will continue long after global temperature has stabilised: sea level rise, for example, is projected to still rise 2–3 metres (7–10 feet) over the coming 2,000 years even if global warming is stabilised at 1.5°C. The faster and the more greenhouse gas emissions are reduced, the more the world can avoid negative impacts and losses and damages.

Large gaps remain between the climate action needed, the action pledged, and the action being taken. The 2023 edition of the United Nations Environment Programme (UNEP) Emissions Gap Report indicated that Nationally Determined Contributions (NDCs), which report efforts by each country to reduce national emissions and adapt to climate change, available at that point in time would only hold global warming to 2.5–2.9°C over the course of the twenty-first century (with 66 per cent *likelihood*). Moreover, domestic climate policies are falling short of achieving the insufficient NDCs and would, without further strengthening, result in global warming of 3.0°C, with catastrophic consequences for people and ecosystems.[2]

Adaptation gaps also exist, between current levels of adaptation and levels needed to respond to impacts and reduce climate risks. Adaptation options, including ecosystem-based and most water-related options, become less effective with increasing warming and require long-term planning to maximise their efficiency. Moreover, there are limits to adaptation, some of which have already been crossed. This means that adaptation, while essential and in need of strengthening, cannot be the only response to tackle climate change; mitigation must be done as well. In addition, action and support are needed to address losses and damages.

The good news is that viable options exist for achieving rapid and dramatic decreases in greenhouse gas emissions. Ensuring that global emissions peak before 2025 and are reduced by at least 40–50 per cent by 2030 is consistent with pathways that limit global warming to 1.5°C with little or no overshoot.

Climate change is a global issue, and everyone has a role to play in halting further changes. Yet, historical contributions to climate change and current capabilities to address it vary significantly within and across regions. To reflect these differences and achieve a just transition, the regional contribution towards reducing global greenhouse gas emissions to achieve net-zero emissions will need to differ too. The IPCC assesses and reports on the literature discussing historical emissions, regional differentiation of efforts, and States' 'fair shares'. However, the IPCC does not recommend one

2 UNEP, 'The Emissions Gap Report 2023' (*UNEP*, 2023) <www.unep.org/resources/emissions-gap-report-2023> accessed 15 April 2024 (UNEP Emissions Gap Report 2023).

specific way of how mitigation efforts can be distributed fairly. The onus is on other various actors to develop mechanisms that address these critical issues around equity. National and regional courts are increasingly being asked to determine such questions relating to climate change and equity, including if the climate actions pledged by States are adequate in relation to their 'fair share' of what is globally required. This is important as it is only in relation to such a 'fair share' that the adequacy of a State's contribution can be assessed in the context of a global collective action problem.

Humanity stands at a crossroads. The scientific evidence is unequivocal: climate change has already caused severe harm to nature and people. The threats it poses to human societies and planetary health are unprecedented in scale and severity. Any further delay in concerted anticipatory global action on adaptation and mitigation will miss a brief and rapidly closing window of opportunity to secure a liveable and sustainable future for all.

## 2.1 INTRODUCTION

Described as the 'biggest threat modern humans have ever faced' by the UN Secretary General António Guterres in 2021,[3] climate change is a complex problem with widespread impacts that are already being felt across the world. These impacts will continue to be felt for millennia – and they are a result of human actions. The extent to which climate change can be limited or stopped depends on the actions taken now and in the coming decades.

This chapter serves as an introduction to the scientific understanding of climate change. It provides an overview of the science behind, the impacts of, and the adaptation and mitigation actions available to limit further changes. It offers a holistic understanding of the complex issue of climate change and its implications for society and the environment. The chapter is based on findings from the Sixth Assessment Report of the IPCC,[4] which was released in 2021–2022, and all key messages have traceable references to specific locations in the relevant reports, for readers who wish to learn more.

As the United Nations body for assessing the science related to climate change, the IPCC has produced reports on climate change for over thirty years. The IPCC contains three main working groups that cover different aspects of climate change: Working Group I looks at the physical climate changes, Working Group II considers the impacts these changes have on people and ecosystems, as well as how we can adapt to our changing climate, and Working Group III examines how climate change can be reduced or stopped (mitigation). The IPCC does not do its own research but bases its reports on the published scientific evidence (scientific literature, data, etc.).

3 'Climate Change "Biggest Threat Modern Humans Have Ever Faced", World-Renowned Naturalist Tells Security Council, Calls for Greater Global Cooperation' (*UN*, 2021) <https://press.un.org/en/2021/sc14445.doc.htm> accessed 15 April 2024.

4 See 'IPCC' <www.ipcc.ch/> accessed 15 April 2024.

Tens of thousands of scientific papers were assessed across the three working groups in its latest (sixth) assessment cycle by almost 1,000 scientists from across the world. Thousands more scientists contributed to the process by reviewing the report drafts.

Since the creation of the IPCC, each assessment cycle has provided input that has underpinned international climate policymaking. The First Assessment Report in 1990, for example, provided evidence that led to the creation of the United Nations Framework Convention on Climate Change (UNFCCC) and the Fifth Assessment Report contributed to the scientific foundation upon which the Paris Agreement was signed.

Each IPCC assessment cycle lasts approximately eight years, within which a set of reports are released. Its sixth cycle, completed in 2023, was the most comprehensive to date, releasing seven assessment reports on climate change and a methodological update to the IPCC Guidelines for National Greenhouse Gas Inventories. These reports are:

- The Special Report on Global Warming of 1.5°C (SR1.5, 2018)
- The Special Report on Climate Change and Land (SRCCL, 2019)
- The Special Report on the Ocean and Cryosphere in a Changing Climate (SROCC, 2019)
- 2019 Refinement to the 2006 IPCC Guidelines for National Greenhouse Gas Inventories (TFI, 2019)
- Working Group I: The Physical Science Basis (WGI, 2021)
- Working Group II: Impacts, Adaptation and Vulnerability (WGII, 2022)
- Working Group III: Mitigation of Climate Change (WGIII, 2022)
- The Synthesis Report (SYR, 2023)

The first IPCC report (1990)[5] concluded that human-caused climate change would soon become apparent but could not yet confirm that it was already happening. With more data and better models, scientists now understand much more about how the atmosphere interacts with the ocean, ice, snow, ecosystems, and land surfaces of the Earth. Computer climate simulations have also improved dramatically, incorporating many more natural processes and providing projections at much higher resolutions. Now, the evidence is overwhelming that human activities have changed the climate.[6]

This introductory section of the chapter continues with an overview of the components of the climate system, the carbon cycle, and the greenhouse gas effect, and exemplifies the natural and manmade causes of climate change. Section 2.2, 'The Scientific Consensus on Anthropogenic Climate Change', looks backwards to show the influence that humans have had on climate change to date – covering greenhouse gas emissions sources and trends, and the attribution of observed climate

5 John Houghton, Geoffrey Jenkins, and John Ephraums (eds), *IPCC* (Cambridge University Press 1990).

6 Frequently Asked Question 1.1, Delian Chen and others, 'Chapter 1: Framing, Context, and Methods' in Valerie Masson-Delmotte and others (eds), *Climate Change 2021: The Physical Science Basis. Contribution of Working Group I to the Sixth Assessment Report of the Intergovernmental Panel on Climate Change* (Cambridge University Press 2021) 147–286.

change and extreme weather events to human influence, as well as the impacts of these changes. Section 2.3, 'Anthropogenic Climate Changes and Impacts', looks at the present situation. It focuses on the current impacts of climate change, highlighting the widespread and unprecedented climate changes and their resulting impacts on ecosystems and societies. Section 2.4, 'Future Climate Change', then looks forward and presents future emissions scenarios and projected warming and impacts, highlighting both fast and slow onset climate changes. This section also discusses the increasing risks associated with climate change, regional variations, and the implications of overshooting a global warming of 1.5°C. Section 2.5, 'Mitigating Climate Change', evaluates progress toward the goals set in the Paris Agreement and explores strategies for stabilising global temperatures, including the concept of net-zero emissions and carbon budgets. Section 2.6, 'Adaptation and Resilience', delves into strategies for adapting to climate change and building resilience against its impacts.

### 2.1.1 *The Major Components of the Climate System*

The Earth's climate system is made up of several major components that are complex and interacting.[7] Together, they govern the Earth's climate patterns and conditions, changing over time.

The *atmosphere* is a protective layer of gases that surround the Earth's surface, which provides the air we breathe, regulates heat to keep the planet warm, and shields us from harmful UV radiation from the sun. The sun's heat and the Earth's rotation create movement in the atmosphere; these circulation patterns redistribute heat and moisture across the planet, influencing weather and climate.

The *biosphere* comprises all living organisms on Earth. It interacts with other climate components through processes like photosynthesis, respiration, and the carbon and nitrogen cycles, which can affect climate through altering greenhouse gas concentrations and the land surface. Together with the ocean, the land absorbs over half of the carbon dioxide emissions emitted by human activities.

The *hydrosphere* includes the liquid surface and subterranean water, such as in oceans, seas, rivers, freshwater lakes, underground water, wetlands, etc. Covering 70 per cent of the world's surface, the ocean has a huge capacity to absorb and hold heat, energy, and carbon dioxide. The ocean stores and transfers heat across the globe through its ocean currents and deepwater circulations, which in turn affects climate and weather patterns.

The *cryosphere* consists of the frozen parts of the Earth such as glaciers, sea ice, ice sheets, and snow. Cryospheric changes can affect other climate components

7 JB Robin Matthews and others (eds), 'IPCC 2021: Annex VII: Glossary' in Valerie Masson-Delmotte and others (eds), *Climate Change 2021: The Physical Science Basis. Contribution of Working Group I to the Sixth Assessment Report of the Intergovernmental Panel on Climate Change* (Cambridge University Press 2021) 2215–2256.

through processes like glacier and ice-sheet melt (impacting sea levels and ocean circulation) or through snow cover melt (impacting the Earth's energy budget by modifying its albedo – the amount of the sunlight reflected off the Earth's surface).

Finally, the *lithosphere* is the upper layer of the solid Earth (continental and oceanic). It can influence the climate through changes in albedo (how much heat a surface absorbs), through the effects of landforms on atmospheric circulation, and through the weathering of rocks that can affect greenhouse gases concentrations such as carbon dioxide.

The climate system is constantly changing with its components interacting with each other. Many other processes – both inside and outside the Earth – affect the climate system, and these are covered later in this chapter.

### 2.1.2 *Different Types of Scientific Evidence*

Scientific understanding of the climate system's features is robust and well established, based on multiple lines of scientific evidence. For centuries, scientists have been measuring and monitoring aspects of the climate system in order to understand how it works, what drives its changes, and to predict future weather. Weather observations of temperature and pressure have been made since the seventeenth century and the first published study that argued carbon dioxide could raise the Earth's temperature was published in the nineteenth century.[8] Observed evidence for carbon dioxide raising global temperatures was first reported in the early twentieth century.[9] The use of weather and climate observational evidence has steadily grown throughout the centuries. By the twentieth century, systematic and wide-ranging measurements were being made, particularly from the 1970s when satellite-based observations were established, offering near global coverage for many climate variables.

This observational evidence offers a powerful understanding of our climate – however, it is just one line of evidence that scientists use to understand the climate system. Using paleoclimate evidence,[10] scientists have reconstructed the Earth's past climate, dating back hundreds of millions of years into the past. For example, the frozen bubbles taken from ice cores hold information on past temperatures and atmospheric gas concentrations from hundreds of thousands of years ago. Similarly, marine sediment from rock cores can provide information on past temperature, ice volume, and sea level over millions of years. As well as giving relative comparisons for today's climate changes, these data tell us that the Earth in the past has experienced prolonged

8 Eunice Newton Foote, 'Circumstances Affecting the Heat of the Sun's Rays' (1865) 22(65) American Journal of Science and Arts 382–383.

9 Guy Stewart Callendar, 'The Artificial Production of Carbon Dioxide and Its Influence on Temperature' (1938) 64(275) Quarterly Journal of the Royal Meteorological Society 223–240.

10 Climate during periods prior to the development of measuring instruments, including historic and geologic time, for which only proxy climate records are available.

periods of elevated greenhouse gas concentrations that caused global temperatures and sea levels to rise. Studying past climate can therefore help us understand future consequences of increasing greenhouse gases in the atmosphere.

A third line of evidence comes from climate models, which are essential tools for scientists to simulate the Earth's complex climate system. Climate models are computer programs that simulate the Earth's climate, based on fundamental laws of physics, chemistry, and biology of the atmosphere, ocean, ice, and land. Some models include more processes, complexity, and detail than others, giving them different strengths and weaknesses, but their results can be tested by comparing them with past observations and paleo evidence. Climate models can be used to identify what has caused these past changes, and also to explore how the climate could change in the future under scenarios (see Section 2.4). Climate model complexity and the methods for projecting future changes have matured over the decades, but the IPCC concluded that the projections from even the early, simple climate models quite accurately projected what was subsequently observed.

Finally, scientific understanding of physical, chemical, biological, and geological processes that underpin how the climate works complement evidence from observations, paleoclimatology, and modelling. Ocean and atmospheric circulation, ice-sheet dynamics, radiative forcing (how substances alter the balance of energy entering and leaving the Earth's atmosphere), cycles such as the carbon or nitrogen cycles, and climate feedbacks (processes that lead to an amplification or a dampening of further climate changes) are all examples of climate processes.

Used together, these multiple lines of evidence provide the backbone of the scientific understanding of climate change. They enable scientists to test hypotheses, attribute the causes of climate change, and inform adaptation and mitigation decision making.[11] Other sources of knowledge, including Indigenous knowledge, can also provide important insight into climate change and its drivers, impacts, and possible responses.[12]

### 2.1.3 *Natural Variability of the Climate*

Today, the climate is warming almost everywhere across the globe. While global surface temperature has varied over millennia, the reason for recent warming is different.

Constructed using the lines of evidence described earlier, Figure 2.1 shows how atmospheric carbon dioxide levels (upper panel) and global surface temperature (lower panel) have varied over the past 60 million years and how they could evolve into the future, to the year 2300. Temperature changes are all relative to a baseline period just before the industrial revolution (1850–1900). There has always been a close relationship between

[11] Section 1.3.3, Chen and others (n 6).

[12] For example, Intergovernmental Panel on Climate Change, *AR6 Synthesis Report: Climate Change 2023* 107 <www.ipcc.ch/report/sixth-assessment-report-cycle/> accessed 15 April 2024.

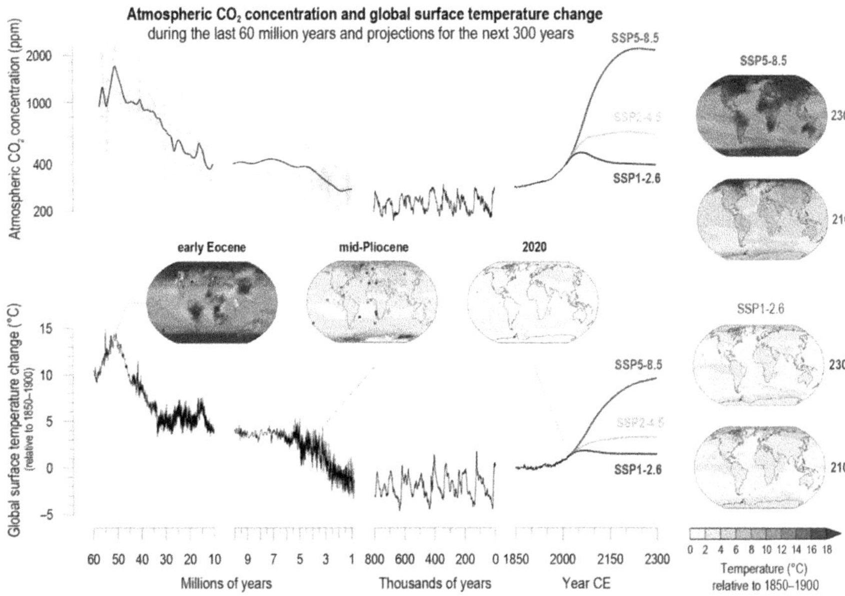


FIGURE 2.1 Historical records of global carbon dioxide concentration levels (parts per million, ppm) and temperature (°C) over the past 60 million years. For context, humans developed around 250,000 years ago, and agriculture only developed 10,000 years ago with a more stable and warmer climate.[13]

carbon dioxide and global temperature but the causes of these changes that are happening now are very different compared to the changes that have occurred in the past.

Natural causes of climate change refer to variations in climate that can be either *externally* driven by natural changes or *internally* generated within the climate system. Figure 2.1 shows how some external natural variability can operate on very long time scales (see the 800,000–0 years axis in Figure 2.1). These temperature and carbon dioxide changes result from changes in the Earth's orbit around the sun. These orbital changes alter the amount of energy absorbed by the Earth from the sun and operate over (very long) time scales of tens-to-hundreds of thousands of years.[14] These orbital shifts alone are not enough to explain the large changes in temperature seen in the past ice ages – global average temperature then was around 4°C cooler than it is today – but they kick-start other processes that further amplify the changes to

[13] Figure TS.1, Paola A Arias and others '2021: Technical Summary' in Valerie Masson-Delmotte and others (eds), *Climate Change 2021: The Physical Science Basis. Contribution of Working Group I to the Sixth Assessment Report of the Intergovernmental Panel on Climate Change* (Cambridge University Press 2021).

[14] Frequently Asked Question 3.2, Veronika Eyring and others, 'Chapter 3: Human Influence on the Climate System' in Valerie Masson-Delmotte and others (eds), *Climate Change 2021: The Physical Science Basis. Contribution of Working Group I to the Sixth Assessment Report of the Intergovernmental Panel on Climate Change* (Cambridge University Press 2021) 423–552.

temperature and carbon dioxide levels. More ice on the Earth's surface causes more of the sun's energy to be reflected back to space, therefore further cooling the Earth. This is one example of what is referred to as climate feedback. More ice in colder temperatures also means lower sea levels, which results in more land area and more growing vegetation that absorb carbon dioxide, thus lowering atmospheric levels. Volcanic eruptions are another example of *external* natural variability, as volcanoes are not part of the climate system but can still cause changes. Large volcanic eruptions can cool the Earth through the particles that they emit, acting as a shield to the sun's rays and reflecting back some incoming radiation. This effect is short-lived: the effect on surface temperature typically fades within a decade after the eruption.

Much like the effects of volcanic eruptions, effects of *internal* natural variability also span over shorter time frames of years to decades. *Internal* natural variability refers to when energy within the climate system redistributes among the different climate components (atmosphere, hydrosphere, etc.). These changes are more clearly observed regionally compared to on the global scale. One example of internal natural variability is El Niño–Southern Oscillation (ENSO), a climate pattern in the tropical Pacific that oscillates between two phases over a period of two to seven years. The ENSO phase influences a variety of weather phenomena around the world, intensifying heat extremes during the El Niño phase, for example.

Natural variability causes major year-to-year or even decadal changes in global surface climate, but over the longer term, it plays a smaller role. Over multiple decades or longer, the oscillations caused by natural variability are clearly discernible from long-term trends caused by human influence. When combined with human-caused climate changes, the consequences of natural variability can be either larger or smaller than initially projected. For those regions affected by ENSO, for example, the human-caused changes to rainfall and wildfires can be a bit larger, or smaller, for that short period of time. There is always a chance that future changes could be a bit stronger (or a bit weaker) than projected – but these natural factors will have little effect on long-term trends.[15]

By comparing today's temperature and carbon dioxide levels with past changes to the climate, it is clear that the recent warming is different from before. Carbon dioxide levels are already their highest in at least two million years. Global temperatures are their highest in at least 100,000 years. The speed of warming over the last 50 years was faster than any other 50-year period over the past 2,000 years. Recent warming reverses a long-term global cooling trend. After the last ice age, global surface temperature peaked around 6,500 years ago, then started to slowly decline. It was not until the mid nineteenth century that the long-term cooling trend started to reverse with now persistent and prominent warming. Today the climate is warming almost everywhere across the globe. Over the past 2,000 years, some regions have always experienced periods of more or less warming than the global average. For example, the North Atlantic region warmed more than many other regions during the tenth

[15] ibid.

and thirteenth centuries, but almost every region of the world is now experiencing sustained warming since the industrial revolution.[16]

The right-hand side of Figure 2.1 shows how global temperatures and carbon dioxide levels could evolve in the coming centuries depending on the choices made by society. Some projected global temperature changes would be larger than the Earth has experienced for over three million years. This is discussed further in Section 2.4.1.

### 2.1.4 *The Greenhouse Effect*

The Earth's energy budget describes the flow of energy within the climate system. Our planet receives vast amounts of energy every day in the form of sunlight. Around a third of the sunlight is reflected back to space by clouds, by tiny particles called aerosols, and by bright surfaces such as snow and ice. The rest is absorbed by the ocean, land, ice, and atmosphere. The planet then emits energy back out to space in the form of thermal radiation. In a world that was not warming or cooling, these energy flows would balance. Some gases in the atmosphere – such as carbon dioxide, methane, and nitrous oxide – warm the Earth by absorbing and then re-radiating some of the energy emitted by the planet as heat. These gases make it harder for heat to be released into outer space. Instead, it is transferred into the climate system.[17]

This effect is called the greenhouse effect, as the same mechanism occurs in a greenhouse, with walls of the greenhouse trapping warmer air inside, making it warmer than its surroundings. Facilitated by greenhouse gases occurring naturally in the atmosphere, the greenhouse effect is a natural process that makes the Earth liveable for humans: without the natural greenhouse effect, the global average temperature would be about 33°C (59°F) colder. However, human activities since the industrial revolution have led to additional, anthropogenic greenhouse gases accumulating in the atmosphere. These emissions result mostly from burning fossil fuels (coal, oil, and gas) but also from agriculture and cutting down forests. These actions have boosted the greenhouse effect, causing global warming and disruption of the climate system. The excess energy is taken up by different parts of the Earth: 91 per cent is absorbed by the oceans, 5 per cent is absorbed by the land, 3 per cent is absorbed by the ice. Only 1 per cent of

[16] Frequently Asked Question 2.1, Sergey K Gulev and others, '2021: Changing State of the Climate System' in Valerie Masson-Delmotte and others (eds), *Climate Change 2021: The Physical Science Basis. Contribution of Working Group I to the Sixth Assessment Report of the Intergovernmental Panel on Climate Change* (Cambridge University Press 2021). See also Sections A.2 & B.1, 'IPCC, 2021: Summary for Policymakers' in Valerie Masson-Delmotte and others (eds), *Climate Change 2021: The Physical Science Basis. Contribution of Working Group I to the Sixth Assessment Report of the Intergovernmental Panel on Climate Change* (Cambridge University Press 2021) (IPCC, 2021: Summary for Policymakers).

[17] Frequently Asked Question 7.1, Piers Forster and others '2021: The Earth's Energy Budget, Climate Feedbacks, and Climate Sensitivity' in Valerie Masson-Delmotte and others (eds), *Climate Change 2021: The Physical Science Basis. Contribution of Working Group I to the Sixth Assessment Report of the Intergovernmental Panel on Climate Change* (Cambridge University Press 2021).

the extra heat is absorbed by the atmosphere. Although the mechanism of the greenhouse effect is relatively simple, the causal mechanisms through which this imbalance in energy manifests itself throughout the climate system, and how these modifications impact societies and ecosystems across the globe, are more complex. The remainder of this chapter will delve into these complexities and unpack a wealth of scientific evidence demonstrating that the impacts of a changing climate have been and will continue to be profound and widespread.[18]

## 2.2 THE SCIENTIFIC CONSENSUS ON ANTHROPOGENIC CLIMATE CHANGE

This section introduces the science which shows that it is now unequivocal that human activities have caused global warming. It presents the sources and trends associated with global warming and shows how we can link that warming and other changes in the climate system to human influence.

### 2.2.1 *Greenhouse Gas Emissions Sources and Trends*

Since 1850, emissions of greenhouse gases into the atmosphere have steadily increased, totalling 2,400 ± 240 $GtCO_2$[19] until the year 2019. Despite the growth rate slowing in the 2010–2019 decade, the average greenhouse gas emissions over this decade were higher than any other previously recorded. Figure 2.2 shows how the net emissions of the major anthropogenic greenhouse gases have changed for the years 1990–2019. The largest amount of net emissions are of carbon dioxide. Emission totals for the year 2019 were calculated to be 59 ± 6.6 $GtCO_2$–eq,[20] which is 12 per cent higher than 2010 levels and 54 per cent higher than 1990 levels. The largest share and growth in greenhouse gas emissions comes from carbon dioxide emissions resulting from fossil fuels combustion and industrial processes (64% of 2019 emissions), followed by methane (18% of 2019 emissions). Of the 2019 emission total, 11 per cent was carbon dioxide emissions associated with land use and land-use change (e.g. deforestation).[21]

Both historically and at present, the regional distribution of emissions across the globe has been very unequal. Figure 2.3 shows the historical contribution (1850–2019) of carbon dioxide per region. Fossil fuel and industry and land use, land-use change, and forestry emissions are shown in panel (a). North America has contributed the highest share of historical carbon dioxide emissions (23%) followed by Europe (16%) and East Asia (12%).

[18] Section A.4, IPCC, 2021: Summary for Policymakers (n 16).

[19] Gt = gigatons. 1 Gt is 1 billion metric tonnes. 2400 $GtCO_2$ = 2,400,000,000,000 tonnes of $CO_2$.

[20] $CO_2$-equivalents ($CO_2$-eq) are calculated to compare different greenhouse gas emissions across a common scale. This calculation can vary depending on which greenhouse gas 'metric' is used. The IPCC report calculated the $CO_2$-eq for each greenhouse gas using the global warming potential with a time horizon of 100 years, or GWP-100.

[21] Section B.1, IPCC, 2021: Summary for Policymakers (n 16).

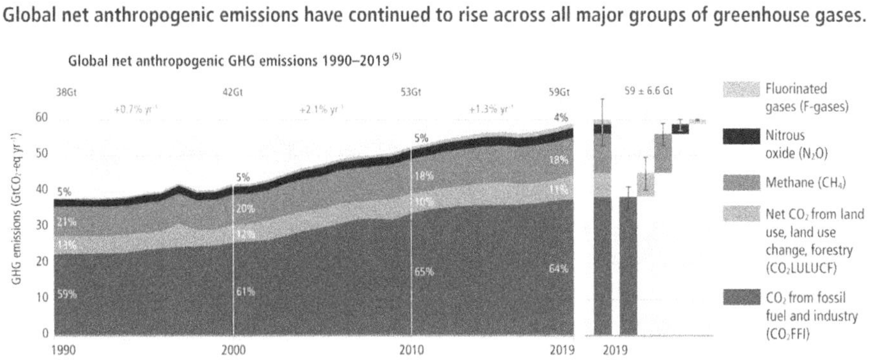


FIGURE 2.2 Global net anthropogenic GHG emissions ($GtCO_2$–eq $yr^{-1}$) 1990–2019. Global net anthropogenic GHG emissions include $CO_2$ from fossil fuel combustion and industrial processes ($CO_2$–FFI); net $CO_2$ from land use, land-use change, and forestry ($CO_2$–LULUCF); methane ($CH_4$); nitrous oxide ($N_2O$); and fluorinated gases (HFCs, PFCs, $SF_6$, $NF_3$). At the right side of the panel, associated uncertainties for each of the components for 2019 are shown.[22]

Panel (b) compliments the historical contributions by showing the 2019 contributions, including other major greenhouse gases, and is weighted by population across the regions, showing the per capita distributions. Taller, narrower rectangles represent regions with lower populations but larger emissions. North America still remains the region with the highest contribution to emissions on a per capita and total population basis.[23]

The global average emissions per person is 6.9 $tCO_2$–eq for the year 2019 (not including land-use-related emissions). Around 35 per cent of the global population live in countries emitting more than 9 $tCO_2$–eq per capita while 41 per cent live in countries emitting less than 3 $tCO_2$–eq per capita, and, of the latter, a substantial share lacks access to modern energy services. LDCs and SIDS have much lower per capita emissions than the global average (1.7 $tCO_2$–eq and 4.6 $tCO_2$–eq, respectively).[24]

Globally, the 10 per cent of households with the highest per capita emissions contribute 34–45 per cent of consumption-based household greenhouse gas emissions, while the bottom 50 per cent contribute 13–15 per cent.[25]

[22] Figure SPM.1, 'IPCC, 2022: Summary for Policymakers' in Priyadarshi Shukla and others (eds), *Climate Change 2022: Mitigation of Climate Change. Contribution of Working Group III to the Sixth Assessment Report of the Intergovernmental Panel on Climate Change* (Cambridge University Press 2022) (IPCC, 2022: Summary for Policymakers WG3).

[23] Section A.1, 'IPCC, 2023: Summary for Policymakers' in Hoesung Lee and others (eds), *Climate Change 2023: Synthesis Report. Contribution of Working Groups I, II and III to the Sixth Assessment Report of the Intergovernmental Panel on Climate Change* (Cambridge University Press 2023) (IPCC, 2023: Summary for Policymakers).

[24] ibid.

[25] ibid. In the IPCC, consumption-based emissions are defined as emissions released to the atmosphere in order to generate the goods and services consumed by a certain entity (e.g. a person, firm, country, or region).

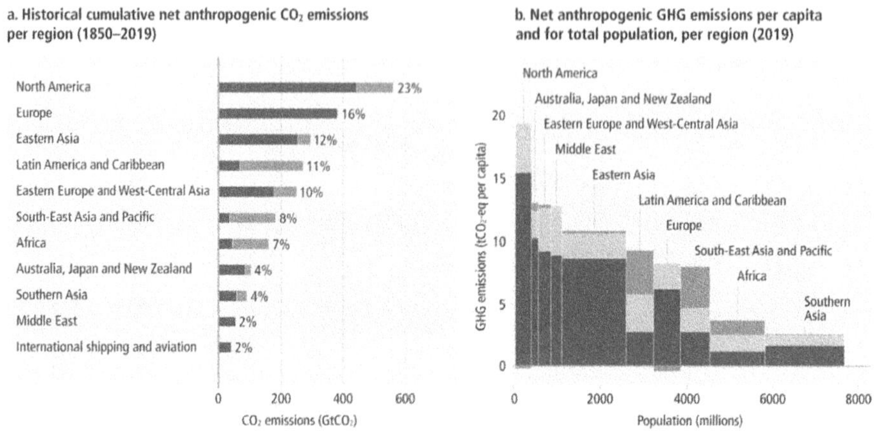


FIGURE 2.3 Regional differentiations of greenhouse gas emissions. **Panel (a)**: Cumulative regional carbon dioxide emissions from 1850 to 2019. **Panel (b)**: Regional GHG emissions in tonnes $CO_2$–eq per capita by region in 2019. Note that emissions from international aviation and shipping are not included. **Key:** Black = $CO_2$ from fossil fuel combustion and industrial processes ($CO_2$–FFI); Dark grey = net $CO_2$ from land use, land-use change, and forestry ($CO_2$–LULUCF); Light grey = Other GHG emissions.[26]

In 2015, countries adopted the Paris Agreement, which set a goal of holding 'the increase in the global average temperature to well below 2°C above pre-industrial levels' and pursuing efforts 'to limit the temperature increase to 1.5°C above pre-industrial levels'.[27] In order to achieve this long-temperature goal, immediate and drastic reductions of greenhouse gas emissions are needed. Regional contributions to these reductions should reflect the principles of 'equity' and 'common but differentiated responsibilities and respective capabilities', to enable a just transition.[28] In contrast to previous reports, the IPCC's Sixth Assessment Report does not provide quantitative indications of how these regional differences could be reflected in mitigation targets. The onus is therefore on other mechanisms and actors to specify equity principles and quantify their implications. National and regional courts are increasingly being asked to determine questions relating to climate change and equity, including if the climate actions pledged by States are adequate in relation to their fair share of what is globally required, as it is only in relation to such a 'fair share' that the adequacy of a State's contribution can be assessed in the context of a global collective action problem.[29]

26 Figure SPM.2, IPCC, 2022: Summary for Policymakers WG3 (n 22).

27 Paris Agreement (entered into force 4 November 2016) 3156 UNTS 79 (Paris Agreement) art 2(1)(a).

28 Box TS.4, Minal Pathak and others, '2022: Technical Summary' in Priyadarshi Shukla and others (eds), *Climate Change 2022: Mitigation of Climate Change. Contribution of Working Group III to the Sixth Assessment Report of the Intergovernmental Panel on Climate Change* (Cambridge University Press 2022).

29 This is discussed further in Chapter 13 on common but differentiated responsibilities and respective capabilities.

### 2.2.2 *Attributing Human Influence on the Climate*

Using the multiple lines of evidence described in this chapter's introduction (Section 2.1), the level of human influence on global warming and many other aspects of changes in the climate system are now known. Attributing the causes of climate change largely refers to three main concepts: the attribution of observed climate change to human influence, the attribution of weather and climate extreme events to human influence, and the attribution of impacts on ecosystems and human systems to changing climate and to human influence. This section provides an overview of the current evidence using attribution methods.[30] The following chapter on attribution science dives deeper into this topic.

#### 2.2.2.1 Attribution of Human Influence to Observed Climate Change

Since 1850–1900, human activities have unequivocally caused global warming, with global surface temperature reaching 1.1°C (2°F) in the decade 2011–2020 (1.09 [0.95 to 1.20]°C). All of the observed global surface temperature increase can be attributed to human activities, as Figure 2.4 shows. This figure uses evidence from 'fingerprint' attribution studies, which synthesise and compare information from climate models and observations. Panel (a) compares observations with climate simulations that take into account only natural drivers or natural and human drivers. It is only when climate model simulations include human-caused greenhouse gases that they can recreate temperature observations. By comparing the total observed warming (panel (b)) with the warming amount from different contributors (panel (c)), it can be seen that greenhouse gas emissions from human activities would have in fact warmed the Earth even more than what has been observed, by about 1.5°C (2.7°F) in total. Their total warming effect has been partly counteracted by emissions of air pollutants called aerosols, which have an overall cooling effect. Carbon dioxide is the greenhouse gas that contributes the most to the warming (~0.8°C), followed by methane (~0.5°C), nitrous oxide (~0.1°C), and fluorinated gases (~0.1°C). Solar and volcanic drivers of the climate changed temperatures by –0.1°C to 0.1°C, and internal variability changed it by –0.2°C to 0.2°C.[31]

Human influence on multiple other changes occurring in the climate system has also been attributed. The IPCC assessment attributes human influence as the 'main driver' (contributing more than 50 per cent) of, or as a contributor to, the following changes. The level that human influence is attributable as the main driver is expressed using a likelihood phrasing that has a probabilistic definition or

[30] Cross-Working Group Box on Attribution in Chen and others (n 6).
[31] Section A.1, IPCC, 2023: Summary for Policymakers (n 23).

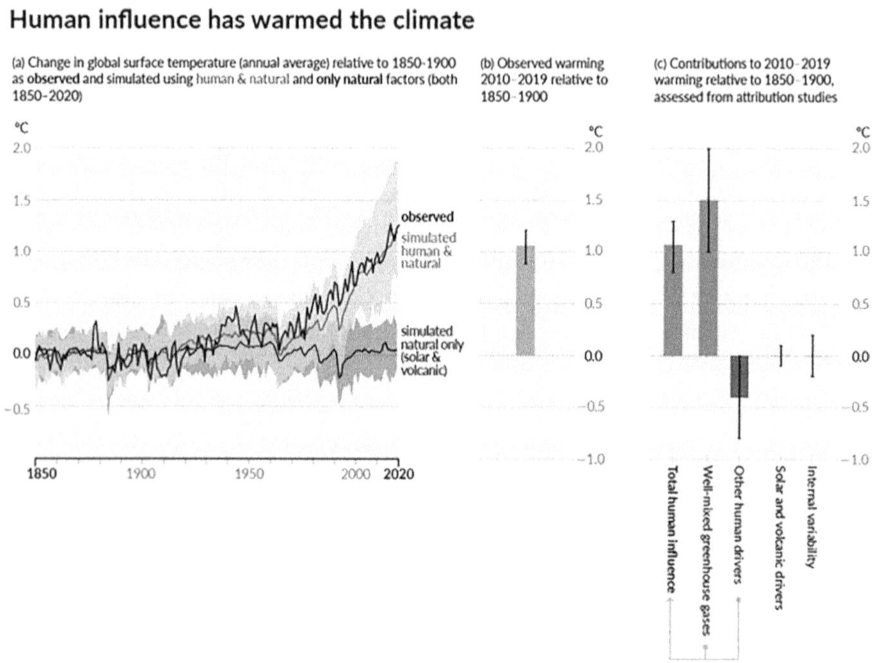


FIGURE 2.4 Observed warming is caused by emissions from human activities, with greenhouse gas warming partly masked by aerosol cooling. **Panel (a)**: Changes in global surface temperature over the past 170 years (thick black line) relative to 1850–1900 and annually averaged, compared to climate model simulations (CMIP6) of the temperature response to both human and natural drivers (dark grey line and shading), and to only natural drivers (solar and volcanic activity) (light grey line and shading). Solid lines show the multi-model average, and shading shows the very likely range of simulations. **Panel (b)**: The bar shows the observed increase of global surface temperature in 2010–2019 relative to 1850–1900 and its uncertainty range (black error bar line). **Panel (c)**: Temperature change in 2010–2019 relative to 1850–1900 attributed to total human influence, change in well-mixed greenhouse gases concentrations, other human drivers (aerosols, ozone, and land-use change), natural drivers (solar and volcanic), and internal climate variability. Whiskers show uncertainty ranges (black error bar lines).[32]

a qualitative phrasing of confidence. Note that if no *confidence* or *likelihood* term is stated in the list then the change has only been observed and not fully attributed. *Confidence* and *likelihood* terms are defined using the IPCC guidelines.[33]

[32] Figure adapted from Figures SPM.1 and SPM.2, IPCC, 2021: Summary for Policymakers (n 16).

[33] All IPCC Sixth Assessment Reports use two variables to communicate the degree of certainty associated with a specific finding: confidence (a qualitative measure based on the amount of evidence and the degree of agreement) and likelihood (a quantitative measure expressed probabilistically). A level of confidence is expressed using five qualifiers: *very low*, *low*, *medium*, *high*, and *very high*. The following terms are used to indicate the assessed likelihood of an outcome or result: *virtually certain* 99–100% probability; *extremely likely* 95–100%; *very likely* 90–100%; *likely* 66–100%; *more likely than not* >50–100%; *about as likely as not* 33–66%; *unlikely* 0–33%; *very unlikely* 0–10%; *extremely*

- The global retreat of glaciers (*very likely* main driver of, since the 1990s).
- The decrease in Arctic sea-ice area (*very likely* main driver of, since the late twentieth century).
- Decreased northern hemisphere spring snow cover (*very likely* main driver of, since 1950).
- The surface melting of the Greenland Ice Sheet (*very likely* main driver of, over the past two decades).
- Global mean sea level rise (*very likely* main driver of, at least since the 1970s), the rate of which has since been accelerating, as ice-sheet and glacier mass loss are now the dominant contributors to rising global mean sea level.
- The warming of the global upper ocean (*extremely likely* main driver of, since the 1970s).
- Global acidification of the surface open ocean (*virtually certain* main driver of).
- Reduced oxygen levels in many upper ocean regions (*medium confidence* contributed to, since the mid twentieth century).
- Changes in near-surface ocean salinity (*extremely likely* contributed to).
- Increased globally averaged precipitation over land (*likely* contributed to, since 1950), with a faster rate of increase since the 1980s.
- The shift of mid-latitude storm tracks polewards in both hemispheres (since the 1980s).
- The poleward shift of the southern hemisphere extratropical jet in austral summer (*very likely* contributed to, since the 1980s).
- A shift polewards of climate biosphere zones in both hemispheres (since the 1970s), and the growing season has on average lengthened in the Northern Hemisphere extratropics (since the 1950s).

#### 2.2.2.2 Attribution of Weather and Climate Extreme Events to Human Influence

It is also now possible to attribute the change in likelihood or characteristics of specific regional weather or climate events or classes of events to underlying drivers, including human influence. Extreme events where an attributable human influence have been identified include hot and cold temperature extremes (including some with widespread impacts), heavy precipitation events, certain types of droughts, and tropical cyclones.[34]

Human-induced climate change is already affecting many weather and climate extremes. In previous IPCC reports, it was not possible to say if or how much human-caused climate change contributed to individual extreme events, but this is now

*unlikely* 0–5%; and *exceptionally unlikely* 0–1%. See 'Guidance Note for Lead Authors of the IPCC Fifth Assessment Report on Consistent Treatment of Uncertainties' <www.ipcc.ch/site/assets/uploads/2018/05/uncertainty-guidance-note.pdf> accessed 15 April 2024.

[34] Cross-Working Group Box on Attribution in Chen and others (n 6).

possible with the development of new scientific methods. For most of these extremes, the extent to which human influence is the main driver of or has contributed to these climate changes can be described using a *likelihood* or *confidence* phrasing.[35]

- Hot extremes have become more frequent and more intense across most land regions (*high confidence* main driver of, since the 1950s). The occurrence of some hot extremes would have been *extremely unlikely* to occur without human influence over the past decade. On a global scale, hot extreme events that used to have a one-in-fifty-year likelihood during the pre-industrial period have now become approximately five times more probable due to human activities. Similarly, events with a one-in-ten-year probability have become almost three times more likely.
- Cold extremes have become less frequent and less severe (*high confidence* main driver of, since the 1950s).
- Increased marine heatwaves (*very likely* contributed to, since at least 2006). Marine heatwaves have approximately doubled in frequency since the 1980s.
- Increased frequency and intensity of heavy precipitation over land where data allows for analysis (*likely* contributed to, since the 1950s).
- Increased agricultural and ecological droughts in some regions due to increased land evapotranspiration (*medium confidence* contributed to, since the 1950s).
- Increased occurrences of the major (Category 3–5) tropical cyclones (since the 1970s).
- Although there has been no overall increase in the annual number of tropical cyclones, they are now *likely* stronger (the proportion of Category 3–5 tropical cyclones has increased since the 1970s) and this cannot be explained by only natural variability.
- Increased heavy precipitation associated with tropical cyclones (supported by attribution studies and physical process understanding but not observed on the global scale due to data limitations).
- Increased chance of compound extreme events (since the 1950s). Compound extreme events are the combination of multiple drivers and/or hazards that contribute to societal or environmental risk and include concurrent heatwaves and droughts, fire weather in some regions of all inhabited continents, and compound flooding.
- Human activities have impacted the global monsoon system, although in this case there is a complex interplay between the influence of climate-warming greenhouse gases and other types of air pollution.

Figure 2.5 is a synthesis of assessed observed and attributable regional changes. It shows that human-caused climate change has already affected *all* inhabited regions around

[35] Section A.3, IPCC, 2021: Summary for Policymakers (n 16).

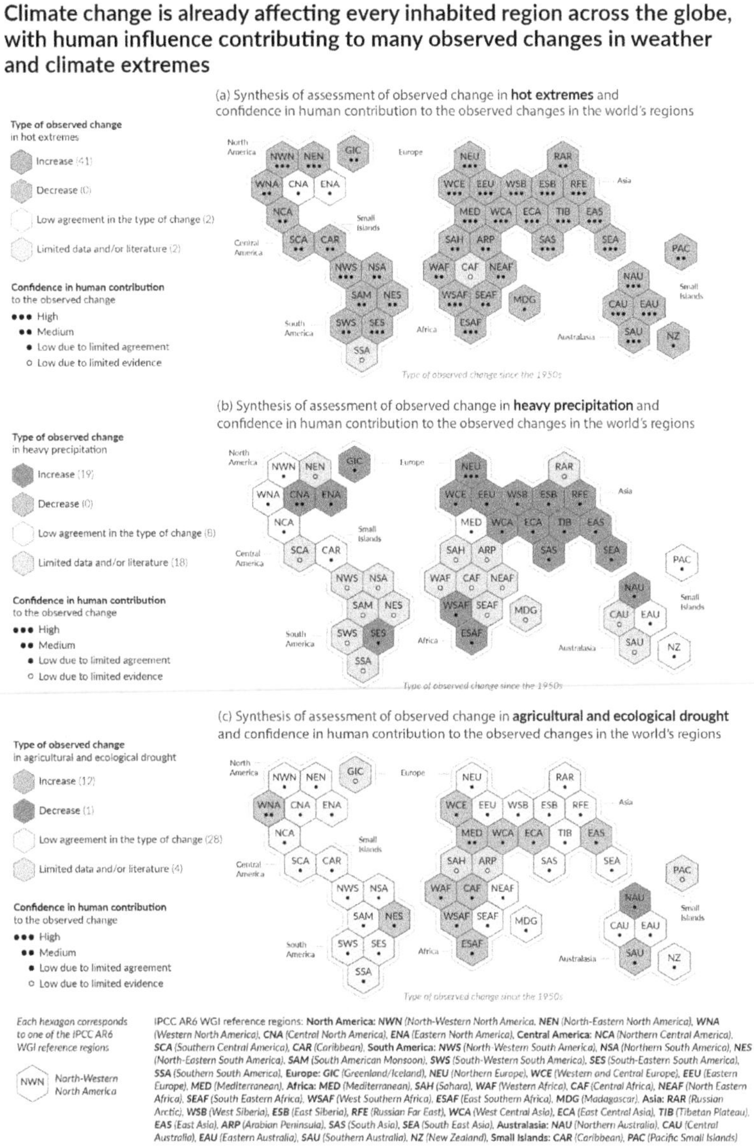


FIGURE 2.5 Synthesis of assessed observed and attributable regional changes for (a) hot extremes (b) heavy precipitation and (c) agricultural and ecological drought. The inhabited regions as defined in the IPCC Working Group I Sixth Assessment Report are displayed as hexagons with identical size in their approximate geographical location. The shading of each hexagon corresponds to observed changes. The dots within each hexagon indicate the level of confidence in the human contribution to these changes. All assessments are made for the 1950s to the present. White and light-grey striped hexagons are used where there is low agreement in the type of change for the region as a whole, and light grey hexagons are used when there is limited data and/or literature that prevents an assessment of the region as a whole.[36]

[36] Figure SPM.3, IPCC, 2021: Summary for Policymakers (n 16).

the world through occurrences of hot extremes, heavy precipitation events, and agricultural and ecological droughts. When the IPCC was first established, it was not possible to confirm that climate change was already happening, but now we are able to actually observe and attribute changes all across the world of human-caused climate change.

## 2.3 ANTHROPOGENIC CLIMATE CHANGES AND IMPACTS

This section highlights the widespread and unprecedented climate changes already being experienced worldwide and the corresponding present-day impacts on ecosystems and societies.

### 2.3.1 *Widespread, Unprecedented Climate Changes*

The influence of human activities is propelling the Earth's climate into uncharted territory. Many of the climate changes being felt across the globe are unprecedented in over hundreds, if not thousands, or even millions, of years. Continued increases in atmospheric greenhouse gas concentrations reached annual averages of 410 parts per million (ppm) for carbon dioxide, 1,866 parts per billion (ppb) for methane, and 332 ppb for nitrous oxide in 2019. These levels were higher than any time in at least two million years for carbon dioxide and 800,000 years for methane and nitrous oxide. Global surface temperatures have increased faster since 1970 than in any other 50-year period over at least the last 2,000 years. Each of the last four decades has been warmer than any previous decade since 1850 and the years 2011–2020 were the warmest decade the world has experienced in at least the last 100,000 years. The area of the Arctic Ocean covered by sea ice in the summer is now 40 per cent smaller than in the 1980s. It is the smallest it has been for at least 1,000 years. The near global retreat of all glaciers since the 1950s is unprecedented in at least the last 2,000 years. By absorbing carbon dioxide from the atmosphere, the ocean is becoming more acidic. The surface water of the ocean is now unusually acidic compared with the last two million years. Global mean sea level has risen ~0.20m between 1901 and 2018. This increase was faster than in any preceding century over the last 3,000 years. The global ocean has warmed faster in the past century than during the end of the last deglacial transition around 11,000 years ago.[37]

### 2.3.2 *Resulting Impacts on Ecosystems and Societies*

Human-induced climate change, including more frequent and intense extreme events, has caused widespread adverse impacts and related losses and damages to nature and people, beyond natural climate variability (Figure 2.6). They manifest as

37 Section A.2, IPCC, 2021: Summary for Policymakers (n 16).

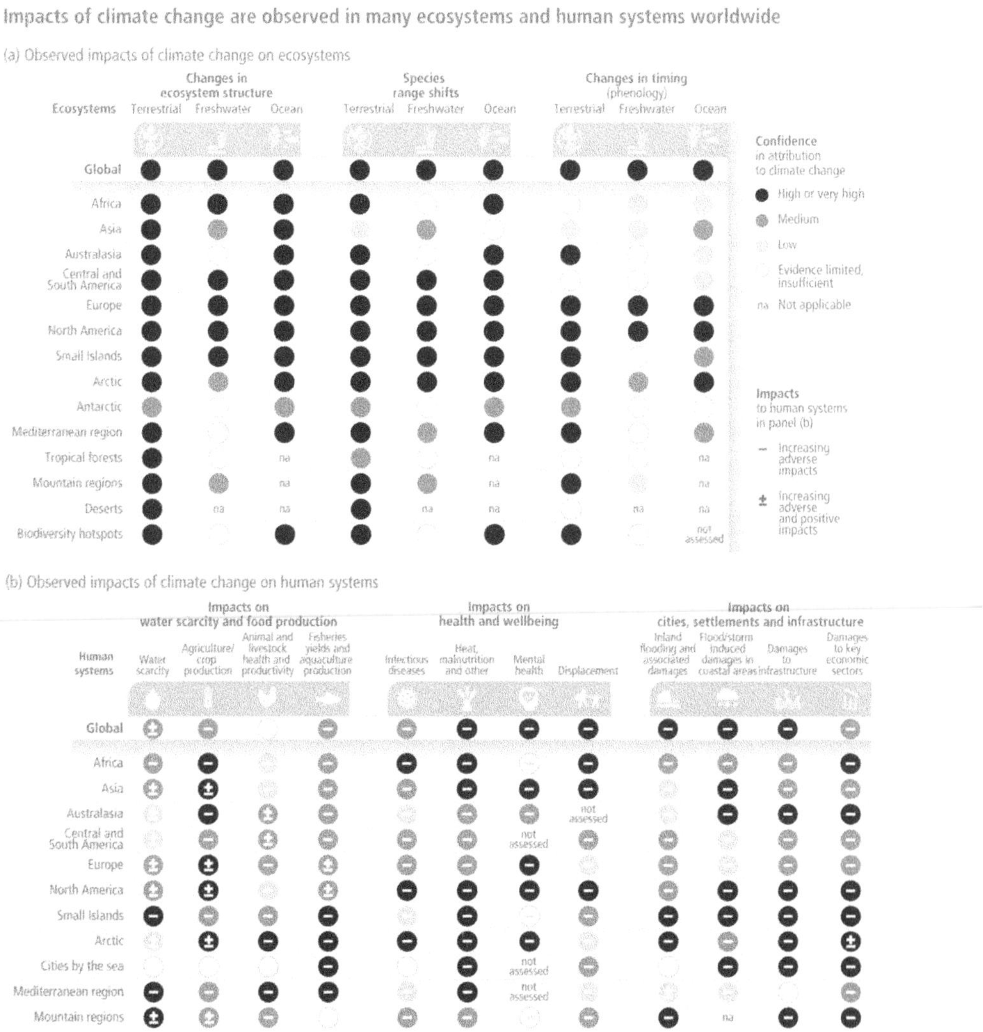


FIGURE 2.6 Observed global and regional impacts on (a) ecosystems and (b) human systems attributed to climate change at global and regional scales. Confidence levels in the attribution of the observed impacts to climate change are given. Global assessments focus on large studies, multi-species, meta-analyses, and large reviews. For that reason, they can often be assessed with higher confidence than regional studies, which often rely on smaller studies that have more limited data. Regional assessments consider evidence on impacts across an entire region. For human systems (b), the + and – symbols indicate the direction of observed impacts, with a – denoting an increasing adverse impact and a ± denoting that, within a region or globally, both adverse and positive impacts have been observed.[38]

[38] Figure SPM.2, 'IPCC, 2022: Summary for Policymakers' in Hans O Pörtner and others (eds), *Climate Change 2022: Impacts, Adaptation, and Vulnerability. Contribution of Working Group II to the Sixth Assessment Report of the Intergovernmental Panel on Climate Change* (Cambridge University Press 2022) (IPCC, 2022: Summary for Policymakers WG2).

the consequence of a spectrum of climatic events, ranging from the sudden intensity of extreme occurrences like heatwaves, floods, storm surges, hurricanes, and cyclones to the gradual onset of phenomena such as increasing temperatures, glacial retreat, prolonged droughts, ocean acidification, and rising sea levels. Impacts on terrestrial, freshwater, and ocean ecosystems include species losses and changes in timing such as flowering and growing seasons.

Climate change has resulted in a wide array of detrimental impacts on human systems, spanning from water security and food production to health and overall well-being, as well as impacts on urban areas, communities, infrastructure, and economies. The most vulnerable countries and communities, which historically are those that have contributed the least to current climate change, are disproportionately impacted with devastating consequences on their lives and livelihoods. Some examples of impacts, detailed in the IPCC WGII report, are given later.

#### 2.3.2.1 Impacts on Ecosystems

Climate change has altered terrestrial, freshwater, and ocean ecosystems. Observed impacts include local species losses and shifts in ecosystem composition, alterations in the geographical distribution of species, pests, and diseases, and changes in the timing of seasonal events (phenology) such as animal migration or plant flowering. Of the thousands of species assessed around the world, approximately half show shifts in geographical distributions towards the poles or to higher elevations on land. At higher latitudes, warming has expanded the available habitable areas but has also altered the timing of biological events such as flowering, breeding, and migrations. This can result in potential mismatches between, for example, plant flowering and pollinator appearance, insect availability, and bird breeding, or plankton blooms and the appearance of young fish.

Losses of local plant and animal populations have been widespread and many are associated with large increases in hottest yearly temperatures and heatwaves on land and in the ocean. Examples of such events include large-scale coral reef bleaching and death, mass mortalities of wildlife such as fruit bats on land and fish in lakes and coastal waters, death of mangroves along tropical coastlines, and increases in forest and grassland area burned by wildfires. Some of these losses are already becoming irreversible as species and ecosystems, such as coral reefs, are pushed beyond their natural abilities to adapt. Species extinctions are an irreversible impact; there is now evidence of two species extinctions driven by climate change.

The close interlinkages between climate, nature, and people mean that climate-driven impacts on ecosystems have consequences for food and water supply, human health, livelihoods, well-being, and other essential aspects of human life. Human communities, particularly Indigenous Peoples and those dependent on the environment for their subsistence and well-being, are already being negatively impacted. In addition, climate change impacts interact with other societal and environmental challenges such as biodiversity loss from overexploitation and habitat destruction, unsustainable land-use change, unsustainable consumption and production, socioeconomic development patterns, and historical and ongoing patterns of inequity; these can reinforce and intensify the impacts of climate change.[39]

### 2.3.2.2 Impacts on Humanity

2.3.2.2.1 FOOD AND WATER SECURITY Many millions of people are experiencing climate change through impacts on food and water security. Changes in the hydrological cycle have exposed more people to the hazards of floods and droughts exacerbating existing water-related vulnerabilities caused by socioeconomic factors. Mortality rates from floods, droughts, and storms were fifteen times higher in highly vulnerable countries compared to less vulnerable ones over 2010–2020. Currently, nearly half of the world's population experiences severe water scarcity for at least one month each year due to climatic and other factors. Approximately half a billion people now reside in areas where precipitation levels have increased to historically unfamiliar levels, mainly in the mid and high latitudes, while around 163 million people live in areas that have become unusually dry.

Droughts, floods, heatwaves including marine heatwaves, and variable rainfall have contributed to reduced food availability and higher food prices, posing significant threats to food and nutrition security and the livelihoods of millions globally. For instance, human-induced global warming has slowed agricultural productivity growth in mid and low latitudes over the past five decades. It has also negatively impacted crop and grassland quality, as well as the stability of harvests. In many regions, direct and indirect impacts of climate change, compounded by overfishing, has resulted in declines in fishery catches. It is estimated that ocean warming has reduced the global sustainable potential catches of several fish populations by 4.1 per cent between 1930 and 2010. The detrimental effects of climate-related extremes on water and food security, nutrition, and livelihoods are particularly severe in sub-Saharan Africa, Asia, small islands, Central and South America, the Arctic, and among small-scale food producers globally.[40]

2.3.2.2.2 DISEASE, ILLNESS, AND DEATH Climate change is causing the expansion of disease-carrying vectors such as ticks, flies, and mosquitoes to new areas, leading to the spread of diseases. Climate-related food-borne and water-borne diseases are rising in some regions. Factors like higher temperatures, heavy rainfall, and flooding are linked to the increased occurrences of diarrheal illnesses such as cholera and other gastrointestinal infections. Increased exposure to wildfire smoke in various

[39] Sections B1 and B2, IPCC, 2022: Summary for Policymakers WG2 (n 38).
[40] ibid.

regions is associated with climate-sensitive cardiovascular and respiratory diseases. Although not well assessed in many regions, there is evidence of impacts on mental health arising from impacts on lives, livelihoods, and culture.

Rising temperatures and heatwaves are causing higher rates of human mortality and morbidity with some regions already experiencing heat stress conditions at or approaching the upper limits for human survival. Impacts vary by age, gender, and socioeconomic factors. A significant proportion of warm-season heat-related mortality in temperate regions is attributed to observed human-induced climate change. However, data limitations make it challenging to establish such attribution in tropical areas. Groups highly vulnerable to heat stress include anyone working outdoors and, especially, those doing outdoor manual labour (e.g. construction and outdoor workers, farming), leading to lost productivity with economic consequences.[41]

2.3.2.2.3 VULNERABILITY AND MIGRATION The most vulnerable and thus the hardest hit by climate change include marginalised groups, Indigenous Peoples, and those living in poverty. About 3.3–3.6 billion people are living in contexts that are highly vulnerable to climate change. Global hotspots of high human vulnerability are found particularly in West, Central, and East Africa; South Asia; Central and South America; SIDS; and the Arctic. There is also increased evidence that extreme events and climate variability act as and compound drivers of involuntary migration and displacement and as indirect drivers through deteriorating climate-sensitive livelihoods. Since 2008, on average, over 20 million people a year have been internally displaced (within national boundaries) by extreme events, in particular storms and floods, with the largest numbers of displaced people in Asia and sub-Saharan Africa. Small island States in the Caribbean and Pacific are highly affected relative to their small population sizes.[42]

2.3.2.2.4 ATTRIBUTING HUMAN-INDUCED CLIMATE CHANGE TO SOCIETAL IMPACTS Attributing human-induced climate change to societal impacts is an accounting of the causes of impacts on human or environmental systems. It encompasses a wide range of methods, both qualitative and quantitative, that connect a change in a natural or human system (e.g. crop yields, species populations, human health) to changes in climate – or environmental – related systems (i.e. temperature change, ocean acidification, sea level rise). It requires accounting for other potential drivers of change. For example, changes in human population patterns, or technological and economic changes in agriculture affecting crop production. Impact attribution does not always involve attribution to human-induced climate change; however, a growing number of studies now include this aspect. Assessment

41 ibid.
42 ibid.

of multiple independent lines of evidence, taken together, can provide rigorous attribution when more quantitative approaches are not available.[43]

## 2.4 FUTURE CLIMATE CHANGE

This section looks ahead and presents the various ways that climate change may evolve in the future.

### 2.4.1 *Climate Scenarios and Future Global Temperatures*

The climate we and the young generations will experience depends on future emissions. Reducing emissions rapidly will limit further changes, but continued emissions will trigger larger changes that will increasingly affect all regions. Many changes will persist for hundreds or thousands of years, so today's choices will have long-lasting consequences.

To study how climate change can evolve into the future, the scientific community often uses scenarios. The IPCC defines scenarios as 'plausible description[s] of how the future may develop based on a coherent and internally consistent set of assumptions about key driving forces and relationships'. In addition, the IPCC notes that scenarios 'are neither predictions nor forecasts, but are used to provide a view of the implications of developments and actions'.[44] The driving forces in the IPCC's definition of scenarios can refer to assumptions about economic and population growth, inequality, technological innovation and costs, or dietary or other societal preferences, amongst many other things.[45] The relationships referred to in the definition indicate that not any combination of assumptions is possible. For example, it is highly unlikely that an unequal world with low educational attainment or low levels of female education would see the highest rates of technological innovation.

Climate change scenarios are created and assessed by different types of scientific models. A first type of model known as Integrated Assessment Models (IAMs) creates emissions scenarios. Emissions scenarios describe how society can meet its future energy, food, and other demands while limiting climate change, and report the implied resulting greenhouse gas emissions. These emissions scenarios are subsequently used by a different type of model, typically referred as climate models, to estimate how these emissions would affect future climate change. These climate models report how temperature, precipitation, or humidity might change in the future, when a specific emissions scenario is followed. Socioeconomic or ecological

43 Renée van Diemen and others (eds), 'IPCC, 2022: Annex I: Glossary' in Priyadarshi Shukla and others (eds), *Climate Change 2022: Mitigation of Climate Change. Contribution of Working Group III to the Sixth Assessment Report of the Intergovernmental Panel on Climate Change* (Cambridge University Press 2022).

44 ibid.

45 ibid.

impacts are then explored by a last type of model, known as impact models. Using climate change scenario information from IAMs and climate models, these specialised models estimate the climate change impact of an emissions scenario for a specific sector or system, be it agriculture, flood risks, human health, and many more.

Because the range of possible futures is large, the scientific community has developed a framework to explore scenarios in a more systematic way. This is known as the framework of the Shared Socioeconomic Pathways or SSPs. The SSPs describe five distinct future socioeconomic contexts (SSP1 to SSP5) that differ between them in the degree to which mitigation and adaptation efforts experience challenges. For example, SSP1, called Sustainability, sketches a future socioeconomic context with reducing inequalities, increasing international collaboration and innovation, and a switch to healthy and environmentally conscious lifestyles. In an SSP1 world, implementing adaptation and mitigation measures is considered to encounter only low challenges. On the contrary, SSP3, called Regional Rivalry, describes a world with resurgent nationalism, exacerbating inequalities both within and between countries, and consequently low levels of technological innovation. Such an SSP3 world reflects a context with high challenges to effectively implement adaptation and mitigation measures. Other SSPs describe other socioeconomic futures with SSP2 covering a middle-of-the-road scenario that continues historical dynamics. For each of these SSP futures, the scientific community then explores how low global warming can be kept or what the implications of global warming are for adaptation and impacts.[46] Despite their usefulness, the SSPs do not exhaustively cover the space of future socioeconomic possibilities. Both the scientific literature and the IPCC therefore make use of scenarios that are entirely independent of the SSPs, for example, exploring strong improvements in energy efficiency and reducing energy demand.[47]

The IPCC also makes use of scenarios to integrate insights across chapters and reports. For example, the Physical Science report (Working Group I) of the IPCC Sixth Assessment uses a selection of five emissions scenarios, discussed later on (see also Figure 2.7). These span a range from very high to very low future greenhouse gas emissions and allow climate change projections from climate models to be easily compared and assessed. In contrast, the Mitigation report (Working Group III) of the IPCC Sixth Assessment is tasked with the assessment of the entire climate scenario literature. They therefore take a different approach. On the one hand, they collect as many emissions scenarios as possible from the published literature in a centralised database that underpins the broader IPCC assessment.[48] The large set of emissions scenarios that is included in this database helps to explore

46 Box SPM.1, IPCC, 2021: Summary for Policymakers (n 16).
47 ibid.
48 Edward Byers and others, 'AR6 Scenarios Database' available at <https://doi.org/10.5281/zenodo.5886912> accessed 15 April 2024.

the many potential strategies that can be pursued for limiting global warming to a specific level. To showcase this variety even more clearly, the IPCC also selected a small set of seven 'illustrative mitigation pathways' which illustrate the diverse strategies that can be followed while reducing greenhouse gas emissions. Finally, IPCC scenario databases are also made freely available online for further use and analysis by others.[49]

Five scenarios showing how carbon dioxide emissions could change in the future are shown in Figure 2.7. These scenarios are based on the five core SSP scenarios referred to earlier. The lower part of Figure 2.7 (panel (a)) depicts the projected warming for each of these emissions scenarios. It shows that global warming continues to rise until at least around 2050 in all of the five scenarios. This is because the human activities that cause greenhouse gas emissions cannot stop immediately. Even with ambitious action, it will take time to implement actions to reduce greenhouse gas emissions, resulting in a continued increase in temperatures before stabilising. Nevertheless, strong reductions in greenhouse gases starting now would slow and reduce the total amount of warming. Projected temperatures look very different after the 2050s, depending on the actions we take now and in the near future. For example, if carbon dioxide emissions are strongly and rapidly reduced starting now and throughout the twenty-first century, warming would be halted by around the middle of the century, reaching around 1.5°C (2.7°F) or 2°C (3.6°F) by the end of the century. On the other hand, if emissions remain the same or increase, temperatures will continue to rise. In scenarios that look at very high levels of greenhouse gas emissions, warming reaches around 4.5°C (8°F) by the end of the century.

These climate scenarios show that the world will most likely reach 1.5°C (2.7°F) global warming within the period 2021–2040.[50] Unless there are rapid, strong, and sustained reductions in greenhouse gas emissions, limiting warming to 1.5°C (2.7°F) or even 2°C (3.6°F) will be impossible.[51] The following section assesses the projected warming associated with countries' current NDCs and climate policies.

### 2.4.2 *Fast and Slow Onset Climate Changes*

Looking ahead, many aspects of climate change will continue to increase or intensify as the Earth becomes warmer. Extremes such as heatwaves, heavy rainfall, and droughts will continue to become more severe and more frequent. Rising temperatures and worsening extreme events are examples of so-called climate change 'fast' responses because they react relatively quickly to rising atmospheric greenhouse

[49] 'AR6 Scenario Explorer and Database hosted by IIASA' available at <https://data.ene.iiasa.ac.at/ar6/> accessed 15 April 2024.

[50] In the IPCC's reports, a level of global warming is defined as the 20-year average global surface temperature change relative to 1850–1900.

[51] Section B.1, IPCC, 2023: Summary for Policymakers (n 23). See also Section 2.5.1.

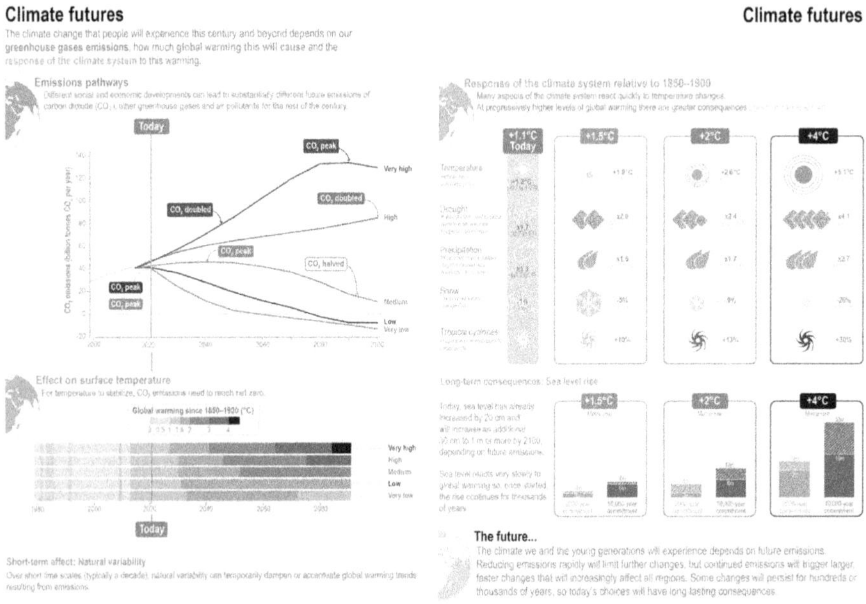


FIGURE 2.7 Linking carbon dioxide emissions, global warming, and effects on the climate systems. **Panel (a):** Top – Annual emissions of carbon dioxide for the five core Shared Socioeconomic Pathway (SSP) scenarios (very low: SSP1–1.9, low: SSP1–2.6, medium: SSP2–4.5, high: SSP3–7.0, very high SSP5–8.5). These scenarios are illustrative, meaning that they are not intended to be predictions of what will happen in the future; instead they serve an informative purpose to see how the Earth will respond to different situations. Bottom – Projected warming for each of these emissions scenarios. This figure is sourced from the Technical Summary Infographic. **Panel (b):** Top – How temperature extremes, droughts, heavy rainfall (precipitation) events, snow cover, and tropical cyclones change at different levels of global warming compared with the late nineteenth century (1850–1900). Today, here is the average over 2011–2020. Bottom – Long term (2,000 and 10,000 years) committed sea level rise for global warming of 1.5°C, 2°C, and 4°C).[52]

gas concentrations. All of these examples respond roughly linearly to rising carbon emissions, meaning that every increment of global warming leads to noticeable and discernible changes and impacts on ecosystems and society. An extreme heatwave that used to happen once in every ten years in the pre-industrial era is now 2.8 times as *likely* to occur, and this will become 5.5 times as *likely* to occur in a 2°C warmer world. Similarly, a heavy precipitation event that used to happen once in every ten years in the pre-industrial era is era is now 1.3 times as *likely* to occur, and this will become 1.7 times as *likely* to occur in a 2°C warmer world. Globally, the intensity of precipitation increases ~7 per cent on average for every degree of global warming. An extreme agricultural and ecological drought that used to happen once in every

[52] Infographic TS.1, Arias and others (n 13).

ten years in the pre-industrial era is now 1.7 times as *likely* to occur, becoming 2.5 times as *likely* to occur in a 2°C warmer world.[53]

The water cycle will intensify and be more variable although not always linearly due to the complex interaction with pollution aerosols as described earlier in this chapter. Rainfall over land, including monsoon rainfalls, will become more variable and intense: some areas will get drier, others will get wetter. Further warming will also amplify the thawing (defrosting) and melting of many frozen parts of the world, such as snow cover, glaciers, frozen ground, and Arctic sea ice. For instance, it is estimated that the Arctic Ocean will be effectively free of sea ice at its lowest point in summer (September) at least once before 2050. Tropical cyclones will get stronger. The differences in severity of some climate changes at 1.5°C (2.7°F), 2°C (3.6°F), and 4°C (7.2°F) global warming are illustrated in Figure 2.7 (panel (b)).[54]

Compound extreme events are the combination of multiple drivers and/or hazards over space and time that contribute to societal or environmental risk. Their probability of occurrence is projected to increase with global warming. They can occur on various spatial scales from sub-national to global and can often impact ecosystems and societies more strongly than when such events occur in isolation. Examples are concurrent heatwaves and droughts in multiple locations, compound flooding (e.g. a storm surge in combination with extreme rainfall and/or river flow), compound fire weather conditions (i.e. a combination of hot, dry, and windy conditions), or concurrent extremes at different locations such as in multiple crop-producing regions. Compound extremes at multiple locations, including in crop-producing areas, become more frequent at 2°C and above compared to 1.5°C global warming.[55]

There are many changes that will continue for hundreds or thousands of years as they react very slowly to rising greenhouse gas emissions and a warming world. Changes like deep ocean warming, Greenland and Antarctica ice-sheet melting, carbon lost from thawing permafrost, and sea level rise are slow to respond to the atmosphere warming but will continue to change for centuries, if not millennia. These changes are deemed irreversible because they would continue to change on these time scales even if greenhouse gases or global temperatures were stabilised or brought back down again. The bottom of panel (a) in Figures 2.7 and 2.8 illustrate the long-term committed changes of sea level rise as a result of climate change: even if global warming can be stabilised at 1.5°C (2.7°F), sea level would still rise 2–3 metres (7–10 feet) over the coming 2,000 years and 6–7 metres (20–23 feet) over the coming 10,000 years. Stabilising at higher levels of global warming will result in increased committed changes and will increase the rate of these changes compared to stabilising at global warming levels like 1.5°C (2.7°F).[56] Figure 2.8

53 Figure SPM.6, IPCC, 2021: Summary for Policymakers (n 16).
54 Section B.2, IPCC, 2021: Summary for Policymakers (n 16).
55 Section C.2, IPCC, 2021: Summary for Policymakers (n 16).
56 Section B.5, IPCC, 2021: Summary for Policymakers (n 16).

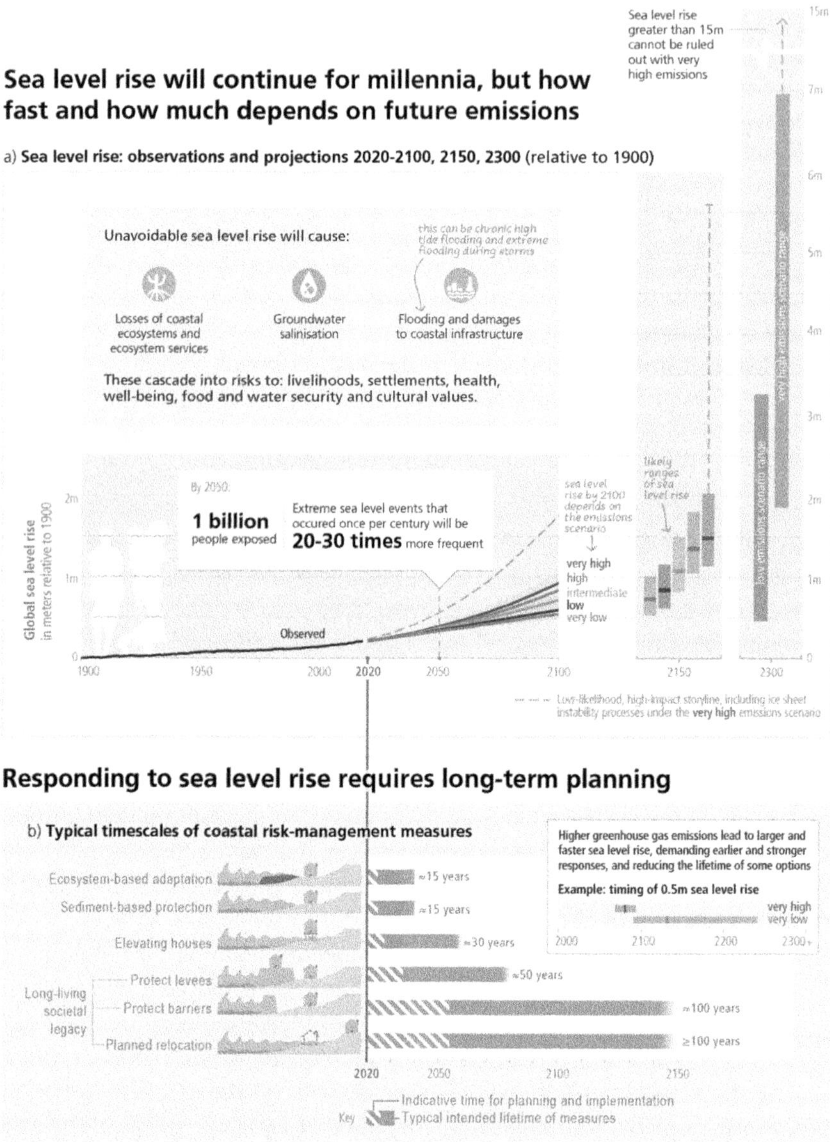


FIGURE 2.8 Observed and projected global mean sea level change and its impacts, and time scales of coastal risk management. **Panel (a):** Global mean sea level change in metres relative to 1900. The historical observed changes (black line) are recorded by tide gauges before 1992 and altimeters afterwards. The future changes from 2020 to 2100 and for 2150 are assessed consistently with observational constraints based on emulation of CMIP, ice-sheet, and glacier models, and median values and *likely* ranges are shown for the considered scenarios. Relative to 1995–2014, the *likely* global mean sea level rise by 2050 is between 0.15 to 0.23 m in the very low GHG emissions scenario (SSP1–1.9) and 0.20 to 0.29 m in the very high GHG emissions scenario (SSP5–8.5); by 2100 between 0.28 to 0.55 m under SSP1–1.9 and 0.63 to 1.01 m under SSP5–8.5; and by 2150

shows how these committed sea level changes compare to timelines of implementing various adaptation options.

### 2.4.3 *Irreversibility, Tipping Points, and Abrupt Changes*

As stated earlier, it is virtually certain that irreversible, committed change is already underway for the slow-to-respond processes as they come into adjustment for past and present emissions. So-called 'tipping points' exist in the climate system where processes undergo sudden shifts, becoming more or less sensitive to change. They are characterised by abrupt changes once a threshold is crossed. Even a return to pre-threshold surface temperatures or to lower atmospheric carbon dioxide concentrations would not guarantee that the tipping elements return to their pre-threshold state. An example would be a major deglaciation, where 1°C range of temperature change might correspond to a large or small ice-sheet mass loss during different stages.

The current levels of scientific understanding around tipping points is limited but scientists cannot rule them out and the likelihood of abrupt and/or irreversible changes increases with higher global warming levels. If they were to occur, the consequences would be extremely serious. Events that are currently termed as low-likelihood, high-impact outcomes include the collapse of the Earth's ice sheets

---

FIGURE 2.8 (cont.)

between 0.37 to 0.86 m under SSP1–1.9 and 0.98 to 1.88 m under SSP5–8.5 (medium confidence). Changes relative to 1900 are calculated by adding 0.158 m (observed global mean sea level rise from 1900 to 1995–2014) to simulated changes relative to 1995–2014. The future changes to 2300 (bars) are based on literature assessment, representing the 17th–83rd percentile range for SSP1–2.6 (0.3 to 3.1 m) and SSP5–8.5 (1.7 to 6.8 m). Dashed lines are showing a low-likelihood, high-impact storyline including ice-sheet instability processes. These indicate the potential impact of deeply uncertain processes and show the 83rd percentile of SSP5–8.5 projections that include low-likelihood, high-impact processes that cannot be ruled out; because of uncertainty surrounding these processes in the projections, this is not included as part of a *likely* range. IPCC AR6 global and regional sea level projections are hosted at https://sealevel.nasa.gov/ipcc–ar6–sea–level–projection–tool. The low-lying coastal zone is currently home to around 896 million people (nearly 11% of the 2020 global population), projected to reach more than one billion by 2050 across all five SSPs. **Panel (b)**: Typical time scales for the planning, implementation (dashed white and grey bars), and operational lifetime of current coastal risk-management measures (fully grey bars). Higher rates of sea level rise demand earlier and stronger responses and reduce the lifetime of measures (inset). As the scale and pace of sea level rise accelerates beyond 2050, long-term adjustments may in some locations be beyond the limits of current adaptation options and could be an existential risk for some small islands and low-lying coasts.[57]

57 Figure 3.4, Hoesung Lee and others (eds), *Climate Change 2023: Synthesis Report. Contribution of Working Groups I, II and III to the Sixth Assessment Report of the Intergovernmental Panel on Climate Change* (Cambridge University Press 2023).

(resulting in a much larger, quicker rise in sea levels) or extensive forest dieback (which would lead to the release of a significant amount of carbon dioxide into the atmosphere and a reduction in the amount being absorbed by nature).

At the regional scale, abrupt responses, tipping points, and even reversals in the direction of change also cannot be excluded. Some regional abrupt changes and tipping points could have severe local impacts, such as unprecedented weather, extreme temperatures, and increased frequency of droughts and forest fires.[58]

### 2.4.4 *Increasing Risks and Limits*

Risks[59] of adverse impacts and related losses and damages[60] escalate as global warming continues to rise, being higher for global warming of 1.5°C than at present, and even higher at 2°C. Expected elevated risks include:

- an increase in heat-related human mortality and morbidity
- food-borne, water-borne, and vector-borne diseases
- mental health challenges
- flooding in coastal and other low-lying cities and regions
- species extinctions and biodiversity loss in land, freshwater, and ocean ecosystems
- a decrease in food production in some regions
- an increase in local flooding impacts from an increased frequency and intensity of heavy precipitation

All these risks are expected to increase within the near term (defined as before 2040) but the extent to which these risks manifest is dependent on the region, the ecosystems, and human systems affected, and the capacity to adapt to already committed climate changes (as well as the capacity to mitigate against future climate changes not yet committed). Hard and soft limits to adaptation have already been reached in some ecosystems and regions and, with increasing global warming, this will continue for both human and natural systems (see Section 2.6 for more information).[61]

Looking beyond 2040, risks will become more widespread and damaging but will depend on the level of global warming reached. For example, in an assessment of tens of thousands of land-based species, 3–14 per cent of them were assessed to *likely* face a very high risk of extinction at global warming levels of 1.5°C. This increases up to 3–18 per cent at 2°C, 3–29 per cent at 3°C, and 3–39

[58] Section C.3, IPCC, 2021: Summary for Policymakers (n 16). See also Box TS.9, Arias and others (n 13).

[59] Risk is defined as the potential for adverse consequences for human or ecological systems, recognising the diversity of values and objectives associated with such systems. In the context of climate change, risks can arise from potential impacts of climate change as well as human responses to climate change.

[60] Losses and damages (lowercase letters) in IPCC reports refer broadly to harm from (observed) impacts and (projected) risks and can be economic or non-economic.

[61] Section B.3, IPCC, 2022: Summary for Policymakers WG2 (n 38).

per cent at 4°C. Similarly, the global aggregated net economic damages are expected to increase non-linearly with higher global warming levels, with significant regional variations in those economic damages. It is estimated that per capita economic damages will be higher in developing countries as a fraction of income compared to in developed countries. Although presently the connection between climate change and forced migration and conflict is relatively weak compared to other driving socioeconomic factors, involuntary migration from regions with high exposure and low adaptive capacity would occur at progressive levels of warming. Displacement, which already occurs today after extreme events, would increase in the mid to long term.[62]

Many other non-climatic drivers of change will interact with the 'physical' climate changes often exacerbating vulnerabilities and risks felt by ecosystems and society. Compound and cascading risks are more complex and difficult to manage. Many are also climate feedbacks, that is, processes that lead to an amplification or a dampening of further climate changes. Positive climate feedbacks (that amplify/further increase global warming) include the destruction of forests – a vital carbon sink – after the result of a combination of climate change and unsustainable human development. Unsustainable agricultural expansion is another. While agricultural development contributes to food security, unsustainable agricultural expansion, driven in part by unbalanced diets, increases greenhouse gas emissions, thereby increasing ecosystem and human vulnerability and leading to competition for land and/or water resources.[63]

By organising the many risks of climate change into five broad categories, the IPCC's Reasons for Concern (RFCs) were created for its Third Assessment Report (released in 2001).[64] They have since become fundamental graphics for many of the report summaries. The RFCs comprise:

1. **RFC1: Unique and threatened systems:** ecological and human systems that have restricted geographic ranges constrained by climate-related conditions and have high endemism or other distinctive properties. Examples include coral reefs, the Arctic and its Indigenous Peoples, mountain glaciers, and biodiversity hotspots.
2. **RFC2: Extreme weather events:** risks/impacts to human health, livelihoods, assets, and ecosystems from extreme weather events such as heatwaves, heavy rain, drought and associated wildfires, and coastal flooding.
3. **RFC3: Distribution of impacts:** risks/impacts that disproportionately affect particular groups due to uneven distribution of physical climate change hazards, exposure, or vulnerability.

62 ibid Section B.4.
63 Section A.2, IPCC, 2023: Summary for Policymakers (n 23).
64 James J McCarthy and others (eds), *Climate Change 2001: Impacts, Adaptation, and Vulnerability, Full Report* (Cambridge University Press 2001).

4. **RFC4: Global aggregate impacts:** impacts to socio-ecological systems that can be aggregated globally into a single metric, such as monetary damages, lives affected, species lost, or ecosystem degradation at a global scale.
5. **RFC5: Large-scale singular events:** relatively large, abrupt, and sometimes irreversible changes in systems caused by global warming, such as ice-sheet disintegration or thermohaline circulation slowing.

While the RFCs represent global risk levels for aggregated concerns about 'dangerous anthropogenic interference with the climate system', they represent a great diversity of risks and, in reality, there is not one single dangerous climate threshold across sectors and regions.

Projected global temperatures for the five different SSP scenarios (discussed earlier) are shown in Figure 2.9 panel (a) with the corresponding risks for the RFCs (see top right side of panel (a)). Known as the burning embers, these diagrams portray four levels of additional risk from undetectable to very high.

- **Undetectable Risk Level:** This level indicates that no impacts can be detected or attributed to climate change. In other words, there is no evidence of climate change-related effects.
- **Moderate Risk Level:** This level signifies that impacts are noticeable and can be linked to climate change with a moderate level of confidence. This assessment takes into account specific criteria used to evaluate significant risks.
- **High Risk Level:** The high risk level points to severe and widespread impacts that are deemed substantial according to one or more key risk assessment criteria. This implies that the effects of climate change are extensive and significant.
- **Very High Risk Level:** This level represents a situation where there is a very high likelihood of severe impacts resulting from climate change. These impacts are accompanied by a notable degree of irreversibility or the persistence of climate-related hazards. Additionally, the ability to adapt to these hazards or risks is limited due to their nature or the resulting consequences.

All five RFCs are already at either moderate or high risk at today's level of warming (1.1°C above 1850–1900 levels). The thinner burning ember placed beside each RFC is a comparison to the state of knowledge in the previous IPCC assessment, which was released in 2014. The risks for all RFCs have become higher since the last assessment; risk reaching high or very high levels will occur at lower levels of warming than previously thought. This update in assessment is due to new observational evidence, improved process understanding, and new knowledge on exposure and vulnerability of human and natural systems. This means that limits to adaptation for some aspects of the RFCs will be reached sooner, if global warming continues to rise.[65]

[65] Section B.2, IPCC, 2023: Summary for Policymakers (n 23).

Burning embers for specific land-based or ocean/coastal-based systems are shown in Figure 2.9 panel (b). Warm-water corals are already at high risk at 1.1°C global warming. They are projected to reach very high risk at a global warming of 1.5°C, declining by 70–90 per cent. This rises to a decline of 90 per cent at 2°C global warming. Moderate risk is given to wildfires at today's level of warming. This transitions to very high risk at 3°C global warming. At over 4°C global warming, for example, an extra 100 million more people will be exposed to wildfires compared to present levels.[66]

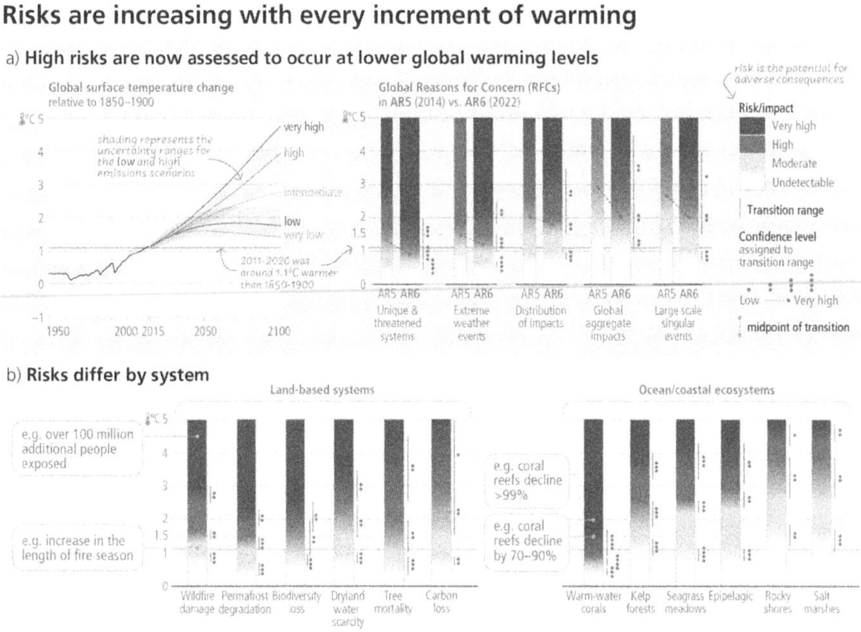


FIGURE 2.9 Synthetic diagrams of global and sectoral assessments and examples of key risks for global warming of 0–5°C global surface temperature change relative to preindustrial period (1850–1900). **Panel (a):** Left – Global surface temperature changes in °C relative to 1850–1900. Very likely uncertainty ranges are shown for the low and high GHG emissions scenarios (SSP1–2.6 and SSP3–7.0). Right – Global Reasons for Concern (RFC), comparing AR6 (thick embers) and AR5 (thin embers) assessments. Risk transitions have generally shifted towards lower temperatures with updated scientific understanding. Diagrams are shown for each RFC, assuming low to no adaptation. Lines connect the midpoints of the transitions from moderate to high risk across AR5 and AR6. **Panel (b):** Selected global risks for land and ocean ecosystems, illustrating general increase of risk with global warming levels with low to no adaptation. The horizontal line denotes the present global warming of 1.09°C which is used to separate the observed, past impacts below the line from the future projected risks above it.[67]

[66] Figure SPM.4, IPCC, 2023: Summary for Policymakers (n 23).
[67] ibid.

### 2.4.5 *Regional Changes and Risks*

Looking ahead, all regions of the world will experience further climate changes – with changes ratcheting up with every increase in global temperatures.[68] The IPCC reports dedicate hundreds of pages towards assessing regional climate changes and risks, which are insufficiently summarised in this chapter. Outreach material, such as the Working Group I and II's Regional Factsheets[69] or the Reports' Technical Summaries provide a much more detailed analysis of regional changes and risks. Additionally, the IPCC Interactive Atlas allows users to explore the different climate changes in regions of their interest.[70]

Each region is unique and affected by climate change in its own way, but every region will increasingly experience multiple and concurrent climate changes: the greater the warming, the larger and more widespread the changes. Changes will be more widespread at 2°C compared to 1.5°C global warming and even more widespread and/or pronounced for higher warming levels.[71]

Figure 2.10 shows projected changes in annual mean temperature (panel (b)), precipitation (panel (c)), and total soil moisture (panel (d)) at 1.5°C, 2°C, and 4°C global warming compared to 1850–1900 baseline levels. It shows that all regions will experience increases in heat-related climate changes such as heatwaves and decreases in cold-related changes such as cold snaps. Across warming levels, land areas warm more than ocean areas, and the Arctic and Antarctica warm more than the tropics. Precipitation is projected to increase over high latitudes, the equatorial Pacific, and parts of the monsoon regions, but decrease over parts of the subtropics and in limited areas of the tropics. A number of regions in North-Western, Central, and Eastern North America, Arctic regions, North-Western South America, Northern and Central Western Europe, Siberia, Central, South, and East Asia, Southern Australia, and New Zealand will experience decreases in snow and ice or increases in pluvial/river flooding. Across warming levels, changes in soil moisture largely follow changes in precipitation but also show some differences due to the influence of evapotranspiration. Many regions in Southern Africa, the Mediterranean, North Central America, Western North America, the Amazon regions, South-Western South America, and Australia will experience increases in drought, aridity, and weather conducive to triggering and sustaining wildfires. This will affect a wide range of sectors, including agriculture, forestry, health, and ecosystems. Currently, there is lower understanding of past and future changes

68 See Figure 2.6 for a list of all the IPCC-defined regions.

69 For WGI, see <www.ipcc.ch/report/ar6/wg1/resources/factsheets/> accessed 15 April 2024. For WGII, see <www.ipcc.ch/report/ar6/wg2/about/factsheets> accessed 15 April 2024.

70 See <https://interactive-atlas.ipcc.ch/> accessed 15 April 2024.

71 Figure SPM.5, IPCC, 2021: Summary for Policymakers (n 16).

in some of the damaging hazards such as hail, ice storms, storms, sand and dust storms, heavy snowfall, mudslides, and avalanches. This does not mean that they will not be affected by climate change. Rather, it means that their impacts are not currently able to be fully resolved by climate or impact models and do not benefit from long and homogeneous observations.[72]

Figure 2.11 gives examples of regional key risks with sufficient data and understanding to assess the risk with at least medium confidence (as characterised by IPCC). In some cases, it is possible to apply a 'burning ember' assessment.[73] Risks in Africa include

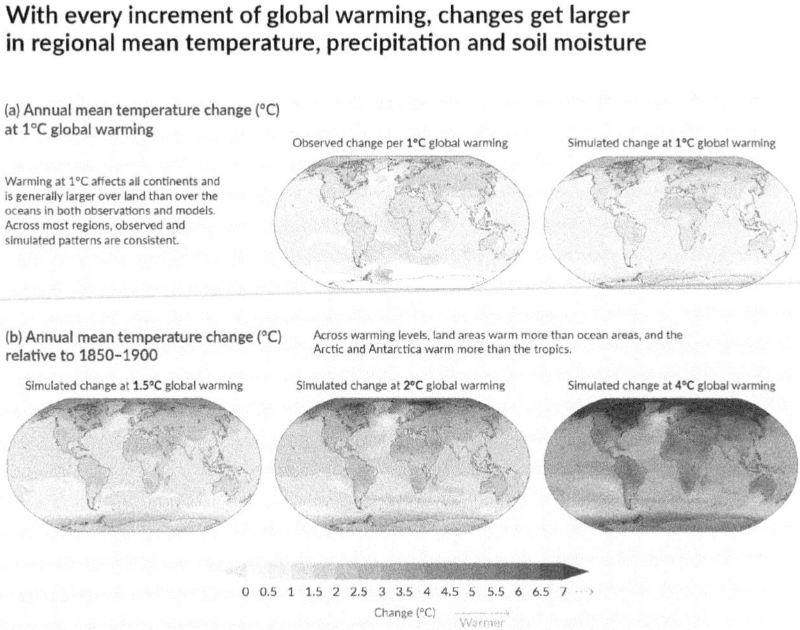


FIGURE 2.10 Changes in annual mean surface temperature, precipitation, and soil moisture. **Panel (a)**: Comparison of observed and simulated annual mean surface temperature change. The left map shows the observed changes in annual mean surface temperature in the period 1850–2020 per °C of global warming (°C). White indicates areas where time coverage was 100 years or less and thereby too short to calculate a reliable magnitude. The right map is based on model simulations and shows change in annual multi-model mean simulated temperatures at a global warming level of 1°C. **Panel (b)**: Simulated annual mean temperature change (°C). **Panel (c)**: Precipitation change (%). **Panel (d)**: Total column soil moisture change at global warming levels of 1.5°C, 2°C, and 4°C.[74]

[72] ibid.

[73] Further detail on regional risks can be found in the WGII Regional chapters and cross-chapter papers. In each region there are additional risks that are less well quantified or understood.

[74] Figure SPM.5, IPCC, 2021: Summary for Policymakers (n 16).

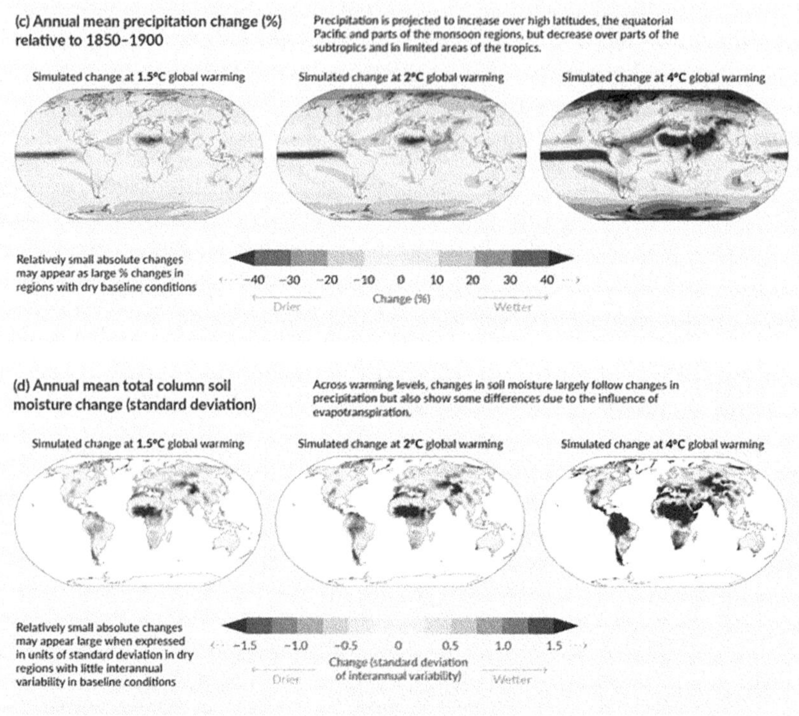


FIGURE 2.10 (cont.)

species extinction, food security risks, marine ecosystem threats, health impacts, and economic decline. Asia risks involve urban infrastructure damage, biodiversity loss, coral bleaching, fishery declines, and food/water security challenges. North America risks encompass health impacts, ecosystem degradation, water scarcity, food security threats, and risks to coastal areas. Central and South America risks include water security, health impacts, coral reef degradation, food security threats, and damages from natural disasters. Australia risks encompass coral reef degradation, coastal loss, agriculture decline, heat-related issues, and loss of alpine biodiversity. Small Islands risks will be biodiversity loss, threats to lives and assets, economic decline, and water security issues. Finally, in Europe, the risks involve flooding, health problems, disruptions to ecosystems, water scarcity, and crop production losses.[75]

### 2.4.6 *Risks Associated with Overshooting Global Warming of 1.5°C*

Every increment of global warming increases climate changes and negative consequences on ecosystems and society. Therefore, if global temperatures were to exceed

[75] Figure SPM.2, IPCC, 2023: Summary for Policymakers (n 23).

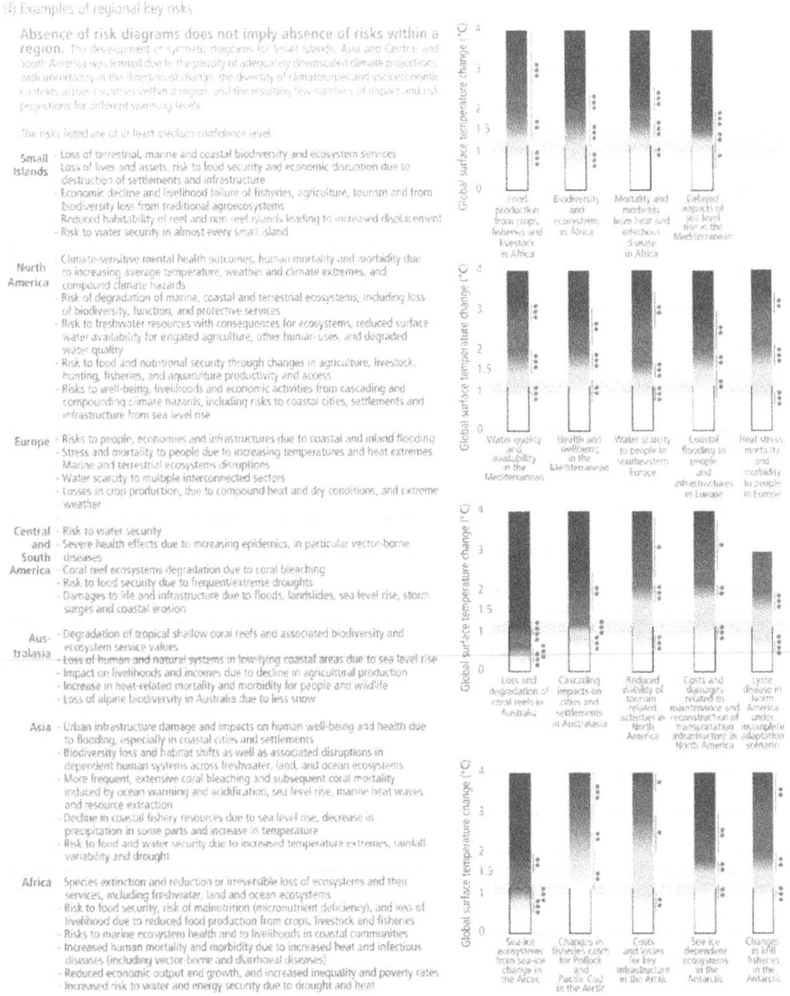


FIGURE 2.11 Synthetic diagrams of regional key risks. Diagrams show the change in the levels of impacts and risks assessed for global warming of 0–5°C global surface temperature change relative to pre-industrial period (1850–1900) over the range. Key risks are identified based on the magnitude of adverse consequences (pervasiveness of the consequences, degree of change, irreversibility of consequences, potential for impact thresholds or tipping points, potential for cascading effects beyond system boundaries); likelihood of adverse consequences; temporal characteristics of the risk; and ability to respond to the risk, for example, by adaptation. The full set of 127 assessed global and regional key risks is given in WGII Chapter 17 Supplementary Material Section SM16.7. The development of synthetic diagrams for Small Islands, Asia, and Central and South America were limited by the availability of adequately downscaled climate projections, with uncertainty in the direction of change, the diversity of climatologies and socioeconomic contexts across countries within a region, and the resulting low number of impact and risk projections for different warming levels. Absence of risks diagrams does not imply absence of risks within a region.[76]

[76] Figure SPM.3, IPCC, 2022: Summary for Policymakers WG2 (n 38).

a warming level, even if only temporarily, many human and natural systems would face additional severe risks compared to a future where global temperatures always remained below that warming level. A temporary overshoot of 1.5°C is a feature of the most ambitious emission pathway (SSP1-1.9, overshooting by ~0.1°C) discussed in Section 2.5. The extent to which severe risks are increased depends on, among other things, the magnitude and duration of a warming level being exceeded. The higher the magnitude or the longer the duration of this 'overshoot', the more ecosystems and societies are exposed to greater and more widespread climate changes, such as higher risks to infrastructure, low-lying coastal settlements, and associated livelihoods. Overshooting 1.5°C will result in severe risks and irreversible impacts in many ecosystems with low resilience, such as polar, mountain, and coastal ecosystems. Affected ecosystems will be impacted by temperature increase and extreme events, ice-sheet melt, glacier melt, or accelerating and higher committed sea level rise. Irreversible impacts include extinction of species, loss of coral reefs, and loss of human life.[77]

Additionally, some of the adverse impacts that occur during a period of overshoot may cause additional warming via feedback mechanisms that would make the return even more challenging. Such impacts and their feedback mechanism include increased wildfires, mass mortality of trees, drying of peatlands, permafrost thawing, weakening natural land carbon sinks, and increasing releases of greenhouses gases.[78]

Temporarily overshooting a global warming level is a relatively new area of research and has limited model-based assessments on how the climate responds to and the impacts of an overshoot. Observations and current understanding of climate processes support the current understanding of the implications of an overshoot but further research would allow assessments to be more robust and comprehensive.

### 2.4.7 *The Role of the Land and Ocean Removing Atmospheric Carbon Dioxide*

Finally, climate change affects the natural removal of carbon from the atmosphere, predominantly by land vegetation and ocean, which removes roughly half of the carbon dioxide that humans emit to the atmosphere. This fraction of carbon dioxide removal has remained relatively stable over the past sixty years (at roughly 56 per cent). While human activities emitted more and more carbon dioxide into the atmosphere, the land vegetation and ocean also removed more carbon dioxide. This has led to the oceans becoming more acidic, because when carbon dioxide dissolves in water, it reacts to make the seawater more acidic. Climate modelling shows, however, that if more and more carbon dioxide is emitted into the atmosphere, the relative amount being naturally removed by the land vegetation and ocean would decline. For example, the scenario where carbon dioxide emissions are ambitiously mitigated and global temperatures are kept to below 1.5°C by the end of the century

77 Section B.7, IPCC, 2023: Summary for Policymakers (n 23).
78 ibid.

(SSP1–1.9) shows a 70 per cent removal of carbon dioxide by the land and ocean. Conversely, the scenario where carbon dioxide emissions remain relatively high in the future (SSP3–7.0) shows that the land and ocean will only remove 44 per cent from the atmosphere. The bottom line is that nature will 'help' less if more carbon dioxide is emitted in the future compared to if emissions in the future are reduced.[79]

## 2.5 MITIGATING CLIMATE CHANGE

This section presents an overview of the mitigation action needed in the coming decades to limit further global warming and its associated impacts.

### 2.5.1 *Paris Agreement: Are We on Track?*

Current emissions reduction pledges under the Paris Agreement, known as countries' NDCs, are 'woefully insufficient' to meet the treaty's long-term temperature goal.[80] The IPCC highlighted in 2022 that NDCs announced before COP26 in 2021 would lead to warming exceeding 1.5°C in the twenty-first century. Unless combined with a rapid acceleration of efforts to reduce emissions after 2030, they would also result in 2°C of warming being exceeded.[81]

Estimating the alignment of NDCs or climate policies with temperature goals is an inherently dynamic exercise, as countries are expected to regularly update their NDCs as part of the Paris Agreement's five-yearly ratcheting cycles and the number of national climate policies can change at any time. The snapshots provided by scientific assessments such as those of the IPCC will therefore only be valid over a limited amount of time. Other authoritative initiatives provide more regular updates. For example, UNEP publishes their Emissions Gap Report yearly,[82] providing a synthesis of the most up-to-date information about where emissions are heading under the NDCs and as a result of policies that countries are implementing domestically.

The 2023 edition of the UNEP Emissions Gap Report indicated that NDCs available at that point in time would only hold global warming to 2.5–2.9°C over the course of the twenty-first century (with 66 per cent *likelihood*). Moreover, domestic climate policies were falling short of achieving these insufficient NDCs and would, without further strengthening, hold global warming to 3.0°C only.[83] This assessment by UNEP is updated annually and is expected to change as new NDCs are submitted, and domestic policies are taken up or rolled back.[84]

79 Section B.4, IPCC, 2021: Summary for Policymakers (n 16).

80 UNEP, 'The Emissions Gap Report 2022' (*UNEP*, 2022) <www.unep.org/resources/emissions-gap-report-2022> accessed 15 April 2024. The emissions gap remained largely unchanged in 2023.

81 Section B.6, IPCC, 2022: Summary for Policymakers WG3 (n 22).

82 See <www.unep.org/resources/emissions–gap–report>.

83 UNEP Emissions Gap Report 2023 (n 2).

84 See (n 82).

### 2.5.2 *How to Stabilise Global Temperature*

#### 2.5.2.1 Net Zero

Greenhouse gas emissions from human activities are the main driver of the global warming our planet is currently experiencing. Carbon dioxide is contributing most to current warming with methane coming second. Carbon dioxide remains in the atmosphere for a very long time – some of it for centuries to millennia. That means that carbon dioxide emissions accumulate in the atmosphere and every addition of carbon dioxide to the atmosphere will cause further warming. There is a near-linear relationship between cumulative anthropogenic carbon dioxide emissions and the global warming they cause. Any continuation of carbon dioxide emissions will therefore result in further warming of the planet.[85]

To stop temperatures from increasing even more, we need to either stop all carbon dioxide emissions from human activities or reach a point where any remaining emissions of carbon dioxide are balanced by activities that remove carbon dioxide from the atmosphere permanently – or at least for many centuries (see Section 2.4.1). This is a direct consequence of the mentioned near-linear relationship between the total amount of carbon dioxide emissions ever emitted by human activities and global warming.

The sum of carbon dioxide emissions and carbon dioxide removals in a given year is referred to as *net* carbon dioxide emissions. A state where anthropogenic emissions and removals are perfectly balanced is therefore referred to as reaching net-zero carbon dioxide emissions. If net-zero anthropogenic carbon dioxide emissions are achieved, global temperatures are projected to stabilise, although this could be at a slightly higher or lower temperature than the level at which net-zero carbon dioxide emissions were achieved.[86] Stabilisation of global warming means that climate change would not worsen, but not that past changes would be reversed.

Carbon dioxide is only one of the human-emitted greenhouse gases that cause global warming. Strong, rapid, and sustained reductions in other greenhouse gases like methane and nitrous oxide are also needed to limit climate change. Achieving net-zero carbon dioxide emissions is different from achieving net-zero greenhouse gas emissions, where all remaining anthropogenic greenhouse gas emissions are balanced with anthropogenic removals. To put different greenhouse gas emissions on a common scale, the scientific community has developed conversion factors known as greenhouse gas metrics. Changing the emissions metric used to calculate net emissions of different greenhouse gases will affect what point in time greenhouse gas emissions are said to reach net zero, and if global warming is projected to be halted by net-zero emissions. Emissions pathways that reach and sustain net-zero greenhouse emissions as reported to

[85] Section B.5, IPCC, 2023: Summary for Policymakers (n 23).
[86] Section D1.8, IPCC, 2021: Summary for Policymakers (n 16).

the UNFCCC are projected to result in a decline in surface temperature after an earlier peak and therefore achieve more than merely a stabilisation of global temperatures.[87]

#### 2.5.2.2 Carbon Dioxide Removal

Global warming can be reversed if permanent anthropogenic removals of carbon dioxide exceed emissions globally. Achieving such a state, however, is highly challenging and very uncertain. All pathways assessed by the IPCC that transition from current emission levels to net-zero carbon dioxide emissions involve some degree of carbon dioxide removal (CDR).

There are two main types of CDR: either enhancing existing natural processes that remove carbon from the atmosphere (e.g. by increasing carbon uptake by trees, soil, or other 'carbon sinks') or using chemical or engineering processes to, for example, capture carbon dioxide directly from the ambient air and store it elsewhere (e.g. underground). All CDR methods are at different stages of development, and some are more conceptual than others, as they have not been tested or proven at scale. The consideration and required scale of CDR in future pathways depend on model assumptions about the feasibility, desirability, and effectiveness of mitigation measures that reduce greenhouse gas emissions and of large-scale CDR.[88] Similar caution is also warranted in connection with speculative technologies such as Solar Radiation Modification measures, which face large uncertainties and knowledge gaps as well as substantial risks.[89] Against this backdrop, it must be underscored that science does not foreclose the existence of 1.5°C compliant pathways that do not rely on CDR, instead envisaging deeper forms of socio-economic transformation than those envisaged in the IPCC pathways.

Clearly thus, depending on their mitigation choices, net-zero strategies can have important differences in their side effects or risks. For example, pursuing deep carbon dioxide emission reductions combined with a limited amount of removals would have significantly lower carbon leakage and sustainability risks than a strategy that combines weak emissions reductions with very large quantities of removals.[90]

#### 2.5.2.3 Carbon Budgets

The near-linear relationship between cumulative anthropogenic carbon dioxide emissions and global warming implies that limiting global temperature increase to a specific level requires limiting overall carbon dioxide emissions to within a carbon

87 ibid Sections D.1 and D.2.

88 IPCC, *Global Warming of 1.5°C* <www.ipcc.ch/site/assets/uploads/sites/2/2022/06/SR15_Full_Report_HR.pdf> accessed 15 April 2024 (Global Warming 1.5°C). See also B.5.4, SPM-19, IPCC, 2022: Summary for Policymakers WG3 (n 22). (Risks arise from some responses that are intended to reduce the risks of climate change, including risks from maladaptation and adverse side effects of some emission reduction and carbon dioxide removal measures (high confidence).)

89 C.1.4, Global Warming 1.5°C (n 88).

90 Section C.11, IPCC, 2022: Summary for Policymakers WG3 (n 22).

budget. Such carbon budgets have been estimated (Table 2.1) and are regularly updated with more recent data.[91] Carbon budget estimates depend critically on the level of global warming that is to be avoided (e.g. 1.5°C, 1.7°C, or 2.0°C), the likelihood with which this level of warming is to be avoided (50 per cent, 66 per cent, 90 per cent, or higher), and assumptions about how deeply other greenhouse gases are

TABLE 2.1 *Historical carbon dioxide emissions and estimates of remaining carbon budgets. Estimated remaining carbon budgets are calculated from the beginning of 2020 and extend until global net-zero $CO_2$ emissions are reached. They refer to $CO_2$ emissions, while accounting for the global warming effect of non-$CO_2$ emissions. Global warming in this table refers to human-induced global surface temperature increase, which excludes the impact of natural variability on global temperatures in individual years.*[92]

| Global warming between 1850–1900 and 2010–2019 (°C) | Historical cumulative $CO_2$ emissions from 1850 to 2019 ($GtCO_2$) |
| --- | --- |
| 1.07 (0.8–1.3; *likely* range) | 2390 (± 240; *likely* range) |

| Approximate global warming relative to 1850–1900 until temperature limit (°C)[a] | Additional global warming relative to 2010–2019 until temperature limit (°C) | Estimated remaining carbon budgets from the beginning of 2020 ($GtCO_2$) *Likelihood of limiting global warming to temperature limit*[b] | | | | | Variations in reductions in non-$CO_2$ emissions[c] |
| --- | --- | --- | --- | --- | --- | --- | --- |
| | | 17% | 33% | 50% | 67% | 83% | |
| 1.5 | 0.43 | 900 | 650 | 500 | 400 | 300 | Higher or lower reductions in accompanying non-$CO_2$ emissions can increase or decrease the values on the left by 220 $GtCO_2$ or more |
| 1.7 | 0.63 | 1450 | 1050 | 850 | 700 | 550 | |
| 2.0 | 0.93 | 2300 | 1700 | 1350 | 1150 | 900 | |

[a] Values at each 0.1°C increment of warming are available in Tables TS.3 and 5.8.
[b] This likelihood is based on the uncertainty in transient climate response to cumulative $CO_2$ emissions (TCRE) and additional Earth system feedbacks and provides the probability that global warming will not exceed the temperature levels provided in the two left columns. Uncertainties related to historical warming (± 550 $GtCO_2$) and non-$CO_2$ forcing and response (± 220 $GtCO_2$) are partially addressed by the assessed uncertainty in TCRE, but uncertainties in recent emissions since 2015 (± 20 $GtCO_2$) and the climate response after net-zero $CO_2$ emissions are reached (± 420 $GtCO_2$) are separate.
[c] Remaining carbon budget estimates consider the warming from non-$CO_2$ drivers as implied by the scenarios assessed in SR1.5. The Working Group III Contribution to AR6 will assess mitigation of non-$CO_2$ emissions.

[91] See Indicators of Global Climate Change, <www.igcc.earth/> accessed 15 April 2024.
[92] Table SPM.2, IPCC, 2021: Summary for Policymakers (n 16).

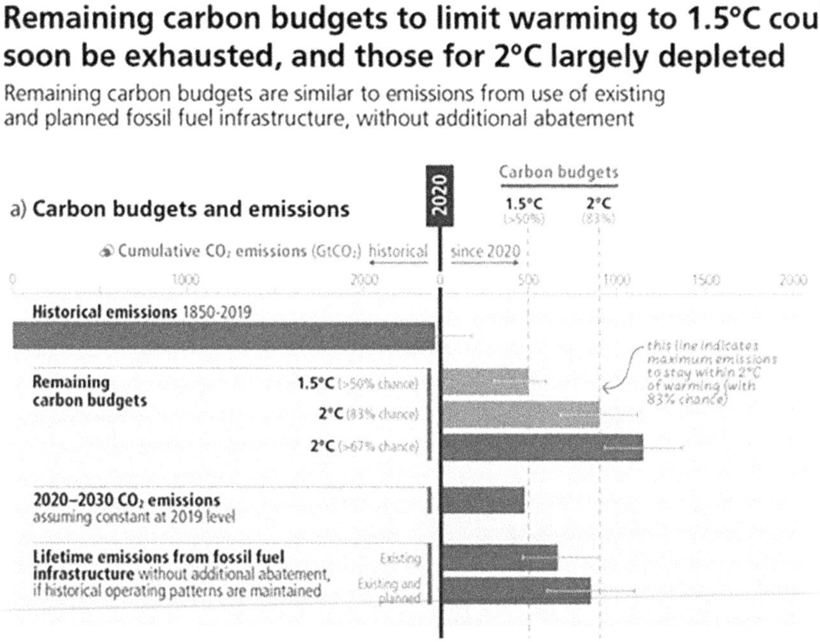


FIGURE 2.12 Visual representation of historical carbon dioxide emissions and estimates of remaining carbon budgets for keeping warming to 1.5°C and 2°C with different levels of probability. The lower bars show how quickly the remaining carbon budgets are depleted if global $CO_2$ emissions do not decline from current (in this case 2019) levels or if all emissions embedded in current and planned fossil fuel infrastructure are considered.[93]

mitigated.[94] Irrespective of the choices that can be made regarding the likelihood of avoiding a given level of warming and the reductions in other greenhouse gas emissions, the remaining carbon budgets for 1.5°C and 2°C are very small.

Figure 2.12 illustrates how a failure to reduce carbon dioxide emissions from today until 2030 will exhaust the remaining carbon budget for keeping warming to 1.5°C with 50 per cent chance entirely.

Carbon budgets describe geophysical limits to how much carbon dioxide society can emit while keeping warming to a specified temperature level. To understand how we can stay within these carbon budget limits, they are used as inputs into analyses of how society can transform while meeting global energy, food, and other needs. The models used to explore these transformations are called IAMs (see Section 2.4.1). These models make assumptions about future socioeconomic developments (which are often structured along a specific SSP) and the level of desired climate change mitigation (often defined by a maximum carbon budget that can be emitted). The socioeconomic assumptions include aspects of economic growth, inequality, and

93 Figure 3.5 from IPCC, 2023: Summary for Policymakers (n 23).

94 Joeri Rogelj and Robin D Lamboll, 'Substantial Reductions in non-$CO_2$ Greenhouse Gas Emissions Reductions Implied by IPCC Estimates of the Remaining Carbon Budget' (2024) 5(35) Communications Earth and Environment.

availability and characteristics of technologies, as well as levels of education or population growth. Conditional on these assumptions, IAMs then create emissions scenarios that are consistent with limiting global warming to a specific level and that are considered technically and economically feasible within the socioeconomic context that was assumed. The IPCC provides further tools to understand the feasibility of emissions scenarios, and highlights that this depends on geophysical, economic, technological, socio-cultural, and institutional aspects.[95] Geophysical, economic, and technological aspects of the feasibility of mitigation scenarios are typically covered better by IAMs than aspects of socio-cultural and institutional feasibility which are more subject to societal willingness and capacity for change.

Table 2.2 gives a detailed overview of the key characteristics of different modelled pathways showing how the world could respond to climate change.[96] The table covers projected carbon dioxide and greenhouse gas emission reductions and net-zero timings. Scenarios are clustered into several categories including:

- **C1: Limit warming to 1.5°C (>50%) with no or limited overshoot (97 scenarios)**. This category refers to scenarios that reach or exceed 1.5°C during the twenty-first century with a likelihood of ≤67%, and limit warming to 1.5°C in 2100 with a likelihood of >50%. Limited overshoot refers to exceeding 1.5°C by up to about 0.1°C and for up to several decades. By limiting the maximum likelihood of exceeding 1.5°C, scenarios in this category simultaneously have a likelihood of close to and more than 90 per cent of limiting peak global warming to 2°C throughout the twenty-first century.
- **C2: Return warming to 1.5°C (>50%) after a high overshoot (133 scenarios)**. This category refers to scenarios that exceed warming of 1.5°C during the twenty-first century with a likelihood of >67%, and limit warming to 1.5°C in 2100 with a likelihood of >50%. High overshoot refers to central warming estimates temporarily exceeding 1.5°C global warming by 0.1°C–0.3°C for up to several decades.
- **C3: Limit warming to 2°C (>67%) (311 scenarios)**. This category refers to scenarios that limit peak warming to 2°C throughout the twenty-first century with a likelihood of >67%.

As risks of global warming increase with every additional 0.1°C of warming and the sustainable scale of CDR technologies needed to reverse warming after an overshoot is still speculative, it is clear that scenarios in the C1 category represent the safest climate future. Even within the C1 category there are, however, scenarios that might be undesirable as some of them rely strongly on mitigation measures which might have other societal side effects, such as a reduction in biodiversity if a scenario

95 Keywan Riahi and others, '2022: Mitigation Pathways Compatible with Long-Term Goals' in Priyadarshi Shukla and others (eds), *Climate Change 2022: Mitigation of Climate Change. Contribution of Working Group III to the Sixth Assessment Report of the Intergovernmental Panel on Climate Change* (Cambridge University Press 2022).

96 Table 2, IPCC, 2022: Summary for Policymakers WG3 (n 22).

TABLE 2.2 *Key characteristics of the modelled global emissions pathways. Summary of projected $CO_2$ and GHG emissions, projected net-zero timings, and the resulting global warming outcomes. Pathways are categorised (C1–C3), according to their likelihood of limiting warming to different peak warming levels in 2100. Values shown are for the median [p50] and 5th–95th percentiles [p5–p95], noting that not all pathways achieve net-zero $CO_2$ or GHGs.*[97]

| p50 [p5–o51] | | | GHG emissions ($GtCO_2$-eqyr-1) | | | GHG emissions reductions from 2019 (%) | | | Emissions milestones | | | |
|---|---|---|---|---|---|---|---|---|---|---|---|---|
| Category [#pathways] | Category/ subject label | WGI SSP & WGIII IPs/IMPs alignment | 2030 | 2040 | 2050 | 2030 | 2040 | 2050 | Peak $CO_2$ emissions (% peak before 2100) | Peak GHG emissions (% peak before 2100) | Net-zero $CO_2$ (% net-zero pathways) | Net-zero GHGs (% net-zero pathways) |
| Modelled global emissions pathways categorised by projected global warming levels. Detailed likelihood definitions are provided in SPM Box 1.<br>The five illustrative scenarios (SSPx yy) considered by AR6 WGI and the Illustrative (Mitigation) Pathways assessed in WGIII are aligned with the temperature categories and are indicated in a separate column.<br>Global emission pathways contain regionally differentiated information. This assessment focuses on their global characteristics. | | | Projected median annual GHG emissions in the year across the scenarios, with the 5th–95th percentile in brackets.<br>Modelled GHG emissions in 2019: 55 [53–58] $GtCO_2$-eq. | | | Projected median GHG emissions reductions of pathways in the year across the scenarios compared to modelled 2019, with the 5th–95th percentile in brackets. Negative numbers indicate increase in emissions compared to 2019. | | | Median 5-year intervals at which projected $CO_2$ & GHG emissions peak, with the 5th-95th percentile interval in square brackets.<br>Percentage of peaking pathways is denoted in round brackets.<br>Three dots (…) denotes emissions peak in 2100 or beyond for that percentile. | | Median 5-year intervals at which projected $CO_2$ & GHG emissions of pathways in this category reach net zero, with the 5th–95th percentile interval in square brackets.<br>Percentage of net-zero pathways is denoted in round brackets.<br>Three dots (…) denotes net zero not reached for that percentile. | |

*(continued)*

TABLE 2.2 *(continued)*

| | p50 [p5–051] | | GHG emissions ($GtCO_2$-eqyr-1) | | | GHG emissions reductions from 2019 (%) | | | Emissions milestones | | | |
|---|---|---|---|---|---|---|---|---|---|---|---|---|
| Category [#pathways] | Category/ subject label | WGI SSP & WGIII IPs/IMPs alignment | 2030 | 2040 | 2050 | 2030 | 2040 | 2050 | Peak $CO_2$ emissions (% peak before 2100) | Peak GHG emissions (% peak before 2100) | Net-zero $CO_2$ (% net-zero pathways) | Net-zero GHGs (% net-zero pathways) |
| **C1 [97]** | **limit warming to 1.5°C (>50%) with no or limited overshoot** | | 31 [21–36] | 17 [6–23] | 9 [1–15] | 43 [34–60] | 69 [58–90] | 84 [73–98] | 2020–2025 (100%) [2020–2025] | | 2050–2055 (100%) [2035–2070] | 2095–2100 (52%) [2050–...]<br>2070–2075 (100%) [2050–2090] |
| C1a [50] | ... with net-zero GHGs | SSP1–1.9, SP LD | 33 [22–37] | 18 [6–24] | 8 [0–15] | 41 [31–59] | 66 [58–89] | 85 [72–100] | | | | ...–... [0%] |
| C1b [47] | ... without net-zero GHGs | Ren | 29 [21–36] | 16 [7–21] | 9 [4–13] | 48 [35–61] | 70 [62–87] | 84 [76–93] | | | | [...–...] |
| C2 [133] | return warming to 1.5°C (>50%) after a high overshoot | Neg | 42 [31–55] | 25 [17–34] | 14 [5–21] | 23 [0–44] | 55 [40–71] | 75 [62–91] | 2020–2025 (100%) [2020–2030] | [2020–2025] | 2055–2060 (100%) [2045–2070] | 2070–2075 (87%) [2055–...] |

| | | | | | | | | | | | |
|---|---|---|---|---|---|---|---|---|---|---|---|
| **C3 [311]** | **limit warming to 2°C (>67%)** | | 44 [32–55] | 29 [20–36] | 20 [13–26] | 21 [1–42] | 46 [34–63] | 64 [53–77] | 2020–2025 (100%) [2020–2030] [2020–2025] | 2070–2075 (93%) [2055–...] | ...–... (30%) [2075–...] |
| **C3a [204]** | **... with action starting in 2020** | SSP1–2.6 | 40 [30–49] | 29 [21–36] | 20 [14–27] | 27 [13–45] | 47 [35–63] | 63 [52–76] | 2020–2025 (100%) [2020–2025] | 2070–2075 (91%) [2055–...] | ...–... (24%) [2080–...] |
| **C3b [97]** | **... NDCs until 2030** | GS | 52 [47–56] | 29 [20–36] | 18 [10–25] | 5 [0–14] | 46 [34–63] | 68 [56–82] | 2020–2025 (100%) [2020–2030] | 2065–2070 (97%) [2055–2090] | ...–... (41%) [2075–...] |

97 Table SPM.2, IPCC, 2022: Summary for Policymakers WG3 (n 22).

relies excessively on biomass for energy production or types of afforestation with poor biodiversity.

Based on global modelled pathways that limit warming to 1.5°C (>50%) with no or limited overshoot and in those that limit warming to 2°C (>67%) and assume immediate action, greenhouse gas emissions will reach their peak sometime between 2020 and, at the latest, before 2025. For these scenarios rapid and deep greenhouse gas emissions reductions continue through 2030, 2040, and 2050. Table 2.2 highlights that net global greenhouse gas emissions need to fall from 2019 levels by 27 per cent by 2030 and 63 per cent by 2050 for category C3a, that is, limit warming to 2°C (>67%) and assuming immediate action. While for category C1, it should reduce by 43 per cent by 2030 and 84 per cent by 2050. In pathways with larger overshoot – C2 – greenhouse gas emissions are reduced by 23 per cent in 2030 and by 75 per cent in 2050. These reduction percentages are median estimates surrounded by ranges that illustrate choices about the distribution of emissions reductions over time (see Table 2.2). If weaker emissions reductions are assumed by 2030, stronger emissions reductions will be required later to remain within the same carbon budget and limit warming below the same temperature limit.

Global net-zero greenhouse gas emissions, when measured in terms of their global warming potential over a 100-year period (GWP–100), are expected to be achieved sometime between 2095 and 2100 for C1. Pathways that reach net-zero greenhouse gas emissions before 2100 (which also includes roughly 90% of pathways that bring global warming back down to 1.5°C after experiencing a high overshoot (>0.1°C) by 2100) typically have a time gap of twelve to fourteen years (7–39) years, between reaching net-zero carbon dioxide emissions and reaching net-zero greenhouse gas emissions.[98]

Global modelled emission pathways, including those based on cost effective approaches, contain regionally differentiated assumptions and outcomes, and have to be assessed with the careful recognition of these assumptions. Most do not make explicit assumptions about global equity, environmental justice, or intra-regional income distribution. See also Section 2.2.1.

### 2.5.3 *Mitigation Actions*

The IPCC defines mitigation as a human intervention to reduce emissions or enhance the sinks of greenhouse gases. Mitigation measures include technologies, processes, or practices that reduce emissions.[99] Modelled pathways that limit warming to 1.5°C with no or limited overshoot assume immediate and ambitious mitigation action this decade. These actions fall broadly into the following categories: deployment of low- or zero-emission technologies, reducing and changing demand through infrastructure design and access, socio-cultural and behavioural changes, and increased technological efficiency and adoption.[100]

98 Section C.1, IPCC, 2022: Summary for Policymakers WG3 (n 22).
99 Section B.3, IPCC, 2022: Summary for Policymakers WG3 (n 22).
100 Section C.3, IPCC, 2023: Summary for Policymakers (n 23).

Figure 2.13 shows that multiple mitigation and adaptation options are already available. These solutions span across a number of sectors, including energy systems, industry, transport, buildings, agriculture, forestry, and land-use, that have been effectively implemented in many parts of the world (see Section 2.6 for more information on adaptation).[101]

Phasing out fossil fuels merits especially urgent attention, as current levels of fossil fuel consumption and new investments in fossil fuels are inconsistent with 1.5°C or even 2°C pathways (see Figure 2.12). Projections show that new investments in fossil fuels are not consistent with meeting the goals of the Paris Agreement and the achievement of Sustainable Development Goals, leading to substantial economic losses from stranded assets while also delaying the development of low carbon sectors and infrastructure.[102] Immediate action to phase out fossil fuels and reduce emissions more broadly would: reduce and avoid the reliance on risky and less known CDR methods; reduce or avoid climate damages from high-temperature overshoot; and bring long-term gains for the economy, as well as earlier benefits of avoided climate change impacts.[103]

Many of the solutions aligned with 1.5°C pathways are transformative. For energy systems, for example, this would imply an ambitious transformation from current polluting systems towards electricity systems that emit no or very low carbon dioxide emissions. This would involve moving away from fossil fuel use, increasing energy conservation and energy efficiency, and increased use of renewable energy and higher electrification.[104] However, such a transition is complex and challenging and may result in distributional consequences within and between countries. Such transitions need to be carefully managed.

Food systems, including agriculture, processing, transport, and consumption of food also have a significant impact on the climate system, as well as on biodiversity, soil quality, and human health. Diets that include high amounts of plant proteins and have low meat and dairy are associated with lower greenhouse gas emissions and bring higher benefits to human health and to the planet. Realising the full mitigation potential from the food system requires change at all stages from producer to consumer and waste management, which can be facilitated through integrated policy packages.[105]

In addition, there is a need to identify policies and actions that can reduce emissions intensive consumption or what is referred to as status consumption. Choices made by policymakers, citizens, the private sector, and other stakeholders all influence societies' development pathways.[106]

101 Figure SPM.7, IPCC, 2023: Summary for Policymakers (n 23).
102 Section C.4 and C.12, IPCC, 2022: Summary for Policymakers WG3 (n 22).
103 ibid.
104 Sections B.4, C.4 and C.6, IPCC, 2022: Summary for Policymakers WG3 (n 22).
105 Section C.9, IPCC, 2022: Summary for Policymakers WG3 (n 22).
106 Table TS.1 and Section TS.6.2, Pathak and others (n 28).

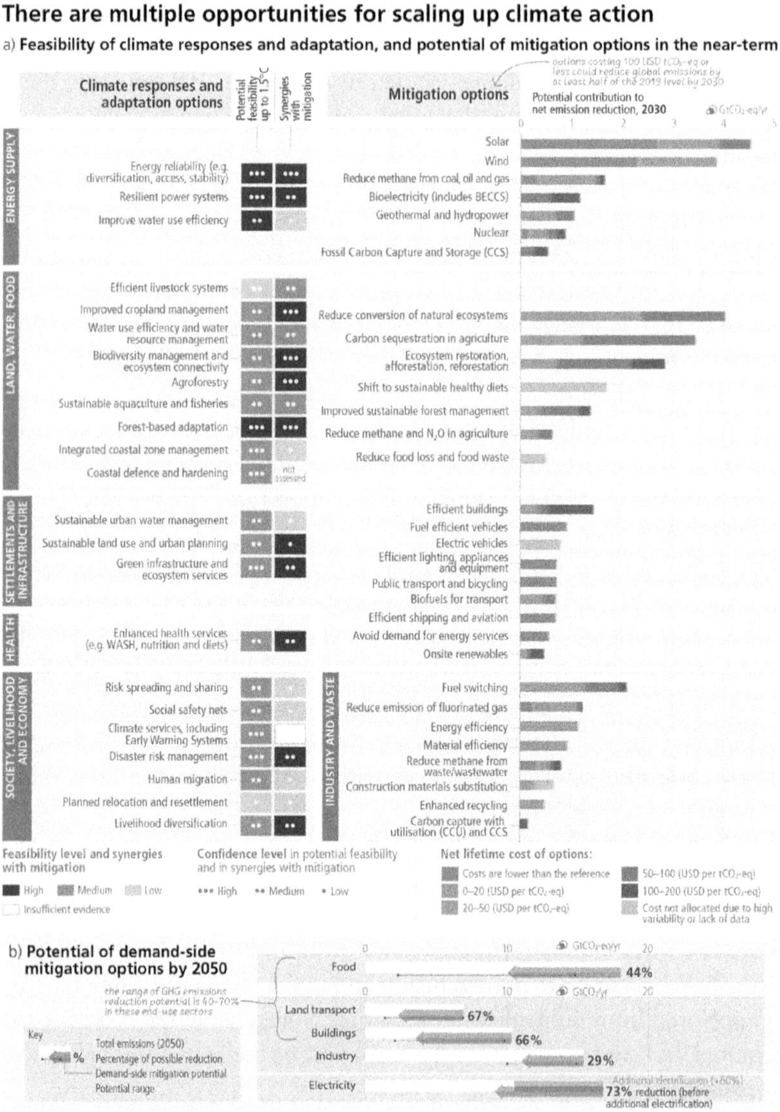


FIGURE 2.13 Multiple opportunities for scaling up climate action. **Panel (a)**: presents selected mitigation and adaptation options across different systems. Left – climate responses and adaptation options assessed for their multidimensional feasibility at global scale, in the near term and up to 1.5°C global warming. Six feasibility dimensions (economic, technological, institutional, social, environmental, and geophysical) were used to calculate the potential feasibility of climate responses and adaptation options, along with their synergies with mitigation. For potential feasibility and feasibility dimensions, the figure shows high, medium, or low feasibility. Synergies with mitigation are identified as high, medium, and low. Right – an overview of selected mitigation options and their estimated costs and potentials in 2030. The potential (horizontal axis) is the quantity of net GHG

### 2.5.4 *Policies, Legislation, and Enabling Conditions*

Many countries, both developed and developing, have announced plans to achieve net-zero greenhouse gas (or carbon dioxide) emissions by or around mid century. These targets now cover 90 per cent of global emissions, compared to 49 per cent in 2010. Direct and indirect climate legislation has also steadily increased and this is supported by a growing list of financial investors. But these targets often lack clear definitions and roadmaps for achievement. The UNFCCC, Kyoto Protocol, and Paris Agreement are supporting rising levels of national ambition and encouraging development and implementation of climate policies, but large gaps remain.[107]

Accelerated international financial cooperation is a critical enabler of low greenhouse gas and just transitions but the current tracked financial flows to achieve mitigation goals across all sectors and regions fall short of the finance levels needed. These gaps are largest in developing countries. Developing countries need increased financial support from developed countries and other sources to enhance their mitigation actions and address financial inequities and impacts related to climate change. Technology transfer and capacity building are also crucial for these countries to transition to low-emission systems.[108]

## 2.6 ADAPTATION AND RESILIENCE

Adaptation is the process of adjustment to actual or expected climate and its effects, in order to moderate harm or exploit beneficial opportunities. Adaptation actions

FIGURE 2.13 (cont.)

emission reduction that can be achieved by a given mitigation option relative to a specified emission baseline. The baseline used consists of current policy (around 2019) reference scenarios from the AR6 scenarios database (25–75 percentile values). Potentials are broken down into cost categories (see Net lifetime of cost options in the bottom right of panel (a)). The uncertainty in the total potential is typically 25–50%. **Panel (b):** displays the indicative potential of demand-side mitigation options for 2050. The left-pointing arrows represent the demand-side emissions reductions potentials. The range in potential is shown by a line connecting dots displaying the highest and the lowest potentials reported in the literature. The bottom row shows how demand-side mitigation options in other sectors can influence overall electricity demand. The dark grey bar shows the projected increase in electricity demand above the 2050 baseline due to increasing electrification in the other sectors. This projected increase in electricity demand can be avoided through demand-side mitigation options in the domains of infrastructure use and socio-cultural factors that influence electricity usage in industry, land transport, and buildings (indicated by the left-pointing arrow).[109]

[107] Section E.3, IPCC, 2022: Summary for Policymakers WG3 (n 22).
[108] Section E.5, IPCC, 2022: Summary for Policymakers WG3 (n 22).
[109] Figure SPM.7, IPCC, 2023: Summary for Policymakers (n 23).

aim to reduce risks from climate change by avoiding or moderating harm. The Paris Agreement established a global goal on adaptation with a view to 'enhancing adaptative capacity, strengthening resilience and reducing vulnerability to climate change'.[110] However, progress is needed to develop methodologies, indicators, data and metrics, monitoring, and evaluation systems to strengthen planning and implementation of adaptation actions.[111] Much adaptation reported to date is small-scale, makes only gradual progress, and is unequally distributed. Adaptation challenges are complicated by unsustainable land-use and land cover change, unsustainable consumption, deforestation, loss of biodiversity, pollution, and rapid urbanisation, among others. Adaptation can thus involve both trade-offs and synergies with mitigation and sustainable development and is closely intertwined with questions of equity and climate justice.

Nature offers potential to reduce climate impacts and risks, deal with the causes of climate change, and improve people's lives and livelihoods. Risks to ecosystems from climate change can be reduced by protection and restoration of ecosystems, and also by a range of targeted actions to adapt conservation practices to take climate change into account. However, nature itself is vulnerable to climate change. For example, coral reefs are already at high risk from ocean warming and marine heatwaves (see Section 2.4.4).[112] Evidence also indicates that there are limits to adaptation, and some systems have already crossed or are approaching limits to adaptation. Above 1.5°C global warming level, some ecosystem-based adaptation measures will lose their effectiveness in providing benefits to people.[113]

Adaptation limits can be 'hard' or 'soft'. For so-called soft limits, adaptation options may exist but are not currently available; however, options may become available in the future by addressing a range of constraints – primarily financial, governance, institutional, and policy. For hard limits, no adaptive actions are possible to avoid intolerable risks. Losses and damages increase with increasing global warming and become more difficult to avoid as additional adaptation limits are reached and are strongly concentrated among the most vulnerable ecosystems and human populations. For instance, the effectiveness of most water-related adaptation options decreases with increasing temperature – as an example, irrigation expansion in agriculture will face increasing limits due to limitations in water availability beyond 1.5°C. For small islands and for regions dependent on glacier and snow melt, beyond 1.5°C warming, reductions in freshwater resources pose potential hard adaptation limits. Some ecosystems are already near hard limits due to human-induced warming to date, such as warm-water coral reefs, coastal

[110] https://unfccc.int/sites/default/files/resource/Global_goal_on_adaptation_0.pdf; Paris Agreement (n 27) art 7(1).
[111] Sections A, C.1, C.4, and C.5, IPCC, 2022: Summary for Policymakers WG2 (n 38).
[112] Section B.4, 'IPCC, 2018: Summary for Policymakers' in Global Warming 1.5°C (n 88).
[113] Sections C.4 and C.5, IPCC, 2022: Summary for Policymakers WG2 (n 38).

wetlands, rainforests, and polar and mountain ecosystems, and will reach or surpass hard limits at 1.5°C and beyond.[114]

Insufficient financing is a key driver of adaptation gaps. Current global financial flows for adaptation are insufficient and constrain implementation of adaptation options, especially in developing countries. Implementing actions can require large upfront investments of human, financial, and technological resources, both for immediate benefits and those that become visible in the next decade or beyond. Enhancing climate change literacy on impacts and possible solutions is also necessary to ensure widespread, sustained implementation of adaptation by State and non-State actors.[115]

Adaptation actions may also result in unintended consequences or 'maladaptation', especially if poorly planned and implemented. Adaptation options can become maladaptive due to their environmental impacts that constrain ecosystem services and decrease biodiversity and ecosystem resilience to climate change, or by causing adverse outcomes for different groups – thereby exacerbating inequity. Climate actions that focus on sectors and risks in isolation and on short-term gains often lead to maladaptation.[116] Maladaptive responses to climate change can create lock-ins of vulnerability, exposure, and risks that are difficult and expensive to change and exacerbate existing inequalities. Maladaptation especially affects marginalised and vulnerable groups adversely (e.g. Indigenous Peoples, ethnic minorities, low-income households, people living in informal settlements). Maladaptation can be avoided by flexible, multi-sectoral, inclusive, and long-term planning and implementation of adaptation actions, building on local knowledge and Indigenous knowledge.[117]

## 2.7 CONCLUSION

An overwhelming body of scientific evidence has provided insight into anthropogenic climate change, including its causes and impacts. It shows that the impacts of climate change on ecosystems, societies, and planetary health are far-reaching and unprecedented. The best available scientific evidence thus suggests that immediate, robust, and sustained global action on both adaptation and mitigation is imperative. The evidence also underscores the urgent need for action and support to address losses and damages from climate change. The time for decisive action is now: every year, choice and fraction of warming matters in shaping a sustainable and resilient future for all.

[114] Section B.2, IPCC, 2023: Summary for Policymakers (n 23).

[115] ibid.

[116] Maladaptation refers to actions that may lead to increased risk of adverse climate-related outcomes, including via increased greenhouse gas emissions, increased or shifted vulnerability to climate change, more inequitable outcomes, or diminished welfare, now or in the future. Most often, maladaptation is an unintended consequence.

[117] Sections 2.3 and 3.2, IPCC, 2023: Summary for Policymakers (n 23).

| IPCC Report | IPCC Figure Number | IPCC Report Chapter | IPCC Report Page Number | Figure number in this chapter of reproduced IPCC figure |
|---|---|---|---|---|
| WGI AR6 | TS.1 | TS | 44 | Figure 2.1 |
| | **Figure TS.1 \| Changes in atmospheric $CO_2$ and global surface temperature** (**relative to 1850–1900**) **from the deep past to the next 300 years**. *The intent of this figure is to show that $CO_2$ and temperature co-vary, both in the past and into the future, and that projected $CO_2$ and temperatures are similar to those only from many millions of years ago*. $CO_2$ concentrations from millions of years ago are reconstructed from multiple proxy records (grey dots are data from Section 2.2.3.1, Figure 2.3 shown with cubic-spline fit). $CO_2$ levels for the last 800,000 years through the mid twentieth century are from air trapped in polar ice; recent values are from direct air measurements. Global surface temperature prior to 1850 is estimated from marine oxygen isotopes, one of multiple sources of evidence used to assess paleo temperatures in this Report. Temperature of the past 170 years is the AR6 assessed mean. $CO_2$ levels and global surface temperature change for the future are shown for three Shared Socioeconomic Pathway (SSP) scenarios through 2300 CE, using Earth system model emulators calibrated to the assessed global surface temperatures. Their smooth trajectories do not account for interannual to inter-decadal variability, including transient response to potential volcanic eruptions. Global maps for two paleo reference periods are based on Coupled Model Intercomparison Project Phase 6 (CMIP6) and pre-CMIP6 multi-model means, with site-level proxy data for comparison (squares and circles are marine and terrestrial, respectively). The map for 2020 is an estimate of the total observed warming since 1850–1900. Global maps at right show two SSP scenarios at 2100 (2081–2100) and at 2300 (2281–2300; map from CMIP6 models; temperature assessed in 4.7.1). A brief account of the major climate forcings associated with past global temperature changes is in Cross-Chapter Box 2.1. (Section TS.1.3, Figure TS.9, Cross-Section Box TS.1, Box TS.2) {1.2.1.2; Figures 1.14 and 1.5; 2.2.3; 2.3.1.1; 2.3.1.1.1; Figures 2.4 and 2.5; Cross-Chapter Box 2.1, Figure 1; 4.5.1; 4.7.1; Cross-Chapter Box 4.1; Cross-Chapter Box 7.1; Figure 7.13} | | | |
| WGIII AR6 | SPM.1 | SPM | 7 | Figure 2.2 |

**Figure SPM.1 | Global net anthropogenic GHG emissions ($GtCO_2$-eqyr–1) 1990–2019**. Global net anthropogenic GHG emissions include $CO_2$ from fossil fuel combustion and industrial processes ($CO_2$-FFI); net $CO_2$ from land use, land-use change, and forestry ($CO_2$-LULUCF)9; methane ($CH_4$); nitrous oxide ($N_2O$); and fluorinated gases (HFCs, PFCs, SF6, NF3). **Panel (a)** shows aggregate annual global net anthropogenic GHG emissions by groups of gases from 1990 to 2019 reported in $GtCO_2$-eq converted based on global warming potentials with a 100-year time horizon (GWP100-AR6) from the IPCC Sixth Assessment Report Working Group I (Chapter 7). The fraction of global emissions for each gas is shown for 1990, 2000, 2010, and 2019; as well as the aggregate average annual growth rate between these decades. At the right side of panel (a), GHG emissions in 2019 are broken down into individual components with the associated uncertainties (90% confidence interval) indicated by the error bars: $CO_2$-FFI ± 8%; $CO_2$-LULUCF ± 70%; $CH_4$± 30%; $N_2O$ ± 60%; F-gases ± 30%; GHG ± 11%. Uncertainties in GHG emissions are assessed in Supplementary Material 2.2. The single-year peak of emissions in 1997 was due to higher $CO_2$-LULUCF emissions from a forest and peat fire event in South-East Asia. **Panel (b)** shows global anthropogenic $CO_2$-FFI, net $CO_2$-LULUCF, $CH_4$, $N_2O$, and F-gas emissions individually for the period 1990–2019, normalised relative to 100 in 1990. Note the different scale for the included F-gas emissions compared to other gases, highlighting its rapid growth from a low base. Shaded areas indicate the uncertainty range. Uncertainty ranges as shown here are specific for individual groups of greenhouse gases and cannot be compared. The table shows the central estimate for: absolute emissions in 2019; the absolute change in emissions between 1990 and 2019; and emissions in 2019 expressed as a percentage of 1990 emissions. {2.2, Figure 2.5, Supplementary Material 2.2, Figure TS.2}

| | | | | |
|---|---|---|---|---|
| WGIII AR6 | SPM.2 panels (b) and (c) | SPM | 10 | Figure 2.3 |

**Figure SPM.2: Regional GHG emissions, and the regional proportion of total cumulative production-based $CO_2$ emissions from 1850 to 2019.**

**Panel (b)** shows the share of historical cumulative net anthropogenic $CO_2$ emissions per region from 1850 to 2019 in $GtCO_2$. This includes $CO_2$ from fossil fuel combustion and industrial processes ($CO_2$-FFI) and net $CO_2$ emissions from land use, land-use change, and forestry ($CO_2$-LULUCF). Other GHG emissions are not included. 6$CO_2$-LULUCF emissions are subject to high uncertainties, reflected by a global uncertainty estimate of ± 70% (90% confidence interval).

*(continued)*

(*continued*)

| IPCC Report | IPCC Figure Number | IPCC Report Chapter | IPCC Report Page Number | Figure number in this chapter of reproduced IPCC figure |
|---|---|---|---|---|
| | **Panel (c)** shows the distribution of regional GHG emissions in tonnes $CO_2$-eq per capita by region in 2019. GHG emissions are categorised into: $CO_2$-FFI; net $CO_2$-LULUCF; and other GHG emissions (methane, nitrous oxide, fluorinated gases, expressed in $CO_2$-eq using GWP100-AR6). The height of each rectangle shows per capita emissions, the width shows the population of the region, so that the area of the rectangles refers to the total emissions for each region. Emissions from international aviation and shipping are not included. In the case of two regions, the area for $CO_2$-LULUCF is below the axis, indicating net $CO_2$ removals rather than emissions. $CO_2$-LULUCF emissions are subject to high uncertainties, reflected by a global uncertainty estimate of ± 70% (90% confidence interval).<br>{1.3, Figure 1.2, 2.2, Figure 2.9, Figure 2.10, Figure 2.11, Annex II} | | | |
| WGI AR6 | SPM.1 panel (a) and SPM.2 panel (a) and (b) | SPM | 6–7 | Figure 2.4 |
| | **Figure SPM.1 \| History of global temperature change and causes of recent warming**<br>**Panel (a) Changes in global surface temperature reconstructed from paleoclimate archives** (solid grey line, years 1–2000) **and from direct observations** (solid black line, 1850–2020), both relative to 1850–1900 and decadally averaged. The vertical bar on the left shows the estimated temperature (*very likely* range) during the warmest multi-century period in at least the last 100,000 years, which occurred around 6500 years ago during the current interglacial period (Holocene). The Last Interglacial, around 125,000 years ago, is the next most recent candidate for a period of higher temperature. These past warm periods were caused by slow (multi-millennial) orbital variations. The grey shading with white diagonal lines shows the *very likely* ranges for the temperature reconstructions.<br>**Figure SPM.2 \| Assessed contributions to observed warming in 2010–2019 relative to 1850–1900**<br>**Panel (a) Observed global warming** (increase in global surface temperature). Whiskers show the *very likely* range.<br>**Panel (b) Evidence from attribution studies, which synthesise information from climate models and observations**. The panel shows temperature change attributed to: total human influence; changes in well-mixed greenhouse gas concentrations; other human drivers due to aerosols, ozone and land-use change (land-use reflectance); solar and volcanic drivers; and internal climate variability. Whiskers show *likely* ranges. | | | |

| | | | | |
|---|---|---|---|---|
| WGI AR6 | SPM.3 | SPM | 10 | Figure 2.5 |
| | **Figure SPM.3 \| Synthesis of assessed observed and attributable regional changes**<br>The IPCC AR6 WGI inhabited regions are displayed as **hexagons** with identical size in their approximate geographical location (see legend for regional acronyms). All assessments are made for each region as a whole and for the 1950s to the present. Assessments made on different time scales or more local spatial scales might differ from what is shown in the figure. The **colours** in each panel represent the four outcomes of the assessment on observed changes. Striped hexagons (white and light grey) are used where there is *low agreement* in the type of change for the region as a whole, and grey hexagons are used when there is limited data and/or literature that prevents an assessment of the region as a whole. Other colours indicate at least *medium confidence* in the observed change. The **confidence level** for the human influence on these observed changes is based on assessing trend detection and attribution and event attribution literature, and it is indicated by the number of dots: three dots for *high confidence*, two dots for *medium confidence* and one dot for *low confidence* (single, filled dot: limited agreement; single, empty dot: limited evidence).<br>**Panel (a) For hot extremes**, the evidence is mostly drawn from changes in metrics based on daily maximum temperatures; regional studies using other indices (heatwave duration, frequency and intensity) are used in addition. Red hexagons indicate regions where there is at least *medium confidence* in an observed increase in hot extremes.<br>**Panel (b) For heavy precipitation**, the evidence is mostly drawn from changes in indices based on one-day or five-day precipitation amounts using global and regional studies. Green hexagons indicate regions where there is at least *medium confidence* in an observed increase in heavy precipitation.<br>**Panel (c) Agricultural and ecological droughts** are assessed based on observed and simulated changes in total column soil moisture, complemented by evidence on changes in surface soil moisture, water balance (precipitation minus evapotranspiration) and indices driven by precipitation and atmospheric evaporative demand. Yellow hexagons indicate regions where there is at least *medium confidence* in an observed increase in this type of drought, and green hexagons indicate regions where there is at least *medium confidence* in an observed decrease in agricultural and ecological drought.<br>For all regions, Table TS.5 shows a broader range of observed changes besides the ones shown in this figure. Note that Southern South America (SSA) is the only region that does not display observed changes in the metrics shown in this figure, but it is affected by observed increases in mean temperature, decreases in frost, and increases in marine heatwaves. {11.9, Atlas 1.3.3, Figure Atlas.2, Table TS.5, Box TS.10, Figure 1} | | | |
| WGII AR6 | SPM.2 | SPM | 10 | Figure 2.6 |

*(continued)*

*(continued)*

| IPCC Report | IPCC Figure Number | IPCC Report Chapter | IPCC Report Page Number | Figure number in this chapter of reproduced IPCC figure |
|---|---|---|---|---|
| | **Figure SPM.2 \| Observed global and regional impacts on ecosystems and human systems attributed to climate change**. Confidence levels reflect uncertainty in attribution of the observed impact to climate change. Global assessments focus on large studies, multi-species, meta-analyses, and large reviews. For that reason they can be assessed with higher confidence than regional studies, which may often rely on smaller studies that have more limited data. Regional assessments consider evidence on impacts across an entire region and do not focus on any country in particular.<br>(**a**) Climate change has already altered terrestrial, freshwater, and ocean ecosystems at global scale, with multiple impacts evident at regional and local scales where there is sufficient literature to make an assessment. Impacts are evident on ecosystem structure, species geographic ranges and timing of seasonal life cycles (phenology) (for methodology and detailed references to chapters and cross-chapter papers see SMTS.1 and SMTS.1.1).<br>(**b**) Climate change has already had diverse adverse impacts on human systems, including on water security and food production, health and well-being, and cities, settlements, and infrastructure. The + and – symbols indicate the direction of observed impacts, with a – denoting an increasing adverse impact and a ± denoting that, within a region or globally, both adverse and positive impacts have been observed (e.g. adverse impacts in one area or food item may occur with positive impacts in another area or food item). Globally, '–' denotes an overall adverse impact; 'Water scarcity' considers, e.g. water availability in general, groundwater, water quality, demand for water, drought in cities. Impacts on food production were assessed by excluding non-climatic drivers of production increases; Global assessment for agricultural production is based on the impacts on global aggregated production; 'Reduced animal and livestock health and productivity' considers, e.g. heat stress, diseases, productivity, mortality; 'Reduced fisheries yields and aquaculture production' includes marine and freshwater fisheries/production; 'Infectious diseases' include, e.g. water-borne and vector-borne diseases; 'Heat, malnutrition and other' considers, e.g. human heat-related morbidity and mortality, labour productivity, harm from wildfire, nutritional deficiencies; 'Mental health' includes impacts from extreme weather events, cumulative events, and vicarious or anticipatory events; 'Displacement' assessments refer to evidence of displacement attributable to climate and weather extremes; 'Inland flooding and associated damages' considers, e.g. river overflows, heavy rain, glacier outbursts, urban flooding; 'Flood/storm induced damages in coastal areas' include damages due to, e.g. cyclones, sea level rise, storm surges. Damages by key economic sectors are observed impacts related to an attributable mean or extreme climate hazard or directly attributed. Key economic sectors include standard classifications and sectors of importance to regions (for methodology and detailed references to chapters and cross-chapter papers see SMTS.1 and SMTS.1.2). | | | |
| WGI AR6 | Infographic TS.1 | TS | 88–89 | Figure 2.7 |

**Infographic TS.1 | Climate Futures**. *The intent of this figure is to show possible climate futures: The climate change that people will experience this century and beyond depends on our greenhouse gas emissions, how much global warming this will cause, and the response of the climate system to this warming.*

**(top left)** Annual emissions of $CO_2$ for the five core Shared Socioeconomic Pathway (SSP) scenarios (very low: SSP1-1.9, low: SSP1-2.6, intermediate: SSP2-4.5, high: SSP3-7.0, very high: SSP5-8.5). **(bottom left)** Projected warming for each of these emissions scenarios. **(top right)** Response of some selected climate variables to four levels of global warming (°C). Changes in the 'Today' column are based on a global warming level of 1°C. **(bottom right)** The long-term effect of each global warming level on sea level. See Section TS.1.3.1 for more detail on the SSP climate change scenarios. This infographic builds from several figures in the Technical Summary: Figure TS.4 (for top left panel), Figure TS.6 (bottom left), Figure TS.12 (top right) and Box TS.4, Figure 1b (bottom right).

| | | | | |
|---|---|---|---|---|
| SYR AR6 | Figure 3.4 | Section 3 | 80 | Figure 2.8 |

**Figure 3.4:** Observed and projected global mean sea level change and its impacts, and time scales of coastal risk management. **Panel (a):** Global mean sea level change in metres relative to 1900. The historical changes (black) are observed by tide gauges before 1992 and altimeters afterwards. The future changes to 2100 and for 2150 (coloured lines and shading) are assessed consistently with observational constraints based on emulation of CMIP, ice-sheet, and glacier models, and median values and likely ranges are shown for the considered scenarios. Relative to 1995–2014, the likely global mean sea level rise by 2050 is between 0.15 to 0.23 m in the very low GHG emissions scenario (SSP1-1.9) and 0.20 to 0.29 m in the very high GHG emissions scenario (SSP5-8.5); by 2100 between 0.28 to 0.55 m under SSP1-1.9 and 0.63 to 1.01 m under SSP5-8.5; and by 2150 between 0.37 to 0.86 m under SSP1-1.9 and 0.98 to 1.88 m under SSP5-8.5 (medium confidence). Changes relative to 1900 are calculated by adding 0.158 m (observed global mean sea level rise from 1900 to 1995–2014) to simulated changes relative to 1995–2014. The future changes to 2300 (bars) are based on literature assessment, representing the 17th–83rd percentile range for SSP1-2.6 (0.3 to 3.1 m) and SSP5-8.5 (1.7 to 6.8 m). Red dashed lines: Low-likelihood, high-impact storyline, including ice-sheet instability processes. These indicate the potential impact of deeply uncertain processes, and show the 83rd percentile of SSP5-8.5 projections that include low-likelihood, high-impact processes that cannot be ruled out; because of low confidence in projections of these processes, this is not part of a likely range. IPCC AR6 global and regional sea level projections are hosted at https://sealevel.nasa.gov/ipcc-ar6-sea-level-projection-tool. The low-lying coastal zone is currently home to around 896 million people (nearly 11% of the 2020 global population), projected to reach more than one billion by 2050 across all five SSPs. **Panel (b):** Typical time scales for the planning, implementation (dashed bars) and operational lifetime of current coastal risk-management measures (blue bars). Higher rates of sea level rise demand earlier and stronger responses and reduce the lifetime of measures (inset). As the scale and pace of sea level rise accelerates beyond 2050, long-term adjustments may in some locations be beyond the limits of current adaptation options and for some small islands and low-lying coasts could be an existential risk. {WGI SPM B.5, WGI C.2.5, WGI Figure SPM.8, WGI 9.6; WGII SPM B.4.5, WGII B.5.2, WGII C.2.8, WGII D.3.3, WGII TS.D.7, WGII Cross-Chapter Box SLR} (Cross-Section Box.2)

*(continued)*

(*continued*)

| IPCC Report | IPCC Figure Number | IPCC Report Chapter | IPCC Report Page Number | Figure number in this chapter of reproduced IPCC figure |
|---|---|---|---|---|
| SYR AR6 | SPM.4 | SPM | 17 | Figure 2.9 |
| | **Figure SPM.4**: Subset of assessed climate outcomes and associated global and regional climate risks. The burning embers result from a literature based expert elicitation. **Panel (a):** Left – Global surface temperature changes in °C relative to 1850–1900. These changes were obtained by combining CMIP6 model simulations with observational constraints based on past simulated warming, as well as an updated assessment of equilibrium climate sensitivity. Very likely ranges are shown for the low and high GHG emissions scenarios (SSP1-2.6 and SSP3-7.0) (Cross-Section Box.2). Right – Global Reasons for Concern (RFC), comparing AR6 (thick embers) and AR5 (thin embers) assessments. Risk transitions have generally shifted towards lower temperatures with updated scientific understanding. Diagrams are shown for each RFC, assuming low to no adaptation. Lines connect the midpoints of the transitions from moderate to high risk across AR5 and AR6. **Panel (b):** Selected global risks for land and ocean ecosystems, illustrating general increase of risk with global warming levels with low to no adaptation. | | | |
| WGI AR6 | SPM.5 | SPM | 16–17 | Figure 2.10 |
| | **Figure SPM.5 \| Changes in annual mean surface temperature, precipitation, and soil moisture** **Panel (a) Comparison of observed and simulated annual mean surface temperature change**. The **left map** shows the observed changes in annual mean surface temperature in the period 1850–2020 per °C of global warming (°C). The local (i.e. grid point) observed annual mean surface temperature changes are linearly regressed against the global surface temperature in the period 1850–2020. Observed temperature data are from Berkeley Earth, the dataset with the largest coverage and highest horizontal resolution. Linear regression is applied to all years for which data at the corresponding grid point is available. The regression method was used to take into account the complete observational time series and thereby reduce the role of internal variability at the grid point level. White indicates areas where time coverage was 100 years or less and thereby too short to calculate a reliable linear regression. The **right map** is based on model simulations and shows change in annual multi-model mean simulated temperatures at a global warming level of 1°C (20-year mean global surface temperature change relative to 1850–1900). The triangles at each end of the colour bar indicate out-of-bound values, that is, values above or below the given limits. | | | |

**Panel (b) Simulated annual mean temperature change (°C), panel (c) precipitation change (%), and panel (d) total column soil moisture change (standard deviation of interannual variability)** at global warming levels of 1.5°C, 2°C and 4°C (20-year mean global surface temperature change relative to 1850–1900). Simulated changes correspond to Coupled Model Intercomparison Project Phase 6 (CMIP6) multi-model mean change (median change for soil moisture) at the corresponding global warming level, that is, the same method as for the right map in panel (a).

In **panel (c)**, high positive percentage changes in dry regions may correspond to small absolute changes. In **panel (d)**, the unit is the standard deviation of interannual variability in soil moisture during 1850–1900. Standard deviation is a widely used metric in characterising drought severity. A projected reduction in mean soil moisture by one standard deviation corresponds to soil moisture conditions typical of droughts that occurred about once every six years during 1850–1900. In panel (d), large changes in dry regions with little interannual variability in the baseline conditions can correspond to small absolute change. The triangles at each end of the colour bars indicate out-of-bound values, that is, values above or below the given limits. Results from all models reaching the corresponding warming level in any of the five illustrative scenarios (SSP1-1.9, SSP1-2.6, SSP2-4.5, SSP3-7.0 and SSP5-8.5) are averaged. Maps of annual mean temperature and precipitation changes at a global warming level of 3°C are available in Figure 4.31 and Figure 4.32 in Section 4.6. Corresponding maps of panels (b), (c) and (d), including hatching to indicate the level of model agreement at grid-cell level, are found in Figures 4.31, 4.32 and 11.19, respectively; as highlighted in Cross-Chapter Box Atlas.1, grid-cell level hatching is not informative for larger spatial scales (e.g. over AR6 reference regions) where the aggregated signals are less affected by small-scale variability, leading to an increase in robustness. {Figure 1.14, 4.6.1, Cross-Chapter Box 11.1, Cross-Chapter Box Atlas.1, TS.1.3.2, Figures TS.3 and TS.5}

| | | | | |
|---|---|---|---|---|
| WGII AR6 | SPM.3 | SPM | 17 | Figure 2.11 |

**Figure SPM.3 | Synthetic diagrams of global and sectoral assessments and examples of regional key risks. Diagrams show the change in the levels of impacts and risks assessed for global warming of 0–5°C global surface temperature change relative to pre-industrial period (1850–1900) over the range.**

*(continued)*

(*continued*)

| IPCC Report | IPCC Figure Number | IPCC Report Chapter | IPCC Report Page Number | Figure number in this chapter of reproduced IPCC figure |
|---|---|---|---|---|
| | (f) Examples of regional key risks. Risks identified are of at least *medium confidence* level. Key risks are identified based on the magnitude of adverse consequences (pervasiveness of the consequences, degree of change, irreversibility of consequences, potential for impact thresholds or tipping points, potential for cascading effects beyond system boundaries); likelihood of adverse consequences; temporal characteristics of the risk; and ability to respond to the risk, e.g. by adaptation. The full set of 127 assessed global and regional key risks is given in SM16.7. Diagrams are provided for some risks. The development of synthetic diagrams for Small Islands, Asia, and Central and South America were limited by the availability of adequately downscaled climate projections, with uncertainty in the direction of change, the diversity of climatologies and socioeconomic contexts across countries within a region, and the resulting low number of impact and risk projections for different warming levels. Absence of risks diagrams does not imply absence of risks within a region. (Box SPM.1) {Figure TS.4, Figure 2.11, Figure SM3.1, Figure 7.9, Figure 9.6, Figure 11.6, Figure 13.28, 16.5, 16.6, Figure 16.15, SM16.3, SM16.4, SM16.5, SM16.6 (methodologies), SM16.7, Figure CCP4.8, Figure CCP4.1 0, Figure CCP6.5, WGI AR6 2, WGI AR6 SPM A.1.2, WGI AR6 Figure SPM.8} | | | |
| SYR AR6 | Figure 3.5 panel (a) | Section 3 | 83 | Figure 2.12 |
| | **Figure 3.5:** Cumulative past, projected, and committed emissions, and associated global temperature changes. **Panel (a)** Assessed remaining carbon budgets to limit warming more likely than not to 1.5°C, to 2°C with a 83% and 67% likelihood, compared to cumulative emissions corresponding to constant 2019 emissions until 2030, existing and planned fossil fuel infrastructures (in $GtCO_2$). For remaining carbon budgets, thin lines indicate the uncertainty due to the contribution of non-$CO_2$ warming. For lifetime emissions from fossil fuel infrastructure, thin lines indicate the assessed sensitivity range. {WGI SPM D.1, WGI Figure SPM.10, WGI Table SPM.2; WGIII SPM B.1, WGIII SPM B.7, WGIII 2.7; SR1.5 SPM C.1.3 | | | |
| SYR AR6 | SPM.7 | SPM | 27 | Figure 2.13 |

**Figure SPM.7:** Multiple Opportunities for scaling up climate action. Panel (a) presents selected mitigation and adaptation options across different systems. Left – climate responses and adaptation options assessed for their multidimensional feasibility at global scale, in the near term and up to 1.5°C global warming. As literature above 1.5°C is limited, feasibility at higher levels of warming may change, which is currently not possible to assess robustly. The term response is used here in addition to adaptation because some responses, such as migration, relocation, and resettlement, may or may not be considered to be adaptation. Forest-based adaptation includes sustainable forest management, forest conservation and restoration, reforestation, and afforestation. WASH refers to water, sanitation, and hygiene. Six feasibility dimensions (economic, technological, institutional, social, environmental, and geophysical) were used to calculate the potential feasibility of climate responses and adaptation options, along with their synergies with mitigation. For potential feasibility and feasibility dimensions, the figure shows high, medium, or low feasibility. Synergies with mitigation are identified as high, medium, and low. Right – an overview of selected mitigation options and their estimated costs and potentials in 2030. Costs are net lifetime discounted monetary costs of avoided GHG emissions calculated relative to a reference technology. Relative potentials and costs will vary by place, context, and time and in the longer term compared to 2030. The potential (horizontal axis) is the net GHG emission reduction (sum of reduced emissions and/or enhanced sinks) broken down into cost categories (coloured bar segments) relative to an emission baseline consisting of current policy (around 2019) reference scenarios from the AR6 scenarios database. The potentials are assessed independently for each option and are not additive. Health system mitigation options are included mostly in settlement and infrastructure (e.g. efficient healthcare buildings) and cannot be identified separately. Fuel switching in industry refers to switching to electricity, hydrogen, bioenergy, and natural gas. Gradual colour transitions indicate uncertain breakdown into cost categories due to uncertainty or heavy context dependency. The uncertainty in the total potential is typically 25–50%. Panel (b) displays the indicative potential of demand-side mitigation options for 2050. Potentials are estimated based on approximately 500 bottom-up studies representing all global regions. The baseline (white bar) is provided by the sectoral mean GHG emissions in 2050 of the two scenarios (IEA-STEPS and IP_ModAct) consistent with policies announced by national governments until 2020. The green arrow represents the demand-side emissions reductions potentials. The range in potential is shown by a line connecting dots displaying the highest and the lowest potentials reported in the literature. Food shows demand-side potential of socio-cultural factors and infrastructure use, and changes in land-use patterns enabled by change in food demand. Demand-side measures and new ways of end-use service provision can reduce global GHG emissions in end-use sectors (buildings, land transport, food) by 40–70% by 2050 compared to baseline scenarios, while some regions and socioeconomic groups require additional energy and resources. The last row shows how demand-side mitigation options in other sectors can influence overall electricity demand. The dark grey bar shows the projected increase in electricity demand above the 2050 baseline due to increasing electrification in the other sectors. Based on a bottom-up assessment, this projected increase in electricity demand can be avoided through demand-side mitigation options in the domains of infrastructure use and socio-cultural factors that influence electricity usage in industry, land transport, and buildings (green arrow). {Figure 4.4}

*(continued)*

*(continued)*

| IPCC Report | IPCC Figure Number | IPCC Report Chapter | IPCC Report Page Number | Figure number in this chapter of reproduced IPCC figure |
|---|---|---|---|---|
| WGI AR6 | Table SPM.2 | SPM | 29 | Table 2.1 |
| | **Table SPM.2 \| Estimates of historical carbon dioxide ($CO_2$) emissions and remaining carbon budgets**. Estimated remaining carbon budgets are calculated from the beginning of 2020 and extend until global net-zero $CO_2$ emissions are reached. They refer to $CO_2$ emissions, while accounting for the global warming effect of non-$CO_2$ emissions. Global warming in this table refers to human-induced global surface temperature increase, which excludes the impact of natural variability on global temperatures in individual years. | | | |
| WGIII AR6 | Table SPM.2 | SPM | 20 | Table 2.2 |
| | **Table SPM.2 \| Key characteristics of the modelled global emissions pathways**. Summary of projected $CO_2$ and GHG emissions, projected net-zero timings, and the resulting global warming outcomes. Pathways are categorised (rows), according to their likelihood of limiting warming to different peak warming levels (if peak temperature occurs before 2100) and 2100 warming levels. Values shown are for the median [p50] and 5th–95th percentiles [p5–p95], noting that not all pathways achieve net-zero $CO_2$ or GHGs. | | | |

# 3

# Attribution Science

## *Insights into Climate Change and Its Consequences*

*Carly A. Phillips, L. Delta Merner, and Friederike Otto**

### 3.1 INTRODUCTION

The consequences of climate change are growing increasingly severe, leading to significant damages and losses globally. As a physical process, the science is overwhelmingly clear – more than a century of burning fossil fuels and degrading ecosystems has led to an accumulation of greenhouse gases in the atmosphere, raising global temperatures, acidifying oceans, and amplifying extreme events.[1] Warming ocean waters and marine heatwaves have led to widespread coral bleaching and mortality. On land, extended droughts have increased tree mortality, while priming forests for severe wildfire.[2] Building on the introduction to climate science in the preceding chapter, this chapter provides an overview of the science establishing these causal links, attribution science, as presented in the Intergovernmental Panel on Climate Change (IPCC), and it further explores three types of attribution science – trend, source, and event – to understand the current state of the science and research findings globally.

The IPCC stands as an authority in the realm of climate attribution science. Through its rigorous evaluations and synthesis of scientific research, the IPCC has brought clarity and consensus to understanding how human actions are directly linked to climatic shifts and extreme weather events. Its comprehensive assessments have solidified and contextualised the role of attribution science as a fundamental aspect of our understanding of climate change. Climate attribution science, which

* Carly A. Phillips is a research scientist with the Science Hub for Climate Litigation at the Union of Concerned Scientists. L. Delta Merner is a lead scientist with the Science Hub for Climate Litigation at the Union of Concerned Scientists. Friederike Otto is a senior lecturer in climate science at the Grantham Institute for Climate Change and the Environment at Imperial College London.

1 'IPCC, 2023: Summary for Policymakers' in Hoesung Lee and others (eds), *Climate Change 2023: Synthesis Report. Contribution of Working Groups I, II and III to the Sixth Assessment Report of the Intergovernmental Panel on Climate Change* (Cambridge University Press 2023).

2 'IPCC, 2022: Summary for Policymakers' in Priyadarshi Shukla and others (eds), *Climate Change 2022: Mitigation of Climate Change. Contribution of Working Group III to the Sixth Assessment Report of the Intergovernmental Panel on Climate Change* (Cambridge University Press 2022).

identifies and quantifies the contribution of human-induced climate change to global trends and extreme events, reveals critical insights about how human-caused climate change has and continues to impact communities worldwide.[3] Event attribution research has been around for about two decades, which makes it a comparatively new scientific endeavour. In that short time, however, the field has made impressive advances and is growing rapidly. By comparing models of Earth's climate with and without human influence as well as weather observations of past and present, studies in this field can now explain how climate change makes a heatwave hotter or a heavy rainfall event more intense.[4]

Source attribution science traces the origin of the pollutants that cause climate change and quantifies their role in driving climate impacts.[5] This research determines the relative contributions of different emission sources, including governments, oil and gas, agriculture, and other sectors, to the overall increase in concentrations of heat-trapping gas in the atmosphere and subsequent impacts like sea level rise and global temperature increase.[6] This research is particularly useful since significant portions of the emissions driving climate change can be traced to a relatively small number of actors.[7]

With this foundation, the chapter will delve into specific regional impacts, showcasing how attribution science has illuminated the ways in which different parts of the world – Africa, the Americas, Europe, the South Pacific, and Asia – are experiencing and responding to the unique challenges posed by a changing climate.

## 3.2 CLIMATE ATTRIBUTION SCIENCE

Climate attribution science is an umbrella term that encompasses distinct yet intertwined scientific research subfields. This section provides context on the integration of attribution science in the IPCC, establishing attribution as a robust scientific field. It further explores three types of attribution science: trend, source, and event. Each represents a critical aspect of our understanding of climate phenomena. Trend attribution systematically analyses long-term climatic shifts, discerning patterns amidst the global climate upheaval. Source attribution rigorously traces the

3 'IPCC, 2023: Section 2.1.2' in Hoesung Lee and others (eds), *Climate Change 2023: Synthesis Report. Contribution of Working Groups I, II and III to the Sixth Assessment Report of the Intergovernmental Panel on Climate Change* (Cambridge University Press 2023).

4 Sonia I. Seneviratne and others, 'Chapter 11: Weather and climate extreme events in a changing climate' in Valerie Masson-Delmotte and others (eds), *Climate Change 2021: The Physical Science Basis. Contribution of Working Group I to the Sixth Assessment Report of the Intergovernmental Panel on Climate Change* (Cambridge University Press 2021).

5 Brenda Ekwurzel and others, 'The rise in global atmospheric $CO_2$, surface temperature, and sea level from emissions traced to major carbon producers' (2017) 144 Climatic Change 579–590.

6 ibid.

7 Richard Heede, 'Tracing anthropogenic carbon dioxide and methane emissions to fossil fuel and cement producers 1854–2010' (2014) 122 Climatic Change 229–241.

genesis of these changes, pinpointing the human and natural factors contributing to our evolving climate. Event attribution, with its focus on acute phenomena, examines specific extreme weather occurrences, elucidating their links to broader climatic trends. By exploring the definitions, scope, methodologies, and examples of studies within each domain, this chapter provides insight into how these three facets of attribution science have evolved in parallel, offering distinct yet complementary perspectives for understanding climate change.

## 3.3 ATTRIBUTION SCIENCE IN THE INTERGOVERNMENTAL PANEL ON CLIMATE CHANGE

The IPCC is an international body that provides the world with objective, scientific information about climate change. Established in 1988 by the World Meteorological Organization (WMO) and the United Nations Environment Programme (UNEP), the IPCC has become the foremost authority on climate science, synthesising research from thousands of scientists across the globe. Its comprehensive assessment reports, released every few years, are critical in informing international policy and debate on climate change. By rigorously analysing and compiling the latest scientific findings, the IPCC plays a vital role in enhancing global awareness and guiding policy decisions aimed at mitigating and adapting to the effects of a warming world.

The IPCC operates through structured assessment cycles that culminate in comprehensive reports. Within each cycle, the IPCC organises its work into three Working Groups, each focusing on a distinct aspect of climate change. Working Group I (WG1) deals with the physical science basis of climate change, synthesising the latest scientific findings on climate processes, changes, and impacts. Working Group II (WG2) addresses climate change impacts, adaptation, and vulnerability, offering insights into how climate change affects natural and human systems and potential ways to adapt. Working Group III (WG3) tackles the mitigation of climate change, exploring strategies and policies for reducing greenhouse gas emissions and mitigating the effects of climate change. Together, these Working Groups produce detailed reports that provide a comprehensive, multidisciplinary understanding of climate change, its implications, and potential responses. The IPCC also produces a synthesis report, which synthesises all information contained in the three reports comprising the most recent IPCC assessment cycle.

According to the IPCC, 'Human-caused climate change is already affecting weather and climate extremes in every region. This has led to widespread adverse impacts and related losses and damages to nature and people (*high confidence*)'.[8]

[8] The statement summarises the findings generated by assessing the literature on extreme event and trend attribution in the WG1 Report, particularly Chapter 11, and impact attribution in WG2. In the WG2 Report, attribution literature is assessed in almost every chapter as one important line of

Quoted from the Summary for Policymakers (SPM) of the IPCC Sixth Assessment (AR6) Synthesis Report, this statement is the second key finding that the report highlights, preceded only by the fact that greenhouse gas emissions from burning fossil fuels have already warmed the climate by over 1°C.

Attribution, and particularly the rapid development of extreme event attribution since the previous IPCC assessment cycle (AR5), has been highlighted as a major new development. The third key finding of the SPM of WG1 in AR6 notes – 'Human-induced climate change is already affecting many weather and climate extremes in every region across the globe. Evidence of observed changes in extremes such as heat waves, heavy precipitation, droughts, and tropical cyclones, and, in particular, their attribution to human influence, has strengthened since AR5' – is one example.[9] Particularly notable is that this is stated without any uncertainty and confidence language, which means it is a fact, carrying the same level of scientific confidence as the statement that human influence has warmed the climate.

In AR5, a chapter was dedicated to attribution in WG1[10] and WG2, respectively,[11] where the attribution of extreme events was introduced. With the science having now matured, attribution science is used as an important additional line of evidence to assess the impacts of human-induced climate change in all regions and for a range of different types of extreme weather events, as detailed in the following section.

Marking a significant milestone in the evolution of climate science, attribution science was highlighted in a 'cross working group box' reproduced in the first chapter of WG reports from AR6 for the first time in the history of the IPCC – underscoring the scientific consensus around its methods and findings. Attribution science was the one topic deemed relevant across all three working groups. Written by authors from different reports, the box provides a brief introduction to attribution science and an overview of the major publications. It also serves as a signpost to all of the chapters throughout the IPCC reports that assess attribution.

evidence and summarised in Chapter 16. See Valerie Masson-Delmotte and others (eds), *Climate Change 2021: The Physical Science Basis. Contribution of Working Group I to the Sixth Assessment Report of the Intergovernmental Panel on Climate Change* (Cambridge University Press 2021) and Brian O'Neill and others, 'Chapter 16: Key risks across sectors and regions' in Hans O. Portner and others (eds), *Climate Change 2022: Impacts, Adaptation and Vulnerability. Contribution of Working Group II to the Sixth Assessment Report of the Intergovernmental Panel on Climate Change* (Cambridge University Press 2022).

9 'IPCC, 2021: Summary for Policymakers' in Valerie Masson-Delmotte and others (eds), *Climate Change 2021: The Physical Science Basis. Contribution of Working Group I to the Sixth Assessment Report of the Intergovernmental Panel on Climate Change* (Cambridge University Press 2021) (IPCC, 2021: Summary for Policymakers).

10 Nathaniel L. Bindoff and others, 'Detection and attribution of climate change: From global to regional' in Thomas F. Stocker and others (eds), *Climate Change 2013: The Physical Science Basis. Contribution of Working Group I to the Fifth Assessment Report of the Intergovernmental Panel on Climate Change* (Cambridge University Press 2013).

11 Wolfgang Cramer and others, 'Chapter 18: Detection and attribution of observed impacts' in Christopher B. Field and others (eds), *Climate Change 2014: Impacts, Adaptation, and Vulnerability. Part A: Global and Sectoral Aspects. Contribution of Working Group II to the Fifth Assessment Report of the Intergovernmental Panel on Climate Change* (Cambridge University Press 2014).

In summary, the IPCC uses attribution as a key line of evidence throughout all assessments dealing with the impacts of the burning of fossil fuels on the climate as well as human and natural systems. This not only provides much more detail on local and regional impacts and losses and damages but also corroborates earlier model projections that have now become reality. Attribution thus brings observations and model projections together in a comprehensive framework reducing uncertainty within climate science overall.

## 3.4 TREND ATTRIBUTION

### 3.4.1 *Definition and Scope of Trend Attribution*

Trend attribution science detects and quantifies the link between human-driven changes to the climate system and key global trends, with early studies focused on indicators like average surface temperature[12] and sea level.[13] Research in this area was the first to fingerprint human influence in the climate system,[14] and it provided the basis for a scientific understanding of climate change. While trend attribution began as a more narrow field, it has since expanded to cover a range of climate impacts including drought, ocean acidification, arctic sea ice loss, and increases in precipitation in mid-high latitudes.[15]

### 3.4.2 *Methodologies and Models Used in Trend Attribution*

Methodologies for trend attribution have evolved since the release of the IPCC's First Assessment report in 1990, leading to more complex global climate models, a more sophisticated representation of system dynamics, and an unequivocal understanding that human influence has warmed the planet and induced rapid, widespread changes across the world.[16] Similar to other types of attribution research, trend attribution studies often use observed historical data alongside the output of models with and without anthropogenic warming. These simulations (currently from the sixth iteration of the Coupled Model Intercomparison Project, i.e. CMIP6)

[12] Simon F. B. Tett and others, 'Causes of twentieth-century temperature change near the Earth's surface' (1999) 399 Nature 569–572.

[13] Veronika Eyring and others, 'Chapter 3: Human influence on the climate system' in Valerie Masson-Delmotte and others (eds), *Climate Change 2021: The Physical Science Basis. Contribution of Working Group I to the Sixth Assessment Report of the Intergovernmental Panel on Climate Change* (Cambridge University Press 2021).

[14] Gabriele C. Hegerl and others, 'Climate change detection and attribution: Beyond mean temperature signals' (2006) 19 Journal of Climate 5058–5077.

[15] Eyring and others (n 13).

[16] Delian Chen and others, 'Chapter 1: Framing, context, and methods' in Valerie Masson-Delmotte and others (eds), *Climate Change 2021: The Physical Science Basis. Contribution of Working Group I to the Sixth Assessment Report of the Intergovernmental Panel on Climate Change* (Cambridge University Press 2021).

provide counterfactual evidence of a climate without the interference of human-caused greenhouse gas emissions and associated impacts, which allows scientists to better tease out the impact of human-caused climate change.

### 3.4.3 *Trend Attribution Studies*

Trend attribution studies span a wide range of climate impacts and can form the basis for other types of attribution science. For example, human-caused climate change has increased global surface temperatures by 1.07°C (0.8°C–1.3°C) since the pre-industrial period and led to a 40 per cent reduction in September Arctic sea ice area since the 1980s.[17] In addition, human influence was the main driver of the rise of 0.2 m (0.15 to 0.25 m) of global mean sea level between 1901 and 2018.[18] On a regional scale, climate attribution of wildfires in forests of western North America found that human-caused climate change led to an additional 4.2 million acres burned between 1984 and 2015.[19]

Recent work has expanded the findings from trend attribution studies to explore how economic and health impacts can be linked to climate change. While still a relatively young field, this 'impact attribution' research can provide key insights into the toll that climate change exacts on society and ecosystems. For example, recent research on the economic impacts of Hurricane Sandy, which hit the East Coast of the United States in 2012, found that roughly $8 billion of the more than $60 billion in overall damages were attributable to 'climate-mediated anthropogenic sea-level rise'.[20] Similarly, a study of global heat exposure found that 37 per cent (20.5%–76.3%) of heat-related deaths during the warm season from 1991 to 2018 are attributable to anthropogenic climate change.[21]

## 3.5 SOURCE ATTRIBUTION

### 3.5.1 *Definition and Scope of Source Attribution*

Source attribution research, which quantifies how emissions from specific sources contribute to a given impact, highlights how industries, states, and ecosystem processes drive climate change and its consequences. These studies allow scientists to pinpoint, for example, how carbon dioxide from the fossil fuel industry, methane from the agricultural sector, or cumulative emissions from an individual country

[17] IPCC, 2021: Summary for Policymakers (n 9).

[18] ibid.

[19] John T. Abatzoglou and A. Park Williams, 'Impact of anthropogenic climate change on wildfire across western US forests' (2016) 113 PNAS 11770–11775.

[20] Benjamin H. Strauss and others, 'Economic damages from Hurricane Sandy attributable to sea level rise caused by anthropogenic climate change' (2021) 12 Nature Communications 2720.

[21] Ana Maria Vicedo-Cabrera and others, 'The burden of heat-related mortality attributable to recent human-induced climate change' (2021) 11 Nature Climate Change 492–500.

like the United States contribute to increases in global temperature or ocean acidification. As a result, such studies provide important information for mitigation and adaptation to climate change.

### 3.5.2 *Methodologies and Models Used in Source Attribution*

Similar to other detection and attribution research, source attribution methodology uses models to simulate Earth's climate with and without emissions from specific sources. The case studies described later in this chapter use a global energy-balance carbon-cycle model to explore scenarios that include and exclude carbon dioxide and methane emissions traced to the eighty-eight largest 'carbon majors', institutions representing investor-owned, state-owned, and nation-state fossil fuel producers and cement manufacturers.[22] This model, derived from the impulse response function approach in the IPCC's Fifth Assessment report (AR5) and other studies,[23] incorporates AR5-consistent parameters for atmospheric residence times of $CO_2$ and methane. It extends the AR5 model to include a term scaling $CO_2$ time constants with global mean surface temperature (GMST) anomaly and cumulative carbon uptake[24] and includes contributions to the climate system from historical, natural, and anthropogenic sources. The contributions of these eighty-eight entities (previously ninety, now eighty-eight due to mergers and acquisitions) represent both Scope 1 and 3 emissions, that is direct emissions from an entity's activities as well as downstream emissions from the use and combustion of their products.[25] To date, the majority of source attribution studies have focused on emissions impacts from the fossil fuel industry because the combustion of fossil fuels is the primary driver of observed increases in Earth's surface temperature.[26]

### 3.5.3 *Source Attribution Studies*

In the past decade, source attribution research has grown rapidly, tracing emissions from eighty-eight 'carbon majors' to rapidly rising temperatures, sea levels, ocean acidification, and wildfires. Indeed, nearly two-thirds of global industrial carbon

22 Heede (n 7).

23 See Gunnar Myhre and others, 'Chapter 8: Anthropogenic and natural radiative forcing supplementary material' in Thomas F. Stocker and others (eds), *Climate Change 2013: The Physical Science Basis. Contribution of Working Group I to the Fifth Assessment Report of the Intergovernmental Panel on Climate Change* (Cambridge University Press 2013); Fortunat Joos and others, 'Carbon dioxide and climate impulse response functions for the computation of greenhouse gas metrics: A multi-model analysis' (2013) 13 Atmospheric Chemistry and Physics 2793–2825.

24 Richard J. Millar and others, 'A modified impulse-response representation of the global response to carbon dioxide emissions' (2017) 17(1) Atmospheric Chemistry and Physics 1–20.

25 Edgar Hertwich and Richard Wood, 'The growing importance of scope 3 greenhouse gas emissions from industry' (2018) 13 Environmental Research Letters 104013.

26 See US Global Change Research Program, *Climate Science Special Report: A Sustained Assessment Activity of the US Global Change Research Program* (Donald Wuebbles and others (eds) 2017).

dioxide and methane emissions since 1751 can be traced to these eighty-eight entities.[27] Such a rapid increase in the concentration of atmospheric greenhouse gases (GHGs) has led to profound changes in Earth's climate, with more than 40 per cent of the GMST increase between 1880 and 2010 being traceable to the combustion of their products.[28] More than 35 per cent of this attributable temperature increase has occurred in the last fifty years,[29] and an even smaller subset of carbon producers have played an outsized role. Emissions traced to the top twenty investor and state-owned companies contributed to nearly 25 per cent of the increase in GMST between 1880 and 2010.[30] In addition to GHGs and temperature, emissions from eighty-eight 'carbon majors' contributed more than 55 per cent of the increase in ocean acidification[31] and 34 per cent of the increase in global sea level rise between 1880 and 2015.[32] When evaluating investor-owned enterprises alone, emissions traced to forty-eight 'carbon majors' contributed 15 per cent of the increase in both global average temperature and ocean acidification.[33]

In 2023, scientists published the first regional source attribution study, pinpointing the contribution of emissions traced to eighty-eight carbon majors to wildfire-prone conditions and burned area in forests of western North America. This research showed that more than a third of burned area between 1986 and 2021 and nearly half of the increase in wildfire-prone conditions since 1901 are attributable to emissions from these eighty-eight companies.[34] These case studies provide additional evidence to underscore the historical and on-going role of major carbon producers and the fossil fuel industry in driving climate change.

## 3.6 EVENT ATTRIBUTION

### 3.6.1 *Definition and Scope of Event Attribution*

Extreme event attribution relies on several different methods[35] to assess and quantify the relative contribution of multiple causal factors, such as anthropogenic

27 Heede (n 7).
28 Ekwurzel and others (n 5).
29 Heede (n 7).
30 Ekwurzel and others (n 5).
31 Rachel Licker and others, 'Attributing ocean acidification to major carbon producers' (2019) 14 Environment Research Letters 2.
32 Ekwurzel and others (n 5).
33 Licker and others (n 31).
34 Kristina A. Dahl and others, 'Quantifying the contribution of major carbon producers to increases in vapor pressure deficit and burned area in western US and southwestern Canadian Forests' (2023) 18(6) Environment Research Letters 1.
35 See Myles Allan, 'Liability for climate change' (2003) 421 Nature 891–892; Sjoukje Philip and others, 'A protocol for probabilistic extreme event attribution analyses' (2020) 6 Advances in Statistical Climatology, Meteorology and Oceanography 177–203; Geert Jan van Oldenborgh and others, 'Pathways and pitfalls in extreme event attribution' (2021) 166 Climatic Change 13.

climate change, to an extreme weather event.[36] Over the past two decades, scientists have released more than 500 event attribution studies,[37] highlighting the strong influence of human-induced climate change across the world. This growing body of evidence is complementary to other analyses that document observed and modelled trends in extremes due to climate change and that project future risk. The evidence from attribution studies adds value by highlighting the role of human-induced climate change as a causal driver in experienced events, which in turn is useful for building future resilience.[38] It also enables the attribution of impacts, which is useful for cost–benefit analysis of mitigation and is a potential avenue for the exploration of drivers of loss and damage from climate-related extremes.[39] Despite the growing breadth of event attribution research, these studies address only a fraction of impactful extreme events occurring any year, and as a result, do not give a comprehensive overview of the attributable impacts of human-induced climate change.[40]

### 3.6.2 *Methodologies and Models Used in Event Attribution Studies*

Event attribution research involves the comparison of a world with and without anthropogenic climate change using both 'probabilistic' and 'storyline' approaches. These methods compare observed historical changes, simulated under observed forcings (i.e. with climate change), to a counterfactual climate simulated in the absence of all or some components of anthropogenic forcing (without climate change).[41] For 'probabilistic' event attribution, such comparisons are made in a quantitative, statistical way, allowing scientists to assess the overall likelihood of an event, as well as whether and to what extent the likelihood and intensity of an event has changed due to anthropogenic climate change.[42] In one study,[43] scientists found that the prolonged heat in Siberia in 2020 was made at least 600 times more likely by human-induced

[36] Friederike E. L. Otto, 'Attribution of extreme events to climate change' (2023) 48 Annual Review of Environment and Resources 813–828.

[37] 'Attributing extreme weather to climate change' (*Carbon Brief*, 4 August 2022) <www.carbonbrief.org/mapped-how-climate-change-affects-extreme-weather-around-the-world/> accessed 18 April 2024.

[38] Emmanuel Raju and others, 'Stop blaming the climate for disasters' (2022) 3 Nature Communications Earth and Environment 1.

[39] Rachel A. James and others, 'Attribution: How is it relevant for loss and damage policy and practice?' in Reinhard Mechler and others (eds), *Loss and Damage from Climate Change: Concepts, Methods and Policy Options* (Springer 2019).

[40] Friederike EL. Otto and Emmanuel Raju, 'Harbingers of decades of unnatural disasters' (2023) 4 Nature Communications Earth and Environment 280.

[41] Otto (n 36).

[42] Seneviratne and others (n 4).

[43] Andrew Ciavarella and others, 'Prolonged Siberian heat of 2020 almost impossible without human influence' (2021) 166 Climatic Change 1–18.

climate change and that an event of the same likelihood as the heat experienced in 2020 (estimated to be approximately a 1-/130-year event) would have been two degrees cooler in a world without climate change.[44] In contrast, 'storyline' attribution studies address the atmospheric dynamics that led to an event, specifically focusing on how an event would have developed with and without human-induced climate change, thereby creating a counterfactual storyline for a given event.[45] Research using a storyline approach might find, for example, that 50 per cent of the magnitude of a given event under the same dynamical conditions as observed can be explained by natural variability,[46] but it does not address the likelihood of an event.

Many studies incorporate elements of both methods,[47] for example, by defining atmospheric conditions that accompany an extreme event and then assessing how the relative frequency of such occurrences has changed. In the case of the Mediterranean storm Apollo of 2021, the frequency of similar situations leading to heavy storms increased significantly in September when the storm occurred.[48] In this way, the primary difference between these event attribution approaches lies in their fine-tuning rather than their underlying process, leading scientists and bodies like the IPCC to assess all attribution studies together[49] rather than separating by methodology.

It is important to note that not all hazards are equally understood or studied with current attribution methods. While there are attribution studies for an increasing number of different types of physical hazards, the main hazards studied to date are heat and cold waves, storms, heavy rainfall and associated flooding, droughts, and wildfires. The focus on these hazards in attribution science stems from their significant impacts, clear scientific links to climate change, data availability, and public and policy relevance. However, the absence of an attribution study does not imply that climate change did not intensify or increase the likelihood of a particular event. Rather, it reflects that the resources and human capacity to conduct these studies are finite, meaning an attribution study for every extreme event is not possible. Here we briefly summarise event attribution studies for key impacts that are strongly attributable to climate change, specifically heat, heavy rainfall, drought, and wildfire.[50]

44 Mathias Hauser and others, 'Methods and model dependency of extreme event attribution: the 2015 European drought' (2017) 5 Earth's Future 1034–1043.

45 Chen and others (n 16); Theodore G Shepherd and others, 'Storylines: an alternative approach to representing uncertainty in physical aspects of climate change' (2018) 151 Climatic Change 555–571.

46 Theodore G. Shepherd, 'A common framework for approaches to extreme event attribution' (2016) 2 Current Climate Change Reports 28–38.

47 Aglaé Jézéquel and others, 'Behind the veil of extreme event attribution' (2018) 149 Climatic Change 367–383.

48 Davide Faranda and others, 'A climate-change attribution retrospective of some impactful weather extremes of 2021' (2022) 3 Weather and Climate Dynamics 1311–1140.

49 Seneviratne and others (n 4).

50 Ben Clarke and others, 'Extreme weather impacts of climate change: an attribution perspective' (2022) 1 Environmental Research Climate 012001.

### 3.6.2.1 Heat

Heat and cold extremes represent the most dramatic changes in extreme weather induced by climate change. The likelihood, duration, and intensity of heat extremes, like heatwaves, are increasing while cold extremes are declining. The IPCC's WG1 2021 report, which represents the global scientific consensus, clearly states that increases in heat on every continent are the result of human-caused climate change:[51]

> A heatwave that would once have had a chance of 1 in 10 to occur in any given year in the pre-industrial climate will now occur 2.8 (1.8–3.2) times more frequently and be 1.2°C hotter. At 2°C of global warming, it will occur 5.6 (3.8–6.0) times more frequently and be 2.6°C hotter. A heatwave that would have had a 1 in 50 chance to occur in any given year in the pre-industrial climate will now occur 4.8 (2.3–6.4) times more frequently and be 1.2°C hotter. At 2°C of global warming, it will occur 13.9 (6.9–16.6) times more frequently and be 2.7°C hotter.[52]

By 2015, the likelihood of moderate heat extremes on land was roughly five times higher than in pre-industrial times and roughly 75 per cent of moderate heat extremes were attributable to human-induced climate change.[53] Globally, previously very rare heat is now just unusual,[54] while extreme heat events today reach temperatures that were formerly all but impossible.[55] Together, heat attribution studies and projections of future heat trends highlight the impacts wrought by each fraction of a degree of warming.

[51] Valerie Masson-Delmotte and others (eds), *Climate Change 2021: The Physical Science Basis. Contribution of Working Group I to the Sixth Assessment Report of the Intergovernmental Panel on Climate Change* (Cambridge University Press 2021).

[52] Clarke and others (n 50).

[53] Erich Fischer and Reto Knutti, 'Anthropogenic contribution to global occurrence of heavy-precipitation and high-temperature extremes' (2015) 5 Nature Climate Change 560–564.

[54] See Markus G. Donat and others, 'Temperature and precipitation extremes in century-long gridded observations, reanalyses, and atmospheric model simulations' (2016) Journal of Geophysics Research Atmospheres 11174; Andrew D. King, 'Attributing changing rates of temperature record breaking to anthropogenic influences' (2017) 5 Earth's Future 1156–1168; Robert Dunn and others, 'Development of an updated global land in situ-based data set of temperature and precipitation extremes: HadEX3' (2020) Journal of Geophysics Research Atmospheres; Min-Gyu Seong and others, 'Anthropogenic greenhouse gas and aerosol contributions to extreme temperature changes during 1951–2015' (2021) 34(3) Journal of Climate 857–870.

[55] See Stefan Rahmstorf and Dim Coumou, 'Increase of extreme events in a warming world' (2011) 108 PNAS 17905–17909; Yukiko Imada and others, 'The July 2018 high temperature event in Japan could not have happened without human-induced global warming' (2019) 15A SOLA 8–12; Sebastian Sippel and others, 'Climate change now detectable from any single day of weather at global scale' (2020) 10 Nature Climate Change 35–41; Alexander Robinson and others, 'Increasing heat and rainfall extremes now far outside the historical climate' (2021) 4 NPJ Climate and Atmospheric Science 45.

### 3.6.2.2 Heavy Rainfall and Associated Flooding

Since the 1950s, human-caused climate change has led to increases in the frequency and intensity of heavy rainfall across most parts of the world.[56] While the evidence and confidence in trends vary geographically, the likelihood of heavy precipitation has not strongly decreased anywhere.[57] Indeed, a previously one-in-ten year rainfall event currently occurs 1.3 (1.2–1.4) times every ten years and is 6.7 per cent wetter. At 2°C of global warming, such an event will occur 1.7 (1.6–2.0) times per ten years and be 14 per cent wetter.[58] Additionally, short-duration extreme rainfall events are intensifying,[59] while regional attribution studies show that downpours are increasing in frequency and intensity, particularly across North America, Asia, and Europe.[60] Data are more sparse in Africa and South America but recent studies do see a strong increase in some events attributable to human-induced climate change.[61]

### 3.6.2.3 Drought

Human-induced climate change is a key driver of increasing drought in several drought-prone regions of the world,[62] as well as globally.[63] While specific categories of drought (meteorological, agricultural, and hydrological) have different drivers

[56] See Fischer and Knutti (n 53); Erich Fischer and Reto Knutti, 'Observed heavy precipitation increase confirms theory and early models' (2016) Nature Climate Change 986–991; Seneviratne and others (n 4).

[57] Table 11.9, Seneviratne and others (n 4).

[58] Valerie Masson-Delmotte and others (eds), *Climate Change 2021: The Physical Science Basis. Contribution of Working Group I to the Sixth Assessment Report of the Intergovernmental Panel on Climate Change* (Cambridge University Press 2021).

[59] Hayley J. Fowler and others, 'Anthropogenic intensification of short-duration rainfall extremes' (2021) 2 Nature Reviews Earth and Environment 107–122.

[60] See Huopo Chen and Jianqi Sun, 'Contribution of human influence to increased daily precipitation extremes over China' (2017) 44 Geophysical Research Letters 2436–2444; Huopo Chen and Jianqi Sun, 'Anthropogenic influence has increased climate extreme occurrence over China' (2021) 66 Science Bulletin (Beijing) 749–752; Seungmok Paik and others, 'Determining the anthropogenic greenhouse gas contribution to the observed intensification of extreme precipitation' (2020) 46 Geophysical Research Letters; Siyan Dong and others, 'Attribution of extreme precipitation with updated observations and CMIP6 simulations' (2021) 34 Journal of Climate 871–881; Qiaohong Sun and others, 'A global, continental, and regional analysis of changes in extreme precipitation' (2021) 34 Journal of Climate 243–258.

[61] See 'Climate change exacerbated heavy rainfall leading to large scale flooding in highly vulnerable communities in West Africa' *(World Weather Attribution)* <www.worldweatherattribution.org/climate-change-exacerbated-heavy-rainfall-leading-to-large-scale-flooding-in-highly-vulnerable-communities-in-west-africa/> accessed 18 April 2024; 'Climate change increased heavy rainfall, hitting vulnerable communities in Eastern Northeast Brazil' (*World Weather Attribution)* <www.worldweatherattribution.org/climate-change-increased-heavy-rainfall-hitting-vulnerable-communities-in-eastern-northeast-brazil/> accessed 18 April 2024.

[62] See Chen and Sun (n 60); Benjamin Cook and others, 'Climate change and drought: From past to future' (2018) 4 Current Climate Change Reports 164–179.

[63] Kate Marvel and others, 'Twentieth-century hydroclimate changes consistent with human influence' (2019) 569 Nature 59–65.

with implications for various parts of society, droughts across the world are complex, powerful events that impact billions of people. All types of drought are connected and broadly refer to a moisture deficit relative to a baseline in either precipitation, soil moisture, or groundwater reservoirs.[64] While drought in some regions, like the Mediterranean and Southern Africa, is due to decreases in precipitation, globally, drought is largely driven by higher temperatures which increase evaporation and decrease snowpack, reducing the contribution of meltwater to surface water flows.[65] In other regions like central Chile and southwest Australia climate change has dried out these ecosystems and communities, which are now more prone to drought.[66] In some regions suffering regularly from drought, such as East Africa, attribution studies have found that while changes in meteorological drought cannot be attributed to climate change, human-caused climate change has a strong impact on agricultural drought, turning periods of low rain that would have been unproblematic in a cooler climate into extreme droughts.[67]

#### 3.6.2.4 Wildfire

Climate change has increased the risk of wildfire across the world, including the western US, Alaska, and Canada,[68] the Mediterranean,[69] Amazonia,[70] southeast Asia,[71] and Australia.[72] Dry and hot conditions prime forests for wildfire, and

64 Cook and others (n 62).
65 ibid.
66 Richard Seager and others, 'Climate variability and change of Mediterranean-type climates' (2019) 32 Journal of Climate 2887–2915.
67 Joyce Kimutai and others, 'Human-induced climate change increased drought severity in Horn of Africa' (2023) UNU-EHS Working Paper.
68 See Simon Allen and others, 'Summary for policymakers' in Christopher B. Fields and others (eds), *Managing the risks of extreme events and disasters to advance climate change adaptation. A Special Report of Working Groups I and II of the Intergovernmental Panel on Climate Change* (Cambridge University Press 2012); Philip E. Dennison and others, 'Large wildfire trends in the western United States, 1984–2011' (2014) 41 Geophysical Research Letters 2928–2933; Jennifer K. Balch and others, 'Switching on the big burn of 2017' (2018) 1(1) Fire 17; Michael Goss and others, 'Climate change is increasing the likelihood of extreme autumn wildfire conditions across California' (2020) 15 Environmental Research Letters 094016.
69 See John T. Abatzoglou and others, 'Global emergence of anthropogenic climate change in fire weather indices' (2019) 46 Geophysical Research Letters 326–336; Renaud Barbero and others, 'Attributing increases in fire weather to anthropogenic climate change over France' (2020) 8 Frontiers in Earth Science; Danielle Touma and others, 'Human-driven greenhouse gas and aerosol emissions cause distinct regional impacts on extreme fire weather' (2021) 12 Nature Communications 212.
70 See Ane Alencar and others, 'Temporal variability of forest fires in eastern Amazonia' (2011) 21 Ecological Applications 2397–2412; Ane Alencar and others, 'Landscape fragmentation, severe drought, and the new Amazon forest fire regime' (2015) 25 Ecological Applications 1493–1505; Abatzoglou and others (n 69); Touma and others (n 69).
71 Touma and others (n 69).
72 See Andrew J. Dowdy, 'Climatological variability of fire weather in Australia' (2018) 57 Journal of Applied Meteorology and Climatology 221–234; Andrew J. Dowdy and Acacia Pepler, 'Pyroconvection

fire risk is particularly pronounced during periods of extreme fire weather, when conditions of low humidity, lack of rain, high temperature, and high windspeed co-occur with dried out vegetation, increasing the likelihood of fire growth and spread.[73] Major wildfire seasons in recent years have illustrated the consequences of this heightened risk. During British Columbia's record-breaking 2017 wildfire season, climate change increased the area burned by a factor of 7–11, and increased the likelihood of the extreme season by a factor of 2–4.[74] In addition, extreme fire risk events in western Canada were made 1.5 to 6 times more likely by climate change, including the 2016 Fort McMurray wildfire event in Alberta, Canada, which burned 600,000 ha and displaced 80,000 people.[75] Climate change also made extensive Swedish forest fires in 2018 10 per cent more likely,[76] the record-breaking Australian bushfire season of 2019 and 2020 at least 30 per cent more likely,[77] and the extreme wildfires in Southern China in 2019 at least seven times more likely.[78] Further, by increasing the drying power of the atmosphere, climate change more than doubled burned area in forests of western North America between 1984 and 2015.[79]

## 3.7 CASE STUDIES: ATTRIBUTION SCIENCE ACROSS CONTINENTS

Attribution studies have been conducted all around the globe. Here, we present studies that exemplify the diverse nature of climate-related impacts and the scientific inquiries being pursued across different regions, notably Africa, the Americas, Asia, Europe, and the South Pacific/Oceania. While not exhaustive, this compilation offers glimpses into the types of findings and conclusions being drawn in each region. It highlights how attribution science is being applied to understand and

risk in Australia: Climatological changes in atmospheric stability and surface fire weather conditions' (2018) 45 Geophysical Research Letters 2005–2013; Sarah Harris and Chris Lucas, 'Understanding the variability of Australian fire weather between 1973 and 2017' (2019) 14 PLOS One.

73 See Van Wagner, *Development and Structure of the Canadian Forest Fire Weather Index System* (Forestry Technical Report 35, Canadian Forestry Service 1987); Andrew J. Dowdy and others, *Australian Fire Weather as Represented by the McArthur Forest Fire Danger Index and the Canadian Forest Fire Weather Index* (The Centre for Australian Weather and Climate Research 2009).

74 Megan Kirchmeier-Young and others, 'Attribution of the influence of human-induced climate change on an extreme fire season' (2019) 7 Earth's Future 2–10.

75 Megan Kirchmeier-Young and others, 'Attributing extreme fire risk in Western Canada to human emissions' (2017) 144 Climatic Change 365–379.

76 Folmer Krikken and others, 'Attribution of the role of climate change in the forest fires in Sweden 2018' (2021) 21(7) Natural Hazards and Earth Systems Sciences 2169.

77 Geert Jan van Oldenborgh and others, 'Attribution of the Australian bushfire risk to anthropogenic climate change' (2020) 21 Natural Hazards and Earth System Sciences 941–960.

78 Jizeng Du and others, 'Attribution of the extreme drought-related risk of wildfires in spring 2019 over Southwest China' (2021) 102 Bulletin of the American Meteorological Society S83–S90.

79 Abatzoglou and Williams (n 19).

address region-specific climate phenomena, and underscores the global reach and relevance of attribution science. As not all regions are equally represented in the attribution literature, the discussion of some regions will review case studies while others will point to trends.

### 3.7.1 *Africa*

Although understudied, attribution science in Africa offers valuable insights into the region's changing climate dynamics. These studies range from drought analysis in the Horn of Africa to the examination of tropical storms and their consequences. Each provides critical evidence of how human-induced climate change influences weather patterns and extreme events in Africa, underscoring the need for targeted adaptation and mitigation strategies. The following are some notable examples of attribution science at work in Africa, demonstrating the significant and varied impacts of climate change across the continent. One study focused on attributing the impacts of a prolonged drought in the Southern Horn of Africa, affecting parts of Ethiopia, Somalia, and Kenya, from 2020 to 2022, to human-induced climate change.[80] The study employed climate models and observational data to demonstrate that low rainfall events during the long rains have become twice as likely due to climate change. Additionally, the research highlighted the role of temperature in exacerbating drought severity, making events like the record-breaking drought in 2020–2022 about 100 times more likely. The study underscores the urgent need for adaptation strategies that address both wet and dry extremes, considering the substantial impacts on agriculture, pastoralism, and vulnerable communities in the region. Furthermore, the findings emphasise the importance of preparing for prolonged droughts in the face of state fragility, conflict, and potential challenges to existing drought management systems.

Another study focused on the impacts of tropical storms Ana and cyclone Batsirai, with flooding identified as the primary cause of damage.[81] Madagascar, Malawi, and Mozambique, already vulnerable due to prior flooding and underlying conditions like conflict and drought, faced compounded challenges. Despite well-forecasted events by meteorological centres, communication breakdowns and damaged infrastructure hindered effective warnings in some areas. Meteorologically, Ana was an extreme event with a one in fifty years return period, while storms like Batsirai occurred more frequently (one in two years over Madagascar). Sparse rainfall data

[80] 'Human-induced climate change increased drought severity in Horn of Africa' (*World Weather Attribution*) <www.worldweatherattribution.org/human-induced-climate-change-increased-drought-severity-in-southern-horn-of-africa/> accessed 18 April 2024.

[81] 'Climate change increased rainfall associated with tropical cyclones hitting highly vulnerable communities in Madagascar, Mozambique & Malawi' (*World Weather Attribution*) <www.worldweatherattribution.org/climate-change-increased-rainfall-associated-with-tropical-cyclones-hitting-highly-vulnerable-communities-in-madagascar-mozambique-malawi/> accessed 18 April 2024.

in the region complicates trend assessments, but qualitative analysis suggests an increase in heavy rainfall associated with tropical cyclones over time. The findings align with future projections, affirming that climate change contributed to the heightened likelihood and intensity of rainfall linked to Ana and Batsirai.

Yet another study focused on drought patterns in the Horn of Africa from 1979 to 2019, employing the Standardized Precipitation Evapotranspiration Index (SPEI).[82] Results indicate an increasing trend in the frequency, duration, and intensity of droughts in the region over the past decades. The most severe drought occurred in the 'short rains' of 2016 and 'long rains' of 2017, with a calculated return period of 250 years based on the SPEI index. While precipitation anomalies alone couldn't explain this extreme drought, statistical analysis revealed that abnormally high temperatures (1.02°C higher than normal) and exceptional evaporation (1-in-131 years event) played crucial roles. The study suggests that compound droughts, exacerbated by the simultaneous occurrence of low precipitation and high temperatures, may become more prevalent in the Horn of Africa due to continuous anthropogenic warming. This underscores the importance of considering combined impacts for accurate future drought predictions and effective adaptation measures in the region.

### 3.7.2 *The South Pacific/Oceania*

While few attribution studies focus on the South Pacific, global studies combined with region-specific research provide compelling evidence of how climate change has amplified extreme events and threatened communities, ecosystems, and livelihoods. For example, climate change has already increased sea levels in the South Pacific by 100 to 200 mm, an increase greater than many other regions globally.[83] As a result, damages from storms are higher than they would have been without human-induced climate change,[84] particularly when it comes to storm surge.[85] Indeed, during Typhoon Haiyan in 2013, storm surge height was made 20 per cent greater due to climate change,[86] a finding that is transferable to other similar events due to the role of sea level rise. Further, the observed poleward migration of tropical cyclones highlights the risks faced by communities in the South Pacific. While scientists have not investigated the role of climate change

[82] Xue Han and others, 'Attribution of the extreme drought in the Horn of Africa during short-rains of 2016 and long-rains of 2017' (2022) 14(3) Water 409.

[83] Hans O. Pörtner and others (eds), *IPCC Special Report on the Ocean and Cryosphere in a Changing Climate* (Cambridge University Press 2019).

[84] ibid.

[85] Kathleen L. McInnes and others, 'Quantifying storm tide risk in Fiji due to climate variability and change' (2014) 116 Global and Planetary Change 115–129.

[86] Izuru Takayabu and others, 'Climate change effects on the worst-case storm surge: A case study of Typhoon Haiyan' (2015) 10 Environmental Research Letters 1.

for individual storms, the overall increase in tropical cyclones is attributable to human-caused climate change.[87]

As with all regions in the world, every heatwave occurring today in the South Pacific has been made more likely to occur, and is hotter and longer due to the burning of fossil fuels.[88] Heatwaves are, in most parts of the world, the deadliest extreme weather events, costing thousands of people their lives every year, with even more deaths likely going uncounted in these totals.[89] Studies on heatwaves in the Global South, including the Pacific Islands, are sparse, but recent research shows that extreme temperatures have increased significantly across the South Pacific region, in line with global trends.[90] Further, extreme temperatures, like those experienced in Indonesia in 2015, are entirely attributable to human-induced climate change.[91] Together with the attribution assessments of extreme heat from the IPCC,[92] this research provides strong evidence of the impact of human-induced climate change on extreme heat in the South Pacific.

The impact of climate change on marine heatwaves is equally pronounced in the South Pacific. These periods of very warm ocean temperatures have devastating impacts on marine ecosystems and the societies depending on them. The increase in frequency and intensity of marine heatwaves has been assessed as a key impact of human-induced climate change by the most recent IPCC report.[93] Globally, including in the South Pacific, human-induced climate change has increased the most severe marine heatwaves by a factor of twenty,[94] while anthropogenic warming in combination with natural drivers of extreme heat in the South Pacific (like El Nino Southern Oscillation) led to the most severe marine heatwaves in the last decade.[95]

Overall, global evidence strongly links human-induced climate change to rising sea levels, intensified storms, and more severe heatwaves.

87 Seneviratne and others (n 4).

88 See Clarke and others (n 50); Ben Clarke and others, 'When don't we need a new extreme event attribution study?' (2023) 176 Climatic Change 60.

89 Kristie L. Ebi and others, 'Using detection and attribution to quantify how climate change is affecting health' (2020) 39 Health Affairs 12.

90 Simon McGree and others, 'Recent changes in mean and extreme temperature and precipitation in the Western Pacific Islands' (2019) 32 Journal of Climate 4919–4941.

91 Andrew David King and others, 'Climate change and El Nino increase likelihood of Indonesian heat and drought' (2018) 97(12) Bulletin of the American Meteorological Society S113–S117.

92 Seneviratne and others (n 4).

93 Baylor Fox-Kemper and others, 'Chapter 9: Ocean, cryosphere and sea level change' in Valerie Masson-Delmotte and others (eds), *Climate Change 2021: The Physical Science Basis. Contribution of Working Group I to the Sixth Assessment Report of the Intergovernmental Panel on Climate Change* (Cambridge University Press 2021).

94 Charlotte Laufkötter and others, 'High-impact marine heatwaves attributable to human-induced global warming' (2020) 369 Science 1621–1625.

95 Neil J. Holbrook and others, 'A global assessment of marine heatwaves and their drivers' (2019) 10 Nature Communications 2624.

### 3.7.3 *The Americas*

Climate change has caused major disruptions to communities, infrastructure, and industry throughout the Americas. Attribution science in this region has primarily focused on understanding the impacts of precipitation, heat, and drought. Studies generally agree on an increase in both precipitation and extreme heat due to climate change, while the attribution of droughts presents a more complex picture.

The frequency and intensity of heavy precipitation and flooding, attributed to climate change, have been a significant focus in the Americas. Research has shown a substantial increase in the risk of extreme rainfall events, as seen in the Uruguay River Basin, leading to widespread flooding and notable social and economic impacts.[96] The exceptionally wet conditions in Peru in March 2017 were estimated to be at least 1.5 times more likely to occur, when compared to pre-industrial times.[97] These examples underline the challenges in managing water resources and protecting vulnerable populations from flood-related hazards.

The region has also witnessed an escalation in temperature extremes due to climate change. The increased risk of heatwave events, like the one Argentina experienced in December 2013, was quantified as being five times greater due to climate change.[98] A clear anthropogenic signal has been identified in temperature extremes across South America, though the specific impacts vary by region.[99] These temperature variations pose significant threats to public health, agriculture, and local ecosystems.

As mentioned previously, the first regional source attribution study was conducted in North America and found that 19.8 million acres burned – 37 per cent of the total area scorched by forest fires in the western United States and southwestern Canada since 1986 – can be attributed to heat-trapping emissions traced to the world's eighty-eight largest fossil fuel producers and cement manufacturers.[100] Emissions from these companies also contributed to nearly half of the observed increase in drying conditions that raise the risk of large, severe forest fires across the region since 1901. The findings provide new data that can advance efforts to hold companies accountable for past, present, and future climate damages and risks.

In South America, particularly in the Andes, the hazard of glacial lake outbursts has emerged as a growing concern due to climate change. The risks these outbursts

[96] Rafael C. de Abreu and others, 'Attribution of detected temperature trends in Southeast Brazil' (2019) 46 Geophysical Research Letters 8407–8414.

[97] Nikolaos Christidis and others, 'The extremely wet March of 2017 in Peru' (2019) 100 Bulletin of the American Meteorological Society S31–S35.

[98] Alexis Hannart and others, 'Causal influence of anthropogenic forcings on the Argentinian heat wave of December 2013' (2015) 96 Bulletin of the American Meteorological Society S41–S45.

[99] Matilde Rusticucci and Natalia Zazulie, 'Attribution and projections of temperature extreme trends in South America based on CMIP5 models' (2021) 1504 Annals of the New York Academy of Sciences 154–166.

[100] Dahl and others (n 34).

pose, especially in regions like Peru, highlight the need for increased attention and research in these areas.[101] The case of Lake Palcacocha, which sits below the summits of Palcaraju and Pucaranra and above the city of Huaraz, exemplifies the increasing hazard from such events, driven by human-induced glacier retreat. An outburst flood in 1941 killed more than 1,800 people and destroyed one-third of the city of Huaraz. A study found that the retreat of Palcaraju glacier to its current state is not solely attributable to natural variability and that the glacier's retreat observed by 1941 likely represents an early consequence of anthropogenic greenhouse gas emissions.[102] This same research highlighted how anthropogenic climate change has continued to drive glacier retreat and glacial lake outburst flood hazard and how it presents a significant threat to the community of Huaraz.

Research on droughts in South America presents contrasting evidence. While a study on the prolonged Northeast Brazil hydrometeorological drought (2012–2016) suggested that climate change was not a significant factor,[103] other research points to the intensification of the dry season and reduced water availability in parts of South America and the northern Andes as consequences of human-induced climate change.[104] This divergence in findings illustrates the complexity in attributing droughts to climate change and highlights the necessity for region-specific investigations.

### 3.7.4 *Asia*

In Asia, a diverse range of attribution studies have focused on the impacts of climate change on extreme weather events, particularly emphasising the increased frequency and intensity of rainfall, flooding, and temperature extremes.

Several studies have concentrated on flooding and extreme rainfall. In the Lancang-Mekong River Basin, climate change has been linked to a 14 per cent increase in the magnitude and a 45 per cent increase in the frequency of floods compared to the baseline period of 1985–2007.[105] Similarly, research on the 2019 rainy season in Southern China and the record-breaking rainfall in Western Japan in July 2018 has shown a substantial increase in the severity and likelihood of such

[101] Caroline Taylor and others 'Glacial lake outburst floods threaten millions globally' (2023) 14 Nature Communications 487.

[102] Rupert Stuart-Smith and others, 'Increased outburst flood hazard from Lake Palcacocha due to human-induced glacier retreat' (2021) 14 Nature Geoscience 85–90.

[103] Eduardo Martins and others, 'A multimethod attribution analysis of the prolonged Northeast Brazil hydrometeorological drought (2012–16)' (2018) 99 Bulletin of the American Meteorological Society S65–S69.

[104] Ryan Padrón and others, 'Observed changes in dry-season water availability attributed to human-induced climate change' (2020) 13 Nature Geoscience 477–481.

[105] Xiaobo Yun and others, 'Impacts of climate change and reservoir operation on streamflow and flood characteristics in the Lancang-Mekong River Basin' (2020) 590 Journal of Hydrology 125472.

events due to human-induced climate change. The certain extreme rainfall events in Western Japan, for instance, now has a return period of 20.7 years, significantly shorter than the 68.0 years under pre-human influence conditions.[106] In China, the detectable anthropogenic influence on summer precipitation has been linked to changes in heavy, moderate, and light precipitation, with future projections suggesting an increase in heavy precipitation.[107]

Contrary to the increased frequency of extreme rainfall events in some parts of Asia, a study in Southern China found that anthropogenic forcings have reduced the likelihood of heavy precipitation events like those experienced in March–July 2019 by about 60 per cent, highlighting regional variability in the impacts of climate change.[108]

The contribution of atmospheric circulation to extreme weather events has been a subject of interest, particularly regarding the record-breaking precipitation and heat events in the middle and lower reaches of the Yangtze River and South China during the Meiyu period in 2020. A study found that the risk of an event reaching or exceeding the 2020 Meiyu amount increased 5.1 times in the current climate, with 80 per cent of this increase attributable to climate change.[109]

In Bangladesh, studies have shown varying impacts of climate change on flooding and extreme pre-monsoon precipitation. While one study suggested a negligible role of climate change in exacerbating 2017's floods, future projections indicate an increased probability of such events. Another study found that climate change had doubled the likelihood of extreme pre-monsoon rainfall. These results do not indicate that the science is unsuitable, but rather that in certain seasons, like the pre-monsoon season in Bangladesh where rainfall is highly variable from year to year, attribution studies need to take future projections into account to complement shorter observed records.[110]

In the 2022 study by Li and Otto,[111] the catastrophic effects of Typhoon Hagibis, which struck the Tokyo metropole region in October 2019, were closely examined to understand the role of human-induced climate change in exacerbating its impacts.

[106] Yukiko Imada and others, 'Advanced risk-based event attribution for heavy regional rainfall events' (2020) 3 NPJ Climate and Atmospheric Science 37.

[107] Chunhui Lu and others, 'Detectable anthropogenic influence on changes in summer precipitation in China' (2020) 33(13) Journal of Climate 5357–5369.

[108] Rouke Li and others, 'Anthropogenic influences on heavy precipitation during the 2019 extremely wet rainy season in Southern China' (2020) Bulletin of the American Meteorological Society S103–S109.

[109] Yangbo Ye and Cheng Qian, 'Conditional attribution of climate change and atmospheric circulation contributing to the record-breaking precipitation and temperature event of summer 2020 in southern China' (2021) 16 Environmental Research Letters 044058.

[110] Ruksana H. Rimi and others, 'Risks of pre-monsoon extreme rainfall events of Bangladesh: Is anthropogenic climate change playing a role?' (2019) 100 Bulletin of the American Meteorological Society S61–S65.

[111] Sihan Li and Friederike EL. Otto, 'The role of human-induced climate change in heavy rainfall events such as the one associated with Typhoon Hagibis' (2022) 172 Climatic Change 7.

The typhoon led to substantial destruction, including significant loss of life and livelihoods, with economic damages surpassing $10 billion USD. The study's findings show an increase in the likelihood of such an extreme rainfall event, ranging from 15 per cent to 150 per cent, directly attributable to anthropogenic climate change. Additionally, the study quantified the fraction of attributable risk to understand impacts, and conservatively estimated that about $4 billion of the total damages could be attributed to the climate change-induced intensification of the rainfall. This research not only highlights the escalating economic toll of climate change but also stresses the urgency for effective adaptation strategies to mitigate the risks associated with such extreme weather events.

### 3.7.5 *Europe*

Heatwaves in Europe have been a significant focus of attribution studies, revealing a trend towards increased frequency and intensity of these extreme weather events. Anthropogenic forcings have markedly influenced European temperature extremes from 1961–2010, contributing to a more frequent occurrence of heatwaves,[112] and were a major contributor to the conditions leading to the 2015 central Europe heatwave.[113] Human-induced climate change significantly increased the likelihood of the unprecedented June–July 2019 Europe heat event, increasing its likelihood by up to twenty-three times since the 1980s.[114] A strong human influence was identified in the extremely warm May of 2020 in western Europe, estimating that such events are now forty times more likely due to human activities.[115] Research from the World Weather Attribution project further supports these findings, indicating clear trends towards more frequent heatwaves in Northern Europe, including Ireland, the Netherlands, and Denmark, with a twofold increase in the likelihood of heatwaves in Dublin, Ireland, and a fourfold increase in Denmark.[116] Climate change significantly amplified the intensity and frequency of the June 2017 heatwave in Portugal and other parts of Europe, making such extremes at least twice as likely in Belgium and up to ten times as likely in Portugal and Spain.[117] Additional research has quantified the proportion of heat-related mortality that can be attributed to climate

[112] Nikolaos Christidis and Peter A. Stott, 'Attribution analyses of temperature extremes using a set of 16 indices' (2016) 14 Weather and Climate Extremes 24–35.

[113] Buwen Dong and others, 'The 2015 European heat wave' (2016) 97 Bulletin of the American Meteorological Society S57–S62.

[114] Feng Ma and others, 'Unprecedented Europe heat in June–July 2019: Risk in the historical and future context' (2020) 47 Geophysical Research Letters.

[115] Stephanie Herring and others (eds), *Explaining Extreme Events of 2020 from a Climate Perspective* (2022) 103(3) Bulletin of the American Meteorological Society S1.

[116] 'Heatwave in northern Europe, summer 2018' (*World Weather Attribution*) <www.worldweatherattribution.org/attribution-of-the-2018-heat-in-northern-europe/> accessed 18 April 2024.

[117] 'Record June temperatures in western Europe' (*World Weather Attribution*) <www.worldweatherattribution.org/european-heat-june-2017/> accessed 18 April 2024.

change, finding that an average of 37 per cent of heat-related deaths between 1991 and 2018 are attributable, and that this trend in mortality is detectable on every continent.[118] These studies collectively underscore the growing impact of anthropogenic climate change on the frequency and severity of heatwaves across Europe.

Drought attribution studies in Europe have shed light on the increasing severity and likelihood of such events in the region. The record-breaking drought that affected western and central Europe from July 2016 to June 2017 serves as a prime example. This event, unusual in its spatial pattern affecting both northern and southern European regions, was identified as the most severe European drought at the continental scale since at least 1979.[119] It caused significant impacts on water supplies, agriculture, hydroelectric power production, and forest fires in Iberia. Additionally, a study on the record low rainfall in western Europe during December 2016 suggests that this extreme event may have been buoyed by an unprecedented reduction of Arctic sea ice, a condition likely driven by anthropogenic climate change.[120] These studies collectively point to a trend of more severe and frequent droughts in Europe, exacerbated by both dynamic atmospheric patterns and thermodynamic processes associated with climate change.

A handful of studies also look at flooding in the region. One study looked at flooding in the aftermath of storm Desmond in December 2015, yielding significant insights into the impact of climate change on such occurrences. The findings revealed that climate change had contributed to increasing the likelihood of similar, single-day precipitation events by approximately 40 per cent. A further, more detailed analysis using additional data and considering a broader event definition indicated an estimated 59 per cent increase in the frequency of such events, albeit with a wider confidence interval.[121] This study exemplifies the growing body of evidence suggesting an enhanced likelihood of severe precipitation and flooding events in Europe, influenced by the on-going shifts in climate patterns.

## 3.8 NAVIGATING ATTRIBUTION SCIENCE

The field of attribution science, while significantly robust, does have limitations and challenges, namely data inequities, misinterpretation of scientific uncertainty, and intrinsic event complexity. The disparity in access to high-quality climatic

[118] Ana Maria Vicedo-Cabrera and others, 'The burden of heat-related mortality attributable to recent human-induced climate change' (2021) 11 Nature Climate Change 492–500.

[119] Ricardo García-Herrera and others, 'The European 2016/17 drought' (2019) 32(11) Journal of Climate 3169–3187.

[120] Stephanie Herring and others (eds), Explaining extreme events in 2017 from a climate perspective (2019) 100(1) Bulletin of the American Meteorological Society S1–S117.

[121] Freiderike E. L. Otto and others, 'Climate change increases the probability of heavy rains in Northern England/Southern Scotland like those of storm Desmond – a real-time event attribution revisited' (2018) 13(2) Environmental Research Letters 024006.

data is profound, particularly in developing countries in the Global South. These countries, often most vulnerable to climate change, suffer from sparse observational networks, leading to significant data gaps. This scarcity hampers the precision of attribution studies and, by extension, the formulation of targeted adaptation strategies. Moreover, the established reliance on *global* climate models, while beneficial for broad-scale analysis, can fall short in capturing localised climatic variations, especially in data-poor regions. Enhancing local data collection capabilities and developing more nuanced, region-specific models are crucial steps towards addressing this inequity.

Attribution science, with its inherent complexities, faces the challenge of distinguishing human-induced changes from natural climatic variability, which – as in all scientific modelling – involves navigating uncertainties. However, the primary issue lies not in the presence of uncertainty, which is a fundamental aspect of scientific inquiry, but rather in effectively communicating these uncertainties within a legal context. In the scientific domain, uncertainty is a measure of our knowledge's depth and precision, a concept crucial to attribution science. It is methodically reported, often via confidence intervals, acknowledging the intrinsic limitations of models while underscoring their value in enhancing our understanding.

Finally, as mentioned earlier, the attribution of specific types of weather events to climate change varies considerably in ease and accuracy. Events such as heatwaves often present a more direct and easily discernible link to climate change, primarily due to their close association with rising global temperatures. Conversely, more complex phenomena like droughts or floods involve intricate interactions with various factors, including local geography, atmospheric conditions, and human activities, making their attribution to climate change more challenging. This complexity is compounded by varying temporal and spatial scales, as some events might exhibit clearer signals of climate change influence over larger areas or extended periods, while others are more perceptible at local scales or in shorter time frames.

Addressing these challenges is essential for the continuous improvement of the field and its application in informing climate litigation and adaptation measures. As research in this area progresses, attribution science is set to play an increasingly crucial role in enhancing our understanding of climate change impacts and guiding global responses.

## 3.9 THE PIVOTAL ROLE OF ATTRIBUTION SCIENCE IN CLIMATE RESPONSE

The emergence and rapid advancement of attribution science marks a transformative moment in our understanding of climate change, offering a powerful tool for quantifying the ties between human actions and shifting climate impacts. Attribution science is well established and accepted by the scientific community, as evidenced by its inclusion and prominence in the latest IPCC assessment.

With its three distinct strands – trend, source, and event – attribution science provides a comprehensive picture of how human activities influence climatic trends, the origin of emissions, and the frequency and intensity of extreme weather events. Each branch of this discipline adds a unique layer to our scientific understanding of the complexities of a rapidly evolving global climate system. These studies not only serve as a testament to the impact of anthropogenic factors on the climate, but also as a clarion call for immediate and decisive action.

As we stand at the crossroads of a climate crisis, the role of attribution science becomes increasingly pivotal. It bridges the gap between abstract climate models and the tangible reality of climate impacts, providing a foundation for informed policy decisions, effective adaptation strategies, and, crucially, climate litigation. The insights derived from attribution science are not just academic exercises; they are tools for accountability and change, guiding us towards a more resilient and sustainable future.

As attribution science continues to evolve, it is poised to play an ever-more critical role in our collective response to climate change. It empowers us with the knowledge to understand the past, address the present, and prepare for the future, forging a path towards a more informed and proactive global response to the climate crisis.

**PART I**

# Preliminary Issues

# 4

# Standing

*Randall S. Abate**

## 4.1 INTRODUCTION

United States (US) Supreme Court Justice Antonin Scalia famously distilled the essence of standing to a four-word inquiry: 'What's it to you?'[1] The law of standing provides standards for evaluating who is a proper party to bring a case to the courts. Standing is a gate-keeping mechanism that seeks to avoid opening the floodgates of litigation and subjecting the courts to frivolous claims. So, in asking, 'What's it to you?' the court is seeking to confirm that only proper parties are permitted to bring claims to help optimise the use of valuable and limited judicial resources.

Standing is jurisdiction-specific. In some jurisdictions, such as the US, a party will not have standing without meeting the requirements of a three-part test. The constitutional origin for this test is the 'cases or controversies' language in Article III, Section 2 of the US Constitution. The three-part test evaluates whether (1) the plaintiff has sustained an 'actual or imminent' injury that is 'concrete and particularized'; (2) the plaintiff's injury is 'fairly traceable' to the action or inaction of the defendant; and (3) a favourable decision by the court is likely to redress the plaintiff's claim.[2] Unlike the restrictive standing requirements in US and other common law jurisdictions around the world, 'universal standing' is the norm in many other jurisdictions, which permits all interested parties to file claims challenging laws that are the alleged sources of their concerns. In some jurisdictions, environmental claims have more relaxed standing requirements than other types of civil claims. There are many other procedural grounds on which the claims may be dismissed, and many ways in which the claims may fail to meet their burdens of proof at trial. Therefore, more permissive standing in climate litigation is important to offer opportunities for

* Randall S. Abate is Assistant Dean for Environmental Law Studies, The George Washington University Law School. The author gratefully acknowledges valuable research assistance from Kelly Hanna, Catherine Hall, Rebecca Hitchiner, and Daniel Conte.

1 Antonin Scalia, 'The Doctrine of Standing as an Essential Element of the Separation of Powers' (1983) 17 Suffolk University Law Review 881, 882.

2 *Lujan v Defenders of Wildlife*, 504 US 555 (1992) [556]–[561].

meritorious claims to proceed in the courts. The courts are an indispensable last resort in climate litigation in jurisdictions that are plagued by inadequate or non-existent legislative or executive action on climate change matters.

The *Urgenda* case is a positive step forward in addressing standing in climate litigation.[3] The standing barrier has precluded many plaintiffs from seeking accountability in the courts from governmental or private sector actors that contribute to climate change.[4] Yet, in *Urgenda*, the Court concluded that the Urgenda Foundation had standing to file a collective action claim under the Dutch Civil Code. The Supreme Court noted that the interests of residents of the Netherlands in relation to climate change are sufficiently identical and can be 'bundled' to secure protection in a collective action suit. Moreover, the State had not disputed standing in that the claim concerned the protection of the interests of the inhabitants of the Netherlands from dangerous climate change. The State did object to Urgenda's asserted standing on behalf of people outside the Netherlands and on behalf of future generations. The Dutch government and the Court's willingness to allow plaintiffs to have standing to bring meritorious climate litigation claims in the courts is a standard towards which the world should aspire in future climate litigation. Ideally, the standard should also include standing on behalf of future generations in climate litigation claims.

Standing is a significant and widely litigated issue in climate litigation around the world and that trend will continue, especially in common law jurisdictions, as the number of these cases continues to rise dramatically.[5] Strict standing barriers need to be reduced in many jurisdictions around the world to promote broader access to the courts in climate litigation because of the urgency of the climate emergency and the difficulty of asserting individualised harm in climate litigation. There are

3 *State of the Netherlands (Ministry of Economic Affairs and Climate Policy) v Stichting Urgenda* [2019] ECLI:NL:HR:2019:2007 (Supreme Court of the Netherlands) (*Urgenda Supreme Court*); See André Nollkaemper and Laura Burgers, 'A New Classic in Climate Litigation: The Dutch Supreme Court Decision in the Urgenda Case' (*EJIL: Talk!*, 6 January 2020) <www.ejiltalk.org/a-new-classic-in-climate-change-litigation-the-dutch-supreme-court-decision-in-the-urgenda-case> accessed 24 February 2024.

4 The reasoning in *Urgenda* was successfully applied in climate litigation against the private sector in 2021 in the groundbreaking *Milieudefensie v Royal Dutch Shell* [2021] ECLR:NL: RBDHA:2021:5339 (District Court of the Hague). For a helpful discussion of the case, see generally Michael Salau and Zita Manzi, 'All Businesses Face the Growing Threat of Climate Litigation' (*Beale & Co*, July 2021) <https://beale-law.com/article/all-businesses-face-the-growing-threat-of-climate-change-litigation> accessed 24 February 2024; McGuire Woods LLP, 'A Change of Climate in the Courts' (*JDSupra*, 16 June 2021) <www.jdsupra.com/legalnews/a-change-of-climate-in-the-courts-7104107> accessed 24 February 2024.

5 For a discussion and accounting of this explosion in global climate litigation, see generally United Nations Environment Programme and Sabin Center for Climate Change, 'Global Climate Litigation Report: 2020 Status Review' (2020) <https://wedocs.unep.org/bitstream/handle/20.500.11822/34818/GCLR.pdf?sequence=1&isAllowed=y> accessed 24 February 2024; Asian Development Bank, 'Coming Soon to a Court Near You: Climate Litigation in Asia and the Pacific and Beyond' (December 2020) <www.adb.org/sites/default/files/publication/659631/climate-litigation-asia-pacific.pdf> accessed 24 February 2024.

two primary obstacles for plaintiffs seeking to secure standing in climate litigation. Under US law, one obstacle is the principle that 'injury to all is injury to none',[6] which means that because of the widespread nature of climate change impacts, it is difficult for plaintiffs to allege that the harm that they suffer is sufficiently 'concrete and particularized'[7] to satisfy the injury element of standing. Another obstacle that is common to plaintiffs in many jurisdictions is causation – the challenge to attribute climate change impacts to the action or inaction of government and private sector defendants. In recent years, climate attribution science has advanced considerably and will help diminish this obstacle,[8] though it remains a challenge for many climate litigation plaintiffs.

This chapter reviews cases in several jurisdictions to reveal how courts have addressed standing in climate litigation to date. Section 2 addresses case studies of standing in climate litigation in the US, New Zealand, the European Union (EU), EU Member States, the Philippines, India, and Australia. It reveals how standing has been a barrier to climate litigation in the US, New Zealand, the EU, and the Philippines, whereas standing barriers either do not exist or exist to a lesser degree in several European Member States, India, and Australia. Section 3 identifies emerging best practices to offer recommendations on how future climate litigation claims may avoid dismissal on standing grounds.

## 4.2 CASE LAW DEVELOPMENTS – STATE OF AFFAIRS

This section describes significant climate litigation cases in several jurisdictions to highlight the range of approaches that courts and tribunals have taken in considering standing in climate litigation. The review of these cases reveals a gap of inconsistent treatment of parties' ability to seek redress for climate litigation claims. Given the urgency of the climate crisis, and because it is unlikely that there will be frivolous cases seeking to raise ambition in addressing climate change or dealing with its consequences, a more liberalised standard for standing in climate litigation is needed to the maximum extent permissible within the constraints of domestic jurisprudence on standing.

There is a broad spectrum of approaches to standing across jurisdictions. The US represents the most restrictive approach to standing, which requires the constitutional minimum of injury, causation, and redressability to be met for a party to be eligible to proceed with a claim. The US approach to standing is arguably the most stringent, formal, and complex in the world. At the other end of the spectrum are jurisdictions like the European Member States discussed in this section that

6 B. S. Mank, 'Is Injury to All Injury to None?' (2005) 35 ELR 1, 29.
7 *Lujan* (n 2) [561].
8 See generally Michael Burger and others, 'The Law and Science of Climate Attribution' (2020) 45 CJEL 57.

have adopted a liberal approach in granting standing to climate litigation plaintiffs. A middle category in this range of approaches to standing is reflected in jurisdictions like Australia that allow a lower standing threshold when cases are filed under certain statutes as compared to the higher standing threshold for common law claims. The diversity of approaches along this spectrum is explored in this section.

### 4.2.1 *United States*

The approach to standing by US courts is the most restrictive, and it therefore falls at one end of the spectrum. Climate litigation in the US has proceeded against federal and state governmental entities and private sector companies. Climate litigation in the US traces its origins to the landmark case *Massachusetts v EPA*.[9] In this case, the US Supreme Court concluded that the state of Massachusetts had standing to seek to compel the Environmental Protection Agency (EPA) to regulate carbon dioxide emissions from new motor vehicles, even when the agency had decided not to do so in the exercise of its administrative discretion. The state of Massachusetts brought its claim on behalf of its citizens to seek a remedy for the loss of coastal land in the state due to sea level rise, which is caused by global climate change. This 'special solicitude' of the state to bring claims on behalf of its citizens was a significant component of the Court's analysis in granting standing in the case.[10]

The Court concluded that this alleged injury was both 'actual' and 'imminent' because it was occurring and was likely to continue to occur. It was also 'concrete and particularized' and not abstract or conjectural because it involved scientifically demonstrable loss of land in the state. The second element, causation, was easily established because the defendant, the EPA, conceded it. The final element, redressability, also was satisfied. The Court concluded that although EPA regulations addressing carbon dioxide emissions from new motor vehicles would not stop the loss of coastal land in Massachusetts from sea level rise, it would help slow the rate of loss of that land ever so slightly, which the Court deemed sufficient to meet the redressability standard.[11]

Since *Massachusetts v EPA*, climate litigation plaintiffs in the US have been plagued by standing barriers in cases against both governmental and private sector defendants. For example, in *Native Village of Kivalina v ExxonMobil Corp.*, the plaintiffs were a traditional Inupiat village of approximately 400 residents living on a remote Arctic strip of land severely compromised by sea level rise and coastal erosion.[12] The community filed a suit against twenty-three of the leading multinational oil and gas companies, seeking damages for their contribution to global

9 *Massachusetts v EPA* 549 US 497 (2007).
10 ibid 520.
11 ibid 521–526.
12 *Native Village of Kivalina v ExxonMobil Corp* 696 F.3d. 849, 868–869 (9th Cir 2012).

climate change, which, in turn, accelerated the demise of this Native village. The US Circuit Court of Appeals for the Ninth Circuit affirmed the District Court's dismissal of the case, holding that the plaintiffs lacked standing to bring the claim and that the Court lacked jurisdiction to hear the case due to the political question doctrine.[13] The Court concluded that the plaintiffs failed on the causation element of standing because they could not show plausible traceability from the defendants' actions to their injuries.[14] The Ninth Circuit did not apply *Massachusetts v EPA* to recognise the unique capacity of the federally recognised Native Village as a quasi-sovereign entity that could benefit from the 'special solicitude' reasoning. The Court also highlighted concerns around causation (as related to standing), although perhaps that would not have been the case if the village had the benefit of the more advanced climate attribution science that supports climate litigation today.[15]

Climate litigation against the US federal government in *Juliana v United States*[16] has also attracted international attention. The youth plaintiffs' litigation theory, known as 'atmospheric trust litigation', asserted an expansive reading of the common law public trust doctrine (to include federal government stewardship of the atmosphere) and the US Constitution (to recognise a right to a stable climate under the Due Process Clause of the Fourteenth Amendment). The plaintiffs in *Juliana* sought a comprehensive injunctive remedy in the case – a climate recovery plan – based on these ambitious common law and constitutional law theories. In denying the federal government's motion to dismiss, Judge Ann Aiken's landmark 2016 decision determined that the atmospheric trust dimensions of the youth plaintiffs' arguments, and the rights-based arguments under the US Constitution, deserved to proceed to trial.[17]

The Ninth Circuit ultimately dismissed the case in January 2020. Although the Court concluded that the plaintiffs met the injury and causation elements of standing, it held that the plaintiffs failed to meet the redressability element. The Court determined that the youth plaintiffs' requested remedy to order the federal government to adopt 'a comprehensive scheme to decrease fossil fuel emissions and combat climate change' would exceed a federal court's remedial authority and thus failed to meet the redressability element of standing.[18]

[13] ibid 854.

[14] ibid 868 (Justice Pro, concurring).

[15] For a discussion of the positive impact of the IPCC's Sixth Assessment report in August 2021 on climate litigation, see Section 4.5.

[16] *Juliana v United States* 947 F.3d 1159 (9th Cir 2020) (*Juliana*).

[17] *Juliana v United States* 217 F.Supp.3d 1224, 1260 (District Court of Oregon 2016).

[18] *Juliana* (n 16) 1171. More recently, see *Held v Montana* No CDV-2020-307 (District Court of Montana 2023) where the Court found that the youth plaintiffs proved standing to bring their claims based on injuries to their physical and mental health, homes and property, recreational, spiritual, and aesthetic interests, tribal and cultural traditions, economic security, and happiness. The trial court granted the plaintiffs' request for declaratory relief, which was upheld by the Montana Supreme Court in December 2024. *Held v Montana* 2024 MT 312 (Supreme Court of Montana).

### 4.2.2 *New Zealand*

New Zealand represents a slightly less restrictive approach to standing but one that still creates a barrier for bringing a climate case to trial. In New Zealand, climate litigation cases have only discussed standing in the context of public nuisance claims, which require a 'special interest' similar to Australia's special interest requirement (discussed later): (1) the harm must be greater than that to the general public, and (2) the harm must also be particular, direct, and substantial.[19] The case of *Smith v Fonterra Co-Operative Group Ltd* illustrates this approach.[20]

Smith, an Indigenous plaintiff who is the climate change spokesman for the Iwi Chairs' Forum, sued several large New Zealand-based companies over their greenhouse gas (GHG) emissions. He asserted three tort-based causes of action – (1) public nuisance; (2) negligence; and (3) breach of an inchoate duty – and sought an injunction to require each defendant to reach zero net emissions by 2030. The plaintiff claimed to have interests in lands and other resources that have customary, cultural, historical, nutritional, and spiritual significance to him. In his public nuisance claim, he asserted that anthropogenic climate change will cause sea levels to rise, which will damage his family's land and interfere with public health, safety, comfort, convenience, and peace.

Under New Zealand law, the Attorney General has standing to sue for an injunction to restrain a public nuisance. The Attorney General can act personally or by way of a relator action in which they act on relation of a private individual or local authority. An individual, meanwhile, can only bring a public nuisance action if they suffer some special damage that is appreciably more serious than that of the general public.[21] Special damage is considered particular, direct, and substantial, and more than merely consequential.[22] In this case, Smith chose not to invite the Attorney General to sue on his behalf and instead sued in his own right.

The court of first instance held that Smith's harm was merely consequential and could not be directly traced to the defendants' actions due to the long chain of traceability. The Court also held that Smith's alleged damage was neither particular nor direct to him. Rather, it was a manifestation of the effects of climate change not only on him but also on very many others.[23]

On appeal, Smith alleged that the special damage rule did not account for his interest in the land, as well as the tikanga Māori and his kaitiaki responsibilities,

[19] For a discussion of legal personhood as a potential strategy to avoid standing barriers in New Zealand, see Mihnea Tanasescu, 'When a River is a Person: From Ecuador to New Zealand, Nature Gets Its Day in Court' (*The Conversation*, 19 June 2017) <https://theconversation.com/when-a-river-is-a-person-from-ecuador-to-new-zealand-nature-gets-its-day-in-court-79278> accessed 25 February 2024.

[20] *Michael John Smith v Fonterra Co-Operative Group Limited and Others* CIV-2019-404-001730 [2020] NZHC 419 (*Smith High Court*).

[21] ibid [59].

[22] ibid [61].

[23] ibid [62].

which he asserted were sufficient to set him apart from the general public.[24] In reevaluating Smith's claims, the Court addressed the special damage rule, noting that there is no universally accepted formulation. Typically, there are two approaches. The first approach is that the 'harm suffered by the individual must not only be appreciably different in degree but also different in kind from that shared by the general public'.[25] The second approach is that 'all that matters is for the injury and inconvenience to be appreciably "more substantial, more direct and immediate" than that suffered by the general public without necessarily differing in its nature'.[26]

Even when applying the second, more liberal approach to the special damage rule, the Court concluded that Smith lacked standing because he had not suffered any special damage greater than that of other members of the general public, given that many places throughout New Zealand are 'sites of historical, nutritional, spiritual and cultural significance that are at risk or under threat'.[27] Smith asked the court to reconsider the special damages rule in its entirety, but the Court reiterated the justifications for the rule, including the prevention of a multiplicity of actions and the premise that the Attorney General is best suited to bring public nuisance claims in accordance with its constitutional role.[28] The Court ultimately did not decide whether the special damage rule should be abolished. The Court also rejected the 'nuisance due to many' argument, wherein defendants who are even partially responsible for damages are held legally accountable based on the extent of their contribution. In rejecting the argument, the Court observed that those principles apply only in cases where there is a 'finite number of known contributors to the harm, all of whom were before the Court'.[29]

### 4.2.3 *European Union*

While the European Court of Justice (ECJ) approach to standing is very specific, it reflects the restrictive approach adopted by the New Zealand courts – and has been subject to extensive criticism. The ECJ recently issued decisions in two significant climate cases that include important standing analysis: *Carvalho v European Parliament* ('The People's Climate Case')[30] and *Sabo v European Parliament*.[31]

[24] *Michael John Smith v Fonterra Co-Operative Group Limited and Others* CA 128/2020 [2021] NZCA 552 (*Smith Court of Appeal*).
[25] ibid [75].
[26] ibid.
[27] ibid [82].
[28] ibid [85]–[86].
[29] ibid [90]–[92].
[30] Case T-330/18 *Carvalho and Others v Parliament and Council* [2018] 2018/C 285/51 (ECJ, 8 May 2019) (*The People's Climate Change Case*).
[31] Case T-141/19 *Sabo and Others v Parliament and Council* [2020] (ECJ, 6 May 2020).

The former challenged legislation that sets the EU's overall climate change targets, whereas the latter challenged legislation that permits a specific measure – reliance on biomass – to meet those targets.

The Treaty on the Functioning of the European Union (TFEU) organises the EU and governs the laws of *locus standi* that citizens of Member States have before the ECJ.[32] TFEU Article 263(4) establishes what constitutes a 'case or controversy' before the ECJ in stating that 'any natural or legal person may … institute proceedings against an act addressed to that person or which is of direct and individual concern to them, and against a regulatory act which is of direct concern to them and does not entail implementing measures'.[33]

The ECJ is tasked with interpreting these standing requirements, and the definition of 'direct' and 'individual' concern has been developed in ECJ case law. The *Plaumann* test is the standard applied to evaluate the applicants' eligibility to challenge the laws at issue. In *Plaumann*, the ECJ set a high bar to establish individual concern for natural or legal persons. The contested act must affect them 'by reason of certain attributes that are peculiar to them or by reason of circumstances in which they are differentiated from all other persons, and by virtue of these factors distinguishes them individually just as in the case of the addressee'.[34] In seeking to meet the *Plaumann* test, the applicants in the two aforementioned climate cases argued that: (1) any violation of human rights is by its very nature unique or, in the alternative, (2) the test should be altered to take account of the reality of climate change.

In *Sabo*, a group of individuals and civil society organisations from Estonia, France, Ireland, Romania, Slovakia, and the US challenged a piece of EU legislation that allows the burning of forest biomass, which is considered a renewable energy source under the law. The applicants came from areas that have been particularly affected by logging.

The applicants sought annulment of EU legislation that was allegedly in breach of Article 191 of TFEU and the EU Charter. They argued that the accelerated forest loss and significant increases in forest logging and, consequently, in greenhouse gas emissions violated their right to respect for private and family life, right to education, rights of the child, right to property, health care, freedom to manifest religion, and right to respect for religious diversity. Even though some applicants were foresters or lived in forest areas, the court dismissed the plaintiffs' claims at the admissibility stage because they failed to establish standing.

In their appeal, the plaintiffs argued that the 'individual concern' requirement should be interpreted in view of the reality of the global climate crisis and that, in cases alleging human rights violations, direct access to the ECJ must be ensured, as

[32] Consolidated Version of the Treaty on the Functioning of the European Union [2009] OJ C-326 (TFEU). *Locus standi* is another term for standing.

[33] ibid art 263(4).

[34] See Case 25/62 *Plaumann & Co v Commission of the European Economic Community* [1963] ECR 95.

long as there are no alternatives. The Court rejected this argument, reasoning that the claim that the acts at issue infringed fundamental rights was not sufficient to establish that the plaintiffs' claims were admissible without rendering the requirements of TFEU Article 263(4) meaningless.[35] It relied on case law in which strict interpretation of Article 263(4) is consistent with the EU Charter, and with the right to an effective remedy under arts 6 and 13 of the European Convention on Human Rights (ECHR). The Court upheld the *Plaumann* test and continued to bar natural or legal persons from contesting EU environmental law.

In *The People's Climate Case*, ten families from Portugal, Germany, France, Italy, Romania, Kenya, Fiji, and the Saami Youth Association, Saminourra, filed a lawsuit against the European Council. The plaintiffs were children and their parents who worked in agriculture and tourism in the EU and abroad and who were increasingly affected by climate change impacts. They argued that three pieces of legislation designed to enable the EU to meet an overall emissions reduction target of 40 per cent compared with 1990 levels were insufficient to protect their lives, livelihoods, and human rights from the impacts of climate change.

The ECJ dismissed the case, holding that the plaintiffs' claims were inadmissible. Given that the legislative acts at issue were not addressed to the plaintiffs, they had to prove that those acts were of direct and individual concern to them. They argued that they suffered from droughts, flooding, heat waves, sea level rise, and the disappearance of cold seasons. According to settled case law, natural or legal persons satisfy the condition of individual concern only when the plaintiffs are affected in a way that is 'peculiar to them or by reason of circumstances in which they are differentiated from all other persons, and by virtue of these factors distinguishes them individually'.[36]

The ECJ held that general claims will always concern some fundamental right of some particular applicant. The Court was concerned that allowing such claims to proceed would confer standing to almost any plaintiff. For an annulment action to be declared admissible, it is therefore not sufficient to simply claim that a legislative act infringes fundamental rights. By invoking their fundamental rights, the applicants tried to infer an individual concern from the mere infringement of those rights, on the ground that the effects of climate change are unique to and different for each individual. The Court disagreed with this approach, stating that the legislative acts at issue did not affect the applicants by reason of attributes which are peculiar to them or by reason of circumstances in which they are differentiated from all other persons.

[35] The Court's interpretation illustrates the high barriers the *Plaumann* formula erects, especially compared to standing requirements on Member State level for individuals. Some Member States, such as Germany or Italy, confer standing if an applicant claims that a subjective right is affected. Even systems such as France that – like the CJEU – follow a so-called de facto concept only require that an applicant is personally and seriously affected.

[36] *The People's Climate Change Case* (n 30) [46].

### 4.2.4 *European Union Member States*

#### 4.2.4.1 Netherlands

The Netherlands confers standing through a unique civil code provision that grants non-governmental organisations (NGOs) access to its courts.[37] In *Urgenda*, the District Court (2015, first instance) held that the Urgenda Foundation met all of the standing requirements to bring the claim, and that it could: a) act on its own behalf, representing the interests of both current and future generations of Dutch citizens; and b) partially rely on the impact of Dutch emissions abroad to establish its own standing, acknowledging the *possibility* for the Dutch NGO to act on behalf of the interests of persons not resident in the Netherlands: '*Urgenda* can partially base its claims on the fact that the Dutch emissions also have consequences for persons outside the Dutch national borders, since these claims are directed at such emissions.'[38] However, the Court did not directly address this point. Finding that Urgenda already established its standing on behalf of Dutch citizens, it concluded that 'no decision needs to be made on whether *Urgenda*'s reduction claim can als[sic] be successful in so far as it also promotes the rights and interests of current and future generations from other countries'.[39] The District Court denied the standing of the individual claimants, on the basis that they did not have sufficient interests besides *Urgenda*'s interest.

The Court of Appeal confirmed the lower court's decision that the Urgenda Foundation had established its own standing, acting on behalf of the current generation of Dutch nationals and individuals subject to the State's jurisdiction.[40] This was because, in the Court's view, 'it is without a doubt plausible that the current generation of Dutch nationals, in particular but not limited to the younger individuals in this group, will have to deal with the adverse effects of climate change in their lifetime if global emissions of greenhouse gases are not adequately reduced'.[41]

#### 4.2.4.2 Germany

The *Neubauer* case concerned a challenge by a group of German youth of the Federal Climate Protection Act. The claimants argued that the target in the Act to reduce GHG emissions by 55 per cent by 2030 from 1990 levels was insufficient

[37] See art 3:305a, Dutch Civil Code; *Urgenda Supreme Court* (n 3) [5.9.2].

[38] *Urgenda Foundation v The State of The Netherlands* [2015] ECLI:NL:RBDHA:2015:7196 (District Court of the Hague) (*Urgenda District Court*) [4.7].

[39] ibid [4.92].

[40] *State of the Netherlands v Stichting Urgenda* [2018] ECLI:NL:GHDHA:2018:2591 (Court of Appeal).

[41] ibid [37]. As the Urgenda Foundation had not appealed the lack of standing of the 886 co-individual claimants, the Court of Appeal did not address this issue. The Dutch Supreme Court (n 3) did not address the issue of standing in any detail.

to limit global warming to 1.5°C compared to pre-industrial levels, in line with the Paris Agreement – and therefore violated their human rights.[42]

The claimants included eight German individuals, including some minors who were residents of Germany. They were joined by fifteen individual claimants living in Bangladesh and Nepal. The Constitutional Court recognised the standing of the foreign plaintiffs, finding: 'The complainants living in Bangladesh and Nepal also have standing in this respect because it cannot be ruled out from the outset that the fundamental rights of the Basic Law also oblige the German state to protect them against the impacts of global climate change.'[43] However, while the Constitutional Court found a breach of fundamental rights in relation to the resident plaintiffs, the Court established that there could not be a breach of fundamental rights in the case of the non-residents. In the Court's view, the reduction target of 55 per cent was *not* itself unconstitutional. However, the Court found that (1) Germany's emissions must stay within 'its' carbon budget; and that (2) its carbon budget would be almost exhausted by 2030 on the basis of the 55 per cent target. The Court therefore found that Germany would need to take *very* drastic reduction measures after 2030 to stay within its carbon budget, and that these measures would necessarily entail severe restrictions on the fundamental freedoms of the youth plaintiffs (who are residents of Germany). On this basis, the Court established that certain provisions of the Act were incompatible with fundamental freedoms, as they failed to adequately specify emission reductions beyond 2030.

It was therefore because the breach stemmed from the restrictive measures that would be needed to drastically reduce Germany's GHG emissions (as opposed to the impacts of climate change) that the Court was able to conclude that the complainants living in Bangladesh and Nepal would *not* be affected *in their own freedom* (as they would not be subject to such measures).[44] Accordingly, the Court concluded that 'no violation of a duty of protection arising from fundamental rights is ascertainable vis-à-vis the complainants who live in Bangladesh and Nepal'.[45] The Court also noted that the task of fulfilling the duties of protection arising from fundamental rights involves a combination of both climate mitigation *and adaptation measures*. The judges concluded that Germany would not be able to provide this level of protection through adaptation abroad.[46]

### 4.2.4.3 Belgium

Under Belgian law, there is a requirement that plaintiffs have a personal and direct interest in the claim. In the case of *Klimaatzaak* – which was modelled on the

[42] *Neubauer and Others v Germany* [2021] 1 BvR 2656/18, 1 BvR 96/20, 1 BvR 78/20, 1 BvR 288/20, 1 BvR 96/20, 1 BvR 78/20 (German Federal Constitutional Court) (*Neubauer*) [1].

[43] ibid [90]. See also ibid [101].

[44] ibid [131]–[132].

[45] ibid [173].

[46] ibid [178].

*Urgenda* case – the District Court held (which was confirmed by the Court of Appeal) that both the individual plaintiffs and the NGO satisfied this requirement:

> ... the diplomatic consensus based on the most authoritative climate science leaves no room for doubt that a real threat of dangerous climate change exists. This threat poses a serious risk to current and future generations living in Belgium and elsewhere that their daily lives will be profoundly disrupted. In this case, the plaintiffs intend to hold the Belgian public authorities partly responsible for the present and future adverse consequences of climate change on their daily lives. In so doing, each of them has a direct and personal interest in the liability action they have brought.[47]

The District Court and Court of Appeal also recognised the standing of the NGO Klimaatzaak to bring the claim, which included rights-based arguments, noting that 'environmental organisations are given a privileged status by the Aarhus Convention'.[48]

#### 4.2.4.4 France

A court in France issued a decision that also confirmed that *Urgenda*-like analysis on standing in climate litigation is possible at the national level in European Member States. The Conseil d'Etat, France's highest administrative court, delivered a powerful decision in *Commune de Grande Synthe I* regarding France's obligation to reduce its greenhouse gas emissions. The decision could inspire other courts across Europe to review more climate litigation cases.

The Court determined that an individual plaintiff's claim, which was filed by the Mayor of the municipality in this case, was inadmissible despite his current residence in an area experiencing climate change impacts. The Conseil d'Etat concluded, however, that the municipality of Grande Synthe had the right to challenge the government's tacit refusal, as its standing resulted from the impact

[47] *VZW Klimaatzaak v l'État Belge* [2021] 2015/4585/A (Tribunal de première instance francophone de Bruxelles, Section Civile) (*VZW Klimaatzaak First Instance*). The Court of Appeal confirmed the District Court's findings on standing in *VZW Klimaatzaak v Kingdom of Belgium and Others* [2023] 2022/AR/891(Cour d'appel de Bruxelles) (*VZW Klimaatzaak Appeal*). In particular, the Court of Appeal confirmed that the admissibility of claims is governed by rules on standing under domestic law and not by standards set by the ECHR or the Treaty on the Functioning of the European Union. It thus dismissed the relevance of the precedent set in the climate case *Carvalho* (dismissed by the Court of Justice of the European Union for lack of standing). See *VZW Klimaatzaak Appeal* [118].

[48] *VZW Klimaatzaak First Instance* (n 47) [51]. See *VZW Klimaatzaak Appeal* (n 47) [25] '[...] insofar as Klimaatzaak invokes, on the one hand, the violation of arts 2 and 8 of the ECHR in that the rights enshrined in these provisions would be affected by the inaction of the public authorities with regard to global warming and, on the other hand, arts 1382 and 1383 of the former Civil Code, in that this inaction would be wrongful and would have caused it or would be likely to cause it damage, it has an interest within the meaning of arts 17 and 18 of the Judicial Code (examination of the existence and scope of the rights thus invoked is not a matter of admissibility but of the basis of the claim)'. The Court of Appeal confirmed the NGO's interest to *also* bring a claim for damage that has not yet materialised (i.e. worsening global warming), see *VZW Klimaatzaak Appeal* [128].

of its 'direct and certain' exposure to climate change, and more particularly, sea level rise. The Conseil d'Etat also granted intervention requests in this case from the Paris and Grenoble municipalities due to their 'very strong' exposure to climate-related risks.

*Commune de Grande Synthe I* is a landmark precedent for climate litigation in France and follows the European pathway that was opened in *Urgenda*. The Conseil d'Etat's ruling may convince the ECJ to take a less restrictive position on standing in climate litigation. A recent challenge by Paris, Brussels, and Madrid against a Commission regulation on nitrogen oxide emissions has been recently admitted by the General Court and is on appeal before the ECJ as of this writing. This case may be the ECJ's opportunity to adopt reasoning similar to the Conseil d'Etat's in *Commune de Grande Synthe I*.[49]

### 4.2.5 *Philippines*

The Philippines is widely regarded for its groundbreaking public interest environmental litigation. Generally speaking, the Philippines falls on the more liberal end of the standing 'spectrum'.

Championed by the noted lawyer and environmentalist Antonio Oposa, this trendsetting jurisprudence traces its roots to the relaxed standing requirements established in the *Minors Oposa* case in 1993.[50] This case was filed as a taxpayers' class action to compel the Secretary of the Department of Natural Resources to cancel existing timber licensing agreements (TLAs) and refrain from approving new applications. The plaintiffs included Oposa, his children, other children and their parents, and unnamed children of the future. They alleged that all citizens of the Philippines are 'entitled to the full benefit, use and enjoyment of the country's virgin tropical forests'[51] and that they enjoy a constitutional right to a healthful and balanced ecology under Section 16, Article II of the Philippines Constitution.[52] The plaintiffs asserted that continued authorisation of TLA holders to deforest the Philippines would cause irreparable injury to the plaintiffs, especially the minors and their successors who may never see, benefit from, and enjoy the country's virgin tropical forests.[53]

49 The Paris Administrative Court also addressed standing based on a particular statutory standard in *Notre Affaire à Tous and Others v France* [2021] No 1904967, 1904968, 1904972 1904976/4-1. In this case, the Court addressed standing based on Article R. 142-1 of the Environment Code, which allows environmental NGOs to bring claims; and the fact that the case was brought by NGOs is a significant part of why the claim was found to be admissible. See ibid [10]. This development resembles Australia's courts providing liberal interpretations of specific environmental statutory standing provisions to ensure that these cases can be heard.

50 *Minors Oposa v Factoran* [1993] GR No 101083, 224 SCRA 792 *(Minors Oposa v Factoran)*.

51 ibid 795.

52 ibid 800.

53 ibid 799.

The Supreme Court of the Philippines concluded that the plaintiffs had standing to bring the class action. It determined that '[t]he subject matter of the complaint is of common and general interest not just to several, but to all citizens of the Philippines. Consequently, since the parties are so numerous, it becomes impracticable, if not totally impossible, to bring all of them before the court'.[54] The Supreme Court also concluded that the parents, on behalf of the children, correctly asserted that the children represented their generation as well as generations yet unborn.[55]

In the wake of the landmark decision in *Minors Oposa*, courts in the Philippines have issued several decisions that have been highly protective of environmental resources on behalf of current and future generations. Notwithstanding this leadership in the Philippines court system on public interest environmental litigation, plaintiffs in climate litigation in the Philippines have encountered standing obstacles in recent decisions.

In *Segovia v Climate Change Commission*,[56] for example, the plaintiffs sought issuance of writs of kalikasan and continuing mandamus. The writ of kalikasan allows persons filing to do so on behalf of inhabitants prejudiced by alleged environmental damage, whereas mandamus is only available to persons directly aggrieved by the unlawful act or omission.

The plaintiffs represented multiple classes of people, including the car-less, the children of the Philippines, the children of the future, and car owners who would rather not have cars if public transportation were 'safe, convenient, accessible, or reliable'. The plaintiffs sought to compel the implementation of several environmental laws and an administrative order known as the 'Road Sharing Principle', which includes a provision calling for the reformation of transportation and collective favouritism of non-motorised locomotion. The plaintiffs alleged multiple violations including violation of the atmospheric trust provided by the Constitution and failure to implement the Road Sharing Principle mandated by EO 774 and the Climate Change Act. Although the government argued that the plaintiffs violated the hierarchy of courts when they filed their complaint, the Court held that kalikasan is available to persons whose life, health, or property are at risk and allows for circumvention of the typical hierarchy requirements. Therefore, the Court had jurisdiction over the case, and had to determine if the standing requirements were met.

The Court ultimately concluded that the plaintiffs lacked standing on the writ of kalikasan because their allegations amounted to nothing more than 'repeated invocation of the constitutional right to health and to a balanced and healthful ecology' and failed to establish 'a causal link or reasonable connection to the actual or threatened violation of the constitutional right to a balanced and healthful ecology of the

54 ibid 802.
55 ibid.
56 *Segovia v Climate Change Commission* [2017] GR No 211020.

magnitude … required of petitions of this nature'.[57] The Court also dismissed the petition for a writ of mandamus on standing grounds because the plaintiffs failed to prove direct or personal injury.

### 4.2.6 *India*

Other jurisdictions in the Global South take a similarly liberal approach to standing. India, for instance, like the Philippines, has a rich history of groundbreaking public interest environmental litigation, which is just starting to serve as a foundation for climate litigation claims in the country. The courts in India analyse standing for public interest litigation with a different lens than traditional private litigation claims. The landmark case on this point, *SP Gupta v Union of India*,[58] contains famous language justifying the reasoning for adopting a lower threshold for standing in public interest cases:

> This question is of immense importance in a country like India where access to justice being restricted by social and economic constraints, it is necessary to democratise judicial remedies, remove technical barriers against easy accessibility to Justice and promote public interest litigation so that the large masses of people belonging to the deprived and exploited sections of humanity may be able to realise and enjoy the socio-economic rights granted to them and these rights may become meaningful for them instead of remaining mere empty hopes.[59]

Because of this relaxed standard for standing in public interest litigation, plaintiffs in climate cases in India have found particular success with constitutional arguments alleging the right to a clean and healthy environment.[60]

### 4.2.7 *Australia*

Australia's standing jurisprudence makes it a favourable jurisdiction for climate litigation that fits somewhere between the restrictive and liberal jurisdictions

57 ibid [6]. For a discussion of how the writ of kalikasan has been a valuable tool to promote environmental protection in other contexts in the Philippines, see generally Purple Romero, 'Hits and Misses for a Legal Tool to Protect the Environment in Philippines' (*Mongabay*, 28 April 2021) <https://news.mongabay.com/2021/04/hits-and-misses-for-a-legal-tool-to-protect-the-environment-in-philippines> accessed 24 February 2024. Despite the plaintiffs' failure to overcome standing barriers in the *Segovia* case, some commentators believe that climate litigation in the Philippines will increase in the coming years. See generally Gregorio Rafael P. Bueta, 'Environmental Jurisprudence from the Philippines: Are Climate Litigation Cases Just Around the Corner?' (*IUCN*, 21 June 2019) <www.iucn.org/news/world-commission-environmental-law/201906/environmental-jurisprudence-philippines-are-climate-litigation-cases-just-around-corner#_ftnref2> accessed 24 February 2024.

58 *SP Gupta v Union of India* AIR 1982 SC 149.

59 ibid.

60 Asian Development Bank (n 5) 57. See also *Court on its own Motion v State of Himachal Pradesh and Ors* Application No 237 (THC)/ 2013 (CWPIL No 15 of 2010).

discussed so far. Unlike the US where Article III standing requirements (injury, causation, and redressability) always apply to plaintiffs, Australian courts apply narrower common law requirements and broader 'open standing' requirements, and their application depends on what statute is at issue. Litigants in Australia enjoy a lower standing threshold when cases are filed under certain statutes as compared to the higher standing threshold for common law claims.

Two statutes that enable lower standing thresholds in Australia are the Environment Protection Act of 1970 (EP Act) and the Environmental Planning and Assessment Act (EPA Act). To secure standing under these statutes, plaintiffs must demonstrate only that their 'interests are affected by the decision'. These 'interests' can include intellectual, emotional, or aesthetic concerns.

By contrast, common law standing (which is controlling in the absence of any relevant statute) in Australia requires that the plaintiff demonstrate a 'special' interest by offering proof of some advantage or disadvantage that the plaintiff will incur as a result of the action. The special interest must be more than an intellectual or aesthetic concern and must set the plaintiff apart from other members of the general public.

Two climate cases in Australia effectively illustrate the lower standing thresholds under the aforementioned statutes: *Dual Gas Pty Ltd and Ors v Environment Protection Authority*[61] and *Haughton v Minister for Planning and Macquarie Generation; Haughton v Minister for Planning and TRUenergy Pty Ltd.*[62] In *Dual Gas*, Australia's EPA issued a work approval for a power station development, to which three NGOs and an individual, Martin Shield, objected. The tribunal held that three of the four plaintiffs, including Shield, had standing.[63] It evaluated the plaintiffs' standing pursuant to a broader definition set forth in the EP Act and the Victorian Courts and Tribunals Act (VCAT Act). Section 33B (1) of the EP Act confers standing to any person whose 'interests are affected by the decision' to approve or deny a work proposal. The VCAT Act defines 'interest' as an interest of *any* kind, not limited to 'proprietary, economic, or financial' and further allows a person to apply to the tribunal whether their interest is 'directly or indirectly affected by the decision and whether or not any other person's interests are also affected by the decision'.[64]

61 *Dual Gas Pty Ltd and Ors v Environment Protection Authority* [2012] VCAT 308.

62 *Haughton v Minister for Planning and Macquarie Generation* [2011] NSWLEC 217.

63 These broad definitions conflict with the narrow definition of 'interest' at common law. Common law typically requires a 'special interest', like a nexus to the protection of a particular segment of the environment involved in the decision. The tribunal explicitly disagreed with court decisions that applied the narrower definitions on the grounds that the interpretation conflicted with the intent of the legislature in enacting the EP Act and the VCAT Act but made sure to mention that the relevant enabling act is critical to a tribunal or court's interpretation of 'interest'.

64 The VCAT Act provision is based on an older law (which is no longer binding) whose legislative history indicated that standing can be conferred to any person with 'genuinely held and articulated intellectual or aesthetic concern' regarding a decision.

The Tribunal considered three factors to determine if each of the plaintiffs had standing: (1) the nature of the particular project proposal under consideration; (2) the materiality of the project's potential environmental impact; and (3) the involvement of the plaintiff in the project approval process. The power station's environmental impact was global in nature as it would increase Victoria's emission profile by 2.9 per cent by emitting 4.2 million tons of GHGs per year.

Two of the plaintiffs, Environment Victoria (EV) and Shield, were heavily involved in the Dual Gas approval process, while a third plaintiff, Doctors for the Environment Australia (DEA), consisted of members who lived and worked in the Latrobe Valley and would be directly affected by the power station's presence. The Tribunal also considered the government's recognition of EV and its wide community constituency, along with Shield's scientific expertise and the DEA's participation in international climate change matters through its parent organisation, in its determination of the plaintiffs' interest in the case. On the other hand, the fourth plaintiff, Locals into Victoria's Environment (LIVE), submitted an affidavit that referenced only the author's personal feelings towards the project. The Tribunal held that LIVE's consistent involvement in opposition to brown coal in general was not enough of an interest to establish standing for this particular case.

The Tribunal provided extensive support for its conclusions. It first noted that the person seeking to establish standing must demonstrate a material connection with the subject matter of the decision under review, that is, a genuine interest. This may arise from a genuinely held and articulated intellectual or aesthetic concern in the particular subject matter of the decision, as opposed to a broader environmental concern generally.[65] Standing under the VCAT Act is wide but not unlimited. Some meaning must be attached to the words 'a person whose interests are affected'. Despite the apparent breadth of s 5 of the VCAT Act, Parliament must have intended that rights of review do not accrue to any person.[66] It is necessary to consider the context of the relevant enabling Act. This requires consideration of the 'subject, scope and purposes' of the legislation under which the decision in question was made, and the nature of the reviewable decision itself.[67]

In *Haughton*, pursuant to the EPA Act, the Minister declared two coal-fired power station project proposals, Bayswater and Mt. Piper, to be 'critical infrastructure projects' necessary to meet the electricity needs in New South Wales.[68] Plaintiff Haughton challenged the declaration and the plan approvals on the grounds that: (1) the Minister erroneously approved the power stations on the basis that they were critical infrastructure projects; (2) the Minister had not fully considered the principles of ecologically sustainable development; and (3) the Minister had not consid-

65 *Dual Gas* (n 61) [129].
66 ibid [128].
67 ibid [127].
68 *Haughton* (n 62) [18].

ered the impact of the projects on climate change, which was required of him based on his duty to protect the public interest.

The Court granted standing to Haughton pursuant to the 'open standing' requirements of s 123 of the EPA Act, which recognises the right of any person to bring proceedings whether or not any right of that person has been infringed.[69] The Court also determined that even if it erred in granting open standing to Haughton, he has 'general (common) law' standing considering his commitment to being an 'environmental activist', his involvement in the approval process via his membership of a small NGO, and his home address location in the floodplain, which will suffer at the hands of the deleterious effects of climate change, exacerbated by the Minister's approval of coal-fired power plants.[70] In recognising Haughton's common law standing, the Court relied on *Onus v Alcoa*[71] and *North Coast Environmental Council*[72] to determine that Haughton had a special interest in anthropogenic effects of climate change beyond that of the interest of a member of the general public.[73] In essence, standing involves the identification of a legal entity entitled to invoke the jurisdiction of a court.[74] The open standing provisions found in s 123 of the EPA Act or in s 80(1)(c) of the Trade Practices Act (Cth) embrace the common foundation that the right of any person to bring proceedings arises whether or not any right of that person has been or may have been infringed.[75]

The *Dual Gas* and *Houghton* cases reveal Australia's sliding scale approach to standing in climate litigation by relaxing the standing threshold for plaintiffs pursuing claims relating to climate change impacts of certain projects. Standing for this class of litigants who can demonstrate that their interests are adversely affected by such projects is broad but with safeguards that make it less than universal standing for all potential plaintiffs.

## 4.3 EMERGING BEST PRACTICE

There are several principles that constitute emerging best practices for standing in climate litigation. The underlying theme is that existing rules already permit for the granting of standing to climate litigation plaintiffs in most cases, based on the

69 ibid [68].

70 ibid [82].

71 *Onus v Alcoa of Australia Ltd* [1981] 149 CLR 27.

72 *North Coast Environment Council Inc v Minister for Resources* [1994] 55 FCR 492, 127 ALR 617.

73 The court's reasoning here resembles the 'vocational nexus' theory that the plaintiffs asserted in a famous environmental standing in the US, *Lujan* (n 2), which involved the potential extraterritorial application of the Endangered Species Act. The US Supreme Court dismissed the case on standing grounds and rejected the vocational nexus theory and other theories that the plaintiffs asserted to support their standing.

74 *Haughton* (n 62) [64].

75 ibid [68].

direct, personal, or special interest such plaintiffs have in the issue at stake in the case. This is illustrated by the approach of the courts in several cases to date, including *Urgenda, Neubauer*, and *Klimaatzaak*. In other cases, increased liberalisation of standing requirements should be undertaken to ensure that these important claims may be considered as widely as possible in courts around the world. Whether a decision to grant standing is perceived as resulting from a liberal approach or as flowing from a textual interpretation of existing rules, what matters most is that such a decision grants access to justice to those who seek to defend the rule of law.

There are several subparts to what emerging best practices on standing in climate litigation might entail. First, there may be an opportunity in some jurisdictions to create climate litigation exceptions. For example, scholars have argued for a climate litigation exception to the *Plaumann* test in the EU. The concern with applying this strict test for standing in climate litigation claims is that due to the global nature of the climate problem, an anomalous reality occurs in seeking to establish individual and direct harm: 'the more serious the harm, the more people affected, the less chance for individual concern – a quite paradoxical outcome'.[76] Scholars in the US have similarly recognised the anomaly of 'injury to all should not mean injury to none' in climate litigation.[77]

In contrast with these suggested approaches, *Sabo* and *The People's Climate Case* represent an unfortunate impediment to much-needed liberalisation of standing requirements to address climate change in the courts. First, the ECJ bypassed an opportunity in these cases to recognise an exception to the *Plaumann* test in the climate litigation context. Second, the *Plaumann* test also should be modified for climate litigation claims because it is inconsistent with the EU's obligation under the Aarhus Convention. Article 9(3) of the Aarhus Convention states that 'members of the public [must] have access to administrative or judicial procedures to challenge acts and omissions by private persons and public authorities which contravene provisions of its national law relating to the environment'. Moreover, in its 2011 and 2017 reports, the Aarhus Convention Compliance Committee already held that the *Plaumann* criteria were 'too strict to meet the criteria of the Convention' because 'persons cannot be individually concerned if the decision or regulation takes effect by virtue of an objective legal or factual situation'. Nevertheless, the ECJ did not grant an exception.[78]

76 See Lena Hornkohl, 'The CJEU Dismissed the People's Climate Case as Inadmissible: The Limit of Plaumann is Plaumann' (*European Law Blog*, 6 April 2021) <https://europeanlawblog.eu/2021/04/06/the-cjeu-dismissed-the-peoples-climate-case-as-inadmissible-the-limit-of-plaumann-is-plaumann> accessed 24 February 2024.

77 See e.g. B. S. Mank (n 6) 1.

78 For further discussion of *The People's Climate Case* and how the CJEU's decision undermines climate justice through its strict standing analysis, see generally Hornkohl (n 76); Molly Quell, 'Top EU Court Rejects Push for Stricter Emissions Rules' (*Courthouse News Service*, 25 March 2021) <www.courthousenews.com/top-eu-court-rejects-push-for-stricter-emissions-rules> accessed

Recent developments in climate litigation jurisprudence from European Member States represent emerging best practice in establishing a more liberal standing in climate litigation. There are several dimensions of emerging best practice from these cases.

First, these cases confirm that the 'injury to all is injury to none' principle should not apply as a barrier to standing for climate litigation claims. For example, in *Neubauer*, the Court reached the following conclusion regarding the standing of the youth plaintiffs: 'The complainants are individually affected in their own freedom. They are themselves capable of experiencing the measures necessary to reduce $CO_2$ emissions after 2030. The fact that the restrictions will affect virtually everyone then living in Germany does not exclude the complainants from being individually affected.'[79] Similarly, in *Klimaatzaak*, there is a requirement under Belgian law that plaintiffs have a personal and direct interest in the claim. In this case, the first instance court concluded (which was confirmed on appeal) that both the individual plaintiffs and the NGO satisfy this requirement. The first instance court noted that '[t]he fact that other Belgian citizens may also suffer their own damage [from the adverse consequences of climate change], in whole or in part comparable to that of the plaintiffs as individuals, is not sufficient to reclassify the personal interest of each of them as a general interest'.[80] The Czech court in *Klimatická* used similar reasoning in establishing the standing of the individual applicants, noting that the individuals 'must have been directly deprived of [their] rights by the interference'.[81] Since climate change, despite being a global issue with many victims, has 'local adverse manifestations', the Court concluded that citing its wide-ranging effects and pointing to the multitude of victims of those effects 'does not in itself preclude a direct impairment of the rights of the applicants, who belong to that group'.[82]

Outside of Europe, in *Future Generations v Ministry of the Environment and Others*, the Colombian Supreme Court determined the standing of the plaintiffs according to four criteria: a) there is a connection between the impairment of the collective and the individual rights; b) the plaintiff is the one directly affected; c) the impairment of the fundamental right must be proven, not hypothetical; and d)

24 Februar 2024; Climate Action Network, 'Press Release: EU Court Turn a Deaf Ear to Citizens Hit by Climate Crisis' (*Climate Action Network*, 25 March 2021) <https://peoplesclimatecase.caneurope.org/2021/03/eu-court-turn-a-deaf-ear-to-citizens-hit-by-the-climate-crisis> accessed 24 February 2024.

79 *Neubauer* (n 42) [131].

80 VZW *Klimaatzaak First Instance* (n 47) [50]. This was confirmed on appeal. See VZW *Klimaatzaak Appeal* (n 47) [131] 'As pointed out by the first judges, the fact that persons other than those who brought the present proceedings may suffer the same damage or violations of their fundamental rights is not sufficient to transform the interest of each individual appellant into a general interest, which is not simply the sum of individual interests'.

81 *Klimatická žaloba ČR v Czech Republic* [2022] No 14A 101/2021 (Prague Municipal Court) [197]. While this decision was overturned on appeal, this conclusion on standing was not.

82 ibid [198].

the judicial order must re-establish the individual guarantees, and not the collective ones. Twenty-five youth plaintiffs filed a tutela, a constitutional claim used to enforce the protection of fundamental human rights. The Supreme Court held that the youth plaintiffs had standing because their enjoyment of their fundamental rights was 'substantially linked and determined by the environment and the ecosystem'.[83]

Second, the fact that the most serious climate-related harms will occur in the future has also not prevented European courts from finding that individual and NGO plaintiffs have standing in climate change cases. For example, in *Urgenda*, the Dutch Supreme Court made some important conclusions regarding the 'threshold test' for the State's obligations under ECHR, which may be useful for establishing standing in other cases:

> … the Court of Appeal concluded, quite understandably, in para. 45 that there was 'a real threat of dangerous climate change, resulting in the serious risk that the current generation of citizens will be confronted with loss of life and/or a disruption of family life'. The Court of Appeal also held, in para. 37, that it was 'clearly plausible that the current generation of Dutch nationals, in particular but not limited to the younger individuals in this group, will have to deal with the adverse effects of climate change in their lifetime if global emissions of greenhouse gases are not adequately reduced'.[84]

With respect to the State's obligations to protect the right to life under Article 2 of the ECHR, the Court concluded: 'The term "immediate" does not refer to imminence in the sense that the risk must materialise within a short period of time, but rather that the risk in question is directly threatening the persons involved. The protection of Article 2 ECHR also regards risks that may only materialise in the longer term.'[85] Similarly, in *Neubauer*, the Court made important conclusions regarding the rights of youth plaintiffs to seek recourse for climate harms that would not fully manifest until later in their lifetimes:

> As things currently stand, global warming caused by anthropogenic greenhouse gas emissions is largely irreversible […]. It cannot be ruled out from the outset that the complainants will see climate change advancing to such a degree in their own lifetimes that their rights protected under Article 2(2) first sentence GG and Article 14(1) GG will be impaired ([…]). The possibility of a violation of the Constitution cannot be negated here by arguing that a risk of future harm does not represent a current harm and therefore does not amount to a violation of fundamental rights. Even provisions that only begin posing significant risks to fundamental rights over the course of their subsequent implementation can fall into conflict with the Basic Law […] This

83 *Future Generations v Ministry of the Environment and Others (Demanda Generaciones Futuras v Minambiente)* [2018] 11001 22 03 000 2018 00319 00 (Supreme Court of Justice of Colombia) (*Demanda Futuras Generaciones*).

84 *Urgenda Supreme Court* (n 3).

85 ibid [5.2.2].

> is certainly the case where a course of events, once embarked upon, can no longer be corrected […] The complainants are not asserting the rights of unborn persons or even of entire future generations, neither of whom enjoy subjective fundamental rights […]. Rather, the complainants are invoking their own fundamental rights.[86]

Third, the special interests of youth and future generations have been recognised in these cases to support standing.[87] The jurisprudence is less clear on whether claims can be brought on behalf of *unborn* future generations; however, there is now extensive research on the adverse climate impacts that young people alive today will face.[88]

Fourth, it is emerging best practice to enable lower standing thresholds in the context of public interest litigation like climate litigation. India and France have embraced this approach and Australia has applied a version of it in authorising relaxed standing when plaintiffs bring claims under certain environmental statutes. The urgency of the climate crisis and the legislative gridlock in many countries on climate change regulation require that the courts be as available as possible to dispense justice related to climate change issues. Reducing standing barriers is an important step toward achieving this objective.

Other measures to lower standing thresholds include the argument in the Philippines that standing is a procedural requirement that the court can waive

[86] *Neubauer* (n 42) [108]–[109] (emphasis added). See also *VZW Klimaatzaak First Instance* (n 47) [50] ('…the plaintiffs intend to hold the Belgian public authorities partly responsible for the present and future adverse consequences of climate change on their daily lives. In so doing, each of them has a direct and personal interest in the liability action they have brought'); *Advocate Padam Bahadur Shrestha v Prime Minister and Office of Council of Ministers and Others* [2018] Order No 074-WO-0283 (2075/09/10 BS) (Supreme Court of Nepal) 11 ('The matter of climate change and threat posed by pollution is directly connected to the well being of citizens who are guaranteed with the right to clean environment and conservation under the Constitution. Such kind of threat to present and future generations posed by climate change affects every citizen hence, the matters raised in the current petition are of public concern. Considering the public nature of concerns raised in the present petition, there is a meaningful relation between the issues and the petitioners'); *Mathur et al v Her Majesty the Queen in Right of Ontario* [2020] ONSC 6918 (Superior Court of Justice) (*Mathur Strikeout*) [251] ('…no injury needs to have been committed in order to determine standing as long as the claimants can show that a potential injury affected them').

[87] See also ibid *Mathur Strikeout* [2020] (n 86) [253]; *Neubauer* (n 42) [131]; *Environnement Jeunesse v Procureur General du Canada* [2018] 500-06-000955-183 (Quebec Superior Court) 76 (*ENJEU*); *VZW Klimaatzaak First Instance* (n 47) [50]; *Demanda Futuras Generaciones* (n 83) [3], [11.2]; *Urgenda Supreme Court* (n 3) [4.7]; *Held* (n 18) [4]–[5]. On a related note in protecting vulnerable populations, emerging best practice on the issue of victim status in climate litigation is reflected in UN Committee on the Rights of the Child, 'Decision adopted by the Committee under the Optional Protocol to the Convention on the Rights of the Child on a Communications Procedure, concerning Communication No 104/2019', UN Doc CRC/C/88/D/104/2019 (*Sacchi*).

[88] Wim Thiery and others, 'Intergenerational Inequities in Exposure to Climate Extremes' (2021) 374(6564) Science 158. By contrast, the Supreme Court of Switzerland concluded that the future nature of climate harms was a barrier to standing for the individual plaintiffs and organisation of senior women in that case. The European Court of Human Rights later granted standing to the organisation of senior women, but not the individual plaintiffs. See *KlimaSeniorinnen Schweiz and Ors v Federal Department of the Environment, Transport, Energy and Communications* [2020] 1C_37/2019 (Federal Supreme Court of Switzerland); *Verein KlimaSeniorinnen Schweiz and Others v Switzerland* App no 53600/20 (ECtHR).

in the exercise of its discretion. Allowing courts to waive standing in meritorious climate cases can promote enhanced access to the courts. Another strategy is the tutela in Colombia, which the youth plaintiffs in *Future Generations v Ministry of the Environment and Others* used to secure standing in a case compelling the Colombian government to ensure zero deforestation and granting legal personhood to the Colombian Amazon.[89]

A jurisdiction that can benefit from this emerging best practice of selective waiver of standing requirements in climate litigation is New Zealand. The special damage rule in public nuisance litigation for climate change issues in New Zealand has prevented meritorious claims from proceeding on standing grounds. A relaxed version of this rule in climate litigation, or waiver of this requirement altogether for climate cases, would be a better approach for New Zealand to adopt in future public nuisance cases for climate change claims so that meritorious cases may proceed to trial to address the climate crisis.

Related to the issue of the special context of standing in climate litigation, the 'vocational nexus' theory is one mechanism that can help broaden who is a proper plaintiff in these cases. The *Dual Gas* and *Houghton* cases in Australia helped underscore that one's profession and demonstrated interest and engagement on climate issues can support standing, even though this argument was rejected in the landmark US decision in *Lujan v Defenders of Wildlife*. Similarly, in *Notre Affaire à Tous*, the Paris Administrative Court afforded more relaxed standing to environmental NGOs.

Another important dimension of the emerging best practice in this area is to recognise who is bringing the claim and what population is the target of the requested protections. Courts should provide special consideration for sovereign and quasi-sovereign entities who bring climate litigation on behalf of their citizens. This approach was embraced in the 'special solicitude' principle in *Massachusetts v EPA*, but was not applied in the *Kivalina* case. Standing should also recognise the unique vulnerability of certain populations that may be seeking redress in these cases such as Indigenous communities or youth plaintiffs. The field of climate justice has emerged on the strength of their advocacy and the law of standing needs to catch up in many jurisdictions to enable these vulnerable populations to be considered proper parties to bring these claims. Deserving plaintiffs such as the Indigenous communities in *Kivalina* (US) and *Smith* (NZ) and the youth plaintiffs in *Juliana* (US), *Pandey* (India), and the *People's Climate Case* (EU) had their claims dismissed on standing grounds.

## 4.4 REPLICABILITY

This section provides some reflections on the replicability or otherwise of the emerging best practice discussed earlier.

[89] See *Demanda Futuras Generaciones* (n 83).

Some strategic considerations for the near term are important to consider. First, European climate plaintiffs are more likely to succeed by bringing their climate claims in national courts rather than to the ECJ, as evidenced by the outcomes in the *Urgenda* (Netherlands) and *Grande Synthe* (France) decisions as compared to *The People's Climate Case* (EU). Second, the Intergovernmental Panel on Climate Change (IPCC) Sixth Assessment Report[90] released in August 2021 also should help lower barriers for climate litigation plaintiffs by providing broader scientific foundations for injuries as well as enhanced support for attributing those injuries to GHG contributions from government and private sector action and inaction.

Recent developments around the world on rights of nature also offer promise. Efforts to protect non-human entities (i.e. wildlife and natural resources) from climate impacts may be enhanced by application of mechanisms such as legal personhood and rights of nature protections. Legal personhood protections would confer standing directly to these entities who would then be represented by human guardians in court. Two examples of success on these theories are the Colombia Supreme Court's assignment of legal personhood in 2018 to the Colombian Amazon to curb deforestation as a primary driver of climate change in a youth climate case[91] and the Ecuador Constitutional Court's decision in 2021 upholding rights of nature protections for Los Cedros Protected Forest.[92] Two other jurisdictions have not yet succeeded in these efforts. The first example is an effort in Australia to confer rights of nature or legal personhood protections to the Great Barrier Reef as leverage to protect it from continued decimation from ocean acidification and ocean warming.[93] In the second example, the Belgian court in *Klimaatzaak* concluded that 'trees are "not subjects of rights"' in Belgium and therefore lacked standing to bring a claim.[94] This case may, however, leave a door open in cases where nature enjoys legal personhood protections in a given jurisdiction.

The Netherlands, as reflected in *Urgenda*, and other jurisdictions around the world recognise universal standing for associations to bring public interest class actions. While universal standing is a plaintiff-friendly standard for climate litigation and a valuable tool to enhance access to the courts for climate litigation plaintiffs, it may not be the right approach in all jurisdictions that seek to apply standing requirements to safeguard judicial economy and separation of powers.

90 UN Intergovernmental Panel on Climate Change, 'Sixth Assessment Report: Climate Change 2021 – The Physical Science Basis' (6 August 2021) <www.ipcc.ch/report/sixth-assessment-report-working-group-i> accessed 24 February 2024.

91 See Randall S. Abate, *Climate Change and the Voiceless: Protecting Future Generations, Wildlife, and Natural Resources* (Cambridge University Press 2019) 74–86.

92 See GARN Communications, 'Ecuador's Constitutional Court Enforced Rights of Nature to Safeguard Los Cedros Protected Forest' (*Global Alliance for the Rights of Nature*, 21 December 2021) <www.garn.org/los-cedros-rights-of-nature> accessed 24 February 2024.

93 Abate (n 91) 155–161.

94 *VZW Klimaatzaak First Instance* (n 47). This aspect of the case was not addressed on appeal.

Proponents of strict standing barriers advance the common argument that such requirements avoid 'opening the floodgates of litigation'. This argument is more of a perceived than real concern in climate litigation. Even more so than many other forms of litigation, climate litigation is a costly, complex, and time-consuming undertaking for plaintiffs that is not pursued on the basis of whims. In addition to these 'self-restraint' barriers that will naturally limit the number of these cases, jurisdictions typically have safeguards in place in their procedural rules to punish frivolous litigation. Finally, even if causation requirements are relaxed for purposes of standing analysis, causation will remain a daunting barrier for climate litigation plaintiffs at trial. Given these three constraints on potential climate litigants, it is unlikely that relaxed standing requirements would overwhelm judicial systems around the world.

A more relevant issue regarding the role of strict standing requirements as a gatekeeping mechanism is the concern over allowing 'generalized grievances' to proceed in the court system. The courts have a specific role in promoting justice – they resolve disputes between parties. There is a danger that relaxed standing requirements could transform the courts into a secondary legislative body to address generalised concerns about the government's policies, which should be taken up directly with the political branches and not addressed in the courts. Climate litigation, however, is not pursued as an end in itself to displace the proper and primary role of political branches in implementing climate governance policy. Rather, it is merely a first step to promote awareness of the need to enhance climate regulation and an opportunity to develop jurisprudence that can better protect litigants from climate change impacts. The ultimate goal of these efforts is to goad future legislative action, not to seek to regulate climate change one case at a time.

Two jurisdictions that require the most reform to enable enhanced standing in climate litigation are the US and the EU. The US maintains that the Article III requirements of injury, causation, and redressability must be met as a constitutional minimum standard in determining who are proper parties in cases or controversies. The EU requires application of the strict *Plaumann* test in determining who is a proper party to challenge the laws of the EU. In both instances, the existing approaches to standing in these countries have had a chilling effect on plaintiffs seeking to bring climate litigation claims in cases like *Juliana* in the US and the *People's Climate Case* in the EU.

## 4.5 CONCLUSION

Standing has been and will remain a controversial feature in climate litigation in the near future in many jurisdictions around the world. While standing upholds important principles of promoting judicial economy, avoiding generalised grievances, and maintaining separation of powers, there is a need to enhance climate litigation plaintiffs' access to the courts to seek redress of their climate regulation concerns. There are many procedural and substantive bases on which climate litigation claims may fail. Allowing more liberalised standing in these cases merely affords these potentially meritorious claims a better opportunity to be heard.

Easing standing burdens in climate litigation can be guided by the following core principles: (1) climate litigation exceptions to standing requirements may be appropriate in some jurisdictions, building on the approach of reducing standing hurdles for public interest litigation in some jurisdictions; (2) sovereign or quasi-sovereign entities bringing climate litigation claims should have enhanced access to the courts to be able to protect their citizens from climate impacts as in *Massachusetts v EPA* (US) and *Grande Synthe* (France); (3) the needs of uniquely vulnerable populations such as Indigenous communities and youth plaintiffs should be considered in evaluating standing thresholds, perhaps similar to international law's consideration of the 'special needs of developing nations'; (4) climate plaintiffs should be able to secure standing based on their professional and circumstantial relationships to climate change concerns as in *Dual Gas* (Australia); and (5) non-human plaintiffs may be able to gain standing in their own right in climate litigation through mechanisms such as legal personhood and rights of nature.

# 5

# Admissibility

*Juan Auz**

## 5.1 INTRODUCTION

Admissibility could be broadly defined as the group of conditions that render a lawsuit or petition worthy of being reviewed by a judicial or quasi-judicial body, either at the national or international level. Admissibility requirements vary according to jurisdiction and type of legal action but generally relate to procedural requirements. The conflation of the term 'admissibility' with similar ones such as 'jurisdiction' and 'standing' tends to be common. However, some tribunals (including arbitral tribunals) and academics make a distinction by which:

> jurisdiction pertains to the ability or power of a [...] tribunal to hear a claim, whereas admissibility relates to the characteristics of a particular claim. Accordingly, a tribunal would have to decide, as a primary issue, whether it has jurisdiction, before determining whether a particular claim is admissible. It thus follows that, once a tribunal has upheld a jurisdictional objection, it would dismiss the case and consequently not decide upon objections to admissibility.[1]

Therefore, if jurisdiction reflects a court's power to adjudicate a dispute, then admissibility pertains to the terms permitting a court to exercise (or decline to exercise) its legal powers. The authorisation to decide whether to adjudicate a dispute which falls under a court's jurisdiction may be explicitly stated in the court's constitutive instruments or implicitly derived from them.[2] Some international legal instruments will also explicitly spell out criteria for admissibility and stress whether the claim before the court constitutes an abuse of legal process

* Dr Juan Auz is an Ecuadorian lawyer and Postdoctoral Researcher at Tilburg University's Law School working on the TransLitigate project. This chapter was made possible by ERC STG TransLitigate. Funded by the European Union. However, views and opinions expressed are those of the author only and do not necessarily reflect those of the European Union or European Research Council.

[1] Tejas Shiroor, 'Admissibility (Procedure)' (*Jus Mundi*, 27 September 2021) <https://jusmundi.com/en/document/wiki/en-admissibility-procedure> accessed 24 February 2024.

[2] Yuval Shany, *Questions of Jurisdiction and Admissibility before International Courts* (Cambridge University Press 2016) 47.

or whether it is well founded.[3] In that sense, courts often find themselves in a position to manage what cases they should or should not dismiss, considering their permanent cautious approach not to arrogate other branches of power's functions and potentially opening the floodgates to complex climate cases that might be better dealt with in the law-making sphere.[4]

The issue of admissibility is highly relevant to climate litigation because it represents one of the first procedural hurdles for plaintiffs seeking climate-related relief. Accordingly, if the case is dismissed at such an early stage of the legal process, then alleged victims of climate change will, at worst, be left without proper access to justice and, at best, be deprived of discussing the merits of their case. For this reason, broadly speaking, a good emerging practice across different jurisdictions is to balance procedural rigour and consideration of applicants' particular circumstances in the context of the climate crisis. This chapter focuses mainly on admissibility issues before international and regional human rights courts and bodies, such as the requirement to exhaust domestic remedies, because the legal discussion is more noticeable in those spheres. Additionally, very few national-level cases have addressed the issue of admissibility in detail.

As of May 2021, the climate litigation databases from the Grantham Institute at the London School of Economics and the Sabin Center at Columbia University reported 1,841 ongoing or concluded climate change litigation cases from around the world.[5] Of these, 1,387 were filed before courts in the United States (US), while the remaining 454 were filed before courts in thirty-nine other countries and thirteen international or regional courts and tribunals (including the courts of the European Union).[6] About 20 per cent of all the cases (369) reached an outcome, of which 58 per cent (215) were favourable to climate change action, 32 per cent (118) had unfavourable outcomes, and 10 per cent (36) had no discernible likely impact on climate policy.[7] We can infer from this empirical evidence that at least 68 per cent of settled cases (favourable and no discernible likely impact outcomes) were not precluded by admissibility barriers because they were decided on the merits. Admissibility may have been a factor in the remaining 32 per cent of cases. However, this hypothesis cannot be empirically assessed due to unavailable specific data. Despite this, it is clear from the available evidence that most courts and tribunals worldwide permit cases to proceed to the merits stage of litigation, where substantial aspects are discussed instead of stalling and rejecting the case altogether based on admissibility grounds.[8]

3 ibid 48.

4 Laura Burgers, 'Should Judges Make Climate Change Law?' (2020) 9 TEL 55, 58.

5 Joana Setzer and Catherine Higham, 'Global Trends in Climate Change Litigation: 2021 Snapshot' (*LSE Grantham Research Institute on Climate Change and the Environment*, July 2021) 10 <www.lse.ac.uk/granthaminstitute/wp-content/uploads/2021/07/Global-trends-in-climate-change-litigation_2021-snapshot.pdf> accessed 24 February 2024.

6 ibid.

7 ibid 19.

8 It is worth noting that cases dismissed at the admissibility stage may, however, be underrepresented in the databases (especially outside the US, where the database coverage is quite patchy).

From the point of view of attaining proactive and protective climate action, this trend suggests that, overall, judges are not interpreting procedural admissibility aspects of a legal case as an immediate barrier but rather are adopting a flexible approach to admissibility. Therefore, emerging best practices in the context of admissibility requirements in climate litigation reflect a careful balancing between a rigorous understanding of procedural rules with a sensitivity to the issues at stake in the climate emergency and an understanding of the role of the judiciary in clarifying existing laws that could further climate ambition and protection.

## 5.2 STATE OF AFFAIRS

Despite the empirical evidence showing that most climate litigation cases succeeded at the admissibility stage, earlier and recent cases have raised important questions about admissibility requirements. These questions, which could play an influential role in the cross-fertilisation of interpretive norms, have been highlighted mainly by international judicial and quasi-judicial bodies specialised in international human rights law. In these cases, the main hurdle has been some established concerns of admissibility requirements, namely the failure of applicants to exhaust domestic remedies, the failure to establish how the alleged facts would characterise a violation of rights, and the failure to clarify the victim's status. This section will, therefore, explore some of these points in case law.

However, before delving directly into the minutiae of case law, it is important to recall some general aspects of admissibility requirements at the international level, which, to some extent, are also present in many domestic jurisdictions. Comparing the number of cases in the three regional human rights systems, it is conspicuously evident that the European human rights system fares better than its African and Inter-American counterparts regarding the number of petitions admitted and eventually resolved.[9] This is, however, the result of barriers to access to formal institutionalised justice at the domestic level in Africa and Latin America, mainly due to racial and socioeconomic inequalities, lack of information on the scope of their rights, language barriers, cumbersome lawyer costs and court fees, excessive formalism, procedural delays, and geographical location of tribunals.[10] After these structural barriers are factored in, admissibility in the regional human rights systems also shows some numeric disparities. In 2014, the European system declared 97 per cent of petitions to be inadmissible; the Inter-American system declared 8 per cent inadmissible; and in the African system, 27 per cent of the cases under consideration were declared inadmissible.[11] This overview demonstrates that a case's likelihood of overcoming admissibility barriers will depend on the regional human rights system in which it is adjudicated.

[9] Françoise Hampson and others, 'Inaccessible Apexes: Comparing Access to Regional Human Rights Courts and Commissions in Europe, the Americas, and Africa' (2018) 16 IJCL 161, 164.

[10] ibid 166.

[11] ibid 171.

In all international human rights bodies, admissibility is determined through a set of criteria that must be fulfilled cumulatively.[12] The admissibility criteria applied by the Inter-American Commission on Human Rights (IACHR) and the Inter-American Court of Human Rights (IACtHR) include criteria related to *ratione personae*,[13] *loci*,[14] *materiae*,[15] and *temporis*;[16] characterisations of the claim; exhaustion of domestic remedies; and non-duplication of procedures.[17] Admissibility criteria for the European Court of Human Rights (ECtHR) are enumerated in Articles 34–35 of the European Convention on Human Rights (ECHR). They are concerned with jurisdictional matters (compatibility of the application or a complaint with the provisions of the ECHR *ratione materiae, personae, temporis, and loci*), procedural matters (six-month rule and exhaustion of domestic remedies), requirements concerned with the substantive elements of the complaint (manifestly ill-founded and no significant disadvantage criteria), and hybrid criteria that consist both of procedural and substantive elements (requirement of non-repetition and prohibition of the abuse of the right of application), or procedural and jurisdictional criteria (prohibition of anonymous applications).[18]

A notable and early example of how admissibility manifests as a relevant issue in climate litigation can be found in the pioneering petition filed by several Inuit Peoples of the Arctic against the United States before the IACHR in 2005.[19] In this petition, the Inuit requested the IACHR to recommend that the United States adopt mandatory measures to limit its greenhouse gas (GHG) emissions, consider the impacts of GHG emissions on the Arctic in environmental impact assessments,

12 Vidan Hadzi-Vidanovic, 'Admissibility: European Court of Human Rights (ECtHR)', *Max Planck Encyclopaedias of International Law* (Oxford University Press 2018) [1].

13 The *Ratione Persona* criterion is related to what the American Convention on Human Rights says about who can lodge a petition before the Inter-American Commission; every human being (art 1(2)), group of persons, or any NGO (art 44) may lodge petitions with the Commission containing denunciations or complaints. See Inter-American Commission on Human Rights, 'Digest of the Inter-American Commission on Human Rights on Its Admissibility and Competence Criteria' (Inter-American Commission on Human Rights 2020) OEA/Ser.L/V/II.175 [43–45].

14 The *Ratione Loci* criterion refers to art 1(1) of the American Convention concerning the obligation of States to respect the rights and freedoms of all persons subject to their jurisdiction. See ibid [58]–[61].

15 The *Ratione Materiae* criterion refers to art 33(a) of the American Convention concerning the competence of both the Commission and the Court to review matters relating to the fulfilment of the commitments made by States to the American Convention and other Inter-American human rights instruments. See ibid [68]–[79].

16 The *Ratione Temporis* criterion refers to the applicability of the American Convention, the American Declaration, and other Inter-American instruments, over facts that took place when the applicable instrument was in force for the respondent State; or when the events began prior to its entry into force and continued after its entry into force. See ibid [62]–[67].

17 James Cavallaro and others, *Doctrine, Practice, and Advocacy in the Inter-American Human Rights System* (Oxford University Press 2019).

18 Hadzi-Vidanovic (n 12) [6].

19 Petition To the Inter-American Commission on Human Rights Seeking Relief from Violations Resulting from Global Warming Caused by Acts and Omissions of the United States [2005] Inter-American Commission on Human Rights 1413–05.

establish and implement a plan to protect Inuit culture and resources, and provide assistance necessary for Inuit to adapt to the impacts of climate change that cannot be avoided.

Applicants addressed a potential dismissal of their claim based on admissibility requirements in their petition. They stressed that Article 31.1 of the IACHR's rules of procedure specifies that the IACHR, to admit the case, 'shall verify whether the remedies of the domestic legal system have been pursued and exhausted in accordance with the generally recognised principles of international law'.[20] They also cited the exemptions to the general rule of admissibility, namely that the exhaustion requirement shall not apply when the domestic legislation of the State concerned does not afford due process of law for the protection of the right or rights that have allegedly been violated.[21] In that vein, the applicants argued that in the US, there are no remedies suitable to address the infringement of their rights, and therefore, the requirement that domestic remedies be exhausted does not apply in their case, meaning consequently that the petition is admissible under the IACHR's rules of procedure.[22]

A year later, the Assistant Executive Secretary of the IACHR answered the applicants in a letter stating that after having completed the study outlined in Article 26 of the IACHR's Rules of Procedure, the IACHR determined that it would not be possible to process the petition because the information it contains 'does not satisfy the requirements set forth in those Rules and the other applicable instruments'.[23] Specifically, the information provided did not 'enable the IACHR to determine whether the alleged facts would tend to characterise a violation of rights protected by the American Declaration on the Rights and Duties of Man'.[24]

Article 26 of the IACHR's Rules of Procedure concerns the initial review of a petition by the Executive Secretariat of the Commission, who shall be responsible for the study and initial processing of petitions lodged before the Commission that fulfil all the requirements. According to the Executive Secretariat, which served as the first filter of a petition, the applicants did not fulfil the requirements and thus declared it unadmitted.

More recently, on October 12, the United Nations Committee on the Rights of the Child (CRC) found the communication submitted by sixteen children inadmissible for failure to exhaust domestic remedies under Article 7 (e) of the Optional Protocol to the Convention on the Rights of the Child. This case began in September 2019, when sixteen children from different countries filed a claim

20 ibid [111], [112].
21 ibid [112].
22 ibid.
23 Response by the Inter-American Commission on Human Rights Executive Secretary, *Petition To the Inter-American Commission on Human Rights Seeking Relief from Violations Resulting from Global Warming Caused by Acts and Omissions of the United States* [2005] Inter-American Commission on Human Rights 1413-05.
24 ibid.

alleging that Argentina, Brazil, France, Germany, and Turkey violated their rights under the UN Convention on the Rights of the Child because they had not been ambitious enough in reducing their GHG emissions. Specifically, the claimants argued that the countries had failed to take necessary preventive and precautionary measures to respect, protect, and fulfil the claimants' rights to life, health, and culture, as guaranteed by the Convention.[25] As a general remark, the CRC recalled that authors must use all judicial or administrative avenues that may offer them a reasonable prospect of redress and that domestic remedies need not be exhausted if they objectively have no prospect of success. For example, in cases where, under applicable domestic laws, the claim would inevitably be dismissed or where established jurisprudence of the highest domestic tribunals would preclude a positive result. However, the CRC noted that mere doubts or assumptions about the success or effectiveness of remedies do not absolve the authors from exhausting them.[26]

In light of this, the CRC found the petitions inadmissible because the authors did not attempt to exhaust all domestic remedies that were reasonably effective and available to them to challenge the alleged violation of their rights under the Convention and that they did not sufficiently substantiate their arguments on the exception under Article 7 (e) of the Optional Protocol that the application of the remedies is unlikely to bring effective relief.[27]

Another impediment to admissibility in climate litigation relates to the status of victim or the jurisdiction *rationae personae*. Here, courts are clear about them not being appropriate fora for the institution of an *actio popularis* and that their task is not usually to review the relevant law and practice *in abstracto* or without a concrete victim but to determine whether how they were applied to or affected the applicant gave rise to a violation of the relevant treaty.[28] Therefore, the notion of 'victim' broadly denotes the person or persons directly or indirectly affected by the alleged violation. Hence, it is not just the direct victim or victims of the alleged violation who are concerned but also any indirect victims to whom the violation would cause harm or who would have a valid and personal interest in seeing it brought to an end. It was precisely this impediment that arose in the *Armando Ferrão Carvalho and Others v The European Parliament and the Council*, in which ten families, including children, from Portugal, Germany, France, Italy, Romania, Kenya, Fiji, and the Swedish Sami Youth Association Sáminuorra, brought an action in the EU General Court seeking to compel the EU to take more stringent GHG emissions reductions.

[25] UN Committee on the Rights of the Child, 'Decision adopted by the Committee under the Optional Protocol to the Convention on the Rights of the Child on a Communications Procedure, concerning Communication No 104/2019', UN Doc CRC/C/88/D/104/2019 (*Sacchi*).

[26] ibid [10.16].

[27] ibid [10.18].

[28] 'Practical Guide on Admissibility Criteria' (*European Court of Human Rights, Council of Europe*, 1 August 2021) <www.echr.coe.int/documents/admissibility_guide_eng.pdf> [17][18] accessed 24 February 2024.

The plaintiffs alleged that the EU's target to reduce domestic GHG emissions by 40 per cent by 2030, compared to 1990 levels, is insufficient to avoid dangerous climate change and threatens plaintiffs' fundamental rights of life, health, occupation, and property. The applicants' inference did not convince the Court that they were individually concerned, given that although all persons may, in principle, each enjoy the same right (such as the right to life or the right to work), the effects of climate change and, by extension, the infringement of fundamental rights is unique to and different for each individual. The Court stressed that the claim that such an act infringes those rules or rights is not sufficient in itself to establish that the action brought by an individual is admissible without running the risk of rendering procedural requirements meaningless, insofar as the alleged infringement does not distinguish the applicant individually, just as in the case of the addressee.[29]

The grounds for annulling a legally binding piece of EU legislation, such as the 'climate package' plaintiffs sought to annul, arise under certain conditions, such as a lack of competence and an infringement of an essential procedural requirement. However, the admissibility requirements for such actions are very strict and include a requisite that an EU act is of 'direct and individual concern' to the person bringing the case. According to EU case law, the notion of direct concern presupposes that the impugned EU legislative act affects the legal situation of the person concerned directly and leaves no discretion to those responsible for its implementation.[30] Furthermore, an EU legislative act will only be of individual concern to a person bringing the action if it meets the criteria of what has become known as the '*Plaumann* test'.[31] This test assesses if the EU law affects a person because of specific attributes that are peculiar to them or because of circumstances in which they are differentiated from all other persons and, under these factors, distinguish them individually. In other words, the threshold to meet these admissibility requirements is relatively high, which explains why plaintiffs failed to convince the Court.

At the national level, some climate litigation cases have also been dismissed due to a lack of admissibility requirements, including the impossibility of drawing the status of victims. For instance, in the Colombian case of *Germán Espinosa Mejía v Colombia* – arguably the first attempt to integrate climate change and human rights arguments in a Latin American court – a narrow approach to legal interpretation and application on admissibility was adopted. The plaintiff filed a constitutional injunction alleging the violation of the right to a dignified life due to a lack of suitable environmental and climate protection policies. The Supreme Court of Colombia dismissed the legal action because the plaintiff could not represent

29 Case T-330/18 *Carvalho and Others v Parliament and Council* [2018] 2018/C 285/51 (ECJ, 8 May 2019).

30 Marc Willers, 'Climate Change Litigation in European Regional Courts: Jumping Procedural Hurdles to Hold States to Account?' in Ivano Alogna, Christine Bakker, and Jean-Pierre Gauci (eds), *Climate Change Litigation: Global Perspectives* (Brill Nijhoff 2021) 298.

31 Case 25/62 *Plaumann & Co v Commission of the European Economic Community* [1963] ECR 95, 107.

an imprecise group of present and future generations.[32] In this case, the outcome demonstrates that no uniform criteria exist across chambers and judges vis-à-vis the requirements to accept or dismiss *tutelas* or constitutional injunctions.

The examples covered in this section are rulings that have ripple effects across the climate law community, who have expressed their views on the possible impacts these precedents might have on interpreting admissibility requirements in other courts.[33] However, as was shown earlier, these instances in which cases are dismissed purely based on admissibility claims are not most cases, which means that most courts are adopting a relatively lenient approach against rigid procedural formalism by extending the interpretation to a systematic integration according to Article 31 of the Vienna Convention on the Law of Treaties.[34] In that vein, in *VZW Klimaatzaak v Kingdom of Belgium and Others*, the Brussels Court of First Instance referred to the Aarhus Convention on Access to Information, Public Participation in Decision-making and Access to Justice in Environmental Matters to interpret admissibility requirements under domestic law – which was confirmed on appeal.[35] Through this reading, the Court admitted the lawsuit and analysed the petition's merits, an approach that could be replicable in other jurisdictions, as will be discussed in subsequent sections.

## 5.3 EMERGING BEST PRACTICE

As evinced in the case law, a best practice approach to admissibility includes a transparent discussion of admissibility criteria; provides effective balancing and in-depth reasons as to why a petition is not admitted; accommodates a fast-tracking procedure; and takes into consideration contextual aspects in the rationale of why the legal action is admitted or not. For instance, in *Shrestha v Office of the Prime Minister et al*, the Supreme Court of Nepal transparently discusses admissibility criteria and engages in a balancing exercise considering the context. Specifically, it did not explicitly disaggregate standing, jurisdiction, and admissibility issues. However, it recognised that, because the claim invoked constitutional rights and, further, the 'threat to present and future generations posed by climate change affects every citizen, hence, the matters raised in the current petition are of public concern', there was 'a meaningful relation between the issues and the petitioners', and it accordingly accepted the case for consideration on the merits.[36] In the case of *Milieudefensie*

[32] *Germán Espinosa Mejía v Government of Colombia* [2014] STP13863-2014 (Supreme Court of Justice of Colombia) [333].

[33] Setzer and Higham (n 5).

[34] Vienna Convention on the Law of Treaties (entered into force 27 January 1980) 1155 UNTS 331 (VCLT).

[35] *VZW Klimaatzaak v l'État Belge* [2021] 2015/4585/A (Tribunal de première instance francophone de Bruxelles, Section Civile) (*VZW Klimaatzaak First Instance*) [47]; *VZW Klimaatzaak v Kingdom of Belgium & Others* [2023] 2022/AR/891(Cour d'appel de Bruxelles) (*VZW Klimaatzaak Appeal*).

[36] *Advocate Padam Bahadur Shrestha v Prime Minister and Office of Council of Ministers and Others* [2018] Order No 074-WO-0283 (2075/09/10 BS) (Supreme Court of Nepal) (*Shrestha v Office of Council of Ministers*).

*et al v Royal Dutch Shell plc*, the 2021 decision from the Hague District Court stressed that the interests of current and future generations of the world's population, as served with the class actions, are not suitable for bundling because, given the difference in effects of climate change across the globe, they fail to properly constitute a 'similar interest'. However, the interests of current and future generations of Dutch residents and the inhabitants of the Wadden Sea area are suitable for bundling because they are sufficiently similar. The claim, therefore, is deemed admissible concerning Dutch residents and the inhabitants of the Wadden region.[37] This could be argued as an example of best practice because the Court considers the context in which the case takes place and is transparent in doing so.

Another example of best practice can be retrieved from the *Teitiota v New Zealand* communication before the UN Human Rights Committee. In 2015, Ioane Teitiota, a citizen of Kiribati, filed a communication with the UN Human Rights Committee claiming that New Zealand had violated his right to life by denying him asylum despite his assertions that climate change made Kiribati uninhabitable.[38] The Committee, in analysing the grounds of admissibility, noted that the author did exhaust all available domestic remedies and confirmed that the matter was not being examined under another international adjudicative procedure, following the Rules of Procedure of the Optional Protocol, thus justifying the Committee's competence to examine the communication.[39] Furthermore, the Committee stated that admissibility of the communication requires that the author justifies not only the victim status, which in cases of deportation or extradition means the imminent decision to remove the individual, but also an imminent harm in the receiving State. The Committee discussed the imminence requirement by accepting the author's argument that climate change leads to impacts in Kiribati, namely lack of potable water, employment possibilities, and a threat of serious violence caused by land disputes.[40] Notwithstanding the Committee's rejection of the communication on the merits, it did justify its position on the admissibility requirements by having considered the precarious environmental reality the author faces in his country of origin due to climate change.

In April 2018, Colombia's Supreme Court of Justice handed down the *Future Generations v Colombia tutela* brought by twenty-five young people who were advised by the national NGO Dejusticia. This case recognised the correlation between deforestation, climate change, and the infringement of human rights of present and future generations.[41] The Supreme Court of Colombia discussed

[37] *Milieudefensie v Royal Dutch Shell* [2021] ECLR:NL: RBDHA:2021:5339 (District Court of the Hague).

[38] UNHR Committee, 'Views Adopted by the Committee under Article 5(4) of the Optional Protocol, concerning Communication No 2728/2016', 24 October 2019, UN Doc CCPR/C/127/D/2728/2016 *(Teitiota)* [2.1]–[2.10].

[39] ibid [8.3].

[40] ibid [8.5].

[41] *Future Generations v Ministry of the Environment and Others (Demanda Generaciones Futuras v Minambiente)* [2018] 11001 22 03 000 2018 00319 00 (Supreme Court of Justice of Colombia) (*Demanda Futuras Generaciones*).

procedural details regarding the *tutela* process. In the first ruling, the District Court determined that the *tutela* was not an appropriate mechanism to file this particular action because of the collective nature of the problem. However, a *tutela* can be filed if (i) it shows the connection between the violation of collective and fundamental or individual rights, (ii) the person filing the *tutela* is the person directly affected, (iii) the violation of a fundamental right is not hypothetical but fully proved, and (iv) the judicial order being sought is oriented towards restoring individual rights and not collective ones.[42] The Supreme Court found that the fundamental rights to life, health, minimum subsistence, freedom, and human dignity are substantially linked and determined by the environment and the ecosystem. Without a healthy environment, subjects of law and sentient beings in general will be unable to survive, much less protect those rights for our children or future generations. Therefore, the Court added that the exceptional proceeding of the *tutela* is sufficiently demonstrated to resolve in depth the problems raised because the jurisprudential assumptions for the lawsuit are met, given the connection of the environment with fundamental rights.[43]

In the Inter-American Human Rights System, the Court and the Commission have considered the particular cultural characteristics of the applicants and tailored admissibility requirements accordingly. For example, in the case of Indigenous peoples, the IACHR has consistently stated that these communities must exhaust only those remedies that contemplate the particular characteristics, either economic or social, of these groups as well as their particular situation of vulnerability, their customary law, values, uses and customs.[44] The African Commission on Human and Peoples' Rights (ACHPR) has given an even more purposive and generous interpretation than other regional systems.[45] Hampson, Martin, and Viljoen have noted the following:

> The ACHPR has consistently held that the requirement that 'domestic remedies, if any' need to be exhausted means that only remedies that are 'available' (which can be pursued without impediment), 'sufficient' (capable of providing the required remedy), and 'effective' (offering a real prospect of success) need

42 ibid [17].

43 ibid.

44 *Diaguita Agricultural Communities of the Huasco-Altinos and the members thereof v Chile, Admissibility* [2009] Report No 141/09, Petition 415-07, Inter-American Commission on Human Rights (30 December 2009) [45]; *Opario Lemoth Morris et al (Miskitu Divers) v Honduras, Admissibility* [2009] Report No 121/09, Petition 1186-04, Inter-American Commission on Human Rights (12 November 2009) [34]; *Kuna of Madungandí and Emberá of Bayano Indigenous Peoples and their Members v Panama, Admissibility* [2009] Report No 58/09, Petition 12-354, Inter-American Commission on Human Rights (21 April 2009) [37].

45 Nsongurua J. Udombana, 'So Far, So Fair: The Local Remedies Rule in the Jurisprudence of the African Commission on Human and Peoples' Rights' (2003) 97 AJIL 1; Frans Viljoen, *International Human Rights Law in Africa* (Oxford University Press 2012) 323–329.

> to be exhausted.[46] The ACHPR has even gone as far as exempting complainants from this requirement in respect of systemic, widespread, and well-publicized violations, on the basis that the purpose of the requirement (namely, that a state should have notice and thus an opportunity to rectify the situation) had been served.[47]

Another best practice adopted by the ECtHR and IACHR is to expedite priority cases where urgent or systemic rights violations are alleged. This allows admissibility to be assessed promptly. On 30 November 2020, the European Court of Human Rights fast-tracked a climate case brought against thirty-three defendant countries, requiring them to respond by the end of February 2021. On 4 February 2021, the Court rejected a motion by the defendant's government asking the Court to overturn its fast-tracking decision. The governments had asked the court to overturn priority treatment of the case and to hear arguments only on the admissibility of the case. The Court sent a letter to the parties rejecting these motions and gave the defendants until 27 May 2021 to submit a defence on admissibility and the case's merits.[48] However, it should be noted that according to the Global Legal Action Network, who are supporting the case, only a tiny minority of cases before the Court are fast-tracked and communicated.[49]

In the Inter-American system, a new rule authorises expediting consideration of a petition due to the age or health condition of the victim, the potential application of the death penalty, the relationship between the petition and precautionary measures already adopted in that case, whether the victim is deprived of liberty, that there is an express intention of the State to enter into a friendly settlement, or when the petition addresses a structural situation. The IACHR had already implemented these rules in practice before they were included in its Rules of Procedure.[50]

## 5.4 REPLICABILITY

The creation of exceptions to ordinary rules of standing is a practice that could be replicated across jurisdictions. These exceptions arguably allow some room for manoeuvre for interpretive purposes in which judges could factor in some best practices mentioned earlier, such as flexibility and sensibility towards the context in which the case is grounded. For instance, in the case of the exhaustion of domestic remedies requirement, judges could employ a more thorough analysis of why

46 *Sir Dawda K Jawara v The Gambia* [2000] Communication Nos 147/95 and 149/96, African Commission on Human and Peoples' Rights (11 May 2000) [32].

47 Hampson and others (n 9) 172.

48 ibid.

49 'Duarte Agostinho and Others v Portugal and 32 Other States' (*Sabin Center for Climate Change Law*, 2020) <https://climatecasechart.com/non-us-case/youth-for-climate-justice-v-austria-et-al/> accessed 24 February 2024.

50 Hampson and others (n 9) 169.

domestic litigation may not be the most optimal avenue for a complex case such as climate change, especially if there are some extraterritorial elements. For instance, some commentators have argued that in the *Sacchi et al v Argentina et al* case, the Committee on the Rights of the Child could have avoided the dismissal of at least certain applicants if it had duly considered the applicant's argument that under 'domestic laws their claims would inevitably be dismissed or that the established jurisprudence of the highest domestic courts would clearly preclude a positive result, then these arguments have to be assessed under the "no prospect of success" test'.[51]

Another factor that enables replicability is the prevalence of interpretation of the law through the principle of systemic integration. According to the Vienna Convention on the Law of the Treaties, systemic integration refers to the importance of contextual elements that should be considered, such as subsequent practice and international law applicable to the treaty parties, when interpreting the normative content of the primary rule.[52] At the domestic level, the essence of systemic integration can also be applied *mutandis mutandi*. In the context of climate litigation and overcoming admissibility hurdles, interpreting the law systematically and integrally implies resorting to those obligations provided by law that facilitate access to justice for environmental issues. In Europe, for instance, the burden of persuasion for victimhood could be lessened if courts seriously apply the provisions of the Aarhus Convention in light of domestic legislation (as in *Milieudefensie* and *VZW Klimaatzaak v Kingdom of Belgium and Others*). The same is true in Latin America, where judges could enable access to justice for applicants if they integrate the Escazu Agreement on Procedural Environmental Rights content. Article 8 of the Agreement affirms that States shall have, considering their circumstances, broad active legal standing (as a proxy to admissibility) in defence of the environment under domestic legislation.[53] Systematic interpretation could also be guided by *amici curiae*, which showcases the opinion of experts in certain areas of law or other disciplines to guide the courts in their decisions. This institution has been used in the context of climate litigation, and expressly, some experts have commented on specific admissibility aspects, as in the *Sacchi* case.[54]

51 Başak Çali, 'A Handy Illusion? Interpretation of the "Unlikely to Bring Effective Relief" Limb of Article 7(e) OPIC by the CRC in Saachi et al' (*EJIL: Talk!*, 1 November 2021) <www.ejiltalk.org/a-handy-illusion-interpretation-of-the-unlikely-to-bring-effective-relief-limb-of-article-7e-opic-by-the-crc-in-saachi-et-al/> accessed 24 February 2024.

52 VCLT (n 34).

53 Regional Agreement on Access to Information, Public Participation and Justice in Environmental Matters in Latin America and the Caribbean (entered into force 22 April 2021) 3397 UNTC 195 (Escazú Agreement).

54 'Amici Curiae Brief of Special Rapporteurs on Human Rights and the Environment on Admissibility', <https://climatecasechart.com/wp-content/uploads/non-us-case-documents/2021/20210901_Communication-No.-1042019-Argentina-Communication-No.-1052019-Brazil-Communication-No.-1062019-France-Communication-No.-1072019-Germany-Communication-No.-1082019-Turkey_na-2.pdf> accessed 24 February 2024.

Another practice that could be replicated irrespective of jurisdiction is for higher courts to take a more flexible approach to admissibility in reviewing lower court decisions. For example, in the *Urgenda Foundation v The Netherlands* case, the District Court of the Hague accepted the government's argument that neither the Urgenda Foundation nor the individual plaintiffs were entitled to invoke the human rights provisions of the ECHR because they did not fulfil the admissibility criteria of Article 34 of that Convention. In particular, the Court found that the individual plaintiffs had not provided evidence that they were actual or potential victims of the alleged violations of their human rights.[55] This conclusion was later reversed by the Court of Appeal, which upheld the State's obligations derived from the ECHR as the principal legal basis for its own judgment.[56]

Similarly, it is also replicable for some courts to vocally unfollow the interpretation of admissibility requirements of other courts. For example, the Brussels Court of First Instance expressly stressed that the fact 'that other Belgian citizens may also suffer their own damage, in whole or in part comparable to that of the plaintiffs as individuals, is not sufficient to reclassify the personal interest of each of them as a general interest'.[57] Insofar as necessary, the Court continued, the teaching of the CJEU's *Carvalho et al* judgment is not relevant, insofar as in that judgment the Court, and the European Union Court before it, ruled on the admissibility of an action for annulment brought by private persons. This difference results from the autonomous interpretation of the admissibility conditions by courts acting within their own spheres of competence.[58]

## 5.5 CONCLUSION

The empirical evidence from the primary databases on climate litigation worldwide shows that climate cases are growing in number and that most cases are successful. This indicates that admissibility requirements, as a procedural aspect, are not commonly deployed by judges to dismiss these cases. The tendency is that judges interpret admissibility criteria in a way that allows the case to move towards the merits stage of litigation, a contentious phase that allows the discussion of substantive matters that enable the clarification of certain climate law lacuna.

Despite the general trend, some courts and tribunals worldwide are still interpreting admissibility requirements in a fashion that impedes climate cases from reaching the merits stage. These precedents, although far from representing a majority practice, could play a role in influencing the criteria of courts with a

55 *Urgenda Foundation v The State of The Netherlands* [2015] ECLI:NL:RBDHA:2015:7196 (District Court of the Hague).

56 ibid.

57 VZW *Klimaatzaak First Instance* (n 35) [51]. The appeal court agreed with this finding.

58 ibid.

common procedural architecture, especially in terms of admissibility requirements. As an example, the fact that the CRC dismissed the children's petition based on lack of exhaustion of domestic remedies could influence the interpretation of the ECtHR vis-à-vis the climate cases that are pending before it, specifically the *Duarte Agostinho and Others v Portugal and 32 Other States* case.

It is nevertheless important to emphasise that best practice across jurisdictions is emerging to counteract specific trends of interpretation of admissibility requirements that might impede the progress of a climate case from reaching the merits stage. If proactive climate action is a moral imperative, and under the premise that a deeper discussion on the merits within the context of climate litigation could fulfil such a moral imperative, then using a rigid and overly formalistic approach to admissibility could obstruct said goal. As a response, judges worldwide use some interpretive techniques that the law provides to overcome a relatively narrow reading of procedural requirements. This approach allows judges to be mindful of not only the contextual elements in which a case is grounded but also the urgency of the challenge of the climate crisis, thereby unveiling the necessity of prioritising justice over forms in a substantiated and rigorous fashion. The legal tools that allow these approaches are replicable across jurisdictions, including transparency of rationale, exceptional provisions to lessen the burden of specific requirements, systemic interpretation, and reinterpretation of the law, which distances itself from other courts in favour of admissibility flexibility.

# 6

# Separation of Powers

*Christina Eckes, Jasmina Nedevska, and Joana Setzer**

## 6.1 INTRODUCTION

In December 2019, a Supreme Court ruling in the Netherlands made headlines worldwide.[1] In *Urgenda Foundation v State of the Netherlands*, the highest national court confirmed the previous lower instance rulings, obligating for the first time a State to reduce general emissions in line with international commitments. The Dutch Supreme Court found that the State's inaction on climate change violated its citizens' rights to life and privacy under Articles 2 and 8 of the European Convention on Human Rights (ECHR), respectively, and ordered the State to cut its greenhouse gas (GHG) emissions by at least 25 per cent by 2020, compared to levels in 1990. By May 2022, over seventy cases worldwide had been filed to challenge the implementation or ambition of climate targets and policies affecting the whole of a country's economy and society.[2]

In such cases, the plaintiffs have a political purpose: they seek societal change, typically (but not necessarily) more ambitious climate protection. Governments are often the defendants in such cases, which increases the political significance

* Christina Eckes is a professor of European law and Director at the Amsterdam Centre for European Law and Governance at the University of Amsterdam. Jasmina Nedevska is a postdoctoral researcher at Uppsala University, her work was funded by the Swedish Research Council (grant number 2020-06345). Joana Setzer is an associate professorial research fellow at the Grantham Research Institute on Climate Change and the Environment at the London School of Economics and Political Science.

1 *State of the Netherlands (Ministry of Economic Affairs and Climate Policy) v Stichting Urgenda* [2019] ECLI:NL:HR:2019:2007 (Supreme Court of the Netherlands) (*Urgenda Supreme Court*); John Schwartz, 'In "Strongest" Climate Ruling Yet, Dutch Court Orders Leaders to Take Action' (*The New York Times*, 20 December 2019) <www.nytimes.com/2019/12/20/climate/netherlands-climate-lawsuit.html> accessed 24 February 2024.

2 Joana Setzer and Catherine Higham, 'Global Trends in Climate Change Litigation: 2022 Snapshot' (*LSE Grantham Research Institute on Climate Change and the Environment*, June 2022) 16 <www.lse.ac.uk/granthaminstitute/wp-content/uploads/2022/08/Global-trends-in-climate-change-litigation-2022-snapshot.pdf> accessed 24 February 2024.

of the litigation.[3] Sometimes national legislation is challenged.[4] The relationship between the three branches and hence the idea of *separation of powers* lies at the core of the debate about strategic climate litigation. While some cases have been dismissed and described as a 'direct attack on the separation of powers',[5] many cases have been upheld, with apex courts issuing decisions that are favourable for climate action. This chapter discusses the relevance of separation of powers in a wide array of climate cases including in terms of the outcome of successful and unsuccessful cases. The purpose is to identify emerging best practice from the case law to date.

Building on the *definitions and methods* in Section 6.2, we ask: 'In climate litigation cases where separation of powers concerns arise, how do courts engage with that matter?' Our overview of *case law development* in Section 6.3 suggests that separation of powers concerns arise at four stages in the adjudicatory process: justiciability; recognising a right or duty; establishing a breach; and determining a specific obligation, respectively. In cases that result in a legally enforceable obligation, furthermore, separation of powers concerns may relate to whether the obligation is procedural or substantive. In some of these cases, courts innovatively provided procedural obligations for a breach of substantive duties. In Section 6.4, we consider conditions for *best practice*. A central element of emerging best practice is that courts provide arguments for the rightfulness of enforcing the limits that the law imposes on the other branches. This includes prominent international norms, including open-textured and, at times, non-binding ones, and human rights norms. Another relevant (and replicable) element is that courts develop legally enforceable standards interpreting open-textured norms in light of best available science, usually found in the reports of the Intergovernmental Panel on Climate Change (IPCC). Lastly, we discuss the conditions for *replicability* (Section 6.5) of climate rulings across jurisdictions.

3 The political significance and issues around separation of powers are even more evident in cases that are brought by one branch of power against another, or one level of government against another. For instance, in Brazil opposition political parties have already filed three climate cases before the Supreme Court against the federal government. See *PSB and others v Brazil* [2022] ADPF 760 (Federal Supreme Court of Brazil); *PSB and others v Brazil* [2022] ADO 59/DF (Federal Supreme Court of Brazil); *PSB and others v Brazil* [2022] ADPF 708 (Federal Supreme Court of Brazil). In France, a municipality sued the French government for insufficient action on climate change; the suit was filed in the Conseil d'Etat, the highest administrative court in France. See *Commune de Grande-Synthe v France* [2020] N°427301 (Conseil d'Etat) (*Grande-Synthe*).

4 *Neubauer and Others v Germany* [2021] 1 BvR 2656/18, 1 BvR 96/20, 1 BvR 78/20, 1 BvR 288/20, 1 BvR 96/20, 1 BvR 78/20 (German Federal Constitutional Court) (*Neubauer*).

5 United States Court of Appeals for the Ninth Circuit, '18-36082 Kelsey Rose Juliana v USA' (4 June 2019) at 01:23 <www.youtube.com/watch?v=DlQR_sqGt5k> accessed 24 February 2024. For academic discussion, see also Lucas Bergkamp and Jaap C Hanekamp, 'Climate Change Litigation against States: The Perils of Court-Made Climate Policies' (2015) 24 European Energy and Environmental Law Review 102; Laura Burgers, 'Should Judges Make Climate Change Law?' (2020) 9 TEL 55.

## 6.2 DEFINITIONS AND METHODS

Separation of powers is considered 'the litmus test of legal and political legitimacy' in constitutional democracies.[6] Yet, there is no one legal or conceptual blueprint of separation of powers. It is concretised in very different ways in different legal orders. In climate litigation, it is precisely a core issue of separation of powers that arises most, namely the boundaries of judicial powers.

The concept of separation of powers applies to the relationships between the legislative, executive, and judicial branches of government, sometimes referred to as the *trias politica*. In this chapter, we focus on the relationship of the judiciary to the other branches. We make sense of separation of powers by distinguishing between the *concept* and different *conceptions*.[7] We take a concept to convey a singular *meaning* or purpose, whereas different conceptions are different views on *what it takes* to achieve that purpose. The concept of separation of powers describes a *constitutional arrangement of branches of government that avoids the concentration of power*. However, jurisdictions apply the concept (realise the purpose) of separation of powers differently, resulting in distinct conceptions of separation of powers.

A *functional* conception of separation of powers entails that the different branches exercise different functions. According to this idea, law-making is the responsibility of parliaments and the execution of laws the responsibility of governments, while courts apply the laws. This account grants the legislature 'an initiating place on the assembly line of law-making/law enforcement' and is associated with 'a principle of legislative supremacy'.[8] This conception relies heavily on the possibility to hold political representatives accountable for their decisions through regular elections. When defendants in climate litigation point to the ideal of separation of powers, this is often the conception they have in mind. Yet, at times, this conception may also figure in support of judicial intervention in climate litigation.

A *relational* conception, by contrast, entails that functions are shared between the different branches. This conception explicitly 'aims to ensure that the tension between law and majoritarian politics is perpetuated and that neither law nor politics dominates the other' over an extended period of time.[9] It characteristically relies on the capacities of the judiciary to control the exercise of powers by the other

6 Andrea Pin, 'Introduction to Part I' in Antonia Baraggia and others (eds), *New Challenges to the Separation of Powers – Dividing Power* (Edward Elgar 2020) 7.

7 While a concept 'marks off the arena of a disputed idea', conceptions fill that arena with 'different content, criteria or conditions'. See Arthur Isak Applbaum, 'Legitimacy without the Duty to Obey' (2010) 38 Philosophy and Public Affairs 216 and see also HLA Hart, *The Concept of Law* (Oxford University Press 1961) 155–159; John Rawls, *A Theory of Justice* (Harvard University Press 1971) 5.

8 Jeremy Waldron, 'Separation of Powers in Thought and Practice' (2013) 54 BCLR 441, referring to John Locke.

9 Christina Eckes and others, 'Conceptual Framework for the Project Separation of Powers for 21st Century Europe (SepaRope)' (2021) Amsterdam Law School Research Paper 2021-06 <https://dx.doi.org/10.2139/ssrn.3777334> accessed 24 February 2024; Christoph Möllers, *The Three Branches: A Comparative Model of Separation of Powers* (Oxford University Press 2013).

branches of government through judicial review. This conception typically appears in support of judicial intervention in climate litigation.

We treat the two conceptions just discussed as theoretical 'ideal types', which we do not expect to be observed in pure form.[10] A strictly functional conception of the separation of powers would exclude that the judicial branch *ever* exercises the powers of another branch; yet, it is accepted that judicial interpretation may also create law. A maximally relational construction would entail that the judicial branch may enjoy *as much* political power as the legislative and executive branches. Yet, even the most relational system among existing jurisdictions affirms basic functional separation. On our account, any legal system could be placed on a scale between a strictly functional enactment of separation of powers to a maximally relational construction.[11] Examples of jurisdictions that tend more toward the functional conception are France, the Netherlands, and Sweden. Examples of more relational jurisdictions include Germany and the United States.

Such a scale can be used for different methodological purposes in a study on climate litigation. When a court exerts less power over climate policy in a single case, we take it to express a more functional conception; when a court exerts more power over climate policy in a single case, we take it to express a more relational conception. As mentioned, this does not exclude that a functional conception is used to justify ruling in favour of full-on enforceable substantive obligation. A prime example is the *Urgenda* case.[12]

To assess how courts handle separation of powers concerns in climate litigation, we have used the dataset of climate litigation cases compiled for this Handbook as the point of departure. We focus on cases where the issue of separation of powers has been reported as salient.

## 6.3 CASE LAW DEVELOPMENT – STATE OF AFFAIRS

The categorisation of adjudicatory stages is divided into four levels and identifies two subcategories of obligations (see Figure 6.1). As any categorisation, it is subjective to an extent. In individual cases, courts may consider separation of powers at one or several of these adjudicatory stages.

### 6.3.1 *Justiciability*

When courts consider whether a climate case is justiciable, separation of powers is the single most decisive underlying principle. Many procedural rules serve

[10] Richard Swedberg, 'How to Use Max Weber's Ideal Type in Sociological Analysis' (2018) 18 Journal of Classical Sociology 181.

[11] Richard Benwell and Oonagh Gay, 'The Separation of Powers' (*House of Commons Library*, 2011) <https://researchbriefings.files.parliament.uk/documents/SN06053/SN06053.pdf> accessed 24 February 2024.

[12] *Urgenda Supreme Court* (n 1).

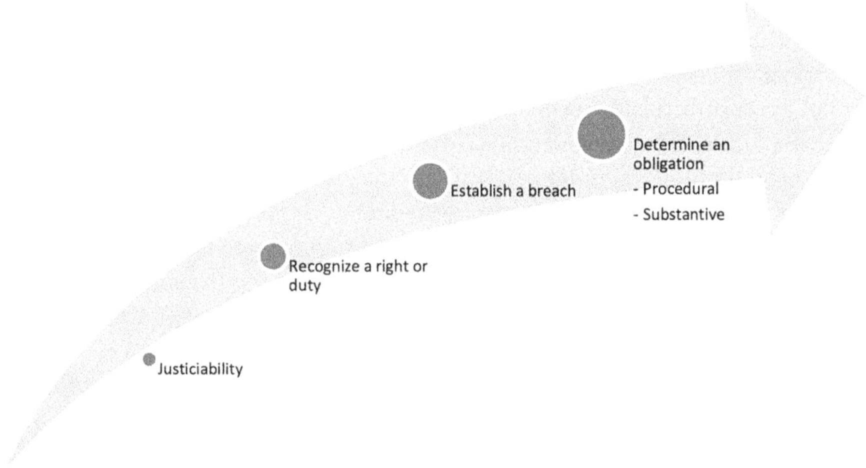


FIGURE 6.1 The four levels and two subcategories of obligations making up the adjudicatory stages where separation of powers concerns arise

the purpose of protecting each branch's core constitutional powers, that is, separation of powers. One could think of standing, availability of legal instruments to require governmental action, or time limits. This subsection considers the judicial reasoning, first, in cases that were found non-justiciable, and second, in cases in which justiciability was the focus of the judicial reasoning and that were found justiciable.

On a more abstract level, judges may be concerned that rulings in strategic climate litigation aiming at mitigation measures could interfere with the core task of elected politicians to prescribe general public policy choices.[13] According to a strict functional view of what separation of powers requires, judges may consider that they cannot decide that general policy choices are necessary and find the case non-justiciable. At the same time, the far-reaching interferences of the climate crisis with the enjoyment of human rights in a concrete and identifiable manner, not just in the future but also in the present, have become apparent. These interferences highlight the failure of the executive and the legislature to take measures that could be seen as adequate in light of established science.[14] Under a more relational conception of separation of powers, it is the task of the judiciary to prompt the other branches to carry out their constitutional mandates when they fail to do so.

[13] In a wider perspective, climate change litigation can be seen as part of a general trend during the late twentieth and early twenty-first century – referred to as the 'judicialization' of politics – to rely on courts to resolve contentious moral matters and public policy issues. See Ran Hirschl, 'The Judicialization of Mega-Politics and the Rise of Political Courts' (2008) 11 ARPS 93. A critique based on a principle of separation of powers could apply to this phenomenon as a whole. Here, however, our focus remains solely with climate litigation.

[14] This was e.g. highlighted by *Neubauer* (n 4).

Furthermore, even non-justiciable cases may have considerable political influence and contribute to the development of legal doctrine. Often, cases are found inadmissible on procedural grounds that serve the purpose of separation of powers but do not necessarily relate to whether judges could generally review climate policy. An example is standing requirements.[15] Our materials reveal that considerations of courts, which ultimately result in dismissals, may also include legal interpretations and doctrinal reasons that may lay the ground for more far-reaching climate policy. In light of the fact that the judiciary has a constitutional duty to 'deliver justice',[16] the logical minimum of reaction, when a case is brought, is declaring a case non-justiciable on specified grounds.

*Juliana v United States* is an example of *a non-justiciable case* from the United States.[17] In this case, a group of child plaintiffs alleged that several United States agencies had continued policies allowing for exploitation of fossil fuels, despite knowing of the hazards for more than fifty years. The plaintiffs claimed that the government thereby violated their constitutional rights, including a right to due process under the Fifth Amendment to a 'climate system capable of sustaining human life'. The Ninth Circuit concluded in a 2-1 decision 'reluctantly' that the plaintiffs' 'impressive case for redress must be represented to the political branches of government, not the judiciary'.[18] In justifying the outcome, the court sided with a more functional conception of separation of powers.

Outside the United States, justiciability has been the focus of climate cases in Australia, Canada, New Zealand, and Pakistan.[19] Similarly, in the supporting judicial reasoning one can pinpoint elements of a more functional conception of separation of powers. In *Sharma and Others v Minister for the Environment*, eight young people, claiming to represent all people under 18, filed a putative class action in Australia's Federal Court to block a coal project. They asserted that it would exacerbate climate change and harm young people in the future. The Federal Court of

[15] See Chapter 5 on Admissibility.

[16] For example the Dutch art 13 AB neergelegde verbod van rechtsweigering (prohibition to deny justice). This is also how 'duty' is read in the famous citation 'It is emphatically the province and duty of the judicial department to say what the law is' from *Marbury v Madison* [1803] 5 US (1 Cranch) 137 (US Supreme Court).

[17] *Juliana v United States* 947 F.3d 1159 (9th Cir 2020). cf see the decision in *Navahine F v Hawai'i Department of Transportation* (First Circuit Court, State of Hawai'i 2023) 6, in which the Court rejects the defendant's claims that the issue is more of a political question and should not be addressed by courts. The Court reaffirms the Court's role in interpreting and defending constitutional rights and guarantees.

[18] ibid 11 (the opening paragraphs of Circuit Judge Hurwitz' Opinion).

[19] *Sharma and others v Minister for the Environment* [2021] FCA 560 (*Sharma First Instance*); *Mathur et al v Her Majesty the Queen in Right of Ontario* [2020] ONSC 6918 (Superior Court of Justice) (*Mathur Strikeout*) and *Mathur v Ontario* [2023] ONSC 2316 (*Mathur Merits*); *Thomson v Minister for Climate Change Issues* [2017] NZHC 733 (*Thomson*); *Michael John Smith v Fonterra Co-Operative Group Limited and Others* [2022] NZSC 35 (*Smith Supreme Court*); *DG Khan Cement Company v Government of Punjab* [2021] C.P.1290-L/2019 (Supreme Court of Pakistan).

Australia established a new duty of care to avoid causing personal harm to children but declined to issue an injunction to force the minister to block the coal mine extension. The judge rejected the minister's argument as to why alleged 'policy reasons' ought to have prevented the recognition of the duty of care. Contrary to the minister's claims, the judge stated that the recognition of this duty would not interfere with the minister's statutory task, nor necessarily render tortious any activity generating GHGs. Despite the Federal Court's decision, the minister granted approval for the proposed mine expansion, and in March 2022 the Full Federal Court of Australia unanimously overturned the primary judge's decision to impose a duty of care on the minister. The three judges had separate reasonings. Chief Justice Allsop found that the duty would require consideration of questions of policy 'unsuitable for the judicial branch to resolve'.[20]

By contrast, the Superior Court of Ontario in Canada found in *Mathur et al v Her Majesty the Queen in Right of Ontario* (preliminary decision) that '[t]he fact that the matter is complex, contentious or laden with social values does not mean that the courts can abdicate the responsibility vested in them by our Constitution to review legislation for Charter compliance when citizens challenge it. In such circumstances, it is the court's obligation to decide the matter'.[21] This case emphasises the functional argument that it is the judiciary's mandate and duty to apply constitutional law.

Equally grappling with issues of justiciability, Justice Mallon argued for the High Court of New Zealand in the case of *Sarah Thomson v The Minister for Climate Change Issues* that:

> The courts have recognised the significance of the issue for the planet and its inhabitants and that those within the court's jurisdiction are necessarily amongst all who are affected by inadequate efforts to respond to climate change. The various domestic courts have held they have a proper role to play in Government decision making on this topic, while emphasising that there are constitutional limits in how far that role may extend. The IPCC reports provide a factual basis on which decisions can be made. Remedies are fashioned to ensure appropriate action is taken while leaving the policy choices about the content of that action to the appropriate state body.[22]

In its reasoning, the Court relied on a relational conception of separation of powers while stressing the importance of functional considerations. It reasoned more

[20] *Sharma First Instance* (n 19).

[21] *Mathur Strikeout* (n 19) [121], quoting *Chaoulli v Québec (Attorney General)* [2005] 1 SCR 791 (Supreme Court of Canada) [107]. Confirmed on the merits, with the exception of the 'fair share' question, see *Mathur Merits* (n 19) [109]. See also *Urgenda Foundation v The State of The Netherlands* [2015] ECLI:NL:RBDHA:2015:7196 (District Court of the Hague) (*Urgenda District Court*) [4.98]; *Thomson* (n 19) [134]; *Environnement Jeunesse v Procureur General du Canada* [2018] 500-06-000955-183 (Quebec Superior Court) 76 (*ENJEU*).

[22] *Thomson* (n 19) [133].

specifically that the 'importance of the matter [climate change] for all and each of us warrants some scrutiny of the public power in addition to accountability through Parliament and the General Elections', yet noted that there are 'constitutional limits' to the role of the judiciary, and that, if a ground of review 'requires the Court to weigh public policies that are more appropriately weighed by those elected by the community', it may be necessary for the Court to 'defer to the elected officials'.[23]

In the case of *Michael John Smith v Fonterra Co-Operative Group Limited and Ors*, the respondent companies are some of New Zealand's largest GHG emitters (including from the dairy and meat industry).[24] In this case the issue was whether tort law could be used to seek wide-ranging private law remedies with respect to climate change. According to one cause of action, the defendants allegedly had a duty to cease contributing to climate change. The High Court found that there were 'significant hurdles' for Smith in persuading the Court that this new duty should be recognised but determined that the relevant issues should be explored at a trial.[25] Invoking a more functional conception of separation of powers, the High Court ultimately decided against any regulation of policy content. It argued that '[t]he Courts are poorly equipped to deal with the issues which Mr. Smith seeks to raise. This country's response to climate change involves policy formation, value judgments, risk analysis, trade-offs and distributional outcomes. These matters are well outside the normal realms of civil litigation'.[26] It further explained that '[i]f the Courts were to reach different conclusions than Parliament, there could be inconsistent and different net zero emission targets and different ways of dealing with the problems thrown up by climate change. That would be highly undesirable and would put significant emitters in a quandary'.[27]

### 6.3.2 *Recognise a Right or Duty*

Separation of powers concerns remain equally present after judges have found a case justiciable and recognise a legal right or duty – positive or negative.[28] Recognising a legal right or duty is an important step in the judicial process including in those cases that determine a particular obligation, with notable examples being *Urgenda*, *VZW Klimaatzaak v Kingdom of Belgium and Others*, *Future Generations v Ministry of the Environment and Others*, *Neubauer and Others v Germany*, *Notre Affaire à*

[23] ibid [134].

[24] The case was decided in three instances: *Michael John Smith v Fonterra Co-Operative Group Limited and Others* CIV-2019-404-001730 [2020] NZHC 419 (*Smith High Court*); *Michael John Smith v Fonterra Co-Operative Group Limited and Others* CA 128/2020 [2021] NZCA 552 (*Smith Court of Appeal*); *Smith Supreme Court* (n 19).

[25] *Smith High Court* (n 24) [98].

[26] ibid [98](g).

[27] ibid [98](h).

[28] See also Lucy Maxwell, Sarah Mead, and Dennis van Berkel, 'Standards for Adjudicating the Next Generation of Urgenda-Style Climate Cases' (2022) 13(1) JHRE 35.

*Tous and Others v France*, and *Shrestha v Office of the Prime Minister and Others*.[29] However, a court may also stop at this level of identifying rights or duties of the parties, for example if it does not establish a breach. These rulings may have a symbolic value in political discourse or obligate the executive or legislative branches to take these rights or duties into consideration.

An example of a case with high constitutional and symbolic value is *Neubauer*.[30] In this case, the German Federal Constitutional Court recognised that the German State had a constitutional duty to address the harm posed by climate change in order to protect the constitutional rights to life and health, protected under the German Constitution and the ECHR, 'by taking steps which […] contribute to stopping human-induced global warming and limiting the ensuing climate change'.[31]

*Urgenda* confirmed in three different instances that climate change fell within the scope of protection of the rights to life and to private and family life, under Articles 2 and 8 ECHR.[32] It also confirmed that the State is subject to a duty of care in tort, which is interpreted in light of these human rights provisions. While the District Court reasoned that the State's *duty of care* in tort, as an open-textured norm, must be interpreted in a manner that is, so far as this is possible, consistent with its obligations under international law.[33] The Dutch government appealed the decision, and *Urgenda* filed a cross-appeal with respect to the ECHR claim. In late 2018, the Court of Appeal upheld the decision of the District Court, while permitting *Urgenda* to make a claim under the ECHR. The Dutch government appealed to the Dutch Supreme Court, which affirmed in December 2019 the order of the District Court and the Court of Appeal's admission of Urgenda's claim under the ECHR. The Supreme Court interpreted the Netherlands' obligations under Articles 2 and 8 ECHR by drawing on non-binding commitments of the Dutch State under the United Nations Framework Convention on Climate Change (UNFCCC), soft law sources such as Conference of the Parties' (COP) decisions, and 'scientific insights and generally accepted standards'.[34]

[29] *Urgenda Supreme Court* (n 1); *VZW Klimaatzaak v Kingdom of Belgium and Others* [2023] 2022/AR/891 (Cour d'appel de Bruxelles) (*VZW Klimaatzaak Appeal*); *Notre Affaire à Tous and Others v France* [2021] No 1904967, 1904968, 1904972 1904976/4-1; *Neubauer* (n 4); *Future Generations v Ministry of the Environment and Others (Demanda Generaciones Futuras v Minambiente)* [2018] 11001 22 03 000 2018 00319 00 (Colombia Supreme Court) (*Demanda Futuras Generaciones*); *Advocate Padam Bahadur Shrestha v Prime Minister and Office of Council of Ministers and Others* [2018] Order No 074-WO-0283 (2075/09/10 BS) (Supreme Court of Nepal) (*Shrestha v Office of Council of Ministers*).

[30] *Neubauer* (n 4).

[31] ibid [144].

[32] *Urgenda Supreme Court* (n 1).

[33] *Urgenda District Court* (n 21).

[34] *Urgenda Supreme Court* (n 1) [5.4.3]; *Demir and Baykara v Turkey* App no 24503/97 (ECtHR, 12 November 2008), which referred to 'The consensus emerging from specialized international instruments and from the practice of contracting States may constitute a relevant consideration for the Court when it interprets the provisions of the Convention in specific cases'.

Building on *Urgenda*, the case of *Milieudefensie et al v Royal Dutch Shell plc* extends the duty of care under tort law (Article 6:162 of the Dutch Civil Code informed by Articles 2 and 8 ECHR) to private companies.[35] The District Court accepted that given the Paris Agreement's goals and the scientific evidence regarding the dangers of climate change, Shell has a duty of care to take action to reduce its GHG emissions.

### 6.3.3 *Establish a Breach*

The next stage at which separation of powers concerns arise is when courts consider whether they recognise a breach, even if that does not necessarily imply that the court orders the defendant to take action. Again, even if such rulings may not prescribe a specific enforceable obligation, they may have high symbolic value in the political discourse and establish important and potentially replicable interpretations of the law.

In *VZW Klimaatzaak*, the Brussels Court of First Instance found a duty and a breach of that duty, but did not establish an enforceable obligation. The Court found the federal state and the three regions jointly and individually in breach of their duties of care for failing to enact good climate governance. However, the Court declined to issue an injunction ordering the government to set the specific emission reduction targets requested by the plaintiffs. The Court found that the separation of powers doctrine limited the Court's ability to set such targets and that doing so would contravene legislative or administrative authority. On appeal, this aspect of the decision was overturned – with the Court of Appeal issuing an order requiring the federal state and regions to adhere to a more ambitious 2030 mitigation target.[36]

There are various other examples where separation of powers has *not* proven to be a barrier in establishing duty and breach. In the *Future Generations* case, the

[35] *Milieudefensie v Royal Dutch Shell* [2021] ECLR:NL: RBDHA:2021:5339 (District Court of the Hague).

[36] *VZW Klimaatzaak v l'État Belge* [2021] 2015/4585/A (Tribunal de première instance francophone de Bruxelles, Section Civile) (*VZW Klimaatzaak First Instance*) and *VZW Klimaatzaak Appeal* (n 29) [227]. The Court of Appeal found

> As already indicated, there is no doubt that the formulation of climate policy is the prerogative of the legislature, which has wide discretionary powers in this area. Nor is it disputable that the 'judge cannot substitute his subjective assessment for that of the democratically elected bodies' or that 'climate policy cannot be pursued in disregard of any other consideration of social cohesion, economic development or other aspects of the environment, for example' (conclusions of the Belgian State, p. 164). As indicated above (paragraph 156), however, the court does not violate the principle of the separation of powers if it confines itself to respecting the minimum requirements laid down by norms of international law which, given their context (in the sense referred to above), have direct effect in the case submitted to it or, in the absence of such norms, if it confines itself to determining, on the basis of data on which there is scientific and political consensus, the minimum requirements.

Supreme Court of Colombia found that the State's failure to prevent deforestation, which exacerbates climate change, violated the claimants' constitutional rights of life, health, and minimum subsistence: 'It is clear that despite several international commitments, legislation, and jurisprudence on the subject, the Colombian State has not efficiently tackled the problem of deforestation in the Amazon'.[37]

An example from Nepal is the *Shrestha* case.[38] In this case, the Supreme Court of Nepal determined that the State's failure to adopt a comprehensive law on climate change and to adequately address the existing impacts of climate change violated the right to life and to live with dignity, as well as the right to a healthy environment under the Nepalese Constitution.[39]

In *Neubauer*, the German Federal Constitutional Court found that the duty to take 'measures that help to limit anthropogenic global warming and the associated climate change' applies despite '[t]he fact that the German State is incapable of halting climate change on its own'.[40] The Court found that this requires the legislature to adopt legislation to reduce GHG emissions in a 'sufficiently prudent manner', without 'offload[ing] reduction burdens onto the future'.[41] The Court established a breach of the rights protected under the German Constitution.[42]

The Municipal Court of Prague found in the first instance in the *Klimatická žaloba* case that the 'far-reaching effects' of climate change posed a threat to the right to a favourable environment, which is protected under the constitution.[43] The constitutional duty to protect human rights thus required the government to develop specific and comprehensive mitigation measures 'without undue delay'.[44] The court found that the government was not doing enough to adequately reduce emissions before 2030, and thus violated its duty to protect human rights. It concluded that '[t]he defendants' failure to act deprived the applicants of their right to a favourable environment'.[45]

In Pakistan, the High Court of Lahore held in *Leghari v Federation of Pakistan* that the State's failure to address the impacts of climate change within the country violated the plaintiff's right to life as well as the right to a healthy environment (among other rights).[46] In this case, Ashgar Leghari, a Pakistani farmer, argued that the government had failed to meet its climate change mitigation and adaptation targets, which had resulted in immediate impacts on the water, food,

37 *Demanda Futuras Generaciones* (n 29) [13].
38 *Shrestha v Office of Council of Ministers* (n 29).
39 ibid [5].
40 *Neubauer* (n 4) [149].
41 ibid.
42 ibid [115].
43 *Klimatická žaloba ČR v Czech Republic* [2022] No 14A 101/2021 (Prague Municipal Court) [223].
44 ibid [278].
45 ibid [327]. This decision was overturned on appeal.
46 *Asghar Leghari v Federation of Pakistan etc* PLD 2018 Lahore 364.

and energy security of Pakistan in a way that interfered with his fundamental right to life. The Court ruled in response that 'the delay and lethargy of the State in implementing the Framework offends the fundamental rights of the citizens which need to be safeguarded'.[47] When establishing the breach, the Court argued that fundamental rights must be guided by the constitutional values of democracy, equality, and social, economic, and political justice, as well as the international environmental principles of sustainable development, the precautionary principle, intergenerational and intragenerational equity, and the doctrine of public trust.

Equally, in *Urgenda*, the first successful strategic climate case aimed at general emission reduction, the Dutch Supreme Court concluded that Dutch climate mitigation efforts were not consistent with IPCC science and the government thus violated its obligation to protect under Articles 2 and 8 of the ECHR.[48]

### 6.3.4 *Determine an Enforceable Obligation*

Finally, a court may impose an enforceable obligation on the parties to the case. These enforceable obligations may be procedural or substantive.[49] From a separation of powers perspective, determining procedural obligations may prima facie be seen as less controversial than determining substantive ones. The principled reasoning of the Supreme Court in *Nature and Youth Norway and others v Norway* may serve as an illustration. The case concerned the validity of a royal decree of 2016 to grant ten petroleum explorations licences in the southern and south-eastern parts of the Barents Sea. The Court did not rule in favour of the plaintiffs but provided extensive reflections in relation to separation of powers. It held that 'decisions involving basic environmental issues often require a political balancing of interests and broader priorities'.[50] Therefore, the Court stated, '[d]emocracy considerations […] suggest that such decisions should be taken by popularly elected bodies, and not by the courts'.[51] Yet, the Court also noted that democratic considerations have less bearing in regard to procedural duties, noting specifically that 'restraint is less required when it comes to assessing the procedure' as 'in reviewing the political balancing of interests'.[52]

47 ibid [8].

48 *Urgenda Supreme Court* (n 1). See also for more details *State of the Netherlands v Stichting Urgenda* [2018] ECLI:NL:GHDHA:2018:2591 (Court of Appeal) (*Urgenda Court of Appeal*) [76].

49 See inter alia Sebastian Oberthür, 'Hard or Soft Governance? The EU's Climate and Energy Policy Framework for 2030' (2019) 7 Politics and Governance 17, 20–21.

50 *Greenpeace Nordic Association v Ministry of Petroleum and Energy* (2020) Case no 20-051052SIV-HRET (Norwegian Supreme Court) (*People v Arctic Oil*) [141].

51 ibid.

52 ibid [182]; see also Pau de Vilchez Moragues and Annalisa Savaresi, 'The Right to a Healthy Environment and Climate Litigation: A Mutually Supportive Relation?' <http://dx.doi.org/10.2139/ssrn.3829114> accessed 24 February 2024.

We treat procedural and substantive obligations in separate subsections later on. We should add, however, that the dividing line between procedural and substantive obligations is at times difficult to draw. A case in point is *Neubauer*, which primarily established *procedural* obligations but also determined that the German Constitution entails a *substantive* constitutional obligation to establish a law with a zero-emission target for 2050. Similarly, in *Friends of the Irish Environment CLG v The Government of Ireland, Ireland and The Attorney General*, the Supreme Court of Ireland ordered the Irish government to return to the drawing board and develop a new National Mitigation Plan, which is a procedural obligation aiming for a substantive outcome.[53]

### 6.3.4.1 Procedural Obligations

Procedural obligations concern processes for governing climate policy without directly regulating the content of such policy. While these rulings do not intervene *substantively* in the decisions of the political branches, procedural remedies may still have an impact on climate policy as imposed institutional structures change the conditions for policy-making.

For example, in *Save Lamu et al v National Environmental Management Authority and Amu Power Co Ltd*, a community-based organisation representing Lamu County and other individual claimants challenged the issuance of a licence by the Kenyan National Environmental Management Authority (NEMA) to a power company for the construction of the first coal-fired power plant in Kenya.[54] The claimants argued that the Kenyan NEMA failed to conduct a proper Environmental Impact Assessment (EIA) and therefore contributed to the adverse effects on human health and biodiversity caused by climate change. The Tribunal set aside the licence issuance and decided that the Kenyan NEMA had violated the EIA regulations by granting it without proper and meaningful public participation in the process. It stated that 'the judicial function of the Tribunal is to examine whether there was compliance with statute. In the present appeal, the procedure was not followed and the process was seriously flawed'.[55]

Similarly, *Neubauer* established a procedural obligation requiring the legislature to return to the drawing board and adopt national legislation in line with constitutionally protected human rights, including for the future, that is, the period after 2030. *Neubauer* did not articulate a particular substantive reduction obligation. Arguably, the latter reflects a degree of judicial self-restraint that relates to the German Federal

[53] *Friends of the Irish Environment CLG v The Government of Ireland, Ireland and the Attorney General* [2020] Appeal no 205/19 (Supreme Court of Ireland).

[54] *Save Lamu et al v National Environmental Management Authority and Amu Power Co Ltd* [2016] Tribunal Appeal No Net 196 of 2016 (Kenya Environmental Tribunal).

[55] ibid [71].

Constitutional Court's self-conception of the role of the judiciary in relation to the other branches. The Court expresses this when emphasising that it is for the legislature to specify the (substantive) emission reduction objectives within what is legal in light of the requirement of climate protection under Article 20(a) GG.[56] The *Neubauer* case is recurrent in our later discussions on emerging best practice and replicability.

### 6.3.4.2 Substantive Obligations

All else being equal, rulings determining substantive obligations usually remain more controversial from a separation of powers perspective. Still, some courts proceed to such measures. Such cases exist from Ireland, the Netherlands, France, and Colombia.[57] Among these, only the Irish case relied on existing parliamentary legislation.

In *Friends of the Irish Environment CLG*, the separation of powers was a key issue. As in the *Neubauer* case, the distinction between a procedural and substantive obligation can be difficult to draw, as the final ruling required a more specific National Mitigation Plan. The High Court ruled against the plaintiffs, holding, *inter alia*, that the State must be given a broad margin of discretion in determining its climate policies, with reference to the separation of powers and the nature, extent, and wording of the statutory obligations in play.[58] In comparison to the High Court, the conception of separation of powers upheld by the Supreme Court can be seen as more relational, as it concluded that 'the issues are justiciable and do not amount to an impermissible impingement by the courts into areas of policy'.[59] Yet, functional separation remained important, as the obligation established by the Court ultimately relied on national legislation, namely the 2015 Climate Action and Low Carbon Development Act.

*Urgenda*, which drew on Articles 2 and 8 of the ECHR, constitutes a different example of where courts imposed a specific substantive obligation (25% emission reduction). In the *Urgenda* case, the Court insisted that there remained a legitimate role for the judiciary in determining 'whether the measures taken by the State are too little in view of what is clearly the lower limit of its share in the measures to be taken worldwide against dangerous climate change'.[60] The Court concluded its judgment by outlining why the order made was appropriate in light of the separation of powers, contrary to the State's argument that the order constituted an impermissible

56 *Neubauer* (n 4) [205].

57 *Friends of the Irish Environment CLG* (n 53); *Urgenda Supreme Court* (n 1); *Notre Affaire à Tous* (n 29); *Demanda Futuras Generaciones* (n 29).

58 *Friends of the Irish Environment CLG v The Government of Ireland, Ireland and the Attorney General* [2019] IEHC 747 (High Court) [62], [65], [87]–[92].

59 *Friends of the Irish Environment CLG* (n 53) [9.1].

60 *Urgenda Supreme Court* (n 1) [6.3].

'order to create legislation'.[61] The *Urgenda* case also recurs in our later discussions on emerging best practice and replicability.

The level of detail in imposing enforceable obligations on the State seems crucial. Courts appear willing to impose even substantive obligations but reserve the details of implementation to the State. This is in line with separation of powers considerations that reserve the making of general policy to the legislature. Examples that illustrate this emerging trend of climate rulings imposing general substantive obligations that reserve further (implementation) details to the policy-maker are *Urgenda* and *Notre Affaire a Tous*. In the latter case, the Administrative Court explicitly acknowledged that the government must be granted a wide margin of discretion when implementing a court order pertaining to GHG emissions targets, while this margin of discretion does not as such prevent the judiciary from ordering the government to adopt stronger climate mitigation measures:

> In the circumstances of this case, it is appropriate to order the Prime Minister and the competent ministers to take all the necessary sectoral measures to compensate for the damage up to the uncompensated share of greenhouse gas emissions under the first carbon budget […]. It is appropriate, as has been said, to order the enactment of such measures within a sufficiently short period of time in order to prevent any worsening of that damage. In the context of the present case, the specific measures to make reparation for the damage may take various forms and consequently express choices which are within the Government's discretion.[62]

## 6.4 EMERGING BEST PRACTICE

Separation of powers has been a central issue in the relatively short but dynamic lifespan of climate litigation. To a certain extent, identifying specific best practices around separation of powers is rendered difficult by the wide range of rules and principles that protect or interact with separation of powers very differently in various legal orders. In all climate litigation, the domestic legal order frames the role of the judiciary and determines what judges can and should do. Nevertheless, emerging best practices regarding the separation of powers can be identified with respect to several issues.

### 6.4.1 *Role of the Judiciary in Applying the Law*

The first emerging best practice results from how judges understand their own role vis-à-vis the other branches of government and provide arguments for this understanding. Several courts have emphasised that it is the role of the judiciary to apply

61 ibid [8].
62 *Notre Affaire à Tous* (n 29) [13].

the law. In other words, when the legislature has adopted a national law this mandates the judiciary to ensure that the legally binding commitments made under that national law are given effect.[63] They also generally emphasised the necessity of judicial review of executive conduct with respect to climate change legislation.[64] This exercise of judicial review renders matters which once might have been reserved to 'politics' a matter of lawful conduct.

*DG Khan Cement Company v Government of Punjab* is illustrative of this practice. In that case, the Supreme Court of Pakistan found that the judiciary is not only able but actually required to adjudicate cases that can help address the dangerous consequences of climate change.[65] The Court argued that '[t]his Court and the Courts around the globe have a role to play in reducing the effects of climate change for our generation and for the generations to come. Through our pen and jurisprudential fiat, we need to decolonize our future generations from the wrath of climate change, by upholding climate justice at all times'.[66]

In Germany, which has a constitutional court that enjoys strong review powers over general laws and exceptionally high public support, including in politics and academia, the judiciary is formally in a position to directly restrain politics (legal constitutionalism). In the *Neubauer* case, a group of youth filed a legal challenge against the Federal Climate Protection Act arguing that the target of reducing GHGs 55 per cent by 2030 from 1990 levels was insufficient. The German Federal Constitutional Court struck down parts of that Act, which is a general federal law, as incompatible with fundamental rights protected under the German Constitution.

For its reasoning, the Court could rely on constitutional provisions that limit the scope for political decision-making to take measures to protect the environment or not. The Court found that Article 20a of the German Constitution obliges the legislature to protect the climate and aim towards achieving climate neutrality. Further, the Court stated that Article 20a 'is a justiciable legal norm that is intended to bind the political process in favour of ecological concerns, also with a view to the future generations that are particularly affected'. Accepting arguments that the legislature must follow a carbon budget approach to limit warming to well below 2°C, and, if possible, to 1.5°C, the Court found that the legislature had not proportionally distributed the budget between current and future generations. Because 'one generation must not be allowed to consume large parts of the $CO_2$ budget under a comparatively mild reduction burden if this would at the same time leave future generations with a radical reduction burden and expose their lives to serious losses

[63] See e.g. *Neubauer* (n 4) and *Friends of the Irish Environment CLG* (n 53).

[64] See *Friends of the Irish Environment CLG* (n 53) [9.1]; *Mathur Merits* (n 19) [132]; *Thomson* (n 19) [101]–[135].

[65] *DG Khan* (n 19).

[66] ibid [19].

of freedom', the Court ordered the legislature to set clear provisions for reduction targets from 2031 onward by the end of 2022.[67]

An example from Canada is *Mathur et al.* Although judicial review is relatively weak in Canada, the Superior Court of Ontario explained that the Constitution 'requires' the Court to decide a climate case, even if 'the matter is complex, contentious and laden with social values'.[68]

In the Netherlands, by contrast with Germany and more like Canada, the judiciary is in a comparatively weak position vis-à-vis the political branches and may not review general laws in light of national constitutional rules or principles. However, this did not stop the courts in three instances (District Court, Court of Appeals, and Supreme Court) from ruling in favour of *Urgenda*, determining that, by failing to reduce GHG emissions by at least 25 per cent by end-2020, the Dutch government was acting unlawfully in contravention of its duty of care. In the higher two instances, the courts relied on Articles 2 and 8 of the ECHR, which enjoy constitutional status and direct enforceability in the Dutch system. Directly addressing the matter of separation of powers, the Dutch Supreme Court concluded

> [D]ecision-making on the reduction of greenhouse gas emissions is a power of the government and parliament. They have a large degree of discretion to make the political considerations that are necessary in this regard. It is up to the courts to decide whether, in availing themselves of this discretion, the government and parliament have remained within the limits of the law by which they are bound.[69]

In respect of a functional separation of powers, the Dutch Supreme Court insisted that it was a legitimate function of the judiciary, as required by the rule of law, to determine whether the State was complying with its legal obligations, and had 'remained within the limits of the law by which they are bound'.[70] The Court argued further that 'this order does not amount to an order to take specific legislative measures, but leaves the State free to choose the measures to be taken in order to achieve a 25% reduction in greenhouse gas emissions by 2020'.[71]

Notably, this was the first decision by any court ordering a State to limit GHG emissions for reasons other than statutory mandates. The Court pointed to 'the severity of the consequences of climate change and the great risk of climate change occurring'.[72] The functional separation of powers arguments put forth by the defendant against justiciability, for example, were rejected 'also because the State violates human rights'.[73]

67 *Neubauer* (n 4) [192].
68 *Mathur Merits* (n 19) [106]. See also *Urgenda District Court* (n 21) [4.98]; *Thomson* (n 19) [134]; *ENJEU* (n 21) [70].
69 *Urgenda Supreme Court* (n 1) [8.3.2].
70 ibid.
71 ibid [8.2.7].
72 ibid [2.3.1].
73 ibid [2.3.2].

### 6.4.2 *Giving Effect to International Norms*

Judges have regularly relied on international law to substantiate their reasoning, either because no national climate legislation existed[74] or because international law further strengthened the case as it illustrated the objectives for which the national climate legislation had been adopted.[75]

France is an illustrative example of a jurisdiction in which several courts have emphasised the relevance of a State's previous commitments to an international legal framework that acknowledges and aims to fight the climate emergency. In *Notre Affaire à Tous*, for example, the Administrative Court of Paris explained in 2021 that, by ratifying the UNFCCC and the Paris Agreement, the French government recognised 'an "emergency" to combat current climate change' and 'recognised its capacity to act effectively on this phenomenon in order to limit its causes and mitigate its harmful consequences'.[76] One year earlier, in *Commune de Grande-Synthe v France*, the Supreme French Administrative Court had established the pre-eminence of the UNFCCC and the Paris Agreement in the context of domestic mitigation action, explaining that the treaties 'must be taken into account in the interpretation of provisions of national law' aimed at reducing GHG emissions.[77]

The status of international law within the domestic legal order is highly relevant to judges' considerations of a State's international commitments. When courts are asked to determine the relevance and meaning of international law in domestic proceedings, they usually enjoy additional discretion. They act as gatekeepers determining which international norms meet the domestic requirements of enjoying direct effect and what the relationship between domestic and international norms is. Hence, reliance on international norms as the basis for a ruling rather than, for example, national constitutional law increases the power of the judiciary vis-à-vis the other branches. At the same time, the legislature does not have the same powers over the creation of international norms as it has over national laws, even if it may be formally involved in the ratification of international agreements. Thus, giving effect to international norms, in particular in relation to national laws, may be prima facie read as disempowering parliament. Separation of powers concerns may increase if decisions rely predominantly on international norms rather than national laws.

Very different constitutional framework conditions establish very different conceptions of separation of powers, for example that the judiciary is given the explicit mandate to review the constitutionality of general laws (Germany) or not (Netherlands). However, this does not exclude replicable best practices from emerging, such as

74 *Urgenda Supreme Court* (n 1).
75 *Neubauer* (n 4) and *Friends of the Irish Environment CLG* (n 53).
76 *Notre Affaire à Tous* (n 29) [21].
77 *Grande-Synthe* (n 3) [12].

reliance on non-binding norms of international law or (repeated) political commitments to substantiate a particular mitigation obligation.

### 6.4.3 A *Matter of Protecting Human Rights*

Where there is a right, there is a remedy.[78] The right to a remedy when one's rights are violated lies at the heart of the rule of law and separation of powers. Generally, human rights are seen as the prime example of rights for which the judiciary must offer remedies to enforce them against the executive and the legislature. In line with this, the Dutch Supreme Court, followed by several other national courts, emphasised that it is for the courts to ensure that the other branches do not overstep the law when exercising their political discretion, *particularly when human rights are at stake*.[79] When assessing the scope of judicial scrutiny in the context of human rights protection, the Municipal Court of Prague in its first instance decision in *Klimatická žaloba* stated that '[i]n accordance with the precautionary principle, persons have the right to be concerned about the quality of their environment and do not have to wait until the climatic conditions are so unfavourable that they do not allow the fulfilment of their basic needs of life'.[80] This line of reasoning appears to broaden the protection of human rights by establishing that persons may enforce their rights before a(n irreversible) situation of severe human rights violation has occurred. This is particularly meaningful in the context of the climate emergency, which is a cumulative global common action problem, that is, every ton of $CO_2$ emitted anywhere in the world creates an irreversible temperature increase that changes life on Earth.

Separation of powers concerns in human rights adjudication play out in different ways. On the one hand, judges may consider that separation of powers weighs in favour of exercising judicial review because (human) rights protection at the end of the legislative cycle lies at the centre of their role within a democratic system.[81] On the other hand, human rights adjudication is seen as a field where judges are necessarily empowered vis-à-vis the other branches because judges need to give meaning to open-textured norms and balance interests.[82] This could support an argument in favour of more judicial restraint. At the same time, it appears relevant whether the rights norms that the court relies on were produced with the democratic legitimation of the domestic law – or even constitution-making process – or whether they emerged from international treaty-making.[83] In the case of the latter,

78 Ubi jus, ibi remedium.
79 *Urgenda Supreme Court* (n 1) [8.3.2]. See also e.g. *ENJEU* (n 21) and *Klimatická žaloba ČR* (n 43).
80 *Klimatická žaloba ČR* (n 43) [211]. This decision was overturned on appeal.
81 See Möllers (n 9).
82 Christina Eckes, 'Tackling the Climate Crisis with Counter-Majoritarian Instruments: Judges between Political Paralysis, Science, and International Law' (2021) 6 European Papers 1307.
83 As an example of the former, see *Neubauer* (n 4). As an example of the latter, see *Urgenda Supreme Court* (n 1).

additional considerations relating to the empowerment of the executive in external relations come into play.

Perhaps the most innovative decision so far has been the decision granted by the High Court of Lahore decision in the *Leghari* case, as it resulted in procedural obligations for a breach of substantive duties.[84] The Court created a Climate Change Commission composed of representatives of key ministries, NGOs, and technical experts to monitor the government's progress in terms of its own climate change policy and implementation framework. In other words, while refraining from imposing higher substantive targets, the Court established the institutional framework to oversee the execution of the State's existing policies.

Another highly relevant point on the judicial mandate to protect human rights was made by the Superior Court of Quebec, when it noted in *ENvironnement JEUnesse* that 'in the case of an alleged violation of the rights guaranteed by the Canadian Charter, a court should not decline jurisdiction on the basis of the doctrine of justiciability'.[85]

The need to exercise judicial review over executive but also legislative action has been particularly recognised as a result of the growing scientific evidence of the ubiquity and intensity of interferences with human rights caused by the climate crisis. This connects to the widely shared understanding that protecting the rights of individuals, including large numbers from foreseeable harm in the future, is the core task of courts under separated powers.

### 6.4.4 *Developing Legally Enforceable Norms from Best Available Science*

The Dutch Supreme Court in *Urgenda* relied heavily on the IPCC reports to argue that 'objective' standards exist against which to review the State's conduct.[86] This highlights the role of courts as independent fora, where impartial judges need to be convinced, not only of what the law is and what legal obligations may flow from it within the particular case but also of the climate science that should underpin any political and judicial decision-making on climate issues.

Generally, many courts have heavily relied on climate science for their reasoning. Examples include the case of *Friends of the Irish Environment*, in which the Irish Supreme Court found that the scientific understanding of the 'safe temperature rise target' in Article 2.1(a) of the Paris Agreement has increasingly gravitated towards 'a lower figure [...] in the region of 1.5°C', as scientific knowledge has developed since the Paris Agreement.[87] Furthermore, the Administrative Court

84 *Asghar Leghari* (n 46).

85 *ENJEU* (n 21) [56]. See also *Urgenda Supreme Court* (n 1) [6.4], [8.3.3]; *Family Farmers and Greenpeace v Germany* [2018] 00271/17/R/SP (Administrative Court of Berlin) [45]; and *Mathur Strikeout* (n 19) [126].

86 *Urgenda Supreme Court* (n 1) [6.4]. See also *Mathur Strikeout* (n 19) [56].

87 *Friends of the Irish Environment CLG* (n 53) [3.4].

of Paris recalled in *Notre Affaire à Tous* the IPCC's findings in the Special Report on 1.5°C (2018) and concluded that 'a warming of 2°C rather than 1.5°C would seriously increase these various phenomena and their consequences'.[88] Similarly, in *Klimaatzaak*, the Court of Appeal pointed out scientific evidence regarding the risks of exceeding the threshold of 1.5°C[89] and, in *Milieudefensie*, the Hague District Court converged towards the same conclusion, establishing that 'in the last couple of years, further insight has shown that a safe temperature increase should not exceed 1.5°C'.[90]

One may conclude that climate litigation necessarily brings science back into the debate, ideally in a rational, non-interest-driven, and fact-checking fashion. By relying on the IPCC reports as reflecting the best available science established in a transparent and inclusive process that vouches for its scientific impartiality, judges vest climate science in the societal debate with *legal* authority.[91] In all climate litigation cases, judges are required to establish the relevant facts underpinning the claims of the parties on what reduction obligations flow from the law. While this point may prima facie appear only indirectly linked to separation of powers, it reinforces the function of the judiciary to rationalise societal conflict pursuant to pre-established procedural rules and, by doing so, offers a procedural mechanism of systematically debunking scientific myths that lacks in the less formal political debate, for example, in parliament.

Judges have also justified why climate issues are justiciable irrespective of the complex science involved, the alleged uncertainties under the scientific models sketching the probable impacts of rising emissions, or the numerous interests affected by the impacts and mitigation measures. On the first aspect, the German Federal Constitutional Court acknowledged in *Neubauer* that, while there are several scientific methods for determining a State's necessary emissions reductions to hold global warming to a particular temperature limit, all of which entail uncertainties, 'this does not make it permissible under constitutional law for Germany's required contribution to be chosen arbitrarily. Nor can a specific constitutional obligation to reduce $CO_2$ emissions be invalidated by simply arguing that Germany's share of the reduction burden and of the global $CO_2$ budget are impossible to determine'.[92] Similarly, the Hague District Court established in *Milieudefensie* that while 'no one single [reduction] pathway is the measure of all things on a global scale', there nevertheless exists 'widely endorsed consensus' regarding the minimum emissions reductions that are required to avert dangerous climate change.[93]

88 *Notre Affaire à Tous* (n 29) [16].
89 *VZW Klimaatzaak Appeal* (n 29) [176] [191].
90 *Milieudefensie* (n 35) [2.3.3].
91 See *Urgenda Supreme Court* (n 1) and *Thomson* (n 19).
92 *Neubauer* (n 4) [225].
93 *Milieudefensie* (n 35) [4.4.29].

It should be added that judges must often decide based on incomplete knowledge and rely on science to substantiate their fact finding.[94] This is not different in climate cases; yet, increasingly detailed science on the impacts of climate change are seen by judges as providing them with the necessary knowledge to give rulings.

## 6.5 REPLICABILITY

Different courts around the world have interpreted the issue of separation of powers in climate litigation in very distinct ways. Ultimately, the extent to which judicial reasoning relating to separation of powers can be replicated depends on the similarities and differences of the relevant legal elements that determine the national conception of separation of powers. In principle, successful litigation requiring a government to do or not do something in relation to climate change is more likely to be observed in countries that have constitutional or national legal provisions protecting a healthy environment and/or climate.[95] The existence of national climate framework laws with clear targets, accountability mechanisms, and, in some cases, an explicit mandate for courts to review the implementation of climate laws also provide clarity in ensuring judicial oversight.[96]

Once the legislature has exercised its core function and adopted a law, the court is not supposed to apply and interpret the law. As pointed out by the Brazilian Superior Court of Justice, in countries that have legislation protecting the environment and/or the climate, 'the judge does not create obligations to protect the environment. Instead, they emanate from the law once they have been examined by the Legislative Branch. For this reason, we do not require activist judges, because activism is found within the law and the constitutional text'.[97]

All four stages of adjudication have a potential for replicability. Even the most far-reaching decisions (level 4) have already been replicated, and, notably, the

[94] Katalin Sulyok, *Science and Judicial Reasoning – The Legitimacy of International Environmental Adjudication* (Cambridge University Press 2021).

[95] See e.g. art 20a of the German Constitution (*Grundgesetz*).

[96] In Benin, Kenya, Uganda, and Papua New Guinea, judicial review provisions are broadly applied to the implementation of all obligations in the law. Uganda's law is particularly interesting, since it allows any concerned citizen to bring an action against either the government or a private entity for actions or omissions that may prove adverse to climate action without the need to prove a specific injury or damage, a requirement that has proved challenging for litigants in climate change cases to meet in other contexts (see, for example, *Verein KlimaSeniorinnen Schweiz and Others v Switzerland* App no 53600/20 (ECtHR)). In Ireland and New Zealand, the relevant provisions instead focus explicitly on government obligations to meet emissions reduction targets. See Catherine Higham and others, 'Accountability mechanisms in climate change framework laws' (*LSE Grantham Research Institute on Climate Change and the Environment*, November 2021) 27 <www.lse.ac.uk/granthaminstitute/wp-content/uploads/2021/11/Accountability-mechanisms-in-climate-change-framework-laws.pdf> accessed 24 February 2024.

[97] *Public Prosecutor's Office v H Carlos Schneider S/A Comércio e Indústria & Others* [2007] 650.728 – SC 2003/0221786-0 (Superior Tribunal de Justicia) [3.2] (own translation).

interpretations used in the *Urgenda* decision have been discussed at length in other cases in the Netherlands and beyond. '*Urgenda*-type' cases have been replicated with the aim of holding governments accountable for reducing GHG emissions in Canada, the United States, Norway, South Korea, Ireland, Colombia, and other countries. The *Urgenda* case was also adapted and replicated as a tort law case in *Milieudefensie* – another decision that could, in principle, be replicated in other jurisdictions with tort law. Furthermore, decisions from other jurisdictions, while not binding, may provide and have provided persuasive arguments.[98] This practice on the part of domestic courts makes explicit what has been termed the 'transnational dimensions of the global climate change case law'.[99]

Even the far-reaching orders of Mansoor Ali Shah in the *Leghari* case were arguably replicated in the *Shrestha* case. This type of decision could potentially be further replicable in jurisdictions where there is a constitutional right to life and a judicial willingness to interpret this right to life as including a right to a healthy environment, a right to clean air, and/or other similar rights enshrined in the country's constitution or human rights law.[100]

While the different expressions of the idea of separation of powers vary tremendously, we see a trend that the justiciability of climate cases against public authorities, as well as the establishment of enforceable obligations, are becoming more widely accepted.[101] Climate litigation has a strong transnational dimension,[102] which strengthens the potential for replicability. It can further be expected that climate cases will continue being brought and hence that courts must continue to engage with climate issues under the conditions of an unfolding global climate emergency.

## 6.6 CONCLUSION

The central aim of the study has been to identify emerging best practice in relation to how separation of powers has been addressed in climate litigation across a wide variety of jurisdictions and doctrinal contexts. Our account suggests that, while judicial engagement is likely to be diverse, the decisions can be understood in a more systematic way. We have identified four stages of adjudication, ranging in intensity from low to high – justiciability, recognising a right or duty, establishing

98 ibid. See the use of *Urgenda Supreme Court* (n 1) in *Neubauer* (n 4).

99 Emily Barritt and Boitumelo Sediti, 'The Symbolic Value of Leghari v Federation of Pakistan: Climate Change Adjudication in the Global South' (2019) 30 KLJ 203. See also Jacqueline Peel and Jolene Lin, 'Transnational Climate Litigation: The Contribution of the Global South' (2019) 113 AJIL 679.

100 Keely Boom and others, 'Climate Justice: The International Momentum Towards Climate Litigation' (*Heinrich-Böll-Stufting & Climate Justice Programme*, 2016) <www.boell.de/en/2016/11/15/climate-justice-international-momentum-towards-climate-litigation> accessed 24 February 2024.

101 Inter alia, Kleoniki Pouikli, 'Editorial: A Short History of the Climate Change Litigation Boom across Europe' (2022) 22 ERA Forum: Journal of the Academy of European Law 569.

102 Barritt and Sediti (n 99); Peel and Lin (n 99).

a breach, and determining enforceable obligations (procedural and/or substantive). Within one and the same case, a lower level of intensity indicates a more functional conception of separation of powers, while a higher level of intensity indicates a more relational conception of separation of powers. Further, we have identified four areas of emerging best practice in progressive climate rulings: the role of the judiciary, giving effect to international norms, human rights protection, and developing norms from science.

Once a climate case is filed, the decision of a court to declare the case justiciable opens a number of avenues for what the court can do and how far it can go within its mandate and in line with the separation of powers. Judges have a choice of establishing a lower or higher level of intervention. Such a choice is bound by a judgment about the institutional competence of the courts. Surely, courts are most likely to respond where the legislature has acknowledged a duty of the State and/or of corporations to act. But judges are also sensitive to the different ways in which separation of powers goals are implicated in a policy domain,[103] as well as to the severity of the problem that they are faced with.

At the same time, climate litigation is a dynamic field, characterised as a 'transnational' phenomenon. As Peel and Lin observe, advocates see their climate litigation work as contributing to the global effort to address climate change, and the cases are often accompanied by campaigns that seek to appeal to an international audience.[104] Litigants take notice of what cases are being filed and what decisions are given in other jurisdictions, and that knowledge often informs the cases they bring. Similarly, judges are following the decisions given by other courts across borders. The *Urgenda* decision has already been cited in judgements by courts in several other climate cases, including cases in Australia, Ireland, and Germany. Bold decisions elsewhere therefore can give additional confidence for judges deciding new cases presented before them.

[103] Aziz Z. Huq and Jon D. Michaels, 'The Cycles of Separation-of-Powers Jurisprudence' (2016) 126 YLJ 346.

[104] Peel and Lin (n 99).

PART II

# Merits

# 7

# Human Rights

*Margaretha Wewerinke-Singh and Lucy Maxwell**

Climate change is a reality that now affects every region of the world. The human implications of currently projected levels of global heating are catastrophic. Storms are rising and tides could submerge entire island nations and coastal cities. Fires rage through our forests, and the ice is melting. We are burning up our future – literally.

Michelle Bachelet, 'Global Update at the 42nd session of the Human Rights Council'

## 7.1 INTRODUCTION

It has been widely recognised that climate change adversely affects the enjoyment of a wide range of human rights, including the rights to life, adequate housing, food, the highest attainable standard of health, and the right to self-determination.[1] Measures taken to respond to climate change also have implications for the enjoyment of human rights.[2] As of December 2023, the United Nations (UN) Human Rights Council has adopted thirteen resolutions on human rights and climate change,[3] and several UN Special Procedure mandate holders have published reports on human rights and climate change.[4] The Paris Agreement refers explicitly

* Margaretha Wewerinke-Singh is an Associate Professor of Sustainability Law at the University of Amsterdam and an Attorney at Blue Ocean Law. Lucy Maxwell is Co-Director of the Climate Litigation Network.

1 Daniel Bodansky, Jutta Brunnée, and Lavanya Rajamani, *International Climate Change Law* (Oxford University Press 2017) 301; Siobhan McInerney-Lankford, Mac Darrow, and Lavanya Rajamani, *Human Rights and Climate Change: A Review of the International Legal Dimensions* (World Bank Studies 2011) 11–19.

2 McInerney-Lankford, Darrow, and Rajamani (n 1) 7; Michael Burger and Jessica A. Wentz, 'Climate Change and Human Rights' (*UNEP and Sabin Center for Climate Change Law*, December 2015) 8–10 <https://wedocs.unep.org/bitstream/handle/20.500.11822/9530/-Climate_Change_and_Human_Rightshuman-rights-climate-change.pdf.pdf> accessed 9 February 2024.

3 'Human Rights Council Resolutions on Human Rights and Climate Change' (*OHCHR*, 2022) <www.ohchr.org/en/climate-change/human-rights-council-resolutions-human-rights-and-climate-change> accessed 9 February 2024.

4 See e.g. 'Special Rapporteur on Human Rights and the Environment' (*OHCHR*, 2022) <www.ohchr.org/en/special-procedures/sr-environment> accessed 9 February 2024; see also n 20.

to human rights in its preamble, calling upon parties to 'respect, promote and consider their respective obligations on human rights'.[5] The link between human rights and climate change was further institutionalised through the creation of a mandate for a Special Rapporteur on Human Rights and Climate Change,[6] who was first appointed in March 2022.[7]

The recognition of the link between climate change and human rights has also inspired litigation, giving rise to an increasingly rich body of jurisprudence clarifying the scope and content of States' human rights obligations in the context of climate change.[8] Recent jurisprudence further suggests that corporations also have obligations to respect human rights in the face of climate change.[9]

In this chapter, we provide a roadmap to this field of climate litigation based on human rights or constitutional rights provisions (rights-based climate litigation). We summarise key jurisprudential developments and identify emerging areas of best practice and replicable jurisprudence.

## 7.2 RIGHTS-BASED CLIMATE LITIGATION AT A GLANCE

Rights-based climate litigation is a dynamic and rapidly evolving field of practice globally.[10] In the past decade, and particularly since the adoption of the Paris Agreement in 2015,[11] courts and tribunals around the world have issued judgments in rights-based climate cases, demonstrating a rising trend in climate litigation.[12] As at the end of 2022, more than a hundred rights-based climate cases have been

5 Paris Agreement (entered into force 4 November 2016) 3156 UNTS 79 (Paris Agreement). See also Alan Boyle, 'Climate Change, the Paris Agreement and Human Rights' (2018) 67 ICLQ 759; John Knox, 'The Paris Agreement as a Human Rights Treaty' in Dapo Akande and others (eds), *Human Rights and 21st Century Challenges: Poverty, Conflict, and the Environment* (Oxford University Press 2020).

6 UNHRC, 'Mandate of the Special Rapporteur on the Promotion and Protection of Human Rights in the Context of Climate Change' UN Doc A/HRC/RES/48/14 (2021).

7 'Special Rapporteur on Climate Change' (*OHCHR*, 2022) <www.ohchr.org/en/specialprocedures/sr-climate-change#:~:text=Mr.,mandate%20on%201%20May%202022> accessed 26 February 2024.

8 César Rodríguez-Garavito, 'Litigating the Climate Emergency: The Global Rise of Human Rights–Based Litigation for Climate Action' in César Rodríguez-Garavito (ed), *Litigating the Climate Emergency: How Human Rights, Courts, and Legal Mobilization Can Bolster Climate Action* (Cambridge University Press 2022); Margaretha Wewerinke-Singh, 'Preventing Climate Harm: The Role of Rights-Based Litigation' (2023) 40 Wisconsin International Law Journal 245. Note that the cases discussed substantively in this chapter are current through November 2023.

9 Andreas Hösli, '*Milieudefensie et al v Shell*: A Tipping Point in Climate Change Litigation against Corporations?' (2021) 11 Climate Law 195.

10 For a systematic review of rights-based climate litigation, see Annalisa Savaresi and Joana Setzer, 'Rights-based Litigation in the Climate Emergency: Mapping the Landscape and New Knowledge Frontiers' (2022) 13(1) JHRE 7–34. The authors draw upon data from the world's most established climate litigation databases (up to May 2021) – those compiled by the Sabin Center for Climate Change Law at Columbia Law School and the Grantham Research Institute on Climate Change and the Environment at the London School of Economics. We refer to their findings in what follows.

11 See ibid 12.

12 See ibid Annex.

identified globally.[13] Predominantly, these rights-based climate cases have been brought against States and public authorities,[14] while a smaller but rapidly growing number of cases filed against corporations.[15] These cases broadly encompass four categories:

a) Systemic or 'framework' mitigation cases that concern a State's (or company's) *overall* efforts to mitigate climate change;
b) Project-based cases that concern the conduct of a State (or its organs) with respect to a specific project or initiative with greenhouse gas (GHG) implications. Most cases are premised on statutory grounds (such as under planning law) and focus on the State's failure to meet requirements of consultation, provision of information, and environmental impact assessment, including contribution to climate change;
c) Adaptation and loss and damage cases that concern actions related to the impacts of climate change, including adaptation and climate-induced migration; and
d) 'Just transition' cases that concern the design or implementation of a State's mitigation measures.

Most rights-based cases determined by courts fall into the systemic mitigation category.[16] The rights relied upon by plaintiffs in such cases include the right to self-determination; the right to life and dignity; the right to the highest attainable standard of health; the right to private and family life; the right to residence, movement, and inviolability of home; the right to a healthy environment; the right to property; cultural rights; and the right to equality and freedom from discrimination. Some rights-based cases invoke the State's obligations with respect to procedural rights such as the right to information, participation, and the right to a remedy.[17] The invocation of procedural rights is particularly common in project-based and 'just transition' cases.[18]

[13] 'Human Rights' (*Sabin Center for Climate Change Law*, 13 July 2023) <http://climatecasechart.com/non-us-climate-change-litigation/> accessed 24 February 2024.

[14] Savaresi and Setzer (n 10) 14.

[15] ibid. For instance, of the 112 rights-based cases that were filed through May 2021, 16 cases were directed against corporations. See e.g. in the Netherlands *Milieudefensie v Royal Dutch Shell* [2021] ECLR:NL: RBDHA: 2021:5339 (District Court of the Hague); in the Philippines *In re Greenpeace Southeast Asia and Others* [2022] Case No CHR-NI-2016-0001 (Commission on Human Rights of the Philippines); in France see Complaint filed in *Friends of the Earth et al v Total* before Nanterre High Court, 2019 <http://climatecasechart.com/non-us-case/friends-of-the-earth-et-al-v-total/> accessed 24 February 2024.

[16] Savaresi and Setzer (n 10) 19. Out of 112 rights-based cases, 83 concern mitigation, 9 concern adaptation, and 20 both mitigation and adaptation.

[17] See ibid 23–34.

[18] See e.g. Case C-524/09 *City of Lyon v French Deposits and Consignments Fund* [2009] ECR-I 14115; 'Access to Information on International GHG Emissions Trading by Ukraine' (*Environment-People-Law*, 27 January 2017) <http://epl.org.ua/en/environment/6599/> accessed 27 February 2024.

With respect to fora, most rights-based climate cases have been filed at the national level, with domestic courts issuing the vast majority of judgments in cases to date.[19] Regional and international courts, tribunals, and human rights bodies have also developed a rich body of norms and principles regarding States' human rights obligations in the context of climate change.[20] At the time of publication, there are pending climate cases before the European Court of Human Rights (ECtHR) and the East African Court of Justice.[21] Moreover, in March 2023, the UN General

[19] Savaresi and Setzer (n 10) 10. Approximately 13 per cent of rights-based cases have been filed before international and regional human rights bodies.

[20] See e.g. UNHR Committee, 'Views Adopted by the Committee under Article 5(4) of the Optional Protocol, concerning Communication No. 2728/2016', 24 October 2019 UN Doc CCPR/C/127/D/2728/2016 (*Teitiota*); UN Committee on the Rights of the Child, 'Decision adopted by the Committee under the Optional Protocol to the Convention on the Rights of the Child on a Communications Procedure, concerning Communication No. 104/2019', UN Doc CRC/C/88/D/104/2019 (*Sacchi*); UNHR Committee, 'Views Adopted by the Committee under Article 5(4) of the Optional Protocol, concerning Communication No 3624/2019', 21 July 2022, UN Doc CCPR/C/135/D/3624/2019 (*Billy*); Case T-330/18 *Armando Ferrão Carvalho and Others v The European Parliament and the Council* [2019] ECLI:EU:T:2019:324; *The Environment and Human Rights (State Obligations in Relation to the Environment in the Context of the Protection and Guarantee of the Rights to Life and to Personal Integrity – Interpretation and Scope of Articles 4(1) and 5(1) of the American Convention on Human Rights)*, Advisory Opinion OC-23, Inter-American Court of Human Rights Series A No 23 (15 November 2017) (IACtHR OC-23/17) [47], [54]; 'African Commission on Human and Peoples' Rights' (*ACHPR*) <www.achpr.org/documentationcenter?search=resolution%20on%20climate%20change%20and%20human%20rights> accessed 24 February 2024; UN Human Rights Committee, 'General comment No 36 (2018) on article 6 of the International Covenant on Civil and Political Rights, on the right to life' (30 October 2018) UN Doc CCPR/C/GC/36 (CCPR General Comment No 36); CEDAW, 'General Recommendation No 37 on Gender-related Dimensions Of Disaster Risk Reduction In The Context of Climate Change', UN Doc CEDAW/C/GC/37; Concluding Observations issued by UN Human Rights Treaty Bodies to States on numerous occasions, as reported in Centre for International Environmental Law and The Global Initiative for Economic, Social and Cultural Rights, see Lucy Mckernan and others, *States' Human Rights Obligations in the Context of Climate Change: 2022 Update* (CIEL and GIESCR 2022). See e.g. OHCHR, 'Joint Statement on "Human Rights and Climate Change"' (16 September 2019) <www.ohchr.org/en/statements/2019/09/five-un-human-rights-treaty-bodies-issue-joint-statement-human-rights-and> accessed 24 February 2024; Statement of the UN Committee on Economic, Social and Cultural Rights (CESCR), 'Climate change and the International Covenant on Economic, Social and Cultural Rights' (*OHCHR*, 8 October 2018) <www.ohchr.org/en/NewsEvents/Pages/DisplayNews.aspx?NewsID=23691&LangID=E> accessed 24 February 2024; OHCHR, Joint Statement of UN Special Mandates on Climate Change (23 September 2019) <www.ohchr.org/EN/NewsEvents/Pages/DisplayNews.aspx?NewsID=25003&LangID=E> accessed 24 February 2024. See e.g. OHCHR, 'Report of the Special Rapporteur on the Issue of Human Rights Obligations Relating to the Enjoyment of a Safe, Clean, Healthy and Sustainable Environment' (2017) UN Doc A/HRC/34/49; OHCHR, 'Report of the Special Rapporteur on the Issue of Human Rights Obligations Relating to the Enjoyment of a Safe, Clean, Healthy and Sustainable Environment' (2019) UN Doc A/74/161.

[21] For the list of cases pending before the European Court of Human Rights, see Council of Europe, 'Factsheet – Climate Change' (*Council of Europe*, February 2023) <www.echr.coe.int/documents/d/echr/FS_Climate_change_ENG#:~:text=There%20are%20currently%20three%20cases,the%20Court%20on%20this%20issue.&text=On%2011%20January%202023%20the,Duarte%20Agostinho%20and%20Others%20v> accessed 24 February 2024. These cases

Assembly adopted a resolution by consensus requesting an advisory opinion from the International Court of Justice on the obligation of States with respect to climate change.[22] Similar advisory opinion requests have also been submitted to the International Tribunal for the Law of the Sea[23] as well as the Inter-American Court of Human Rights.[24]

In terms of outcomes, courts have issued a range of remedies in rights-based cases. These include declaratory relief;[25] determinations that provisions of legislation are unconstitutional;[26] injunctive relief[27] (including orders imposing particular emission-reduction targets[28] or requiring that existing targets to be met);[29] quashing orders for emission-intensive projects;[30] and particular types of adaptation support and relief. The next section will explore the expansive scope of rights-based case law in greater detail.

include Complaint filed in *Duarte Agostinho and Others v Portugal and 32 Other States* (ECtHR) <http://climatecasechart.com/climate-change-litigation/wp-content/uploads/sites/16/non-us-case-documents/2020/20200902_3937120_complaint.pdf> accessed 24 February 2024; Application filed in *Union of Swiss Senior Women for Climate Protection v Swiss Federal Council and Others* (ECtHR) <http://climatecasechart.com/climate-change-litigation/non-us-case/union-of-swiss-senior-women-for-climate-protection-v-swiss-federal-parliament/> accessed 24 February 2024; Petition filed in *Greenpeace Nordic Association v Ministry of Petroleum and Energy* (ECtHR) <http://climatecasechart.com/non-us-case/greenpeace-nordic-assn-v-ministry-of-petroleum-and-energy-ecthr/> accessed 24 February 2024; Complaint filed in *Mex M v Austria* (ECtHR) <http://climatecasechart.com/climate-change-litigation/non-us-case/mex-m-v-austria/> accessed 24 February 2024; Complaint filed in *Uricchio v Italy and 32 other States* (ECtHR) <http://climatecasechart.com/non-us-case/uricchio-v-italy-and-32-other-states/> accessed 24 February 2024; Application for injunction in *Center for Food and Adequate Living Rights et al v Tanzania and Uganda* (East African Court of Justice) <http://climatecasechart.com/climate-change-litigation/wp-content/uploads/sites/16/non-us-case-documents/2020/20201106_12737_application.pdf> accessed 24 February 2024.

22 Obligations of States in Respect of Climate Change (Request For Advisory Opinion) <http://climatecasechart.com/wp-content/uploads/sites/16/non-us-case-documents/2023/20230420_18913_order.pdf> accessed 24 February 2024.

23 Request for an Advisory Opinion of 12 December 2022 <www.itlos.org/fileadmin/itlos/documents/cases/31/Request_for_Advisory_Opinion_COSIS_12.12.22.pdf> accessed 24 February 2024.

24 Petition filed in *Request for an Advisory Opinion on the Scope of the State Obligations for Responding to the Climate Emergency* (IACtHR) <http://climatecasechart.com/non-us-case/request-for-an-advisory-opinion-on-the-scope-of-the-state-obligations-for-responding-to-the-climate-emergency/> accessed 24 February 2024.

25 *Billy* (n 20).

26 See the judgment in *Neubauer and Others v Germany* [2021] 1 BvR 2656/18, 1 BvR 96/20, 1 BvR 78/20, 1 BvR 288/20, 1 BvR 96/20, 1 BvR 78/20 (German Federal Constitutional Court) (*Neubauer*); *Notre Affaire à Tous and Others v France* [2021] No 1904967, 1904968, 1904972 1904976/4-1.

27 See ibid *Neubauer*; *VZW Klimaatzaak v Kingdom of Belgium and Others* [2023] 2022/AR/891 (Cour d'appel de Bruxelles) (*VZW Klimaatzaak Appeal*); *Center for Food and Adequate Living Rights et al v Tanzania and Uganda* (n 21).

28 See e.g. *State of the Netherlands (Ministry of Economic Affairs and Climate Policy) v Stichting Urgenda* [2019] ECLI:NL:HR:2019:2007 (Supreme Court of the Netherlands) (*Urgenda Supreme Court*).

29 *Notre Affaire à Tous* (n 26).

30 See e.g. *Pro Public and Others v Godavari Marble Industries Pvt Ltd and Others* 068–WO–0082 (Supreme Court of Nepal); *In re Hawai'i Electric Light Co* No SCOT-22-0000418 (Supreme Court of Hawai'i) (majority and concurring opinions).

## 7.3 CASE LAW DEVELOPMENT

Legal norms governing States' human rights obligations in the context of climate change have matured greatly in many jurisdictions around the world in recent years. Emerging jurisprudence further suggests that corporations have obligations to respect human rights in the face of climate change, including the alignment of their policies and conduct with the goals of the Paris Agreement. This selection provides a summary of developments across the four categories of rights-based climate cases. While the most significant developments have occurred in decisions issued in 'systemic' mitigation cases against governments, relevant principles are also starting to emerge from jurisprudence in other categories of rights-based climate cases.

### 7.3.1 *Systemic Mitigation Cases*

Systemic mitigation cases challenge a State's (or company's) *overall* efforts to mitigate climate change. The central allegation in such cases is that the State has failed to adopt reasonable and appropriate measures to mitigate climate change through the rapid reduction of GHG emissions, and that this failure constitutes a violation of its obligation to protect human rights, given the severe and foreseeable harm caused by climate change, of which the State knows or ought to have known.[31] Most such cases have been brought against governments in the Global North. Additionally, there is a small but growing number of cases that challenge a corporation's contribution to climate change and inadequate mitigation measures.[32]

Judgments issued in systemic mitigation cases to date include those by: the Dutch courts in *Urgenda v the Netherlands*;[33] the German Constitutional Court

[31] Most cases are premised on jurisprudence regarding the State's obligations to protect the human rights of persons within its jurisdiction against a foreseeable and serious risk of harm. See sources listed in Lucy Maxwell, Sarah Mead, and Dennis van Berkel, 'Standards for Adjudicating the next Generation of Urgenda-Style Climate Cases' (2022) 13(1) JHRE 35, 40.

[32] See e.g. in the Netherlands, *Milieudefensie v Royal Dutch Shell* [2021] ECLR:NL: RBDHA:2021:5339 (District Court of the Hague); in France, *Friends of the Earth et al v Total* (n 15) (pending); Complaint filed in *Notre Affaire a Tous and others v Total* before Nanterre District Court <http://climatecasechart.com/climate-change-litigation/wp-content/uploads/sites/16/non-us-case-documents/2020/20200128_NA_complaint.pdf> accessed 24 February 202 (pending). See Complaint filed in *Envol Vert et al v Casino* before Saint-Étienne Judicial Court <http://climatecasechart.com/climate-change-litigation/non-us-case/envol-vert-et-al-v-casino/> accessed 24 February 2024; in Italy see Summary of Complaint filed in *Rete Legalità per il Clima (Legality for Climate Network) and others v ENI* before National Contact Point of the OECD <https://climate-laws.org/geographies/italy/litigation_cases/rete-legalita-per-il-clima-legality-for-climate-network-and-others-v-eni> accessed 24 February 2024 (pending); in Germany see Petition filed in *Deutsche Umwelthilfe (DUH) v Bayerische Motoren Werke AG (BMW)* before Regional Court of Munich <https://climate-laws.org/geographies/germany/litigation_cases/deutsche-umwelthilfe-duh-v-bayerische-motoren-werke-ag-bmw> accessed 24 February 2024 (pending); the Philippines, *In re Greenpeace Southeast Asia and Others* (n 15). For further detail, see Savaresi and Setzer (n 10) 24–27.

[33] *Urgenda Supreme Court* (n 28).

in *Neubauer et al v Germany*;[34] the District Court of the Hague in *Milieudefensie v Royal Dutch Shell*;[35] and by courts in Belgium,[36] Canada,[37] Colombia,[38] France,[39] Ireland,[40] Switzerland,[41] the United States,[42] Nepal,[43] and Brazil[44] in cases which, like *Urgenda*, concern the lawfulness of the State's overall mitigation efforts. The decisions have all been issued since 2015, which marks the beginning of the wave of systemic mitigation cases globally.[45] Until the UN Human Rights Committee issued its views on *Billy et al v Australia*, no regional or international court or tribunal had issued a decision on the merits in such a case.[46] We discuss this decision – which remains the only one of its kind – later on.

34 See *Neubauer* (n 26).

35 *Milieudefensie* (n 32).

36 *VZW Klimaatzaak Appeal* (n 27).

37 *La Rose v Her Majesty the Queen* T-1750-19 [2020] (Federal Court of Canada) (on a preliminary point); *La Rose v His Majesty the King* A-289-20, A-308-20 [2023] (Federal Court of Appeal); Judgment in *Environnement Jeunesse v Procureur General du Canada* [2018] 500-06-000955-183 (Quebec Superior Court) (*ENJEU*), which was affirmed on appeal by the Supreme Court of Canada in July 2022; Judgement in *Mathur v Ontario* [2023] ONSC 2316 (*Mathur Merits*).

38 *Future Generations v Ministry of the Environment and Others (Demanda Generaciones Futuras v Minambiente)* [2018] 11001 22 03 000 2018 00319 00 (Colombia Supreme Court) (*Demanda Futuras Generaciones*).

39 *Notre Affaire à Tous* (n 26) (albeit that the court upheld the case on the basis of the tort of ecological damage, rather than human rights provisions). *Commune de Grande-Synthe v France* [2020] No 427301 (Conseil d'Etat) (*Grande-Synthe*). The Supreme Administrative Court of France upheld the case on grounds other than human rights provisions.

40 *Friends of the Irish Environment CLG v The Government of Ireland, Ireland and the Attorney General* [2020] Appeal no 205/19 (Supreme Court of Ireland) (albeit that the court upheld the case on the basis of administrative law, rather than human rights provisions).

41 *Swiss Senior Women* (n 21).

42 See e.g. *Juliana v United States* 947 F.3d 1159 (9th Cir 2020); Order in *Barhaugh v Montana* (Montana Supreme Court) <http://climatecasechart.com/case/2436/> accessed 27 February 2024; Order in *Held v Montana* (District Court Montana) <http://climatecasechart.com/wp-content/uploads/sites/16/case-documents/2021/20210804_docket-CDV-2020-307_order.pdf> accessed 27 February 2024; *Alec v McCarthy* (Court of Appeals for District of Columbia) <http://climatecasechart.com/case/alec-l-v-mccarthy/> accessed 27 February 2024.

43 *Advocate Padam Bahadur Shrestha v Prime Minister and Office of Council of Ministers and Others* [2018] Order No 074-WO-0283 (2075/09/10 BS) (Supreme Court of Nepal) (*Shrestha v Office of Council of Ministers*).

44 *PSB and others v Brazil* [2022] ADPF 708 (Federal Supreme Court of Brazil).

45 For discussion of this 'wave' of climate litigation, see e.g. Priyadarshi R. Shukla and others (eds.), *Climate Change 2022: Mitigation of Climate Change. Contribution of Working Group III to the Sixth Assessment Report of the Intergovernmental Panel on Climate Change* (Cambridge University Press 2022) [13.4.2].

46 Previous cases were dismissed on admissibility grounds. These include cases before: UN Committee on the Rights of the Child (UN CRC); Inter-American Court of Human Rights; Court of Justice of the European Union. The UN CRC has issued decisions in five systemic mitigation cases brought by a number of children against five Respondent States (*Sacchi* (n 20)). Each communication was deemed inadmissible, but the Committee did make important remarks in its views: it noted that States have cross-border obligations to protect children from climate harm; *Carvalho* (n 20); see also *Petition To the Inter-American Commission on Human Rights Seeking Relief from Violations Resulting from Global Warming Caused by Acts and Omissions of the United States* [2005] Inter-American Commission on Human Rights 1413-05.

Systemic mitigation cases have led to a range of notable developments in jurisprudence.[47] For instance, many jurisdictions – including courts in the Netherlands,[48] Germany,[49] Belgium,[50] Canada,[51] Colombia,[52] and Nepal[53] – have recognised the justiciability of systemic mitigation cases, which is an important threshold issue, as described in greater detail in the Admissibility chapter.[54] Although some courts in North America have declined to hear systemic mitigation cases on admissibility grounds,[55] many courts elsewhere in the world have recognised that the State has a legal obligation under existing human rights law to undertake mitigation efforts, through GHG emissions reduction, in light of the harm caused by climate change. Finally, a smaller number of courts have proceeded to assess whether a State's overall mitigation efforts are sufficient to discharge its human rights obligations.[56] These significant judgments include *Urgenda* and *Neubauer* (as well as a recent appeal decision in the Belgian *Klimaatzaak case*), which we explore in Section 7.4.

A small but growing number of rights-based climate cases have been filed against corporations. A landmark case in this category is the Carbon Majors inquiry of the Commission on Human Rights of the Philippines (CHRP), also known as *In re Greenpeace Southeast Asia and Others*,[57] which focused on the responsibility of fossil fuel companies for human rights violations resulting from climate change. The inquiry resulted in a groundbreaking report in which the CHRP documented the contribution of fossil fuel companies' products and operations to climate change and the resulting loss and damage.[58] The report also provided evidence that these companies were aware of the climate risks from their products for several decades, but misled investors, regulators, and the public about the nature and severity of these risks.[59]

The District Court of the Hague in *Milieudefensie v Royal Dutch Shell* built on the findings of the CHRP report and reached its own landmark holding in 2021. The court issued the first decision globally that found that a corporation had a

47 For further details, see Maxwell, Mead, and Van Berkel (n 31).
48 *Urgenda* (n 28).
49 *Neubauer* (n 26); *Family Farmers and Greenpeace v Germany* [2018] 00271/17/R/SP (Administrative Court of Berlin).
50 *VZW Klimaatzaak Appeal* (n 27).
51 *Mathur Merits* (n 37). But contrast *ENJEU* (n 37) (appeal).
52 *Demanda Futuras Generaciones* (n 38).
53 *Shrestha v Office of Council of Ministers* (n 43).
54 See Chapter 5 on Admissibility.
55 See e.g. *Juliana* (n 42); *ENJEU* (n 37).
56 For details, see Maxwell, Mead, and Van Berkel (n 31) 46 Part 3.3.
57 *In re Greenpeace Southeast Asia and Others* (n 15).
58 Commission on Human Rights of the Philippines, 'National Inquiry on Climate Change Report' (CHRP December 2022).
59 ibid. See also Annalisa Savaresi and Jacques Hartmann, 'Using Human Rights Law to Address the Impacts of Climate Change: Early Reflections on the Carbon Majors Inquiry' in Jolene Lin and Douglas A. Kysar (eds) *Climate Change Litigation in the Asia Pacific* (Cambridge University Press 2020); Savaresi and Setzer (n 10).

legal obligation, pursuant to tort law, to adopt additional Scope 1, 2, and 3 GHG emission-reduction measures. The judgment determined that Royal Dutch Shell's obligations in tort law must be read in light of human rights law, including the UN Guiding Principles on Business and Human Rights, Articles 2 and 8 of the European Convention on Human Rights (ECHR), and Articles 6 and 17 of the International Covenant on Civil and Political Rights (ICCPR), which we expand on later.[60]

### 7.3.2 *Project Cases*

Project cases can trigger human rights guarantees in several ways. First, they may invoke 'procedural' human rights, such as those enshrined under the *Aarhus Convention* and *Escazú Agreement*, which include the right of access to information, the right to a fair hearing, and the right to an effective remedy. Secondly, they may rely on 'substantive' human rights, such as the rights to life and health. In the latter type of cases, the argument is similar to those made in 'systemic' mitigation cases: that the approval of the project is contrary to the duty to adopt reasonable and appropriate measures to protect human rights from the harm posed by climate change. It is important to note that there is a small body of jurisprudence regarding rights-based project cases and a larger body that does *not* relate to human rights arguments.[61] These cases concern a range of matters, including: the decision to permit exploration for new fossil fuel reserves;[62] permission for a new coal-fired power plant;[63] approval of an airport extension;[64] and the sale of state-owned coal-fired power plants.[65]

Jurisprudence in rights-based project cases has produced a mixed picture to date. For example, courts in South Africa have upheld two project-based cases with rights arguments, including the express constitutional right to a healthy environment. In *EarthLife*, the High Court found that the minister's failure to consider the proposed mine's contribution to global climate change rendered the approval unlawful,

60 *Milieudefensie* (n 32).

61 See e.g. *Gloucester Resources Limited v Minister for Planning* [2019] NSWLEC 7 (*Gloucester Resources*); *Minister for the Environment v Sharma* [2022] FCAFC 35 (*Sharma*); *Friends of the Earth v Haaland* (2022) <http://climatecasechart.com/case/friends-of-the-earth-v-haaland/> accessed 24 February 2024; *ClientEarth v Secretary of State* (2021) <http://climatecasechart.com/non-us-case/clientearth-v-secretary-of-state/> accessed 24 February 2024.

62 *Greenpeace Nordic* (n 20); Complaint filed in *OAAA v Araucaria Energy SA* before Federal Court of Mercedes <http://climatecasechart.com/non-us-case/oaaa-v-araucaria-energy-sa/> accessed 24 February 2024; *Waratah Coal Pty Ltd v Youth Verdict Ltd* [2022] QLC 21.

63 *EarthLife Africa Johannesburg v Minister of Environmental Affairs and Others* [2017] 65662/16 <http://climatecasechart.com/wp-content/uploads/sites/16/non-us-case-documents/2017/20170306_Case-no.-6566216_judgment-1.pdf> accessed 27 March 2023.

64 See e.g. *In re Vienna-Schwechat Airport Expansion* (2018) Bundesverwaltungsgericht W109 2000179-1/291E.

65 *PUSH Sweden, Nature and Youth Sweden and Others v Government of Sweden* (Stockholm District Court) <http://climatecasechart.com/climate-change-litigation/non-us-case/push-sweden-nature-youth-sweden-et-al-v-government-of-sweden/> accessed 24 February 2024.

despite no express reference to climate change in the relevant legislation.[66] In *Sustaining the Wild Coast NPC and others*, the High Court granted an injunction to prevent seismic surveying for offshore fossil fuel reserves due to the defendants' failure to meaningfully consult the applicants, as well as the risk of harm from the seismic survey, which would promote extraction of fossil fuels and adversely impact climate change, the applicant communities' cultural practices, ocean conservation, and the spiritual and sustainable use of ocean for healing and fishing purposes.[67]

Similarly, in Australia, in the *Waratah Coal* case, the Queensland Land Court recommended to the relevant government minister that an application for a new coal mine should be rejected.[68] The Court took into account a range of factors in reaching this decision, including the contribution of the mine to climate change, the economic and social benefits and costs, and the impacts on human rights.[69] The Court found that the project would limit a range of human rights, including the right to property, privacy, and home for the owners of the local area, and in relation to climate change, the cultural rights of First Nations Peoples, the rights of children, the right to property and to privacy and home, the right to enjoy human rights equally, and the right to life.[70] The final approval of the project depends on the decision of the government minister, but this court decision sets an important precedent for challenges to mining projects on public interest and human rights grounds.

Likewise, in *Marangopoulos Foundation for Human Rights v Greece*, the European Committee on Social Rights underscored the need for a holistic assessment of States' environmental law obligations on the one hand and its human rights obligations on the other.[71] The Committee found that Greece violated the right to a clean environment (Article 11 of the European Social Charter ('the Charter')), the right to just conditions of work (Article 2 of the Charter), and the right to safe and healthy working conditions (Article 3 of the Charter) as a result of the nature of the State's defective oversight and partial ownership of several lignite coal mines and coal-fired power plants.[72] The violations stemmed from the State's failure to prepare adequate environmental impact assessments, lax enforcement of pollution control measures, failure to achieve reductions in the emission of conventional pollutants and GHGs, and a lack of effective labour protections. In establishing these violations, the Committee observed that Greece had not managed to strike a reasonable

66 *EarthLife* (n 63) [81]–[83].

67 *Sustaining the Wild Coast NPC and Others v Minister of Mineral Resources and Energy and Others* (High Court of South Africa) <http://climatecasechart.com/climate-change-litigation/non-us-case/sustaining-the-wild-coast-npc-and-others-v-minister-of-mineral-resources-and-energy-and-others/> accessed 24 February 2024.

68 *Waratah Coal* (n 62).

69 ibid.

70 ibid [1795].

71 *Marangopoulos Foundation for Human Rights (MFHR) v Greece* (Decision on the Merits) (6 December 2006), ECSR Complaint No 30/2005, Resolution CM/ResChS (2008).

72 ibid [240].

balance between the interests of persons living in the mining areas and the general interests,[73] and that it had failed to provide precise and plausible information on measures taken to ensure the enforcement of regulations on health and safety.[74] These findings show that even provisions of human rights treaties that grant national authorities a considerable margin of discretion must be interpreted in a manner that makes the relevant human rights safeguards practical and effective.

By contrast, courts in other jurisdictions have dismissed project-based cases featuring human rights arguments. This jurisprudence includes legal challenges to airport extensions in Austria[75] and in England and Wales;[76] oil drilling in Argentina[77] and Norway;[78] and the sale of a state-owned coal-fired power plant in Sweden.[79] The dismissal of these cases, which attempted to leverage human rights arguments to deter projects with significant deleterious impacts on the climate system, underscores the intricate challenge of applying traditional legal frameworks to the complex, global, and systemic nature of the climate crisis. Further, they highlight the pressing need for more expansive legal approaches to ensure that these legal frameworks remain fit for purpose in the face of the evolving climate crisis.

The section on emerging best practice will highlight instances where judicial innovation and adaptability have paved the way for rulings capable of offering protection of the climate system. These emerging best practices offer a beacon of hope, demonstrating the potential of the judiciary to grapple with climate change through a human rights lens. As we examine these cases, we can draw valuable insights on how courts can evolve their interpretations and applications of legal frameworks to better address the multifaceted human rights issues posed by the climate crisis.

### 7.3.3 *Adaptation and Loss and Damage Cases*

Several cases concerning States' human rights obligations in the context of climate change adaptation hail from the Global South.[80] For instance, the leading judgment in this category is that of the Lahore High Court in *Leghari v Pakistan* in 2015.[81] There, the High Court found that the State had failed to take appropriate action with

73 ibid [221].
74 ibid [231].
75 *In re Vienna-Schwechat Airport Expansion* (n 64).
76 *R (on the application of Plan B Earth and others) v Heathrow Airport Ltd (Heathrow Expansion)* [2020] UKSC 52. See [113] for consideration of the human rights arguments, which were dismissed.
77 See also proceedings in *Greenpeace Argentina et al v Argentina et al* before courts in Argentina <http://climatecasechart.com/climate-change-litigation/non-us-case/greenpeace-argentina-et-al-v-argentina-et-al/> accessed 24 February 2024.
78 *Greenpeace Nordic* (n 20).
79 *PUSH Sweden* (n 65).
80 See also Sudha Kavuri and Anjana Ramanathan, 'Climate Change Litigation: Chronicles from the Global South: A Comparative Study' (2022) 28 Comparative Law Review 169.
81 *Asghar Leghari v Federation of Pakistan etc* PLD 2018 Lahore 364.

respect to climate change adaptation and that this infringed the petitioner's right to life and the right to human dignity under Pakistan's Constitution.[82] The Court ordered the State to effectively implement its existing adaptation policies, including allocating a specified budget to climate change adaptation in order to guarantee an effective protection to constitutional rights. Another relevant case is *Advocate Padam Bahadur Shrestha v Prime Minister and Office of Council of Ministers and Others*. In this decision from the Supreme Court of Nepal, the petitioner secured an order directing the relevant authorities to actively implement national adaptation plans and policies and to formulate an effective implementation plan for adaptation and mitigation to protect people's lives and livelihoods from direct and indirect effects of climate change.[83]

In other cases, courts have ordered States to adopt new laws or policies pertaining to adaptation. Of particular note is the decision of the Colombian Supreme Court in *Future Generations v Ministry of the Environment and Others* (*Future Generations*). In addition to measures relating to the protection of the Amazon, the Supreme Court ordered the formulation and implementation of national, regional, and local implementation strategies of a preventative, mandatory, corrective, and pedagogical nature, directed towards climate change adaptation.[84] Likewise, in *Notre Affaire à Tous and others v France* (*Notre Affaire*), the plaintiffs sought an order enjoining the Government of France, amongst other things, to take the necessary measures to adapt the national territory to the effects of climate change.[85] While the Administrative Court of Paris deferred the decision on whether to issue an injunction, it did issue a decision recognising that the State's failure to take adequate climate action had resulted in ecological damage.[86] Finally, of particular note is the decision of the UN Human Rights Committee in *Billy et al v Australia*, in which the Committee found that Australia's 'failure to adopt timely adequate adaptation measures' violated the First Nation authors' rights to privacy and home (Article 17 ICCPR) and cultural rights (Article 27 ICCPR), which we outline in more detail in Section 7.4.3.

Few cases to date have addressed questions related to loss and damage from climate change.[87] In the earliest of these cases, *Pro Public and Others v Godavari Marble Industries Pvt Ltd and Others* (*Pro Public*), the petitioners sought, among

82 ibid [8].
83 *Shrestha v Office of Council of Ministers* (n 43).
84 *Demanda Futuras Generaciones* (n 38) [10]–[11].
85 See Complaint in *Notre Affaire à Tous* (n 26). See also *Grande-Synthe* (n 39) in which the commune of Grande Synthe and Mr Damien Careme ask the Council of State to put in place immediate measures to adapt to climate change.
86 ibid *Notre Affaire à Tous*.
87 The potential of this climate litigation strategy, however, represents an emerging area of scholarship. Patrick Toussaint, 'Loss and Damage and Climate Litigation: The Case for Greater Interlinkage' (2021) 30 RECIEL 16; Jacob Wise, 'Climate Change Loss and Damage Litigation: Infeasible or a Useful Shadow?' (2021) 38 Wisconsin International Law Journal 687.

others, orders that would hold the respondent accountable for paying the costs of restoring the Godavari area in Nepal to its earlier condition prior to the operation of the mines in question.[88] While the Supreme Court of Nepal did not grant the requested compensation, it did quash the Department of Mines and Geology's decision to extend the lease to the respondent company with another ten years so as to avoid further damage.[89] Similarly, in *Notre Affaire*, the plaintiff NGOs demanded the symbolic sum of one euro in compensation for moral damage they claimed to have suffered as a result of the climate crisis, and another one euro in compensation for environmental damage linked to climate change. The Administrative Court of Paris found that France's failure to take ambitious climate action had indeed resulted in environmental damage from climate change and awarded the plaintiffs the requested amount of one euro in compensation for moral damage. However, it declined to issue compensatory damages for environmental harm as it found that the plaintiffs had failed to show that the government was unable to repair the harm caused by its inaction.[90]

To date, there have been no rights-based cases that address the obligations of developed countries to provide climate finance pursuant to the UN Framework Convention on Climate Change (UNFCCC)[91] and Paris Agreement.[92] However, three domestic cases concerned developed countries' obligations to provide legal protection to people fleeing the impacts of climate change. The earliest of these was a claim before Australia's Refugee Review Tribunal filed by a citizen of Kiribati, which argued that the destruction of their main livelihood in Kiribati because of climate change gave rise to protection obligations for Australia under the Refugee Convention.[93] Citizens of Tuvalu[94] and Kiribati[95] filed similar protection claims before courts and tribunals in New Zealand. All these claims were dismissed for various reasons, including that the harm alleged did not constitute 'persecution' under refugee law. In *Ioane Teitiota v The Chief Executive of the Ministry of Business, Innovation and Employment*, however, the Supreme Court of New Zealand noted that its decision did not rule out the possibility 'that environmental degradation resulting from climate change or other natural disasters could create a pathway into the Refugee Convention or protected person jurisdiction'.[96] As discussed later, the case was subsequently brought before the UN Human Rights Committee as *Ioane*

88 *Pro Public* (n 30).

89 ibid.

90 *Notre Affaire à Tous* (n 26).

91 United Nations Framework Convention on Climate Change (entered into force 21 March 1994) 1771 UNTS 107 (UNFCCC) arts 4(3), 4(4).

92 Paris Agreement (n 5) art 9(1).

93 0907346 [2009] RRTA 1168.

94 *In re: AD (Tuvalu)* [2014] Cases 501370-371.

95 *Ioane Teitiota v Chief Executive of the Ministry of Business, Innovation and Employment* [2015] NZSC 107.

96 ibid.

*Teitiota v New Zealand* (*Teitiota*),[97] where the question before the Committee was whether New Zealand's decision to deport Mr Teitiota constituted a violation of his right to life under the ICCPR.

### 7.3.4 *Just Transition Cases*

Finally, a small but growing number of rights-based cases challenge the design or implementation of a State's mitigation measures. These are known as 'just transition' or 'mal-adaptation' cases,[98] the majority of which are brought by Indigenous Peoples. In general, plaintiffs allege that the State has failed to take into account their human rights in designing or adopting mitigation measures, such as the development of wind farms. As most of these cases remain pending, they are not included in the 'best practice' analysis. However, their potential to create positive obligations on States in this arena is worthy of attention in future scholarship.

## 7.4 EMERGING BEST PRACTICE

Having reviewed the current state of play in rights-based climate litigation, it is clear that courts and tribunals around the world are increasingly recognising the need to address the human rights implications of climate change. From the judgments and decisions rendered to date, we can distil several areas of emerging best practice in rights-based climate jurisprudence. These best practices fall into three broad categories: interpretative techniques, recognition of the impacts of climate change on human rights, and recognition of States' obligations or corporations' responsibilities to protect human rights in the face of the climate crisis. In this section, we will explore each of these areas in more detail and highlight some of the key cases and decisions that have contributed to their development.

### 7.4.1 *Interpretive Techniques*

National courts and UN human rights bodies have recognised that, in interpreting States' obligations to protect human rights in the context of climate change, it is instructive to refer to norms of international environmental law and best available science.[99] This is particularly important as most human rights instruments do not

[97] *Teitiota* (n 19).

[98] Joana Setzer and Catherine Higham, 'Global Trends in Climate Change Litigation: 2021 Snapshot' (*LSE Grantham Research Institute on Climate Change and the Environment*, July 2021) 15 <www.lse.ac.uk/granthaminstitute/wp-content/uploads/2021/07/Global-trends-in-climate-change-litigation_2021-snapshot.pdf> accessed 24 February 2024; Savaresi and Setzer (n 10) 29–30.

[99] See further Maxwell, Mead, and Van Berkel (n 31) 47–49 [footnotes 76 and 89]. Regarding international law, see e.g. *Urgenda Supreme Court* (n 28) as discussed below; CCPR General Comment

expressly refer to climate change. Furthermore, as mentioned earlier, States' obligations to protect human rights are usually framed by reference to open-textured standards of 'reasonableness' and 'appropriateness'.[100] International law, as it pertains to climate change, environmental protection, transboundary harm, and human rights, has thus been a crucial source for many courts and UN human rights institutions in interpreting States' obligations in the context of climate change.[101] Many courts have referred to the near-universally ratified UNFCCC and Paris Agreement as central sources of applicable legal norms.[102] For instance, the ultimate objective of the UNFCCC, as cited by the Dutch Supreme Court in *Urgenda*, is 'to stabilise greenhouse gas concentrations in the atmosphere at a level that would prevent dangerous human induced interference with the climate system'.[103] The principles and commitments contained in the UNFCCC are discussed in more detail in the chapter on international law.[104]

Turning now to courts' application of these sources in practice, the Dutch Supreme Court in *Urgenda* has also provided the most extensive explanation of its interpretive method. The interpretive method itself, as well as the Dutch Supreme Court's sense of transparency in the process of establishing a legal duty with far-reaching implications, is indicative of emerging best practice.[105] Pursuant to Article 31(1) of the Vienna Convention on the Law of Treaties, the Court determined that the ECHR must be interpreted so as to render its provisions 'practical and effective' in light of its object and purpose as a treaty to protect individual human beings.[106] This required a consideration of 'the relevant rules of international law',[107] the practice of European States,[108] and 'scientific insights and generally

No 36 (n 20) [62]. See also Sarah Mead and Lucy Maxwell, 'Climate Change Litigation: National Courts as Agents of International Law Development' in Edgardo Sobenes, Sarah Mead, and Benjamin Samson (eds), *The Environment through the Lens of International Courts and Tribunals* (Asser 2022); Regarding best available science, see *Urgenda Supreme Court* (n 28) (referring to the reports of the IPCC at [4.4], [4.5], [7.2.1] and reports of the UN Environment Program at [4.6]). *Neubauer* (n 26) [16] and following referring to the IPCC; Joint Statement of Five UN Human Rights Treaty Bodies (n 20).

100 See Maxwell, Mead, and Van Berkel (n 31).

101 Benoit Mayer, 'Climate Change Mitigation as an Obligation Under Human Rights Treaties?' (2021) 115 AJIL 409.

102 The UNFCCC has 197 parties. Out of 197 Parties to the Convention, 191 are Parties to the Paris Agreement. See <https://treaties.un.org/>.

103 *Urgenda Supreme Court* (n 28) [5.7.3].

104 See Chapter 12 on International Law.

105 *Urgenda Supreme Court* (n 28) [5.6.3]; Cf Judgement in *Plan B Earth and Ors v Prime Minister and Ors* <https://climate-laws.org/geographies/united-kingdom/litigation_cases/plan-b-earth-and-others-v-prime-minister> [5] ('The fundamental difficulty which the Claimants face is that there is no authority from the European Court of Human Rights on which they can rely, citing the Paris Agreement as being relevant to the interpretation of the ECHR, arts 2 and 8.').

106 *Urgenda Supreme Court* (n 28) [5.4.1].

107 ibid [5.4.2].

108 ibid.

accepted standards'.[109] The Court's approach consciously reflected the ECtHR's 'common ground'[110] doctrine,[111] which enables the European court to interpret the Convention 'in the light of present day conditions' and on the basis that it is a 'living instrument'.[112] The common ground approach, furthermore, ensures that human rights instruments remain relevant in light of evolving threats to human rights. Accordingly, the Supreme Court then drew upon international law in a number of stages in its judgment, as we discuss later.[113]

Numerous other national courts have engaged closely with international law in adjudicating rights-based climate cases. The Lahore High Court stated in *Leghari* that '[o]ur environmental jurisprudence … has weaved our constitutional values and fundamental human rights with the international environmental principles'.[114] This built on the understanding of the court that:

> fundamental rights, like the right to life … which includes the right to a healthy and clean environment and right to human dignity … read with constitutional principles of democracy, equality, social, economic and political justice include within their ambit and commitment, the international environmental principles of sustainable development, precautionary principle, environmental impact assessment, inter and intra-generational equity and public trust doctrine. Environment and its protection has taken a center stage in the scheme of our constitutional rights. … The existing environmental jurisprudence has to be fashioned to meet the needs of something more urgent and overpowering i.e., Climate Change. From Environmental Justice, which was largely localized and limited to our own ecosystems and biodiversity, we need to move to Climate Change Justice. Fundamental rights lay at the foundation of these two overlapping justice systems. Right to life, right to human dignity, right to property and right to information … read with the constitutional values of political, economic and social justice provide the necessary judicial toolkit to address and monitor the Government's response to climate change.[115]

In *Milieudefensie v Shell*, the Hague District Court of the Netherlands extended this reasoning to corporations, finding that Royal Dutch Shell had an obligation under Dutch tort law to reduce its emissions in accordance with the long-term temperature goal enshrined in the Paris Agreement and in accordance with the best available scientific evidence as laid down in the reports of the Intergovernmental Panel on Climate Change (IPCC). Significantly, Shell's

[109] ibid [5.4.3].
[110] *Demir and Baykara v Turkey* App no 34503/97 (ECtHR, 12 November 2008).
[111] See *Urgenda Supreme Court* (n 28) [5.4.1]–[5.4.3] and [6.3]. For application of the method to the facts, see [7.2.1]–[7.2.11], in particular [7.2.11].
[112] ibid.
[113] See further Mead and Maxwell (n 99).
[114] *Asghar Leghari* (n 81) [20].
[115] ibid [7].

duty of care under Dutch tort law was construed in light of the rights to life and respect for private and family life, as enshrined in the ECHR and in the ICCPR. While recognising that these human rights treaties do not directly bind corporations, the Court highlighted 'the widespread international consensus that human rights offer protection against the impacts of dangerous climate change and that companies must respect human rights'.[116] The Court explicitly relied on the UN Guiding Principles on Business and Human Rights (UNGP) in its understanding of businesses' responsibilities to respect human rights, noting that since 2011, 'the European Commission has expected European businesses to meet their responsibilities to respect human rights, as formulated in the UNGP'.[117] For this reason, the UNGP 'are suitable as a guideline in the interpretation of the unwritten standard of care' contained in Dutch national law.[118] The Court's willingness to draw from these guidelines and other relevant human rights law can thus be considered an emerging best practice with respect to corporations' responsibilities to address the climate crisis.

In another rights-based case focused on both mitigation and adaptation, the Supreme Court of Colombia in *Future Generations* contributed to emerging best practice by drawing extensively upon principles of international law.[119] The Court outlined that its judgment would be guided by 'the legal environmental principles of (i) precaution; (ii) intergenerational equity; and (iii) solidarity' (the latter reflecting the 'no harm' principle of customary international law).[120] The Court then drew upon the precautionary principle in assessing the severity of the harm posed by climate change, and referred to the risk and irreversibility of the damage posed by climate change.[121] Citing the principle of intergenerational equity, the Court adopted a broad understanding of the persons and things to whom the State's duty to protect fundamental rights extends, including future generations and persons outside Colombia's borders:[122] 'In terms of intergenerational equity, the transgression is obvious', given that 'future generations, including the children who brought this action, will be directly affected, unless our present generation reduces the deforestation rate to zero'.[123] The Colombian State thereby has a 'co-responsibility' to protect the Amazon as a global resource, not only for Colombian people, but 'other people

[116] *Milieudefensie* (n 32) [4.1.3].

[117] ibid [4.4.11].

[118] ibid.

[119] *Demanda Futuras Generaciones* (n 38); Catalina Vallejo Piedrahíta and Siri Gloppen, 'The Quest for Butterfly Climate Adjudication' in César Rodríguez-Garavito (ed), *Litigating the Climate Emergency: How Human Rights, Courts, and Legal Mobilization Can Bolster Climate Action* (Cambridge University Press 2022) 128.

[120] *Demanda Futuras Generaciones* (n 38) [27].

[121] ibid [11.1].

[122] ibid [6.3], [6.4]. Danai Spentzou, 'Climate Change Litigation as a Means to Address Intergenerational Equity and Climate Change' (2021) 2 QMLJ 153, 168–169.

[123] *Demanda Futuras Generaciones* (n 38) [11.2].

who inhabit and share the Amazon [in] foreign territory' and the world's population in general,[124] on the basis of the solidarity principle. Finally, the Court found that the State's failure to reduce deforestation was inconsistent with its commitments under the Paris Agreement, which strengthened its finding regarding the State's violation of the claimants' constitutional rights.[125]

The views of the UN Committee on the Rights of the Child (CRC) in *Sacchi* also demonstrated the relevance of international environmental law in interpreting international human rights law. Citing the *Advisory Opinion OC-23/17* of the Inter-American Court of Human Rights, the Committee stated that the obligation to prevent transboundary environmental damage or harm is an obligation recognised by international environmental law, under which States may be held responsible for any significant damage caused to persons outside their borders by activities originating in their territory or under their effective control or authority.[126] The Committee also referenced the principles of intergenerational equity and the precautionary principle, as well as the Paris Agreement and the UNFCCC, as sources informing its interpretation of the Convention on the Rights of the Child.[127] This approach can be considered an emerging best practice, as the Committee not only emphasised the criticality of these environmental instruments and norms in ensuring children's rights but also suggested the potential of these agreements to inform the broader landscape of human rights law.[128]

### 7.4.2 *Impacts of Climate Change on Human Rights*

Emerging best practice in climate litigation also shows judicial recognition of the impacts of climate change on human rights, both in general and on particular groups. National[129] and regional[130] courts and UN human rights institutions[131] have

[124] ibid [10], [11.3]. See also Manuela Niehaus, 'Protecting Whose Children? The Rights of Future Generations in the Courts of Germany and Colombia' (*Völkerrechtsblog*, 23 March 2022) <https://voelkerrechtsblog.org/protecting-whose-children/> accessed 24 February 2024.

[125] *Demanda Futuras Generaciones* (n 38) [11], [11.3].

[126] *Sacchi* (n 20) 11.

[127] ibid; Aoife Nolan, 'Children's Rights and Climate Change at the UN Committee on the Rights of the Child: Pragmatism and Principle in *Sacchi v Argentina*' (*EJIL: Talk!*, 20 October 2021) <www.ejiltalk.org/childrens-rights-and-climate-change-at-the-un-committee-on-the-rights-of-the-child-pragmatism-and-principle-in-sacchi-v-argentina/> accessed 24 February 2024.

[128] See also Leslie-Anne Duvic-Paoli and Mario Gervasi, 'Harm to the Global Commons on Trial: The Role of the Prevention Principle in International Climate Adjudication' (2022) RECIEL 1, 4; Yusra Suedi, 'Litigating Climate Change before the Committee on the Rights of the Child in Sacchi v Argentina et al: Breaking New Ground?' (2022) 40(4) Nordic Journal of Human Rights 549.

[129] See *Urgenda Supreme Court* (n 28); *Neubauer* (n 26); *VZW Klimaatzaak Appeal* (n 27); *Leghari* (n 81); *Demanda Futuras Generaciones* (n 38); *Shrestha v Office of Council of Ministers* (n 43). See also Maxwell, Mead, and Van Berkel (n 31) 44 [footnote 59].

[130] See e.g. IACtHR OC-23/17 (n 20).

[131] ibid.

recognised that climate change is *already* having, and *will* have, a significant impact on the enjoyment of a wide range of human rights.

National courts, in particular, have repeatedly emphasised the far-reaching impacts of climate change on human rights. This emerging best practice is illustrated in several landmark decisions. For example, the court in *Leghari*, found that:

> Climate Change is a defining challenge of our time and has led to dramatic alternations in our planet's climate system. For Pakistan, these climatic variations have primarily resulted in heave floods and droughts, raising serious concerns regarding water and food security. On a legal and constitutional plane this is clarion call for the protection of fundamental rights of the citizens of Pakistan, in particular, the vulnerable and weak segments of the society who are unable to approach this Court.[132]

As a result, the Court emphasised that 'the delay and lethargy of the State in implementing [its climate policies] offends the fundamental rights of the citizens which need to be safeguarded'.[133] Similarly, the Dutch Supreme Court in *Urgenda* held that the harm posed by climate change triggered the State's obligations to protect the rights to life and to private and family life under the ECHR, in particular due to the precautionary principle.[134] According to the Court:

> The fact that this risk will only be able to materialise a few decades from now and that it will not impact specific persons or a specific group of persons but large parts of the population does not mean – contrary to the State's assertions – that Articles 2 and 8 ECHR offer no protection from this threat [...]. *This is consistent with the precautionary principle* ... The mere existence of a sufficiently genuine possibility that this risk will materialise means that suitable measures must be taken.[135]

The *Urgenda* decision has inspired plaintiffs in other jurisdictions to pursue more ambitious climate action from their governments. In many of these instances, courts in Europe have followed the Dutch courts' lead and relied on climate impacts on human rights in their decisions. For example, in *Klimaatzaak*, the Court of First Instance of Brussels in Belgium recognised that 'there can no longer be any doubt that there is a real threat of dangerous climate change with a direct negative effect on the daily lives of current and future generations of Belgium's inhabitants'.[136] In a recent decision, the Court of Appeal of Brussels affirmed this decision (and expanded on several aspects of the lower court's reasoning).[137] In *Neubauer*, the German Federal Constitutional Court highlighted that '[h]uman health is particularly vulnerable to climate change' and listed a range of ways in which health is

[132] *Asghar Leghari* (n 81) [6].
[133] ibid [8].
[134] *Urgenda Supreme Court* (n 28) [5.3.2].
[135] ibid [5.6.2] (emphasis added).
[136] *VZW Klimaatzaak v l'État Belge* [2021] 2015/4585/A, 61 (Tribunal de première instance francophone de Bruxelles, Section Civile) (*VZW Klimaatzaak First Instance*).
[137] *VZW Klimaatzaak Appeal* (n 27).

impacted by climate change. Apart from impacting physical health, these climate impacts 'can increase social and psychological pressures and trigger disorders such as stress, anxiety attacks and depression'.[138]

Shifting focus to the regional and international level, five UN treaty bodies have recognised, in a joint statement, that 'climate change poses significant risks to the enjoyment of the human rights', including 'the right to life, the right to adequate food, the right to adequate housing, the right to health, the right to water and cultural rights'.[139] The health impacts of climate change were given specific attention by the Inter-American Court of Human Rights in its advisory opinion,[140] and by the UN CRC in *Sacchi v Argentina*. The UN CRC, in particular, gave serious thought to the disproportionate impact of climate change on children as a group. In its deliberation, the Committee highlighted that as children, the authors were particularly impacted by the adverse effects of climate change. This impact arises not just from the unique ways in which they already experience these effects but also from the increasingly serious long-term impact climate change could have on them, particularly if immediate action is not taken.[141] Building on this, and noting the explicit recognition by State parties to the Convention that children are entitled to special safeguards, including appropriate legal protection, it found that States have heightened obligations to protect children from foreseeable harm resulting from climate change.[142] This finding more broadly suggests that States are obliged to take urgent, proactive measures to ensure the rights of vulnerable groups who are disproportionately impacted by climate change.

Judicial emphasis on climate impacts and the human rights of Indigenous Peoples also emerges from the UN Human Rights Committee's views in the case *Billy et al v Australia*. The communication was filed by eight First Nations Peoples and their children, who are nationals of Australia and residents of the Torres Strait region (islands to the north of Australia). The authors alleged that the measures (or lack thereof) adopted by Australia with respect to both mitigation and adaptation were insufficient to protect their rights to life (Article 6 ICCPR) and respect for family and home (Article 17 ICCPR) and their cultural rights (Article 27 ICCPR) (among others) from the impacts caused by climate change, in particularly due to sea level rise. In its decision, the Committee focused upon the conduct of Australia with respect to adaptation, finding that there was 'delay in seawall construction with respect to the islands where the authors live',[143] that climate change had led to a 'reduction of marine resources used for food, and the loss of crops and fruit

[138] *Neubauer* (n 26) [23].
[139] See Joint Statement of Five UN Human Rights Treaty Bodies (n 20). See also CCPR General Comment No 36 (n 20) [62].
[140] IACtHR OC-23/17 (n 20).
[141] *Sacchi* (n 20) [10.13].
[142] ibid.
[143] *Billy* (n 20) [8.12].

trees',[144] and that the authors 'experience anxiety and distress owing to erosion that is approaching some homes in their communities'[145] and gave evidence that 'their lives have been adversely affected by flooding and inundation of their villages and ancestral burial lands'.[146] On this basis, the Committee concluded that:

> the State party's failure to adopt timely adequate adaptation measures to protect the authors' collective ability to maintain their traditional way of life, to transmit to their children and future generations their culture and traditions and use of land and sea resources discloses a violation of the State party's positive obligation to protect the authors' right to enjoy their minority culture. Accordingly, the Committee considers that the facts before it amount to a violation of the authors' rights under article 27 of the Covenant.[147]

The Committee reached a similar finding with respect to the right to respect to family and home (Article 17 ICCPR). It did not uphold the alleged violation of the rights to life (Article 6 ICCPR), and did not consider it necessary to assess the other alleged violations.

By way of orders, the Committee outlined Australia's obligation to provide the authors with an 'effective remedy' (under Article 2(3)(a) ICCPR), which it indicated requires Australia to:

> provide adequate compensation, to the authors for the harm that they have suffered; engage in meaningful consultations with the authors' communities in order to conduct needs assessments; continue its implementation of measures necessary to secure the communities' continued safe existence on their respective islands; and monitor and review the effectiveness of the measures implemented and resolve any deficiencies as soon as practicable.[148]

The Committee's views also suggest that the forced relocation of Indigenous Peoples due to the impact of climate change may constitute a violation of their rights under the ICCPR.[149] This decision highlights the need for affirmative measures to ensure the rights of Indigenous Peoples and other vulnerable groups who are disproportionately affected by climate impacts.

In addition to the developments in climate litigation outlined earlier, the Philippines Human Rights Commission's report on the Carbon Majors inquiry documented a range of human rights violations caused by climate change.[150]

144 ibid.
145 ibid.
146 ibid.
147 ibid [8.14].
148 ibid [11].
149 ibid [4.8]. Sarah Joseph, 'Climate Change and the Torres Strait Islands: UN Condemns Australia' (*Law Future Centre*, 26 September 2022) <https://blogs.griffith.edu.au/law-futures-centre/2022/09/26/climate-change-and-the-torres-strait-islands-un-condemns-australia/> accessed 24 February 2024.
150 *In re Greenpeace Southeast Asia* (n 15).

In relation to the Carbon Majors' assertion that the Commission lacked jurisdiction to investigate their responsibility for climate change-related human rights violations, the Commission stated: 'Stripped of legal niceties, the contentious issue was that our Commission, or, indeed the Philippine State … may only inquire into the conduct of corporate entities operating within Philippine territory, even if the corporations' operations outside our territory were negatively impacting the rights and lives of our people. We cannot accept such a proposition.'[151] Thus, based on the Commission's constitutional mandate 'to investigate and inquire into allegations of human rights violations suffered by our people', the Commission found that it had jurisdiction, and the communication was admissible.[152] The Commission further made important findings on non-economic losses, stating how climate change impacts 'dehumanise' the human person as 'the combination of loss of lives, deprivation of basic needs, material loss, emotional trauma and hopelessness that these survivors experience strip them of their dignities'.[153]

The inquiry's findings reflect evidence from survivors of Super Typhoon Haiyan, one of the strongest storms ever recorded.[154] For example, one individual recounted how 'one moment people were reaching above the water, fighting for their lives, and the next moment, they were gone'.[155] The Commission found that these human rights impacts were directly linked to the conduct of the Carbon Majors, which are not only responsible for the lion's share of atmospheric emissions but also 'engaged in wilful obfuscation of the climate science, which has prejudiced the right of the public to make informed decisions about their products'.[156] This responsibility for climate change and related human rights impacts gave rise to a duty to 'provide for or cooperate in the remediation of those impacts';[157] an obligation which extends to 'all business enterprises in each of the Carbon Majors' respective value chains'.[158] Furthermore, the Commission recommended that States 'fulfil climate finance commitments and device new mechanisms for loss and damage from climate change-related events' including to 'compensate victims'.[159]

All in all, the inquiry as a whole can be viewed as a form of emerging best practice as it has generated the world's largest and most comprehensive body of formal eyewitness and expert testimonies, documentary evidence, and legal analysis relating to responsibility for climate loss and damage, with the report synthesising and

[151] ibid 4.
[152] ibid.
[153] ibid 32.
[154] Meagan Singer, '2013 State of the Climate: Record-Breaking Super Typhoon Haiyan' (Climate.gov, 13 July 2014) <www.climate.gov/news-features/understanding-climate/2013-state-climate-record-breaking-super-typhoon-haiyan> accessed 24 February 2024.
[155] *In re Greenpeace Southeast Asia* (n 15) 34.
[156] ibid 98.
[157] ibid 113.
[158] ibid.
[159] ibid 124; 121.

drawing normative conclusions from these sources. While the report as such is not binding, the Commission's analysis could inspire courts around the world to address questions of responsibility for loss and damage through the lens of human rights. Moreover, it is likely to inspire further development of cases focused on the responsibility of private actors such as fossil fuel companies for contributing to climate change-related loss and damage. The report itself indicates an emerging recognition of the need for reparations and compensation for loss and damage suffered because of climate change, and suggests that the legal landscape for climate justice is gradually shifting.

In summary, emerging jurisprudence in climate litigation and the recognition of the impacts of climate change on human rights demonstrate a growing understanding that climate change is not only an environmental problem but also a human rights issue. This understanding has important legal implications. As the following sections will show, judges around the world are starting to clarify and enforce human rights obligations relating to climate change so that human rights are effectively protected in the face of climate change.

### 7.4.3 *Recognition of the State's Obligations in the Context of Climate Change*

On the basis of the harm posed by climate change, courts and UN treaty bodies have recognised that States must adopt a wide range of actions in order to protect human rights.[160] This position reflects emerging best practice as it demonstrates an understanding of the ambition necessary to address the expansive nature of climate change within the human rights sphere.

One can find this emerging best practice in the 2019 UN joint statement on human rights and climate change referenced in the previous subsection.[161] The statement is significant as it comes from five different treaty bodies with an interest in human rights: the Committee on the Elimination of Discrimination against Women, the Committee on Economic, Social and Cultural Rights, the Committee on the Protection of the Rights of All Migrant Workers and Members of Their Families, the CRC, and the Committee on the Rights of Persons with Disabilities. The obligation is articulated as follows:

> Failure to take measures to prevent foreseeable harm to human rights caused by climate change, or to regulate activities contributing to such harm, could constitute a violation of States' human rights obligations. In order for States to comply with their human rights obligations, and to realize the objectives of the Paris

[160] Kumaravadivel Guruparan and Harriet Moynihan, 'Climate Change and Human Rights-Based Strategic Litigation' (*Chatham House*, November 2021) <www.chathamhouse.org/2021/11/climate-change-and-human-rights-based-strategic-litigation/introduction> accessed 27 February 2024.

[161] Joint Statement of Five UN Human Rights Treaty Bodies (n 20).

> Agreement, they must adopt and implement policies aimed at reducing emissions, which reflect the highest possible ambition, foster climate resilience and ensure that public and private investments are consistent with a pathway towards low carbon emissions and climate resilient development.[162]

The statement, moreover, outlines developed countries' human rights obligations with respect to providing financial aid to developing States. This includes, '[a]s part of international assistance and cooperation towards the realization of human rights', support for 'adaptation and mitigation efforts in developing countries by facilitating transfers of green technologies and by contributing to financing climate mitigation and adaptation'.[163]

As discussed earlier, the UN Human Rights Committee's views in the case *Billy et al v Australia* represent emerging best practice with respect to the obligations of States regarding climate change adaptation.

UN treaty bodies have also analysed States' human rights obligations regarding the use of fossil fuel reserves,[164] including as part of dialogues with States during their periodic reviews. For example, in 2020, the Committee on Economic Social and Cultural Rights recommended that Norway 'reconsider its decision to increase oil and natural gas exploitation and take its human rights obligations as a primary consideration into its natural resource exploitation and export policies'.[165]

At the domestic level, several national courts have articulated States' human rights obligations regarding climate change mitigation through GHG emissions reductions.[166] For instance, in *Urgenda*, the Dutch Supreme Court found that 'no other conclusion can be drawn but that the State is required pursuant to the rights to life and to private and family life under Articles 2 and 8 ECHR to take measures to counter the genuine threat of dangerous climate change',[167] and that such measures must be 'reasonable and suitable', and consistent with 'due diligence'.[168] The Court held that the State had an *individual* responsibility to mitigate climate change based on its commitments under the UNFCCC, the '*no harm*' principle contained therein, and principles of proportionate liability under international and national law. The Court also drew on provisions of the UNFCCC and the Paris Agreement – including the principles of equity and common but

162 ibid [10]–[11].
163 ibid [17].
164 See Mckernan and others (n 20).
165 ibid 13.
166 Note that, in addition to the *Neubauer* and *Urgenda* cases, the recent decision of the Brussels Court of Appeal in the *VZW Klimaatzaak* case in November 2023 is another significant articulation of States' mitigation obligations pursuant to human rights law (there, the ECHR). However, it falls outside the cut-off period for inclusion in this chapter.
167 *Urgenda Supreme Court* (n 28) [5.6.2].
168 ibid. This was also the conclusion of the Court in *VZW Klimaatzaak First Instance* (n 136). It was affirmed by the Brussels Court of Appeal in *VZW Klimaatzaak Appeal* (n 27).

differentiated responsibilities and respective capacities (CBDR-RC) – to formulate the State's duty to contribute its '*fair share*' of global emissions reductions,[169] as follows:[170] 'The UNFCCC is based on the idea that climate change is a global problem that needs to be solved globally. Where emissions of greenhouse gases take place from the territories of all countries and all countries are affected, measures will have to be taken by all countries. Therefore, all countries will have to do the necessary.'[171] Likewise, the German Constitutional Court in *Neubauer* analysed the alleged failure of the State to reduce GHG emissions in the short-term as a potential violation of the State's obligation to protect the constitutional rights to life and health (among others), as well as its obligation to refrain from disproportionately restricting the plaintiffs' constitutional freedoms through future drastic GHG emission reductions. The Court determined that, pursuant to existing constitutional jurisprudence, '[t]he state's duty of protection [of fundamental rights] … includes the duty to protect life and health against the risks posed by climate change'.[172] The Court ultimately upheld the plaintiffs' challenge on the basis that the legislator's proposed reduction of GHG emissions violated the plaintiffs' fundamental freedoms by effectively offloading the burden to reduce emissions onto future generations.[173]

Other important mitigation cases concern the protection of carbon sinks, most notably forests, or other ecosystems essential to climate protection. Perhaps the most well-known success in this category is *Future Generations*, in which the Supreme Court of Colombia granted the youth plaintiffs an order on the Government of Colombia to formulate and implement an 'intergenerational pact for the life of the Colombian Amazon' to adopt measures aimed at reducing deforestation and GHG emissions to zero.[174] And in *Sheikh Asim Farooq v Federation of Pakistan etc.*, the Lahore High Court granted an order requesting the Government of Pakistan to adopt steps to increase the forest cover to 20–25 per cent in order to achieve a balanced economy.[175] Further, in *Pro Public*, the petitioners sought an order declaring the Godavari area as a prohibited area for mineral activities and to establish the area as an Environmental Protection Area pursuant to national laws. The Court agreed on the first count while ruling on the second count that a committee be established to determine if a designation of the area as protected is appropriate.[176]

169 See ibid [6.3] and [6.5] on the 'fair share'.
170 ibid [5.7.1].
171 ibid [5.7.2].
172 *Neubauer* (n 26). The court did not find a breach of the duty to protect, but did find that the manner in which the legislator had discharged this duty violated fundamental freedoms by offloading the burden to reduce emission onto future generations.
173 See further Petra Minnerop, 'The First German Climate Case' (2020) 22(3) ELR 215.
174 *Demanda Futuras Generaciones* (n 38).
175 *Sheikh Asim Farooq v Federation of Pakistan etc* WP No 192069/2018 (Lahore High Court).
176 *Pro Public* (n 30).

Crucially, in all of these instances, national courts and UN treaty bodies have determined that States' human rights obligation exists *notwithstanding* that climate change is a global problem, which cannot be solved by any individual country.[177] The Dutch Supreme Court in *Urgenda*, for instance, determined that the State must do 'its part' in order to prevent dangerous climate change, and expressly rejected the State's defence that its emissions were negligible in absolute terms. The German Constitutional Court in *Neubauer* similarly found: 'The fact that the German state is incapable of halting climate change on its own and is reliant upon international involvement because of climate change's global impact and the global nature of its causes does not, in principle, rule out the possibility of a duty of protection arising from fundamental rights.'[178] Finally, on the issue of States' human rights obligations regarding climate-induced displacement, emerging best practice can be distilled from the UN Human Rights Committee's views on *Teitiota v New Zealand*. As discussed earlier, this case resulted from New Zealand's denial to grant asylum to the author despite his assertions that climate change had made his home country, Kiribati, uninhabitable. In the case before the UN Human Rights Committee, the author sought a declaration that his right to life had been violated because of this denial and his subsequent deportation to Kiribati.[179] To support this claim, the author presented evidence that sea level rise in Kiribati resulting from climate change had created scarcity of habitable space, resulting in violent land disputes, and environmental degradation including saltwater contamination of the freshwater supply.

While the Human Rights Committee did not find a violation of the author's rights, it did make an important pronouncement that represents emerging best practice. That is, States can incur international responsibility for returning individuals who face life-threatening climate impacts in their home States.[180] As Committee member Laki points out, this recognition reflects 'a significant step … toward the recognition of climate refugees, especially as regards *non refoulement* obligations under human rights law and the ICCPR' while also highlighting the importance of international assistance to States adversely affected by climate change.[181] The decision could therefore serve as a stepping-stone for the realisation of the right to a remedy for those who have suffered climate losses.[182]

177 See cases referred to in Maxwell, Mead, and Van Berkel (n 32) 45.

178 *Neubauer* (n 26) [149], [199]–[202]. Note that these issues intersect with other critical areas of climate litigation. See Chapters 13, 15, and 16 on Common but Differentiated Responsibilities and Respective Capabilities, State Responsibility, and Causation, respectively.

179 *Teitiota* (n 20).

180 ibid [9.14].

181 Duncan Muhumuza Laki, 'The Case of Ioane Teitiota v New Zealand at the Human Rights Committee: A Common-Sense Approach' (2022) Proceedings of the ASIL Annual Meeting 162.

182 See further 'Historic UN Human Rights Case Opens Door to Climate Change Asylum Claims' (*OHCHR*, 21 Jan 2020) <www.ohchr.org/EN/NewsEvents/Pages/DisplayNews.aspx?NewsID=25482> (quoting Human Right Committee expert Yuval Shany as saying 'this ruling sets forth new standards that could facilitate the success of future climate change-related asylum claims').

## 7.5 REPLICABILITY

Replicability stands as a pivotal concern in the evolution of the field of rights-based climate litigation. The core question with regard to replicability is to what extent and how the legal principles and reasoning developed in one jurisdiction can be replicated in others, and to what extent they are context- or jurisdiction-specific.

An analysis of existing judicial practice suggests that rights-based reasoning can often be replicated across jurisdictions. The *Urgenda* decision from the Dutch courts serves as a quintessential illustration. Since the first decision in 2015, courts around the world have relied upon the principles established in the *Urgenda* decisions within their own climate case adjudications. This includes judiciaries in France, Belgium, Germany, and Ireland recognising a number of the central tenets of the *Urgenda* decisions. In every instance, the courts found that the State had failed to comply with its legal obligations and that existing legal standards and scientific evidence could be used to assess compliance. These cases follow earlier decisions of the Supreme Courts in Nepal and Colombia, which applied similar principles and found the States in breach of their human rights obligations.

Further instances of replicability of rights-based reasoning across jurisdictions include the *Leghari* decision in Pakistan, which has been cited in courts in Brazil and the Philippines.[183] The decision of the UN Human Rights Committee in the case of *Teitiota v New Zealand* has also been cited in a number of subsequent cases, including by the Administrative Court of Paris in its decision in *Grande-Synthe v France*,[184] while the Supreme Court of Norway has cited the *Urgenda* decision in *People v Arctic Oil*.[185] These examples demonstrate that the principles established in one jurisdiction can be applied and relied upon in other jurisdictions, and thereby contribute to the development of a consistent and coherent body of international climate law.

At the same time, judges have found it important to highlight certain differences between jurisdictions and have insisted that legal principles and reasoning may need to be adapted to the specific legal and social context. For example, in the Philippines, the Human Rights Commission's report on the Carbon Majors inquiry found that the specific historical and social context of the country, including its high vulnerability to climate change impacts, made it necessary to develop a distinct approach to rights-based climate litigation.[186] Similarly, the *Billy et al v Australia* case before

[183] See *Institute of Amazonian Studies v Brazil* <http://climatecasechart.com/non-us-case/institute-of-amazonian-studies-v-brazil/> accessed 24 February 2024; *In re Greenpeace Southeast Asia* (n 15); Joana Setzer and Délton Winter de Carvalho, 'Climate Litigation to Protect the Brazilian Amazon: Establishing a Constitutional Right to a Stable Climate' (2021) RECIEL 197, 203.

[184] See *Luca Salis et al v State of Sachsen-Anhalt* <http://climatecasechart.com/non-us-case/luca-salis-et-al-v-state-of-sachsen-anhalt/> accessed 24 February 2024.

[185] *Greenpeace Nordic* (n 20).

[186] *In re Greenpeace Southeast Asia* (n 15).

the UN Human Rights Committee raised specific issues relating to the impacts of climate change on Indigenous Peoples in Australia, which required a nuanced analysis of the legal principles and standards applicable to the case.[187] These examples suggest that although the core legal principles and reasoning developed in one jurisdiction are often replicable, it is nevertheless important for judges to consider the specific legal and social context of each case and adapt their reasoning accordingly.

Furthermore, the replicability of rights-based reasoning is not limited to climate litigation alone. Lessons learned from the application of rights-based reasoning in climate cases can be applied to other areas of law, such as biodiversity and environmental protection. The recognition of the interconnectedness of human rights and the environment has the potential to shape legal practice in other areas of law and contribute to the development of a more holistic and integrated approach to environmental protection.

In conclusion, the replicability of rights-based reasoning across jurisdictions is a crucial factor in the development of a consistent and coherent body of 'transnational' climate law. While appreciating the nuances inherent in differing legal and social contexts, the application of fundamental legal principles and reasoning can catalyse a more comprehensive and integrated approach towards climate change mitigation and adaptation.

## 7.6 CONCLUSION

Rights-based climate litigation has emerged as a crucial instrument in holding States and corporations accountable for their respective human rights obligations in the face of climate change. The recognition of the intricate link between human rights and climate change has progressively permeated institutional frameworks, leading to its invocation of human rights in climate litigation at the national, regional, and international levels. An increasingly substantial body of legal precedent now underscores the potential of litigation to drive climate action while safeguarding human rights.

This chapter has provided a comprehensive and discerning overview of prevailing trends and emerging best practices in rights-based climate litigation. We reviewed the diverse subjects, fora, and remedies involved in such cases. Although jurisdictional disparities exist, the growing corpus of jurisprudence demonstrates the adaptability and replicability of rights-based reasoning, thereby contributing to the establishment of a consistent and coherent framework for 'transnational' climate law.

The expanding body of jurisprudence in rights-based climate litigation, alongside the ongoing refinement of the interplay between climate change and human rights, underscores the vital role played by courts and tribunals in holding

[187] *Billy* (n 20).

governments and corporations accountable for their actions – or lack thereof – in addressing the climate crisis. As judicial bodies assume this critical role, they also shape the evolution of climate law, both within individual jurisdictions and across borders. We hope that the roadmap presented in this chapter will be leveraged to further enhance the legal robustness and efficacy of rights-based climate litigation, ensuring that it continues to drive meaningful change while safeguarding human rights.

# 8

# Extraterritoriality

*Mark Gibney**

## 8.1 INTRODUCTION

There are at least two ways in which 'territory' plays an essential role in issues related to climate change. The first involves the *Trail Smelter* principle,[1] reaffirmed in Principle 21 of the Stockholm Declaration,[2] which requires states to ensure that activities within their territory and control do not cause damage to those who are outside their borders. This case revolved around smelter factories in Canada that were emitting pollutants which landed in the United States (US). In response, the US brought a case against Canada and was successful in an arbitration hearing. According to the Tribunal:

> under the principles of international law, as well as the law of the United States, no State has the right to use or permit the use of its territory in such a manner as to cause injury by fumes in or to the territory of another or the properties or persons therein, when the case is of serious consequence and the injury is established by clear and convincing evidence.[3]

At first glance, applying the reasoning presented in Trail Smelter to greenhouse gas (GHG) emissions might seem a natural extension of the principle. There are, however, key differences between the localised pollution in Trail Smelter and GHG emissions that complicate the step. Not only does every country produce GHG, albeit at vastly different levels, but all states have already been

* Mark Gibney is the Belk Distinguished Professor of Humanities and Professor of Political Science at the University of North Carolina-Asheville.

[1] *Trail Smelter (US v Canada)* (1938) 3 RIAA 1905.

[2] UNEP 'Declaration of the United Nations Conference on the Human Environment' (1972) UN Doc A/CONF/48/14 (Stockholm Declaration) principle 21 'States have, in accordance with the Charter of the United Nations and the principles of international law, the sovereign right to exploit their own resources pursuant to their own environmental policies, and the responsibility to ensure that activities within their jurisdiction or control do not cause damage to the environment of other States or of areas beyond the limits of national jurisdiction'.

[3] *Trail Smelter* (n 1).

negatively affected by ever-increasing levels of carbon dioxide and methane in the atmosphere. Furthermore, while the pollutants in *Trail Smelter* could be traced back to the operation of the smelter plants in Canada, there is much less certainty with GHG emissions. Or to use a concrete example, and as a reversal of the *Trail Smelter* situation, the GHG emissions now harming Canadian citizens are not only produced within Canada but from any number of other countries, including the US.[4]

The second way in which 'territory' plays an important role in relation to climate litigation is with respect to the scope of human rights obligations. Although human rights are declared to be 'universal', the dominant interpretation of international human rights law has been 'territorial' in scope, which is to say that a state's obligations extend only as far as its own national borders. There are two main reasons for this reading of international human rights law. The first is the international law principle that states are to honour the sovereignty of other states. In that way, a state that seeks to protect the human rights of the citizens of another state might be viewed as interfering with the sovereignty of that other state.

The second reason for the predominance of the 'territorial' interpretation of international human rights law comes from the language of the law itself. Nearly all human rights instruments make reference to either 'territory' or 'jurisdiction', and oftentimes both. One example is the International Covenant on Civil and Political Rights (ICCPR), which provides: 'Each State Party to the present Covenant undertakes to respect and to ensure to all individuals within its *territory* and subject to its *jurisdiction* the rights recognized in the present Covenant ....'.[5] Yet, even human rights treaties that make no mention of either 'territory' or 'jurisdiction' – for example, the International Covenant on Economic, Social and Cultural Rights (ICESCR)[6] – are commonly interpreted in a 'territorial' manner.

One of the biggest hurdles facing courts is that while climate change is extraterritorial in the sense that GHG emissions do not respect national borders, both domestic and international law are generally tethered to national territory. As John Knox, the first Independent Expert (and later Special Rapporteur) on Human Rights and the Environment, has pointed out:

> The more fundamental problem with applying environmental human rights principles to climate change is that the principles were developed primarily to address environmental harm that does not cross international borders. Almost all

4 Among her list of transboundary cases, Maria Banda makes reference to a report that over 50 percent of the air pollution in the Province of Ontario – and more than 90 percent in some municipalities – originates in the United States. Maria L. Banda, 'Regime Congruence: Rethinking the Scope of State Responsibility for Transboundary Environmental Harm' (2019) 103 Minnesota Law Review 1879.

5 International Covenant on Civil and Political Rights (entered into force 23 March 1976) 999 UNTS 171 (ICCPR) art 2(1).

6 International Covenant on Economic, Social and Cultural Rights (entered into force 3 January 1976) 993 UNTS 3 (ICESCR).

of the regional jurisprudence, in particular, arises from cases in which the benefits and costs of the environmental harm are felt within the domestic jurisdiction of one State.[7]

Perhaps not surprisingly, a substantial portion of the climate change cases to date have been 'domestic' or 'internal' in the sense that they involve citizens of one state bringing a suit against their own government seeking a judicial order to reduce GHG emissions. *Urgenda* is typical of this approach.[8] In this case a group of Dutch citizens and civil society organisations brought a suit against the government of the Netherlands, and in a landmark ruling the Supreme Court ordered the Dutch government to reduce its GHG emissions. Thus, for all its novelty and the important role it has played as a legal precedent, *Urgenda* is consistent with a 'territorial' reading of international human rights law.

The present chapter explores how, based on emerging best practice, courts may be able to go beyond the traditional, territorial understanding and grapple with the 'extraterritorial' aspects of climate change that have arisen in litigation to date. Noting the 'grave threats' to the enjoyment of human rights due to transboundary environmental harm, Knox acknowledges the necessity of addressing climate change from a transnational perspective, but also the uncertainty that may arise in this context. 'There is no obvious reason why a State should not bear responsibility for actions that otherwise would violate its human rights obligations, merely because the harm was felt beyond its borders. Nevertheless, the application of human rights obligations to transboundary environmental harm is not always clear.'[9] Judicial practice can play a critical role in reducing this uncertainty and clarify states' obligations in the context of advisory proceedings or dispute settlements.

## 8.2 THE EXTRATERRITORIAL DIMENSION

Section 8.2 is divided into three sub-sections broken down by geographic scope. The first sub-section (Section 8.2.1) provides examples of how *domestic* courts have addressed various extraterritorial issues. The second sub-section (Section 8.2.2) focuses on *regional* human rights institutions, with a particular focus on the 2017 Advisory Opinion of the Inter-American Court of Human Rights (IACtHR). The third and final sub-section (Section 8.2.3) moves the analysis to the *international* plane by examining how the International Court of Justice (ICJ) has approached transnational environmental claims.

7 John Knox, 'Human Rights Principles and Climate Change' (2014) Wake Forest University Legal Studies Paper No 2523599, 9.

8 *State of the Netherlands (Ministry of Economic Affairs and Climate Policy) v Stichting Urgenda* [2019] ECLI:NL:HR: 2019:2007 (Supreme Court of the Netherlands) (*Urgenda Supreme Court*).

9 UN Human Rights Council, 'Report of the Independent Expert on the issue of human rights obligations relating to the enjoyment of a safe, clean, healthy and sustainable environment' (30 December 2013) UN Doc A/HRC/25/53 [63].

### 8.2.1 *Domestic*

As the term indicates, 'extraterritorial' refers to something that occurs outside of a state's own national borders. Yet, extraterritorial issues can arise in a number of ways. The present section provides examples of how domestic courts in three countries – Germany, the Netherlands, and Norway – have addressed different kinds of extraterritorial issues. *Neubauer et al v Germany* involves a situation where foreign nationals brought a claim against a state other than their own. In *Milieudefensie and Others v Royal Dutch Shell*, while the claimants are all citizens of one state, the judicial order applies domestically as well as internationally. Finally, *People v Arctic Oil* addresses the issue of whether a state's responsibility to protect the environment is to be limited to the GHG emissions produced domestically or if it should include extraterritorial emissions as well.

#### 8.2.1.1 Foreign Plaintiffs

*Neubauer*[10] is a case brought by a group of German citizens, joined by claimants from Bangladesh and Nepal, against the German state on the grounds that the government's reduction target of 55 per cent by the year 2030 will be insufficient to stay within the country's carbon budget, thereby necessitating the adoption of drastic measures that would violate the fundamental freedoms of all Germans alive in 2030 and thereafter. Taking an intergenerational approach, the Federal Constitutional Court held that: 'one generation must not be allowed to consume large portions of the $CO_2$ budget while bearing a relatively minor share of the reduction effort, if this would involve leaving subsequent generations with a drastic reduction burden and expose their lives to serious losses of freedom'.[11] The Court ordered the legislature to set clear reduction targets from 2031 onward to the end of 2022. And in response to the ruling, federal lawmakers passed new legislation that requires, at a minimum, a reduction of 65 per cent in GHG emissions from 1990 levels by 2030.

Aside from the result itself, the most noteworthy aspect of *Neubauer* is that the Nepalese and Bangladeshi plaintiffs were given standing. The Court did draw a distinction, however, between the German and foreign claimants. Because the state's breach stemmed from the restrictive measures that would be needed to drastically reduce Germany's GHG emissions, as opposed to the impacts of climate change generally, the Court concluded that the complainants living in Bangladesh and Nepal would not be affected in their own freedoms in the same way as German citizens. According to the Court:

[10] *Neubauer and Others v Germany* [2021] 1 BvR 2656/18, 1 BvR 96/20, 1 BvR 78/20, 1 BvR 288/20, 1 BvR 96/20, 1 BvR 78/20 (German Federal Constitutional Court) (*Neubauer*).

[11] ibid [192].

> The situation is different with regard to the complainants ... who live in Bangladesh and in Nepal. They are not individually affected in this respect. In their case, it can be ruled out from the outset that a violation of their fundamental freedoms might arise from potentially being exposed someday to extremely onerous climate action measures because the German legislator [sic] is presently allowing excessive amounts of greenhouse gas emissions with the result that even stricter measures would then have to be taken in Germany in the future. The complainants ... live in Bangladesh and Nepal and are thus not subject to such measures.[12]

In addition, the Court drew a distinction between adaptation measures undertaken in Germany as opposed to those the German government might attempt to take elsewhere:

> With regard to people living abroad, the German state would not have the same options at its disposal for taking any additional protective action. Given the limits of German sovereignty under international law, it is practically impossible for the German state to afford protection to people living abroad by implementing adaptation measures there. Rather it is the task of the states concerned to select and implement the necessary measures.[13]

While this reading of international law is certainly correct, it leaves the question open as to whether, if Nepal, Bangladesh, and other states harmed by German GHG emissions were to demand assistance in the form of adaptation measures or otherwise, Germany would have a legal obligation to provide it.[14]

#### 8.2.1.2 Extraterritorial Judicial Orders

*Milieudefensie*,[15] handed down by the Hague District Court in 2021, illustrates a different kind of extraterritorial issue. In the aftermath of *Urgenda*, a group of civil society organisations filed suit against Royal Dutch Shell (RDS), a Dutch-based multinational corporation. The District Court ruled in favour of the plaintiffs and ordered a 45 per cent reduction of the company's GHG emissions by 2030 against 2019 levels.

In some respects, *Milieudefensie* is a classic 'domestic' case. The plaintiffs consisted of several Dutch civil society organisations, while the court excluded ActionAid (an international non-governmental organisation) from the proceedings on the grounds that its activities were not wholly geared toward Dutch citizens and interests. The court explained its position:

[12] ibid [132].
[13] ibid [178].
[14] This obligation exists in principle under Article 4(4) of the United Nations Framework Convention on Climate Change. See United Nations Framework Convention on Climate Change (entered into force 19 June 1993) 1771 UNTS 107 (UNFCCC) art 4(4).
[15] *Milieudefensie v Royal Dutch Shell* [2021] ECLR:NL: RBDHA: 2021:5339 (District Court of the Hague).

> The court is of the opinion that the interests of current and future generations of the world's population, as served principally with the class actions, is not suitable for bundling. Although the entire world population is served by curbing dangerous climate change, there are huge differences in the time and manner in which the global population at various locations will be affected by global warming caused by $CO_2$ emissions. Therefore, this principal interest does not meet the requirement of 'similar interest' under [Dutch law].[16]

In addition to the Dutch claimants, the defendant, RDS, is a Dutch-based multinational corporation. Thus, all of the parties involved are Dutch. This raises the question of whether the court would have arrived at a similar result if suit had also been brought against a foreign corporation, such as Total (France) or Exxon (US), two oil companies that conduct a considerable amount of business in the Netherlands and elsewhere.

Leaving this issue aside, for the purposes of our present discussion, the most noteworthy aspect of this case is that the court's order applied not only to RDS's operations within the Netherlands but the company's entire worldwide operations. Furthermore, the order applied not only to RDS's own emissions, but the emissions from the use by other entities of the oil RDS produces. The ruling therefore raises the additional question of whether the Dutch District Court – or any domestic court for that matter – can monitor and enforce a decree with such extraterritorial applications.

#### 8.2.1.3 Extraterritorial GHG Emissions

*Arctic Oil*,[17] decided by the Norwegian Supreme Court in late December 2020, presents yet another type of extraterritorial issue. The plaintiffs consisted of various environmental groups challenging oil drilling licences that had been issued by the Norwegian government in 2013 on the grounds that such actions violated Article 112(1) of the Norwegian Constitution, which provides: 'Every person has the right to an environment that is conducive to health and to a natural environment whose productivity and diversity are maintained. Natural resources shall be managed on the basis of comprehensive long-term considerations which will safeguard this right for future generations as well.' By way of background, Norway's GHG emissions, at least domestically, are relatively small.[18] In addition, under the Norwegian Climate Act of 2017, the government is legally obligated to achieve a 40 per cent reduction of GHG emissions by the year 2030. On the other hand, as the third largest exporter of

[16] ibid [4.2.3].

[17] *Greenpeace Nordic Association v Ministry of Petroleum and Energy* (2020) Case no 20-051052SIV-HRET (Norwegian Supreme Court) (*People v Arctic Oil*).

[18] See generally Christina Voigt, 'The First Climate Change Judgment before the Norwegian Supreme Court: Aligning Law with *Politics*' (2021) 33 JEL 697.

natural gas and the fifteenth largest oil exporter, Norway's GHG emission footprint is enormous, and it is estimated that emissions resulting from exported petroleum are 95 *per cent higher* than territorial emissions in Norway.[19]

The Oslo District Court sided with the government Ministry on the grounds that the national Parliament had considered, but rejected, several proposals to review the previous licensing decision in light of Norway's accession to the 2015 Paris Agreement.[20] According to the District Court, the involvement of the Parliament was sufficient to indicate that the constitutional duty to protect environmental rights had been fulfilled, holding that '[e]missions of $CO_2$ abroad from oil and gas exported from Norway are irrelevant when assessing whether the Decision entails a violation of Article 112'.[21]

The plaintiffs appealed the decision to the Court of Appeals, arguing that the District Court had interpreted Article 112 of the Constitution too narrowly. Finding that Norway is only responsible for GHG emissions emitted on Norwegian territory, they argued, wrongly limits the territorial scope of the government's duty to guarantee the right to a healthy environment. The Court of Appeals upheld the District Court's ruling,[22] although it interpreted Article 112 as requiring that environmental damage from exported petroleum products be considered. However, the Court of Appeals held that the granting of exploration licences, by itself, will not necessarily lead to an increase of GHG emissions.

This ruling was appealed to the Norwegian Supreme Court where the plaintiffs added to their previous complaint that the granting of these licences would also violate the right to life (Article 2) and the right to respect for private and family life (Article 8) of the European Convention on Human Rights (ECHR), which had been the basis of the Dutch Supreme Court's ruling in *Urgenda*. Although the Norwegian Supreme Court readily recognised the severe nature of climate change and acknowledged that Article 112 protects citizens from environmental and climate harms, it also viewed the role of the judiciary as being quite limited.

In terms of the geographic scope of Article 112, the Supreme Court took what might best be described as a 'quasi-territorial' approach:

> A final question is whether it is relevant to consider greenhouse gas emissions and effects outside Norway. Is it only emissions and effects on Norwegian territories that are relevant under Article 112 of the Constitution, or must the assessment also include emissions and effects in other countries? Article 112 does not provide general protection against actions and effects outside the realm. However, if Norway is

19 *People v Arctic Oil* (n 17) [155].

20 *Greenpeace Nordic Association v Ministry of Petroleum and Energy* Case (2018) Case no 16-166674TVI-OTIR/06 (Oslo District Court) (*People v Arctic Oil District Court*).

21 ibid [20].

22 *Greenpeace Nordic Association v Ministry of Petroleum and Energy* (2020) Case no 18-060499ASD-BORG/03 (Borgarting Court of Appeal) (*People v Arctic Oil Court of Appeal*).

> affected by activities taking place abroad that Norwegian authorities may influence directly on or take measures against, this must also be relevant to the application of Article 112. An example is combustion of Norwegian-produced oil or gas abroad, when this causes harm also in Norway.[23]

And later: 'When it comes to greenhouse gas emissions from combustion abroad after Norwegian petroleum export, I believe one must accept that the Storting and the Government build their Norwegian climate policy on the division of responsibilities between states in accordance with international agreements. Here, the clear principle is that each state is responsible for combustion on its own territory.'[24] The Norwegian Supreme Court's narrow interpretation of their extraterritorial obligations is a setback for climate litigation in Norway, but jurisprudence from other European states has shown the possibilities for a more global approach to emissions, even on the national level. This section has presented examples of cases in which domestic courts addressed various extraterritorial issues related to climate change. *Neubauer* dealt with the inclusion of foreign plaintiffs and *Milieudefensie* with the extraterritorial application of the judicial order. Finally, *Arctic Oil* addressed the issue of whether a government was obligated to protect against environmental harms from oil and gas produced domestically but which would be burned in other lands. Although the rulings differ in their interpretations, the courts, particularly in *Milieudefensie*, have opened the door to more inclusive consideration of what constitutes a state's extraterritorial obligations.

### 8.2.2 *Regional*

The 2017 Advisory Opinion by the IACtHR has already achieved landmark status.[25] The Advisory Opinion resulted from a case concerning various construction projects in wetland areas across Colombia that would have posed a serious environmental impact on the Wider Caribbean Region. Colombia, in its request for the opinion, suggested that 'this problem is of interest not only to the States of the Wider Caribbean Region whose coastal and insular population may be directly affected by the environmental damage suffered by this region, but also to the international community'.[26] The Court responded by noting that 'this Opinion constitutes one of the first opportunities that the Court has had to refer extensively to the State obligations arising from the need to protect the environment under the American Convention'.[27]

23 *People v Arctic Oil* (n 17) [149].
24 ibid [159].
25 *The Environment and Human Rights (State Obligations in Relation to the Environment in the Context of the Protection and Guarantee of the Rights to Life and to Personal Integrity – Interpretation and Scope of Articles 4(1) and 5(1) of the American Convention on Human Rights)*, Advisory Opinion OC-23, Inter-American Court of Human Rights Series A No 23 (15 November 2017) (IACtHR OC-23/17).
26 ibid [9].
27 ibid [46].

The essential issue addressed by the Court is the geographic scope of states' human rights obligations. Article 1 of the American Convention on Human Rights provides:

> The States Parties to this Convention undertake to respect the rights and freedoms recognized herein and to ensure to all persons *subject to their jurisdiction* the free and full exercise of those rights and freedoms, without any discrimination for reasons of race, color, sex, language, religion, political or other opinion, national or social origin, economic status, birth, or any other social condition.[28]

Unlike the European Court of Human Rights (ECtHR), which has equated 'jurisdiction' with 'territory', the IACtHR unequivocally took the position that the two are not coterminous.

> The Court recalls that the fact that a person is subject to the jurisdiction of a State does not mean that he or she is in its territory. According to the rules for the interpretation of treaties, as well as the specific rules of the American Convention [...] the ordinary meaning of the word 'jurisdiction', interpreted in good faith and taking into account the context, object and purpose of the American Convention, signifies that it is not limited to the concept of national territory, but covers a broader concept that includes certain ways of exercising jurisdiction beyond the territory of the State in question.[29]

Applying this principle to environmental harm, the Court ruled that:

> In cases of transboundary damage, the exercise of jurisdiction by a State of origin is based on the understanding that it is the State in whose territory or under whose jurisdiction the activities were carried out that has the effective control over them and is in a position to prevent them from causing transboundary harm that impacts the enjoyment of human rights of persons outside its territory. The potential victims of the negative consequences of such activities are under the jurisdiction of the State of origin for the purposes of the possible responsibility of that State for failing to comply with its obligation to prevent transboundary damage. That said, not every negative impact gives rise to this responsibility...[30]

The Court then outlined an approach to jurisdiction that is not purely based on geographic boundaries:

> Accordingly, it can be concluded that the obligation to prevent transboundary environmental damage or harm is an obligation recognized by international environmental law, under which States may be held responsible for any significant damage caused to persons outside their borders by activities originating in their territory or under their effective control or authority. It is important to stress that this obligation

28 American Convention on Human Rights (entered into force 18 July 1978) 1144 UNTS 123 (emphasis added).
29 IACtHR OC-23/17 (n 25) [74].
30 ibid [102].

> does not depend on the lawful or unlawful nature of the conduct that generates the damage, because States must provide prompt, adequate and effective redress to the persons and States that are victims of transboundary harm resulting from activities carried out in their territory or under their jurisdiction, even if the action which caused this damage is not prohibited by international law. That said, there must always be a causal link between the damage caused and the act or omission of the State of origin in relation to activities in its territory or under its jurisdiction or control.[31]

Thus, rather than defining the limits of a state's jurisdiction by its physical borders, the IACtHR allows a state's actions to determine the extent of jurisdiction. If a state's actions or omissions cause harm that impedes the enjoyment of human rights of people in another territory, that original state is found to have effective control over those people and is therefore considered to exercise jurisdiction over them.

The importance of such an extraterritorial interpretation of jurisdiction cannot be overstated with regard to climate litigation. It should be noted that the IACtHR's Advisory Opinion comes in contrast to the approach taken by the ECtHR. As the Committee on the Rights of the Child (CRC) noted in *Sacchi et al v Argentina et al*, discussed later, the approaches may not be compatible, and the IACtHR's approach to jurisdiction seems the most suitable for addressing climate-related human rights harm.[32] Similar to the American Convention, the ECHR references 'jurisdiction' but not 'territory'. Article 1 of the ECHR provides: 'The High Contracting Parties shall secure to everyone within their jurisdiction the rights and freedoms defined in [the Convention]'.[33] The original draft of Article 1 did include the term 'territory', but this was removed from the final draft.

Prior to 2001, both the European Commission for Human Rights and the ECtHR had interpreted the Convention in an extraterritorial fashion.[34] However, beginning with the ECtHR's ruling in *Bankovic et al v Belgium et al*,[35] the European Court has given the Convention a 'territorial'– or what it has described as a 'primarily'[36] or 'essentially'[37] territorial – interpretation. Under this approach, the Convention is intended to only protect those within the territorial borders of the contracting states. At the same time, the ECtHR has extended the protections of the Convention to

[31] ibid [103].

[32] UN Committee on the Rights of the Child, 'Decision Adopted by the Committee under the Optional Protocol to the Convention on the Rights of the Child on a Communications Procedure, concerning Communication No 104/2019', UN Doc CRC/C/88/D/104/2019 (*Sacchi*) [10.7].

[33] European Convention for the Protection of Human Rights and Fundamental Freedoms (entered into force 4 Nov 1950) 213 UNTS 222 (European Convention on Human Rights).

[34] For an extensive history see generally Erik Roxstrom and others, 'The NATO Bombing Case (Bankovic et al v Belgium et al) and the Limits of Western Human Rights Protection' (2005) 23 Boston University International Law Journal 55.

[35] *Bankovic et al v Belgium et al* App no 52207/99 (ECtHR, 21 December 2001).

[36] ibid [59].

[37] ibid [61], [63], and [67].

non-contracting states in two circumstances. First, when agents of a European state operating outside of the territorial borders of that state exercise some degree of personal control over a foreign national. Second, when one of the European powers is exercising 'effective control' over some portion of the land mass of a foreign state. The ECtHR's territorial interpretation in *Bankovic* and in subsequent cases faced a great deal of criticism, including from within the court's own ranks, denouncing the rulings as unprogressive and inconsistent.[38] Although the court has begun returning to their pre-*Bankovic* interpretation, the IACtHR remains ahead of the European court in clearly outlining extraterritorial obligations.

The IACtHR explained its divergence in interpretation from ECtHR case law by underscoring how climate change litigation differs from the kinds of extraterritorial cases taken up by its European counterpart. Cases before the ECtHR tend to involve 'military action or actions by State security forces that indicate "control", "power" or "authority" in the execution of the extraterritorial conduct'.[39] Contrasting these cases with the environmental issue before it, the IACtHR stated 'these are not the situations described by the requesting State and do not correspond to the specific context of environmental obligations referred to in the request for an advisory opinion'.[40]

The IACtHR Advisory Opinion already has played an important role in the climate change debate as evidenced by the *Sacchi* decision issued by the United Nations (UN) CRC, which will be discussed later. Whether it will also serve as a guiding precedent if and when other regional adjudicatory bodies take this issue up remains to be seen.

### 8.2.3 *International*

To date, the ICJ has not issued a ruling on climate change specifically. However, in dealing with transnational environmental cases it has reinforced the customary law principle that one state is not to use its territory to bring about harm to some other state. An example of the Court's jurisprudence on this matter was *Pulp Mills*,[41] which involved a dispute between Argentina and Uruguay over Uruguay's decision to build a pulp-processing plant on the river Uruguay. Citing two of its landmark decisions, the ICJ held that:

> …the principle of prevention, as a customary rule, has its origins in the due diligence that is required of a State in its territory. It is 'every State's obligation not to allow knowingly its territory to be used for acts contrary to the rights of other States' (*Corfu Channel (United Kingdom v Albania)*). A State is thus obliged to use all the

[38] *Al-Skeini and Others v UK* App no 55721/07 (ECtHR, 7 July 2011) (Concurring opinion of Judge Bonello).

[39] IACtHR OC-23/17 (n 25) [80].

[40] ibid.

[41] *Pulp Mills on the River Uruguay (Argentina v Uruguay)* (Merits) [2010] ICJ Rep 14.

means at its disposal in order to avoid activities which take place in its territory, or in any area under its jurisdiction, causing significant damage to the environment of another State. This Court has established that this obligation 'is now part of the corpus of international law relating to the environment' (*Legality of the Threat or Use of nuclear weapons*, Advisory Opinion).[42]

In 2018, the ICJ reaffirmed the principle of transboundary harm in its first environmental compensation claim, *Costa Rica v Nicaragua*.[43] The case originated from a territorial dispute involving a three-kilometre area of wetlands in the border area between the two countries. In 2015, the Court had decided the sovereignty question in favour of Costa Rica, thereby rendering Nicaragua's presence on this land unlawful, giving rise to Costa Rica's claims to reparations. When the two countries were not able to reach agreement on this matter, the issue was brought before the Court.

Two aspects of this case are particularly noteworthy with regard to climate change litigation. One involves the lack of certainty in determining damages, although this did not deter the ICJ: 'In respect of the valuation of damage, the Court recalls that the absence of adequate evidence as to the extent of material damage will not, in all situations, preclude an award of compensation for that damage'.[44]

The second issue involves causation. The Court reaffirmed the principle that there must be a causal link between the wrongful act and the injury suffered,[45] and it also acknowledged the inherent problems in environmental damage claims due to the myriad of concurrent causes as well as the lack of scientific certainty in establishing the necessary causal link.[46] These caveats notwithstanding, the ICJ proceeded to issue a series of rulings in favour of Costa Rica, thus reaffirming the principle that a state is violating international law when it causes environmental harm in some other state.

## 8.3 EMERGING BEST PRACTICES

As noted earlier, one of the biggest hurdles facing judges in this area is the disjuncture between climate change, which on one hand is widely recognised as a global phenomenon, and law that so often has been interpreted and applied in a territorial fashion, on the other. This chapter, however, identifies four emerging best practices that could serve to reconcile law with the global reality of climate change: 1) the growing recognition of extraterritorial obligations; 2) the issue of standing,

42 ibid [101].
43 *Certain Activities Carried Out by Nicaragua in the Border Area (Costa Rica v Nicaragua)* (Compensation owed by the Republic of Nicaragua to the Republic of Costa Rica) [2018] ICJ Rep 15.
44 ibid [35].
45 ibid [32].
46 ibid [34].

especially the inclusion of more victims' voices; 3) holding multinational corporations responsible; and 4) establishing greater accountability for the production of GHG emissions.

### 8.3.1 *The Growing Recognition of Extraterritorial Obligations*

Although human rights are declared to be 'universal', the obligation to protect and enforce these rights has in large part been territorially based. One of the more telling examples of this was a country study of Sweden conducted by Paul Hunt in his capacity as the Special Rapporteur on the Right to Health.[47] Sweden has long been recognised as one of the most 'generous' countries in the world in terms of the amount of foreign aid it provides per capita. However, when Hunt asked government officials whether Sweden, as a state party to the International Covenant on Economic, Social and Cultural Rights, particularly in light of the 'international assistance and cooperation' language in the treaty, was legally obligated to provide foreign aid, government officials demurred. In his report, Hunt took strong exception to this reading of human rights law: 'If there is no legal obligation underpinning the human rights responsibility of international assistance and cooperation, inescapably all international assistance and cooperation is based fundamentally upon charity. While such a position might have been tenable 100 years ago, it is unacceptable in the twenty-first century.'[48] Despite the resistance of states to acknowledge their human rights obligations outside their own national borders, the 'territorial' interpretation of international human rights law is increasingly being challenged, if not discarded altogether. The 2017 IACtHR Advisory Opinion is a particularly salient example, where the Court held that a state that brings about harm to individuals in other lands is thereby exercising 'jurisdiction' over these individuals.

Similarly, the African Commission on Human and People's Rights has interpreted the provision relating to the right to life in the African Charter on Human and People's Rights as follows:

> A State shall respect the right to life of individuals outside its territory. A State also has certain obligations to protect the right to life of such individuals. The nature of these obligations depends for instance on the extent that the State has jurisdiction or otherwise exercises effective authority, power, or control over either the perpetrator or the victim (or the victim's rights) or exercises effective control over the territory on which the victim's rights are affected, or whether the State engages in conduct which could reasonability be foreseen to result in an unlawful deprivation of life.[49]

[47] OHCHR, 'Report of the Special Rapporteur on the right of everyone to the enjoyment of the highest attainable standard of physical and mental health' (2015) UN Doc A/HRC/29/33.

[48] ibid [28].

[49] African Commission, 'General Comment No 3 on the African Charter on Human and Peoples' Rights: The Right to Life (Article 4)' (18 November 2015) [14].

The UN treaty bodies have added their own authoritative interpretation of international human rights law as well.[50] The Committee on Economic, Social and Cultural Rights (CESCR) in its General Comment 24 states 'The extraterritorial obligation to respect requires States parties to refrain from interfering directly or indirectly with the enjoyment of the Covenant rights by persons outside their territories'.[51] More recently, in October 2018, the CESCR released a statement on climate change affirming that states parties are required to respect, protect, and fulfil all human rights for all people and that '[t]hey owe such duties not only to their own populations, but also to populations outside their territories, consistent with … the [UN] Charter'.[52]

Similarly, the Human Rights Committee (HRC) it its General Comment 36 (Right to Life) interpreted the term 'jurisdiction' in Article 2 of the ICCPR in functional terms, referring to the ability of one state to affect the 'enjoyment' of the right to life of a person living in another state:

> A State party has an obligation to respect and to ensure the rights under article 6 [right to life] of all persons who are within its territory and all persons subject to its jurisdiction, that is, all persons over whose enjoyment the right to life it exercises power or effective control. This includes persons located outside any territory effectively controlled by the State, whose right to life is nonetheless impacted by its military or other activities in a direct and reasonably foreseeable manner.[53]

In terms of climate change more specifically, in 2019 five UN human rights treaty bodies – responsible for, respectively, the Convention on the Elimination of All Forms of Discrimination Against Women, the International Convention on the Protection of the Rights of all Migrant Workers and Members of Their Families, the Convention on the Rights of the Child, the Convention on the Rights of Persons with Disabilities, and the ICESCR – issued the following joint statement: 'State parties have obligations, including extra-territorial obligations, to respect, protect and fulfill all human rights of all people. Failure to take measures to prevent foreseeable human rights harm caused by climate change or to regulate activities contributing

[50] This, of course, is not meant to slight the significant contributions made by a host of UN Special Rapporteurs regarding the geographic scope of international human rights law.

[51] UN Committee on Economic, Social and Cultural Rights, 'General Comment No 24 (2017) on State Obligations under the International Covenant on Economic, Social and Cultural Rights in the Context of Business Activities' (10 August 2017) UN Doc E/C.12/GC/24 (CESCR General Comment No 24) [29].

[52] UN Committee on Economic, Social and Cultural Rights, 'Climate Change and the International Covenant on Economic, Social and Cultural Rights' (8 October 2018) <www.ohchr.org/en/statements/2018/10/committee-releases-statement-climate-change-and-covenant> accessed 24 February 2024.

[53] UN Human Rights Committee, 'General Comment No 36 (2018) on Article 6 of the International Covenant on Civil and Political Rights, on the Right to Life' (30 October 2018) UN Doc CCPR/C/GC/36 (CCPR General Comment No 36) [63].

to such harm, could constitute a violation of States' human rights obligations.'[54] Finally, special mention should be made of the CRC's extensive analysis of the scope of states' human rights obligations in its communication in *Sacchi*. The case involved sixteen children from five different states claiming that the respondents were responsible for perpetuating climate change through their own inaction and in so doing had acted in violation of the Convention on the Rights of the Child. Of particular note, the CRC adopted wholesale the IACtHR's interpretation of the term 'jurisdiction':

> Having considered the above, the Committee finds that the appropriate test for jurisdiction in the present case is that adopted by the Inter-American Court of Human Rights in its Advisory Opinion of the Environment and Human Rights. This implies that when transboundary harm occurs, children are under the jurisdiction of the State on whose territory the emissions originated for the purposes of article 5 (1) of the Optional Protocol if there is a causal link between the acts or omissions of the State in question and the negative impact on the rights of children located outside its territory, when the State of origin exercises effective control over the sources of the emissions in question. The Committee further considers that [...] the alleged harm suffered by the victims needs to have been reasonably foreseeable to the State party at the time of its acts or omissions even for the purpose of establishing jurisdiction.[55]

Despite the CRC's expansive view of states' human rights obligations, the Committee ultimately ruled that the communication was inadmissible on the grounds that the children had not exhausted domestic remedies in the relevant countries.

### 8.3.2 *Standing*

It is commonplace to refer to climate change as a global phenomenon in the sense that, in one manner or another, all states contribute to this problem. Yet, as noted by the UN Special Rapporteur on Human Rights and the Environment, three-quarters of global emissions are produced in only twenty states.[56] Unfortunately, those states that produce the lowest amounts of GHG emissions, while oftentimes bearing the brunt of the harms caused by climate change, typically have no seat at the table, both in political negotiations and in the judicial treatment of the issue.

In that vein, one of the emerging best practices is that standing requirements are being loosened, at least to some degree. Because of this, new voices (and new

54 OHCHR, 'Joint Statement on "Human Rights and Climate Change"' (16 September 2019) <www.ohchr.org/en/statements/2019/09/five-un-human-rights-treaty-bodies-issue-joint-statement-human-rights-and> accessed 24 February 2024.

55 *Sacchi* (n 32) [10.7].

56 OHCHR, 'Report of the Special Rapporteur on the Issue of Human Rights Obligations Relating to the Enjoyment of a Safe, Clean, Healthy and Sustainable Environment' (2019) UN Doc A/74/161, 14.

generations) are beginning to be heard, and even more importantly, more avenues for redress are being opened up as well. In the *Neubauer* case, the German plaintiffs were joined by litigants from Nepal and Bangladesh, and although the nature of the claim presented allowed the court to differentiate between these two groups, the more important consideration is that foreign nationals from the Global South were granted standing to pursue a claim against a state from the Global North.

*Sacchi* is another case in point. This communication to the CRC was made by sixteen children from somewhat geographically dispersed countries: Argentina, Brazil, France, Germany, and Turkey. In their communication, the children all claimed to be within the 'jurisdiction' of each of the other four states, which was not contested by the CRC. This raises the question that if these children were within the 'jurisdiction' of each of the other four states, there would be no reason why each one would not also be within the 'jurisdiction' of every country that produces GHG emissions – which is to say every country in the world.

The IACtHR's expansive reading of the term 'jurisdiction' in its 2017 Advisory Opinion should also allow more voices to be heard and more states to be held accountable. Although the biggest shortcoming is that such claims can currently only be filed against other state parties to the American Convention, the trend of emerging case law suggests that more courts will be adopting similarly expansive views of jurisdiction.

### 8.3.3 *Private Actors*

Under international human rights law, states have three different sets of obligations. One is the obligation to *respect* human rights, which means that a state is not to violate human rights principles itself. The second is an obligation to *protect* human rights, which means that a state also has an obligation to ensure that private actors, such as multinational corporations, do not violate human rights standards. Finally, states have an obligation to *fulfil* human rights, which means that if individuals cannot protect their own human rights, the state has an obligation to offer such protection.

Within a state's domestic realm, such obligations largely go unquestioned. However, the same is not true outside a state's national borders. An issue that has been especially contentious is whether a state's duty to protect extends beyond its territorial borders. This issue has commonly been raised in the context of harms caused by the actions or omissions of multinational corporations. In a situation where the 'host' state is either unable or unwilling to regulate the harmful behaviour of the corporation, does the 'home' state have a legal obligation to do so in its stead?

The UN Guiding Principles on Business and Human Rights (UNGP)[57] has taken the position that 'States are not generally required under international human rights

[57] OHCHR, 'Guiding Principles on Business and Human Rights: Implementing the United Nations "Protect, Respect and Remedy" Framework' (2011) HR/PUB/11/04.

law to regulate the extraterritorial activities of businesses domiciled in their territory and/or jurisdiction'.

The Maastricht ETO Principles,[58] however, have a much different interpretation of existing international law. According to these principles, not only does the 'home' state have a duty to act in such situations, but so do other states that can exert a 'decisive influence' over egregious corporate behaviour.

Although it is not possible to establish which of these two presents a sounder reading of international law, the UN treaty bodies – including the ICESCR,[59] the Committee interpreting the International Convention on the Elimination of All forms of Racial Discrimination (CERD),[60] and the CRC[61] – are increasingly willing to recognise that a state's obligation to protect extends outside its national borders. For example, in General Comment 36, the HRC determined that states' obligations include regulation of activities by private actors, noting:

> States must also take appropriate legislative and other measures to ensure that all activities taking place in whole or in part within their territory and in other places subject to their jurisdiction, but having a direct and reasonably foreseeable impact on the right to life of individuals outside their territory, including activities taken by corporate entities based in their territory or subject to their jurisdiction, are consistent with article 6 [right to life], taking due account of related international standards of corporate responsibility, and of the right of victims to obtain an effective remedy.[62]

A slightly different question is whether multinational corporations have human rights obligations that are separate and distinct from the obligations of states. In *Milieudefensie*, the District Court relied extensively on the UNGP, particularly the second pillar: the obligation of corporations to 'respect' human rights. The Court explained the difference between state and non-state responsibilities:

> The differences between states and businesses RDS emphasizes are expressed in the UNGP in the different responsibilities for states and businesses, between which no inevitable tension needs to exist – as follows from the quotation given

58 Maastricht Principles on Extraterritorial Obligations of States in the Area of Economic, Social and Cultural Rights (28 September 2011) <www.ciel.org/wp-content/uploads/2015/05/Maastricht_ETO_Principles_21Oct11.pdf> accessed 24 February 2024.

59 CESCR General Comment No 24 (n 51) [29]; UN Committee on Economic, Social and Cultural Rights, 'General Comment No 15 (2003) on The Right to Water (Arts 11 and 12 of the Covenant)' (20 January 2003) UN Doc E/C.12/2002/11 (CESCR General Comment No 15) [31].

60 CERD Committee, 'Concluding Observations on the Combined Tenth to Twelfth Reports of the United States of America' (2008) UN Doc CERD/C/USA/CO/6 [30]; CERD Committee, Concluding Observations on the Combined Nineteenth and Twentieth Reports of Norway' (2011) UN Doc CERD/C/NOR/CO/19-20 [17].

61 Committee on the Rights of the Child, 'General Comment No 16 (2013) on State Obligations Regarding the Impact of the Business Sector on Children's Rights' (17 April 2013) UN Doc CRC/C/GC/16 [43].

62 CCPR General Comment No 36 (n 53) [22].

> by RDS. The responsibility of business enterprises to respect human rights, as formulated in the UNGP, is a global standard of expected conduct for all business enterprises wherever they operate. It exists independently of States' abilities and/or willingness to fulfill their own human rights obligations and does not diminish those obligations. And it exists over and above compliance with national laws and regulations protecting human rights. Therefore, it is not enough for companies to monitor developments and follow the measures states take; they have an individual responsibility.[63]

The Court then underscored what a global standard of conduct for businesses looks like:

> Business enterprises should respect human rights. This means that they should avoid infringing on the human rights of others and should address adverse human rights impacts with which they are involved. Tackling the adverse human rights impacts means that measures must be taken to prevent, limit and, where necessary, address these impacts. It is a global standard of expected conduct for all businesses wherever they operate.... [T]his responsibility of businesses exists independently of states' abilities and/or willingness to fulfil their own human rights obligations and does not diminish those obligations. It is not an optional responsibility for companies. It applies everywhere, regardless of the local legal context ...[64]

The importance of *Milieudefensie* in the context of addressing climate change cannot be overstated. One of the major shortcomings of climate change litigation to date has been its piecemeal approach. As important as 'domestic' cases such as *Urgenda* happen to be, ultimately, they only address the climate change problem in one state. In contrast, the judicial order in a case like *Milieudefensie* applies not only to RDS's domestic operations but to the entirety of its worldwide operations, and not only its own emissions but those from the use of its product by other entities.

The final point relates to the National Inquiry on Climate Change, a report issued by the Commission on Human Rights of the Philippines (CHRP) in 2022.[65] Not only did the Commission address the contributions to climate change of both state and non-state actors, it also included in the scope of its work foreign corporations that did not operate within the territorial boundaries of the Philippines, but whose overseas operations were nevertheless having a harmful effect on Filipino nationals. To quote at some length from the Commission report:

> Many of the respondent oil companies also raised the issue of *territoriality* – they questioned the power of our Commission to inquire into their activities, since they did not operate within the territory of the Philippines. Stripped of legal

63 *Milieudefensie* (n 15) [4.4.13].
64 ibid [4.4.15].
65 Commission on Human Rights of the Philippines, 'National Inquiry on Climate Change Report' (CHRP December 2022).

> niceties, the contention was that our Commission, or, indeed, the Philippine State, in general, may only inquire into the conduct of corporate entities operating within Philippine territory, even if the corporations' operations outside our territory were negatively impacting the rights and lives of our people. We cannot accept such a proposition.[66]

The report is particularly notable for the extraterritorial perspective that the CHRP champions. Under this progressive approach, protecting the human rights of Philippine citizens would take priority over rigid 'technicalities' and eventually become international law:

> The CHRP is mandated by the Philippine Constitution with the duty to investigate and inquire into allegations of human rights violations suffering by our people. Our Commission decides on how it must perform its constitutional duty. And the performance of this duty is neither constrained by nor anchored on the principle of territoriality alone. The challenge of NHRIs [National Human Rights Institutions] is to test boundaries and create new paths; to be bold and creative, instead of timid and docile; to be more idealistic, or less pragmatic; to promote soft laws into becoming hard laws; to see beyond technicalities and establish guiding principles that can later become binding treaties; in sum, to set the bar of human rights protection to higher standards.[67]

### 8.3.4 *Establishing Greater Accountability for the Production of GHG Emissions*

The final emerging practice is the growing understanding that a purely 'domestic' approach to climate change will only address a small segment of what truly is a global problem. One issue involves how contributions to GHG emissions are to be measured. Is it simply the GHG emissions that are produced within a state? Or, instead, should courts take a much broader approach?

This issue was raised directly in the *Arctic Oil* litigation, bringing forth a variety of judicial responses, none of which are satisfactory. The Oslo District Court took a 'territorial' approach, holding that although GHG emissions from exported oil and gas are some ninety-five times greater than that which are produced domestically, the government's only responsibility relates to emissions produced within Norway's territorial borders. The Court of Appeals took the opposite position. However, it ruled that it would be premature to consider extraterritorial GHG emissions from the granting of a drilling licence alone.

The Supreme Court attempted to split the difference by holding that the Norwegian government's obligations generally only extend to the national borders

66 ibid [4].
67 ibid [4]–[5].

of that country, but that it also had obligations regarding extraterritorial emissions that would have a negative effect on Norwegian citizens. One problem with this is that it would be difficult, if not impossible, to determine when this would arise. However, there is an even bigger problem, which is that *all* GHG emissions will have a negative effect on Norwegian citizens – and the citizens of all other states as well. The larger point is that Norway's domestic GHG emissions do not come anywhere close to capturing the extent to which that country is contributing to climate change, and any judicial treatment of this issue must recognise and deal with this.

Fortunately, other institutions have begun to take a broader perspective. The Human Rights Commission of the Philippines not only concerned itself with GHG emissions from corporations operating abroad, but it has also underscored the importance of considering the role that a host of actors, including financiers and insurance companies, play in supporting environmentally harmful projects.[68]

As mentioned earlier, the judicial decree in *Milieudefensie* was extraordinarily sweeping in that it applied not only to RDS's domestic operations, but those it was engaged in outside the Netherlands as well. This approach challenges the unstated assumption that RDS's domestic GHG emissions are somehow different than those it produces outside the Netherlands. But it also challenges the assumption that the Dutch government can only regulate RDS's domestic operations.[69]

Finally, in *Duarte Agostinho and Others v Portugal and Others*, which is currently before the ECtHR, the children bringing the case against their own state (Portugal) as well as thirty-two states parties to the European Convention argue that there are four aspects of GHG emissions and each needs to be considered: 1) domestic production; 2) GHG emissions from exports as well as 3) imports, and finally, 4) GHG emissions due to overseas financial investments. Cases like these can serve as a starting point for future litigation emphasising the need for governments and national courts to consider all emissions that may result from an action, even if those emissions are not produced within the state's borders.

## 8.4 REPLICABILITY

The best emerging practices are certainly replicable. For example, the ECtHR (as well as other regional adjudicatory bodies) could easily recognise the unique nature of climate change and interpret the term 'jurisdiction' in Article 1 of the European Convention as applying extraterritorially, thereby allowing individuals in one state to pursue an action against one of the other state parties. Yet, even if the Court were

68 ibid [132].

69 For a compelling argument that 'home' states have a legal obligation to regulate the foreign operations of its multinational corporations, see Dalia Palombo, *Business and Human Rights: The Obligations of the European Home States* (Cambridge University Press 2019).

to adopt such a reading in *Agostinho*, it is essential to note that the case was only brought against other state parties to the Convention. What is equally important is understanding that if children in Portugal are within the 'jurisdiction' of the other parties to the European Convention due to the GHG emissions from these states, children living in other parts of the globe are likely to be as well. The same is true of the Inter-American Court. While its Advisory Opinion is certainly a landmark ruling, there is no reason why extraterritorial jurisdiction should only be limited to the state parties to the American Convention.

It is already clear that a case like *Urgenda* is replicable, as similar judgments have now been issued by courts in other countries. While such rulings serve as important precedents, it is also essential to understand the inherent limitation of 'domestic' cases, where citizens of a state are seeking a judicial order limiting GHG emissions by that one country. Although the inclusion of foreign nationals in *Neubauer* is encouraging, what is unclear is how willing other domestic courts will be in entertaining claims brought by foreign nationals. The key is in recognising that the GHG emissions produced in one state can (and will) have a decidedly negative effect on the enjoyment of human rights in other states.

A case like *Milieudefensie* is also replicable. There is nothing that would prevent a French court from hearing a case against Total, a French-based multinational corporation, or a Norwegian court from hearing a case brought against Statoil, and so on. Yet, there is also no reason why domestic courts should only take up cases against domestic corporations. That is, there is no reason why a Dutch court should not also take up a case against 'foreign' corporations such as Total and Exxon as well. These multinational corporations not only produce GHG emissions that are harming Dutch citizens, but both corporations do extensive business in the Netherlands, thus providing a direct jurisdictional link.

One last scenario involves an offshoot of the *Trail Smelter* situation mentioned earlier. However, in this scenario Canada is not bringing a case against the US for the harmful GHG emissions produced in the US (although it could), nor are Canadian citizens bringing a case against the US. Rather, Canadian citizens could bring a case against their own government due to its failure to take action against the US as a way of preventing GHG emissions from entering Canadian airspace.[70]

It should be clear that not only are many of the emerging best practices replicable, but the more important point is that extraterritorial climate change litigation has only started to scratch the surface. The key to all this is to act both efficiently, expeditiously, and fairly. This will only be achieved if as many voices can be heard as possible – while all those responsible for the earth's rapid warming are held to account.

[70] Banda (n 4) lays out various extraterritorial scenarios such as this.

## 8.5 CONCLUSION

One of the more noteworthy aspects of the surge in climate change cases over just the past few years is that judges the world over have shown a great willingness to fill the vacuum left by the inadequate policies and practices of domestic and international political actors. On the other hand, as shown in this chapter, courts have struggled with the various extraterritorial elements that raise questions of culpability and responsibility. Given the long history of territorial grounding of law, perhaps climate change litigation will proceed down the same path. It is clear, however, that not only is this an inefficient way of addressing what is inherently a global problem, but one of the biggest shortcomings of such an approach is the great likelihood of creating enormous gaps in protection.

As we have seen here, some courts have recognised the extraterritorial dimension of climate change and issued rulings that reflect it. There is no question that the IACtHR's 2017 Advisory Opinion is a landmark ruling. Much like the call of the various UN treaty bodies, the Court has given an extraterritorial reading to the term 'jurisdiction' in Article 1 of the American Convention. The legal force of the opinion remains limited, however, to the state parties to the Convention, which does not include the US, the second-largest emitter in the world. Likewise, even if the ECtHR rules in favour of the Portuguese children in *Agostinho*, this ruling would only allow a citizen of one European state to proceed with a claim against one of the other states parties to the European Convention. These children could still not bring an action against China or the US, the two largest producers of GHG. The larger lesson, perhaps, is that even regional human rights institutions can be hampered by territorial limitations.

In recognition of this, what would make an enormous difference would be an Advisory Opinion by the International Court of Justice detailing the responsibilities and obligations of all states – and not simply those of a fairly limited number of states.[71] Yet, there are also things that states could do themselves – immediately. The most obvious, of course, is for states to meet their nationally determined contributions under the Paris Agreement. Some governments might do this on their own, but many more will need some form of judicial guidance. Notwithstanding historic rulings such as *Urgenda*, to paraphrase the district court ruling in *Juliana*,[72]

[71] Ralph Wilde, 'Human Rights Beyond Borders at the World Court: The Significance of the International Court of Justice's Jurisprudence on the Extraterritorial Application of International Human Rights Law Treaties' (2013) 12 CJIL 639 (arguing that the ICJ is uniquely positioned to address extraterritorial claims).

[72] *Juliana v United States* 947 F.3d 1159 (9th Cir 2020). *Juliana* was a suit brought by Our Children's Trust based on the grounds that the US government's failure to protect present and future generations from climate change resulted in a violation of the United States Constitution. While the district court sided with the plaintiffs, this ruling was overturned on appeal. The plaintiffs have since amended their complaint and the district court has ruled that their case can proceed. *Juliana v United States* No 6:15-cv-01517-AA (District Court of Oregon 2023) (Opinion and Order).

judges have tended to be much too conservative in climate change cases and the earth has suffered for this. Given the amorphous nature of climate change itself – but also what is at stake – courts should provide a liberal interpretation of both procedural (i.e. standing, exhaustion of domestic remedies) as well as substantive (i.e. causation) requirements. Above all else, it is imperative to acknowledge that climate change is an extraterritorial problem affecting all states and all people in all states. Attempting to deal with this by a 'territorial' interpretation of the law will simply not work.

# 9

# Duty of Care

*Christina Voigt and Joe Udell**

## 9.1 INTRODUCTION

One central aspect of climate litigation in recent years has been the recognition by courts that States – and now corporations – have a duty of care to address global warming. This development has occurred in both civil and common law jurisdictions, as judges have notably ordered governments to adopt more comprehensive climate policies with greater boldness and regularity based on this norm. This chapter will examine important trends in climate litigation with respect to the duty of care, identify emerging best practices from a range of cases, and analyse the potential for these emerging best practices to be replicated in other jurisdictions.

## 9.2 DUTY OF CARE IN CLIMATE LITIGATION

In a number of recent cases, climate litigants have successfully grounded their claims in a variety of tort law, constitutional rights, and statutory provisions.[1] This has included the tort of hazardous negligence under the Dutch Civil Code in *Urgenda Foundation v The State of The Netherlands*,[2] negligent conduct as applied to public authorities under the Belgian Civil Code in *VZW Klimaatzaak v Kingdom of Belgium and Others*,[3] and ecological damage under the French Civil Code in *Notre Affaire à Tous and Others v France*.[4] Courts have also found duty of care

* Christina Voigt is Professor of Law at the University of Oslo and Chair of the IUCN World Commission on Environmental Law. Joe Udell is a legal associate at the Climate Litigation Network.

1 United Nations Environment Programme and Sabin Center for Climate Change, 'Global Climate Litigation Report: 2020 Status Review' (2020) <https://wedocs.unep.org/bitstream/handle/20.500.11822/34818/GCLR.pdf?sequence=1&isAllowed=y> accessed 24 February 2024.

2 *Urgenda Foundation v The State of The Netherlands* [2015] ECLI:NL:RBDHA:2015:7196 (District Court of The Hague) (*Urgenda District Court*).

3 *VZW Klimaatzaak v l'État Belge* [2021] 2015/4585/A (Tribunal de première instance francophone de Bruxelles, Section Civile) (*VZW Klimaatzaak First Instance*); *VZW Klimaatzaak v Kingdom of Belgium & Others* [2023] 2022/AR/891(Cour d'appel de Bruxelles) (*VZW Klimaatzaak Appeal*).

4 *Notre Affaire à Tous and Others v France* [2021] No 1904967, 1904968, 1904972 1904976/4-1.

violations under the rights to life and to private and family life of Articles 2 and 8 of the European Convention on Human Rights (ECHR) in *Urgenda*,[5] as well as various constitutional rights in *Neubauer and Others v Germany*,[6] *Future Generations v Ministry of the Environment and Others (Demanda Generaciones Futuras v Minambiente)*,[7] *GroundWork Trust and Vukani Environmental Justice Alliance Movement in Action v Minister of Environmental Affairs and Others*,[8] *PSB et al v Brazil*,[9] *Klimatická žaloba ČR v Czech Republic*,[10] *In re Greenpeace Southeast Asia and Others*,[11] and *Mathur and others v Her Majesty the Queen in Right of Ontario*.[12] This section will examine how courts in various jurisdictions have interpreted the duty of care owed by a State or corporation, their focus on minimum reasonableness standards, and their response to common defences.

### 9.2.1 *Interpreting the Standard of Care*

When a State's duty of care to mitigate climate change is an unwritten and/or open-standard norm, courts have relied on a range of sources to determine the contours of that standard, including international law such as the Paris Agreement, the best available science from the Intergovernmental Panel on Climate Change (IPCC), and international soft law, such as guidance from the United Nations (UN) and the Organisation for Economic Co-operation and Development (OECD).

#### 9.2.1.1 International Climate Change Law

Courts have consistently referred to the Paris Agreement when considering a State's duty of care, including several landmark decisions described later such as *Urgenda* and *Neubauer*. Close to 200 nations came to a consensus on the historically ambitious treaty in December 2015, which aims to strengthen the global response to the threat of climate change by (1) holding the increase in the global average temperature to well below 2°C above pre-industrial levels and pursuing efforts to limit the

5 *State of the Netherlands (Ministry of Economic Affairs and Climate Policy) v Stichting Urgenda* [2018] ECLI:NL:GHDHA:2018:2610 (Hague Court of Appeal) (*Urgenda Court of Appeal*).

6 *Neubauer and Others v Germany* [2021] 1 BvR 2656/18, 1 BvR 96/20, 1 BvR 78/20, 1 BvR 288/20, 1 BvR 96/20, 1 BvR 78/20 (German Federal Constitutional Court) (*Neubauer*).

7 *Future Generations v Ministry of the Environment and Others (Demanda Generaciones Futuras v Minambiente)* [2018] 11001 22 03 000 2018 00319 00 (Supreme Court of Justice of Colombia) (*Demanda Futuras Generaciones*).

8 *Trustees for the time being of Groundwork Trust and Another v Minister of Environmental Affairs and Others* [2019] SAFLII 208 (ZAGPPHC) (*Groundwork Trust*).

9 *PSB and others v Brazil* [2022] ADPF 708 (Federal Supreme Court of Brazil).

10 *Klimatická žaloba ČR v Czech Republic* [2022] No 14A 101/2021 (Prague Municipal Court).

11 *In re Greenpeace Southeast Asia and Others* [2022] Case No CHR-NI-2016-0001 (Commission on Human Rights of the Philippines).

12 *Mathur et al v Her Majesty the Queen in Right of Ontario* [2020] ONSC 6918 (Superior Court of Justice) (*Mathur Strikeout*).

temperature increase to 1.5°C above pre-industrial levels; (2) increasing the ability to adapt to the adverse impacts of climate change and foster climate resilience and low greenhouse gas (GHG) emissions development, in a manner that does not threaten food production; and (3) making finance flows consistent with a pathway towards low GHG emissions and climate-resilient development.[13] The instrument has been called 'the most important international agreement in history'[14] and a 'monumental triumph'[15] that 'sets the stage for progress in ending poverty, strengthening peace, and ensuring a life of dignity and opportunity for all'.[16]

The treaty espouses an equitable approach to climate change, with each Party communicating every five years nationally determined contributions (NDCs) that are considered the 'heart of the Paris Agreement'[17] and its long-term temperature goal. The language of Article 4(3) outlines a duty of care that requires each Party's NDC to 'represent a progression beyond the Party's then current [NDC] and reflect its highest possible ambition, reflecting its common but differentiated responsibilities and respective capabilities, in the light of different national circumstances'.[18] As Article 4(3) requires each NDC to reflect a Party's 'highest possible ambition'[19] and reflect 'its common but differentiated responsibilities and respective capabilities, in the light of different national circumstances',[20] the relative content demanded of NDCs creates a due diligence standard of conduct that differs for each Paris Agreement party,[21] while the treaty's largely procedural reporting requirements establish obligations of result.

In addition to the Paris Agreement, national courts have referred to other international law instruments to determine a State's appropriate climate duties. For example, in *Thomson v Minister for Climate Change Issues*, the High Court of

13 Paris Agreement (entered into force 4 November 2016) 3156 UNTS 79 (Paris Agreement) art 2(1)(a)–(c); UNFCCC Secretariat, 'COP 21 – Historical Paris Agreement Adopted' <https://unfccc.int/timeline/> accessed 27 February 2024.

14 'IGOs, Development Banks and UN Agencies React to Paris Agreement' (*IISD*, 7 January 2016) <https://sdg.iisd.org/news/igos-development-banks-and-un-agencies-react-to-paris-agreement/> accessed 27 February 2024.

15 William Brittlebank, 'UN Chief Hails "Monumental" COP21 Climate Deal' (*Climate Action*, 14 December 2015) <www.climateaction.org/news/un_chief_hails_new_cop21_climate_deal> accessed 27 February 2024.

16 ibid.

17 UNFCCC Secretariat, 'Nationally Determined Contributions (NDCs)' <https://unfccc.int/process-and-meetings/the-paris-agreement/nationally-determined-contributions-ndcs/nationally-determined-contributions-ndcs> accessed 28 February 2024.

18 Paris Agreement (n 13) art 4(3).

19 ibid.

20 ibid. For a discussion on the duty of care established by art 4(3) of the Paris Agreement, see Christina Voigt, 'The Paris Agreement: What is the Standard of Conduct for Parties?' (2016) 26 QIL 17; Christina Voigt and Felipe Ferreira '"Dynamic Differentiation": The Principles of CBDR-RC, Progression and Highest Possible Ambition in the Paris Agreement' (2016) 5 TEL 285.

21 Christina Voigt, 'The Power of the Paris Agreement in International Climate Litigation' (2023) 32(2) RECIEL 237–249.

New Zealand noted that, as a matter of statutory interpretation, the power to set GHG emissions reduction targets under s 224(2) of the country's Climate Change Reduction Act 2002 'must be interpreted consistently with New Zealand's international obligations'[22] established by the UN Framework Convention on Climate Change (UNFCCC), the Kyoto Protocol, and the Paris Agreement.

In *Urgenda*, the Hague District Court held that the plaintiff environmental organisation could not directly rely on the no-harm principle, the UNFCCC, or the Kyoto Protocol in its claim.[23] Nevertheless, the court acknowledged that international law obligations have a '"reflex effect" in national law'.[24] As such, courts in the Netherlands will consider these obligations 'when applying and interpreting national-law open standards and concepts',[25] such as social proprietary, reasonableness and propriety, the general interest, or certain legal principles. On appeal, the Dutch Supreme Court similarly applied the 'common ground' method articulated by the European Court of Human Rights in *Demir and Baykara v Turkey* to ascertain the State's positive obligations under Articles 2 and 8 of the ECHR.[26] The Dutch Supreme Court held that 'an interpretation of the ECHR must also take into account the relevant rules of international law referred to in Article 31(3)(c) of the Vienna Convention on the Law of Treaties'.[27] Under the common ground method, the Court also considered scientific insights and soft law.[28]

The Hague District Court, moreover, has indirectly relied on international law within the context of a corporation's duty of care to mitigate climate change. In the landmark *Milieudefensie v Royal Dutch Shell (RDS)* case,[29] which marked the first time that a climate mitigation duty was imposed on a corporate actor, the court considered in the context of the duty of care 'what is needed to prevent dangerous climate change' under the Paris Agreement.[30] It explained that although certain provisions of the Paris Agreement are non-binding on the private actor (in this case RDS), they nevertheless 'represent a universally endorsed and accepted standard that protects the common interest of preventing dangerous climate change'.[31] The court followed this reasoning in its interpretation of the 'unwritten' duty of care in this case, as Book 6, Section 162 of the Dutch Civil Code prohibits acts or omissions

22 *Thomson v Minister for Climate Change Issues* [2017] NZHC 733 (High Court) (*Thomson*).
23 *Urgenda District Court* (n 2).
24 ibid [4.4.3].
25 ibid.
26 *State of the Netherlands (Ministry of Economic Affairs and Climate Policy) v Stichting Urgenda* [2019] ECLI:NL:HR:2019:2007 (Supreme Court of the Netherlands) (*Urgenda Supreme Court*) [5.4.2].
27 ibid.
28 ibid [5.4.3], [7.2.11].
29 *Milieudefensie v Royal Dutch Shell* [2021] ECLR:NL: RBDHA:2021:5339 (District Court of the Hague) [5.3].
30 ibid [4.4.27].
31 ibid.

that conflict with 'proper social conduct'.[32] Accordingly, the court ordered RDS to reduce the Scope 1, 2, and 3 emissions[33] of the Shell group by net 45 per cent by 2030 relative to 2019 levels.[34]

France's *Conseil d'État* (Council of State), the highest administrative court in the country, has also indirectly relied on the Paris Agreement as well as the UNFCCC. In *Commune de Grande-Synthe v France*,[35] the Grande-Synthe municipality, a low-lying coastal area that is particularly susceptible to global warming, sought a court order in January 2019 that would force the government to implement climate measures and prohibit actions likely to increase GHG emissions.[36] The court held in November 2020 that it could not issue a ruling on the merits of the dispute. France was instead given three months to prove that it could meet its emission reduction target of 40 per cent by 2030 compared to 1990 levels without additional measures.[37] Although the plaintiffs could not directly invoke the Paris Agreement or the UNFCCC, the court acknowledged that 'they must nevertheless be taken into consideration in the interpretation of provisions of national law'.[38]

Beyond treaty law, courts have drawn on a broad range of international law norms in climate cases to give meaning and content to the duty of care, including general principles of international environmental law and international human rights law. In *PSB*, Brazil's Federal Supreme Court drew a direct connection between these norms in holding that the Paris Agreement is a human rights treaty because '[t]reaties on environmental law are a species of the genus human rights treaties'.[39] As such, the climate treaty enjoys supranational status under the constitution and 'there is no legally valid option of simply omitting to combat climate change'[40] in the country. Similarly, in *Urgenda*, the Dutch Supreme Court referred to the UNFCCC, the ECHR, Conference of the Parties (COP) decisions, the precautionary principle, the principle of due diligence, the no-harm principle, the law of state responsibility, and the notion of intergenerational equity.[41]

32 Burgerlijk Wetboek book 6, s 162 (Netherlands).

33 Scope 1 emissions are direct GHG emissions from sources owned or controlled by the reporting entity. Scope 2 emissions are indirect GHG emissions associated with the production of electricity, heat, or steam purchased by the reporting entity. Scope 3 emissions are all other indirect emissions, such as those emissions associated with the extraction and production of purchased materials, fuels, and services. Contribution of Working Group III to the Fifth Assessment Report of the Intergovernmental Panel on Climate Change, *Climate Change 2014: Mitigation of Climate Change* 1260 <www.ipcc.ch/site/assets/uploads/2018/02/ipcc_wg3_ar5_full.pdf> accessed 9 February 2024.

34 *Milieudefensie* (n 29) [5.3].

35 *Commune de Grande-Synthe v France* [2020] N°427301 (Conseil d'Etat).

36 ibid [1].

37 ibid [6].

38 ibid [12].

39 *PSB* (n 9) [17].

40 ibid.

41 *Urgenda Supreme Court* (n 26).

### 9.2.1.2 IPCC and Other Forms of best Available Science

Courts have relied on the reports from the IPCC when examining the scope or standard of the duty of care of a State or a corporation. These scientific findings provide best scientific assessments of the current and projected impacts of climate change, as well as the emissions reductions that are required to prevent climate change. For example, *Thomson* shows how the work of the IPCC has provided helpful guidelines for interpreting national commitments:

> The IPCC reports provide the most up to date scientific consensus on climate change. New Zealand accepts this. To give effect to the Act and what New Zealand has accepted, recognised and committed to under the international instruments, and in light of the threat that climate change presents to humankind and the environment, I consider the publishing of a new IPCC report requires the Minister to consider whether a target set under s 224 should be reviewed. That is, it is a mandatory relevant consideration in whether an existing target should be reviewed under s 224(2).[42]

Other climate cases that cite these reports include *Urgenda*,[43] *Neubauer*,[44] *Klimaatzaak*,[45] *In re Greenpeace Southeast Asia*,[46] *Klimatická žaloba ČR*,[47] *Mathur*,[48] *Notre Affaire à Tous*,[49] *Milieudefensie*,[50] and *Future Generations*.[51]

Courts have also drawn on reports from national science institutions. In particular, the German Constitutional Court referred to evidence from the German Advisory Council on the Environment throughout its decision in *Neubauer*. In *Notre Affaire à Tous*, the Administrative Court of Paris drew from the findings of the High Council for the Climate and the Centre Interprofessionnel Technique d'études de la Pollution, an independent national scientific body and a State operator, respectively, to determine that France 'substantially exceeded its first carbon budget'.[52] Finally, the Irish Supreme Court in *Friends of the Irish Environment v Ireland* expressly gave 'significant weight'[53] to the views of the domestic Climate Change Advisory Council before quashing the government's National Mitigation Plan.

42 *Thomson* (n 22) [94].
43 *Urgenda Supreme Court* (n 26).
44 *Neubauer* (n 6).
45 *VZW Klimaatzaak Appeal* (n 3).
46 *Greenpeace* (n 11).
47 *Klimatická žaloba ČR* (n 10).
48 *Mathur Strikeout* (n 12).
49 *Notre Affaire à Tous* (n 4) [16].
50 *Milieudefensie* (n 29).
51 *Demanda Futuras Generaciones* (n 7).
52 *Notre Affaire à Tous* (n 4) [30].
53 *Friends of the Irish Environment CLG v The Government of Ireland, Ireland and the Attorney General* [2020] Appeal no 205/19 (Supreme Court of Ireland).

The growing sophistication of climate change science will likely present courts with novel opportunities to interpret State duty of care responsibilities and add to existing jurisprudence in the future. As plaintiffs articulate the impact that individual States and private actors have on global warming with greater particularity, it will be easier to determine if a defendant's action or inaction violated an affirmative climate duty. Courts will continue to play an essential role in determining the contours of those duties in accordance with new scientific advancements.

### 9.2.2 *Minimum Standard*

Courts have tended to focus on whether States have met the minimum standard of care in light of the risk of climate harm when assessing the scope of States' duty of care. In *Urgenda*, the Dutch Supreme Court issued a binding order requiring the Netherlands to set the minimum reduction level at 25 per cent by 2020 against 1990 levels, which could 'be regarded as an absolute minimum'.[54] In *VZW Klimaatzaak*, the Court of Appeal of Brussels ordered Belgium and two of its regional governments via an injunction to reduce their emissions by 55 per cent by 2030 against 1990 levels.[55] In *Neubauer*, the German Constitutional Court noted that a violation of a duty of protection occurs 'if no precautionary measures whatsoever have been taken, or if the adopted provisions and measures prove to be manifestly unsuitable or completely inadequate for achieving the required protection goal, or if the provisions and measures fall significantly short of the protection goal'.[56] This reflects the reasoning in the *German Family Farmers* case, in which the Administrative Court of Berlin considered whether the government's emissions reduction target violated 'the constitutionally required minimum level of climate protection, even if it is a global problem'.[57]

### 9.2.3 *Soft Law*

Soft law has increasingly helped courts conduct its duty of care analyses for State and non-State actors. In *Urgenda*, for example, the Supreme Court referred to numerous non-binding COP decisions as evidence of 'a high degree of consensus in the international community'[58] on the need for developed countries to reduce their GHG emissions by 25–40 per cent by 2020 compared to 1990 levels.[59] In *Milieudefensie*, soft law instruments, like the UN Guiding Principles on Business and Human Rights (UNGP), OECD Guidelines for Multinational Enterprises, and the UN Global

54 *Urgenda Supreme Court* (n 26) [7.5.1].
55 *VZW Klimaatzaak Appeal* (n 3).
56 *Neubauer* (n 6) [152].
57 *Family Farmers and Greenpeace v Germany* [2018] 00271/17/R/SP (Administrative Court of Berlin).
58 *Urgenda Supreme Court* (n 26) [7.2.7].
59 ibid [7.2.1]–[7.2.3].

Compact, were particularly instructive. Even though RDS endorsed the UNGP on its website, the court noted that such explicit support is actually 'irrelevant' given the 'authoritative' and 'universally endorsed content' of the instrument, as well as the European Commission's expectation that all European businesses adhere to the document's human rights guidance.[60] As a result, the court upheld the UNGP's suitability 'as a guideline in the interpretation of the unwritten standard of care'[61] under Dutch law. Such decisions reinforce the notion that, despite its non-binding nature, soft law has an essential role to play in establishing climate obligations.

### 9.2.4 *Defences*

One prominent argument that climate respondents make is that 'the GHG emissions from a particular activity are but a "drop in the ocean" in global terms and hence cannot be said to cause climate change harm'.[62] This defence stems in part from the 'single-entity focus of traditional regulatory and governance approaches'[63] and 'denies the complex nature of the climate change problem as one that arises because of the *cumulative* effect over time and space of numerous emissions of GHGs from a range of sources'.[64]

Courts have nevertheless upheld a State's duty to mitigate climate change despite its global nature and the fact that no one action can solve the issue. In *Massachusetts v Environmental Protection Agency (EPA)*, one of the earliest climate cases, the EPA argued that its decision not to regulate GHG emissions was because they contribute 'so insignificantly to petitioners' injuries that the Agency cannot be hauled into a federal court to answer for them.[65] The Supreme Court of the United States, however, held that the EPA has the statutory responsibility under the Clean Air Act to regulate emissions as an 'air pollutant', reasoning that agencies 'do not generally resolve massive problems in one fell swoop, but instead whittle away over time, refining their approach as circumstances change and they develop a more nuanced understanding of how best to proceed'.[66]

Courts have continued to disregard the 'drop in the ocean' defence in recent climate cases. *Thomson*, for example, observes that the subject of climate change is not a '"no-go area" for courts around the world, even if the 'problem is a global one and one country's efforts alone cannot prevent harm to that country's people and their environment'.[67] In *Urgenda*, the Dutch Supreme Court held that the State is

60 *Milieudefensie* (n 29) [4.4.11].
61 ibid.
62 Jacqueline Peel, 'Issues in Climate Change Litigation' (2011) 5 CCLR 15, 16.
63 ibid.
64 ibid.
65 *Massachusetts v EPA* 549 US 497, 517 (2007).
66 ibid 524.
67 *Thomson* (n 22) [133].

'obliged to do "its part" in order to prevent dangerous climate change, even if it is a global problem'.[68] The Brussels Court of First Instance expressly agreed with this holding in *VZW Klimaatzaak*, pointing out that the 'global dimension of the problem of dangerous global warming does not exempt the Belgian public authorities from their pre-described obligation under Articles 2 and 8 of the ECHR'.[69] Finally, *Neubauer* emphasises the importance of trust and cooperation between nations in the fight against climate change:

> [T]he particular reliance on the international community gives rise to a constitutional necessity to actually implement one's own climate action measures at the national level – in international agreement wherever possible. It is precisely because the state is dependent on international cooperation in order to effectively carry out its obligation to take climate action under Article 20A GG that it must avoid creating incentives for other states to undermine this cooperation. Its own activities should serve to strengthen international confidence in the fact that climate action – particularly the pursuit of treaty-based climate targets – can be successful while safeguarding decent living conditions, including in terms of fundamental freedoms. In practice, resolving the global climate problem is thus largely dependent on the existence of mutual trust that others will also strive to achieve the targets.[70]

Defendants in climate litigation have also argued that finding a duty of care could open the floodgates of litigation. As a result, some courts have hesitated to recognise novel duties of care in the climate context. For instance, in *Michael John Smith v Fonterra Co-Operative Group Limited*, a tort-based lawsuit in New Zealand, the country's High Court acknowledged that common law 'is capable of creating new principles and causes of action',[71] but establishing these duties involves clearing 'significant hurdles'[72] and matters of public policy, such as the potential for creating 'issues of indeterminate liability':[73]

> [I]t is unlikely that the class could be limited to the owners of coastal property. The claimed duty would be owed to anybody who can claim damage as a result of the widespread effects of climate change. In a very real sense, everyone is a polluter, and therefore a tortfeasor, and everyone is a victim and therefore a potential claimant. If a duty of the kind alleged were recognised, every New Zealander would be liable to suit from every other New Zealander.[74]

68 *Urgenda Supreme Court* (n 26) [5.7.1].

69 *VZW Klimaatzaak First Instance* (n 3) [61]. The Court of Appeal of Belgium echoed this sentiment, asserting that 'the fact that the measures adopted by the respondent parties would not suffice, taken in isolation, to prevent dangerous global warming, cannot relieve them of their positive obligations'. *VZW Klimaatzaak Appeal* (n 3) [160].

70 *Neubauer* (n 6) [202].

71 *Michael John Smith v Fonterra Co-Operative Group Limited and Others* CIV-2019-404-001730 [2020] NZHC 419 (*Smith High Court*).

72 ibid [102].

73 ibid [98(b)].

74 ibid.

The Court of Appeal agreed with this rationale, noting that the recognition of a novel climate duty 'would create a limitless class of potential plaintiffs as well as a limitless class of potential defendants'.[75] Defendants, as a result, 'would be subjected to indeterminate liability and embroiled in highly problematic and complex contribution arguments on an unprecedented scale potentially involving overseas emitters as well as New Zealand emitters'.[76] However, the Supreme Court of New Zealand has since overturned the Court of Appeal's decision and will allow all three claims to proceed to trial.[77] In so doing, the Supreme Court countered the notion that novel climate duties would result in a deluge of lawsuits. Rather, a defendant's actions or omissions 'must amount to a substantial and unreasonable interference with public rights'.[78] This limitation 'creates a significant threshold for plaintiffs' and '[o]nly some emitters will cross it'.[79]

In *Milieudefensie*, RDS raised a similar floodgates defence, asserting that '[e]very person creates significant greenhouse gas emissions'[80] in their daily lives, including the 'countless'[81] people who drive cars on a daily basis and the millions of Dutch people who fly each year.[82] As such, if the court were to impose a duty of care on RDS, that 'would have the undesirable result of opening the door to claims, "from all, against all"'.[83] However, as the next section will discuss, this argument was dismissed because there was 'no room for weighted interests'.[84]

## 9.3 EMERGING BEST PRACTICES

As climate jurisprudence continues to evolve with respect to duty of care obligations, a range of emerging best practices have developed in courts around the world. This section examines several representative best practices with an eye towards informing judges of complex issues that commonly arise in climate litigation.

### 9.3.1 *Hybrid Duty of Care Arguments*

The hybrid nature of climate litigation is perhaps best represented by the landmark *Urgenda* case. As has been pointed out, human rights arguments were 'technically

75 *Michael John Smith v Fonterra Co-Operative Group Limited and Others* CA 128/2020 [2021] NZCA 552 (*Smith Court of Appeal*).
76 ibid.
77 *Michael John Smith v Fonterra Co-Operative Group Limited and Others* [2024] NZSC 5 (*Smith Supreme Court*).
78 ibid [168].
79 ibid.
80 *Milieudefensie* (n 29) (Statement of Defense) [485].
81 ibid.
82 ibid.
83 ibid [463].
84 *Milieudefensie* (n 29) [4.5.3].

peripheral to grounds of the case',[85] which centred around the Dutch Civil Code, but 'they ended up being decisive to the result as they were utilised by the court to fill in the content of due diligence standards owed under the duty of care considered by the court'.[86] Accordingly, *Urgenda* is a 'progressive example'[87] of how courts can 'actively use the substantive and procedural provisions of international human rights law, together with soft law provisions such as targets agreed under the Paris framework, to interpret domestic law, and to bridge the gap between the international law obligations of the state concerned and its domestic law'.[88]

In *Urgenda*, the Dutch Supreme Court affirmed a District Court order that the Netherlands has a duty of care to reduce its GHG emissions by at least 25 per cent by 2020 compared to 1990 levels.[89] This responsibility stems from the unwritten rule pursuant to the aforementioned Book 6, Section 162 of the Dutch Civil Code, which prohibits acts or omissions that conflict with 'proper social conduct',[90] as well as Articles 2 and 8 of the ECHR, which protect the right to life and the right to respect for private and family life, respectively. When analysing potential violations of this tort provision before *Urgenda*, judges in the Netherlands considered 'general social notions of what may be expected from a legal person acting reasonably'.[91] In this case, the court held that the Netherlands has a duty under Articles 2 and 8 of the ECHR to 'take appropriate steps'[92] to address the 'real and immediate risk'[93] of climate change.

*Urgenda* represents an emerging best practice in part because of its forward-looking assessment of climate change impacts and its willingness to frame the State's duties around the uncertainty of that crisis. For example, the court emphasised that the Netherlands has a responsibility to take climate action even if the impacts of climate change will not materialise for decades or impact specific persons.[94] Similarly, the fact that there is uncertainty surrounding the potential materialisation of climate change impacts in the future does not relieve the State of its duty of care in the present.[95] Rather, the 'sufficiently genuine possibility'[96] of this risk materialising

85 Kumaravadivel Guruparan and Harriet Moynihan, 'Climate Change and Human Rights-Based Strategic Litigation' (*Chatham House*, November 2021) www.chathamhouse.org/2021/11/climate-change-and-human-rights-based-strategic-litigation/introduction> accessed 27 February 2024.

86 ibid.

87 ibid.

88 ibid.

89 *Urgenda Supreme Court* (n 26) [9].

90 Burgerlijk Wetboek book 6, s 162 (Netherlands).

91 *Access to Justice: Human Rights Abuses Involving Corporations – The Netherlands* (International Commission of Jurists 2013).

92 *Urgenda Supreme Court* (n 26) [5.3.2].

93 ibid [5.6.2].

94 ibid.

95 ibid [5.3.2].

96 ibid [5.6.2].

requires 'that suitable measures'[97] be taken. Although the Netherlands still has 'discretion in choosing the steps to be taken',[98] they need to be 'reasonable and suitable'[99] given the seriousness of climate change.

### 9.3.2 *Duty of Care Derived from Constitutional Rights*

The German Federal Constitutional Court's analysis in *Neubauer* represents emerging best practice in relation to how far-reaching climate obligations can be derived from constitutional provisions. The case was brought by a large group of youth plaintiffs from Germany, Nepal, and Bangladesh, who argued that Germany's Federal Climate Protection Act (Klimaschutzgesetz – KSG) violated several of their fundamental rights contained in the Basic Law (constitution).[100] The KSG sets a climate neutrality ('net-zero emission') target for 2050. Although KSG specified annual GHG emissions allowed up to 2030, emissions reductions for the post-2030 period needed for reaching climate neutrality in 2050 were undetermined. The court held that this ambiguity and its potential for immense reduction burdens after 2030 unconstitutionally jeopardised the future freedoms of the young plaintiffs.[101]

Under Articles 2(2) and 14(1) of the Basic Law, Germany must safeguard freedom rights and the fundamental right to life and physical integrity,[102] as well as property, respectively.[103] The court notably determined that both these duties encompass climate obligations. For example, Article 2(2) places an obligation on Germany to protect the life and health of current and future generations from the 'considerable risks'[104] brought on by 'increasingly severe climate change',[105] such as heat waves, flooding, and hurricanes. The State, accordingly, has a duty to engage in international treaty negotiations, establish national mitigation measures, and implement adaptation strategies to protect current and future generations from the effects of climate change.[106] Similarly, unmitigated climate change will cause houses and entire settlements in Germany to become uninhabitable due to flooding and rising sea levels.[107] The court reasoned that because the loss of property might 'be accompanied by a loss of stable community ties within the

97 ibid.
98 ibid [5.3.2].
99 ibid. The Court of Appeal of Belgium similarly found that the State breached its duty to take climate action based on Articles 2 and 8 of the ECHR and Articles 1382 and 1383 of the Belgian Civil Code. *VZW Klimaatzaak Appeal* (n 3).
100 *Neubauer* (n 6).
101 ibid [266].
102 ibid [99].
103 ibid [171].
104 ibid [148].
105 ibid.
106 ibid [148]–[150].
107 ibid.

local environment',[108] these ties must be taken into consideration under Article 14(1) GG, which grants 'a certain degree of protection to social environments that have matured to the point of being "communities"'.[109] The court found a violation of the claimants' freedom rights because of the discriminatory allocation of climate measures after 2030.[110] Those measures infringed upon the freedom rights of the young claimants by locking them into a carbon-intensive future that would inevitably require burdensome mitigation measures.

Another example of this dynamic can be found in *In re Court on its own motion v State of Himachal Pradesh*, in which India's National Green Tribunal (NGT) mandated that all visitors to Rohtang Pass – a popular tourist destination in the Himalayas – must pay a tax that addresses the presence of black carbon in the area and the 'need to tackle global warming'.[111] The holding in this case stems from several constitutional Articles that do not mention global warming, but which the NGT interpreted 'in a way that compels governments to support and encourage more effective climate change adaption efforts'.[112] For instance, Article 21 of the country's constitution protects the right to life and personal liberty, which the Supreme Court of India has liberally interpreted to encompass the right to a healthy environment.[113] Article 48A, similarly, places an obligation on the State 'to protect and improve the environment and to safeguard the forest and wildlife in the country'.[114]

*State of Himachal Pradesh* is thus rooted in rights that the court interpreted as 'being compromised by a combination of changing environmental circumstances and government inaction'.[115] Accordingly, Articles 21 and 48A provide the primary legal basis for Himachal Pradesh's duty to 'ensure due protection to the forests and environment of the country'.[116] To fulfil this duty, the tribunal held that the government must implement policy that weighs 'the need for development of industry, irrigation resources, power projects'[117] as well as the sanctity of life, public health,

108 ibid.

109 ibid.

110 ibid [266].

111 *Court on its own Motion v State of Himachal Pradesh and Ors* Application No 237 (THC)/ 2013 (CWPIL No 15 of 2010) *(State of Himachal Pradesh)* [31], [38]. 'Black carbon, or unburned fuel from vehicles, is a "major causative factor for rapid melting of glacier[s] in the Himalayan region" and a significant contributor to global warming.' ibid [3].

112 'The Status of Climate Change Litigation: A Global Review' (*UNEP*, 2017) <https://wedocs.unep.org/bitstream/handle/20.500.11822/20767/climate-change-litigation.pdf?sequence=1&isAllowed=y> accessed 9 February 2024.

113 *State of Himachal Pradesh* (n 111) [13].

114 ibid [11], [20]. The Tribunal also noted that art 51A of the constitution requires citizens to protect and improve the natural environment. As such, 'even the citizens must realize their responsibility towards restoring the degraded environment of one of the most beautiful zones of the country as well as preventing further damage'.

115 ibid.

116 ibid [14].

117 ibid [17].

and ecology.[118] These considerations form a '"reasonable person's" test'[119] involving both factors, with environmental protection ultimately having priority over unemployment and loss of revenue.[120] Himachal Pradesh's failure to properly restrict development in Rohtang Pass thereby violated its duty of care and prompted the tribunal to issue the visitor tax.

In the United States, the Due Process Clause of the country's constitution does not normally impose an obligation on the government to act, even if such action is necessary to prevent the loss of life, liberty, or property.[121] However, an exception applies when government conduct places a person in peril in deliberate indifference to their safety.[122] This 'danger creation' allows plaintiffs to bring forward a substantive due process claim, which the twenty-one youth plaintiffs in *Juliana v United States* invoked against the national government in Oregon's district court.

The *Juliana* plaintiffs contended that the government 'played a unique and central role'[123] in the creation of global warming and 'contributed to the crisis with full knowledge of the significant and unreasonable risks posed by climate change'.[124] As a result of these actions, the Due Process Clause allegedly 'imposes a special duty on defendants to use their statutory and regulatory authority to reduce greenhouse gas emissions'.[125] At the motion to dismiss stage, the court accepted the allegations as true and allowed the substantive due process challenge to proceed.[126]

The district court again considered the danger creation exception claim on motion for summary judgment,[127] with the plaintiffs presenting extensive evidence dating back to the 1960s that demonstrated a question of material fact regarding the government's 'knowledge, actions, and alleged deliberate indifference'[128] to climate change. The court acknowledged the 'complicated and novel questions about standing, historical context, and constitutional rights'[129] and denied the defendants' motion for summary judgment. This provided an opportunity for the plaintiffs to cultivate 'the most exhaustive record possible during a trial'[130] with an understanding that there was still a 'very high bar to ultimately succeed'.[131] The Ninth Circuit ultimately dismissed the plaintiffs' case for lack of standing without examining the

118 ibid.
119 ibid [12].
120 ibid.
121 *Juliana v United States* 217 F.Supp.3d 1224, 1260 (District Court of Oregon 2016).
122 ibid.
123 ibid.
124 ibid.
125 ibid.
126 ibid.
127 *Juliana v United States* 339 F. Supp. 3d 1062 (District Court of Oregon 2018).
128 ibid 1099–1101.
129 ibid 1101.
130 ibid.
131 ibid.

danger creation argument. However, the *Juliana* plaintiffs' efforts to distinguish an affirmative State duty presents an intriguing approach to climate mitigation responsibility in the United States, and the Oregon district court's willingness to allow the plaintiffs to develop a comprehensive record can be regarded as an emerging best practice for substantive due process claims in climate litigation.

### 9.3.3 *Future Emissions Targets and Future Generations*

In recent years, climate change activists, environmental organisations, and the general public have spearheaded strategic litigation aimed at the sufficiency of national climate policies.[132] This trend will likely continue with plaintiffs relying on courts to scrutinise the NDCs that countries must produce every five years under the Paris Agreement. As such, the Paris Administrative Court's recognition in *Notre Affaire à Tous* that a State cannot escape its immediate duty of care obligations by potentially meeting future emissions targets is reflective of emerging best practice.

The four plaintiff environmental organisations in *Notre Affaire à Tous* argued that France has a general duty to fight climate change based on, *inter alia*, the UNFCCC, the Paris Agreement, Articles 2 and 8 of the ECHR, and its domestic law.[133] They posited that France violated this duty by not adopting 'sufficient measures to ensure the application of the legislative and regulatory framework it has set itself to combat climate change'[134] and failing to set 'targets for the reduction of greenhouse gas emissions which do not allow the rise in the global average temperature of the atmosphere to be limited to 1.5°C'.[135] Over 2.3 million citizens signed a petition submitted with the court filings, which represents the greatest level of public support for a climate case at the time of this writing.[136]

The court highlighted how France's international and domestic commitments recognise 'the existence of an "emergency" to combat the ongoing climate change'[137] as well as 'its capacity to act effectively on this phenomenon in order to limit its causes and mitigate its harmful consequences'.[138] The country's corresponding actions include its treaty-based climate obligations to the international community and a domestic 'public policy to reduce greenhouse gas emissions … by specific and successive deadlines'.[139] France thereby accepted a duty of care to take reasonable

[132] Joana Setzer and Catherine Higham, 'Global Trends in Climate Change Litigation: 2021 Snapshot' (*LSE Grantham Research Institute on Climate Change and the Environment*, July 2021) 10 <www.lse.ac.uk/granthaminstitute/wp-content/uploads/2021/07/Global-trends-in-climate-change-litigation_2021-snapshot.pdf> accessed 24 February 2024.
[133] *Notre Affaire à Tous* (n 4) [4].
[134] ibid [17].
[135] ibid.
[136] Setzer and Higham (n 132) 16.
[137] *Notre Affaire à Tous* (n 4) [21].
[138] ibid.
[139] ibid.

political steps and address climate change. However, when the country substantially exceeded its first carbon budget, which took place during 2015 to 2018, it 'failed to carry out the actions that it had itself recognized as likely to reduce greenhouse gas emissions'.[140] Notably, the court held that France's potential to reach its national targets and reduce GHG emissions by 40 per cent in 2030 compared with 1990 levels as well as achieve carbon neutrality by 2050 'does not exonerate it from its liability'.[141] This is because France's climate mitigation missteps have resulted in additional emissions that will aggravate existing ecological damage over their lifetime in the atmosphere.[142]

In addition to *Notre Affaire à Tous*, *Neubauer* can also help judges examine a State's comprehensive climate mitigation plans and evaluate periodic implementation efforts with an eye towards intergenerational equity. In *Neubauer*, the court found that Article 20(a) of the Basic Law, which requires Germany to protect the natural foundations of life for future generations, also establishes an affirmative obligation to take climate action with the aim of achieving climate neutrality.[143] Due to the global nature of climate change, Article 20(a) 'thus contains a duty that necessarily looks beyond the domestic legal system under the sole responsibility of the individual state, and must be understood as also pointing towards the level of international activity'.[144] This obligation to act goes beyond the pursuit of climate treaties and 'extends to the implementation of agreed solutions'.[145] The court interpreted Article 20(a) in light of the goals of the Paris Agreement, and stated that 20(a) required net-zero emissions by 2050. This requirement was implemented into the KSG and thereby legally binding, but not with the needed specificity of mitigation measures for 2031–2050.

As Article 20(a) is uniquely concerned with 'how environmental burdens are spread out between different generations',[146] Germany's duty of care involves 'treat[ing] the natural foundations of life with such care … that future generations who wish to carry on preserving these foundations are not forced to engage in radical abstinence'.[147] Translated to the climate context, it is imperative that the State 'prevent[s] an overly short-sighted and thus one-sided distribution of freedom and reduction burdens to the detriment of the future'.[148] The court held that the emissions allowed before 2030 'are capable of giving rise to substantial burdens to reduce emissions'[149] beyond that time period, which creates

[140] ibid [30].
[141] ibid [31].
[142] ibid.
[143] *Neubauer* (n 6) [197]–[198].
[144] ibid [200].
[145] ibid.
[146] ibid [193].
[147] ibid.
[148] ibid [194].
[149] ibid [142].

a significant risk of impairment to fundamental rights.[150] Germany thereby violated its duty to ensure that the reduction of GHG emissions is 'spread out over time in a forward-looking'[151] and proportional manner that respects the rights of those that are young today in the future in an 'intertemporal' extension of their rights. As young plaintiffs will likely continue to rely on courts to hold States accountable for their climate actions on behalf of future generations, *Neubauer* provides insight into how courts can evaluate the long-term ambition and impacts of national climate policies.

### 9.3.4 *Duty of Care for Corporations*

The Hague District Court's historic ruling in *Milieudefensie* against RDS represents an emerging best practice for how courts should apply duty of care obligations to private actors. As mentioned earlier, by holding that RDS must reduce the Scope 1, 2, and 3 emissions of the global Shell group by net 45 per cent by 2030 relative to 2019 levels, the case marked the first time that a court ordered a corporation to adopt climate policies that are aligned with the Paris Agreement.[152] As such, it provides a potential template for judges who must consider the legal responsibility that corporate defendants have for their GHG emissions.

The main legal issue in *Milieudefensie* was whether RDS owed a duty of care to mitigate climate change based on the same unwritten notion in the Dutch Civil Code from *Urgenda*. The court ultimately sided with the plaintiffs and held that RDS has a duty to take climate action because Book 6, Section 162 of the Dutch Civil Code implies an obligation not to act in conflict with what is generally regarded as proper social conduct according to unwritten law.[153] Interpreting the nuances of this duty called 'for an assessment of all circumstances of the case in question',[154] including international law, soft law, the company's own policies, and the best available science.

Although the plaintiffs could not directly invoke the Paris Agreement and human rights established in the relationship between states and citizens – in this case, Articles 2 and 8 of the ECHR and Articles 6 and 17 of the International Covenant on Civil and Political Rights – the court nevertheless acknowledged that those rights 'may play a role in the relationship'[155] between the plaintiffs and RDS due to the fundamental interest of human rights and the value for society they embody as a

150 ibid [245].
151 ibid [243].
152 Daniel Boffey, 'Court Orders Royal Dutch Shell to Cut Carbon Emissions by 45% by 2030' (*The Guardian*, 26 May 2021) <www.theguardian.com/business/2021/may/26/court-orders-royal-dutch-shell-to-cut-carbon-emissions-by-45-by-2030> accessed 26 February 2024.
153 *Milieudefensie* (n 29) [4.4.1].
154 ibid.
155 ibid [4.4.9].

whole. It thus factored in human rights and the values they embody in its interpretation of the unwritten standard of care: ‘From the Urgenda ruling it can be deduced that Articles 2 and 8 ECHR offer protection against the consequences of dangerous climate change due to $CO_2$ emissions induced global warming’.[156] The court concluded that ‘RDS’ argument that the human rights invoked by Milieudefensie et al. offer no protection against dangerous climate change therefore does not hold. The serious and irreversible consequences of dangerous climate change in the Netherlands and the Wadden region … pose a threat to the human rights of [the claimants]’.[157]

The court also relied on the ‘universally endorsed’[158] – although non-binding – UNGP to distinguish the different responsibilities that States and businesses have in the protection of human rights. The obligation of States under international human rights law is binding and requires them to ‘prevent, investigate, punish and redress’ human rights abuses in their territory through ‘effective policies, legislation, regulations and adjudication’.[159] However, corporations must also ‘avoid infringing on the human rights of others’ and take proactive steps ‘to prevent, limit and, where necessary, address’ such abuses.[160] This duty exists independently of States’ abilities to meet their human rights obligations and ‘applies everywhere, regardless of the local legal context’.[161] As part of its duty of care, RDS thus has a responsibility to respect human rights across its entire value chain,[162] from the business relations of the Shell group, which it has a policy-setting influence over as the top holding company, to the emissions of its end-users.[163]

To ascertain what is needed from RDS to reduce GHG emissions, the Paris Agreement provided crucial guidance. The treaty, according to the court, ‘is supported by widespread international consensus’[164] and ‘represent[s] the best available scientific findings in climate science’.[165] Those findings indicate that limiting global warming to 1.5°C will require reduction pathways aiming for net 45 per cent by 2030, relative to 2010 levels, and net 100 per cent by 2050.[166] Although the instrument does not bind private actors such as RDS,[167] there is ‘broad international consensus that each company must independently work towards

156 *Miljeudefensie* (n 29) [4.4.10].
157 ibid.
158 ibid [4.4.11].
159 ibid [4.4.12].
160 ibid [4.4.15].
161 ibid.
162 ibid [4.4.17].
163 ibid [4.4.18], noting that ‘business relations’ includes places where the Shell group ‘purchases raw materials, electricity and heat’.
164 ibid.
165 ibid [4.4.27].
166 ibid [4.4.29].
167 ibid [4.4.26].

achieving net zero emissions by 2050'[168] and, similar to the *Urgenda* decision, 'RDS may be expected to do its part'.[169]

In specifying RDS's duty of care, the court set an obligation of result and a 'significant best-efforts obligation'.[170] The company's responsibility to lower the $CO_2$ emissions of the Shell group by net 45 per cent relative to 2019 levels is an obligation of result. RDS, however, has leeway to differentiate the respective reductions in Scope 1, 2, and 3 emissions, as long as it achieves the overall target reduction amount.[171] This rationale is consistent with *Urgenda's* willingness to grant the Netherlands discretion in the steps taken to meet its emissions target.[172]

On the other hand, RDS's best-efforts obligation concerns the business relations of the Shell group, including the Scope 3 emissions of its end-users. The court declared that RDS may need to take 'necessary steps' to prevent the serious risks from their $CO_2$ emissions, and to 'use its influence to limit any lasting consequences as much as possible'.[173] It is unclear how RDS should go about exerting this pressure on its value chain, but a possible consequence could be that the company 'forgo[es] new investments in the extraction of fossil fuels' or 'limit[s] its production of fossil resources'.[174] Future jurisprudence will thus be crucial to addressing this gap in climate litigation with respect to corporations.

### 9.3.5 *Environmental Impact Assessments*

As mentioned earlier, one of the difficulties of climate litigation is that the single-entity regulatory focus of governments often overlooks the complex, cumulative nature of climate change. However, international law maintains that projects with the potential for significant transboundary harm must go through the Environmental Impact Assessment (EIA) process. This procedural requirement is supported by International Law Commission scholarship[175] and International Court of Justice case law, particularly *Pulp Mills on the River Uruguay (Argentina v Uruguay) (Pulp*

[168] ibid [4.4.36].
[169] ibid [4.4.26]. The court chose not to discuss whether RDS qualifies as a 'non-Party stakeholder' to the Paris Agreement as discussed at the 25th Conference of the Parties to the UNFCCC in Madrid. Instead, it noted that 'the reduction of $CO_2$ emissions and global warming cannot be achieved by states alone' and 'there has been broad international consensus about the need for non-state action'.
[170] ibid [4.4.55].
[171] ibid [4.4.38]–[4.4.39]. Per the plaintiffs' claims, the court set 2019 as the base year, instead of 2010, because that was the year the summons was issued.
[172] *Urgenda Supreme Court* (n 26) [5.3.2].
[173] *Milieudefensie* (n 29) [4.4.39].
[174] ibid.
[175] ILC, 'Draft Articles on Responsibility of States for Internationally Wrongful Acts, with commentaries' (2001) UN Doc A/RES/56/83 (2001), 53 UN GAOR Supp (No 10) at 43, Supp (No 10) A/56/10 (IV.E.1) 154.

*Mills*), a 2010 dispute in which the court held that States should determine EIA requirements and ensure that the assessment is conducted with due diligence before a project's commencement.[176]

*Save Lamu et al v National Environmental Management Authority and Amu Power Co Ltd* provides insight into the role of an EIA in climate litigation and how these international norms can play out in domestic courts.[177] Kenya adheres to international law by requiring coal plant developers to secure an EIA before construction begins on a project. This obligation is cemented in its national constitution, the Environmental Management and Coordination Act, 1999, the Environmental (Impact Assessment and Audit) Regulations, and the Energy Act, 2019.[178] Public participation is an essential part of Kenya's EIA process and, although an agency is not required 'to accept the view given as dispositive',[179] it does create 'a duty for the government agency or Public Official involved to take into consideration, in good faith, all the views received'.[180] Likewise, it is not necessary for every person to support a project or for a proponent to 'address every unreasonable demand and suggestion',[181] but 'even the most feeble of voices [must] be heard'.[182]

In *Save Lamu*, the National Environmental Tribunal revoked Amu Power Company's EIA licence for a two-billion-dollar coal facility because the National Environmental Management Authority issued it without 'proper and effective public participation'.[183] The tribunal held that the National Environmental Management Authority 'owed a duty to properly supervise and ensure there had been compliance'[184] with EIA requirements, but the agency's efforts were inadequate.[185] The fact that the public did not have information on the project's potential climate impacts before providing testimony was regarded as particularly troubling.[186] Although Amu Power's EIA was ultimately an 'impressive piece of literal work',[187] it was 'devoid of public consultation content, in the manner prescribed by the law, thus rendering it ineffective and at best only of academic value'.[188]

176 *Pulp Mills on the River Uruguay (Argentina v Uruguay)* (Merits) [2010] ICJ Rep 14 [205].
177 *Save Lamu et al v National Environmental Management Authority and Amu Power Co Ltd* [2016] Tribunal Appeal No Net 196 of 2016 (Kenya Environmental Tribunal).
178 ibid [18], observing the Energy Act 2019 (Kenya) art 107(2)(d) requires a Strategic Environment Assessment and Social Impact Assessment.
179 ibid [25] (quoting *Mui Coal Basin Local Community and 15 others v Permanent Secretary Ministry of Energy and 17 others* [2015] eKLR (*Mui Coal Basin*) [97]).
180 ibid.
181 ibid [50].
182 ibid.
183 ibid [151].
184 ibid [71].
185 ibid.
186 ibid [69].
187 ibid [73].
188 ibid.

As States continue to rely on fossil fuels to meet their domestic power needs, *Save Lamu* underscores how an EIA can be a powerful procedural requirement.[189] In fact, it may be the only way for plaintiffs to successfully challenge the construction of projects with significant emissions in some jurisdictions. In Kenya, for example, 'if the requisite conditions are met with respect to environmental matters including the due and proper preparation of an EIA study … coal fired power plants remain, for the time being, a lawful option'.[190] The *Save Lamu* tribunal's willingness to uphold the normative value of those procedural conditions can thus be considered an emerging best practice.

*Earthlife Africa Johannesburg v Minister of Environmental Affairs and Others*[191] can also be seen as a companion case to *Save Lamu* with respect to EIA considerations. South Africa's High Court in Pretoria determined that 'climate change impacts of coal-fired power stations are relevant factors that must be considered before granting environmental authorisation'.[192] The environmental authorisation in *Earthlife* was granted by the Chief Director of the Department of Environmental Affairs to the Thabametsi Power Company Limited for a proposed 1200-megawatt coal-fired plant station in Limpopo Province.[193] Under South Africa's constitution, courts interpreting legislation 'must prefer any reasonable interpretation'[194] consistent with international law 'over any alternative interpretation that is inconsistent with international law'.[195] Thus, international agreements on climate change are relevant to the proper interpretation of the National Environmental Management Act (NEMA) that governs environmental authorisations in South Africa.[196]

[189] Other cases of note that focus on procedural failures include *WildEarth Guardians v Zinke* 368 F.Supp.3d 41 (District Court of Columbia) and *Philippi Horticultural Area Food & Farming Campaign, et al v MEC for Local Government, Environmental Affairs and Development Planning: Western Cape, et al* [2020] High Court of South Africa (Western Cape Division) 39724/2019. In *WildEarth Guardians* [75] the United States District Court for the District of Columbia found that the Bureau of Land Management (BLM) violated the National Environmental Policy Act when it failed to take a hard look at the climate impacts from its oil and gas leases in three states. The court held that although BLM 'may determine that each lease sale individually has a de minimis impact on climate change', it 'must also consider the cumulative impact of GHG emissions generated by past, present, or reasonably foreseeable BLM lease sales in the region and nation'. In *Philippi Horticultural Area Food & Farming Campaign* [4.2.1] South Africa's High Court in Cape Town required the city to reconsider 'any report(s) which detail the impacts' of a proposed aquifer development 'in the context of climate change and water scarcity'.

[190] *Save Lamu* (n 177) [19].

[191] *Earthlife Africa Johannesburg v Minister of Environmental Affairs and Others* [2017] 65662/16 <http://climatecasechart.com/wp-content/uploads/sites/16/non-us-case-documents/2017/20170306_Case-no.-6566216_judgment-1.pdf> accessed 27 March 2023.

[192] ibid [91].

[193] ibid [1]–[2].

[194] ibid [83].

[195] ibid.

[196] ibid.

The *Earthlife* court noted that the absence of an express provision requiring a climate change impact assessment 'does not entail that there is no legal duty to consider climate change'.[197] Rather, NEMA impliedly imposes a peremptory statutory duty on the Chief Director to 'thoroughly investigate climate change impacts'[198] with national and international consequences.

Even if new coal-fired power stations are permitted by the Paris Agreement and South Africa's NDC, a climate change impact assessment is 'necessary and relevant'[199] to the EIA process. This is because the assessment ensures that the proposed development fits South Africa's peak, plateau, and decline trajectory outlined in its NDC as well as 'its commitment to build cleaner and more efficient' coal plants.[200] Ascertaining if a climate assessment has been made involves a narrow examination of conduct: 'A formal expert report on climate change impacts will be the best evidentiary means of establishing that this relevant factor in its multifaceted dimensions was indeed considered, while the absence of one will be symptomatic of the fact that it was not'.[201] Since the Chief Director did not consider any expert climate report before granting Thabametsi an environmental authorisation, the court determined that he overlooked relevant considerations.[202]

*Earthlife* highlights the notion that a national environmental assessment statute can implicitly create climate mitigation duties through the EIA process. This duty affects the State agencies that oversee environmental authorisations as well as the companies carrying out EIAs for compliance purposes. *Earthlife* is therefore significant because it represents a progression from the *Save Lamu* decision and promotes a more robust standard of conduct incorporating treaty-based climate commitments and international law obligations. The case may be especially relevant to dualist systems, where judges must consider a State's responsibilities to the global community and their relationship to domestic environmental legislation.

A recent example of the importance of comprehensively evaluating climate impacts in an EIA assessment can be found in *Greenpeace Nordic and Nature & Youth v Energy Ministry*.[203] The Oslo District Court held that the Norwegian Energy Ministry's approval of three oil and gas fields in the North Sea was invalid because the EIAs did not include combustion (Scope 3) emissions data from the oil and gas produced. This failure went against the idea that EIAs 'must be objective and so comprehensive and complete' that authorities are properly aware of potential environmental harms and the public can gain 'real insight into the climate effects of

[197] ibid [88].
[198] ibid [124].
[199] ibid [90].
[200] ibid.
[201] ibid [88].
[202] ibid [101].
[203] *Greenpeace Nordic and Nature & Youth v Energy Ministry* [2024] Case no 23-099330TVI-TOSL/05 (Oslo District Court).

the combustion emissions'.[204] This rationale is reflective of emerging best practice as it underscores the crucial role Scope 3 emissions data plays in informing both administrative decisionmakers and the public.

### 9.3.6 *Drop in the Ocean Defence*

As described earlier, *Massachusetts v EPA* remains notable in part for the United States Supreme Court's response to the drop in the ocean defence invoked by the EPA. The court disagreed with the agency's assertion that 'gas emissions from developing nations, particularly China and India, are likely to offset any marginal domestic decrease'[205] from its regulation of vehicle emissions. The court reasoned that the possibility that other developing countries may increase GHG emissions in the future is irrelevant since a 'reduction in domestic emissions would slow the pace of global emissions increases, no matter what happens elsewhere'.[206] It is not only this forward-looking rationale that is reflective of emerging best practices; so, too, is the court's willingness to assert its jurisdiction by declaring that, even if 'regulating motor-vehicle emissions will not by itself *reverse* global warming',[207] it still has the ability to determine whether the EPA has the 'duty to take steps to *slow* or *reduce* it'.[208] Such boldness will likely be required of courts in the future as complex climate issues continue to arise with governments and regulatory agencies serving as defendants.

Over a decade and a half later, the line of reasoning in *Massachusetts v EPA* that countered the EPA's drop in the ocean defence continues to play a crucial role in climate cases. This is noticeably apparent in the *Urgenda* decision, in which the Dutch Supreme Court points out that the failure of other States to take climate action is not an excuse for the Netherlands to neglect its duty of care obligations.[209] Even if those countries continue to emit large amounts of pollutants, the Netherlands is still responsible for 'its part'[210] in the climate crisis, as 'no reduction [in GHG emissions] is negligible'.[211] The *Neubauer* court similarly explained that Germany 'may not evade its responsibility here by pointing to greenhouse gas emissions in other states'.[212] Instead, '[i]t's own activities should serve to strengthen

[204] ibid [98]–[99].
[205] *Massachusetts v EPA* (n 65) [524].
[206] ibid.
[207] ibid [525].
[208] ibid.
[209] *Urgenda Supreme Court* (n 26) [5.7.7].
[210] ibid [5.7.1].
[211] ibid [5.7.8]. The *VZW Klimaatzaak* court also cited this logic in reaching its holding, see *VZW Klimaatzaak First Instance* (n 3) [61] ('the global dimension of the problem of dangerous global warming does not exempt the Belgian public authorities from their pre-described obligation under Articles 2 and 8 of the ECHR. In this respect, the Court agrees with the view of the Dutch Supreme Court in the *Urgenda* case').
[212] *Neubauer* (n 6) [202].

international confidence'[213] as addressing climate change is 'largely dependent on the existence of mutual trust that others will also strive to achieve the[ir] targets'.[214] In *Klimatická žaloba ČR*, the Czech court declared that 'the individual responsibility of the States Parties to the Paris Agreement cannot be excluded by reference to the level of emission contributions of other States'[215] since this 'approach would make effective legal protection impossible where the State in question is not a significant emitter of greenhouse gases on a global scale'.[216] Accordingly, the willingness of courts to uphold individual duty of care obligations – irrespective of the comparative emissions of others – is reflective of emerging best practices in what is ultimately a collective effort against climate change.

### 9.3.7 *Floodgates Defence*

The Hague District Court's rejection of the floodgates defence in *Milieudefensie* reflects an emerging best practice that will become more important as duty of care jurisprudence evolves in climate litigation. The court rebutted RDS's floodgates argument by asserting that the 'policy, policy intentions and ambitions'[217] of RDS for the Shell group were 'incompatible'[218] with its reduction obligation. This incompatibility thereby 'implie[d] an imminent violation'[219] of RDS's reduction obligation and, as such, it was not necessary for the court to consider if it was appropriate to impose a climate duty on a single private party or 'whether or not this invites everyone in global society to lodge claims against each other'.[220] In future cases, courts that choose to address the merits of the floodgates defence may opt to do so through a fact-specific inquiry.[221]

213 ibid.

214 ibid. Note that the Court of Appeal of Belgium expressly referenced *Urgenda* and *Neubauer* in its rejection of the government's drop in the ocean defence. *VZW Klimaatzaak Appeal* (n 3) [160].

215 *Klimatická žaloba ČR* (n 10) [325]. Note, however, that the Supreme Administrative Court of the Czech Republic overturned this decision in February 2023. *Klimatická žaloba ČR v Czech Republic* 9 As 116/2022 – 166 (Supreme Administrative Court).

216 ibid.

217 *Milieudefensie* (n 29) [4.5.3].

218 ibid.

219 ibid.

220 ibid.

221 In *Sharma and others v Minister for the Environment*, the Federal Court of Australia substantively dismissed the defendant's floodgates argument as a 'false premise' in ruling that the Minister for the Environment had a duty of care to children when considering a coal expansion project. See *Sharma and others v Minister for the Environment* [2021] FCA 560 (*Sharma First Instance*). According to the court, '[I]t does not follow from the recognition of a duty of care based on the relationship between the Minister and the Children that the Minister owes a duty of care to others or that anyone else involved in contributing to greenhouse gas emissions owes the same duty'. ibid [488]. As the relationship between the Minister and the Children is distinctly 'unique to them', any novel climate duties considered by the court in the future would require a unique multi-factorial assessment. Even though the decision was later overturned, the handling of the floodgates defence displays how the judiciary is well-equipped to sift through frivolous climate claims on a case-by-case basis.

## 9.4 REPLICABILITY

As climate litigation cases grow in complexity and across geographic regions, there is a good probability that a more developed jurisprudence will form around State duty of care obligations. National climate change laws and policies, which have doubled roughly every four years since the adoption of the Kyoto Protocol in 1997,[222] are 'by far the most commonly cited sources of climate obligations'.[223] At the time of this writing, there are more than 2,250 such laws and policies around the world.[224] This steadily expanding stock of climate legislation will provide plaintiffs with increased flexibility to hold States and private actors accountable for their respective duties of care.

Similarly, the Paris Agreement will remain a valuable source of international law that will help courts contextualise Parties' domestic mitigation obligations within their larger commitments to the global community. The communication and implementation of Parties' NDCs, in particular, will likely be a starting point for future legal arguments centred around duties of care and the 'highest possible ambition' requirement of Article 4(3). As each NDC must represent a progression in relation to the previous one,[225] plaintiffs will have important comparative reference points.

Whether a climate case concerns substantive domestic policy or the ambition of an NDC, the emerging best practices detailed in the last section offer insight into when a duty of care violation may have occurred. In this respect, *Urgenda* may be particularly useful in situations that call for a hybrid legal strategy relying on a mix of tort, international, and domestic law. Former UN High Commissioner for Human Rights Michelle Bachelet has not only cited the importance of *Urgenda*, she has emphasised the 'even greater importance of it being swiftly replicated in other countries'.[226] Although tort law will vary by jurisdiction, the rights-based aspect of the decision should bolster its replicability, particularly in nations that are Parties to the ECHR. This dynamic can be observed in cases such as *Notre Affaire à Tous* and *Friends of the Irish Environment*.

*Neubauer*, on the other hand, may be more relevant when plaintiffs aim to invoke constitutional protections or the rights of future generations when challenging national climate plans. In particular, the willingness of the German Federal Constitutional Court to derive a State's duty to allocate fairly over time the burden

[222] Michal Nachmany and others, 'Global Trends in Climate Change Legislation and Litigation' (*LSE Grantham Research Institute on Climate Change and the Environment*, 2017) 8 <http://archive.ipu.org/pdf/publications/global.pdf> accessed 24 February 2024. In 1997, there were only sixty climate laws in existence.

[223] Global Climate Litigation Report 2020 (n 1) 47.

[224] 'Climate Change Laws of the World' <https://climate-laws.org/> accessed 27 February 2024.

[225] Paris Agreement (n 13) art 4(3).

[226] 'Bachelet Welcomes Top Court's Landmark Decision to Protect Human Rights from Climate Change' (*OHCHR*, 20 December 2019) <www.ohchr.org/EN/NewsEvents/Pages/DisplayNews.aspx?NewsID=25450&LangID=E> accessed 26 February 2024.

associated with climate action from constitutional provisions that protect certain freedom rights appears ripe for duplication.[227] This common denominator could thereby serve as the basis for future claims in the climate context with parallels made to the German Constitutional Court's interpretation of Article 2(2). Similarly, given the disastrous impacts of climate change on ecosystems, the right to a healthy environment, which is enshrined in constitutional or legislative provisions of over 150 States and recognised by the UN General Assembly and UN Human Rights Council, could also provide a legal basis for future climate litigants.[228]

*Neubauer* even opens the possibility that Germany and other States could have a constitutional duty to protect individuals outside its borders from climate impacts. The German Constitutional Court granted the plaintiffs living in Bangladesh and Nepal standing because impacts on those plaintiffs could not 'be ruled out from the outset'.[229] However, although such a duty is 'conceivable in principle',[230] the court declined to address it substantively since the scope of protections abroad are context-specific and not codified in the KSG.[231] One possible factor that could establish this climate duty is if 'the severe impairments already or potentially faced by the complainants due to climate change are caused to some – albeit small – extent by greenhouse gas emissions emanating from Germany'.[232] This obligation would be limited by the difficulty of implementing adaptation measures in other countries[233] and, therefore, Germany's theoretical duty to residents abroad would 'not have the same content'[234] as its domestic equivalent. Nevertheless, the court's willingness to consider the possibility of a climate duty to individuals outside its borders lays an intriguing foundation for future claims in Germany and beyond.

Another emerging best practice that appears to be ripe for replication is the *Milieudefensie* court's reasoning in imposing a climate duty on a corporate actor. It has been argued that it 'is hard to overstate the consequences of a decision that is already being hailed as a turning point for big oil'.[235] Accordingly, 'the replicability of the arguments and the international standards and common facts that comprise'

227 John Sprankling, 'The Global Right to Property' (2014) 52 Columbia Journal of Transnational Law 464, 491.
228 OHCHR, 'Report of the Special Rapporteur on the Issue of Human Rights Obligations Relating to the Enjoyment of a Safe, Clean, Healthy and Sustainable Environment' (2019) UN Doc A/HRC/43/53 [13]; UNHCR, 'The Human Right to a Clean, Healthy and Sustainable Environment' in 'Resolution Adopted by the Human Rights Council on 8 October 2021' (2021) UN Doc A/HRC/RES/48/13; UNGA, 'The Human Right to a Clean, Healthy and Sustainable Environment' (2022) UN Doc A/76/L.75.
229 *Neubauer* (n 6) [90].
230 ibid [174].
231 ibid [175].
232 ibid.
233 ibid [178].
234 ibid.
235 Tessa Khan, 'Shell's Historic Loss in The Hague Is a Turning Point in the Fight against Big Oil' (*The Guardian*, 1 June 2021) <www.theguardian.com/commentisfree/2021/jun/01/shell-historic-loss-hague-fight-big-oil> accessed 27 February 2024.

the case 'will inspire a wave of similar actions around the world'.[236] Thus, the *Milieudefensie* court's use of international instruments, such as the UNGP and the Paris Agreement, will likely be instructive beyond the Netherlands' judicial system as climate litigants shift their attention towards corporations.

## 9.5 CONCLUSION

In interpreting the appropriate duty of care, courts have relied on international law and best available science, such as reports from the IPCC, international soft law, and national climate bodies. These cases have largely shied away from ascertaining the exact scope of a State's duty of care and instead looked at whether the appropriate measures reasonably required to mitigate climate change were adopted. In the process, a range of emerging best practices have taken shape, from the derivation of climate duties from constitutional provisions to the notion that States must each do their best and take climate action no matter their national emissions. Some of these emerging best practices will be more replicable than others, particularly in jurisdictions that share common legal systems as well as similar laws and international commitments with the cases analysed in this chapter. Considering the number of landmark decisions that have addressed duty of care owed by States and corporations in recent years – not to mention advisory opinions on climate change from the International Court of Justice, Inter-American Court of Human Rights, and the International Tribunal for the Law of the Sea in the near term[237] – this is a particularly dynamic area of climate jurisprudence that should continue to evolve rapidly as more cases come to trial.

[236] ibid.

[237] Obligations of States in Respect of Climate Change (Request For Advisory Opinion) <www.icj-cij.org/sites/default/files/case-related/187/187-20230412-app-01-00-en.pdf> accessed 24 February 2024; Petition filed in Request for an advisory opinion on the scope of the state obligations for responding to the climate emergency (IACtHR) <www.corteidh.or.cr/docs/opiniones/soc_1_2023_en.pdf> accessed 24 February 2024; Request for an Advisory Opinion of 12 December 2022 <www.itlos.org/fileadmin/itlos/documents/cases/31/Request_for_Advisory_Opinion_COSIS_12.12.22.pdf> accessed 24 February 2024.

# 10

# International Atmospheric Trust

*Rachel M. Pemberton and Michael C. Blumm**

## 10.1 INTRODUCTION

Climate change litigation is surging in the face of scientific consensus that Earth's warming over the past century is dramatically interfering with human and natural systems.[1] Given the complexity of the problem, climate change plaintiffs often bring creative claims using 'unconventional' legal tools outside the realm of environmental statutes.[2] One such tool is the public trust doctrine, an ancient doctrine rooted in the writings of Justinian that exemplifies the democratic principle of anti-monopolisation over public resources.[3] The public trust doctrine recognises that sovereigns have an inherent duty as an incident of their sovereignty to act as a trustee over public resources.[4] Although the doctrine was traditionally invoked to protect navigable waters for public use[5] – particularly in England and

* Rachel M. Pemberton is a practicing attorney in the State of Oregon and an honours graduate of Lewis & Clark Law School. Michael C. Blumm is the Jeffrey Bain Faculty Scholar and Professor of Law at Lewis & Clark Law School. An earlier version of this chapter appeared in (2022) Utah Law Review 941. Professor Blumm is co-author of the only casebook on public trust law, cited below in n 28, which includes excerpts from and commentary on many of the cases discussed in this chapter.

1 'Scientific Consensus: Earth's Climate Is Warming' (NASA *Global Climate Change*, 2022) <https://climate.nasa.gov/scientific-consensus/> accessed 24 February 2024 (stating that at least 97% of climate scientists agree that climate change is 'extremely likely due to human activities').

2 See Mary Christina Wood and Charles W. Woodward IV, 'Atmospheric Trust Litigation and the Constitutional Right to a Healthy Climate System: Judicial Recognition at Last' (2016) 6 WJELP 633, 643–645 (describing the need for a 'macro approach' to climate change litigation and distinguishing such an approach from climate change litigation relying on statutory or nuisance law).

3 See generally Michael C. Blumm and Aurora Paulsen Moses, 'The Public Trust as an Antimonopoly Doctrine' (2017) 44 Boston College Environmental Law Affairs Review 1.

4 See Karl S. Coplan, 'Public Trust Limits on Greenhouse Gas Trading Schemes: A Sustainable Middle Ground?' (2010) 35 Columbia Journal of Environmental Law 311 ('Public trust principles have been described as an essential attribute of sovereignty across cultures and across millennia').

5 See Charles F. Wilkinson, 'The Headwaters of the Public Trust: Some Thoughts on the Source and Scope of the Traditional Doctrine' (1989) 19 Environmental Law 425, 428–430. ('A great many countries have legal rules that, in one fashion or another, give special treatment to major bodies of water' with roots including ancient Roman and Chinese law, medieval Spanish and French law, and Muslim and Native American cultures.)

the United States[6] – courts across the globe have expanded the doctrine's scope in numerous contexts.[7] This ancient doctrine's continuing relevance to natural resources law demonstrates its adaptable nature.[8]

Plaintiffs bringing atmospheric trust[9] claims often face issues of justiciability that do not normally arise when courts apply the public trust doctrine to long-recognised, 'traditional' public trust resources – navigable waterways.[10] Nonetheless, understanding the impending threats posed by climate change, several courts have concluded that the atmosphere is within the doctrine's scope.[11] Numerous other courts have at least recognised the public's strong interest in a properly functioning climate system.[12] This chapter identifies and explores two analytical frameworks evident in international atmospheric trust jurisprudence as emerging best practices: constitutional recognition tied to intergenerational equity and inter-resource affectation.[13] International jurists can and should continue to employ these frameworks when they evaluate atmospheric trust claims.

This chapter will show that the public trust doctrine protects the atmosphere whenever constitutional language establishes public rights in or the sovereign's responsibility for air and climate, a healthy environment, or natural resources

[6] See e.g. *Ill Cent RR Co v Illinois* 146 US 387 (1892) (upholding a state legislature's invalidation of a former legislative grant of submerged lands beneath Chicago harbour to a private railroad company as inconsistent with the sovereign trust over navigable waters), but see *Georgia v Tenn Copper Co* 206 US 230, 237 (1907) (explaining, in a suit by one state to enjoin noxious gas discharges from another state, that each 'state has an interest independent of and behind the titles of its citizens, in all the earth and air within its domain').

[7] See Section 10.1.1.

[8] See Ved P. Nanda and William K. Ris Jr, 'The Public Trust Doctrine: A Viable Approach to International Environmental Protection' (1976) 5 Ecology Law Quarterly 291, 296 ('The doctrine has qualities of breadth and flexibility that make it particularly useful to the solution of complex international environmental problems').

[9] In this chapter, we refer to application of the public trust doctrine to the atmosphere as an 'atmospheric trust'. Cf Michael C. Blumm and Mary Christina Wood, 'No Ordinary Lawsuit: Climate Change, Due Process, and the Public Trust Doctrine' (2017) 67 American University Law Review 1, 21–30, 67–83 (detailing atmospheric trust litigation); Mary Christina Wood, 'Atmospheric Trust Litigation' in William C. G. Burns and Hari M. Osofsky (eds), *Adjudicating Climate Change: State, National and International Approaches* (Cambridge University Press 2009) 99.

[10] See e.g. *Clean Air Council v United States* 362 F.Supp.3d 237 (District Court of Pennsylvania) (dismissing plaintiffs' atmospheric trust suit for lack of standing and, in the alternative, as alleging a non-justiciable political question); *La Rose v Her Majesty the Queen* [2020] 2020 FCR 1008 [102] (Federal Court of Ontario) (granting government's motion to dismiss because 'the public trust doctrine, while justiciable, does not disclose a reasonable cause of action') (*appeal pending*, A-289–20).

[11] See Section 10.2.2.

[12] See Section 10.1.4.

[13] One expert noted that 'an increasing number of domestic courts around the world are considering the issue of climate change and citing to … the decisions of the courts of other countries'. Tiffany Challe-Campiz and Michale B. Gerrard, 'Taking Climate Change to the International Court of Justice: Legal and Procedural Issues' (*Sabin Center*, 2021) <http://blogs.law.columbia.edu/climatechange/2021/09/29/taking-climate-change-to-the-international-court-of-justice-legal-and-procedural-issues/> accessed 27 February 2024.

generally. Many courts have rooted their support for an atmospheric trust in constitutional language, even absent an explicit reference to air or climate, where the relevant constitution establishes common rights in a healthy environment or natural resources.[14] Judicial embrace is strongest when the relevant constitutional provision also speaks to principles of intergenerational equity.[15] Thus, courts appear to be sensitive to the long-term challenges inherent in natural resource management and recognise that the sovereign is in the best position to ensure the continued viability of those resources by exercising its trust duties.

This chapter also illustrates that the atmosphere is subject to the public trust doctrine whenever plaintiffs allege, with supporting scientific evidence, that climate change has impaired their use of traditional public trust resources.[16] Although courts have not always held that the atmosphere itself is a public trust resource, several courts have concluded that threats to non-traditional public trust resources are intricately tied to traditional public trust resources.[17] In at least one court's view, the connection between the atmosphere and navigable waters is sufficient to bring the atmosphere within the public trust doctrine's scope as a matter of inter-resource affectation.[18] Likewise, some courts have expanded the public trust doctrine to include groundwater as a trust resource – relying on the scientific consensus that ground and surface waters are interconnected – to hold that when groundwater use affects surface waters, the groundwater must be managed consistent with the public trust.[19] This basic reasoning applies with equal force to the atmosphere, the degradation of which has scientifically demonstrable effects on navigable surface waters.[20]

The chapter proceeds as follows. Section 10.1 provides additional context and background on the public trust doctrine. Subsequent sections explore the doctrine's application to the atmosphere. Section 10.2 discusses developments in atmospheric trust case law; Section 10.3 presents the emerging best practices associated with applying the public trust doctrine to the atmosphere in the context of climate change litigation; and Section 10.4 provides guidance on key issues of replicability. The chapter concludes that the public trust doctrine, when analysed by courts under either of the frameworks discussed, gives rise to an atmospheric trust that the sovereign must manage in the public interest and safeguard against substantial impairment.[21]

14 See Sections 10.2.2.2–10.2.2.3.
15 See Section 10.3.1.
16 See Section 10.1.3 (identifying navigable waterways as the traditional public trust resources).
17 See Sections 10.2.3 and 10.3.2.
18 See Section 10.3.2.
19 See Section 10.2.3.
20 See e.g. Maggie Fox and Vickie Allen, 'Climate Change Drying Up Big Rivers, Study Finds' (*Reuters*, 21 April 2009) <www.reuters.com/article/us-climate-rivers/climate-change-drying-up-big-rivers-study-finds-idUSTRE53K4MR20090421> accessed 27 February 2024.
21 See *Ill Cent RR Co* (n 6) [452][53] (holding that any improvements to public trust property may 'not substantially impair the public interest' because the state may not relinquish 'control of property in which the public has an interest').

### 10.1.1 *The Nature of the Public Trust Doctrine*

'The public trust [doctrine] is a dual concept of sovereign right and responsibility.'[22] As courts see it, 'public trust claims are unique because they concern inherent attributes of sovereignty'[23] and do not depend on regulations, statutes, or even constitutions for their force.[24] One court in the United States explained that 'in its broadest sense, the term 'public trust' refers to the fundamental understanding that no government can legitimately abdicate its core sovereign powers'.[25] Indeed, 'the public trust imposes on the government an obligation to protect the *res* of the trust', and 'a defining feature of that obligation is that it cannot be legislated away'.[26] In other words, with respect to 'essential natural resources', 'the sovereign's public trust obligations prevent it from depriving a future legislature of the natural resources necessary to provide for the well-being and survival of its citizens'.[27] Since it is both a sovereign right and responsibility, the public trust doctrine empowers the sovereign to hold essential natural resources in trust for the public and also requires the sovereign to ensure those resources remain available for public use and enjoyment.

### 10.1.2 *Basic Trust Principles*

'A trust is a type of ownership in which one party manages property for the benefit of another party'.[28] The premise of the trust relationship, therefore, is that 'the trustee is under a fiduciary obligation to manage the assets for the sole benefit of the

22 *In re Water Use Permit Applications for Waiāhole Ditch*, 9 P.3d 409, 447 (Supreme Court of Hawai'i).

23 *Juliana v United States* 947 F.3d 1159 (9th Cir 2020). See also ibid *Waiāhole Ditch* 443 (stating that 'history and precedent have established the public trust as an inherent attribute of sovereign authority'); *Parks v Cooper*, 676 N.W.2d 823, 837 (Supreme Court of South Dakota 2004); *Butler ex rel Peshlakai v Brewer* No. 1 CA-CV 12-0347, 2013 WL 1091209, at [4] (Court of Appeals for Arizona 2013) (explaining that the public trust doctrine is derived 'from the inherent nature of Arizona's status as a sovereign state'); *Mineral Cnty v Lyons Cnty* 473 P.3d 418, 425 (Supreme Court of Nevada 2020) (characterising the public trust doctrine as being 'derive[d] from inherent limitations on a state's sovereign powers').

24 See *Minors Oposa v Factoran* [1993] GR No 101083, 224 SCRA 792 *(Minors Oposa v Factoran)* (holding that 'the right to a balanced and healthful ecology' belongs to a unique category of basic rights, 'for it concerns nothing less than self-preservation and self-perpetuation … the advancement of which may even be said to predate all governments and constitutions').

25 *Juliana District Court* (n 27) 1252 (citing *Stone v Mississippi* 101 US 814, 820 (1879)).

26 ibid 1260. See also *Ill Cent RR Co* (n 6) (explaining that 'legislative acts concerning public interests are necessarily public laws' and holding that 'the legislature could not give away nor sell the discretion of its successors').

27 *Juliana v United States* 217 F.Supp.3d 1224, 1253 (District Court of Oregon 2016) (*Juliana District Court*). See also *Ill Cent RR Co* (n 6) (explaining that 'every succeeding legislature possesses the same jurisdiction and power as its predecessor' and that 'every legislature must, at the time of its existence, exercise the power of the state in the execution of the trust devolved upon it').

28 Michael C. Blumm and Mary C. Wood, *The Public Trust Doctrine in Environmental and Natural Resources Law* (Carolina Academic Press 2021) 3.

beneficiaries'.[29] These basic principles apply in private and sovereign contexts; 'in the case of the public trust, the beneficiaries are the citizens'.[30] The implication is that if a public asset – such as the atmosphere – does indeed fall within the *res* of a public natural resources trust, the sovereign trustee must manage that public asset for the sole benefit of the citizen beneficiaries.

As noted by a US court, 'the natural resources trust operates according to basic trust principles, which impose upon the trustee a fiduciary duty to 'protect the trust property against damage or destruction'.[31] Because 'the trustee owes this duty equally to both current and future beneficiaries of the trust',[32] the natural resources trust is necessarily intergenerational. Moreover, once 'the existence of a fiduciary duty on the part of the State to protect a public resource' has been established, 'the duty would not seem to depend on the source of the threatened harm'.[33] In other words, the sovereign owes a public trust duty regardless of whether the sovereign is involved in bringing about harm or a threat of harm to the public trust *res*.

The public trust doctrine imposes three categories of restrictions on the sovereign's authority to administer the natural resources trust.[34] First, trust property must 'be used for a public purpose' and must also 'be held available for use by the general public'.[35] Second, trust property may never be sold.[36] Third, trust property 'must be maintained for particular types of uses'.[37] Although 'the "traditional" public trust litigation model … centers on the second restriction, the prohibition against alienation of a public trust asset', a wave of modern public trust litigation asserts that 'state and national governments have abdicated their responsibilities under the public trust doctrine'.[38] Under this modern approach: 'plaintiffs assert that [sovereigns] have violated their duties as trustees by nominally retaining control over trust assets while actually allowing their depletion and destruction, effectively violating the first and third restrictions by excluding the public from use and

[29] ibid.

[30] ibid.

[31] *Juliana District Court* (n 27) 1254 (citing George Gleason Bogert, George Taylor Bogert, and William K. Stevens, *The Law of Trusts and Trustees* s 582 (2016)).

[32] ibid (citing American Law Institute, *Restatement of the Law Second, Trusts* (American Law Publishers 1959)).

[33] *Kanuk Kanuk v State Department Natural Resources* 335 P.3d 1088, 1095 (Supreme Court of Alaska 2014) (*Kanuk*) (denying declaratory relief because such relief would not 'settle' the legal relations at issue and thus would not advance plaintiffs' interests).

[34] Joseph L. Sax, 'The Public Trust Doctrine in Natural Resource Law: Effective Judicial Intervention' (1970) 68 Michigan Law Review 471, 477.

[35] ibid.

[36] ibid. See also *Waiāhole Ditch* (n 22) 450 ('Although its purpose has evolved over time, the public trust has never been understood to safeguard rights of exclusive use for private commercial gain. Such an interpretation, indeed, eviscerates the trust's basic purpose of reserving the resource for use and access by the general public without preference or restriction').

[37] Sax (n 34) 477.

[38] *Juliana District Court* (n 27) 1254.

enjoyment of public resources.'[39] In addition to applying the public trust doctrine to new resources, modern public trust litigation emphasises the public rights that sovereigns have a fiduciary obligation to protect.[40]

### 10.1.3 *Historical Scope of the Doctrine*

The public trust doctrine is rooted in ancient Roman legal principles that described certain natural elements – particularly bodies of water – as belonging to the public as a whole. These principles were incorporated into several modern legal systems, including several European countries and England, but nowhere so prominently as in the United States, where it became a cornerstone of public rights in waterways and is evolving to protect public rights in other natural resources.

In the United States, the public trust doctrine has traditionally protected 'coastlines, harbors, and major rivers and lakes',[41] or, simply put, navigable waterways. According to Professor Charles Wilkinson, 'whether valued in terms of economics, recreation, beauty, or spirituality', these resources are 'among our most valuable'.[42] In *Illinois Central Railroad Co v Illinois*, the seminal public trust doctrine case, the US Supreme Court held that Illinois, like all sovereigns, holds title to lands beneath its navigable waters 'in trust for the people of the state', so that 'they may enjoy the navigation of the waters, carry on commerce over them, and have liberty of fishing therein freed from the obstruction or interference of private parties'.[43] Thus, since its original invocations, the scope of the US public trust doctrine has been closely associated with navigable waters and the values they provide as public resources.

Outside of the US, judicial pronouncement of the public trust doctrine occurred later,[44] but has been far less tethered to navigable waterways.[45] For example, in *M C Mehta v Kamal Nath*, the Supreme Court of India explained that 'the public trust doctrine primarily rests on the principle that certain resources like air, sea, waters and the forests have such a great importance to the people as a whole that it would be wholly unjustified to make them a subject of private ownership'.[46]

Interestingly, the court cited the 'ecological' reasoning employed in both state and federal cases from the United States to conclude that there is 'no reason why the public trust doctrine should not be expanded to include all eco-systems operating in

39 ibid.
40 ibid.
41 Wilkinson (n 5) 426.
42 ibid.
43 See *Ill Cent RR Co* (n 6).
44 See Michael C. Blumm and Rachel D. Guthrie, 'Internationalizing the Public Trust Doctrine: Natural Law and Constitutional and Statutory Approaches to Fulfilling the Saxion Vision' (2012) 45 UC Davis Law Review 741, 746–748.
45 See generally ibid (exploring the relatively broader scope of the public trust doctrine in certain jurisdictions outside of the United States).
46 *M C Mehta v Kamal Nath* (1996) 1 SCC 388.

our natural resources'.[47] Although courts in the United States have accepted such ecologically based arguments to extend the public trust *res* primarily in the context of waters,[48] international courts have shown a greater willingness to apply this reasoning to other natural resources, including whole ecosystems.[49]

### 10.1.4 *The Rise of an Atmospheric Trust*

The rise of atmospheric trust litigation has, in part, been the product of an increased understanding within the international judiciary of the threats posed by climate change and the courts' role in addressing those threats. For example, the Lahore High Court of Pakistan has recognised that 'climate change is a defining challenge of our time and has led to dramatic alterations in our planet's climate system'.[50] In Pakistan, 'these climatic variations have primarily resulted in heavy floods and droughts, raising serious concerns regarding water and food security'.[51] Similarly, as one Washington lower court summarised:

> Washington and the Pacific Northwest have experienced long-term warming, a lengthening of the frost-free season, and more frequent nighttime heat waves. Sea level is rising on most of Washington's coast. Coastal ocean acidity has increased. Glacial area and spring snowpack have declined, and peak stream flows in many rivers have shifted earlier. In addition, climate extremes (floods, droughts, fires, and landslides) are already costly to Washington's [sic] State.[52]

## 10.2 CASE LAW DEVELOPMENT

This section explores the developments in natural resource public trust case law. Section 10.2.1 describes the interpretive process and the judicial role in evaluating natural resource public trust claims. Section 10.2.2 discusses the constitutional recognition framework, under which many courts have rooted their support for an atmospheric trust in constitutional language establishing public rights in or the sovereign's responsibility for air, climate, a healthy environment, or natural resources generally. Finally, Section 10.2.3 introduces what this chapter terms the inter-resource affectation framework, which has been used by courts to bring non-traditional public trust resources under the public trust doctrine's protection.

47 ibid (discussing *National Audubon Society v Superior Court, Alpine County* 658 P.2d 709 (Supreme Court of California 1983) and *Phillips Petroleum Co v Mississippi* 484 US 469 (1988)).
48 See Section 2.3.
49 See *M C Mehta* (n 46).
50 *Asghar Leghari v Federation of Pakistan* PLD 2018 Lahore 364.
51 ibid.
52 *Foster v Washington Department of Ecology* No 14-2-25295-1 SEA, 2017 WL 9772318 [2] (Superior Court of Washington 2017).

### 10.2.1 *Judicial Interpretation of the Public Trust Doctrine*

Courts and scholars have recognised that 'in natural resources cases, the trust property consists of a set of resources important enough to the people to warrant public trust protection'.[53] Nonetheless, perhaps the greatest challenge for courts reviewing claims brought under the public trust doctrine is determining when – that is, to which resources – the doctrine applies. According to the Supreme Court of Hawai'i, 'the public trust, by its very nature, does not remain fixed for all time, but must conform to changing needs and circumstances'.[54] Professor Joseph Sax, the father of the modern public trust doctrine, explained, 'certainly the principle of the public trust is broader than its traditional application indicates'.[55] As new threats to natural resources arise and the public responds by invoking their rights to the continued use and enjoyment of those resources, the public trust doctrine is sure to evolve.

The judiciary's role in this evolution is straightforward. As the Arizona Court of Appeals declared in *Butler v Brewer*, 'it is up to the judiciary to determine the scope of the doctrine'.[56] In *Butler*, which concerned an atmospheric trust claim, the Arizona court reasoned that when 'precedent does not address the measures by which a resource may be determined to be a part of the public trust or a framework for analyzing such contentions', it is appropriate for the court to 'assume without deciding that the atmosphere is a part of the public trust subject to the doctrine'.[57] Consequently, 'the fact that the only Arizona cases directly addressing the doctrine did so in the context of lands underlying navigable watercourses does not mean that the doctrine in Arizona is limited to such lands'.[58] Instead, 'any determination of the scope of the doctrine depends on the facts presented in a specific case'.[59] Thus, public trust cases require courts to engage in a fact-intensive inquiry to determine when the doctrine applies.

Not only must courts 'determine the threshold question of whether a particular resource is a part of the public trust subject to the doctrine, but the courts must also determine whether based on the facts there has been a breach of the trust'.[60]

53 *Juliana District Court* (n 27) 1254 (citing Mary Christina Wood, A *Nature's Trust; Environmental Law for a New Ecological Age* (Cambridge University Press 2014) 167–175.

54 *Waiāhole Ditch* (n 22) 447.

55 Sax (n 34) 557.

56 *Butler* (n 23) 3.

57 ibid 6.

58 ibid. However, see *Chernaik v Brown*, 475 P.3d 68 (Supreme Court of Oregon 2020) 79–80 (declining to expand the scope of Oregon's public trust beyond the state's obligation 'to protect the public's ability to use navigable waters for identifiable uses' despite acknowledging that, 'for over a century', the Oregon Supreme Court 'has recognized that the public trust doctrine is a forward-looking doctrine that is flexible enough to accommodate future uses and to protect against unforeseen harms to the public's ability to use public trust resources').

59 *Butler* (n 23) 6.

60 ibid 5.

In *Kanuk v State*, which also concerned an atmospheric trust claim, the Supreme Court of Alaska explained that because Alaskan courts 'interpret the public trust doctrine in a constitutional context', the judiciary 'has the constitutionally mandated duty to ensure compliance with the provisions of the Alaska Constitution' when it reviews public trust claims.[61] The court held that 'whether the State has breached [its fiduciary] legal duty is a question we are well equipped to answer' once 'the extent of the State's duty' has been judicially determined based on the facts of the case.[62] If it were not up to the courts to evaluate when a sovereign has abdicated its public trust duties, such an inquiry would have no proper forum.

In fact, although the public trust doctrine is not explicitly laid out in Colombia's constitution, the Supreme Court of Colombia has held that the fundamental principle of protecting natural resources for the benefit of the population is enshrined in the constitutional right to a healthy environment.[63] In *Future Generations v Ministry of Environment and Others*, twenty-five youth plaintiffs filed suit against the Colombian government for violating their fundamental rights to a healthy environment, life, health, food, and water by failing to curtail deforestation in the Amazon. The court concluded that the protection of fundamental rights is inextricably linked with the protection of nature, and further, that natural resources such as the Amazon Rainforest belong to all inhabitants of the planet, including those as yet unborn.[64] This recognition of the interconnectedness of fundamental human rights and the rights of nature, and of the shared use by present and future generations of natural resources, are the same basic principles that underpin the protection of natural resources under the public trust doctrine.

Similarly, in *Advocates Coalition for Development and Environment (ACODE) v Attorney General*,[65] ACODE sued the Ugandan government for failing to fulfil its duty as trustee of the Butamira Forest Reserve by granting a private permit to harvest firewood from the forest. The High Court of Uganda determined that the Attorney General had failed in his obligations under Article 237(2)(b) of the Ugandan Constitution, which lays out the government's duty to hold rivers, lakes, and forest reserves, inter alia, in trust for the Ugandan people. By granting the harvesting permit without conducting an environmental impact assessment and without consulting the local communities who rely on the Butamira Forest Reserve for their livelihoods and spiritual practices, the government violated its duty as trustee, and failed in 'its constitutional and statutory duty to conserve the environment and

61 *Kanuk* (n 33) 1099.

62 ibid 1100.

63 *Future Generations v Ministry of the Environment and Others (Demanda Generaciones Futuras v Minambiente)* [2018] 11001 22 03 000 2018 00319 00 (Supreme Court of Justice of Colombia) (*Demanda Futuras Generaciones*) [20].

64 ibid.

65 *Advocates Coalition for Development and Environment (ACODE) v Attorney General* (2005) Miscellaneous Cause No 0100 of 2004 (High Court of Uganda).

natural resources equitably and for the benefit of both the present and future generations'.[66] In this case, therefore, the public trust doctrine was applied not only to natural resource protection, but also to the protection of cultural and religious traditions associated with the resource in question.

This jurisprudence suggests that the public trust doctrine, even in the absence of explicit 'public trust' language, may apply more broadly to important natural resources and is flexible enough to evolve with changing societal needs. If so, the judiciary's role is to determine both when a particular resource falls within the doctrine's scope and when the sovereign has violated or failed to meet its public trust duties concerning public trust resources.

### 10.2.2 *The Constitutional Recognition Framework*

Several courts have rooted their support for an atmospheric trust in constitutional language establishing public rights in, or the sovereign's responsibility for, air, climate, a healthy environment, or natural resources generally. Some experts 'observe that cases advancing constitutional theories of climate obligation are swiftly gaining ground in the world's domestic courts'.[67] Judicial embrace is strongest when the relevant constitutional provision also speaks to principles of intergenerational equity, which this chapter identifies as an emerging best practice. Judicial recognition of a broad public trust capable of including the atmosphere illustrates that the doctrine is subject to expansion.

#### 10.2.2.1 Air and Atmosphere

An atmospheric trust exists where constitutional language establishes public rights in, and the sovereign's duty over, air and climate. For example, Article I Section 27 of the Pennsylvania Constitution unequivocally states that 'the people have a right to clean air'.[68] That section declares that 'Pennsylvania's public natural resources are the common property of all the people, including generations yet to come', and requires the state, 'as trustee of these resources', to 'conserve and maintain them for the benefit of all the people'.[69] The state constitution, therefore, embodies two of the three categories of restrictions on the sovereign's authority to administer the natural resources trust: Trust property must be held available for public use and maintained for public uses.

66 ibid [22].

67 Mary Christina Wood, '"On the Eve of Destruction": Courts Confronting the Climate Emergency' (2022) 97 Indiana Law Journal 239, 286 (citing James R. May and Erin Daly, 'Global Climate Constitutionalism and Justice in the Courts' in Jordi Jaria-Manzano and Susana Borràs (eds), *Research Handbook on Global Climate Constitutionalism* (Edward Elgar 2019) 235.

68 Pennsylvania Constitution art 1(27).

69 ibid.

In *Funk v Wolf*, the Pennsylvania Commonwealth court explained that the first provision of Section 27 'endows the people of Pennsylvania with the *right* to the described resources', thereby 'prevent[ing] the state from acting in ways that would infringe upon such rights'.[70] By placing Pennsylvania's natural resources – including clean air – in trust for the people,[71] the second provision enables citizens to bring a legal challenge against government actions and inactions infringing on the rights recognised in the first provision, proceeding upon either or both of two theories: 'the government has infringed upon citizens' rights' or 'has failed in its trustee obligations'.[72] The court thereby properly recognised the two categories of restrictions imposed by the Pennsylvania Constitution.

Similarly, in *Sanders-Reed v Martinez*, the New Mexico Court of Appeals concluded that the state's constitution 'recognizes that a public trust duty exists for the protection of New Mexico's natural resources, including the atmosphere, for the benefit of the people'.[73] Section 21 of Article XX of the New Mexico Constitution provides that 'the protection of the state's beautiful and healthful environment is hereby declared to be of fundamental importance to the public interest' and requires the state to 'provide for control of pollution and control of despoilment of the air' and other natural resources 'for the maximum benefit of the people'.[74] Thus, the court held, 'the State has a duty to protect the atmosphere' pursuant to its clear 'constitutional mandate'.[75] The court recognised the same two categories of restrictions in the New Mexico Constitution – the sovereign must hold natural resources in trust for public use and maintain those resources consistent with public uses.

The Supreme Court of Hawai'i in *In re Application of Gas Co* recently explained that 'a state agency must perform its functions in a manner that fulfils the State's affirmative obligations under the Hawai'i constitution', including its obligations as a trustee of 'all public natural resources'.[76] The Hawai'i Constitution provides that, '[f] or the benefit of present and future generations, the State … shall conserve and protect Hawaii's natural beauty and all natural resources, including land, water, air, and

70 *Funk v Wolf* 158 A.3d 642 (Supreme Court of Pennsylvania 2017) (denying declaratory relief for lack of practical effect).

71 ibid (citing *Pennsylvania Environment Defense Foundation. v Commonwealth* 108 A.3d 140, 167 (Commonwealth Court of Pennsylvania 2015)).

72 ibid (quoting *Robinson Township v Commonwealth*, 83 A.3d 901, 950–951 (Supreme Court of Pennsylvania 2013)).

73 *Sanders-Reed ex rel Sanders-Reed v Martinez* 350 P.3d 1221, 1225 (Court of Appeals for New Mexico 2015) (affirming summary judgment in favour of the State because plaintiffs failed to allege a constitutional violation, instead of requesting judicial review and intervention as a matter of a 'common law public trust doctrine').

74 ibid 1225 (quoting New Mexico Constitution, art 20 s 21).

75 ibid 1226–1227.

76 *In re Gas Co LLC* 465 P.3d 633, 654 (Supreme Court of Hawai'i 2020) (vacating and remanding to the State Public Utilities Commission to 'consider its constitutional obligations' in light of the court's opinion).

other resources'.[77] Thus, the court concluded that 'the state has a *continuing* duty to monitor the use of trust property, even if the use of the property has not changed', and that a state agency's 'constitutional obligations are ongoing'.[78]

These cases illustrate that where the relevant constitution speaks to public rights in, and the sovereign's duty over, air or climate, courts have embraced the atmosphere as within the scope of the public trust *res*. Nevertheless, many other courts have reached the same conclusion where such explicit constitutional language about air or climate is lacking.

#### 10.2.2.2 A Healthy Environment

Several courts have rooted their recognition of an atmospheric trust in constitutional language that establishes public rights in, and the sovereign's duty over, a healthy environment. Moreover, according to these courts, the right to a healthy environment is inherent in other, constitutionally enumerated fundamental rights. By extension, the sovereign's maintenance and preservation of a healthy atmosphere are essential to fulfilling the public's fundamental rights.

As the Supreme Court of the Philippines explained, 'the right to a balanced and healthful ecology carries with it the correlative duty to refrain from impairing the environment'.[79] The right to a healthy environment, therefore, mandates not only that the state hold trust property – in this context, the environment as a whole – available for public use, but also that the state maintain the environment's health to ensure the continued viability of the public's use of trust property. Although the court did not explicitly reference the public trust doctrine in its ruling, the reasoning in the decision is grounded in the idea that natural resources are held in trust by the state. In this way, the right to a healthy environment embodies the first and third categories of restrictions on the sovereign's authority to administer the natural resources trust: Trust resources must be held open for public use and maintained consistent with public uses.[80]

In *Sher Singh v State of Himachal Pradesh*, the National Green Tribunal of India unequivocally declared that 'the citizens of the country have a fundamental right to a wholesome, clean and decent environment' under India's constitution.[81] Citing judgments by the Supreme Court of India from the 1980s onward,[82] the

77 ibid (quoting Hawai'i Constitution art 11(1)).
78 ibid (citing *Ching v Case* 449 P.3d 1146, 1175–1176 (2019)).
79 *See Minors Oposa v Factoran* (n 24).
80 *See* Sax (n 34) 477.
81 *Court on its own Motion v State of Himachal Pradesh and Ors* Application No 237 (THC)/ 2013 (CWPIL No 15 of 2010) (*State of Himachal Pradesh*) [5].
82 *See Rural Litigation and Entitlement Kendra, Dehradun v State of Uttar Pradesh* 1985 SCR (3) 169; *Virender Gaur v State of Haryana* 1998 (1) CTC 143.

court concluded that 'Article 21 of [India's] constitution[83] has been expanded to take within its ambit the right to a clean and decent environment' as part of a broader 'right to life and personal liberty'.[84] The court explained that the 'wide dimensions' of Article 21 have consistently been construed by Indian courts 'in the larger public interest'.[85] Therefore, the court held that the public interest demands that 'the most vital necessities, namely air … cannot be permitted to be misused or polluted so as to reduce the quality of life of others'.[86] The court also made clear that when the sovereign enacts environmental statutes and regulations, it must do so consistent with its role as 'the trustee of all natural resources which are by [their] nature meant for public use and enjoyment' and of which 'the public at large is the beneficiary'.[87] Thus, the court signalled its willingness to review legislation for consistency with the public trust doctrine.[88]

Similarly, the Lahore High Court of Pakistan in *Asghar Leghari* began its decision by recognising that 'climate change is a defining challenge of our time and has led to dramatic alterations in our planet's climate system'.[89] Against this backdrop, the court determined that '[o]n a legal and constitutional plane', climate change presents a 'clarion call for the protection of fundamental rights of the citizens of Pakistan'.[90] Thus, the court pointed to 'fundamental rights' in Pakistan's constitution, emphasising that such rights 'read with constitutional principles of democracy, equality, [and] social, economic and political justice'.[91] The court focused on Article 9,[92] the right to life, 'which includes the right to a healthy and clean environment', and Article 14,[93] the right to human dignity.[94]

The *Leghari* court concluded that these fundamental rights also 'include within their ambit and commitment' numerous environmental principles such as 'inter and intra-generational equity and [the] public trust doctrine'.[95] In fact, according to the court, environmental protection has taken 'center stage' in Pakistan's scheme of constitutional rights.[96] The court was thus satisfied that the fundamental rights

83 Constitution of India, art 21 ('No person shall be deprived of his life or personal liberty except according to procedure established by law').
84 *State of Himachal Pradesh* (n 81).
85 ibid [7].
86 ibid [9]–[10].
87 *M C Mehta* (n 46).
88 ibid.
89 *Asghar Leghari* (n 50) [5].
90 ibid.
91 ibid [5]–[6].
92 Constitution of Pakistan, art 9 (No person shall be deprived of life or liberty save in accordance with law').
93 Constitution of Pakistan, art 14(1) ('The dignity of man and, subject to law, the privacy of home, shall be inviolable').
94 *Asghar Leghari* (n 50) [5]–[6].
95 ibid.
96 ibid.

articulated in Articles 9 and 14, bolstered by Article 23's right to property and Article 19(A)'s right to information, provided 'the necessary judicial toolkit to address and monitor the Government's response to climate change'.[97] Therefore, the court held that, concerning climate change measures, the sovereign could not continue on its course of 'delay and lethargy' and thereby 'offend … the fundamental rights of the citizens which need to be safeguarded'.[98]

Finally, in *Foster v State Department of Ecology*, a Washington lower court accepted petitioners' characterisation that where the public's 'rights to a healthy environment' are constitutionally protected, those rights are actually protected 'by the Public Trust Doctrine embodied therein'.[99] In other words, the court accepted the proposition that a constitutional right to a healthy environment is actually the recognition of inherent public rights in the environment.[100] The court explained that it allowed petitioners' case to proceed 'due to the emergent need for coordinated science[-]based action by the State of Washington to address climate change before efforts to do so are too costly and too late'.[101] By recognising that petitioners were entitled to an opportunity to 'show evidence and argue that their government has failed and continues to fail to protect them from global warming',[102] the court embraced its judicial role to determine when the sovereign has failed to meet its public trust duties.[103]

These cases show that where the relevant constitution speaks to public rights to, and the sovereign's duty over, a healthy environment, courts have concluded that the atmosphere is within the scope of the public trust *res*. This right to a healthy environment is inherent in other, constitutionally enumerated fundamental rights. This trend – which has a robust presence in international jurisprudence outside of the United States – indicates that courts understand a stable climate system as necessary to environmental health and well-being.

#### 10.2.2.3 Natural Resources

Some courts have grounded their recognition of an atmospheric trust in constitutional language that establishes public rights in, and the sovereign's duty over, natural resources generally, even absent an explicit reference to air or climate. As the Pennsylvania Supreme Court noted, when 'natural resources' appears, unqualified,

97 ibid.

98 ibid.

99 *Foster* (n 52) [1] (allowing petitioners to supplement and amend their petition against the State for its lack of climate change action).

100 ibid.

101 ibid.

102 ibid [3].

103 The *Foster* decision was overturned by the Washington court of appeals in 2017 without addressing the lower court's findings on the public trust doctrine.

in constitutional language, 'the term fairly implicates relatively broad aspects of the environment, and is amenable to change over time to conform, for example, with the development of related legal and societal concerns'.[104] Indeed, the public trust doctrine is a versatile legal tool for natural resource protection.

Some courts, however, have been unwilling to expand the traditional scope of the doctrine to include natural resources more broadly. For example, in *Aji P v State*,[105] youth plaintiffs contended that they had 'alleged valid public trust doctrine claims' in their complaint against the state of Washington for its reliance on fossil fuels because 'navigable waters and the atmosphere are intertwined'.[106] In the plaintiffs' view, 'to argue a separation of the two, or to argue that [greenhouse gas] emissions do not affect navigable waters', would be 'nonsensical' on the state's part.[107] However, looking to the Washington State Constitution, which enumerates the traditional definition of state ownership over the beds and shores of navigable waters, the Washington Court of Appeal disagreed.[108]

The court concluded that the 'complaint alleges a violation of the public trust doctrine in relation to the climate system as a whole, including the atmosphere', whereas 'Washington has not yet expanded the public trust doctrine to encompass the atmosphere'.[109] Although the plaintiffs maintained that they 'alleged impairment to traditional Public Trust Resources such as navigable waters and submerged lands', the court was unpersuaded.[110] In fact, the court deemed this a 'recharacterization' of plaintiffs' allegations, paying particular attention to plaintiffs' assertion in their complaint that 'the overarching public trust resource is the climate system, which encompasses the atmosphere, waters, oceans, and biosphere'.[111] In short, by framing the 'effect on the public's ability to use, access, enjoy and navigate the state's tidelands, shorelands, and navigable waters' as a consequence of climate change,[112] the plaintiffs were unable to satisfy the court's restrictive reading of the public trust doctrine in the context of narrow constitutional language.

In contrast, some courts have accepted that the doctrine applies to all natural resources, including the atmosphere. In *Bonser-Lain v State Commission on Environmental Quality*, a Texas lower court held that 'the public trust doctrine includes all natural resources of the State including the air and atmosphere'.[113] The

[104] *Robinson Township* (n 72) [950]–[951].
[105] *Aji Pexrel Piper v State* 480 P.3d 438 (Court of Appeals for Washington 2021) (*Aji P*).
[106] ibid.
[107] ibid.
[108] ibid [457].
[109] ibid.
[110] ibid.
[111] ibid.
[112] ibid.
[113] *Bonser-Lain v Texas Commission on Environment Quality* No D-1-GN-11-002194, 2012 (District Court of Texas 2012) (holding that the state commission nonetheless had discretion not to proceed with plaintiffs' request for rulemaking), vacated by *Texas Commission on Environment Quality v Bonser-Lain*

court was unpersuaded by the state commission's contention that 'the public trust doctrine in Texas is exclusively limited to the conservation of the State's waters', finding this argument 'legally invalid'.[114] The court reasoned that the doctrine had been incorporated into section 59 of Article XVI of the Texas Constitution, which provides that the conservation, development, and preservation 'of all of the natural resources of this State' are 'declared public rights and duties', and which therefore recognises an expansive public trust *res*.[115]

In *Held v State*, a Montana district court held that the state's practice of ignoring climate change when approving energy projects may implicate the plaintiffs' constitutional rights.[116] Following Montana Supreme Court precedent, the court concluded that 'a clean and healthful environment is a "fundamental right" under Article IX of the Montana Constitution',[117] and that this right is linked to the state's obligation 'to prevent unreasonable degradation of natural resources'.[118] While not explicitly using 'public trust' language, the court recognised that the inclusion of a state duty over natural resources in the Montana Constitution provides 'protections which are both anticipatory and preventative'.[119] Indeed, the Montana Constitution does not force the state into allowing a 'degree of environmental degradation which can be conclusively linked to ill health or physical endangerment' before the state's 'farsighted environmental protections can be invoked'.[120] Instead, the state has an affirmative duty to protect natural resources from substantial impairment.[121]

These cases demonstrate that where the relevant constitution speaks to public rights in, and the sovereign's duty over, natural resources, courts have interpreted such language to recognise resources beyond those traditionally associated with the public trust doctrine – including the atmosphere – as within the scope of the public trust *res*. Although language referencing 'natural resources' does not bring about the same clear reference to the atmosphere as language concerning the air or climate,

438 S.W.3d 887 (Court of Appeals for Texas 2014) (vacating on the ground that plaintiffs lacked a right to judicial review of an agency's refusal to adopt rules under Texas State law).

114 ibid.

115 ibid.

116 *Held v Montana* No CDV-2020-307 (District Court of Montana 2021) (*Held v Montana*) (allowing plaintiffs' claim for declaratory relief to proceed while denying a claim for injunctive relief).

117 ibid [13]–[14] (quoting *Montana Environmental Information Control v Department of Environmental Quality* 988 P.2d 1236, 1246 (Supreme Court of Montana 1999)). See also Constitution of the State of Montana, art 9(1)(1) ('The state and each person shall maintain and improve a clean and healthful environment in Montana for present and future generations').

118 ibid Constitution of Montana art 9(1)(3) ('The legislature shall provide adequate remedies for the protection of the environmental life support system from degradation and provide adequate remedies to prevent unreasonable depletion and degradation of natural resources').

119 ibid [15] (quoting *Montana Environmental Information Control*).

120 ibid [14] (quoting *Montana Environmental Information Control*).

121 *Held v Montana* (n 116). In August 2023, a Montana District Court held that by prohibiting analysis of GHG emissions and climate impacts during the project-approval process, the state violated the plaintiffs' right to a clean and healthful environment. See *Held v Montana* No CDV-2020-307 (District Court of Montana 2023).

broad constitutional language may allow for greater judicial flexibility as the public trust doctrine continues to be applied to new resources and challenges. Moreover, several courts have recognised that the state has affirmative obligations to protect trust resources.

### 10.2.3 *The Inter-Resource Affectation Framework*

Although courts have not always concluded that the atmosphere itself is a public trust resource, several have concluded that threats to non-traditional public trust resources are intricately connected to traditional public trust resources. In those courts' view, this relationship – which this chapter terms 'inter-resource affectation' – brings plaintiffs' claims within the scope of the public trust doctrine. In this way, courts can recognise an atmospheric trust without explicitly defining the scope of the public trust *res*. Several cases reflect this framework; they primarily arise in the United States where a federalist system of dual sovereigns, the federal government and the states, has produced different definitions of the public trust in different jurisdictions.

The principle of inter-resource affectation is perhaps best illustrated by courts' recognition of groundwater as within the scope of the public trust doctrine, even though groundwater is not a traditional public trust resource. For example, in *In re Water Use Permit Applications for Waiāhole Ditch*, the Supreme Court of Hawai'i concluded that there was 'little sense in adhering to artificial distinctions' between groundwater and surface waters – a distinction not 'borne out in the present practical realities of this state'.[122] The court reasoned that 'in other states, the "purposes" or "uses" of the public trust have evolved with changing public values and needs', including recognition of a 'distinct public interest in resource protection'.[123] Moreover, the court recognised that 'modern science and technology have discredited the surface-ground[water] dichotomy' and instead acknowledge 'the unity of the hydrological cycle'.[124] Therefore, the court deferred to a state commission's invocation of the precautionary principle[125] to protect instream water uses, agreeing that 'public trust purposes' (public use of the public trust *res*) should prevail over diversionary interests.[126] In reaching its decision, the court was persuaded by the underlying scientific consensus that certain natural resources – here, ground and surface waters – form two parts of a larger, interconnected system.

122 *Waiāhole Ditch* (n 22) 447.
123 ibid 448.
124 ibid 447.
125 The precautionary principle posits that '[w]here there are threats of serious or irreversible damage, lack of full scientific certainty shall not be used as a reason for postponing cost-effective measures to prevent environmental degradation'. See United Nations, 'Declaration of the United Nations Conference on Environment and Development' (1992) 31 ILM 874 (Rio Declaration).
126 *Waiāhole Ditch* (n 22) 466–467.

Similarly, in *Environmental Law Foundation v State Water Resources Control Board*, the California Court of Appeal affirmed a trial court's holding that the public trust doctrine applies to groundwater if extraction 'adversely impacts a navigable waterway'.[127] In other words, where 'the removal of water will have an adverse impact on navigable water clearly within the public trust', the court was satisfied that it could evaluate groundwater pumping for compliance with the public trust doctrine.[128] Given judicial embrace of an inter-resource affectation framework in the groundwater context, courts have paved the way for this framework to apply to other non-traditional public trust resources, including the atmosphere, where their degradation impairs navigable waterways clearly within the traditional public trust *res*.

## 10.3 EMERGING BEST PRACTICES

This section explores the emerging best practices in atmospheric trust case law. Section 10.3.1 discusses the emerging best practice of constitutional recognition coupled with language that speaks to intergenerational equity. Section 10.3.2 discusses the emerging best practice of applying the inter-resource affectation framework to the atmosphere. Finally, Section 10.3.2 discusses how the inter-resource affectation framework may be most successfully applied when plaintiffs' claims are grounded in a fundamental constitutional right, such as substantive due process.

### 10.3.1 *Constitutional Recognition and Intergenerational Equity*

Constitutional language that speaks to intergenerational equity – in addition to air, climate, a healthy environment, or natural resources – strengthens a court's application of the public trust doctrine to non-traditional public trust resources, such as the atmosphere. Intergenerational constitutional protection establishes a temporal relationship that mirrors basic trust principles. Because a trustee traditionally owes a duty 'equally to both current and future beneficiaries of the trust',[129] the sovereign owes its duties to current and future generations and cannot sanction substantial impairment of the trust *res* solely to serve present-day needs.[130] Even when courts have not used 'public trust' language, their discussion of the sovereign's intergenerational duties with respect to natural resources fits within public trust doctrine jurisprudence.

[127] *Environmental Law Foundation v State Water Resources Control Board* 237 Cal Rep 3d 393, 402 (Court of Appeals for California 2018).

[128] ibid.

[129] *Juliana District Court* (n 27) 1254 (citing *Restatement* (n 32) s 183).

[130] Constitution of Montana (n 119) art 1(1) (mandating a 'healthful environment in Montana for present and future generations').

In *Urgenda Foundation v The State of The Netherlands*, the Hague District Court held that 'Article 21 of the Dutch Constitution[131] imposes a duty of care on the State relating to the liveability of the country and the protection and improvement of the living environment'.[132] The court engaged in a two-part inquiry to determine whether the sovereign was 'taking sufficient mitigation measures' to meet its duty of care with respect to climate change.[133] First, it asked whether there was an 'unlawful hazardous negligence on the part of the State'; second, the court assessed the government's actions in light of 'the State's discretionary power'.[134] Simply put, the court sought to discern whether the state's duty of care had been triggered and, if so, what actions the state needed to take to meet that affirmative duty.[135]

The *Urgenda Foundation* court determined that the 'high risk of dangerous climate change with severe and life-threatening consequences for man and the environment' triggered the state's 'obligation to protect its citizens from [climate change] by taking appropriate and effective measures',[136] including mitigation, as plaintiffs had requested.[137] In other words, the imminence and dangerousness of climate change triggered the state's duty of care.[138] Stressing that 'the possibility of damages for those whose interests Urgenda represents, including current and future generations of Dutch nationals, is so great and concrete', the court ruled that 'the State must make an adequate contribution … to prevent hazardous climate change' consistent with its 'duty of care'.[139] Thus satisfied that the state's duty of care was triggered, the court held that the state was obliged to take effective mitigating and remedial measures.[140]

Similarly, in *Neubauer and Others v Germany*, the Federal Constitutional Court of Germany held that 'the fundamental right to the protection of life and health enshrined in' Article 2 of Germany's Constitution[141] 'imposes on the state a general duty of protection of life and physical integrity', and therefore 'obliges the state to afford protection against the risks of climate change'.[142] According to the court, this fundamental right 'encompasses the state's duty to protect and promote the legal interests of life and physical integrity and to safeguard these interests against

[131] Constitution of the Kingdom of Netherlands, art 21 ('It shall be the concern of the authorities to keep the country habitable and to protect and improve the environment').
[132] *State of the Netherlands (Ministry of Economic Affairs and Climate Policy) v Stichting Urgenda* [2019] ECLI:NL:HR:2019:2007 (Supreme Court of the Netherlands) (*Urgenda Supreme Court*).
[133] ibid 43.
[134] ibid.
[135] ibid.
[136] ibid 47.
[137] ibid 49.
[138] ibid.
[139] ibid 50.
[140] ibid.
[141] Constitution of the Federal Republic of Germany, art 2(2) ('Every person shall have the right to life and physical integrity. Freedom of the person shall be inviolable. These rights may be interfered with only pursuant to a law').
[142] *Neubauer and Others v Germany* [2021] 1 BvR 2656/18, 1 BvR 96/20, 1 BvR 78/20, 1 BvR 288/20, 1 BvR 96/20, 1 BvR 78/20 (German Federal Constitutional Court) (*Neubauer*).

unlawful interference by others'.[143] In this way, the court equated the state's obligation to protect against climate change with the sovereign's public trust duty to safeguard against substantial impairment to the public trust *res*.[144]

The *Neubauer* court emphasised that the state's duty 'does not take effect only after violations have already occurred', but is instead an affirmative duty 'oriented towards the future' that can also be invoked 'to protect future generations'.[145] The protection required of the state, the court continued, 'encompasses protection against impairments and degradation of constitutionally guaranteed interests caused by environmental pollution, regardless of who or what circumstances are the cause.[146] The intergenerational scope of this protection, the court reasoned, was necessary '[i]n view of the considerable risks' posed by 'increasingly severe climate change'[147] and the burden on future generations who will be forced to grapple with amplified climate effects.

Although affording protection to both present and future generations, the *Neubauer* court distinguished between present and future climate change and the sovereign's duties to address each.[148] As to present climate change that 'is not preventable or has already taken place', the court held that the state must 'address the risks by implementing positive measures aimed at alleviating the consequences of climate change'.[149] As to future climate change, on the other hand, the court held that the state is obligated 'to afford protection by taking measures that help to limit anthropogenic global warming and associated climate change'.[150] The court's reasoning reflected its understanding of the disproportionate climate effects future generations will face, leading the court to distinguish present-day remedial measures from mitigation designed to slow additional climate change.[151]

Prior to *Neubauer*, the German legislature had set interim goals with gradual steps to reduce greenhouse gas emissions[152] and an overall goal 'of achieving climate neutrality in the foreseeable future'.[153] Although the court concluded that the legislative provisions challenged by plaintiffs had not clearly violated the state's duty of protection to the present generation,[154] the court nonetheless concluded that those

[143] ibid.
[144] ibid.
[145] ibid.
[146] ibid.
[147] ibid 43.
[148] ibid.
[149] ibid.
[150] ibid.
[151] ibid.
[152] ibid 44–45.
[153] ibid 49.
[154] ibid 43–44 (noting that in a potential future case, the court would 'find a violation of a duty of protection' to the present generation 'if no precautionary measures whatsoever have been taken, or if the adopted provisions and measures prove to be manifestly unsuitable or completely inadequate for achieving the required protection goal, or if the provisions and measures fall significantly short of the protection goal').

provisions did violate the state's duty of protection to future generations.[155] The court faulted the legislature for 'failing to take sufficient precautionary measures to manage the obligations to reduce emissions in ways that respect fundamental rights-obligations that could be substantial in later periods due to the emissions allowed by law until 2030'.[156] Thus, while meeting its obligation to the present generation, the German legislature's climate goals were insufficient to meet the sovereign's obligation to future generations.[157]

These cases illustrate that, where the relevant constitution speaks to intergenerational equity in connection with the sovereign's duties to the public, courts have used this language to aid their embrace of an atmospheric trust. Given the long-term, far-reaching threats posed by climate change and the degradation of an inherently 'public' resource – the air we breathe – these courts also appear to impose a high burden of proof on the sovereign to show that it is complying with its public trust duties to present *and* future generations.

### 10.3.2 *Applying the Inter-Resource Affectation Framework to the Atmosphere*

The decision of the Oregon Federal District Court in *Juliana v United States* offers a persuasive application of the inter-resource affectation framework in the atmospheric trust context.[158] In *Juliana*, twenty-one youth plaintiffs argued that numerous government entities[159] 'violated their obligation to hold certain natural resources in trust for the people and for future generations' by deliberately allowing atmospheric carbon dioxide concentrations to reach unprecedented levels.[160] The plaintiffs' complaint alleged that the government defendants 'violated their duties as trustees by failing to protect the atmosphere, water, seas, seashores, and wildlife'.[161] The defendants countered that 'plaintiffs' public trust claims fail because the complaint focuses on harm to the atmosphere, which is not a public trust asset'.[162] The court, however, decided it was unnecessary 'to determine

155 ibid 53.
156 ibid.
157 ibid.
158 *Juliana District Court* (n 27) 1254. This was reversed and remanded for lack of redressability as required for plaintiffs to satisfy art III standing, see *Juliana* (n 23).
159 These entities included then-President of the United States Barack Obama, the Council on Environmental Quality, the Office of Management and Budget, the Office of Science and Technology Policy, the Department of Energy, the Department of the Interior, the Department of Transportation, the Department of Agriculture, the Department of Commerce, the Department of Defense, the Department of State, and the Environmental Protection Agency. See ibid *Juliana District Court* (n 27) 1233–1234.
160 *Juliana District Court* (n 27) 1233.
161 ibid 1255.
162 ibid.

whether the atmosphere is a public trust asset' given that plaintiffs had 'alleged violations of the public trust doctrine in connection with the territorial sea',[163] a traditional public trust resource.

The federal district court of Oregon concluded that 'because a number of plaintiffs' injuries relate to the effects of ocean acidification and rising ocean temperatures', plaintiffs had 'adequately alleged harm to public trust assets'.[164] The court was satisfied that harm to the atmosphere, when it impairs long-recognised public trust resources, implicates the public trust doctrine, effectively applying the inter-resource affectation framework.[165] This reasoning is consistent with prior judicial practice of looking past artificial distinctions between natural resources (such as ground and surface waters) to expand the application of the public trust doctrine beyond those resources traditionally within the public trust *res*.[166]

### 10.3.3 *Inter-Resource Affectation with Constitutional Grounding*

Although viable in its own right, the inter-resource affectation framework may find its strongest application when coupled with a constitutional grounding. Unlike constitutional language establishing public rights in air, climate, a healthy environment, or natural resources, a constitutional grounding refers to the public's fundamental right to engage in the judicial process to hold the sovereign accountable for its exercise of sovereign duties.

For example, the federal court in *Juliana* included the atmosphere in the public trust doctrine's scope as a matter of inter-resource affectation.[167] But in *Juliana*, the court also considered plaintiffs' claims on constitutional grounds rooted in the US Constitution's Due Process Clause.[168] Because the court

163 ibid.

164 ibid 1256. The Ninth Circuit dismissed the plaintiffs' case on appeal for lack of standing (based on redressability grounds) without disturbing the public trust interpretations of the district court. *See* *Juliana* (n 23) 1169–1175. The plaintiffs have since amended their complaint and the district court has ruled that their case can proceed. *Juliana v United States* No 6:15-cv-01517-AA (District Court of Oregon 2023) (Opinion and Order).

165 ibid. See also *Foster v Washington Department of Ecology* No 14-2-25295-1 SEA, 2015 WL 7721362 [4] (Superior Court of Washington 2015) (explaining that 'current science makes clear that global warming is impacting the acidification of the oceans to alarming and dangerous levels, thus endangering the bounty of our navigable waters'), abrogated by *Aji P* (n 107). *Luis Armando Tolosa Villabona* [2018] 11001-22-03-000-2018-00319-01 (Supreme Court of Justice of Colombia) (explaining that deforestation in the Amazon leads to rampant emissions of carbon dioxide ($CO_2$) into the atmosphere, producing the greenhouse gas effect, which in turn transforms and fragments ecosystems, altering water sources and the water supply for population centres).

166 Section 10.2.2.

167 Section 10.3.2.

168 *Juliana District Court* (n 27) 1250–1251.

determined that public trust rights were implicit in due process,[169] this constitutional grounding provided the court with a catalyst to vindicate plaintiffs' public trust rights. Although the sovereign's public trust duties exist independent of any constitutional recognition, where plaintiffs (and courts) point to a constitutional provision that contemplates the public's right to enforce those duties, such constitutional grounding can act as a vehicle for judicial recognition of public trust rights.

In *Juliana*, the youth plaintiffs argued, in addition to their public trust claims, that numerous government entities were violating plaintiffs' 'substantive due process rights to life, liberty, and property' by deliberately allowing atmospheric carbon dioxide concentrations to reach unprecedented levels.[170] The court agreed, holding that plaintiffs had 'adequately alleged infringement of a fundamental right'.[171] According to the court: 'Where a complaint alleges governmental action is affirmatively and substantially damaging the climate system in a way that will cause human deaths, shorten human lifespans, result in widespread damage to property, threaten human food sources, and dramatically alter the planet's ecosystem, it states a claim for a due process violation.'[172] As the court saw it, 'to hold otherwise would be to say that the Constitution affords no protection against a government's knowing decision to poison the air its citizens breathe or the water its citizens drink'.[173] In other words, these fundamental rights need not be explicitly stated in a constitution to benefit from constitutional protection.

The federal district court proceeded to rule that 'plaintiffs' public trust rights both predated the [US] Constitution and are secured by it, although plaintiffs' right of action to enforce the government's obligations as trustee arises from the Constitution'.[174] The court explained that 'the Due Process Clause's substantive component safeguards fundamental rights that are "implicit" in the concept of ordered liberty' or 'deeply rooted in this Nation's history and tradition'.[175] According to the court, '[p]laintiffs' public trust rights, related as they are to inherent aspects of sovereignty and the consent of the governed from which the United States' authority derives, satisfy both tests'.[176] In other words, the Due Process Clause – and its protection of fundamental rights – acted as a vehicle for the court to consider plaintiffs' fundamental public trust rights.[177]

169 ibid 1261 ('[P]laintiffs' public trust claims are properly categorized as substantive due process claims').
170 ibid 1233.
171 ibid 1250.
172 ibid.
173 ibid.
174 ibid 1260–1261.
175 ibid 1261 (citing *McDonald v Chicago*, 561 US 742, 761, 767 (2010)).
176 ibid.
177 This is not to suggest that the court could not have considered the plaintiffs' public trust claim independent of a constitutional claim.

## 10.4 REPLICABILITY

As noted earlier, even in countries where the public trust doctrine is not explicitly enshrined in the legal tradition, constitutional protection to a healthy environment, natural resources, or intergenerational equity, may offer an avenue for courts to apply the principles of the public trust doctrine. Given the protection afforded these rights in constitutions around the world, this feature of emerging best practice appears to be highly replicable.

However, unlike the constitutional recognition framework – an emerging best practice that is well represented in international case law – the inter-resource affectation framework is ripe for further development. The takeaways from *Juliana* and *Aji P* illustrate how plaintiffs and judges can engage in that development.

The *Juliana* court's discussion of substantive due process indicates that where the relevant constitution does not contain express language establishing public rights in or the sovereign's responsibility for air, climate, a healthy environment, or natural resources, the strength of a plaintiff's atmospheric trust claim can rest upon the ties the plaintiff establishes between climate change and traditional public trust resources – that is, upon inter-resource affectation. Although the court in *Aji P* failed to apply the inter-resource affectation framework, it does not foreclose atmospheric trust claims more explicitly rooted in the impairment of traditional public trust resources. Referring to climate change impacts 'on already-recognized public trust resources such as water, shorelines, wildlife, and fish', the Supreme Court of Alaska has recognised that '[a]llegations that the State has breached its duties with regard to the management of these resources do not depend on a declaratory judgment about the atmosphere'.[178] Therefore, a court need not decide that the atmosphere is a public trust resource to consider the effects of climate change on traditional public trust resources under the inter-resource affectation framework.

Had the *Aji P* plaintiffs claimed that greenhouse gases, particularly dissolved carbon dioxide, create higher river and stream temperatures that impair the public's ability to fish and recreate in those waters, the court would have been more likely to see this injury as directly tied to plaintiffs' use of traditional public trust resources. Likewise, the navigability of traditionally navigable waters has been and continues to be threatened by climate change.[179] Because climate change stresses water availability and thereby alters the structure of rivers and streams,[180] a claim of impairment to navigability could bolster an atmospheric trust claim where a plaintiff cannot assist her position with helpful constitutional language. In other words, alleging impairment to navigable waterways as a result of climate change, rather

[178] *Kanuk* (n 33) 1103.
[179] Fox and Allen (n 20).
[180] ibid.

than alleging impairment to the climate that in turn affects navigable waterways, frames the issue in terms more closely aligned with a limited reading of a narrow state doctrine.

## 10.5 CONCLUSION

Courts around the world have applied the public trust doctrine to the atmosphere in the context of climate change litigation using two analytical frameworks: constitutional recognition and inter-resource affectation. Under the first framework, constitutional recognition, sovereigns recognise – and courts enforce – the ecological importance of protecting air, climate, a healthy environment, and natural resources based on constitutional language establishing public rights to and the sovereign's duty over such resources. Constitutional recognition is strongest when the relevant constitutional language also speaks to principles of intergenerational equity, an emerging best practice. Under the second framework, inter-resource affectation, courts recognise the inherent ecological ties between navigable waters and other resources. Using this approach, at least one court has held that the atmosphere falls within the public trust doctrine's scope even when the atmosphere is not defined as an asset within the public trust *res*, another emerging best practice.

Judicial invocation of either of the discussed frameworks gives rise to an atmospheric trust that the sovereign must manage in the public interest consistent with trust principles. Once courts recognise the atmosphere as within the scope of the public trust *res*, the sovereign can no longer shirk its fiduciary duty to 'protect the trust property against damage or destruction'[181] by allowing climate change to progress unabated.

[181] *Restatement* (n 32) s 183.

# 11

# Rights of Nature

*Susana Borràs-Pentinat**

## 11.1 INTRODUCTION: TOWARDS AN ECOCENTRIC APPROACH WITHIN CLIMATE LITIGATION

The protection of Nature[1] is one of the most effective ways to face climate change and must be an essential part of all plans to reduce global warming. Nature-based solutions to climate change, sometimes called 'natural climate solutions', involve the conservation, restoration, and better management of ecosystems to help remove carbon dioxide ($CO_2$) from the atmosphere. Effective use of nature-based solutions would make it possible to reduce global greenhouse gas emissions by up to a third by 2030.[2] The Working Group II contribution to the Intergovernmental Panel on Climate Change Sixth Assessment Report provides new and valuable insights into the importance of supporting natural pathways to reduce climate risks and, at the same time, improve people's lives.[3] Natural ecosystems not only contribute to reducing climate change by capturing $CO_2$ from the air and sequestering it in plants, soils, and sediments but also provide a wide range of other important benefits, such as cleaner air and water, economic benefits, and increased biodiversity, thereby bolstering our human rights and existence.

* Susana Borràs-Pentinat is Associate Professor of Public International Law and International Relations at the Universitat Rovira i Virgili (Tarragona-Spain) (ORCID: 0000-0002-8264-1252) and former Marie Skłodowska-Curie postdoctoral fellow at the Università degli Studi di Macerata. This work is part of the CLIMOVE Project with funding from the European Union's Horizon 2020 research and innovation programme under the Marie Skłodowska-Curie grant agreement (H2020-MSCA-IF-2020) No 101031252 from the Università degli Studi di Macerata (Italy). This work reflects only the author's view and the European Research Executive Agency (REA) is not responsible for any use that may be made of the information it contains.

1 The word 'Nature' is capitalised as recognised and incorporated in UNGA Res 73/235, preamble twenty-ninth paragraph, and in the Report of the Secretary-General on Harmony with Nature, UN Doc A/74/236.

2 Lera Miles and others, 'Nature based Solutions for Climate Change Mitigation' (*UNEP* 2021).

3 Hans O. Pörtner and others (eds), *Climate Change 2022: Impacts, Adaptation and Vulnerability* (Cambridge University Press 2022).

Therefore, it is not surprising that Nature has emerged in some climate cases as a core (or collateral) element to be protected and a novel aspect for judicial discussions on climate change.

Likewise, the recognition of the rights of Nature and the ecocentric reinterpretation of the legal framework through climate cases contribute to reinforcing the rights of human beings to live in a healthy and clean environment, as well as granting Nature its own rights.[4] The 'ecocentric' perspective holds that the Earth's ecology and ecosystems (including its atmosphere, water, land, and all forms of life) have intrinsic value and seeks to protect environmental organisms even if they cannot be used by humans as resources. An ecocentric interpretation of law therefore places importance on the natural world, and although it may not involve the direct recognition of the rights of Nature, it is a step in that direction. In this chapter, the focus is particularly on an ecocentric interpretation as a transition to interpretations that ultimately uphold the rights of Nature in the context of the climate emergency. This interpretation is particularly critical in light of the debate regarding the appropriateness and ability of human rights to protect the environment from human impact.[5]

In fact, the personification of the environment through ecocentric legal interpretations continues to grow in popularity worldwide because it is an idea that ordinary people and communities can understand and support. This legal interpretation establishes scaffolding to shift the way humans see Nature from property to an understanding of the interconnected relationships between trees, lakes, and rivers. This view is not new for many Indigenous peoples around the world who see Nature not as separate from humans but rather as made up of beings in relation to themselves.

Therefore, the objective of this chapter is to identify emerging best practice in climate litigation on the topic of rights of Nature in judicial decisions to date. Section 11.2 analyses how courts have dealt with arguments relating to rights of Nature or incorporate an ecocentric perspective. Section 11.3 focuses on how courts have progressively introduced this ecocentric interpretation into climate litigation, contributing to emerging best judicial practice. Finally, Section 11.4 outlines the possibility of replicating some of the best practices in future litigation.

## 11.2 STATE OF AFFAIRS: RIGHTS OF NATURE BEFORE COURTS

Nature has traditionally been afforded legal protection because of the simple material, genetic, or productive utility it represents for human beings. In many countries, however, particularly in the Global South, rights of Nature have been recognised due to the relationship of particular populations with their local environments.

4 Susana Borràs, 'New Transitions from Human Rights to the Environment to the Rights of Nature' (2016) 5(1) TEL 113.

5 Rolston Holmes III, 'Rights and Responsibilities on the Home Plane' (1993) 18 YJIL 251. See also Conor Gearty, 'Do Human Rights Help or Hinder Environmental Protection?' (2010) 1 JHRE 7.

This recognition stems from an understanding of the inherently exceptional value of certain natural resources, as well as from the ecological and cultural dependence of some populations on Nature for subsistence. For many Indigenous communities, Nature is not simply a resource for survival but also a source of spirituality and sacredness, forming a basis for traditional cultures rooted in the interconnectedness of all living beings. However, modern levels of overexploitation and domination leave ecological systems and human cultures in critical condition. This vulnerability is aggravated by the climate emergency, which highlights the need to approach environmental protection from a more ecocentric perspective, rather than the traditional anthropocentric rule of law.

The rights of Nature have been commonly understood as 'the rights of the non-human species, elements of the natural environment and … inanimate objects for a continuous existence not threatened by human activities'.[6] Some jurisdictions go even further. The Ecuadorian Constitution of 2008 states in Article 71 that: '[t]he nature or Pacha Mama' is 'where life is realized' and that 'she has the right to have her existence fully respected and the maintenance and regeneration of [her] vital cycles, structure, functions and evolutionary processes'. In addition, the Constitution provides that '[e]very person, community, people or nationality may require the public authority to comply with the rights of nature' and, in Article 72, Nature is granted the right to restoration.[7]

Some judicial bodies in the Global South have recently linked the climate question to the ecological perspective, recognising constitutional protection for other forms of life beyond human life and acknowledging that an ecologically balanced environment is indispensable if fundamental rights are to be preserved. Recognition of the human rights dimensions of climate change is no longer sufficient to secure life in the climate emergency. Therefore, the new ecocentric interpretation of law qualifies as emerging best judicial practice, as it highlights Nature's right to be protected, directly or indirectly, as an important element for consideration in climate litigation.[8]

Ecuador, Bolivia, New Zealand, Bangladesh, Brazil, Colombia, and Mexico, among other countries,[9] have either issued court decisions, enacted laws, or

6 David Boyd, *The Rights of Nature: A Legal Revolution That Could Save the World* (ECW Press 2017) 137. Several authors from around the world contributed, significantly, to this ecocentric interpretation of law including Christopher Stone in the United States, Godofredo Stutzin in Chile, and Cormac Cullinan in South Africa.

7 ibid 293.

8 Eduardo Gudynas, 'Los derechos de la naturaleza en serio. Respuestas y aportes desde la ecología política' in Alberto Acosta and Esperanza Martínez (eds), *La naturaleza con derechos. De la filosofía a la política* (Abya Yala 2011).

9 Legal provisions recognizing the Rights of Nature, sometimes referred to as Earth Jurisprudence, include constitutions, national statutes, and local laws. See an exhaustive compilation at the UN Harmony with Nature website <www.harmonywithnatureun.org/rightsOfNature/> accessed 24 February 2024.

amended constitutions recognising the legal rights of Nature. Panamá recently enacted a 'Rights of Nature Law', guaranteeing the natural world's right to exist, persist, and regenerate.[10]

The recognition of the rights of Nature's different elements has proliferated in various jurisdictional venues. A good example is Ecuador, where two individuals brought an 'Accion de Proteccion' against the Provincial Government of Loja 'in favour of Nature, particularly in favour of the Vilcabamba River'.[11] The Criminal Chamber of the Court ruled that the government had violated the constitutional rights of the Vilcabamba River to exist and maintain its life cycles, structure, functions, and evolutionary processes by conducting excavation for the construction of a new provincial road. This case was the first success story of the rights of Nature under Article 71 of the Ecuadorian Constitution. The Chamber accepted that 'the action for protection is the only suitable and effective way to put an end to and immediately remedy focused environmental damage'. The judges applied the precautionary principle:

> [U]ntil it is objectively demonstrated that there is no probability or certain danger that the work carried out in a certain area will produce pollution or cause environmental damage, it is the duty of the constitutional judges to immediately protect and make effective the judicial protection of the rights of Nature, carrying out whatever is necessary to prevent it from being polluted, or to remedy it. Note that we even consider that in relation to the environment, we do not only work with the certainty of damage, but we aim at the probability[12]

The Chamber also recalled that the Constitution:

> without precedent in the history of humanity, recognises nature as a subject of rights …; it assumes as an evident and indisputable fact the 'importance of Nature', to such an extent that it considers 'that any argument in this respect is succinct and redundant', incorporating in the decision the idea that the damage caused to it is 'generational damage', which it defines as 'that which by its magnitude has repercussions not only on the current generation but that its effects will have an impact on future generations'[13]

The global case law to date has covered not only the protection of Nature itself, but also the protection and preservation of intangible and spiritual assets, such as sacred sites or ancestral knowledge. For example, in 2017, the High Court of the Indian state of Uttarajand ruled that the Ganges and its main tributary, the Yamuna, both considered sacred by millions of Hindus, were living beings and,

[10] Asamblea Nacional Ley No 287 Gaceta Oficial No 29484-A <www.gacetaoficial.gob.pa/pdfTemp/29484_A/GacetaNo_29484a_20220224.pdf> accessed 24 February 2024.

[11] *Wheeler v Director de la Procuraduría General* [2011] No 11121-2011-00010 (Provincial Criminal Court for Loja).

[12] ibid [5].

[13] ibid [7].

as such, had the right to be legally protected and not to be harmed and could be parties to disputes.[14]

Through this ruling, the Court explicitly recognised the rivers' legal personality. The Court ordered that the two rivers be represented by the director of the National Clean Ganga Mission, a government body that oversees projects and conservation of the river, as well as by the state's chief secretary and advocate general. This order served to protect the rivers from increasing pollution caused by both locals and thousands of visitors to this Himalayan region.[15] However, the Court stayed the ruling on appeal.

Similarly, New Zealand has declared the Whanganui River a living entity and appointed two guardians to protect its interests. While New Zealand has not yet formally adopted Nature's rights in any statutory or constitutional law, the nation has already recognised that Nature can have inherent rights by granting legal personality to lands and rivers. Thus, in 2013, the Tūhoe people and the New Zealand government agreed upon the Te Urewera Act, giving the Te Urewera National Park 'all the rights, powers, duties, and liabilities of a legal person'.[16]

In other countries, the rise of an ecocentric interpretation of law has taken the form not of the attribution of rights to Nature, but rather of obligations to protect Nature. Countries such as Switzerland, Portugal, France, Colombia, and Brazil have specified a set of governmental obligations to Nature and its protection. Colombia, in fact, offers a key example of the possibilities. In one decision, the Colombian Constitutional Court described the ecocentric interpretation as follows: 'It is a principle that radiates through the entire legal order corresponding to the State responsibility to protect the natural wealth of the Nation; 2. It is a constitutional (fundamental and collective) right held by all people through various judicial channels; and 3. It is an obligation of the authorities, society and individuals, by involving qualified duties of protection.' In addition, the Constitution establishes 'environmental sanitation as a public service and fundamental purpose of state activity'.[17]

The Constitutional Court refined this interpretation in the Atrato River case,[18] in which ethnic communities sued Colombia for illegal mining in the department of Chocó. The Court recognised the 'attribution of rights to Nature' and the obligation

14 *Mohd Salim v State of Uttarakhand and others* Writ Petition (PIL) No 126 of 2014 (Uttarakhand High Court).

15 The Indian Supreme Court later overturned the decision on the basis that declaring the rights of rivers was 'legally unsustainable'. See 'India's Ganges and Yamuna Rivers Are "Not Living Entities"' (*BBC*, 7 July 2017) <www.bbc.com/news/world-asia-india-40537701> accessed 27 February 2024.

16 See Te Uruwera Act 2014, s 14 <www.legislation.govt.nz/act/public/2014/0051/latest/DLM6183601.html> accessed 27 February 2024. Also see Te Awa Tupua Act 2017 <www.legislation.govt.nz/act/public/2017/0007/latest/whole.html#DLM6831458> accessed 27 February 2024.

17 Sentence C-449 (Constitutional Court of Colombia 2015) [4.1].

18 *The Atrato River Case*, Sentence T-622 (Constitutional Court of Colombia 2016).

to guarantee the protection, conservation, maintenance, and restoration of the Atrato River and Nature in general. The Court declared that the environment's 'integral elements … can be protected per se and not simply because they are useful or necessary for the development of human life', and therefore that 'the protection of the environment goes beyond the mere utilitarian notion'.[19] The Court also extended the protection to include 'biocultural rights': rights to life, health, water, food security, a healthy environment, and, importantly, to the culture and territory of the ethnic communities (Black and Indigenous) that inhabit the Atrato River basin and its tributaries.

The Court stated:

> [J]ustice with nature must be applied beyond the human scenario and must allow nature to be the subject of rights. It is under this understanding that the chamber considers it necessary to take a step forward in jurisprudence towards the constitutional protection of one of our most important sources of biodiversity: the Atrato River. This interpretation finds full justification in the superior interest of the environment, which has been widely developed by constitutional jurisprudence and which is made up of numerous constitutional clauses that constitute what has been called the 'Ecological Constitution' or 'Green Constitution'. This set of provisions makes it possible to affirm the importance of a healthy environment and the interdependent link between human beings and the State.[20]

Following the trend of recognising rights of Nature and reinterpreting the different normative frameworks, the Advisory Opinion of the Inter-American Court of Human Rights (OC-23/17) stated:

> The Court considers it important to stress that, as an autonomous right, the right to a healthy environment, unlike other rights, protects the components of the environment, such as forests, rivers and seas, as legal interests in themselves, even in the absence of the certainty or evidence of a risk to individuals. This means that it protects nature and the environment, not only because of the benefits they provide to humanity or the effects that their degradation may have on other human rights, such as health, life or personal integrity, but because of their importance to the other living organisms with which we share the planet that also merit protection in their own right. In this regard, the Court notes a tendency, not only in court judgments, but also in Constitutions, to recognize legal personality and, consequently, rights to nature.[21]

19 Sentence C-123 (Constitutional Court of Colombia 2014) Section 1.

20 ibid [12].

21 See *The Environment and Human Rights (State Obligations in Relation to the Environment in the Context of the Protection and Guarantee of the Rights to Life and to Personal Integrity – Interpretation and Scope of Articles 4(1) and 5(1) of the American Convention on Human Rights)*, Advisory Opinion OC-23, Inter-American Court of Human Rights Series A No 23 (15 November 2017) (IACtHR OC-23/17) [59].

## 11.3 EMERGING BEST JUDICIAL PRACTICE: NATURE PROTECTION TO FACE CLIMATE CHANGE

In climate litigation, arguments to recognise the ecocentric interpretation of law or even rights of Nature have begun to appear in different judicial cases worldwide as an important avenue through which to address climate change. The appearance of those novel elements in environmental court cases has allowed the development of certain judicial good practices to protect the rights of both humans and Nature against environmental degradation. Arguments constituting best practice have emerged by asking judges to consider an ecological interpretation of law when a particular activity has been found to be unacceptably harmful to the environment and living things. In other cases, courts have addressed the importance of the ecological integrity and intrinsic value of Nature, moving away from the utilitarian protection of Nature purely for the benefit of humans.[22] Another novel argument has been to prioritise the protection of vulnerable ecosystems over the expansion of carbon-based and greenhouse gas-generating activities, which compromise not only the well-being of Nature but also climate goals. Finally, certain cases have sought recognition of the right to a safe and stable climate based on the protection of the atmosphere as a common public good. It should be noted, however, that although all these practices incorporate an ecocentric interpretation of law, some still favour the rights of humans over those of Nature.[23]

In cases where emerging best practice has been identified, judges have focused their arguments on the rights that some legal systems already attribute to Nature, thus approaching an ecocentric interpretation of the law. Judges have especially relied on the right to integral conservation, the right to restoration, precaution against extinction of species and non-introduction of genetically modified organisms, and non-appropriation of environmental services. This practice is particularly innovative where the legal systems in question do not expressly recognise the rights of Nature.[24]

The following analysis will attempt to identify emerging best practice in the introduction of the rights of Nature to climate jurisprudence. The evolution of an ecocentric interpretation of law can be observed in several stages, beginning with the assumption of environmental degradation and its impact on human rights, followed by the recognition of the integrity per se of natural elements, and ultimately legal recognition of the rights and subjectivity of Nature or at least of some of its elements.

[22] Rafi Youatt, 'Personhood and the Rights of Nature: The New Subjects of Contemporary Earth Politics' (2017) 11(1) International Political Sociology 39.

[23] Burns H. Weston and Tracy Bach, 'Recalibrating the Law of Humans with the Laws of Nature: Climate Change, Human Rights, and Intergenerational Justice' (2009) Vermont Law School Research Paper 10–106.

[24] Kirsten Anker and others, *From Environmental to Ecological Law* (Routledge 2020).

### 11.3.1 *Reparation of Ecological Harm*

The need to repair and restore the ecological harm done to certain natural elements that are important for life can be identified as emerging best practice in climate litigation to date. Nature conservation and protection is not only a matter of ensuring the well-being of future human generations, but also a matter of doing justice to non-human living beings, who are equally affected by climate change. Hence, the ecocentric interpretation of law has developed in such a way as to promote ecojustice or ecological justice. This section will discuss several cases in which the argument of reparation of ecological harm was used successfully.

In Australia, in the case of *Bulga Milbrodale Progress Association Inc v Minister for Planning and Infrastructure and Warkworth Mining Limited*,[25] the Court rejected the cost–benefit analysis presented by Warkworth Mining Limited in its appeal. This cost–benefit analysis sought to estimate, in monetary terms, the costs of the main intangible environmental, cultural, and social impacts of the expansion of the Warkworth Mine. The Court found that the analysis did not consider issues of equity or distributive justice by failing to give adequate regard to the entities on whom the mine's burdens would fall. Among the entities identified were threatened fauna in the area of disturbance and other components of biological diversity (such as ecological communities). The Court found that the integrity, stability, and beauty of these environmental components would be unacceptably impacted by the mine. This argument focuses not only on the benefits of biodiversity and ecosystem services for humans, but also on the additional concept of biodiversity and its elements as entities that have intrinsic value.[26]

The ecocentric interpretation of law in terms of ecojustice has been used not only to force reparation of ecological harm, but also as a moral argument to respect biodiversity. In *Shrestha v Prime Minister's Office of Nepal and others*,[27] the plaintiff's main request was for the government to enact a new climate law. The case presents, among other arguments, the severe impacts of environmental degradation, including climate change, on non-human life forms, biodiversity, wildlife, and ecosystems. Accordingly, the Nepalese Supreme Court declared:

> Climate change, exploitation of natural resources and environmental pollution have posed a threat to the existence of ecology and biodiversity. Such threats do not just affect the organisms living today but also cause irreversible damage to nature and pose an imminent threat to future generations. The matter of climate change

[25] *Bulga Milbrodale Progress Association Inc v Minister for Planning and Infrastructure and Warkworth Mining Limited* [2013] NSWLEC 48.

[26] See Anil Markandya, 'Cost Benefit Analysis and the Environment: How to Best Cover Impacts on Biodiversity and Ecosystem Services' (2016) OECD Environment Working Papers.

[27] *Advocate Padam Bahadur Shrestha v Prime Minister and Office of Council of Ministers and Others* [2018] Order No 074-WO-0283 (2075/09/10 BS) (Supreme Court of Nepal).

> and [the] threat posed by pollution is directly connected to the well-being of citizens who are guaranteed the right to clean environment and conservation under the Constitution.[28]

The Court thus recognised the need for moral, balanced, and responsible usage of the ecological resources that sustain humans and the lives of other organisms.

The concept of 'ecological harm' and arguments in favour of ecojustice are also found in the case *Notre affaire à tous and Others v France (L'affaire du siècle)*.[29] The plaintiffs argued for the recognition of a new general principle of law relating to the right to live in a sustainable climate system, also based on the concept of pure ecological damage ('préjudice écologique') as recognised in the French Civil Code. The court ruled that compensation for 'ecological damage'[30] was admissible and declared that the state 'should be held liable for part of this damage if it had failed to meet its commitments to reduce greenhouse gas emissions'. The recognition of 'pure' ecological damage, suffered exclusively by Nature, allows for an expansion of the system of civil liability for environmental damage, which was traditionally based on indirect damage suffered by the environment (damage to property, economic loss, and personal injury), as a mere instrument or object rather than the 'victim'.[31]

Reparation of ecological harm, therefore, abstractly represents the rights of Nature, or at least an ecocentric interpretation of law, because it allows plaintiffs to claim pure ecological harm, a harm that only affects ecosystems. It represents a significant step towards a kind of 'punitive ecology', which imposes measures and sanctions to bring about changes that respond to environmental damage and favour environmental protection.

### 11.3.2 *Preservation of Ecological Integrity and the Intrinsic Value of Nature*

In some climate litigation cases that have adopted an ecocentric approach, judges have based their decisions on another argument: the intrinsic value of natural elements. This argument recognises Nature's inherent value, its naturalness and wildness, and its degree of independence from human influence.[32] From this perspective, the

28 ibid.

29 *Notre Affaire à Tous and Others v France* [2021] No 1904967, 1904968, 1904972 1904976/4-1.

30 The concept of 'ecological damage' was formally recognised in French Civil Code art 1247, which states that 'Ecological damage consisting of non-negligible damage to the elements or functions of ecosystems or to the collective benefits derived by man from the environment shall be compensable', and supported by 'anyone liable for ecological damage'.

31 See Ivano Alogna, 'Environmental Law of France' in Nicholas Robinson and others (eds), *Comparative Environmental Law and Regulation* (Thomson Reuters 2018) [38].

32 The concept of the intrinsic value of Nature appeared in a case in France, where the Tribunal de Grande Instance de Lyon did not limit its consideration to the impact of climate change on humanity but also noted the impact on non-humans. See No 19168000015 (2019).

extension of Nature's rights to ecosystems and species is a form of protection of Nature itself.

This argument is included in one of the first pieces of climate change litigation in Brazil, *PSB and others v Brazil (on Climate Fund)*,[33] filed on 5 June 2020, as a Direct Action of Unconstitutionality for Omission before the Brazilian Federal Supreme Court. The action challenged the Federal Union's failure, and specifically the lack of efforts by the National Climate Change Fund (Fundo Clima), to adopt administrative measures with the goal of supporting projects, studies, and financial activities aimed at climate change mitigation and adaptation. In a preliminary decision the court recognised the interconnections between the right to a healthy environment and other human rights (right to life, health, food security, labour), as well as the impacts of ecological disequilibrium on the livelihoods and cultural identity of traditional communities and Indigenous peoples.[34]

The Supreme Court found that the Federal Union, through its lack of action, had violated its obligation to protect Nature, as established in the Brazilian Constitution and in accordance with the precautionary principle.[35] The Court based its argumentation mainly on article 225 of the Constitution, which is the ecological matrix of the Brazilian legal system.[36] The article imposes a set of positive and negative duties on the state related to environmental protection: preserve and restore ecological processes; promote the ecological management of ecosystems; define special protected territorial spaces and their components; and protect fauna and flora.[37] The Supreme Court incorporates a kind of constitutionalisation of climate change, as it admits its importance in the constitutional protection of not

33 *PSB and others v Brazil* [2022] ADPF 708 (Federal Supreme Court of Brazil) (*PSB ADPF 708*).

34 ibid.

35 ibid.

36 See Constitution of the Federative Republic of Brazil art 225, 'Everyone has the right to an ecologically balanced environment, which is a public good for the people's use and is essential for a healthy life. The Government and the community have a duty to defend and to preserve the environment for present and future generations'.

37 See ibid art 225(1), 'In order to ensure the effectiveness of this right, it is incumbent upon the Government to: I – preserve and restore the essential ecological processes and provide for the ecological treatment of species and ecosystems; II – preserve the diversity and integrity of the genetic patrimony of the country and to control entities engaged in research and manipulation of genetic material; III – define, in all units of the Federation, territorial spaces and their components which are to receive special protection, any alterations and suppressions being allowed only by means of law, and any use which may harm the integrity of the attributes which justify their protection being forbidden; IV – demand, in the manner prescribed by law, for the installation of works and activities which may potentially cause significant degradation of the environment, a prior environmental impact study, which shall be made public; V – control the production, sale and use of techniques, methods or substances which represent a risk to life, the quality of life and the environment; VI – promote environment education in all school levels and public awareness of the need to preserve the environment; VII – protect the fauna and the flora, with prohibition, in the manner prescribed by law, of all practices which represent a risk to their ecological function, cause the extinction of species or subject animals to cruelty'.

only human life but also non-human life, due to its intrinsic value and the essential contribution of an ecologically balanced environment to the effectiveness of other fundamental rights.[38]

The Brazilian Supreme Court cited two important decisions of the Inter-American Court of Human Rights (IACHR) to connect the State's duty to protect biodiversity with the rights of Nature.[39] In the IACHR Advisory Opinion No. 23/2017, the Court established that the right to a healthy environment is a fundamental human right[40] and further stated that it is a state's duty to protect Nature because of Nature's inherent importance, distinct from its importance to humans.[41] The second decision mentioned is the judgment in *Indigenous Communities of the Lhaka Honhat Asociation (Our Land) v Argentina*,[42] where the IACHR stated that a state has the duty to 'respect', 'guarantee', and 'prevent' damage to the environment, as well as the responsibility for ensuring the right to food security and access to water, in particular for Indigenous communities.[43]

Referencing these arguments, the Brazilian Supreme Court in *PSB and others* recognised that 'the damage caused to the environment compromises biodiversity, fauna and flora, which represent enormous economic potential and a differential for the country. They undermine Brazil's credibility internationally and its ability to raise funds to fight deforestation and reduce greenhouse gases'.[44]

Another case pending before the Federal Supreme Court in Brazil is the *Political Parties v Union (Brasil) (on deforestation and human rights)*,[45] through Direct Action of Unconstitutionality by Omission to denounce the deforestation. The case raises the compliance of the Action Plan for the Prevention and Control of Deforestation in the Amazon (PPCDAm) and the lack of ambition of Brazil's Nationally Determined Contribution (NDC) to sanction illegal deforestation, as well as to achieve an 80 per cent reduction in the rate of deforestation. It also alleges non-compliance with Article 225 of the 1998 Federal Constitution (CF/88), concerning the ecological balance of the environment, and calls for urgent precautionary measures.

38 *PSB ADPF 708*.

39 *PSB and others v Brazil* [2022] ADO 59/DF (Federal Supreme Court of Brazil) (*PSB ADO 59/DF*).

40 IACtHR OC-23/17 (n 22) [59].

41 ibid [62].

42 *The Indigenous Communities of the Lhaka Honhat (Our Land) Association v Argentina* Inter-American Court of Human Rights Series C No 400 (6 February 2020) [71].

43 See *The Saramaka People v Suriname* Inter-American Court of Human Rights Series C No 172 (28 November 2007) [82]. 'Land means more than merely a source of livelihood for them; it is also a necessary source for the continuity of life and cultural identity of the members of the Saramaka people. The lands and resources of the Saramaka resources of the Saramaka people are part of their social, ancestral and spiritual essence. In this territory, the Saramaka people hunt, fish and harvest, and collect water, plants for medicinal purposes, oils, minerals and timber'.

44 *PSB ADO 59/DF* (n 40).

45 *PSB and others v Brazil* [2022] ADPF 760 (Federal Supreme Court of Brazil).

Although not found in an express provision on the constitutional level in the European Union (EU), the intrinsic value of Nature is contained in directives and case law on Nature conservation. The assessment of significant effects on the integrity of 'Natura 2000' sites had relevance in case C-404/09, *European Commission v Kingdom of Spain*.[46] The European Commission alleged that Spain approved two open-cast coal-mining projects within protected areas of the Natura 2000 network without properly evaluating the environmental impacts of the mines. An investigation confirmed not only the existence of several open-pit coal-mining operations, but also that the open-pit mining activity was going to continue through newly authorised operations and those in the process of authorisation.

The Court of Justice of the European Union determined that the possible effects on the most vulnerable species had not been taken into account during the authorisation procedure, as required by the provisions of Directive 85/337 on Environmental Impact Assessment. This Directive requires the description and assessment of the important environmental effects of the disputed projects, including 'the direct, indirect and cumulative effects in the short, medium and long term … permanent or temporary' on all plant and animal life, soil, water, air, climate and the landscape, material assets and cultural heritage, as well as the interaction between them. With regard to the EU Directive 92/43 on habitats, the Court held that the consequences of these mining operations on grouse and brown bear cannot only be assessed in terms of direct destruction of critical areas, but must also be assessed with consideration for the greater fragmentation, deterioration, and destruction of potentially suitable habitats for their recovery, as well as the increase in disturbances for these species due to development.[47]

In *Save Lamu et al v National Environmental Management Authority and Amu Power Co. Ltd*,[48] the appellants challenged the issuance of an environmental and social impacts assessment (ESIA) licence to a coal-fired power plant that was to be located in the coastal Lamu County in Kenya.[49] Incorporating environmental and human welfare considerations, the Kenyan National Environmental Tribunal found, through the implementation of the precautionary principle, that such a project could increase the possibility and potential for acid rain, thereby killing fish and plants, as well as causing other adverse effects on forests, soil, and vegetation as a whole. Therefore, the tribunal ruled that if Amu Power Co. chose to continue with the project, it would have to carry out a new ESIA to prevent ecological damage.

46 Case C-404/09 *European Commission v Kingdom of Spain* [2011] ECLI:EU:C:2011:768.
47 ibid [197].
48 *Save Lamu et al v National Environmental Management Authority and Amu Power Co Ltd* [2016] Tribunal Appeal No Net 196 of 2016 (Kenya Environmental Tribunal).
49 See ESIA report <https://naturaljustice.org/wp-content/uploads/2021/01/Copy-of-the-EIA-Study-Report_merged.pdf> accessed 27 February 2024.

Although climate change is not at the centre of the Tribunal's analysis in these cases, mining activities have a significant impact on the Earth's climate system. Therefore, environmental impact assessment of these activities has a very important contribution to make to safeguarding the ecological integrity of natural areas and preventing further climate impacts.

### 11.3.3 *Recognition of Rights of Nature and the Protection of Fundamental Rights*

Best practice has also emerged in cases where courts have relied on fundamental rights to recognise the rights of Nature. The first successful climate case introducing the personhood of natural resources in Colombia was before the Supreme Court, in the case *Future Generations v Ministry of the Environment and Others*.[50] In its ruling, the Supreme Court adopted an ecocentric conception of the rule of law by recognising the rights of Nature. The Court declared the Amazon, as an ecological region and as an entity, a 'holder of protection, conservation, maintenance, and [restoration] from the State and its territorial entities'.[51] It further described the Amazon as a 'vital ecosystem for the global future', and stated that, in order to protect it, the Amazon is recognised as an entity 'subject of rights'.[52]

The Court based its decision on arguments focused on alterity and solidarity not only for every human on the planet in both present and future generations, but also for animals and plants, based '(i) [on the] ethical solidarity duty of the species and (ii) in the intrinsic value of nature'.[53]

In addition, the inherent meaning of ecojustice is evident in this case. The main reason for the Court's decision and ecocentric approach was the fact that deforestation of the Amazonian forest had already generated an increase in greenhouse gas emissions and temperature. In the view of the Court, these increases violated the rights of present and future generations. The absence of necessary efforts to prevent global warming also affected the ecological integrity of the ecosystem and the survival of other species. The Supreme Court went beyond the anthropogenic perspective and reiterated the ecocentric perspective, adopting a 'green' reading of constitutional postulates. In particular, the Court held that the concentration of greenhouse gas emissions in the atmosphere due to the deforestation of the Amazon causes imminent and serious damage not only to the plaintiffs but to all

[50] *Future Generations v Ministry of the Environment and Others (Demanda Generaciones Futuras v Minambiente)* [2018] 11001 22 03 000 2018 00319 00 (Supreme Court of Justice of Colombia) (*Demanda Futuras Generaciones*).

[51] ibid 45.

[52] About the case, see Paola Andrea Acosta Alvarado and Daniel Rivas-Ramíres, 'A Milestone in Environmental and Future Generations' Rights Protection: Recent Legal Developments before the Colombian Supreme Court' (2018) 30 JEL 519 (2018).

[53] *Demanda Futuras Generaciones* (n 51) 19.

the inhabitants of the Colombian territory and of the entire planet. This argument includes recognition of extraterritoriality and a collective consideration of the right to a healthy environment. In this sense, the Court explains:

> The principle of solidarity, for the specific case, is determined by the duty and co-responsibility of the Colombian State in stopping the causes that cause GHG emissions caused by the abrupt reduction forest of the Amazon, being imperative to adopt immediate mitigation measures, protecting the right to environmental well-being, both to the guardians, like the other people who inhabit and share the Amazonian territory, not only the national, but the foreign, along with all the inhabitants of the globe, including ecosystems and living beings.[54]

The constitutional parameters invoked in this case by the plaintiffs are the same as in the Atrato River case (right to life, health, and a healthy environment). However, the major difference between the two cases is that, here, the principle of solidarity applies to Nature for the benefit of future generations, in the sense that the claimants are recognised as having rights as representatives of future generations who will be primarily affected by climate change.[55]

The Colombian Supreme Court's decision in this case represents a significant step from an anthropocentric model of environmental law to a more 'anthropic ecocentric' model. This transition is evident when the Court recognises that the 'fundamental rights of life, health, the minimum subsistence, freedom, and human dignity are substantially linked and determined by the environment and the ecosystem'.[56] In addition, the Court underlines the need to establish a relationship of intragenerational equity between species based on the ethical duty of solidarity that must exist between humans and Nature.[57] Ultimately, the Court declared that the Colombian Amazon was entitled to protection, conservation, maintenance, and restoration, and ordered the government to develop and implement action plans to halt deforestation.

Other cases in Ecuador reflect an ecocentric perspective to confront the climate crisis, although some of these cases do not appear in climate litigation databases. The Ecuadorian courts have considered the rights of Nature in various cases centred on mining activities, oil, and energy production that influence climate governance.[58]

54 ibid 37.

55 César Rodríguez-Garavito, 'Human Rights: The Global South's Route to Climate Litigation' (2020) 114 AJIL Unbound 40.

56 *Demanda Futuras Generaciones* (n 51) 13.

57 ibid 20.

58 For example, cases of the mining concessions in the Los Cedros Biological Reserve (Case No 1149-19-JP) and the cases of mining in areas of ecological interest in the Upper Nangaritza region (Cases Nos 1232-19-JP and 2917-19-EP), pending before the Constitutional Court. Other cases are those involving violation of constitutional guarantees and rights of the nature and the Cofán de Sinangoe people (Process No 21333-2018-00266, judged by the Single Chamber of the Provincial Court of Justice of Sucumbios); the Waorani people (Process No 16171-2019-00001, judged by the Multi-competent Chamber of the Provincial Court of Pastaza) and the case of violation of the rights of nature due to the execution of the project of infrastructure for the supply of energy from the Dulcepamba river, pending before the Constitutional Court (Case No 502-19-JP).

A lawsuit filed by several Indigenous girls from the Ecuadorian Amazon sought to eliminate more than 400 gas-burning lighters associated with the exploitation of crude oil in that region – which caused the plaintiffs to suffer severe chronic diseases.[59] The action was initially denied. On appeal, however, the court ruled in favour of the plaintiffs.[60]

The decision recognises the violation of the rights of health, Nature, and a healthy environment, as well as the systematic failure of the Ecuadorian state to comply with international obligations on climate change. According to the Court, 'it is the obligation of the State, to put into mobility, the application of the precautionary principle that is based on the scientific doubt of this or that reaction caused by the activity of gas flaring in the so-called lighters'. The Court also states that 'nature is being affected, and its constitutional rights are being violated … since the burning of gas affects the air, biodiversity, due to the fact that this activity directly sends greenhouse gas emissions' and that 'with the burning of gas resulting from the hydrocarbon extractive activity, the constitutional rights of the inhabitants living in the area of influence of the aforementioned activity are not recognised'.[61]

A similar case was filed by civil society organisations and members of the Waorani Indigenous people of Miwaguno[62] in northeastern Ecuador, seeking to hold the Chinese oil company PetroOriental[63] that operates in the Amazon accountable for the burning and venting of gas in lighters during oil extraction and the consequent atmospheric pollution and direct effects on climate change. The plaintiffs argue that the company's actions constitute a permanent violation of human and Nature's rights. This lawsuit was the first in Ecuador to exclusively appeal to the relationship

59 *Valentina and others v Minister of Environment and others* Process No 21201-2020-00170 <www.derechosdelanaturaleza.org.ec/wp-content/uploads/2021/05/3.-CASO-MECHEROS-SENTENCIA-PRIMERA-INSTANCIA.pdf> accessed 24 February 2024.

60 ibid.

61 The plaintiffs base their position on the IACtHR, which has ruled that the state, as the party responsible for environmental damage, is obliged to specify the extent of the reparations and the scope of reparations and the manner in which they are to be carried out. However, according to the plaintiffs, the measures decreed by the Court's Judgement under the heading of 'integral reparation' are far from compliant with the established and required parameters. Therefore, the case is now before the Constitutional Court by an extraordinary action. See *The Kaliña and Lokono Peoples v Suriname* Inter-American Court of Human Rights Series C No 309 (25 November 2015).

62 Acción Ecológica, together with the International Federation for Human Rights (FIDH), the Union of People Affected by Texaco (UDAPT), and the Waorani community of Miwaguno. See 'Ecuador: Waorani Community Sues Fossil Fuel Company for Contributing to Climate Change' (*International Federation for Human Rights*, 10 December 2020) <www.fidh.org/en/region/americas/ecuador/ecuador-waorani-community-sues-fossil-fuel-company-for-contributing> accessed 27 February 2024.

63 PetroOriental operates exploration blocks 14 and 17 in Orellana province, which yield about 10,000 barrels of oil per day. See 'Ecuador: Pueblo Waorani demanda a la empresa china PetroOriental por cambio climático debido a la contaminación del aire de torres petroleras en la Amazonía' (*Centre for Business and Human Rights*, 17 December 2020) <www.business-humanrights.org/fr/derni%C3%A8res-actualit%C3%A9s/ecuador-pueblo-waorani-demanda-a-la-empresa-china-petrooriental-por-cambio-clim%C3%A1tico-debido-a-la-contaminaci%C3%B3n-del-aire-de-torres-petroleras-en-la-amazon%C3%ADa/> accessed 27 February 2024.

between human and environmental rights and climate change.[64] The Court considered that protecting Nature and preventing and mitigating the effects of climate change are necessary to guarantee the constitutional rights of the inhabitants of the affected communities and to prevent future violations in similar circumstances. The constitutional rights of Indigenous peoples are violated by the significant contribution of greenhouse gas emissions to climate change, especially carbon dioxide, methane, soot, nitrous oxide, ozone, and water vapour. This violation of human rights comes in tandem with, and because of, a violation of the right of Nature to be protected, demonstrating the vital interdependence between the two.

In an unprecedented case, the Constitutional Court of Ecuador applied the constitutional provision on the rights of Nature. In the case *Reserva Los Cedros v Ecuador*,[65] the Court recognised the rights of Nature to safeguard the Los Cedros cloud forest from mining concessions. The Court ruled that the government of Ecuador is obligated to apply Article 73 of the Ecuador Constitution, which requires precautionary and restrictive measures be taken to prevent the extinction of species:

> It's not about a college or a conditioned option, but from a constitutional obligation derived from the intrinsic valuation that the Constitution makes of the existence of species and ecosystems, through the rights of nature. Indeed, the risk in this case is not necessarily related to affectations to human beings, although they can be included, but to the extinction of species, destruction of ecosystems or permanent alteration of natural cycles or other types of serious or irreversible damage to nature, regardless of such damage.

Based on the UN Framework Convention on Climate Change and other international norms, the Court also acknowledged: 'The Constitution expressly adds as part of this right to have a pollution-free environment, since pollution is one of the forms of human intervention in the environment that accelerates its degradation and makes it uninhabitable for himself and other living beings.' Consequently, the Court ruled that mining and all kinds of extractive activities in the Los Cedros Protected Forest would violate the constitutional rights of nature and are therefore prohibited in the forest. To enforce the ruling, the Court revoked the governmental authorisations granted to mining corporations to operate in Los Cedros. The Court also declared that the application of the constitutional rights of Nature is not limited to protected areas, such as Los Cedros, rather, as with any other constitutional

[64] See on the case 'Sobre el litigio climático contra PetroOriental' (*Accion Ecologica*, April 2021) <www.accionecologica.org/sobre-el-litigio-climatico-contra-petrooriental/> accessed 27 February 2024 and 'Organizaciones y comunidad Waorani demandan a la empresa PetroOriental ante jurisdicción ecuatoriana por su contribución al cambio climático' (*Accion Ecologica*, 10 December 2020) <www.accionecologica.org/wp-content/uploads/boletin-prensa-waorani-ESP.pdf> accessed 27 February 2024. Also see *Nixon and others v Minister of Environment and others*, Process No 22281-2020-00201.

[65] See *Reserva Los Cedros v Ecuador*, Case No 1149-19-JP/20 <http://esacc.corteconstitucional.gob.ec/storage/api/v1/10_DWL_FL/e2NhcnBldGE6J3RyYW1pdGUnLCB1dWlkOic2MmE3MmIxNy1hMzE4LTQyZmMtYjJkOS1mYzYzNWE5ZTAwNGYucGRmJ30=> accessed 27 February 2024.

right, it applies in the entire territory of the country. This case sets a precedent that is important not only for Ecuador but also for the international community to protect the integrity of forests and their biodiversity.

Another case of 'personifying the environment' can be found in the class action of the *Civil Association for Environmental Justice and others v Province of Entre Ríos and others*, filed in 2020 in the Argentinian Supreme Court against a government and municipality in Argentina for their alleged failure to protect environmentally sensitive wetlands. The plaintiffs brought the complaint with the aim of preserving the wetlands of the Paraná Delta, arguing that the Delta has its own rights.[66] The case was merged with *Equística Defensa del Medio Ambiente v Provincia de Santa Fe y ots*,[67] as both claim that this essential wetland ecosystem has the right to government measures for climate change mitigation and adaptation, due to the ecosystem services it provides. The Court in the latter case united recognition of the intrinsic value of biological diversity with consideration of the precautionary principle[68] and national jurisprudence regarding the principle of *in dubio pro natura*.[69] In order to safeguard the ecological integrity of the Paraná Delta, the Supreme Court, following the Climate Change Adaptation and Mitigation Law, ordered the establishment of an Environmental Emergency Committee to adopt effective precautionary measures to prevent and put out irregular fires in the area.

Both the precautionary and *in dubio pro natura* principles are also used by the Supreme Court of Pakistan, in the case of *D. G. Khan Cement Company v Government of Punjab*.[70] The Supreme Court of Pakistan upheld a decision by the Punjab provincial government prohibiting the construction of new or expanded cement plants in

66 *Asociación Civil Por La Justicia Ambiental y otros v Entre Ríos* CSJ 487/2020. See <www.cij.gov.ar/nota-38022-La-Corte-Suprema-ordena-constituir-un--Comit--de-Emergencia-Ambiental--para-detener-y-controlar-los-incendios-irregulares-en-el-Delta-del-Paran-.html> accessed 27 February 2024.

67 *Equística Defensa del Medio Ambiente Asociación Civil v Santa Fe, Provincia de y otros* CSJ 468/2020. See <https://cdh.defensoria.org.ar/wp-content/uploads/sites/3/2020/08/EQUISTICA-DELTA-DEL-PARANA.pdf> accessed 27 February 2024.

68 The precautionary principle, reflected in United Nations 'Declaration of the United Nations Conference on Environment and Development' (1992) 31 ILM 874 (Rio Declaration) principle 15. The principle provides, 'where there are threats of serious or irreversible damage, lack of full scientific certainty shall not be used as a reason for postponing cost-effective measures to prevent environmental degradation'.

69 This emerging environmental principle is declared as Principle 5 of the IUCN World Declaration on the Environmental Rule of Law (2016) 'in cases of doubt, all matters before courts, administrative agencies, and other decision-makers shall be resolved in a way most likely to favour the protection and conservation of the environment, with preference to be given to alternatives that are least harmful to the environment. Actions shall not be undertaken when their potential adverse impacts on the environment are disproportionate or excessive in relation to the benefits derived therefrom'.

70 *DG Khan Cement Company v Government of Punjab* [2021] C.P.1290-L/2019 (Supreme Court of Pakistan). See also Joana Setzer and Catherine Higham, 'Global Trends in Climate Change Litigation: 2021 Snapshot' (*LSE Grantham Research Institute on Climate Change and the Environment*, July 2021) 10 <www.lse.ac.uk/granthaminstitute/wp-content/uploads/2021/07/Global-trends-in-climate-change-litigation_2021-snapshot.pdf> accessed 24 February 2024.

environmentally fragile areas. The decision emphasises the need to protect the rights of Nature itself: '[m]an and his environment each need to compromise for the better of both and this peaceful co-existence requires that the law treats environmental objects as holders of legal rights'. The decision also justifies the personification of the environment, saying 'the environment needs to be protected in its own right. There is more to protecting nature than a human centred rights regime'.

Therefore, the Lahore Tribunal emphasised the obligation of courts to treat the environment as a subject of law, because of the intrinsic value of nature and its natural elements, and to protect and preserve natural resources, because of their importance in reducing the effects of climate change. As a result, the Supreme Court rejected the company's challenges and upheld the government's ruling that new or expanded cement plants could cause further depletion of groundwater and other harmful environmental impacts. The arguments were based on the government's duty to uphold the precautionary principle in protecting the rights to life, sustainability, and dignity of the communities surrounding the project areas.

### 11.3.4 *Protecting the Atmospheric Commons through the Public Trust and the Right to a Stable Climate*

Following the global trend, human rights now play a central role in climate litigation. In fact, the cases described earlier in this chapter demonstrate how the 'greening' or 'ecocentric approach' to human rights and the collective consideration of the human right to a healthy environment offer a good starting point for rebuilding harmonious relationships between human beings and Nature.

As developed in Chapter 10, another emerging best practice is consideration of the atmosphere as a common good, as part of public trust.[71] The public trust principle, which is well established in US case law, is the proposition that the sovereign holds certain natural resources in trust for the public.[72] More than two dozen cases have been brought around the world based on 'public trust' arguments, each arguing that the state has a duty to protect public resources from harm.

This argument is closely linked to the anthropocentric idea that the fundamental right to life is inextricably tied to the right to a healthy environment, including a stable climate, as put forth in the ruling of *Clean Air Council v United States*.[73]

Following an expansive interpretation of the traditional public trust doctrine, these lawsuits are potentially important in terms of emerging best judicial practices. Both characterise the government as a public trustee – that is, the manager

[71] Mary Christina Wood, *Nature's Trust: Environmental Law for a New Ecological Age* (Cambridge University Press 2014).

[72] Joseph Sax, 'The Public Trust Doctrine in Natural Resource Law: Effective Judicial Intervention' (1969) 68 Michigan Law Review 471, 484 (1969).

[73] *Clean Air Council v United States* 362 F.Supp.3d 237 (District Court of Pennsylvania 2019).

of those natural resources – including the atmosphere, air, and water – that are subject to the public trust. Therefore, the government has a fiduciary duty to protect and preserve those vital natural resources in trust for the people and for future generations.[74] Under the public trust doctrine, the government has a high, solemn, and perpetual duty to protect these special commons and the public's use of them from impairment, subordination, or alienation for private control. This trust establishes a legal relationship, just like a trust created with a bank as trustee, between the trustee, beneficiaries, and the commons in Nature. The public trust doctrine has connections derived from the due diligence principle or duty of care discussed in the *Urgenda* case.[75]

As in the legal or judicial recognition of the rights of Nature, the public trust doctrine calls for respect for the beingness or personhood of Nature, and at the same time ensures a citizen's right to bring an action to protect this personhood and the essential protected use of water or ecosystems. Therefore, if the government breaches or fails in its duty as trustee to protect the rights or beingness of Nature, citizens, as legal beneficiaries, have a right and standing to bring civil action against the government.

This doctrine is especially important because the protection of the atmosphere for the common good would result in the recognition and new constitutionalisation of the right to a stable climate, thus firmly establishing a government's fundamental duty to maintain climate stability. The recognition of the right to a stable climate to protect Nature is found in the case of *Institute of Amazonian Studies (IEA) v Brazil*.[76] The lawsuit alleges that the federal government has failed to comply with Brazilian emissions and annual Amazon deforestation rate reduction targets set out in the National Law on Climate Change Policy and fundamental rights, and calls for recognition of the explicit fundamental right to a stable climate for present and future generations under Article 225 of the Brazilian Constitution.[77] In order to remedy this situation, the plaintiffs ask the government to reforest an area equivalent to what was deforested to fulfil the duty of the state to protect the Amazon Forest.[78] The case was transferred to the Amazonas Court, due to an alleged connection between this case and the case of the *Federal Public Ministry against IBAMA*, a case in which the Public Ministry asked the government to put in place monitoring bases in ten critical areas of the Amazon to combat deforestation, as set out in the PPCDAm.

74 *Juliana v United States* No 6:15-cv-01517-TC (District Court of Oregon 2016).

75 *Urgenda Foundation v The State of The Netherlands* [2015] ECLI:NL:RBDHA:2015:7196 (District Court of the Hague).

76 *Institute of Amazonian Studies (IEA) v Brazil* No 5033746-81.2021.4.04.0000.

77 Lei 12187/09 Política Nacional de Mudança do Clima. See <www.planalto.gov.br/ccivil_03/_ato2007-2010/2009/lei/l12187.htm> accessed 27 February 2024.

78 See Joana Setzer and Délton Carvalho, 'IEA v Brazil: Rights-based Climate Litigation to Protect the Brazilian Amazon' (*OxHRH Blog*, April 2021) <https://ohrh.law.ox.ac.uk/iea-v-brazil-rights-based-climate-litigation-to-protect-the-brazilian-amazon/> accessed 27 February 2024.

Both cases concern illegal deforestation in the Amazon, which aggravates the climate crisis and is directly linked to violations of the fundamental rights of traditional peoples and Indigenous communities. It is therefore understood that the right to a stable climate can only be guaranteed by preserving the Amazon rainforest, which is essential for both human life and ecological balance,[79] with clear intergenerational and global implications justifying the recognition of the right to a stable climate.[80]

After analysing these cases, judges see climate change, ecosystem degradation, and biodiversity loss as interdependent questions. Ecosystem degradation is caused by and exacerbates climate change, which is already one of the main drivers of biodiversity loss globally. Thus, the recognition of the right to a stable climate can play a key role in addressing the combined climate and biodiversity crises while contributing to accelerating transformative change towards Nature protection.

## 11.4 REPLICATION OF JUDICIAL BEST PRACTICES FROM THE ECOCENTRIC APPROACH

As the previous sections demonstrate, constitutional and legislative advances in terms of 'greening' the law are in different stages across different jurisdictions. Despite distinct normative realities, it is possible to recognise common characteristics in judicial discussions to confront the climate crisis. Recognition of the intrinsic value and autonomous specific rights of ecosystems essential for the balance of climate and biodiversity is the first step, followed by the expansion of 'personhood' and the 'personification of the environment' to move away from a human-centred rights regime towards an approach that includes elements of Nature such as plants, animals, and rivers.

The attribution of legal rights to Nature follows two basic lines of reasoning. First, that the legal and moral foundations for human rights rely in part on the belief that rights emanate from the simple fact of human existence, which implies that the same inherent rights should also apply to the natural world. A second and more pragmatic argument claims that humanity's very survival depends on healthy ecosystems and that protecting the rights of Nature is tantamount to protecting human rights and well-being. This last reason can be accommodated by both civil and common law systems. From this perspective, most cases present powerful examples of the increasing relevance of rights-based claims of environmental protection in the context of the climate emergency.

The cases discussed in this chapter are judicial responses to public interest litigation that require governments to take climate action to protect all natural

79 *IEA v Brazil* (n 77).
80 ibid.

life, including humans, from the worst impacts of climate change. While adopting ecocentric arguments, these court cases have had an impact on the protection of Nature.

Through mandates such as prevention, preservation, regeneration, and restoration, these cases provide the following elements of replicability, which can be modulated according to the greater or lesser proximity of judges and courts to the ecocentric interpretation of the legal framework (Nature-centred approach):

- Equating damage to Nature with damage to humans, which is a significant change from the way environmental law has traditionally protected Nature by limiting itself to regulating human impacts.
- Recognising the importance of ecosystems for climate change mitigation and adaptation, recognising the existing vulnerabilities and risks produced by the biodiversity lost.
- Safeguarding the human rights of present and future generations by requiring the protection of Nature as a life support. Although the protection of Nature may be a secondary consequence, Nature is central to guarantee human rights in the context of the climate emergency. The cases in Brazil could provide vital guidance to other courts interpreting the constitutional right to a healthy environment, including the right to a safe climate and the right to healthy ecosystems and biodiversity and in benefit of humans and non-humans.
- Recognising the personality and rights of Nature as having intrinsic value *per se* and recognising the eco-dependence of humans on Nature. A growing number of climate lawsuits related to ecosystem rights could set a precedent, even if their legal systems do not yet explicitly recognise those rights.

In particular, the use of substantive 'eco-principles' can help judges in different jurisdictions approach this reorientation of climate litigation from an ecocentric interpretation of the law. Principles such as precaution or *in dubio pro natura* play a fundamental role in the protection of the rights to life and sustainability, thus promoting a new ecocentric approach to climate litigation.

In this sense, courts in different countries are beginning to maintain a jurisprudential dialogue, applying the ecocentric perspective through these principles of law to act for the conservation of biodiversity by opposing extractive projects that contribute to exacerbating climate change through the destruction of natural ecosystems.

The serious risks posed by climate change and the essential importance of Nature in addressing climate impacts call for new legal perspectives that protect Nature to protect life, and that means overturning the overwhelming legal protection of the human interest that currently exists in law.

Achieving this reinterpretation of the law within the climate litigation can also benefit the protection of Nature in different degrees, through judges' recognition of:

- An 'ecocentric punitive and restorative approach of law': by shifting environmental protection out of the exclusive domain of public law and creating access to the remedies available in private law, such as compensation for damages, mandatory precautionary restoration measures, among others, promoting the so-called 'punitive ecology' and 'restorative ecology'.[81]
- An 'ecocentric utilitarianism of Nature approach of law': A preventive approach, judicially recognising the rights of Nature in order to protect human rights, including the human right to a healthy environment. At the same time, human rights-based approaches provide a powerful framework of analysis and basis for recognising the rights of Nature, granting protection beyond the realm of public law and empowering Nature protectors to proactively seek private legal solutions.
- A 'pure ecocentric approach of law': by recognising the interdependence and interconnectedness of Nature, asserting the intrinsic value of Nature and the right to be protected from climate change and degradation. This could imply granting 'personality', legally recognising Nature as a living being, equal to humans. Likewise, it supposes creating a fiduciary duty of all interested parties starting with States, companies, and society in general.

As a result, these cases have the potential to influence both environmental law and human rights law on a much broader scale than the jurisdiction of the courts. In particular, the legal pluralism that characterises these numerous cultural contexts produces greater interpretive flexibility in the mindset of judges, especially in relation to environmental law. Therefore, the replicability of the ecocentric interpretation of law to other jurisdictions depends not on the existence of a legal framework that expressly recognises the rights of Nature, nor on the influence of Indigenous peoples, but on recognising the importance of Nature in responding to the climate emergency.

## 11.5 CONCLUSIONS: FROM CLIMATE LITIGATION TO ECOLOGICAL JUSTICE

As global warming accelerates, ecosystems are being pushed towards collapse, bringing the human right to a healthy environment and other fundamental rights down with them. The anthropocentric conception of environmental protection is not enough to combat the effects of climate change.

81 In particular, the application of the exclusively French concept of 'pure ecological damage' to the field of climate change is an important legal development and a new way to challenge government and corporate acts that are detrimental to climate change mitigation. This application may allow the expansion of the right to a healthy environment to include certain duties with respect to Nature and the recognition of a general climate obligation based on general principles of law. This argument could be extrapolated to other jurisdictions as a call for an approach that pairs the right to a clean environment with the duty to care for elements of Nature and ecosystems as a whole.

Climate litigation worldwide raises awareness of the importance of Nature and the development of more Nature-centred solutions as key to both protecting Nature and increasing societal resistance to climate change. This 'ecocentric' approach to climate litigation has developed mainly in the Global South, where most of the world's biodiversity is concentrated. Climate change, however, is a universal concern, and therefore the experience from the Global South can contribute to Global North climate litigation and strengthen the ecocentric perspective on rights.

Some courts have made Nature legally visible by reinterpreting and expanding the meaning of certain norms and legal institutions historically used for different purposes. Even so, recognition of the rights of ecosystems remains rare because recognition of the rights of Nature was seen as collateral to the climate litigation and because the ecocentric approach is still not widely used, compared to the traditional rule of law.

Nevertheless, recognition of the importance of an ecocentric perspective in climate litigation has been steadily growing, not only because it is a solution that can help save us from the climate emergency but also because of increasing respect for the existence of non-human life forms and greater understanding of their vulnerability to the effects of anthropogenic climate change. This growing recognition is important because, in many cases, the changing climate is not the centre of legal demands but is instead integrated into litigation as an issue that aggravates pre-existing environmental and socioeconomic problems. The treatment of climate change as merely an add-on threatens the realisation of fundamental rights and the preservation of carbon sinks.

Recognition of the rights of Nature allows people to view Nature as a being or life form connected to themselves and worthy of protection, thereby strengthening the relationship between humans and Nature. When this happens, people are more likely to fight to protect that relationship when Nature is harmed or threatened, and they will expect the law to recognise it as the status quo of a viable and sustainable being. Courts will then be more receptive and understanding, and they will therefore be more likely to articulate new interpretations of law and pass new laws and constitutional provisions that ensure the protection of Nature. Perhaps equally important, if not more so, people will become more likely to see Nature, ontologically speaking, as beingness and a concern of all humankind, surpassing the idea of Nature as exclusively a question of the culture and spirituality of Indigenous peoples. In this way, people can bring civil actions to insist that those new rights of Nature be protected, and the burden shifts to those who threaten these rights of Nature to prove that there is no likely harm to its elements.

The main arguments, which allow the ecocentric approach of global warming in climate litigation, are focused on the protection of essential ecosystems in order to maintain balance within the climate system. The approach to the climate crisis based on intergenerational and interspecies equity and solidarity allows the progressive recognition of the legal personality and rights of ecosystems threatened by climate change. While all cases bring a different legal argumentation depending on the jurisdictional level, there is a common element between international, national, and local norms of how the climate, human rights, and children can only benefit from the application of clear ecological standards, thus allowing for greater ambition on climate and the protection of the ecological integrity of ecosystems.

In sum, the ecocentric interpretation of law is one of the promising emerging trends in climate litigation in that it centres ecosystems and other elements of Nature and considers the impacts and root causes of climate change, as well as life projects and ecological functions. The 'ecocentric climate litigation' reaches the causes and consequences of the climate emergency, unlike other cases of climate litigation. That is, responsibility towards Nature, offering prevention, repair, and accountability to address climate change. All of these allow a reinterpretation of the legal framework without the need to introduce a reform recognising the legal personhood of Nature and its inherent value and rights, while still protecting human rights and climate objectives. In this way, climate litigation can serve as a critical means of fostering ecological justice.

# PART III

# Regime Interaction and Interpretation

# 12

# International Law

*Sarah Mead and Meinhard Doelle**

## 12.1 INTRODUCTION

The nature of climate change as an urgent global problem renders international law a logical source of guidance in climate litigation. A survey of case law to date reveals that litigants and courts frequently draw on international law, particularly the UN Framework Convention on Climate Change (UNFCCC or the Convention) and the Paris Agreement, in climate change litigation. This has fostered a global judicial dialogue regarding the interpretation of States' obligations under international law.

This chapter explores how courts around the world have treated international law in climate litigation. Beginning with an introduction to the international legal instruments most frequently invoked in climate litigation and their usage by courts, the chapter proceeds with a descriptive section on general trends and approaches (Section 12.2), followed by an analytical section that identifies emerging best practices and explains why it qualifies as such (Section 12.3). Subsequently, the chapter discusses the issue of replicability (Section 12.4) and concludes with some final thoughts.

In line with the overall approach of the Handbook, this chapter focuses on case law that offers helpful lessons for judges and litigants. For this chapter, such a selective approach is also necessitated by the sheer volume of potentially relevant case law. The primary focus is on how courts have engaged with international environmental law, particularly international climate change law. While international human rights law is also frequently invoked in climate litigation, it is addressed in detail in Chapter 7.

* Sarah Mead is Co-Director of the Climate Litigation Network. Meinhard Doelle was Professor of Law at the Schulich School of Law at Dalhousie University. He sadly passed away on 17 September 2022. This chapter was therefore completed posthumously.

### 12.1.1 *International Climate Change Law*

International climate change law encompasses a 'complex web of principles, rules, regulations and institutions'.[1] At its core sit three treaties: the UNFCCC,[2] the Kyoto Protocol,[3] and the Paris Agreement. These treaties are supplemented by a vast array of principles that comprise international environmental law and intersect with various other fields of international law, in particular international human rights law. This section provides a brief overview of the two main treaties now in operation – the UNFCCC and the Paris Agreement – to provide context for the subsequent discussion.

Adopted in 1992, the near universally ratified UNFCCC aims 'to achieve, in accordance with the relevant provisions of the Convention, stabilization of greenhouse gas concentrations in the atmosphere at a level that would prevent dangerous anthropogenic interference with the climate system'.[4] The Convention sets out various commitments for States towards achieving this objective,[5] such as developing national inventories of greenhouse gas (GHG) emissions and formulating national and regional programmes to mitigate GHG emissions and facilitate adaptation.[6] Additionally, developed countries 'commit themselves specifically' to adopting national policies and taking measures to reduce GHG emissions.[7] The Convention establishes several principles to guide State action 'to achieve the objective of the Convention and to implement its provisions'[8] including common but differentiated responsibilities (CBDR), intergenerational equity, precaution, the special circumstances of developing countries, and sustainable development.[9]

The Paris Agreement, adopted in 2015, seeks to enhance the implementation of the Convention and 'strengthen the global response to the threat of climate change'.[10] To that end, it aims to hold 'the increase in the global average temperature to well below 2°C above pre-industrial levels and pursu[e] efforts to limit the temperature

[1] Daniel Bodansky, Jutta Brunnée, and Lavanya Rajamani, *International Climate Change Law* (Oxford University Press 2017) 10.

[2] United Nations Framework Convention on Climate Change (entered into force 21 March 1994) 1771 UNTS 107 (UNFCCC).

[3] Kyoto Protocol to the United Nations Framework Convention on Climate Change (entered into force 16 February 2005) UN Doc FCCC/CP/L7/Add1. The Kyoto Protocol set internationally binding targets for developed country parties for the period 1990–2012 to reduce GHG emissions. The Doha Amendment extended the Protocol to 31 December 2020.

[4] UNFCCC (n 2) art 2. See UNFCCC – Status of Ratification <https://treaties.un.org/Pages/ViewDetailsIII.aspx?src=IND&mtdsg_no=XXVII-7&chapter=27&Temp=mtdsg3&clang=_en> accessed 9 February 2024.

[5] ibid UNFCCC art 4.

[6] ibid art 4(1)(a).

[7] ibid art 4(1).

[8] ibid art 3.

[9] ibid.

[10] Paris Agreement (entered into force 4 November 2016) 3156 UNTS 79 (Paris Agreement) art 2.

increase to 1.5°C above pre-industrial levels'.[11] The Agreement covers several action areas: mitigation, adaptation, loss and damage, and finance,[12] but it is the provisions relating to mitigation that have proven most relevant to climate litigation to date. Under the Agreement, State parties 'must prepare, communicate and maintain successive nationally determined contributions' (NDCs) and pursue domestic mitigation measures 'with the aim of achieving the objectives' of their NDCs.[13] In terms of content, NDCs are to reflect parties' 'highest possible ambition' towards achieving the Agreement's objectives,[14] with developed country parties continuing to take the lead by setting economy-wide absolute emission reduction targets and providing support for developing country parties.[15] Setting the regime's 'direction of travel',[16] the Agreement also requires that updates of NDCs 'represent a progression' over time in terms of ambition, taking into account the outcome of the global stocktake.[17]

In addition to these treaties, climate litigation frequently invokes international environmental law principles such as harm prevention,[18] precaution,[19] intergenerational equity,[20] and sustainable development.[21]

### 12.1.2 *International Law Before National Courts*

The treatment of international law by national courts formally depends on the legal system within which the litigation takes place. Legal systems are often categorised as monist or dualist. A monist system treats international law as automatically

11 ibid art 2(1).
12 ibid art 2(1).
13 ibid art 14(2).
14 ibid art 4(2), 4(3) and 4(9)
15 ibid art 4(4).
16 Lavanya Rajamani, 'Ambition and Differentiation in the 2015 Paris Agreement: Interpretative Possibilities and Underlying Politics' (2016) 65 ICLQ 493, 496.
17 Paris Agreement (n 10) arts 4(2) and 14(3).
18 See Chapter 15 on State Responsibility. The harm prevention principle imposes a responsibility on states 'to ensure that activities within their jurisdiction or control do not cause damage to the environment of other States or of areas beyond the limits of national jurisdiction'. See United Nations, 'Declaration of the United Nations Conference on the Human Environment' (1972) 11 ILM 1416 principle 21; United Nations 'Declaration of the United Nations Conference on Environment and Development' (1992) 31 ILM 874 (Rio Declaration) principle 2; UNFCCC (n 2) preamble, eighth paragraph.
19 The precautionary principle states that if there are 'threats of serious or irreversible damage, lack of full scientific certainty shall not be used as a reason for postponing cost-effective measures to prevent environmental degradation'. See ibid Rio Declaration principle 15; UNFCCC (n 2) art 3(3).
20 See Chapter 14 on Intergenerational Equity. The principle of intergenerational equity articulates a concept of fairness among generations in the use and conservation of the environment and its natural resources. See UNFCCC (n 2) art 3(1); Paris Agreement (n 10) art 2(2) (equity).
21 The principle of sustainable development is defined as development 'that meets the needs of the present generation without compromising the ability of future generations to meet their own needs'. See UNGA 'Our Common Future: Brundtland Report' UN Doc A/42/427 (1987); Rio Declaration (n 18) principle 3; UNFCCC (n 2) art 3(4); Paris Agreement (n 10) art 2(1).

incorporated into national law (incorporation), while a dualist system treats international law as an external body of law that requires transformation into national law, typically through legislative action (transformation).[22] In practice, this distinction is more nuanced: various rules, including those applied by courts, modify how international law is received into the domestic legal system.[23] The result is a 'moderation of the opposing main positions of incorporation and transformation', softening the stark contrast between the two approaches and yielding similar outcomes despite differences in local constitutional set-ups.[24]

An evolution in the nature of international law has expanded the role of national courts in interpreting and applying international law. Traditionally, international law primarily focused on relations between States, leaving a limited role for national courts.[25] Modern international law, by contrast, is often described as 'inward-looking' as it concerns the internal affairs of States.[26] This shift is most evident in international human rights law but can also be seen in the field of international environmental law. The so-called 'bottom up' structure of States' mitigation obligations under the Paris Agreement, whereby contributions are 'nationally determined', showcases this shift.[27] As Wegener explains:

> Although the Paris Agreement does not contain substantive provisions comparable with the mitigation provisions of the Kyoto Protocol, it nonetheless sets up a normative architecture of internationally agreed standards and expectations. These are in need of translation into domestic governance and, finally, domestic action. While this may be primarily a task for legislatures, domestic courts can contribute by 'holding their governments to account, and … ensuring that … commitments are given practical and enforceable effect'. Rather abstract provisions, such as the collective temperature goal, which are not directly justiciable, are given practical effect when invoked in domestic courts… Moreover, by referring to the non-binding standards set by the Paris Agreement and NDCs, national courts help to strengthen the legitimacy of those standards.[28]

22 Study Group on Principles on the Engagement of Domestic Courts with International Law, 'Mapping the Engagement of Domestic Courts with International Law – Final Report' in International Law Association Report of the Seventy-Seventh Conference (International Law Association, London 2016) (ILA Domestic Courts and International Law Final Report) 8.

23 ibid [16].

24 ibid [29].

25 Eyal Benvenisti and George W. Downs, 'National Courts, Domestic Democracy, and the Evolution of International Law' (2009) 20 EJIL 59, 62; ILA Domestic Courts and International Law Final Report (n 22) 5.

26 ILA Domestic Courts and International Law Final Report (n 22); Antonios Tzanakopoulos and Christian J. Tams, 'Introduction: Domestic Courts as Agents of Development of International Law' (2013) 26 LJIL 531.

27 Bodansky, Brunnée, and Rajamani (n 1) 214.

28 Lennar Wegener, 'Can the Paris Agreement Help Climate Change Litigation and Vice Versa?' (2020) 9(1) TEL 35, citing Lord Robert Carnwath, 'Climate Change Adjudication after Paris: A Reflection' (2016) 28(1) JEL 9.

## 12.2 CASE LAW DEVELOPMENT: STATE OF AFFAIRS

A review of the case law to date demonstrates that courts usually rely on international law indirectly in climate litigation to interpret standards under national law, rather than applying international law directly. The most common source of norms are the UNFCCC and the Paris Agreement, specifically the collective goals, principles, and individual mitigation commitments contained therein. Often looking beyond whether a commitment or obligation is binding *per se* in international law, courts are asking questions such as:

- Has the government committed (in law or policy) to implementing the commitment or obligation?
- Is the commitment or obligation relevant in defining the government's duty to its citizens under domestic tort law, human rights law, or environmental law?
- Is the commitment or obligation helpful in defining the powers, duties, and functions of government decision-makers when making policy or decisions that might support or hinder efforts to meet the commitment?

The case law also shows an emerging distinction – whether justified or not – between common and civil law courts in the treatment of international law.

The *Urgenda* case illustrates how courts can draw on international law both directly and indirectly in the context of climate litigation.[29] In 2019, the Supreme Court of the Netherlands ruled that the Dutch government must take measures to reduce emissions in the country by at least 25 per cent below 1990 levels by 2020. The Court relied directly on international law in the form of the European Convention on Human Rights (ECHR), which has a direct effect in the Netherlands, as the source of the breached obligation.[30] After determining that climate change poses a real and foreseeable risk of harm under Articles 2 and 8 of the ECHR, the Court concluded that the State had a positive obligation to take reasonable and adequate measures to address that risk.

The Supreme Court indirectly utilised various norms of international law to determine the scope of the State's obligation under the ECHR. For example, the Court referred to international law (i.e. the UNFCCC, the no harm principle, and the international law on state responsibility) to determine that the State had an individual responsibility to mitigate climate change, despite it being a global problem.[31]

29 For a more detailed discussion of how the courts in the *Urgenda* case engaged with international law see Sarah Mead and Lucy Maxwell, 'Climate Change Litigation: National Courts as Agents of International Law Development' in Edgardo Sobenes, Sarah Mead, and Benjamin Samson (eds), *The Environment through the Lens of International Courts and Tribunals* (Asser Springer 2022).

30 Pursuant to arts 93 and 94 of the Dutch Constitution, Dutch courts must apply every provision of the ECHR that is binding on all persons.

31 *State of the Netherlands (Ministry of Economic Affairs and Climate Policy) v Stichting Urgenda* [2019] ECLI:NL:HR:2019:2007 (Supreme Court of the Netherlands) *(Urgenda Supreme Court)* [5.6.1]–[5.8].

The Court then drew on both hard and soft norms of international law to determine the minimum amount by which the State must reduce its GHG emissions as a way of 'concretising' the obligation, including UNFCCC provisions, Conference of the Parties (COP) decisions, Intergovernmental Panel on Climate Change (IPCC) reports, EU law, and international environmental law principles such as the precautionary principle.[32] The Supreme Court concluded that 'there is a high degree of consensus in the international community on the need for … Annex 1 countries to reduce greenhouse gas emissions by 25 per cent to 40 per cent by 2020',[33] with the lower limit representing the 'absolute minimum' for the State to discharge its positive obligations under Articles 2 and 8 of the ECHR.[34]

The approach of drawing on international law indirectly to interpret open standards at the national level is particularly evident in European case law. For example, the Brussels Court of First Instance in the Belgian case of *Klimaatzaak* drew on a range of international law norms to determine whether the respondent governments had breached their obligations under the ECHR – as per the Dutch courts in *Urgenda*.[35] The Council of State in the French case of *Grande-Synthe* did the same. The case, which was brought by a coastal municipality (Grande-Synthe) and its mayor, argued that the French Government was not doing enough to combat climate change. The Council of State ultimately limited its review to whether the State was complying with its own climate mitigation target to reduce GHG emissions by 40 per cent by 2030 compared to 1990. This was based on its view that the plaintiffs could not rely directly upon the UNFCCC and the Paris Agreement to challenge the government's inaction. The Council of State nevertheless was clear that the State's obligations under international law were relevant to interpreting national law. The Council of State explained:

> According to these stipulations and provisions, the European Union and France, as signatories of the UNFCCC and the Paris Agreement, have committed to combating the harmful effects of climate change caused notably by the increase, during the industrial era, in greenhouse gas emissions attributable to human activities, by implementing policies aimed at reducing the level of these emissions in gradual stages, in order to assume, based on the principle of an equitable contribution by all states parties to the objective of reducing greenhouse gas emissions, their common but differentiated responsibilities according to their contribution to the level of emissions and their capacity and resources for reducing them in the future, in light of their level of economic and social development. While the stipulations of the UNFCCC and the Paris Agreement cited in point 9 require further actions to be taken to produce effects in respect of individuals and accordingly, do not have

[32] ibid [6.1]–[7.3.6].
[33] ibid [7.2.7].
[34] ibid [7.5.1].
[35] *VZW Klimaatzaak v l'État Belge* [2021] 2015/4585/A (Tribunal de première instance francophone de Bruxelles, Section Civile).

any direct effect, they must nevertheless be taken into consideration in interpreting the provisions of national law, notably those cited in point 11, which, in referring to the targets they set, are specifically aimed at their implementation.[36]

Civil law courts outside of Europe have engaged with international law in a similar way. The Supreme Court of Colombia in the case of *Future Generations* identified a broad range of 'hard and soft law' instruments 'which constitute a global ecological public order and serve as guiding criteria for national legislation'.[37] Among the most relevant instruments identified were the International Covenant on Economic, Social and Cultural Rights, the Stockholm Declaration, and the Paris Agreement. The decisions in *Leghari* and *Shrestha*, two landmark cases from Pakistan and Nepal respectively, also draw liberally on international environmental law to inform the interpretation of the relevant domestic law provisions of human rights law – as discussed in more detail in Section 12.1.2.[38]

By contrast, common law courts have taken a more cautious approach to using international law in the context of climate litigation. This is evident in the Australian case of *Sharma*. The case was brought by eight young people who sought an injunction to prevent the Minister from approving a coal mine extension. Reversing the first instance decision, the Full Federal Court of Australia ultimately found that the Minister did not owe the youth plaintiffs a duty of care. In coming to its decision, the Court (in three separate judgments) did not consider the climate treaty regime relevant to determining the standard of care. While acknowledging that the relevant Act 'is founded in significant part on the translation of international agreements into Commonwealth law', Allsop CJ reasoned that the relevant international agreements had not been 'translate[d]' into domestic law – referring to the dualist orientation of the Australian legal system.[39]

The UK Supreme Court in the *Heathrow Extension* case adopted a similar approach. The case challenged the legality of the UK Government's Airport National Policy Statement, which gave in-principle support to the extension of Heathrow Airport. Among the claims, Plan B argued that the Government's

36 *Commune de Grande-Synthe v France* [2020] N°427301 (Conseil d'Etat) [12].

37 *Future Generations v Ministry of the Environment and Others (Demanda Generaciones Futuras v Minambiente)* [2018] 11001 22 03 000 2018 00319 00 (Supreme Court of Justice of Colombia) (*Demanda Futuras Generaciones*).

38 *Asghar Leghari v Federation of Pakistan etc* PLD 2018 Lahore 364; *Advocate Padam Bahadur Shrestha v Prime Minister and Office of Council of Ministers and Others* [2018] Order No 074-WO-0283 (2075/09/10 BS) (Supreme Court of Nepal) (*Shrestha v Office of Council of Ministers*).

39 *Sharma and others v Minister for the Environment* [2021] FCA 560 [5] (Allsop CJ). The decision of the New Zealand Court of Appeal in *Smith v Fonterra* also contains very limited references to international law beyond acknowledgement of the existing framework of international law (including the UNFCCC, the Kyoto Protocol, and the Paris Agreement). The Court noted that the existence of international obligations was a 'crucial factor telling against a duty'. See *Michael John Smith v Fonterra Co-Operative Group Limited and Others* CA 128/2020 [2021] NZCA 552 (*Smith Court of Appeal*).

commitment to the Paris Agreement was part of 'government policy', and that the Government had therefore breached Section 12.5(8) of the Planning Act. The Court found that the reference to 'government policy' in the Planning Act excluded the Paris Agreement, noting:

> The fact that the United Kingdom had ratified the Paris Agreement is not itself a statement of Government policy in the requisite sense. Ratification is an act on the international plane. It gives rise to obligations of the United Kingdom in international law which continue whether or not a particular government remains in office and which, as treaty obligations, 'are not part of UK law and give rise to no legal rights or obligations in domestic law'.[40]

The distinction between civil and common law courts does not, however, provide clear direction as to how national courts approach international law. In the New Zealand case of *Thomson*, the High Court applied the presumption of consistency to interpret the scope of the Minister's discretion in setting the country's emissions reduction targets.[41] Under the Climate Change Response Act, the Minister had the power to set, amend, or revoke New Zealand's climate targets at any time. The plaintiff challenged the Minister's failure to review the 2050 target following the release of the IPCC's Fifth Assessment Report (AR5). The Court ultimately dismissed the application for judicial review. However, it found that the Minister was required to review the 2050 target following the release of AR5 in order to 'give effect to the Act, and what New Zealand ha[d] accepted, recognised and committed to under the international instruments'.[42] In doing so, it made an important pronouncement:

> The Paris Agreement has been entered into in 'pursuit of' the Convention's objective and guided by its principles. As a matter of statutory interpretation, s 224(2) can and therefore must be interpreted consistently with New Zealand's international obligations under these instruments. I consider s 224(2) is also to be interpreted consistently with matters that New Zealand has recognised and accepted in these instruments, as these aid in interpreting our obligations.[43]

[40] *R (on the application of Plan B Earth and others) v Heathrow Airport Ltd (Heathrow Expansion)* [2020] UKSC 52 [108]. See also *Plan B Earth and others v Prime Minister and others* [2021] EWHC 3469 (Admin), in which the Court denies permission for judicial review of the UK Government's policies relating to climate change. Among the reasons for dismissing the claim, the High Court notes that: 'claims based on breaches of the Paris Agreement were hopeless because the Courts have no jurisdiction to determine whether the Government has acted in breach of its obligations under an unincorporated international treaty'.

[41] *Thomson v Minister for Climate Change Issues* [2017] NZHC 733. For a more in-depth discussion on the *Thomson* case and international law, see Mead and Maxwell (n 29). Among the purposes of the Act is to provide a framework to guide the development of policies to 'contribute to the global effort under the Paris Agreement to limit the global average temperature increase to 1.5° Celsius above pre-industrial levels'. Art 3(1)(aa)(i). However, the 'presumption of consistency' as applied by courts in New Zealand is not dependent on this. See Section 12.4 for further discussion.

[42] ibid [94].

[43] ibid [88].

In the Australian case of *Rocky Hill*,[44] the Court similarly considered the Paris Agreement as a factor to be considered when deciding whether to grant approval for the proposed mine. In reaching its decision to deny approval for the mine, the Court noted that – although the Paris Agreement did not prohibit new coal mine approvals –:

> the exploitation and burning of a new fossil fuel reserve, which will increase GHG emissions, cannot assist in achieving the rapid and deep reductions in GHG emissions that are necessary in order to achieve 'a balance between anthropogenic emissions by sources and removals by sinks of greenhouse gases in the second half of this century' (Article 4(1) of the Paris Agreement) or the long term temperature goal of limiting the increase in global average temperature to between 1.5C and 2C above pre-industrial levels (Article 2 of the Paris Agreement).[45]

In a limited number of cases, there is a conspicuous lack of references to the role of international law. For example, in the United States, neither the majority nor dissenting opinions in the appeal judgment in the *Juliana* case refer to international law in their reasoning, despite its obvious relevance.[46]

## 12.3 EMERGING BEST PRACTICE

### 12.3.1 *Utilising International Law to Interpret National Law Standards*

The most important element of emerging best practice in case law to date is the critical role international law, including non-binding soft law norms, can play in shaping domestic law through the act of interpretation. Where the duty of care being invoked in a case involves an open standard or open-textured norm, jurisprudence shows how courts have employed international law to provide substance or content to those standards. Although the source of the duty differs from case to case, a consistent factor is the use of international law norms to establish the standard against which the act or omission in question is assessed.

The *Urgenda* case exemplifies this. While the District Court ruled that Urgenda could not rely on international law directly, it recognised that international law still has a 'reflex effect' in national law, in this instance, to interpret the standard of care related to the tort of hazardous negligence. The Court explained:

> [I]t follows that an international-law standard – a statutory provision or an unwritten legal standard – may not be explained or applied in a manner which would mean that the state in question has violated an international-law obligation, unless no

[44] *Gloucester Resources Limited v Minister for Planning* [2019] NSWLEC 7 (*Gloucester Resources*).

[45] ibid [527]. The case was an appeal of a ministerial decision where the court reached its own conclusion, as opposed to a judicial review. The Court therefore effectively concluded that the Paris Agreement was relevant in making its own decision about whether to approve the mine, rather than finding that the original decision-maker was reasonable in considering international law.

[46] *Juliana v United States* 947 F.3d 1159 (9th Cir 2020).

> other interpretation or application is possible. This is a generally acknowledged rule in the legal system. This means that when applying and interpreting national-law open standards and concepts, including social proprietary, reasonableness and propriety, the general interest or certain legal principles, the court takes account of such international-law obligations.[47]

The Supreme Court also utilised a broad range of international law norms to interpret the ECHR, which formed the basis of its decision. In the Court's view, any interpretation of the ECHR 'must ... take into account ... relevant rules of international law' and state practice, in accordance with the jurisprudence of the European Court of Human Rights.[48] This was consistent with Article 31(3) of the Vienna Convention on the Law of Treaties which notes that 'any relevant rules of international law applicable in the relations between the parties' shall be taken into account when interpreting a treaty. The District Court and the Supreme Court therefore ultimately used international law to similar effect, despite the different bases for their decisions.[49]

### 12.3.2 *International Law and the 'Greening' of Human Rights*

The interconnected nature of international environmental law and international human rights law is well established in national, regional, and international jurisprudence. As human rights law increasingly forms the basis for climate cases, courts are adopting the best practice of drawing on international environmental law to define the scope and content of those human rights obligations.

In the *Asghar Leghari* case, a Pakistani farmer complained that the Government had failed to implement its own climate change policies, which constituted a breach of his constitutional rights. In its judgment, the Court drew on a variety of international environmental law principles to interpret the scope of the relevant rights. The Court explained:

> Fundamental rights, like the right to life (Article 9) which includes the right to a healthy and clean environment and right to human dignity (Article 14) read with constitutional principles of democracy, equality, social, economic and political

47 *Urgenda Foundation v The State of The Netherlands* [2015] ECLI:NL:RBDHA:2015:7196 (District Court of the Hague) (*Urgenda District Court*) [4.43].

48 *Urgenda Supreme Court* (n 31) [5.4.2].

49 See further *Advisory Opinion on Cassation Appeal of the Procurator General in the Matter between the Netherlands v Urgenda* ECLI:NL:PHR:2019:1026 No 19/00135 (Supreme Court of the Netherlands 2019) [2.30] ('The common ground method is somewhat comparable to the reflex effect that national courts, in implementing open standards into national law, can attribute to treaty provisions and 'soft law' that have no direct effect. This explains why the Court of Appeal in its contested judgment reached the same conclusion on the basis of arts 2 and 8 ECHR as the District Court did on the basis of art 6:162 (Dutch Civil Code): for the concrete implementation of the reduction obligation, the District Court and the Court of Appeal sought to draw on the same climatological insights, objectives of international climate policy and principles of international law'). See also [2.7.2].

> justice include within their ambit and commitment, the international environmental principles of sustainable development, precautionary principle, environmental impact assessment, inter and intra-generational equity and public trust doctrine. Environment and its protection has taken a center stage in the scheme of our constitutional rights. It appears that we have to move on. The existing environmental jurisprudence has to be fashioned to meet the needs of something more urgent and overpowering ie Climate Change.[50]

Similarly, in the case of *Shrestha*, the Supreme Court referred to the UNFCCC, the Kyoto Protocol, and the Paris Agreement when determining that the State had not fulfilled its constitutional obligations to protect the petitioner's right to life with dignity and a clean environment.[51] The case was brought by a Nepalese lawyer, Padam Bahadur Shrestha, who alleged that the Government's failure to set and implement adequate climate law and policies breached his rights under the Constitution and violated Nepal's commitments under the UNFCCC and the Paris Agreement. Finding in favour of the plaintiff, the Court found that 'a new law dealing with climate change adaptation and mitigation, ensuring environmental justice while taking measures for maintaining clean environment with environmental conservation, and regulating production that causes impact on food, species, and ecosystem, and health seems imperative'. In addition to being necessary to protect constitutional rights, the Court noted that such a law 'would also facilitate in effectuating the commitments under the Paris Agreement on Climate Change, 2015'.[52]

The Brazilian case, *PSB et al v Brazil (on Climate Fund)*, represents a significant development in the greening of human rights. The case concerned the administration of the National Climate Fund (Fundo Clima) which had been created by law but inoperative for several years. The Supreme Court found that the executive branch has a constitutional duty to execute and allocate the funds of the Climate Fund to mitigate climate change, based on both the separation of powers and the constitutional right to a healthy environment. In this context, it determined that environmental treaties, including the Paris Agreement, 'are a species of the genus human rights treaties and enjoy, for this reason, supranational status'.[53] This means that any Brazilian law or decree that contradicts the Paris Agreement, including the NDC, may be invalidated. In coming to this view, the decision recalls the statement made by a UN Environment Programme representative during the hearing that '[t]here are no human rights on a dead or sick planet'.[54]

The interconnected relationship between environmental protection and human rights is also reflected in the jurisprudence at the regional and international levels.

50 *Asghar Leghari* (n 38) [12].

51 *Shrestha v Office of Council of Ministers* (n 38) [5].

52 ibid [12].

53 *PSB et al v Brazil (on Climate Fund)* [2022] ADPF 708 (Federal Supreme Court of Brazil) [17].

54 ibid.

The Inter-American Court of Human Rights (IACtHR), in its landmark Advisory Opinion No 23, noted 'the existence of an undeniable relationship between the protection of the environment and the realization of other human rights, in that environmental degradation and the adverse effects of climate change affect the real enjoyment of human rights'.[55] It accordingly concluded that it could 'avail itself of the principles, rights and obligations of international environmental law' when determining the scope of the State's obligations under the American Convention.[56]

Turning to the international level, the Committee on the Rights of the Child similarly drew on international environmental law in its *Sacchi* decision. The complaint was brought by sixteen children from around the world who alleged that their rights under the Convention on the Rights of the Child had been violated due to insufficient mitigation and adaptation action on the part of the respondent States. The Committee ultimately found the complaint to be inadmissible for failing to exhaust domestic remedies. The Committee's decision nevertheless shows the relevance of international environmental law to interpreting international human rights law. For instance, in determining the State's individual responsibility for the harm that may arise as a result of its GHG emissions, the Committee drew on the Paris Agreement and the principle of CBDR.[57] The Committee also pointed to the UNFCCC and the Paris Agreement as evidence that the respondent States were aware of the potential harm associated with their GHG emissions.[58]

### 12.3.3 *Range of International Law Norms, Including Soft Law*

Emerging best practices in climate litigation involve courts relying on a broad range of international law norms when adjudicating climate cases. These norms include international treaty law (e.g. the UNFCCC and the Paris Agreement), general principles of international environmental law (e.g. the principles of precaution and no harm), and soft law instruments (e.g. decisions of COP and the UN Guiding Principles).

A groundbreaking aspect of the *Shell* decision was its use of human rights law, including soft law, to interpret the standard of care applicable to a company in its global operations – in this case, Royal Dutch Shell. The plaintiff, a Dutch NGO called Milieudefensie, relied on the same provision of the Dutch Civil Code in

55 *The Environment and Human Rights (State Obligations in Relation to the Environment in the Context of the Protection and Guarantee of the Rights to Life and to Personal Integrity – Interpretation and Scope of Articles 4(1) and 5(1) of the American Convention on Human Rights)*, Advisory Opinion OC-23, Inter-American Court of Human Rights Series A No 23 (15 November 2017) (IACtHR OC-23/17) [47].

56 ibid [55].

57 UN Committee on the Rights of the Child, 'Decision Adopted by the Committee under the Optional Protocol to the Convention on the Rights of the Child on a Communications Procedure, concerning Communication No 104/2019', UN Doc CRC/C/88/D/104/2019 (*Sacchi*) [10.10].

58 ibid [10.11].

combination with Articles 2 and 8 of the ECHR as in the *Urgenda* case. The case alleges that Royal Dutch Shell has violated its duty of care by failing to adopt policies that will reduce the company's emissions in line with the Paris Agreement's long-term temperature goal. Finding in favour of the plaintiffs, the Court ordered Shell to reduce its emissions by 45 per cent by 2030 relative to 2019 (roughly in line with the global average) across all of its activities, including both its own emissions and end-use emissions.[59] In its interpretation of the standard of care, the Court treated the non-binding goals of the Paris Agreement as 'a universally endorsed and accepted standard that protects the common interest of preventing dangerous climate change'.[60] It also considered the protections afforded by international human rights law, including the International Covenant on Civil and Political Rights and the ECHR. While acknowledging that human rights law does not give rise to binding obligations on Shell (as a non-State actor), the Court considered human rights to be important – also given the extent of Royal Dutch Shell's emissions which exceed that of the Netherlands. The Court noted that '[d]ue to the fundamental interest of human rights and the value for society as a whole they embody, human rights may play a role in the relationship between Milieudefensie et al. and RDS. Therefore, the court will factor in the human rights and the values they embody in its interpretation of the unwritten standard of care'.[61] The Court also cited various soft law instruments, including the UN Guiding Principles on Business and Human Rights (UNGPs), to support its finding that companies must respect human rights. The reliance on these sources did not depend on the company having endorsed them, nor a finding that these sources were binding on the jurisdictions in which Shell operates.

The Commission on Human Rights of the Philippines adopted a similar approach in its decision relating to the *Carbon Majors* inquiry.[62] The inquiry assessed the responsibility of the 'Carbon Majors' – i.e. those corporations that have historically contributed the most to climate change – for human rights violations arising from climate impacts in the Philippines. In its decision, the Commission found that enterprises 'must comply with the Nationally Determined Commitments of States who are parties to the Paris Agreement', as a result of their obligations under the UNGP to respect the principles of international human rights.[63] The Commission therefore relied on the UNGP to establish not only the responsibility of enterprises towards human rights but also the duty of States to regulate the activities of enterprises in accordance with international human rights obligations.

[59] *Milieudefensie v Royal Dutch Shell* [2021] ECLR:NL: RBDHA:2021:5339 (District Court of the Hague). The Court of Appeal of the Hague overturned this decision in November 2024, following the completion of this manuscript.

[60] ibid [4.4.27].

[61] ibid [4.4.9].

[62] *In re Greenpeace Southeast Asia and Others* [2022] Case No CHR-NI-2016-0001 (Commission on Human Rights of the Philippines).

[63] ibid [98].

### 12.3.4 *International Law as Relevant to Determining the Minimum Standard*

It is emerging best practice for courts to use a combination of international law and the best available science to determine the minimum standard (of care) that, for example, a government must meet to fulfil its legal duties. This is particularly relevant in cases which require a court to determine whether a State's mitigation policies are sufficient to meet its 'fair share' of global emissions reductions. Courts have generally acknowledged that the UNFCCC, the Paris Agreement, and the IPCC science reports do not themselves set a precise standard against which to assess States' mitigation policies. Nevertheless, courts have been willing to set conservative minimum standards based on the international consensus reflected in these sources.[64]

The German *Neubauer* case serves as a useful illustration of this emerging best practice. The case concerned a legal challenge to Germany's Federal Climate Protection Act on the basis that the mitigation target contained therein violated the youth plaintiffs' human rights, as protected under the German Constitution. The Court approached the complaint from two angles: firstly, asking whether the Act violated the State's duty to protect (i.e. as a breach of a positive duty) and secondly, asking whether the Act violated the State's duty not to interfere with fundamental freedoms (i.e. a breach of a negative duty).[65] In relation to the first question, the Court found that the dangers presented by climate change are sufficiently real and serious to give rise to a duty to protect under the German Constitution. Given the wide margin afforded the State in relation to positive duties, however, the Court did not consider that any such duty had been breached in the present case as the approach adopted in the German Act was not 'manifestly unsuitable or completely inadequate'.[66] The Court did, however, find that the State had breached its negative duty not to interfere with the fundamental freedoms of the complainants in the future. In the Court's view, Article 20a of the Constitution concerning the protection of the natural foundations of life and animals requires the government to take climate action.[67] While the government has 'considerable leeway' to design the content of its climate action, the Court considered that its role was to 'review whether the boundaries of Article 20a are respected'.[68] International law played a key role in determining those boundaries. The temperature limit set out in the Act – which

[64] See Lucy Maxwell, Sarah Mead, and Dennis van Berkel, 'Standards for Adjudicating the next Generation of Urgenda-Style Climate Cases' (2022) 13(1) JHRE 35.

[65] For an explanation of this distinction in the context of German Constitutional law, see Petra Minnerop, 'The "Advance Interference-Like Effect" of Climate Targets: Fundamental Rights, Intergenerational Equity and the German Federal Constitutional Court' (2021) JEL 41, 42–43.

[66] *Neubauer and Others v Germany* [2021] 1 BvR 2656/18, 1 BvR 96/20, 1 BvR 78/20, 1 BvR 288/20, 1 BvR 96/20, 1 BvR 78/20 (German Federal Constitutional Court) (*Neubauer*) [152].

[67] ibid [206].

[68] ibid.

reflected that in the Paris Agreement – was identified 'as providing fundamental orientation for climate action'.[69] The Court explained:

> Rather than being purely an expression of political will, the chosen temperature limit must indeed also be understood as being a specification of the climate action required under constitutional law. This is primarily supported by the fact that the climate target specified in [the Act] is the internationally agreed temperature limit of Article 2(1)(a) Paris Agreement, which the legislator has deliberately and explicitly taken as a basis. Its constitutional law significance goes beyond the consent given by the German legislator to the Paris Agreement in passing the act of approval. The fact that the Paris target is explicitly named as the basis of Germany's Federal Climate Change Act is closely related to the obligation to take climate action arising from Article 20(a) GG. Due to the genuinely global dimension of climate change, the state can ultimately achieve the objective of slowing down climate change enshrined in Article 20(a) GG only through international cooperation. It has taken action to this end by ratifying the Paris Agreement, which provides the framework within which it is now also fulfilling its more extensive climate action obligations arising from Article 20(a) GG [...]. By adopting the temperature limit of Article 2(1)(a) Paris Agreement, the legislator has set the fundamental course of national climate change law in a direction that gives the German state an opportunity to effectively fulfil its constitutional mandate to take climate action through its own efforts embedded within an international framework.[70]

Reliance on best available science when assessing obligations relating to climate change can also be considered a requirement derived from international law. The Paris Agreement's preamble recognises 'the need for an effective and progressive response to the urgent threat of climate change on the basis of the best available scientific knowledge', while Article 4(1) refers to the need for emissions to peak and for parties 'to undertake rapid reductions thereafter in accordance with best available science'.[71] The Glasgow Climate Pact (2021) further recognises 'the importance of the best available science for effective climate action and policymaking'[72] and the need for 'accelerated action in this critical decade, on the basis of the best available scientific knowledge and equity'.[73]

The New Zealand case of *Thomson* (discussed earlier) linked the need to rely on best available science with the government's obligations under international law. Under the Climate Change Response Act, there was no express requirement for the

69 ibid [208]. Section 1 of the relevant Act noted 'The basis of the Act is the obligation according to the Paris Agreement, under the United Nations Framework Convention on Climate Change, to limit the increase in the global average temperature to well below two degrees Celsius and, if possible, to 1.5 degrees Celsius, above the pre-industrial level'.

70 ibid [209].

71 Paris Agreement (n 10) art 4(1).

72 UNFCCC, Glasgow Climate Pact, FCCC/PA/CMA/2021/10/Add.1 1/CMA 3 (13 November 2021) [1].

73 ibid [23]; ibid [18].

Minister to review the 2050 target following the release of a new IPCC Assessment Report. However, the Court found that there was an implied mandatory consideration to give effect to the Act and New Zealand's international commitments.[74] In the Court's view, the provisions of the climate treaty regime together 'underline the pressing need for global action, that global action requires all Parties individually to take appropriate steps to meet the necessary collective action, and that Parties should do so in light of relevant scientific information and update their individual measures in light of such information'.[75] The Court therefore concluded:

> The IPCC reports provide the most up to date scientific consensus on climate change. New Zealand accepts this. To give effect to the Act and what New Zealand has accepted, recognised and committed to under the international instruments, and in light of the threat that climate change presents to humankind and the environment, I consider the publishing of a new IPCC report requires the Minister to consider whether a target set under s 224 should be reviewed. That is, it is a mandatory relevant consideration in whether an existing target should be reviewed under s 224(2).[76]

### 12.3.5 *International Law as Relevant to Interpreting Statutory Discretion*

Finally, courts have shown a willingness to draw on international law when interpreting the scope of a statutory discretion – whether afforded to the State or one of its representatives such as a Minister – usually with a narrowing effect. This can also be treated as an element of emerging best practice.

In *EarthLife Africa*, South Africa's High Court was asked to determine whether the climate-related impacts of a new coal-fired power station needed to be taken into account before approval for the project was granted.[77] The Court acknowledged that the relevant legislation did not expressly refer to climate change. However, with reference to the Paris Agreement, the Court held that climate change was a 'necessary and relevant' consideration for the environmental review of the project, and that the failure to take it into account rendered the approval process for the project unlawful. The Court noted:

> The respondents further argued that the power station project is consistent with South Africa's NDC under the Paris Agreement, which envisages that South Africa's emissions will peak between 2020 and 2025. Again I agree with EarthLife that this contention misses the point. The argument is not whether new coal-fired

[74] *Thomson* (n 41) [94].
[75] ibid [91].
[76] ibid [94].
[77] *EarthLife Africa Johannesburg v Minister* [2017] 65662/16 <https://climatecasechart.com/wp-content/uploads/non-us-case-documents/2017/20170306_Case-no.-6566216_judgment-1.pdf> accessed 27 March 2023.

> power stations are permitted under the Paris Agreement and the NDC. The narrow question is whether a climate change impact assessment is required before authorising new coal-fired power stations. A climate change impact assessment is necessary and relevant to ensuring that the proposed coal-fired power station fits South Africa's peak, plateau and decline trajectory as outlined in the NDC and its commitment to build cleaner and more efficient than existing power stations.[78]

The Canadian Supreme Court in *Greenhouse Gas Pollution Pricing Act* is similarly illustrative of the role that international law can play in interpreting statutory discretion.[79] The case concerned the constitutional validity of Canada's Greenhouse Gas Pollution Pricing Act (GGPPA) in light of the division of power between the federal and provincial levels of government in Canada.[80] In considering the respective governments' powers, the Court referred to the urgent need to reduce GHG emissions, Canada's obligations under the UN climate treaty regime, and the reference to the Paris Agreement in the preamble of the GGPPA. This led the majority of the Court to find that climate change is a global challenge that cannot be left exclusively to the provinces to address. A carbon pricing backstop was an effective way for the Federal Government to ensure progress on its commitments under the Paris Agreement, while still leaving room for provinces to develop their own mitigation policies.

## 12.4 REPLICABILITY

Many aspects of how courts have engaged with international law in climate litigation to date are replicable in other jurisdictions, including the emerging best practices identified earlier. There are two key reasons for this. Firstly, the most relevant international treaties – the UNFCCC and the Paris Agreement – enjoy almost universal ratification, providing litigants and judges with a common source of norms in the context of climate litigation.[81] Consequently, interpretations and applications of these instruments by courts in one jurisdiction may offer valuable guidance to courts in other jurisdictions, even in the absence of any formal binding effect. Secondly,

78 ibid [90].

79 *Saskatchewan et al v Greenhouse Gas Pollution Pricing Act* (2021) SCC 11 (*Saskatchewan and others*). See also the District Court decision in *Urgenda*, where the Court noted that – while the relevant norms of international law cannot be relied on directly – they help determine 'what degree of discretionary power the State is entitled to in how it exercises the tasks and authorities given to it' and thus 'constitute an important viewpoint in assessing whether or not the State acts wrongfully', *Urgenda District Court* (n 47) [4.52].

80 In Canada, provinces have primary jurisdiction over many of the activities that contribute to Canada's GHG emissions, while the Federal Government has the power to negotiate and ratify treaties such as the Paris Agreement.

81 See United Nations Treaty Collection <www.treaties.un.org>.

the primary way in which international law has been invoked in the jurisprudence (i.e. indirectly) lends itself to replicability. This is because *how* and *to what extent* the applicable international law norm is formally incorporated into the national legal system is less relevant.

Each legal system has its own rules regarding the reception of international law which operate to regulate how courts engage with international law. However, as noted in Section 12.1.2, various rules and practices have the effect of blunting or moderating the rules that dictate whether a particular legal system is considered 'monist' or 'dualist'. New Zealand, for example, is a dualist system – requiring international law to be translated into domestic law via legislation for it to become part of the domestic legal system. Still, the presumption of consistency applied by New Zealand courts favours an interpretation of statutory law that is consistent with international law where possible. This is similar to the 'reflex effect' described by the Dutch District Court in the *Urgenda* case, despite the Netherlands being a monist system. Writing extrajudicially, the current Chief Justice and two Judges of the Supreme Court of New Zealand noted that:

> New Zealand courts apply a presumption to the interpretation of statutes that Parliament did not intend to legislate contrary to New Zealand's international obligations. We anticipate that international treaties in the climate change area will increasingly be used in this way in litigation and it may be that courts will, as they respond to the magnitude of the issue, seek to strengthen the presumption.[82]

There is therefore considerable scope – even accounting for how different legal systems receive international law – for courts to draw on how courts from other traditions have treated international law in climate litigation.

## 12.5 CONCLUSION

A survey of the relevant case law to date highlights the extent to which courts across diverse jurisdictions have drawn on international law in adjudicating climate cases. This is unsurprising given the inherently global nature of climate change. As explained by the Canadian Supreme Court in its decision in *Greenhouse Gas Pollution Pricing Act* regarding the unique features of climate change:

> First, [climate change] has no boundaries; the entire country and entire world are experiencing and will continue to experience its effects. Second, the effects of climate change do not have a direct connection to the source of GHG emissions. Provinces and territories with low GHG emissions can experience effects of climate change that are grossly disproportionate to their individual contributions to

[82] Helen Winkelmann, CJ, Susan Glazebrook, and Ellen France, 'Climate Change and the Law' (2019) Asia-Pacific Judicial Colloquium <www.courtsofnz.govt.nz/assets/speechpapers/ccw.pdf> accessed 9 February 2024.

> Canada's and the world's total GHG emissions.... Third, no one province, territory or country can address the issue of climate change on its own. Addressing climate change requires collective national and international action. This is because the harmful effects of GHGs are, by their very nature, not confined by borders.[83]

The most important conclusion to be drawn from the cases reviewed is that international law can significantly influence domestic law interpretation to help overcome obstacles litigants face when seeking recourse for climate change-related harms. The details will vary from jurisdiction to jurisdiction, but the trend is clear and important. Even non-binding sources of international law offer important context for helping to shape domestic law to fairly and effectively deal with climate cases. The legitimacy of legal systems depends on this, which serves to encourage courts to draw on international law in their deliberations and legal analysis.

The role of international courts and tribunals in addressing climate change is also receiving increasing attention. At the time of writing, the International Tribunal for the Law of the Sea,[84] the IACtHR,[85] and the International Court of Justice have each received requests seeking an advisory opinion seeking to clarify the obligations of States in light of the climate crisis.[86] Each opinion will serve as a critical opportunity for these international courts to build on the foundation established by national courts in emerging best practices. Clearly, courts at all levels have important roles to play in further clarifying and enforcing the obligations of States and non-State actors in the context of the climate crisis.

[83] *Saskatchewan and others* (n 79) [12].

[84] On 16 December 2022, the Commission of Small Island States on Climate Change and International Law requested an advisory opinion from the International Tribunal for the Law of the Sea. The request seeks the Tribunal's opinion on the obligations of State Parties to the UN Convention on the Law of the Sea (UNCLOS) in relation to certain provisions of the Convention in light of climate change.

[85] On 9 January 2023, Chile and Colombia requested an advisory opinion from the Inter-American Court of Human Rights aiming to clarify States' human rights obligations in light of the climate emergency.

[86] On 29 March 2023, the General Assembly of the United Nations requested an advisory opinion from the International Court of Justice on the obligations of States with respect to climate change. The question seeks the Court's opinion on both the obligations of States under international law in relation to climate change, and the legal consequences for States where they, by their act and omissions, have caused significant harm to the climate system.

# 13

# Common but Differentiated Responsibilities and Respective Capabilities

*Patricia Galvao Ferreira**

## 13.1 INTRODUCTION

This chapter examines how domestic courts have considered the principle of 'common but differentiated responsibilities and respective capabilities' (CBDR-RC) when deciding lawsuits alleging violations of domestic statutory obligations, constitutional rights, or common law duties by governments in the context of efforts to mitigate climate change. Although CBDR-RC emerged first as a principle of international law to guide State-to-State relations (outward-looking), national courts are increasingly relying on CBDR-RC to help interpret the scope of national climate obligations (turning this principle 'inward-looking').[1]

A growing number of courts are relying on CBDR-RC when analysing a country's individual obligation to do their 'fair share' of global mitigation efforts under the United Nations (UN) climate regime or when defining the scope of each country's unique due diligence standard of protection in the face of global climate risks. Courts are using CBDR-RC as part of a set of hard and soft international environmental law standards to help determine what level of political discretion governments have when deciding whether to reduce emissions in their territories, how much to reduce, and by what timeline.

* Patricia Galvao Ferreira is an associate professor at the Schulich School of Law at Dalhousie University.

[1] Study Group on Principles on the Engagement of Domestic Courts with International Law, 'Mapping the Engagement of Domestic Courts with International Law – Final Report' in International Law Association Report of the Seventy-Seventh Conference (International Law Association, London 2016) (ILA Domestic Courts and International Law Final Report).

It is worth noting that while some courts are more explicit in their application of the CBDR-RC principle, others are doing so implicitly, by engaging with related concepts such as a country's obligation to do their part and contribute their 'fair share' of global climate efforts. This chapter therefore includes examination of decisions where courts explicitly referred to CBDR-RC as a relevant principle when setting the legal standards applicable to the adjudication, articulated reasonings related to the concepts of fair distribution of climate responsibilities, invoked CBDR-RC in the interpretation of specific legal obligations, or engaged with concepts directly related to the principle. Thus far, CBDR-RC has featured primarily in climate mitigation cases, particularly but not exclusively in lawsuits challenging the legality of overall efforts of a State to mitigate climate change.

Although the CBDR-RC jurisprudence is still nascent and at times inconsistent, it holds relevance due to the important role this principle plays in the effectiveness of the international climate change regime, and in worldwide efforts by those most affected by climate impacts to promote climate justice. As discussions on each country's 'fair share' of global climate efforts pick up pace in the context of the 2015 Paris Climate Agreement's (PA) iterative process of pledge and review of national contributions, aimed at closing the emissions gap to achieve the temperature goal of 'well below 2°C' and striving to remain at '1.5°C', we expect the CBDR-RC jurisprudence to expand over time. There is an expectation that more judicial decisions will engage with the principle, following plaintiffs invoking CBDR-RC in complaints before international human rights bodies such as the Committee on the Rights of the Child (CRC), the Human Rights Committee (HRC), and the European Court of Human Rights. CBDR-RC also features in the upcoming Advisory Opinion (AO) by the Inter-American Court of Human Rights (IACtHR) on the scope of State obligations to respond to human rights implications of climate threats. With courts' engagement with CBDR-RC becoming more established, it is also possible to predict that it will appear in future climate litigation related to climate finance, adaptation, or loss and damage.

In the balance of this chapter, Section 13.2 introduces a background discussion on two issues that are central to understanding how courts are finding legal content in the emerging concept of national 'fair shares' of global climate efforts: a) the evolution of the CBDR-RC principle in the international climate regime; and b) the scientifically backed international political consensus on the global average temperature goals needed to avoid dangerous climate impacts, as well as the associated concepts of remaining global carbon budgets and fair allocation of national carbon budgets. Section 13.3 then reviews the CBDR-RC case law development; Section 13.4 highlights emerging best practices; Section 13.5 analyses the potential for replicability; Section 13.6 concludes with a few observations.

## 13.2 RELEVANT BACKGROUND ISSUES

### 13.2.1 *CBDR-RC in International Climate Law*

CBDR-RC is foundational to international environmental law[2] and is deeply embedded in the UN climate regime.[3] The principle has two separate elements: the common responsibility of States to respond to the global climate change challenge; and the need to differentiate which 'fair share' of the common responsibility should be assigned to each individual country according to a series of possible equity benchmarks.[4] These equity benchmarks have never been enumerated in the text of international climate law agreements. In climate negotiations and in decisions of the Conference of the Parties (COP) to the UN Framework Convention on Climate Change (UNFCCC), we find reference to the following criteria: individual responsibilities for the climate problem (e.g. historic or current greenhouse gas (GHG) emissions, absolute emissions, or *per capita* emissions); capabilities to take climate action (financial, technological, or institutional capacities); and/or stages of development.[5]

Climate action has been long recognised as a common responsibility of all countries. As an international problem of 'common concern', climate change can only be confronted via multilateral cooperation.[6] As the Intergovernmental Panel on

[2] United Nations, 'Declaration of the United Nations Conference on Environment and Development' (1992) 31 ILM 874 (Rio Declaration) principle 7. Some authors (e.g. Owen McIntyre, 'The Role of Customary Rules and Principles of International Environmental Law in the Protection of Shared International Freshwater Resources' (2006) 46 Natural Resources Journal 157; David Tacaks, 'Carbon Into Gold: Forest Carbon Offsets, Climate Change Adaptation, and International Law' (2009) 15 Hastings West-Northwest Journal of Environmental Law and Policy 39) argue that CBDR-RC can already be recognised as an emerging principle of customary IEL, although there are dissenting opinions (e.g. Daniel Bodansky, Jutta Brunnée, and Lavanya Rajamani, *International Climate Change Law* (Oxford University Press 2017); Philippe Cullet, 'Differentiation' in Lavanya Rajamani and Jacqueline Peel (eds), *The Oxford Handbook of International Environmental Law* (Oxford University Press 2021). See also Daria Shapovalova, 'In Defence of the Principle of Common but Differentiated Responsibilities and Respective Capabilities' and Thomas Leclerc, 'The Notion of Common but Differentiated Responsibilities and Respective Capabilities: A Commendable but Failed Effort to Enhance Equity in Climate Law' in Benoît Mayer and Alexander Zahar (eds), *Debating Climate Law* (Cambridge University Press 2021).

[3] References to CBDR-RC appear in the preamble and in several operative provisions of the 1992 UNFCCC and the 2015 Paris Agreement and in dozens of decisions adopted by the Conference of the Parties to the UNFCCC (COPs) and the COP serving as the Meeting of the Parties to the Paris Agreement (CMA); ibid Bodansky, Brunnée, and Rajamani (n 2) 27.

[4] See Philippe Sands and Jacqueline Peel, *Principles of International Environmental Law* (Cambridge University Press 2018) 244.

[5] Bodansky, Brunnée, and Rajamani (n 2) 26. For a detailed discussion on how countries have engaged with these equity benchmarks for differentiation in their NDCs and a critical analysis of which benchmarks are aligned with IEL principles see Lavanya Rajamani and others, 'National "Fair Shares" in Reducing Greenhouse Gas Emissions Within the Principled Framework of International Environmental Law' (2021) 21 Climate Policy 983, 984.

[6] All members of the United Nations are Parties to the United Nations Framework Convention on Climate Change (as of 2023).

Climate Change (IPCC) noted in its 2014 Assessment Report 5 (AR5), international cooperation is crucial to address 'global commons' challenges such as climate change, characterised by having 'multiple actors that are diverse in their perceptions of the costs and benefits of collective action; emissions sources that are unevenly distributed; heterogenous climate impacts that are uncertain and distant in space and time; and mitigation costs that vary'.[7] States have consistently reaffirmed their common responsibility, including in the latest COP 27 decision in which they reiterated 'the critical role of multilateralism … including in the context of the implementation of the Convention and the Paris Agreement, and the importance of international cooperation for addressing … climate change'.[8]

Although there is also consensus on the general need to differentiate each individual State's 'fair share' of global climate efforts, the relative importance of the various possible equity benchmarks for differentiation, and on how exactly differentiation should be implemented in a world where contributions to GHG emissions, financial and technological capabilities, and development indicators are in flux, has remained under political dispute. The differentiation element of CBDR-RC can thus be considered an open standard of international climate law, a standard whose normative content is currently being defined by State practice, judicial interpretation, and continuous international negotiations.

Despite the lack of consensus on specific equity benchmarks, it is possible to identify a significant level of agreement over a set of normative expectations that have been at the core of differentiated responsibilities since the inception of the international climate regime. One normative expectation is that developed countries must 'take the lead' in the international climate response, and a second normative expectation is that differentiation must be guided by equity considerations.[9] The allocation of differentiated climate responsibilities along a North–South (developed countries–developing countries) axis has been a constant element of CBDR-RC in the text of various climate legal agreements and

7 Ottmar Edenhofer and others, 'International Cooperation: Agreements & Instruments' in Ottmar Edenhofer and others (eds), *Climate Change 2014: Mitigation of Climate Change, Contribution of Working Group III to the Fifth Assessment Report of the Intergovernmental Panel on Climate Change* (Cambridge University Press 2015) 1008.

8 UNFCCC, Sharm el-Sheikh Implementation Plan, FCCC/CP/2022/10/Add.1 (20 November 2022) (Sharm-el-Sheikh Implementation Plan) preamble, first paragraph.

9 United Nations Framework Convention on Climate Change (entered into force 21 March 1994) 1771 UNTS 107 (UNFCCC) art 3(1). The UNFCCC regime has also consistently provided for special treatment to countries that are particularly vulnerable to the adverse effects of climate change, expressly citing low-lying and other small island countries, and other developing countries prone to floods, droughts, and desertification. The UNFCCC additionally differentiates the forty-nine Parties classified as least developed countries (LDCs) by the United Nations, giving them special consideration on account of their limited capacity to respond to climate change and to adapt to its adverse effects. There is therefore a normative expectation that these countries will receive international support as part of global efforts to address climate change. This aspect of differentiation may become relevant in future climate litigation related to finance or adaptation.

decisions. The UNFCCC preambular language recognises that industrialised countries are the source of most past and current (in 1992) GHG emissions and should assume greater responsibility.[10] Operative provisions of the UNFCCC also contain a directive that developed countries should 'take the lead' in combating climate change and its adverse effects.[11]

The PA represents a new approach to international equity in the climate regime, replacing the top-down structure and binary Annex I/non-Annex I distinction of the Kyoto Protocol with a bottom-up, self-differentiation approach to the formulation of 'Nationally Determined Contributions' (NDCs). CBDR-RC remains, however, a fundamental principle, expressly appearing in the preamble and in provisions relating to the Agreement's purpose, progression, and long-term low GHG emissions development strategies, besides various references in specific operative provisions, including on mitigation, finance, and adaptation.[12] Despite its significantly altered form, including the added expression 'in light of different national circumstances', the two basic normative expectations associated with CBDR-RC remain: developed countries must play a 'leadership role'; and each NDC is expected to represent a country's 'fair share' of global efforts according to their contributions and/or capabilities and national circumstances.[13]

In other words, the *common* aspect of CBDR-RC was thus strengthened, but the normative expectation of differentiation based on equity considerations remains, including a North–South distinction based on 'leadership' of developed countries. Without international consensus on which equity benchmarks should be considered (and given which weight) when defining individual 'fair shares', and on what exactly should the concept of 'leadership' of developed countries mean in practice, there are various parallel normative discussions on what constitutes each country's 'fair share' taking place.[14] In addition, discussions about the precise

10 Sharm-el-Sheikh Implementation Plan (n 8).

11 UNFCCC (n 9) art 3(2).

12 Paris Agreement (entered into force 4 November 2016) 3156 UNTS 79 (Paris Agreement) art 2(2) states that the Agreement 'will be implemented to reflect equity and the principle of common but differentiated responsibilities and respective capabilities, in the light of different national circumstances'; Christina Voigt and Felipe Ferreira, '"Dynamic Differentiation": The Principles of CBDR-RC, Progression and Highest Possible Ambition in the Paris Agreement' (2016) 5 TEL 285.

13 Lavanya Rajamani, 'Ambition and Differentiation in the 2015 Paris Agreement: Interpretive Possibilities and Underlying Politics' (2016) 65 ICLQ 493, 506; Voigt and Ferreira (n 12); UNFCCC (n 9) arts 4(2), 4(3), 4(5); Joanna Depledge, 'Foundations for the Paris Agreement' in Daniel Klein and others (eds), *The Paris Agreement on Climate Change* (Oxford University Press 2017); Patricia Galvao-Ferreira, 'Differentiation in International Environmental Law' in Neil Craik and others (eds), *Global Environmental Change and Innovation in International Law* (Cambridge University Press 2018); Lavanya Rajamani and Emmanuel Guerin, 'Central Concepts in the Paris Agreement and How They Evolved' in Daniel Klein and others (eds), *The Paris Agreement on Climate Change* (Oxford University Press 2017). References to special treatment for countries that are most vulnerable to adverse effects of climate change and LDCs were also maintained in the Paris Agreement.

14 Kate Dooley and others, 'Ethical Choices behind Quantifications of Fair Contributions under the Paris Agreement' (2021) 11 (4) Nature Climate Change 300–305.

content of developed countries' obligations with respect to finance and technology transfer are ongoing.[15]

The operationalisation of differentiation in Article 4 of the PA, on mitigation, is especially relevant to this chapter, as thus far all climate lawsuits invoking CBDR-RC relate to mitigation. In Article 4, Parties agreed to peak emissions as soon as possible and to undertake progressive and rapid emissions reductions in order to achieve net zero emissions by 2050.[16] They have also agreed that emissions will take longer to peak in developing countries than in developed countries.[17] The language indicates that Parties have certain leeway when defining the scope of their mitigation actions under their NDCs. This flexibility is, however, bounded by certain directives, including that: a) the sum of individual contributions must be sufficient to achieve the PA long-term temperature goals; b) each successive NDC 'will represent a progression [over the preceding one] and reflect its highest possible ambition'; and c) the NDC will reflect the country's 'common but differentiated responsibilities and respective capabilities, in light of different national circumstances'.[18]

There is no mechanism to review the adequacy of each individual State's contribution to the long-term goals, or the 'fairness' of these contributions. The PA relies instead on two main mechanisms. The first is an enhanced transparency framework whereby each country has the legal obligation to regularly report on their progress in contributing their share to meet the global goals.[19] The second is the global stocktake, whereby Parties to the PA will periodically review the sum of reductions pledged in the NDCs to assess the collective progress towards the global temperature goals and to identify what added levels of effort are still needed.[20]

The normative expectations that NDCs will reflect a country's 'fair share' to the collective effort, based on differentiated responsibilities and capabilities in light of national circumstances, and that developed countries will continue to 'take the lead' are vital for building international trust in the PA iterative process. The 2018 Paris Rulebook requires countries to provide narrative justification for the ambition and fairness of their NDCs when regularly reviewing and updating them, including how they are addressing the normative expectations of developed country leadership, progression, and highest possible ambition.[21] Despite the lack of international consensus on equity benchmarks, a country's justification of how they arrived at

[15] See e.g. Yulia Yamineva, 'Climate Finance in the Paris Outcome: Why Do Today What You Can Put Off till Tomorrow?' (2016) RECIEL 25(2) 174–185.

[16] Paris Agreement (n 12) art 4(1).

[17] ibid.

[18] ibid art 4(3); See Rajamani and Guerin (n 13) 85.

[19] Yamide Dagnet and Kelly Levin, 'Transparency (Article 13)' in Daniel Klein and others (eds), *The Paris Agreement on Climate Change* (Oxford University Press 2017).

[20] Jurgen Friedrich, 'Global Stocktake (Article 14)' in Daniel Klein and others (eds), *The Paris Agreement on Climate Change* (Oxford University Press 2017).

[21] Rajamani and others (n 5) 984.

their proposed 'fair share' can be – and has been – politically scrutinised by other countries and by non-State actors.[22] And now domestic courts are also finding normative content on these international legal concepts of 'common responsibility' and 'differentiated fair share'.

Before examining concrete examples of courts' engagement with CBDR-RC, the chapter briefly reviews the scientifically backed political consensus (reflected in COP decisions and the Paris Agreement) on the need to keep the global average temperature between 1.5°C and 2°C, as well as calculations of the remaining global carbon budget based on this temperature goal, as they are key to understanding the use of CBDR-RC as an interpretive tool in climate litigation.

### 13.2.2 *Long-term Temperature Goal and Carbon Budgets*

Courts around the world have recognised the best available climate science assessed in IPCC reports as part of the undisputed factual basis informing their adjudication of climate lawsuits.[23] Virtually all climate decisions include reference to IPCC reports on the state of climate science to demonstrate, inter alia: estimates of global temperature levels that would avoid catastrophic impacts; and pathways for emissions reductions that would ensure the world keeps global temperature rise below agreed limits. The IPCC 1.5°C Special Report and Assessment Report Six (AR6) have strengthened the scientific consensus (already reflected in the temperature goal of the Paris Agreement) on the risks of allowing global average temperatures to exceed 1.5°C.[24]

The concept of global carbon budgets has closely followed the consensus on maximum temperature goals based on climate science. A global carbon budget has been defined as 'the maximum amount of cumulative global emissions to the atmosphere that may be "allowable", based on the physical properties of the climate system, in order to stay below a politically agreed warming limit'.[25] Scientists have been able to estimate which maximum global carbon budgets will increase the likelihood of meeting the PA temperature goal. Carbon budgets featured prominently in IPCC

22 ibid.

23 On IPCC see Shardul Agrawala, 'Context and Early Origins of the Intergovernmental Panel on Climate Change' (1998) 39(4) Climatic Change 605–620; Mike Hulme and Martin Mahony, 'Climate Change: What Do We Know about the IPCC?' (2010) 34(5) Progress in Physical Geography 705–718; Alison Shaw and John Robinson, 'Relevant but not Prescriptive? Science Policy Models within the IPCC' (2004) 48 Philosophy Today 106–117.

24 Valerie Masson-Delmotte and others, 'Summary for Policy Makers' in Global Warming of 1.5°C (2018) <www.ipcc.ch/sr15/chapter/spm/#:~:text=A%20wide%20range%20of%20adaptation,knowledge)%2C%20the%20risks%20of%20sea> accessed 23 February 2024; See also the earlier Intergovernmental Panel on Climate Change, Fourth Assessment Report (2007), which informed the Paris Agreement's temperature goal.

25 Bård Lahn, 'A History of the Global Carbon Budget' (2020) 11(3) Wiley Interdisciplinary Reviews Climate Change 2.

AR4, IPCC Special 1.5°C Report (SR5), and again in IPCC AR6.[26] The PA does not include a specific reference to carbon budgets. However, in the 2021 Glasgow Climate Pact, States expressed 'alarm and utmost concern that … carbon budgets consistent with achieving the Paris Agreement temperature goals are now small and being rapidly depleted',[27] while in the 2022 Sharm el-Sheikh Implementation Plan they affirmed their resolve to 'pursue further efforts to limit the temperature increase to 1.5°C'.[28] The concept of carbon budgets has also been invoked in various policy debates, either to support specific policy proposals at the national level, to advocate for burden-sharing of climate efforts based on equity considerations, or to guide financial investments.[29] This policy uptake comes despite IPCC reports indicating residual scientific uncertainty about the size of remaining carbon budgets, depending on several factors.[30]

The unsettled political debate on which equity markers should drive the distribution of shares of remaining global carbon budgets among countries makes it more challenging for the IPCC to estimate scenarios of specific remaining carbon budgets for each country or even groups of countries. Courts need to navigate this complex science-policy interface when trying to determine the existence and scope of domestic legal obligations in light of the normative framework of the international climate regime. The next section examines how courts are relying on CBDR-RC not to directly derive rights or legal duties but rather as an interpretive tool to help establish the scope of domestic legal obligations.

## 13.3 STATE OF AFFAIRS: CASE LAW DEVELOPMENT

Citizen groups that are particularly vulnerable to climate impacts have increasingly invoked CBDR-RC across jurisdictions as part of their claims either that governments are *setting* emissions reductions targets that are too low in light of what should constitute their 'fair share' of global mitigation efforts, or that governments are failing to meet their obligations to effectively *implement* their legislated 'fair share' targets. These citizen groups argue that it is now possible to identify minimum legal standards of 'fair share' contributions for individual countries, based on the concept of a remaining global carbon budget in light of the PA temperature goal and other norms and principles of international climate law, particularly CBDR-RC. They argue that courts must therefore consider these minimum international legal standards when interpreting the scope of domestic constitutional, statutory, or common law legal obligations in the context of addressing climate risks.

26 ibid.
27 UNFCCC, Glasgow Climate Pact, FCCC/PA/CMA/2021/10/Add.1 1/CMA 3 (13 November 2021) [2].
28 Sharm-el-Sheikh Implementation Plan (n 8) [4].
29 Lahn (n 25) 1.
30 Masson-Delmotte and others (n 24) [C.1.3].

### 13.3.1 *Common Responsibility*

A number of courts have now relied on the 'common responsibility' element of CBDR-RC – explicitly or implicitly – to help establish that States are under a legal obligation to do 'their part' to address the climate challenge. The starting points for courts when engaging with the common element of the CBDR-RC principle is the recognition of the significant risks and impacts posed by climate change, the global nature of the threat, and the inexorable need for a coordinated international response. In *Urgenda*,[31] *Grande-Synthe*,[32] *Neubauer*,[33] and *Klimaatzaak*,[34] the courts took judicial notice that the global dimension of climate change requires governments in each country to engage in a collective response through international cooperation, if they are to protect their citizens from the significant dangers of climate change. By reproducing relevant provisions of the UNFCCC and the PA, the Dutch, French, German, and Belgian courts either explicitly or implicitly recognise that by joining the international climate regime under the UNFCCC, governments acknowledge their common, albeit differentiated, responsibility over this global response.

Courts either explicitly reason[35] or infer that by joining an international regime that explicitly affirms the need for global cooperation, governments incur a legal obligation to fulfil their part of shared global efforts as part of their duty of care to protect citizens against significant climate risks and impacts. This is an important development in climate litigation. Courts are using the 'common responsibility' aspect of CBDR-RC to reject a prominent defence which governments have advanced against climate lawsuits over the years: that their nationally determined emissions reduction targets and other climate plans are not legally binding under international law or national law and, therefore, are discretionary political acts that should be exempt from judicial review. This is also an important development in international environmental law, as national courts are now expanding on

[31] *Urgenda Foundation v The State of The Netherlands* [2015] ECLI:NL:RBDHA:2015:7196 (District Court of the Hague) (*Urgenda District Court*); *State of the Netherlands (Ministry of Economic Affairs and Climate Policy) v Stichting Urgenda* [2019] ECLI:NL:HR:2019:2007 (Supreme Court of the Netherlands) (*Urgenda Supreme Court*) [2.2.1].

[32] *Commune de Grande-Synthe v France* [2020] N°427301 (Conseil d'Etat) (*Grande-Synthe*) [12].

[33] *Neubauer and Others v Germany* [2021] 1 BvR 2656/18, 1 BvR 96/20, 1 BvR 78/20, 1 BvR 288/20, 1 BvR 96/20, 1 BvR 78/20 (German Federal Constitutional Court) (*Neubauer*) [197].

[34] *VZW Klimaatzaak v Kingdom of Belgium and Others* [2023] 2022/AR/891 (Cour d'appel de Bruxelles) (*VZW Klimaatzaak Appeal*) [283] 'The national contributions of each of the States party to the UNFCCC, including Belgium, to reducing GHG emissions are the world's main tool for preventing and mitigating the risk of dangerous global warming. These international agreements are based on the mutual trust of the States that are party to them in the fact that each will contribute to the effort required to achieve the desired result, and it is in this way that the contribution of each State, including a "small" State like Belgium (on a global scale), plays a decisive role in the fight against global warming'.

[35] See *Urgenda Supreme Court* (n 31) [5.7.1]–[5.7.9]; *Neubauer* (n 33) [199]–[204].

a principle of international (State–State) cooperation to give it normative content when interpreting obligations owed to individuals.

This reasoning can be seen as distinct from and additional to the arguments used to reject another common defence advanced by governments (and corporations) against climate lawsuits: lack of causation or 'de minimis' / 'drop in the ocean' contributions.[36] The argument in the lack of causation defence is that governments and corporations have an obligation to do their part by reducing emissions under their control, no matter how small their share of contributions. This argument is anchored in the fact that climate change is caused by the combination of a myriad of sources that, even if insignificant in isolation, jointly become a significant problem.[37] Independent of what others are doing, a government or corporation can be found to have an obligation to act in order to minimise the danger by reducing emissions that they can control. This legal debate can be linked to concepts of causation in tort law and the need to identify relevant contributors to a collective legal wrong or problem.

The reasoning based on the 'common responsibility' element of CBDR-RC is different, as it places the focus not on causation or contribution but rather on remedy or redress. Distinct from the causation defence, the redressability defence in climate litigation relates to arguments that the creation and implementation of domestic climate policies are impervious to judicial review, as a judicial decision mandating a country to set a certain minimum level of GHG emissions, or to implement emissions reduction targets, will not be able to effectively redress plaintiffs' harms or reduce their risks. Under this argument, due to the global nature of climate change, an effective remedy to plaintiffs' injuries or risks depends on the uncertain or speculative response from various other governments and actors, something courts have no power to influence; in other words, it is a political rather than a legal question. This debate appeared in *Massachusetts v EPA*, where the US Supreme Court found the redressability requirement satisfied because the requested relief for EPA to regulate $CO_2$ emissions from American motor vehicles, even if not alone solving global climate change, would likely slow or reduce impacts or risks significantly.[38] In the case *Juliana v United States*, the Ninth Circuit panel declared the lawsuit non-justiciable in part because the requested injunction for the US to develop and implement a plan to do its part to reduce emissions would not solve global climate change. In other words, the case was dismissed on redressability grounds.[39]

36 See Chapter 16 on Causation; see also Nataša Nedeski and André Nollkaemper, 'A Guide to Tackling the Collective Causation Problem in International Climate Litigation' (*EJIL: Talk!*, 15 December 2022) <www.ejiltalk.org/a-guide-to-tackling-the-collective-causation-problem-in-international-climate-change-litigation/> accessed 24 February 2024.

37 Nedeski and Nollkaemper (n 36).

38 *Massachusetts v EPA* 549 US 497, 517 (2007).

39 *Juliana v United States* 947 F.3d 1159 (9th Cir 2020) 1171; Matt Lifson and others, 'Redressability of Climate Change Injuries after Juliana' (*Legal Planet*, 12 June 2020) <https://legal-planet.org/2020/06/12/guest-contributors-matt-lifson-camila-bustos-and-natasha-brunstein-redressability-of-climate-change-injuries-after-juliana/> accessed 24 February 2024.

When using CBDR-RC to help interpret the scope of legal obligations, courts are taking judicial notice that each country has politically and legally agreed, by ratifying the UNFCCC and the PA, that they depend on the actions by the rest of the international community if they are to afford any level of protection to their citizens from the impacts and dangers of global climate change. Therefore, national courts in the Netherlands,[40] Germany,[41] France,[42] and Belgium[43] have concluded that since addressing climate risks is a common responsibility of all States, there is at least a normative command, if not a legal obligation, for each country to do their part, by contributing their 'fair share' to the multilateral efforts on climate change, as the only way to offer a measure of effective redress.

Courts are recognising that even those countries that contribute minimal emissions are equally (or often disproportionately more) vulnerable to climate impacts. These countries are highly dependent on the success of the international response to protect their citizens. Governments cannot argue that there is no legal obligation to do their part of the common response, because it will not offer sufficient or effective redress for a problem that is global and collective, when their lack of action is actively undermining global efforts and essentially making any potential measure of redress more difficult or impossible.

### 13.3.2 *Differentiated Responsibilities and Capabilities*

The second way in which courts are engaging with CBDR-RC relates to the 'differentiated' aspect of the principle, which more directly relates to the 'fair share' concept. Various plaintiffs have challenged the legality of current emissions targets set by States for being too low to represent their 'fair share' of global efforts and therefore inadequate to offer an effective contribution to the global response to the dangers of climate change.[44] When courts engage with the concept of a country's minimum 'fair share' they are again considering that countries have politically agreed to the PA temperature goal and often legalised this goal by referencing it in national climate law. Courts are also noting that a global target temperature goal allows for scientific calculations of remaining global carbon budgets with limited or no overshoot, even when lingering scientific uncertainties make exact calculations of this budget elusive.[45]

40 *Urgenda Supreme Court* (n 31).

41 *Neubauer* (n 33).

42 *Grande-Synthe* (n 32).

43 *VZW Klimaatzaak Appeal* (n 34).

44 Lucy Maxwell, Sarah Mead, and Dennis van Berkel, 'Standards for Adjudicating the next Generation of Urgenda-Style Climate Cases' (2022) 13(1) JHRE 35.

45 See e.g. *Neubauer* (n 33) [209]–[210] 'By adopting the temperature limit of art 2(1)(a) Paris Agreement, the legislator has set the fundamental course of national climate change law in a direction that gives the German state an opportunity to effectively fulfil its constitutional mandate to take climate action through its own efforts embedded within an international framework. (b) The legislator is not entirely free in how it specifies the obligation to take climate action under [constitutional law]'; and *Neubauer* (n 33) [215] on carbon budget.

Courts address the normative expectation that a country's individual 'part' must represent its 'fair share' of global efforts when they engage with the range of equity benchmarks articulated in the effort-sharing negotiations and principles of the climate regime or in the literature. For example, various courts have taken judicial notice of a country's contributions to global emissions in absolute or *per capita* terms or of its levels of socio-economic development achieved in part due to historic emissions.[46] As part of their exercise to decide whether the 'differentiated' element of CBDR-RC carries legal meaning, a small number of courts have also engaged with the normative expectation that developed countries should 'take the lead' in global climate efforts, when identifying what would be a legal minimum 'fair share' of the remaining global carbon budget for each individual country.[47]

Enduring disputes among countries over how to translate the differentiated element of CBDR-RC into concrete effort-sharing standards in the international climate regime, and the Paris Agreement bottom-up model of self-differentiation via NDCs, have left courts struggling to identify a core normative content from the evolving CBDR-RC principle.[48] Courts are arriving at different conclusions as to what extent the CBDR-RC principle has or has not curtailed the level of discretion of legislative and administrative bodies to set their own mitigation targets, or to meet these targets, based on the concepts of 'fair share', differentiation, and 'leadership role' for developed countries. Some courts, like in the cases of *Grande-Synthe*,[49] *Notre Affaire à Tous*,[50] and *Klimaatzaak*,[51] make references to CBDR-RC in their decisions in the context of discussing countries' 'fair shares', yet they do not articulate whether (and how) they considered the different CBDR-RC equity benchmarks when interpreting the scope of national climate obligations. These courts merely assert that the Paris Agreement left it to each individual country to propose their individual 'fair share' contributions to the international climate response.

In *Urgenda* and *Neubauer*, the courts also relied on the CBDR-RC principle (explicitly or implicitly) to grapple with the question of the degree of discretion governments have in determining their individual 'fair share' of global efforts to address climate change. These courts found that although there is no legal standard determining the exact scope of individual emissions reductions targets or timelines, they could assess whether the State has adopted the minimum reasonable measures to fulfil their duty of care to protect against the dangers of global climate change, based on existing international climate law principles and

46 For example, *Neubauer* (n 33) [29]; *Urgenda Supreme Court* (n 31) [2.1].

47 *Urgenda Supreme Court* (n 31) [2.1]; *Grande-Synthe* (n 32) [9].

48 Gerry Liston, 'Enhancing the Efficacy of Climate Change Litigation: How to Resolve the "Fair Share Question" in the Context of International Human Rights Law' (2020) 9(2) CILJ 241.

49 *Grande-Synthe* (n 32) [9].

50 *Notre Affaire à Tous and Others v France* [2021] No 1904967, 1904968, 1904972 1904976/4-1 [26]–[27].

51 *VZW Klimaatzaak Appeal* (n 34) [169].

standards, including CBDR-RC, but also cooperation, the precautionary principle, and intergenerational equity. A more detailed examination of the courts' reasoning is included in the next section.

As part of this discussion, the Dutch courts have considered whether the CBDR-RC directive that developed countries play a leadership role in global climate efforts has normative value when determining the degree of discretion States hold when defining their minimum 'fair share'. The Hague Court took notice that by agreeing, under international climate law, to take the lead in climate action with other developed countries, the Netherlands has 'therefore committed to a more than proportional contribution to reduction, in view of a fair distribution between industrialized and developing countries'.[52] The discretionary power of the State to decide its 'fair share' was thus limited by the legal norms and principles of the international climate regime, including CBDR-RC.

The implication is that the political discretion of the Dutch government to choose among the broad array of equity benchmarks when defining its 'fair share' for the Netherlands is not unlimited. The Dutch courts are indicating, if implicitly, that as a developed country that needs to do a more than proportional contribution to reductions, the Netherlands is entitled to a smaller piece of the remaining global carbon budget than if calculated based on global emissions per capita (GEC). In contrast, the German courts in *Neubauer*[53] and *German Family Farmers*[54] found that the German government still keeps the wide political discretion to choose among equity benchmarks when defining a 'fair share', including by choosing to use the GEC *benchmark*, therefore apparently dismissing a normative role for the concept of developed countries' leadership role under the CBDR-RC principle.[55]

Judicial engagement with the CBDR-RC element of 'leadership role' for developed countries has begun to spread outside European jurisdictions. The New South Wales Court in *Gloucester Resources Limited v Minister for Planning*[56] invoked this concept when rejecting the market substitution argument advanced by the mining company against the denial of their permit to expand a coal operation due to increased carbon emissions, namely that developing countries with weaker regulations would

52 *Urgenda District Court* (n 31) [4.76].

53 *Neubauer* (n 33) [225].

54 Rajamani and others (n 5) [20].

55 *Urgenda Supreme Court* (n 31) [7.3.4], 'Moreover, the Court of Appeal rightly held in para. 60 that it would not be obvious for a lower reduction rate to apply to the Netherlands as an Annex I country than to the Annex I countries as a whole. As the Court of Appeal considered in para. 66, the Netherlands is one of the countries with very high per capita emissions of greenhouse gases. In the above agreements at EU level, the reduction percentage agreed upon for the Netherlands is, accordingly, one of the highest reduction percentages applicable to the EU Member States (Annex II to the Effort Sharing Decision). It can be assumed that this high percentage corresponds to the possibilities and responsibilities of the Netherlands. As the Court of Appeal established in para. 60, the State has not substantiated why a lower percentage should apply'.

56 *Gloucester Resources Limited v Minister for Planning* [2019] NSWLEC 7 (*Gloucester Resources*).

fill the gap in coal production if Australia left coal on the ground.[57] The Philippines Human Rights Commission also addressed the 'leadership role' of developed countries in their Carbon Majors report. The Commission found that although all States have the responsibility to contribute to the response to climate change, whether they have contributed no GHG emissions or half of current emissions, highly industrialised countries that have benefited from historic emissions 'bear a larger share in providing solutions to the problems they have created'.[58]

The matter has also recently been addressed at the international level in the recent General Comment issued by the CRC. The Committee establishes a strong link between climate inaction and human rights violations and elaborates on what this means in terms of mitigation. It calls 'for urgent collective action by all States to mitigate greenhouse gas emissions, in line with their human rights obligations', noting that 'historical and current major emitters should take the lead in mitigation efforts'.[59] It further specifies:

> When determining the appropriateness of their mitigation measures in accordance with the Convention, and also mindful of the need to prevent and address any potential adverse effects of those measures, States should take into account the following criteria:
>
> (a) Mitigation objectives and measures should clearly indicate how they respect, protect and fulfil children's rights under the Convention. …
>
> (b) States have an individual responsibility to mitigate climate change in order to fulfil their obligations under the Convention and international environmental law, including the commitment contained in the Paris Agreement to hold the increase in the global average temperature to well below 2°C above pre-industrial levels and to pursue efforts to limit the temperature increase to 1.5°C above pre-industrial levels by 2030. Mitigation measures should reflect each State party's fair share of the global effort to mitigate climate change, in the light of the total reductions necessary to protect against continuing and worsening violations of children's rights. Each State, and all States working together, should continuously strengthen climate commitments in line with the highest possible ambition and their common but differentiated responsibilities and respective capacities. High-income States should continue to take the lead by undertaking economy-wide absolute emission reduction targets, and all States should enhance their mitigation measures in the light of their different national circumstances in a manner that protects children's rights to the maximum possible extent.[60]

57 ibid [539].

58 Sharm-el-Sheikh Implementation Plan (n 8) [117].

59 Committee on Rights of the Child, 'General Comment No 26 on Children's Rights and the Environment with a Special Focus on Climate Change' (22 August 2023) UN Doc CRC/C/GC/26.[95].

60 ibid [98].

## 13.4 EMERGING BEST PRACTICES

In the context of a yet fledgling jurisprudence on CBDR-RC, many courts are still struggling to navigate the complexity of this multifaceted and evolving principle. It is, however, possible to identify a few examples of emerging best practices (EBPs). Since plaintiffs will most likely continue to invoke CBDR-RC in climate litigation, this section highlights some EBPs, while also discussing some missteps that courts can avoid when called to examine the normative value of CBDR-RC as an interpretive tool to delimit the scope of obligations or rights in the context of foreseeable climate risks and impacts.

The German Constitutional Court offered the most comprehensive treatment of the legal consequences of the 'common responsibility' element of CBDR-RC in *Neubauer*, if implicitly. After referencing CBDR-RC in the Paris Agreement as part of the relevant international law framework it was taking into consideration,[61] the Court declared that the global nature of climate change does not invalidate the national obligation to take climate action, instead being 'significant for determining the content of the duty of climate change related protection' under German Constitutional law.[62] The Constitutional Court held that the global nature of climate change compels the State to engage in internationally oriented activities to tackle climate change, requiring it to promote climate action within the international framework.[63] According to the Court, the State is under a constitutional obligation to take steps to protect citizens against climate risks, 'with the help of international involvement'.[64]

The German Court went on to say that the international engagement aspect of the constitutional obligation includes two distinct elements. First, international engagement requires negotiation and participation in international agreements to promote the collective international action needed to offer effective protection to German citizens. Second, international engagement requires effectively implementing individual contributions agreed to in the international climate regime. In the Constitutional Court's words, 'the international dimension of the obligation to take climate action [under the German Constitution] is not confined to the task of seeking to resolve the climate problem at the international level and ideally reaching some agreement to that effect. Rather, the constitutional obligation to take climate action also extends to the implementation of agreed solutions.'[65] It is reasonable to affirm that the Constitutional Court has thus set one obligation of conduct (to negotiate and to participate in good faith in international agreements to deliver a global

61 *Neubauer* (n 33) [8].
62 ibid [149].
63 ibid [144].
64 ibid.
65 ibid [200].

response to climate change) and one obligation of results (to effectively implement whatever contribution it has agreed to at international level, to avoid undermining the success of the collective efforts). This was the first time that a national court made this linkage, that as part of their 'common responsibility' to address global climate change through international cooperative efforts, a State is under an obligation to implement their NDCs once they are defined and set in national law.

To be clear, the Constitutional Court did not explicitly articulate that it was using CBDR-RC to help interpret this obligation to participate in the elaboration and to implement international obligations. The 'common responsibility' element of CBDR-RC, however, is the one that manifests the scientifically backed international political consensus that climate change is an environmental problem of 'common concern' that evades unilateral or plurilateral action, necessarily requiring a multilateral or global coordinated response.

Unlike the traditional outward treatment of the principle of cooperation under international environmental law, which sets State-to-State obligations to cooperate to respond to problems of 'common concern' (in order to prevent or address transboundary harm to each other), here the Court is applying the 'common responsibility' element of CBDR-RC inward: to help interpret the scope of constitutional obligations of protection for German citizens against the risks of climate change, which require international coordination. To protect German citizens, the government must participate in good faith in the international regime by doing its part of the global response, which should represent the country's 'fair share' to keep the legitimacy and trust of the collective response. This is an EBP because it addresses the problematic State defence accepted by some courts that, because climate action in one country cannot redress the risks or impacts of climate change, climate obligations are non-justiciable or defy judicial responses.

It is worth noting that the Constitutional Court was careful not to overstep the division of powers, refraining from deciding on the precise scope of an obligation to participate in good faith in the international climate legal regime.[66] It set instead minimum standards [very low, critics may say] affirming that a violation of a duty of protection occurs 'if no precautionary measures whatsoever have been taken, or if the adopted provisions and measures prove to be manifestly unsuitable or completely inadequate for achieving the required protection goal, or if the provisions and measures fall significantly short of the protection goal'.[67] The Court concluded that by ratifying the PA and adopting its temperature limits under German law, the legislator had set the country in a direction that 'gives the German state an opportunity to effectively fulfil its constitutional mandate to take climate action through its own efforts *embedded within an international framework*'.[68] The Court

66 See Chapter 6 on Separation of Powers.
67 *Neubauer* (n 33) [152].
68 ibid [210].

concluded that the State was not in violation of this obligation at the time. Despite this low standard, the logical conclusion is that the German Constitutional Court established that the State does not have the unlimited discretion to withdraw from international cooperative regimes, or to arbitrarily decide on its own climate actions, thereby ignoring the international regime's principles and standards.

In other words, the German Court granted the legislator significant leeway when deciding the allocation of global mitigation efforts that represents Germany's 'fair share'. However, as discussed later, it affirmed that the necessity to engage internationally generates an obligation for the State to participate in the international legal regime in good faith, by both considering relevant international climate law principles (including differentiated responsibilities and capabilities) when determining these national targets, and effectively implementing these nationally determined targets in order to build trust, as mutual trust is key to the success of international climate efforts.

The Dutch Court decisions in the *Urgenda* case best illustrate how courts can engage with the various elements of the CBDR-RC: the common responsibilities element[69] as well as the two angles of differentiated responsibilities and respective capabilities, in light of national circumstances (leadership role for developed countries and self-differentiation based on equity benchmarks). The Dutch Court decisions represent EBP when clearly articulating the potential normative value of the 'leadership role' of developed countries under the CBDR-RC principle. As the 'leadership role' of developed countries is an important element of CBDR-RC and is fundamental to maintain trust in international cooperative efforts to address climate change, it is essential that courts in developed countries tackle this normative concept when analysing the scope of legal obligations to contribute their 'fair share'.

The *Urgenda* decisions found that this leadership role requires developed countries to contribute a 'more than proportionate share' of global mitigation efforts.[70] The evident conclusion, although not stated with these exact words by the Dutch courts, is that the 'leadership role' element of CBDR-RC constrains the political discretion of developed countries to define their 'fair share' exclusively based on options such as 'emissions per capita rights' (EPC).[71] EPC approaches to determining a 'fair share' of the remaining global carbon budget take the *status quo* of highly unequal past levels of emissions, and other equity benchmarks such as financial and technological capacity or socio-economic development needs, for granted. The Dutch courts did not identify a specific equity formula that governments were legally required to use to define 'fair share', recognising that there is not yet a politi-

69 Similar to the German Constitutional Court, although not as well developed.

70 *Urgenda District Court* (n 31) [4.76].

71 Keith Williges and others, 'Fairness Critically Conditions the Carbon Budget Allocation across Countries' (2022) 74 Global Environmental Change 102481.

cal consensus on equitable allocation formula enshrined in international or Dutch law. Although governments retain political discretion to define specific fair shares based on ethical assumptions and political choices, they have to be consistent with the principles and norms of the UNFCCC and Paris Agreement. Current research broadly acknowledges that EPC and grandfathering approaches do not distribute global efforts in a fair manner, according to CBDR-RC, rather benefiting countries with a comparably current high share of emissions and placing developing countries at disadvantage.[72]

The Dutch courts in *Urgenda* also offer the most comprehensive discussion of CBDR-RC equity benchmarks, when deciding whether there is a duty of care to contribute a minimum fair share.[73] First, the courts explicitly deliberate on the Netherlands' differentiated responsibility based on its contributions to GHG atmospheric concentration. For example, the District Court (first instance) discussed the country's absolute and per capita emissions in comparison with other developed countries (particularly EU and the USA) but also the BRIC emerging economies (Brazil, Russia, India, and China).[74] The District Court explicitly states that developed countries accepted to take the lead in global climate efforts because '[f]rom a historical perspective the current industrialized countries are the main causers of the current high greenhouse gas concentration in the atmosphere and that these countries also benefit from the use of fossil fuels, in the form of economic growth and prosperity'.[75] Besides historic contributions, the District Court also considered the capabilities equity indicator by stating that this prosperity also means that '[developed] countries have the most means available to take measures to combat climate change'.[76]

The Dutch Court of Appeal (second instance) equally considered contributions (responsibilities) and capabilities as relevant in the context of the leadership role: 'taking into account their *per capita* emissions, the long history of their emissions and their resource bases, the Annex I countries must take the lead in fighting climate change'.[77] The Court of Appeal went on to consider that the Netherlands has relatively high *per capita* emissions, even when compared to other developed countries. In absolute emissions, the Court noted that the Netherlands ranks 34th out of 208 countries and 'of the 33 countries with even higher emissions, only nine have a higher per capita emission and not a single one is an EU Member State'.[78] The district courts returned to responsibilities and capabilities indicators when rejecting the State's defence that the timeframe to comply with the decision is too

72 Dooley and others (n 14) [300]–[305].
73 *Urgenda District Court* (n 31).
74 ibid [2.27]–[28].
75 ibid [4.57].
76 ibid.
77 *Urgenda Supreme Court* (n 31) [9].
78 ibid [28].

short, noting not only that the State has officially acknowledged the severity of the climate crisis but that:

> It deserves further attention that the Netherlands as a highly developed country has profited from fossil fuels for a long time and still ranks among the countries with the highest per capita greenhouse gas emissions in the world. It is partly for this reason that the state should assume its responsibility, a sentiment that was also expressed in the UNFCCC and the PA.[79]

The Dutch Supreme Court (apex decision) confirmed the lower courts' decisions, stating that although the distribution of global efforts should not be based solely on historic emissions, they must be taken into consideration alongside capabilities.[80] Rejecting the argument that the IPCC AR4 emissions reduction range of 25–40 per cent was calculated for developed countries as a group, and should not be used to determine the Netherlands individual contribution, the Supreme Court reiterated that considering Dutch high *per capita* emissions and capabilities even when compared to other developed countries, 'it would not be obvious for a lower reduction rate to apply to the Netherlands…'[81] Although the Supreme Court concluded that the exact 'fair share' was still to be determined by political bodies, it made clear that they are bound by the set of equity benchmarks from the international climate regime when making this determination, shifting the burden to the State to justify why a lower reduction rate would apply to the Netherlands in light of equity benchmarks or other international climate law norms. This is in line with the interpretation the CRC made on the scope of developed countries' 'fair share' obligations in their General Comment 26, as reproduced in Section 13.3.

The German Constitutional Court also showed best practice when articulating that the government is required to formulate its individual national contribution to global efforts in a way that will build trust among members of the collective response. Although not stated explicitly in the *Neubauer* decision, this articulation has two important normative implications that other courts can equally recognise. First, although governments retain leeway when deciding what constitutes their individual 'fair share', in the absence of clear international agreement on valid fairness benchmarks, they must justify how their calculation aligns with the principles and standards of the UN climate regime, particularly CBDR-RC. Shifting the burden to the State to justify the 'fairness' of their proposed contribution to global efforts to address climate risks and impacts is an EBP for minimum legal standards that courts can replicate. As noted in the IPCC AR6, the Paris Rulebook obliges Parties to provide information on fairness considerations in their NDCs,

79 ibid [66].
80 ibid [5.7.6].
81 ibid [7.3.4].

including reflecting equitable principles of the climate regime (CBDR-RC being a key principle).[82]

The Dutch courts also showed EBP when they separated the 'leadership role' for developed countries from considerations of the set of CBDR-RC equity benchmarks that should guide governments in determining their 'fair share', even if the differentiated elements of CBDR-RC are interrelated (with the Dutch courts explicitly linking the 'leadership role' normative expectation to historic emissions, per capita emissions, and capabilities). CBDR-RC is likely to appear in future climate litigation in developing countries, including in high emitting emerging economies. Courts in the Global South will thus be urged to consider the normative role of the various equity benchmarks related to the principle in international climate law to determine the respective differentiated fair share, without engaging with the 'leadership role' exclusive to developed countries. It is important to clarify that the differentiated element of the CBDR-RC principle applies to the determination of responsibilities in all Parties to the UNFCCC, not only to developed countries.

By signalling that there is a distinct normative role for the CBDR-RC equity benchmarks for identifying minimum fair shares, the *Urgenda* decisions help to repel the mistaken view that CBDR-RC serves only to establish greater obligations to developed countries, with developing countries getting from the principle only a right to receive support for their climate action. Another mistaken view that the separate judicial treatment of the various elements of CBDR-RC, including the 'common responsibility' and the equity benchmarks, can help dispel is the one that proposes that the principle allows developing countries to concentrate only on climate adaptation rather than mitigation. As part of their common responsibility to pursue the temperature goal of the PA, all countries must propose their differentiated nationally determined contribution to emissions reductions. All countries must therefore do their part, however small, and justify why their NDC represents their 'fair share' of global efforts according to disclosed equity benchmarks.

Although not explicitly articulating it as a legal consequence of the CBDR-RC principle, the German Constitutional Court in *Neubauer* illustrates EBP in engaging with the 'common responsibilities' aspect of CBDR-RC, related to the global nature of the climate challenge. The Constitutional Court indicates that a blatant refusal to participate in global cooperative climate efforts to tackle climate dangers, or a patently inadequate contribution to such efforts, constitutes a constitutional violation. Other courts can now follow this best practice if their governments and parliaments decide, for example, to withdraw from the Paris Agreement without offering valid alternatives for global climate action.

[82] Anthony Patt and others, 'Chapter 14: International Cooperation' in Priyadarshi R. Shukla and others (eds), *Climate Change 2022: Mitigation of Climate Change, Contribution of Working Group III to the Sixth Assessment Report of the Intergovernmental Panel on Climate Change* (Cambridge University Press 2022) 1468.

## 13.5 REPLICABILITY

As the jurisprudence on CBDR-RC is still recent, there are questions related to its replicability. A flurry of pending cases in which CBDR-RC was either part of the plaintiffs' claims or where related concepts of 'fair shares' and equity in light of international climate law have been considered indicates that it is very likely that other courts will engage with the principle in their reasoning. CBDR-RC plays a noticeable role in recent climate proceedings launched against Italy and Poland. In A *Sud et al v Italy*,[83] the plaintiffs argue that Italy's proposed emissions reduction targets do not represent its 'fair share' based on a report prepared by Climate Analytics which 'assesses the contribution of the Italian State towards meeting the Paris Agreement's long-term temperature goal, in line with the principles of equity and common but differentiated responsibilities as enshrined in that agreement, so that its climate commitments represent a "fair share" towards achieving that goal'. Polish citizens, with support from the NGO ClientEarth, also relied on a Climate Analytics report on fair shares when they brought forward five similar cases questioning Poland's decisions to allow GHG emissions in excess of their fair share.[84]

Despite most of the decisions featuring CBDR-RC or related concepts of 'fair share' in light of international climate law equity principles and norms being concentrated in European jurisdictions, the principle or related concepts appear in courts' reasonings in cases in Australia[85] and Canada.[86] In *Do-Hyun Kim et al v South Korea*,[87] which is still pending, a group of youth activists filed a complaint before South Korea's Constitutional Court challenging the central government for their 'inadequate' climate policies. Although the plaintiffs did not explicitly invoke CBDR-RC, they engaged with related concepts of carbon budget and fair shares.

While all the cases reviewed in this chapter were presented before courts in developed countries, courts in the Global South will most likely be called to deliberate on

[83] *A SUD and others v Italy* [2021] (Civil Court of Rome) <https://climatecasechart.com/non-us-case/a-sud-et-al-v-italy/#:~:text=Summary%3A,a%20stable%20and%20safe%20climate> accessed 24 February 2024.

[84] *ClientEarth v Poland (on Behalf of MG)* [2021] <https://climatecasechart.com/non-us-case/clientearth-v-poland-acting-on-behalf-of-mg/#:~:text=Summary%3A,worsening%20effects%20of%20climate%20change.> accessed 24 February 2024; *ClientEarth v Poland (on Behalf of MO)* [2021] <https://climatecasechart.com/non-us-case/clientearth-v-poland-on-behalf-of-mo/#:~:text=Summary%3A,worsening%20effects%20of%20climate%20change> accessed 24 February 2024; *ClientEarth v Poland (on Behalf of MS)* [2021] <http://climatecasechart.com/non-us-case/clientearth-v-poland-on-behalf-of-ms/> accessed 24 February 2024; *ClientEarth v Poland (on behalf of PN)* [2021] <http://climatecasechart.com/non-us-case/clientearth-v-poland-on-behalf-of-pn/> accessed 24 February 2024; *ClientEarth v Poland (on behalf of PR)* [2021] <http://climatecasechart.com/non-us-case/clientearth-v-poland-on-behalf-of-pr/> accessed 24 February 2024 (all pending).

[85] *Gloucester Resources* (n 56); *Waratah Coal Pty Ltd v Youth Verdict Ltd and Others* (No 6) [2022] QLC 21.

[86] *Mathur v Ontario* [2023] ONSC 2316.

[87] *Do-Hyun Kim et al v South Korea* [2020] Constitutional Court of South Korea (pending).

the normative content of both the common element of CBDR-RC, and the equity benchmarks of responsibilities and capabilities. Plaintiffs in the Global South can use CBDR-RC arguments to challenge the legality of either timid targets or the failure to meet targets, based on each individual country's obligation to contribute their 'fair share' to meet the temperature goal of the PA.[88]

CBDR-RC has also been invoked in pending individual complaints related to climate rights before international bodies such as the CRC and the HRC and in the cases against Austria and Switzerland currently pending at the European Court of Human Rights.[89] The principle also appears prominently in the Portuguese children's case against thirty-three European States (*Duarte Agostinho v Portugal et al*) before the European Court of Human Rights.[90] In *Duarte Agostinho*, the youth plaintiffs invoke CBDR-RC as part of the international legal framework to help challenge the emissions reduction targets from key European countries for not representing their 'fair share' of global efforts. In anticipation of arguments that, because there is currently no international agreement on a set of equity criteria to guide fair allocation of a remaining carbon budget, definition of a 'fair share' remains a political question and therefore impervious to judicial review, they argue that 'fair share' ambiguity should be resolved in their favour since this ambiguity 'is a direct consequence of the failure by states (globally) to agree a clearly defined approach to sharing the burden of mitigating climate change'.

In January 2023, Chile and Colombia included five questions related to common but differentiated responsibilities as part of their request for an AO by the IACtHR[91] which was called to clarify the scope of State obligations to respond to human rights implications of climate threats. This AO may generate new insights on how courts throughout Latin America will engage with CBDR-RC in climate litigation in the near future. Considering the evolution of the CBDR-RC principle in the PA, moving towards a more nuanced differentiation, we expect that plaintiffs from countries in different stages of development, but particularly from emerging economies with growing emissions, to engage with this principle in their climate litigation strategies.

Although all CBDR-RC cases have thus far been in civil law jurisdictions, there is no apparent obstacle for courts in common law countries to examine the normative value of CBDR-RC as an interpretive tool to help establish and define the scope of open common law concepts, or of statutory law in common law jurisdictions.

88 For an analysis of the potential of using a 'fair share' approach to climate litigation, in light of CBDR-RC, against Brazil, see Maria Antonia Tigre, 'The "Fair Share" of Climate Mitigation: Can Litigation Increase National Ambition for Brazil?' (2023) JHRP <https://academic.oup.com/jhrp/advance-article-abstract/doi/10.1093/jhuman/huad032/7261647> accessed 24 February 2024.

89 Rajamani and others (n 5) [984].

90 *Duarte Agostinho v Portugal and 32 other States* App no 39371/20 (ECtHR).

91 'Request for an Advisory Opinion on the Scope of the State Obligations for Responding to the Climate Emergency' (2023) <www.corteidh.or.cr/docs/opiniones/soc_1_2023_en.pdf> accessed 24 February 2024.

Because courts are clear that they are using CBDR-RC as interpretive tools to help establish the content of open standards based on national law (rather than international legal obligations that may potentially generate rights), the jurisprudence discussed in this chapter can be replicated in countries that adopt a monist model or a dualist model of international law incorporation into national law.

Thus far, litigation invoking CBDR-RC has been restricted to cases related to climate mitigation. Yet the principle is also very relevant to questions related to international climate finance. It is fair to anticipate, for example, cases arguing that developed countries have a constitutional or duty of care obligation to provide a 'fair share' of climate finance to developing countries as part of their common but differentiated responsibility to effectively contribute to international climate efforts in a way that builds trust among other countries. Since developed countries as a group have an obligation to provide climate finance to developing countries under the UN climate regime, it is possible that similar arguments related to whether individual developed countries are contributing their 'fair share' of this collective financial obligation be raised in national or international courts. With the evolution of CBDR-RC from an outward-looking principle of international law (State-to-State) to an inward-looking principle (influencing the scope of obligations within jurisdictions), we should expect other innovative litigation strategies related to climate adaptation and loss and damage. Courts around the world should thus be prepared to properly address CBDR-RC arguments in the future.

## 13.6 CONCLUSION

The 2022 IPCC Sixth Assessment Report states with 'high confidence' that 'issues of equity remain of central importance in the UN climate regime, notwithstanding shifts in the operationalization of [CBDR-RC] from Kyoto to Paris'.[92] Yet, the same IPCC report has also recognised the challenge of determining 'fair shares' in a system based on voluntary, self-determined contributions and noted the low political feasibility of States agreeing on equity benchmarks within the UNFCCC regime at the moment.[93] As a result, actors and mechanisms outside the UNFCCC regime will continue to shoulder the burden of developing such equity benchmarks, as 'it is only in relation to such a "fair share" that the adequacy of a state's contribution can be assessed in the context of a global collective action problem'.[94]

92 Patt and others (n 82).

93 ibid [14.3.2.3].

94 ibid. For initiatives proposing methodologies to identify fair shares of various countries, see e.g. 'Climate Equity Reference Project' <https://climateequityreference.org/> accessed 24 February 2024; 'Friends of the Earth Climate Fair Shares' <www.foei.org/what-we-do/climate-justice-and-energy/climate-fair-shares/> accessed 24 February 2024; 'Climate Action Tracker Fair Shares' <https://climateactiontracker.org/methodology/cat-rating-methodology/fair-share/> accessed 24 February 2024; 'Climate Analytics' <https://climateanalytics.org/publications/2020/fair-share-carbon-dioxide-removal-increases-major-emitter-responsibility/> accessed 24 February 2024. For reviews of literature on equitable methods for effort-sharing see Rajamani and others (n 5) [1021] and Dooley and others (n 14).

In this context, courts will undoubtedly feature among the actors increasingly facing questions related to fair effort-sharing in light of CBDR-RC in the context of climate litigation. The momentum of 'fair share' climate litigation shall pick up pace as Parties provide their narrative justification for the ambition and fairness of their NDCs, as required by the Paris Rulebook, as they are pressured to provide more rigorous information on their adopted equity considerations, and as the scientific community continues to work on reducing uncertainties over the remaining global carbon budget.

Furthermore, as the impacts and dangers of climate change become more evident, and questions on who should bear the costs of dealing with such impacts and risks become more prominent, plaintiffs will likely prompt courts to deliberate on the normative content of CBDR-RC when interpreting the scope of a country's obligation to contribute its 'fair share' under the international climate regime in relation to adaptation, loss and damage, and finance, besides mitigation. This chapter offers some thoughts to inform what promises to be thriving legal debates in courts around the world in the years to come.

# 14

# Intergenerational Equity

*Sam Bookman and Margaretha Wewerinke-Singh**

## 14.1 INTRODUCTION

Intergenerational equity is a legal principle reflected in international treaties[1] and soft law instruments,[2] and recognised by many international and domestic tribunals.[3] It encapsulates the idea that '[t]he present residents of the earth hold the earth in trust for future generations and at the same time the present generation is entitled to reap benefits from it'.[4] Thus, the principle demands a just balance between the needs of present and future generations. Like other equitable principles, intergenerational equity reflects the need for flexibility and fairness. In the context of climate change, it demands consideration of *justice*: decisionmakers must pay attention to the distributive consequences of climate harms, government policies, and lack of action.[5] Further, as the High Court of South Africa put it, intergenerational justice in the context of climate change involves 'a rejection of short-termism as it requires the state to consider the

* Sam Bookman is a postdoctoral fellow at Harvard Law School. Margaretha Wewerinke-Singh is Associate Professor of Sustainability Law and Co-Founder of SEVEN, the University of Amsterdam's climate institute; Adjunct Professor of Law at the University of Fiji; and Of Counsel at Blue Ocean Law.

1 See United Nations Framework Convention on Climate Change (entered into force 19 June 1993) 1771 UNTS 107 (UNFCCC) art 3, 'The Parties should perfect the climate system for the benefit of present and future generations, on the basis of equity and in accordance with their common but differentiated responsibilities and capabilities'.

2 See e.g. UNEP, 'Declaration of the United Nations Conference on the Human Environment' (1972) UN Doc A/CONF/48/14 (Stockholm Declaration) principle 1, [humankind] 'bears a solemn responsibility to protect and improve the environment for present and future generations … The natural resources of the earth, including the air, water, land, flora and fauna and especially representative samples of natural ecosystems, must be safeguarded for the benefit of present and future generations through careful planning or management, as appropriate'.

3 Lydia Slobodian, 'Defending the Future: Intergenerational Equity in Climate Litigation' (2020) 32 GELR 569.

4 Werner Scholtz, 'Equity' in Lavanya Rajamani and Jacqueline Peel (eds), *The Oxford Handbook of International Environmental Law* (Oxford University Press 2021) 339. See also Edith Brown Weiss, *In Fairness to Future Generations* (Brill 1989).

5 See ibid Brown Weiss.

long-term impact of pollution on future generations'.[6] As a *principle*, intergenerational equity is rarely a standalone basis for decision-making. Rather, it informs the interpretation and application of legal doctrine, with implications for many areas of climate law. This includes issues discussed elsewhere in this volume, such as standing, admissibility, public trust,[7] and the precautionary principle. Judges already frequently refer to 'intergenerational equity',[8] 'intergenerational responsibility',[9] 'intergenerational justice',[10] or the broad interests of 'future generations'[11] when considering the obligations owed by States and other actors. While terminology and doctrine may be jurisdiction-specific, the general animating principle – of considering the future interests of children and unborn generations – has travelled widely across borders.

Intergenerational equity is especially important in the context of climate change. As the UN Committee on the Rights of the Child (CRC) has observed, children are impacted by climate change more than adults in the 'manner in which they experience such effects as well as the potential of climate change to affect them throughout their lifetime'.[12] This reflects two related dynamics. The first is future oriented. Climate change distributes benefits and burdens unequally over time: the failure by existing adults to mitigate greenhouse gas emissions and invest in adaptation infrastructure means that current children and future generations will experience greater harms.

The second dynamic relates to present, existing harms to children and young people. The dangers of climate change are not an abstract future proposition – they are already felt globally. As the Intergovernmental Panel on Climate Change (IPCC) has recognised, children are at particularly high risk of harm from the physical consequences of climate change (such as food and water security),[13] as well as

6 *Trustees for the time being of Groundwork Trust and Another v Minister of Environmental Affairs and Others* [2019] SAFLII 208 (ZAGPPHC) (*Groundwork Trust*) [41]; See also the decision of the Gauteng High Court in *Earthlife Africa Johannesburg v Minister of Environmental Affairs and Others* [2017] 65662/16 <http://climatecasechart.com/wp-content/uploads/sites/16/non-us-case-documents/2017/20170306_Case-no.-6566216_judgment-1.pdf> accessed 27 March 2023.

7 *Fomento Resorts & Hotels and Another v Minguel Martins and Ors* [2009] Civil Appeal No 4154 OF 2000 with Civil Appeal Nos 4155 and 4156 of 2000 [32].

8 *Advocate Padam Bahadur Shrestha v Prime Minister and Office of Council of Ministers and Others* [2018] Order No 074-WO-0283 (2075/09/10 BS) (Supreme Court of Nepal) (*Shrestha v Office of Council of Ministers*).

9 See e.g. *Minors Oposa v Factoran* [1993] GR No 101083, 224 SCRA 792 (*Minors Oposa v Factoran*).

10 *Groundwork Trust* (n 6).

11 See e.g. *Neubauer and Others v Germany* [2021] 1 BvR 2656/18, 1 BvR 96/20, 1 BvR 78/20, 1 BvR 288/20, 1 BvR 96/20, 1 BvR 78/20 (German Federal Constitutional Court) (*Neubauer*); *Future Generations v Ministry of the Environment and Others (Demanda Generaciones Futuras v Minambiente)* [2018] 11001 22 03 000 2018 00319 00 (Supreme Court of Justice of Colombia) (*Demanda Futuras Generaciones*).

12 UN Committee on the Rights of the Child, 'Decision Adopted by the Committee under the Optional Protocol to the Convention on the Rights of the Child on a Communications Procedure, concerning Communication No 104/2019', UN Doc CRC/C/88/D/104/2019 (*Sacchi*) [10.13].

13 Hans O. Pörtner and others, 'IPCC 2022: Summary for Policymakers' in Hans O. Pörtner and others (eds), *Climate Change 2022: Impacts, Adaptation and Vulnerability* (Cambridge University Press 2022) (IPCC) B.1.3.

mental health impacts such as anxiety and stress.[14] Furthermore, children and young people are rendered more vulnerable by their lack of political power – in particular, their inability to vote. Young people have highlighted these dynamics in cases across several jurisdictions, including Australia,[15] the Philippines,[16] Germany,[17] Nepal,[18] Colombia,[19] and the United States.[20]

The ongoing significance of intergenerational equity in climate litigation is evident in international and regional litigation. In the forthcoming case before the European Court of Human Rights (ECtHR), *Duarte Aghostinho and others v Portugal and 32 other States*, six Portuguese children have brought thirty-three member States of the Council of Europe before the ECtHR for alleged violations of Articles 2, 8, and 14 of the European Convention for the Protection of Human Rights and Fundamental Freedoms (ECHR) due to failure to take sufficiently ambitious climate action. In their claim, the applicants rely on intergenerational equity as a principle that must inform the interpretation of States' obligations under the ECHR. The ECtHR recognised the importance of intergenerational equity in this claim by including a question on intergenerational equity in their invitation to the respondent States to react to the application: it asked whether 'the defendant States [have] performed the obligations incumbent upon them …, read in the light of the pertinent provisions and principles, such as the principles of precaution and intergenerational equity, contained in international environmental law, including in the international treaties to which they are a Party'.[21] Furthermore, the recent advisory opinion submitted to the International Court of Justice by the United Nations General Assembly calls on that court to provide guidance concerning obligations owed to future generations, a question which will undoubtedly require consideration and enumeration of intergenerational equity.[22]

Against this backdrop, this chapter contributes to the debate on intergenerational equity and climate change. Like the other chapters in this Handbook, it is divided into a descriptive section and a normative section that identifies emerging best practice. In the first, descriptive section, we analyse how the principle of intergenerational equity has been applied in judicial decisions on climate change, specifically in decisions on cases initiated by children and youth. We survey three

[14] ibid B.4.4.
[15] *Minister for the Environment v Sharma* [2022] FCAFC 35 (*Sharma*).
[16] See e.g. *Minors Oposa v Factoran* (n 9).
[17] See e.g. *Neubauer* (n 11).
[18] See *Shrestha v Office of Council of Ministers* (n 8).
[19] See *Demanda Futuras Generaciones* (n 11).
[20] See e.g. *Juliana v United States* 947 F.3d 1159 (9th Cir 2020) (*Juliana*).
[21] *Duarte Agostinho v Portugal and 32 other States* App No 39371/20 (ECtHR, Statement of 13 November 2020).
[22] Request for an Advisory Opinion of the International Court of Justice on the Obligations of States in Respect of Climate Change, UNGA Res 77/276 (29 March 2023).

broad areas of jurisprudence: normative obligations owed by States; procedural mechanisms to ensure courtroom participation of children, young people, and representatives of future generations; and future-focused judicial remedies. These themes are often contained in one and the same judgment. By organising the section thematically, we create an overview of the state of play of climate change jurisprudence in connection with each of these themes across jurisdictions.

The second, normative part of the chapter pulls out judicial practice that could serve as a source of inspiration for legal reasoning in future cases. We consider such practices to be those which best give legal effect to the principle of intergenerational equity, or that best allow for judicial consideration of the principle in a courtroom setting. Continuing rapid emissions of greenhouse gases and failure to invest in climate adaptation infrastructure constitutes an injustice to future generations perpetrated by (some members of) the present. Normatively, only ambitious and equitable climate mitigation and adaptation policies and measures can be consistent with intergenerational equity.[23]

Zooming in on the existing case law, we then identify six areas of emerging best practice. First, best practice entails recognising that based on intergenerational equity, States owe obligations to children, young people, and future generations, such as the development of mitigation and adaptation plans and targets which distribute obligations fairly within and across generations.[24] Second, emerging best practice includes cases where judges have ensured that decisionmakers must account for intergenerational equity in planning and consent decisions which may have negative long-term climate impacts or downstream consequences.[25] Another substantive emerging best practice is the recognition of children, young people, and future generations as classes which may experience discrimination because of insufficiently ambitious climate policy.[26] Furthermore, intergenerational equity considerations are dependent on effective representation in court. Emerging best practice recognises the importance of children's participation both as representative of future generations (understood, as per the High Court of South Africa, as 'a broad concept which can mean posterity, or those whose birth is imminent')[27] and as vulnerable parties in the here and now. Ensuring such participation requires an open approach to issues such as standing, separation of powers, and certification of class actions. It may also require procedural innovations to facilitate courtroom participation

23 See e.g. Simon Caney, 'Climate Change, Intergenerational Equity and the Social Discount Rate' (2014) 13(4) Politics, Philosophy and Economics 320.

24 See *Neubauer* (n 11).

25 See e.g. Australian cases such as *Gloucester Resources Limited v Minister for Planning* [2019] NSWLEC 7 (*Gloucester Resources*).

26 *Mathur et al v Her Majesty the Queen in Right of Ontario* [2020] ONSC 6918 (Superior Court of Justice) (*Mathur Strikeout*). See to the contrary, however, the merits decision of the same court in *Mathur v Ontario* [2023] ONSC 2316 (*Mathur Merits*).

27 *Groundwork Trust* (n 6) [82.4].

and communicate judicial decisions.[28] Finally, emerging best practice incorporates the principle of intergenerational equity in crafting remedies that ensure long-term oversight and enforcement of judicial decisions.[29]

## 14.2 CASE LAW DEVELOPMENTS

### 14.2.1 *Development of the Principle in International Law*

Intergenerational equity forms part of the basis of international environmental law (IEL). The Stockholm Declaration of 1972 – widely recognised as one of IEL's founding documents – observes that humans bear 'a solemn responsibility to protect and improve the environment for present and future generations'.[30] Similarly, the United Nations Framework Convention on Climate Change (UNFCCC) requires States to 'protect the climate system for the benefit of present and future generations, on the basis of equity and in accordance with their common but differentiated responsibilities and respective capabilities'.[31] The principle of intergenerational equity has been extensively developed by the scholar Edith Brown Weiss, who argued that these (and other) statements of international law give rise to three obligations on States: to conserve options (ensuring future generations have a resource base they can use to 'satisfy their own values'); to conserve quality ('ensuring the quality of the environment on balance is comparable between generations'); and to conserve access (meaning 'non-discriminatory access among generations to the Earth and its resources').[32] The interests of future generations are also reflected in the principle of sustainable development. Principle 3 of the 1992 Rio Declaration on Environment and Development – a non-binding but highly influential international law instrument – provides that '[t]he right to development must be fulfilled so as to equitably meet developmental and environmental needs of present and future generations'.[33]

The most recent definition of intergenerational equity by a major international tribunal was recently provided by the UN CRC in its General Comment 26. In that Comment – and drawing on extensive consultation with children – the Committee noted that 'children constantly arriving are also entitled to the realization of their human rights to the maximum extent', and that 'States bear the responsibility for

[28] *Sacchi* (n 12).

[29] *Asghar Leghari v Federation of Pakistan* PLD 2018 Lahore 364; *Demandas Futuras Generaciones* (n 11).

[30] *Stockholm Declaration* (n 2) principle 1. See also *AP Pollution Control Board v Prof M V Nayudu (Retd) and Others* 1994 (3) SCC 1.

[31] UNFCCC (n 1) art 3.

[32] Edith Brown Weiss, 'Climate Change, Intergenerational Equity, and International Law' (2008) 9 VJEL 615, 616.

[33] United Nations, 'Declaration of the United Nations Conference on Environment and Development' (1992) 31 ILM 874 (Rio Declaration) principle 3.

foreseeable environment-related threats arising as a result of their acts or omissions now, the full implications of which may not manifest for years or even decades'.[34]

Intergenerational equity has been developed and recognised by judges of the International Court of Justice (ICJ). In its 1996 *Advisory Opinion on the Legality of the Threat or Use of Nuclear Weapons*, the ICJ observed that

> the environment is not an abstraction, but represents the living space, the quality of life and the very health of human beings, including generations unborn. The existence of the general obligation of States to ensure that activities within their jurisdiction and control respect the environment of other States or of areas beyond control is now part of the corpus of international law relating to the environment.[35]

Separate and dissenting ICJ judges have gone as far as suggesting that the principle gives rise to *rights* held by unborn generations.[36] For example, in a separate opinion in *Pulp Mills on the River Uruguay*, Judge Cançado Trindade observed that 'it can hardly be doubted that the acknowledgment of inter-generational equity forms part of conventional wisdom in international environmental law', and that the principle demanded that international law be interpreted and applied with reference to the 'long-term temporal dimension', 'displaying concern for seeking to secure the welfare not only of present but also of future generations'.[37]

### 14.2.2 *Development of the Principle in Domestic Courts in the Climate Context*

#### 14.2.2.1 Obligations Owed by States

14.2.2.1.1 EQUITABLE CLIMATE MITIGATION POLICY The principle of intergenerational equity is frequently referred to in climate litigation. Sometimes, this is framed in terms of the 'rights' or 'interests' of future generations.[38] Despite

[34] Committee on Rights of the Child, 'General Comment No 26 on Children's Rights and the Environment with a Special Focus on Climate Change' (22 August 2023) UN Doc CRC/C/GC/26 (General Comment 26).

[35] *Legality of the Threat or Use of Nuclear Weapons* (Advisory Opinion) [1996] ICJ Rep 226 [29].

[36] See e.g. the dissenting opinion of Judge ad hoc Sir Geoffrey Palmer in *Request for an Examination of the Situation in Accordance with Paragraph 63 of the Court's Judgment of 20 December 1964 in the Nuclear Tests (Australia v France)* (Judgment) [1974] ICJ Rep 253 (*Request for an Examination – Nuclear Tests*) [114]–[115]. See also the dissenting opinion of Judge Weeramantry in *Legality of the Threat or Use of Nuclear Weapons* (Advisory Opinion) [1996] ICJ Rep 226 [455], the dissenting opinion of Judge Weeramantry in *Request for an Examination – Nuclear Tests* (especially [341]), and the separate opinion of Judge Weeramantry in *Gabčíkovo-Nagymaros Project (Hungary/Slovakia)* (Judgment) [1997] ICJ Rep 7 [106]–[108].

[37] *Pulp Mills on the River Uruguay (Argentina v Uruguay)* (Merits) (Separate Opinion of Judge Cançado Trindade) [2010] ICJ Rep 14 [114]–[124].

[38] Unfortunately, these terms are used interchangeably in both jurisprudence and academic literature. In this chapter we do not attempt to provide a perfect conceptual distinction between these terms, but we consider legal reasoning concerning the rights of future generations as (potential) manifestations of the principle of intergenerational equity.

some conceptual variation, the principle has shaped judicial decisions which recognise the substantive obligations of States to equitably mitigate the future effects of climate change, and to recognise environmental rights possessed by children, young people, and future generations. The Inter-American Court of Human Rights has observed that the right to a healthy environment – recognised in more than 100 national constitutions and recently by the UN Human Rights Council and the UN General Assembly[39] – includes an individual dimension, as well as a 'collective dimension' as a 'universal value that is owed to both present and future generations'.[40] The Supreme Court of Colombia has observed in 2018 that 'without a healthy environment, subjects of law and sentient beings will not be able to survive, much less protect those rights for our children or future generations'.[41] Relatedly, at least one United States appellate judge has interpreted a 'perpetuity principle' as 'structural and implicit' in the United States Constitution, requiring a guarantee of a stable climate to 'all future generations'.[42] India's National Green Tribunal has interpreted intergenerational equity consistently with sustainable development, requiring the State to 'balance' the objectives of environment protection and development as part of the government's constitutional environmental duty.[43] Similarly, the High Court of South Africa has highlighted the link between sustainable development and the 'principle of "intergenerational justice"' which involves 'a rejection of short-termism as it requires the state to consider the long-term impact of pollution on future generations'.[44]

One of the first courts to recognise rights and obligations derived from intergenerational equity was the Supreme Court of the Philippines in 1993 in *Minors Oposa v Factoran*.[45] In that ground-breaking case, a group of children sought orders that the government cancel all existing timber licence agreements in the country and cease issuing new ones. The case was brought following decades of massive deforestation. The Court acknowledged the climate implications of the

39 UNHCR, 'The Human Right to a Clean, Healthy and Sustainable Environment' in 'Resolution Adopted by the Human Rights Council on 8 October 2021' (2021) UN Doc A/HRC/RES/48/13; UNGA, 'The Human Right to a Clean, Healthy and Sustainable Environment' (2022) UN Doc A/76/L.75.

40 *The Environment and Human Rights (State Obligations in Relation to the Environment in the Context of the Protection and Guarantee of the Rights to Life and to Personal Integrity – Interpretation and Scope of Articles 4(1) and 5(1) of the American Convention on Human Rights)*, Advisory Opinion OC-23, Inter-American Court of Human Rights Series A No 23 (15 November 2017) (IACtHR OC-23/17) [59]. See also the decision of the District Court in *Greenpeace Mexico v Ministry of Energy and Others* [2020] Amparo No 372/2020 (*Greenpeace Mexico*), where the Court observes that the failure to preserve resources for future generations constitutes a violation of the 'collective dimension' of the right to a healthy environment.

41 *Demanda Futuras Generaciones* (n 11).

42 Dissenting opinion of Judge Staton in *Juliana* (n 20).

43 *Court on its own Motion v State of Himachal Pradesh and Ors* Application No 237 (THC)/ 2013 (CWPIL No 15 of 2010) [14], [18].

44 *Groundwork Trust* (n 6) [41].

45 *Minors Oposa v Factoran* (n 9).

case, observing that deforestation resulted in 'the reduction of the earth's capacity to process carbon dioxide gases'.[46] Drawing on the obligation contained in the Philippines Constitution requiring the State to 'protect and advance the right of the people to a balanced and healthful ecology in accord with the rhythm and harmony of nature', the Court found in favour of the plaintiff children.[47] From this, the Court derived an obligation of 'inter-generational responsibility' and 'inter-generational justice'. The Court interpreted 'rhythm and harmony of nature' as incorporating a duty to ensure:

> [the] judicious disposition, utilization, management, renewal, and conservation of the country's forest, mineral, land, waters, fisheries, wildlife, offshore areas and other natural resources to the end that their exploration, development and utilization be equitably accessible to present as well as future generations. Needless to say, every generation has a responsibility to the next to preserve that rhythm and harmony for the full enjoyment of a balanced and healthful ecology. Put a little differently, the minors' assertion of their right to a sound environment constitutes, at the same time, the performance of their obligation to ensure the protection of that right for the generations to come.[48]

The obligation was further developed in 2008 by the Supreme Court in *Metropolitan Manila Development Authority v Concerned Residents of Manila Bay*.[49] In that case the Court affirmed mandamus relief[50] requiring the appellant to repair environmental damage to Manila's badly polluted harbour, observing that '[e]ven assuming the absence of a categorical legal provision specifically prodding petitioners to clean up the bay, they and the men and women representing them cannot escape their obligations to future generations of Filipinos to keep the waters of the Manila Bay clean and clear as humanly possible. Anything less would be a betrayal of the trust reposed in them.'[51]

In other cases, courts have drawn on intergenerational equity in fixing State obligations to take more aggressive action on climate mitigation. In 2021 in *Neubauer v Germany*, the Federal Constitutional Court of Germany considered a challenge to Germany's national climate legislation.[52] Plaintiffs – including several children – challenged the constitutionality of national legislation which set a 55 per cent reduction target in Germany's greenhouse gas emissions by 2030, and a goal of climate

46 ibid [3].

47 Constitution of the Philippines, art II.16. Like art 20A at issue in the German *Neubauer* case, this provision is not textually phrased as an explicit objective right. The *Minors Oposa* Court nevertheless interpreted it is as implying a subjective environmental right.

48 *Minors Oposa v Factoran* (n 9) [8].

49 *MMDA et al v Concerned Residents of Manila Bay* GR No 171947-48 (18 December 2008) (*MMDA v Concerned Residents of Manila Bay*).

50 A mandamus relief is an obligation imposed by a court on a lower court or civil servant to execute their respective tasks adequately.

51 *MMDA v Concerned Residents of Manila Bay* (n 49).

52 *Neubauer* (n 11).

neutrality by 2045.[53] The Act set out concrete annual targets up until 2030, but no specific post-2030 targets. Plaintiffs pointed out that the relatively modest cuts in greenhouse gas emissions prior to 2030 implied that significant cuts would be necessary in the following fifteen years to meet Germany's 2045 net-zero goal. The plaintiffs argued that this uneven distribution violated the government's constitutional obligation in Article 20A of the German Federal Basic Law (*Grundgesetz*), which provides that 'Mindful also of its responsibility towards future generations, the state shall protect the natural foundations of life and animals by legislation and, in accordance with law and justice, by exclusive and judicial action, all within the framework of the constitutional order'.[54] The plaintiffs further argued that the deferral of drastic climate mitigation measures to the future meant that the future fundamental freedoms of future generations would be strongly curtailed, especially relative to those enjoyed by existing adult generations.

The Court accepted the latter of these arguments. It found that Article 20A set a baseline obligation on the government to mitigate climate change, and that the deferral of significant action would create 'advance interference-like effects' (*Eingriffsähnliche Vorwirkung*) which would prevent young people from enjoying their rights and freedoms in the future. Thus, 'fundamental rights have nonetheless been violated because the emission amounts allowed by [the Act] in the current period are capable of giving rise to substantial burdens to reduce emissions in later periods … [t]he duty to afford protection against risks to life and health can also establish a duty to protect future generations'.[55] Although such generations 'do not yet carry any fundamental rights in the present',[56] '[u]nder certain conditions, the *Grundgesetz* imposes an obligation to safeguard fundamental freedom over time and to spread the opportunities associated with freedom proportionately across generations. As intertemporal guarantees of freedom, fundamental rights afford the complainants protection against [burdens] … being unilaterally offloaded onto the future'.[57]

The decision thus pays close attention to the question of *who* is required to mitigate climate change. The Court found that the State had an obligation to distribute those obligations – concretised in Germany's legislated 'carbon budget' – in a fair and equitable manner. This consideration of the distributional consequences of climate action is closely aligned to the principle of intergenerational equity. However, the granular level of analysis applied in *Neubauer* has not been employed in all

53 The summary of the case draws heavily on the author's summary of the case elsewhere. See Sam Bookman, 'Creativity and Climate Rights in "Commonwealth Model" Jurisdictions', Public Law Conference, Dublin, 6–8 July 2022.

54 Grundgesetz art 20A, as translated by the Constitute Project. See <https://constituteproject.org/constitution/German_Federal_Republic_2014?lang=en> accessed 9 February 2024.

55 *Neubauer* (n 11) [142]–[146].

56 ibid [146].

57 ibid [183].

climate cases concerning the interests of future generations. In other instances, courts have paid greater deference to governments' own assessments of justice. For example, in 2015 in *Foster v Washington Department of Ecology*, the Supreme Court of the US State of Washington found that although the state owed public trust obligations to '[p]reserve, protect and enhance the air quality for future generations', this obligation was adequately discharged simply by engaging in a rulemaking process to establish climate regulations.[58]

Intergenerational equity was also discussed in the Dutch *Urgenda* judgments of the District Court of the Hague (2015), Court of Appeal of the Hague (2018), and the Supreme Court (2019).[59] These judgments confirmed that the risks resulting from dangerous climate change can translate into violations of the right to life (Article 2 ECHR) and the right to private and family life (Article 8 ECHR). These risks result in a duty of care by the State to do its 'fair share' to mitigate climate change. The court of first instance, the District Court of the Hague, ruled that this duty of care applies to both current and future generations. Furthermore, the District Court based its decision explicitly on the principle of fairness laid down in Article 3 of the UNFCCC. According to the District Court, this principle entails that a State's climate policy 'should not only start from what is most beneficial to the current generation at this moment, but also what this means for future generations, so that future generations are not exclusively and disproportionately burdened with the consequences of climate change'.[60] The Court of Appeal and the Supreme Court, however, did not dwell upon the question of the State's eventual obligations towards future generations, as the risks for current generations were sufficient to establish a breach of the duty of care.[61] Thus, no answer was given to the question whether rights derived from the ECHR also apply to future generations, nor was the intergenerational element of the principle of fairness further touched upon.

14.2.2.1.2 PERMITTING AND CONSENT DECISION-MAKING Intergenerational equity has also played a role in shaping the procedural climate obligations owed by States. Specifically, courts have found intergenerational equity and the interests of future generations to be a factor that decisionmakers must take into account

[58] *Foster v Washington Department of Ecology* No 14-2-25295-1 [2015] (Supreme Court of Washington) (*Foster v Washington*) [6]. The public trust doctrine has its origins in Roman law that was introduced into, among others, the US legal order, through common law. The doctrine entails that the (sovereign) State manages and controls natural resources for future generations.

[59] *Urgenda v the Netherlands* [2015] ECLI:NL:RBDHA:2015:7145 (District Court of the Hague) (*Urgenda District Court*); *Urgenda v the Netherlands* [2018] ECLI:NL:GHDHA:2018:2591 (The Hague Court of Appeal) (*Urgenda Court of Appeal*); *State of the Netherlands (Ministry of Economic Affairs and Climate Policy) v Stichting Urgenda* [2019] ECLI:NL:HR:2019:2007 (Supreme Court of the Netherlands) (*Urgenda Supreme Court*).

[60] ibid *Urgenda District Court* [4.57].

[61] *Urgenda Court of Appeal* (n 59) [37].

when setting government policy or deciding whether to permit the development of carbon-emitting projects (such as mines or power plants). For instance, in 2013, the Supreme Court of India ordered an Environmental Impact Assessment study on capping iron ore excavations in the State of Goa, taking into account the principles of intergenerational equity and sustainable development.[62] The Supreme Court of Sri Lanka observed in 2000 that the principle 'should be regarded as axiomatic in the decision-making process concerning the natural resources and the environment'.[63]

Intergenerational equity is referred to in several pieces of Australian environmental and planning legislation.[64] In a series of cases, courts and tribunals in Australia have directed decisionmakers to consider the interests of future generations based on this principle. In *Gloucester Resources v Minister for Planning*, the New South Wales Land and Environment Court (NSWLEC) upheld the decision of the Minister of Planning to refuse permission to develop a proposed coal mine. The Court observed that '[t]he principle of inter-generational equity provides that the present generation should ensure that the health, diversity and productivity of the environment are maintained for future generations'.[65] In this case, '[t]he economic and social benefits of the Project will last only for the life of the Project (less than two decades), but the environmental, social and economic burdens of the project will continue for long after'.[66] The Court further drew on the principle of intergenerational equity in concluding that the responsible minister was required to consider the potential climate impacts of the mine before allowing the development to go ahead,[67] including indirect, downstream' emissions – that is, emissions generated by burning the mined coal, which would subsequently be supplied to energy generators.[68]

The NSWLEC in *Gloucester* embarked on an extensive cost–benefit analysis before arriving at the same conclusion as the responsible minister. In other cases, courts have determined that, at a minimum, decisionmakers have a procedural obligation to turn their minds to intergenerational equity. In 2006 in *Gray v Minister for Planning*, the NSWLEC considered a challenge to the defendant's decision to permit the development of the Anvil Hill Coal Mine.[69] One of the issues for the Court to consider was whether the responsible minister had fulfilled his statutory duty

62 *Goa Foundation v Union of India and Ors* Writ Petition (Civil) No 435 Of 2012 [8]. See also *Intellectuals Forum, Tirupathi v State of Andhra Pradesh and Ors* Appeal (Civil) 1251 of 2006.

63 *Bulankulama and Others v Secretary, Ministry of Industrial Development and others* [2000] LKSC 18 (Supreme Court of Sri Lanka).

64 See e.g. Protection of the Environment Act 1991 s 6(2)(b) (NSW); Environment Protection and Biodiversity Conservation Act 1999 s 6A(c) (Cth).

65 *Gloucester Resources* (n 25).

66 ibid [415].

67 ibid [498].

68 ibid [499].

69 *Gray v The Minister for Planning, Director-General of the Department of Planning and Centennial Hunter Pty Ltd* [2006] NSWLEC 720.

to consider the principles of 'ecologically sustainable development', which included the principle of 'inter-generational equity'.[70] The Court concluded that the principle demands that decisionmakers consider the *cumulative* impacts of proposed activities, rather than any single event. A cumulative approach 'must include the effect on future generations'.[71] In light of this requirement, the Court concluded that the planning process had been deficient. Specifically, the Court considered that the environmental impact assessment requirements – which set the terms of the mine's environmental assessment – failed to take into account Scope 3 emissions resulting from the development.[72] This omission amounted to a 'failure of a legal requirement to take into account the principle of intergenerational equity'.[73] As in other cases (such as the 2019 decision of the Chilean Supreme Court in *Chauhan Chauhan*),[74] the Court linked the principle of intergenerational equity to the precautionary principle: both suggest a need for caution in the face of future uncertainty. Permission for the mining development was accordingly set aside. By contrast, in 2011 in *Haughton v Minister for Planning and Macquarie Generation*, the minister's decision to allow the construction of a power station was upheld in part because the minister had considered the intergenerational implications of climate change, albeit at a high level of generality.[75]

This jurisprudence was recently applied by the Queensland Land Court in the 2022 case of *Waratah Coal v Youth Verdict*.[76] In that case, the Court recommended against approvals for the development of a new coal mine in an ecologically sensitive area. The Court observed that:

> The intergenerational aspect of climate change risks makes the rights of children paramount. The year 2100 is the reference point for the Paris Agreement long-term temperature goal. My generation of decision makers will be long gone, but a child born this year will be 78 in 2100. The principle of intergenerational equity places responsibility with today's decision makers to make wise choices for future generations. The children of today and of the future will bear both the more extreme effects of climate change and the burden of adaptation and mitigation in the second half of this century. Their best interests are not served by actions that narrow the options for achieving the Paris Agreement temperature goal. This weighs the balance against approving the applications.[77]

[70] ibid [260]–[261], citing the Environmental Planning and Assessment Act 1979 ss 4 and 5(a)(vii).

[71] ibid [279].

[72] That is, downstream emissions resulting from the activities of other parties. In this case, this would include energy producers burning the coal extracted from the Anvil Hill Mine. For a definition of Scope 3 emissions, see >https://ghgprotocol.org/sites/default/files/standards_supporting/FAQ.pdf> accessed 9 February 2024.

[73] *Gray v The Minister for Planning* (n 68) [294].

[74] *Chauhuan Chauhuan v Empresa Nacional de Petroleos, ENAP SA* Rol 5888-2019 (Excelentisima Corte Suprema, 2019).

[75] *Haughton v Minister for Planning and Macquarie Generation* [2011] NSWLEC 217.

[76] *Waratah Coal Pty Ltd v Youth Verdict Ltd* [2022] QLC 21.

[77] ibid [1603].

In another recent Australian case, *Sharma v Minister for the Environment* in 2021, a group of children challenged the minister's decision to approve the expansion of a coal mine. Rather than alleging a failure to fulfil a statutory duty, the plaintiffs argued that the minister owed them a tortious common law duty of care. The plaintiffs were successful in the first instance. The Federal Court Judge concluded that it was 'reasonably foreseeable' that the extension of the mine would lead to greater harms faced by the children in the future and that the responsible minister had 'substantial control' over such harm.[78] The decision, however, was overturned on appeal.[79] The most important basis for the minister's appeal was the reasoning of the federal court that formulating climate policy is a task not of judges but of democratically chosen parliaments together with the government. This issue will be discussed further in Section 14.3 below.

14.2.2.1.3 NON-DISCRIMINATION The third context in which intergenerational equity has shaped the obligations owed by States is in equality and non-discrimination challenges brought by children and young people against governments. In this context, child and young person plaintiffs have pointed to the current and future harms that climate change will impose on their generation. Scientific research confirming the presence of such harms and their significance has played an important role in the evolving jurisprudence.[80] Such harms are significant – as the first instance court in *Sharma* observed in factual findings that were upheld on appeal, present children are at a heightened risk of many climate harms (such as heat waves and mental health harms), while in the future, they are more likely to experience greater health, quality of life, and financial harms.[81] The extent of this risk and danger depends partly on the effectivity of the measures taken to counter climate change and to protect children from its consequences.

Despite these uneven impacts, some courts have refused to consider equality challenges brought by children and young people. These claims are particularly prolific in North America. In *ENJEU v Procurer General du Canada*, the Quebec Superior Court declined to certify an equality rights claim brought on behalf of Quebecers under the age of 35, finding the identification of such a group to be 'arbitrary'.[82] In *Aji P*, the Court of Appeals of Washington State determined that children

78 *Sharma and others v Minister for the Environment* [2021] FCA 560 *(Sharma First Instance).*

79 *Sharma* (n 15).

80 See e.g. Wim Thiery and others, 'Intergenerational inequities in exposure to climate extremes' (2021) Science 158; Caroline Hickman and others, 'Climate anxiety in children and young people and their beliefs about government responses to climate change: a global survey' (2021) 5(12) Lancet Public Health 863.

81 ibid. See *Sharma First Instance* (n 78), where the Court estimated that the average child would lose $41–85,000 in family wealth and $170,000 in lost income over the course of their lives as a result of climate change.

82 *Environnement Jeunesse v Procureur General du Canada* [2018] 500-06-000955-183 (Quebec Superior Court) 123 (*ENJEU*).

were not a 'suspect class' that attracted equal protection rights under the United States Constitution.[83] This finding was based on three reasons drawn from United States equal protection jurisprudence: childhood is not an immutable characteristic; the alleged harms were not imminent; and 'the aggregate acts of the State do not show any discrimination or discriminatory intent'.[84] The equal protection claim was accordingly rejected.

Other courts, however, have been more open to such challenges. In the 2020 *Mathur v Ontario* case, the Supreme Court of Ontario allowed an equality claim against the provincial government to proceed to a full merits hearing. Plaintiffs alleged that the replacement of previous climate mitigation targets with less ambitious ones constitutes age discrimination prohibited by section 15 of the Canadian Charter of Rights and Freedoms. The Court decided that the section 15 claim 'self-evidently' met the threshold test of having a 'reasonable prospect of success', given that 'most, if not all of [the plaintiffs] will be proportionately [sic] affected by the impacts of climate change and will suffer the most of all generations; but more importantly, these impacts will exacerbate their pre-existing vulnerability and disability'.[85] Despite this initial success, however, the claim was unsuccessful at the merits stage.[86] While the Court accepted that 'climate change has disproportionate impacts on young people and indigenous peoples',[87] it nonetheless found that the government did not have a positive obligation to bridge 'a gap between group and non-group members'.[88] The Court further found that the differentiated impact was not between people of different ages, but rather, 'a temporal distinction', and therefore not a ground protected or recognised by Canadian human rights law.[89]

Recently, the UN Human Rights Committee addressed a claim brought by a number of indigenous Torres Strait islanders alleging that Australia's failure to take effective climate mitigation and adaptation measures violated their rights under the International Covenant on Civil and Political Rights (ICCPR). In this case, known as *Daniel Billy v Australia*,[90] the question at hand was not discrimination against future generations in general but the specific consequences of climate policy for the indigenous groups of which the claimants were members. Substantially, the complaint involved alleged violations of the right to life and the right to privacy, family, and home life, as well as minority rights, rather than age discrimination. Nevertheless, the Committee's jurisprudence may have important implications for

83 *Aji Pexrel Piper v State* 480 P.3d 438 (Court of Appeals for Washington 2021) (*Aji P*).
84 ibid [29].
85 *Mathur Strikeout* (n 26) [178].
86 *Mathur Merits* (n 25).
87 ibid [25], [178].
88 ibid [178].
89 ibid [180].
90 UNHR Committee, 'Views Adopted by the Committee under Article 5(4) of the Optional Protocol, concerning Communication No 3624/2019', 21 July 2022, UN Doc CCPR/C/135/D/3624/2019 (*Billy*).

age discrimination claims. The ground-breaking views of the Committee confirmed the violation of Articles 17 and 27 of the ICCPR, concerning the right to private and family life and the right of minority groups to enjoy their own culture. The Committee considered the right to culture through an intergenerational lens: it recognised that the 'the State party's failure to adopt timely adequate adaptation measures to protect the authors' collective ability to maintain their traditional way of life, to transmit to their children and future generations their culture and traditions and use of land and sea resources discloses a violation of the State party's positive obligation to protect the authors' right to enjoy their minority culture'.[91] This ruling illustrates how intergenerational equity can be effectively integrated into human rights law, thus ensuring that the rights of both present and future generations are protected through the adoption of effective climate policies.

14.2.2.1.4 COURTROOM PROCEDURE In addition to the obligations outlined earlier, intergenerational equity plays a role in considerations of courtroom procedure and access to justice. Many judges have considered that procedural innovations are necessary in order to allow claims of intergenerational equity to be presented in court. In particular, judges have been required to consider *who*, if anyone, may be permitted to represent the interests of future generations; and in particular, whether children may do so. As many judges have noted, these interests are unrepresented in the political process – neither children nor future generations can vote.[92] The Supreme Court of Pakistan observed in 2021 that intergenerational justice requires that 'the Court should be mindful that its decisions also adjudicate upon the rights of the future generations of this country', a 'silent majority' which 'is rendered powerless and needs a voice'.[93] And the High Court of South Africa has found that the right to a healthy environment as protected under section 24 of the Constitution of South Africa 'may be invoked purely for the benefit of future generations' even if violations of the right of present generations cannot be demonstrated.[94]

These considerations are central to decisions concerning standing and the certification of class actions. In *Minors Oposa*, the Court recognised the standing not only of the child plaintiffs to be represented in Court by their litigation guardians but for the children to 'sue on behalf of the succeeding generations … based on the concept of intergenerational responsibility'.[95] The Court later observed that the children had standing not just as parties in themselves but also to 'represent their

[91] ibid [8.14].

[92] *Sharma First Instance* (n 78) [296], 'vulnerability of the children is partly a function of the magnitude of the potential risk of harm they face but is also a function of their powerlessness to avoid that harm', and 'children have no choice but to live in the environment which will be bequeathed to them'.

[93] *DG Khan Cement Company v Government of Punjab* CP 1290-L/2019 (Supreme Court of Pakistan) [19].

[94] *Groundwork Trust* (n 6) [82.4].

[95] *Minors Oposa v Factoran* (n 9) [7].

generation as well as generations yet unborn'.[96] The Court formally certified the children as representatives of a class action, finding that 'since the parties are so numerous, it becomes impracticable if not totally impossible, to bring all of them before the court. We likewise declare that the plaintiffs therein are numerous and representative enough to ensure the full protection of all concerned interests'.[97]

The wide-reaching approach of the *Oposa* court has been influential in Filipino law. Since the 1993 decision, the Philippines has introduced writs of *kalikasan*, designed to streamline and liberalise standing requirements in environmental cases.[98] Nevertheless, the approach has encountered resistance in some quarters. Subsequent courts have been concerned that the approach presupposes that a single group of plaintiffs could speak for entire present and future generations, counterproductively resulting in the court making decisions on their behalf that actually preclude the full range of future decision-making. In *Arigo v Swift*, the Court observed that:

> [w]hile 'intergenerational responsibility' is a noble principle, it should not be used to obtain judgments that would preclude future generations from making their own assessment based on their actual concerns. The present generation must restrain itself from assuming that it can speak best for those who will exist at a different time, under a different set of circumstances. In essence, the representative suit will inevitably result in preventing future generations from protecting their own rights and pursuing their own interests and decisions. It reduces the autonomy of our children and our children's children. Even before they are born, we again restricted their ability to make their own arguments.[99]

Judge Leonen suggested in his concurring opinion to *Resident Marine Mammals of the Protected Seascape Tanon Strait v Reyes* that standing and class action certification of groups on behalf of future generations should be restricted only to cases where:

> a) … there is a clear legal basis for the representative suit; b) there are actual concerns based squarely upon an existing legal right; c) there is no possibility of any countervailing interest existing within the population represented or those that are yet to be born; and d) there is a threat of catastrophe so imminent that an immediate protective measure is necessary.[100]

'Better still', the Court suggested, referring to the *Minors Oposa* case, 'in light of its costs and risks, we abandon the precedent altogether'.[101]

96 ibid [2].
97 ibid [7].
98 *See* Hilario G. Davide, 'The Environment as Life Sources and the Writ of Kalikasan in the Philippines' (2012) 29 PELR 592, 597–598.
99 *Arigo v Swift* [2014] GR No 206510, 743 Phil 8.
100 *Resident Marine Mammals of the Protected Seascape Tanon Strait v Reyes* GR No 180771 [2015] (Supreme Court of Philippines), Conflicting Opinion of Judge Leonen.
101 ibid.

This tension is evident elsewhere in the world. Many courts have followed the path forged by *Minors Oposa* in liberalising participation requirements to facilitate the presentation of arguments on behalf of future generations. In *Demanda Futuras Generaciones*, the Supreme Court of Colombia took a flexible approach to standing, permitting climate claims to be brought on behalf of children and future generations through the streamlined *tutela* procedure.[102] In 2023 in the Belgian case of *VZW Klimaatzaak*, the Court of Appeal reviewed relevant human rights standards on the right to participate in environmental decision-making, and in particular, the Convention on Access to Information, Public Participation and Access to Justice in Environmental Matters ('Aarhus Convention'). The Court concluded that the plaintiffs were entitled to bring claims on behalf of future generations, especially in light of the impacts that climate change has on the entire present and future population.[103]

In the United States, plaintiffs face especially restrictive standing requirements. Plaintiffs must generally demonstrate the existence of a particularised injury; caused by the defendant; and redressable by the Court. Some child and youth plaintiffs have met these requirements, particularly before state (rather than federal) courts. In *Funk v Wolf*, the Commonwealth Court of Pennsylvania ultimately rejected a state constitutional law challenge to the state's failure to develop a comprehensive mitigation plan, but it accepted that at least one child plaintiff had experienced harms that could be distinguished from the general population for the purposes of standing requirements.[104] The Court further recognised that the claim met the causation requirement for the purposes of standing, namely the requirement that there is a causal relationship between the defendant's conduct and the injury suffered. The Court observed that '[t]he zone of interests protected by the [state constitution's environmental provision] is the rights of all people in the Commonwealth, including future generations'.[105] The Court, however, rejected the claim on substantive grounds. Youth plaintiffs in at least two other state court claims – *Held v Montana* and *Kanuk v Alaska* – have likewise overcome standing restrictions. In *Kanuk v Alaska*, the Supreme Court of Alaska found that Alaskan state courts do not deny 'injured persons standing on grounds that others are also injured … to require dismissal of … lawsuits because all possible viewpoints cannot be represented would create unacceptable barriers to the courts'.[106] And in *Held v Montana*, a trial court found that youth plaintiffs had standing because they

[102] *Demanda Futuras Generaciones* (n 11). The tutela-procedure facilitates accessibility to the courts through accessible requirements for filing an application that alleges a violation of a constitutional right.

[103] *VZW Klimaatzaak v Kingdom of Belgium and Others* [2023] 2022/AR/891 (Cour d'appel de Bruxelles) (*VZW Klimaatzaak Appeal*).

[104] *Funk v Wolf* 158 A.3d 642 (Supreme Court of Pennsylvania 2017).

[105] ibid [29].

[106] *Kanuk v State* 335 P.3d 1088 (2014) [11]. It should be noted, however, that the Court nevertheless dismissed the claim on political question grounds.

experienced not only speculative future harms but already manifest harms of climate change, such as anxiety-related mental health harms.[107]

Other courts have been more circumspect in relation to standing and class certification. In the Dutch *Urgenda* case, the Supreme Court did not touch upon the question whether interest groups can litigate on behalf of future generations. In the German *Neubauer* case discussed earlier, the standing of child plaintiffs was recognised, but only as existing persons – not as representatives of future generations. The Court observed that '[t]he complainants are not asserting the rights of unborn persons or even of entire future generations, neither of whom enjoy subjective fundamental rights. Rather, the complaints are invoking their own fundamental rights'.[108] In the *ENJEU* case also discussed earlier, the breadth of climate impacts was considered a reason to *restrict* the standing of plaintiffs purporting to represent all young people, and instead reserve the matter for the political branches.[109] In addition to these specific concerns related to young people and future generations, as discussed elsewhere in this volume, some courts have drawn on general separation of powers concerns or the political question doctrine to preclude judicial consideration of claims related to intergenerational equity. Such decisions are particularly common in North America.[110]

Finally, it should be noted that child and youth participation may extend beyond formal matters such as standing and class action certification, to issues related to the accessibility and age-appropriateness of procedures. In *Sacchi* for example, the CRC considered a communication brought by children from several countries who argued that inaction on climate change violated their rights under the UN Convention on the Rights of the Child. The communication was unsuccessful on the basis that the children had failed to exhaust domestic remedies, a prerequisite for the Committee to consider the complaint.[111] Nevertheless, the Committee engaged with the complainants by communicating their decision in a plain-language document, intended to be legible to the child complainants, while also adopting a closed-door hearing procedure that allowed the child petitioners to address the Committee directly. Moreover, the complainant Chiara Sacchi and other children were invited to participate in a special advisory team on climate and children's rights. The Committee also organised an online consultation among children and youth to gain a better understanding of the ways in which children's rights are affected by climate change and environmental degradation. These measures suggest the potential for greater innovation in facilitating the access of children and young people to judicial decision-making on climate issues.

107 *Held v Montana* No CDV-2020-307 (District Court of Montana 2023) [87].
108 *Neubauer* (n 11) [109].
109 *ENJEU* (n 82) [35].
110 See e.g. *Juliana* (n 20); *La Rose v Her Majesty the Queen* T-1750-19 [2020] (Federal Court of Canada); *Lho'imggin et al v Her Majesty the Queen* 2020 FC 1059 [2020] (Federal Court of Canada); *Aji P* (n 83).
111 See Chapter 5 on Admissibility.

14.2.2.1.5 REMEDIES Intergenerational equity concerns may play a role in remedies awarded in climate cases. The principle suggests that remedies must be effective over a long-term horizon, rather than satisfying the short-term demands of the parties.

Tailoring judicial remedies to the needs of future generations is no easy task. Courts have referred to the need for such tailoring, but explicitly crafted remedies remain rare. In the 2018 *Shrestha v Prime Minister* case, the Supreme Court of Nepal found that the Nepali government owed a constitutional obligation to legislate a comprehensive climate mitigation and adaptation policy. It ordered the government to 'make legal arrangements to ensure ecological justice and environmental justice to the future generation', but gave little guidance as to how such an outcome could be achieved.[112] In *VZW Klimaatzaak*, the Belgian Court in the first instance explicitly declined to specify a remedy, despite finding that the government had violated plaintiffs' rights.[113] More extensive guidance was provided by the Federal Constitutional Court of Germany in *Neubauer*. Although it was left to the legislature to amend the challenged legislation, the Court set out principles to guide that amendment, including a requirement that annual emission amounts and reduction targets be set out in greater detail.[114] The Dutch *Urgenda* judgments show a thoroughly considered level of detail with the District Court of the Hague partly basing its emission reduction order on the principle of intergenerational equity.

A more novel and comprehensive scheme was set out by the Supreme Court of Colombia in *Demanda Futuras Generaciones*. In that case, youth plaintiffs challenged the government's failure to control logging in the Amazon Rainforest, in part because of logging's effect on climate change. The Court recognised the Amazon Rainforest as a subject of rights (*sujeto de derecho*), effectively recognising the rainforest as a legal person. It also ordered several government agencies, together 'with the active participation of the plaintiffs, affected communities, scientific organizations or environmental research groups, and interested populations in general', to develop an 'intergenerational pact for the life of the Colombian Amazon' that includes 'measures aimed at reducing deforestation to zero and greenhouse gas emissions' and has 'national, regional and local implementation strategies of a preventative, mandatory, corrective and pedagogical nature, directed toward climate change adaptation'.[115] The Court further set out a process for judicial oversight to monitor the implementation of the remedy. It should be noted that many groups, including the plaintiffs, have complained that the remedy has not been implemented by the Colombian government.[116] Similar remedy mechanisms are available elsewhere, such as in the

[112] *Shrestha v Office of Council of Ministers* (n 8) [13].

[113] *VZW Klimaatzaak v l'État Belge* [2021] 2015/4585/A (Tribunal de première instance francophone de Bruxelles, Section Civile) [2.3.1]–[2.3.2]; *VZW Klimaatzaak Appeal* (n 103).

[114] *Neubauer* (n 11) [254]–[261].

[115] *Demanda Futuras Generaciones* (n 11) [14].

[116] Alex Guillau, 'The Colombian Government Has Failed to Fulfil the Supreme Court's Landmark Order to Protect the Amazon' (*Dejusticia*, 15 April 2019) <www.dejusticia.org/en/

Philippines, where the writ of continuing mandamus has been applied in environmental cases to ensure long-term court oversight and action plans.[117]

Another novel remedy in the environmental context was awarded in the Argentinian case of *Fischer v Comune Dique Chico*. The case concerned an agricultural school which challenged the government's decision to allow inorganic fumigation and fertilisation to take place in the surrounding area. The Court found the decision to be unconstitutional and emphasised the importance of environmental education, finding that children should be taught about the importance of intergenerational equity. As part of the remedies awarded in the case, the Court ordered the judgment to be taught in nearby schools for 'pedagogical-environmental purposes'.[118] The Court observed that was 'a cultural way of strengthening generational equity', demonstrating that 'present generations should not – we must not – adopt environmental decisions that irreversibly compromise them as future generations … [f]or this reason, the corresponding copies [of this decision] will be sent to them'.[119]

Lastly, the UN Human Rights Committee has issued extensive recommendations in the previously mentioned *Billy* case. The Committee determined that the State has an obligation to effectively remedy the damage suffered by the victims of the established human rights violations. This obligation entails among others an obligation to make full reparation and to provide adequate compensation for the harm suffered and to 'engage in meaningful consultations with the authors' communities in order to conduct needs assessments; continue its implementation of measures necessary to secure the communities' continued safe existence on their respective islands'.[120]

## 14.3 EMERGING BEST PRACTICE

We consider 'emerging best practices' to be those judicial practices which best give practical effect to the principle of intergenerational equity, or which ensure adequate application of the principle in judicial decisions. The principle requires consideration of the obligations owed by the present to future generations. One overriding obligation is clear: intergenerational equity requires that States introduce policies to ensure rapid decarbonisation and climate mitigation, and to adapt to current and future effects of climate change. The absence of such policies is fundamentally inconsistent with the principle of intergenerational equity.[121] When cast in terms of intergenerational distribution, the rapid emission of greenhouse gases into the

the-colombian-government-has-failed-to-fulfill-the-supreme-courts-landmark-order-to-protect-the-amazon/> accessed 12 February 2023.

[117] See the decision in *MMDA v Concerned Residents of Manila Bay* (n 49) [598]–[599].

[118] *Fischer v Comuna Dique Chico* (2020) [23].

[119] ibid.

[120] *Billy* (n 90) [11].

[121] See e.g. the decision in *Shrestha v Office of Council of Ministers* (n 8), where the complete absence of any climate legislation was found to be inconsistent with the Constitution of Nepal. The Court referenced the principle of intergenerational equity in reaching this conclusion.

atmosphere amounts to one generation imposing hardship and burdens on another. The adoption of an expressly distributional approach in *Neubauer* fundamentally exposed this. The intergenerational injustice of climate change is clear, whether approached expressly from the standpoint of a right to a healthy environment (as in *Minors Oposa v Factoran*), or through general principles and obligations (as in the dissenting opinion of Judge Staton in the 2020 case of *Juliana v United States*).

In addition to this high-level, overriding obligation, we set out six more specific emerging best practices: (1) consideration of the distributional impacts of climate policies; (2) requiring consideration of long-term and downstream climate effects in planning and permitting decisions; (3) recognising and admitting age discrimination cases that relate to climate change; (4) a flexible approach to the standing and class certification; (5) fostering children and young people's participation in courtrooms; and (6) crafting judicial remedies which promote long-term and participatory implementation.

Best practice involves paying attention to the fair distribution of climate obligations. The approach taken in the *Neubauer* decision is a strong instantiation of intergenerational equity. The Court went beyond Germany's high-level climate policy targets and conducted a distributional assessment of who would bear the burden of reaching them. The analysis reveals how climate policies, in addition to climate change itself, have distributional consequences. The Court drew on well-established constitutional jurisprudence in finding that the State could not unduly interfere with children's rights and freedoms in the development of climate mitigation policies, requiring the German parliament to revisit its approach. This distributional assessment reflects best practice. Such an approach is particularly crucial in jurisdictions which recognise an explicit right to a healthy environment,[122] but it may be applied – as in *Neubauer* – even in jurisdictions where no such subjective right exists. By contrast, we consider that it is insufficient for courts to simply note that a government has, or is considering, a climate mitigation policy, even where such a policy may be ambitious in absolute terms (such as a long-term net-zero target).[123] Such an approach fails to apply considerations of fairness and justice as demanded by the principle of intergenerational equity.

Secondly, emerging best practice involves the application of intergenerational equity considerations in permitting and planning decisions. Depending on the overall decision-making framework and the task of the reviewing court, such applications may be either substantive or procedural. At a minimum, decisionmakers should be expected to turn their minds to the long-term impact of greenhouse gas emitting projects (such as mines, power plants, and airports) and the renewal of infrastructure necessary for climate adaptation. This includes downstream consequences, such

[122] As the Inter-American Court of Human Rights has recognised, such a right includes a collective dimension which is held by future generations.

[123] See e.g. the approach taken in *Foster v Washington* (n 58), where the Court was satisfied that the state government had fulfilled its duty simply by beginning a climate rulemaking process.

as the Scope 3 emissions considered in *Gray v Minister for Planning*. More ambitiously, judges could consider whether to recognise supra-statutory obligations owed by decisionmakers to young people, as the trial court did in *Sharma*. Where a court is entrusted with reviewing the merits of planning decisions, judges themselves should inquire into downstream climate consequences. The *Gloucester Resources* and *Waratah Coal* cases discussed earlier demonstrate how judges can apply the principle of intergenerational equity when engaging in cost–benefit analysis or merits review of permitting decisions.

Thirdly, emerging best practice reinforces the relevance of anti-discrimination and equal protection law. As numerous scientific and judicial bodies have recognised, children and young people face existing and future vulnerabilities as a result of climate change policies.[124] These consequences are entirely the fault of prior generations but will be borne by subsequent ones. This should be recognised as a form of substantive age discrimination, regardless of intent.[125] Alternatively, some have suggested a new ground of discrimination of 'birth cohort' discrimination – that is, differentiated impact that will arise in the future as a result of the timespan in which a cohort of people have been born.[126] The preliminary decision of the Supreme Court of Ontario in the *Mathur* decision is an example of emerging best practice and demonstrates the importance of recognising the differentiated impact of climate change. The subsequent decision on the merits, which rejected the existence of a positive obligation on governments to remediate age-based differentiated impact, should not be considered emerging best practice. By contrast, the *Billy* decision of the UN Human Rights Committee shows how protection of the rights of those who suffer the most from the consequences of climate change can be ensured while keeping in mind the intergenerational dimension of the right to culture.

Fourthly – and relatedly – emerging best practice demonstrates a flexible approach to standing and class certification. Courts should consider the fact that children and young people are generally excluded from the political process, most obviously by being unable to vote. Courts may thus offer one of the few options for children and young people to participate in climate decision-making. This judicial role was forcefully articulated in *Minors Oposa v Factoran*. Courts should be careful not to erect too many barriers to children's access to the courtroom. This does not necessarily imply that judges should exceed the bounds of their proper constitutional role. As Filipino courts have suggested in cases since the *Minors Oposa* decision (such as *Arigo v Swift* and the *Marine Mammals* case), it will often be appropriate for judges to inquire whether child plaintiffs in the particular case are appropriately representative of a

[124] See *Sharma* (n 15) [11]; UNCRC in *Sacchi* (n 12) [10.13]; IPCC (n 13); Commission on Human Rights of the Philippines, 'National Inquiry on Climate Change Report' (CHRP December 2022) [53]–[55].

[125] The intent requirement presents particular difficulties in the United States, where it has long been necessary to prove intent in order to establish an equal protection violation. See *Aji P* (n 83) [28].

[126] See Refia Kaya, 'Environmental Vulnerability, Age and the Promises of anti-Age Discrimination Law' (2019) 1 RECIEL 162.

broader class of children, or of future generations more generally. But where interests are broad and collective – such as where courts are called upon to review the validity of continuing national climate policies – child plaintiffs may play an important role in articulating the long-term interests at stake. Furthermore, as the trial court recognised in *Held v Montana*, harm to children is not merely speculative: it is already manifest, thus meeting the requirement for many injury-based standing tests in national law. The scale of the climate crisis should not be used as a reason to preclude such standing, as occurred in the *Juliana* decision. Judges can play a role in climate governance through more modest declaratory remedies concerning the validity of particular laws and policies, as recognised in the preliminary decision in *Held v Montana*.

Fifthly, once admitted into the courtroom, judges could consider how to facilitate children and young people's ability to participate in judicial decision-making. Rights of participation and access to justice are broadly recognised in IEL and international human rights law and could be better reflected in domestic courtroom processes.[127] The CRC's decision in *Sacchi v Argentina* suggests some basic possibilities, such as the use of closed-door hearings or presentation of evidence, and plain-language communication of decisions. Such procedures will not be appropriate in all cases – indeed, open justice considerations may preclude the possibility of closed-door hearings. Where local rules of procedure permit, judges could consider other mechanisms through which to foster youth participation. This issue was canvassed in the CRC's General Comment No 26 on children's rights and the environment with a special focus on climate change, which in turn clarified the relevance of the UN Convention on the Rights of the Child to climate litigation.[128]

Finally, emerging best practice suggests the importance of remedies that will promote the long-term interests of children and young people. This is a challenging task for any court. Even carefully structured remedies mandating judicial oversight, such as those crafted in *Demanda Futuras Generaciones*, may fail in implementation. But where such remedies are available – as in the Philippines, which permits the use of continuing mandamus remedies in environmental matters – they may offer opportunities for children to play a role in future decision-making and governance. More novel approaches, such as the pedagogical orders made by the Argentinian court in *Fischer*, may also foster children's participation in environmental and climate governance. Recognising the Rights of Nature, as occurred in *Demanda Futuras Generaciones*, may also facilitate children's participation where they are accompanied by participatory governance structures to make decisions on Nature's behalf.

[127] See e.g. Convention on the Rights of the Child (entered into force 2 September 1990) 1577 UNTS 3 (CRC) art 3; Convention on Access to Information, Public Participation in Decision-Making and Access to Justice in Environmental Matters (entered into force 30 October 2001) 2161 UNTS 447 (Aarhus Convention); Regional Agreement on Access to Information, Public Participation and Justice in Environmental Matters in Latin America and the Caribbean (entered into force 22 April 2021) 3397 UNTC 195 (Escazú Agreement).

[128] General Comment 26 (n 34).

Even where such remedies are not available and implementation will necessarily be left to the political branches, clearly specifying the requirements of intergenerational justice in judicial orders can help to integrate intergenerational equity in subsequent legislative and policy decisions. Moreover, the recommendations in the UN Human Rights Committee's *Billy* case suggest that reparations can be used in order to remedy climate damage that has already occurred and reverse, as far as possible, its consequences. Together with measures to mitigate future damage, this remedy could play an important role in ensuring intergenerational equity before the courts.

## 14.4 REPLICABILITY OF BEST PRACTICES

Intergenerational equity is an increasingly recognised principle of IEL. As such, all States have an obligation to integrate it into their domestic frameworks. The precise form of such integration, however, will inevitably vary between jurisdictions. Where a right to a healthy environment is recognised, such a right should be interpreted as incorporating the principle of intergenerational equity into domestic law. This has been recognised by the Supreme Court of the Philippines in *Minors Oposa*,[129] the Inter-American Court of Human Rights,[130] and the Mexican District Court in *Greenpeace Mexico*.[131] In other instances, such as Australia, intergenerational equity will be referenced in domestic legislation. Even where it is not explicitly referenced in domestic law, it may operate as an interpretive principle or relevant consideration.

Furthermore, the form and extent of implementation will be dictated by doctrine and rules of procedure. In some jurisdictions, judges and rule makers have already integrated principles of intergenerational equity in relaxed standing requirements (as in *Minors Oposa* and subsequent development of the writ of *kalikasan* in the Philippines) or allowing environmental matters to be brought under more streamlined judicial procedures (as reflected in the Supreme Court of Colombia permitting the *Demanda Futuras Generaciones* case to be brought as a *tutela* action). In systems with relatively strict or inflexible procedural requirements, the principle of intergenerational equity may not permit judicial innovation on issues such as standing, remedies, and certification of class actions.

Nevertheless, judges will often be able to develop the law to better reflect the evolving obligations of States to incorporate intergenerational equity into domestic decision-making. We consider that all of the best practices identified in this chapter are in some way applicable to the legal systems of most States. Whatever the *form* in which intergenerational equity is applied, its *function* should permeate all aspects of judging in the context of climate change.

129 In that case, the Court concluded that the existence of an environmental directive principle in the national constitution entailed a correlative right, which in turn included obligations of intergenerational equity.

130 IACtHR OC-23/17 (n 40).

131 *Greenpeace Mexico* (n 40).

## 14.5 CONCLUSION

In this chapter we have canvassed judicial practice from a wide range of jurisdictions. We have underscored the importance of intergenerational equity as a principle of international and domestic law, emphasising that it demands ambitious action on climate change. The principle introduces a distributional framework that judges can apply when considering claims, especially those made by children, young people, and representatives of future generations. Emerging best practice recognises that the principle entails a set of obligations that States owe to children and young people, including fairness in overall climate policy, consideration of future interests in decision-making, and recognition of the generationally differentiated impacts of climate change. Furthermore, such practice often involves flexibility and innovation in judicial procedure and remedies. Intergenerational equity is a cross-cutting legal principle which is likely to play a growing role as youth-led climate litigation continues to proliferate across the world. By applying this principle in their decisions, judges can ensure that future generations are not left to bear the burden of the current generation's failure to take appropriate action on climate change.

**PART IV**

# Liability and Evidence

# 15

# State Responsibility

*Annalisa Savaresi**

## 15.1 INTRODUCTION

State responsibility is increasingly invoked in climate change litigation. It typically arises when an action or omission that is attributable to a State breaches an international obligation. However, as the International Court of Justice (ICJ) has noted, compliance with domestic law and compliance with international law are different questions.[1]

International courts typically apply the general law of State responsibility as codified and elaborated by the International Law Commission.[2] Conversely, national courts tend to apply domestic rules when they consider arguments concerning a breach of an international obligation and pay limited attention to what the law of State responsibility says on these matters.[3] The ICJ recognised this inconsistency when it stated that 'what is a breach of treaty may be lawful in the municipal [domestic] law and what is unlawful in the municipal law may be wholly innocent of violation of a treaty provision'.[4] As this chapter explains, however, the distinction between domestic and international law is sometimes blurred, especially in the dynamic field of climate change litigation.

Generally, domestic courts' engagement with international law obligations is on the rise. This reflects a shift in the nature of international law itself, which has historically been concerned with 'outward-looking' State-to-State obligations to be implemented through conduct on the international plane. Now, the focus is increasingly turning towards 'inward-looking' obligations – whereby States are required to undertake certain conduct within their own jurisdiction, such as

* Annalisa Savaresi is a professor of international environmental law at the University of Eastern Finland, and a professor of environmental law at the University of Stirling.

1 *Elettronica Sicula S.p.A. (ELSI) (US v Italy)* [1989] ICJ Rep 1551 (*ELSI*) [73].

2 ILC, 'Draft Articles on Responsibility of States for Internationally Wrongful Acts, with commentaries' (2001) UN Doc A/RES/56/83 (2001), 53 UN GAOR Supp (No 10) at 43, Supp (No 10) A/56/10 (IV.E.1) (ILC Draft Articles).

3 André Nollkaemper, 'Internationally Wrongful Acts in Domestic Courts' (2007) 101 AJIL 760, 761.

4 *ELSI* (n 1) 73.

adopting a specific legal framework, according certain rights, or abstaining from taking particular actions.[5] The latter type of international obligations are common in international environmental and human rights law. It is therefore not a surprise that international law obligations concerning environmental and human rights protection are, more and more, being invoked before national courts,[6] especially in the context of climate change litigation.[7] Domestic courts have thus inadvertently found themselves on the frontline of the enforcement of international obligations concerning climate change. There is, however, no uniform approach to the treatment of international obligations in general, and to the use of the law of State responsibility in particular, in domestic judicial practice.

This chapter expounds the fundamental tenets of the law of State responsibility, with a view to clarifying how this set of norms is used in the context of climate litigation. It starts with a succinct introduction to the law of State responsibility, illustrating its constituting elements and how they may apply to climate change. The chapter then considers how State responsibility has been framed in national judicial practice so far and what may be regarded as emerging best practice. This chapter does not consider legal redress that may be provided once responsibility for injury arising from a failure to fulfil that legal obligation has been established. The matter of damages is instead addressed in another chapter of this Handbook.[8]

## 15.2 THE LAW OF STATE RESPONSIBILITY

State responsibility typically arises when an action or omission that is attributable to a State breaches an international obligation,[9] regardless of the origin or character of that obligation.[10] As such, State responsibility requires neither fault nor damage.

Any 'injured' State, whose rights have been violated by said breach, may invoke State responsibility in an international dispute.[11] This may occur in a *bilateral* setting – for the breach of an obligation owed by one State to another – or in a *multilateral* setting – for the breach of an obligation due to multiple States, or indeed to all States.[12] The latter includes the possibility that the breach is 'of such a character

[5] See Study Group on Principles on the Engagement of Domestic Courts with International Law, 'Mapping the Engagement of Domestic Courts with International Law – Final Report' in International Law Association Report of the Seventy-Seventh Conference (International Law Association, London 2016) (ILA Domestic Courts and International Law Final Report) 12.

[6] ibid.

[7] Lucy Maxwell, Sarah Mead, and Dennis van Berkel, 'Standards for Adjudicating the next Generation of Urgenda-Style Climate Cases' (2022) 13(1) JHRE 35.

[8] See Chapter 18 on Remedies.

[9] ILC Draft Articles (n 2) art 2.

[10] ibid art 12.

[11] ibid art 42.

[12] Christian Dominicé, 'The International Responsibility of States for Breach of Multilateral Obligations' (1999) 10 EJIL 353, 361.

as radically to change the position of all the other States to which the obligation is owed with respect to the further performance of the obligation'.[13] In both instances, an injured State must be specifically affected by the breach of an international obligation, for example because the wrongful act was committed against its citizens or on its territory.[14] The remedies available under the law of State responsibility range from cessation of the wrongful act, to assurances of non-repetition, restitution, compensation, and satisfaction.[15]

In addition, any State may invoke State responsibility for the breach of obligations in the collective interest (so-called *erga omnes* or *erga omnes partes* obligations), even where it is not itself specifically affected.[16] Thus, in the case of *erga omnes* obligations – such as, for example, the prohibition of genocide – the law of State responsibility may be invoked for wrongful acts committed against the citizens of another State and on the territory of another State.[17] In these instances, however, the applicant State can only demand cessation of the internationally wrongful act and the performance of the duty to make reparation for the benefit of any injured States.[18]

In order to instigate a dispute for a breach of an international obligation concerning climate change, therefore, a set of conditions need to materialise:

1. A State has international obligations that directly or indirectly concern climate change;
2. One or more of these obligations have been breached, through an act or omission by the same State;
3. The breach is attributable to said State;
4. One or more States have been injured by said breach *or* the breached obligation is *erga omnes/erga omnes partes.*

The remainder of this section considers how the conditions to instigate an inter-State dispute for a breach of an international obligation concerning climate change may be fulfilled.

### 15.2.1 *International Obligations Concerning Climate Change*

As other chapters in this volume explain in further detail,[19] there are several international law obligations concerning climate change. These obligations are primarily – though not exclusively – enshrined in international climate treaties, namely,

[13] ILC Draft Articles (n 2) art 42(2).
[14] Robert Kolb, *International Law of State Responsibility: An Introduction* (Edward Elgar 2018) 196.
[15] ILC Draft Articles (n 2) arts 30–31.
[16] ibid art 48.
[17] See for example *Application of the Convention on the Prevention and Punishment of the Crime of Genocide (The Gambia v Myanmar)* [2022] ICJ Rep 477.
[18] ibid.
[19] See Chapter 9 on Duty of Care and Chapter 12 on International Law.

the 1992 United Nations Framework Convention on Climate Change (UNFCCC), the 1997 Kyoto Protocol, and the 2015 Paris Agreement.[20] The numerous bodies created by these treaties have produced secondary rules that further articulate and substantiate parties' obligations. While formally not legally binding, decisions of bodies like the Conference of the Parties (COP) to the UNFCCC provide authoritative guidance on the interpretation of climate treaties. States normally implement these decisions and regard them as part and parcel of the obligations under said treaties.[21]

Other international treaties, however, also provide obligations that are relevant to climate change.[22] For example, the Multilateral Environmental Agreements (MEAs) on matters such as air quality, the protection of the ozone layer, biodiversity, and the conservation of the marine environment. Similarly, international law-making bodies other than those established under the climate treaties – like the International Civil Aviation Organisation and the International Maritime Organization – have produced international norms on specific climate related matters – such as, for example, emissions from aviation or maritime transport.[23]

Similarly, climate change triggers States' human rights obligations. It is by now widely recognised that climate change affects the enjoyment of virtually all human rights,[24] as well as that measures to respond to climate change can have significant human rights implications. The preamble of the Paris Agreement specifies that parties 'should, when taking action to address climate change, respect, promote and consider their respective obligations on human rights'.[25] The UN Human Rights Council has adopted a series of resolutions emphasising the relevance of human rights obligations to climate change action, and the need to systemically interpret States' obligations and corporate responsibilities in this connection, both at the national and international levels.[26]

[20] United Nations Framework Convention on Climate Change (entered into force 19 June 1993) 1771 UNTS 107 (UNFCCC); Kyoto Protocol to the United Nations Framework Convention on Climate Change (entered into force 16 February 2005) UN Doc FCCC/CP/L7/Add1 (Kyoto Protocol); Paris Agreement (entered into force 4 November 2016) 3156 UNTS 79 (Paris Agreement).

[21] Robin R. Churchill and Geir Ulfstein, 'Autonomous Institutional Arrangements in Multilateral Environmental Agreements: A Little-Noticed Phenomenon in International Law' (2000) 94 AJIL 623; Jutta Brunnée, 'COPing with Consent: Law-Making under Multilateral Environmental Agreements' (2002) 15 LJIL 1.

[22] See for example the review of practice in Rosemary Rayfuse and Shirley Scott, *International Law in the Era of Climate Change* (Edward Elgar 2012); Harro van Asselt, *The Fragmentation of Global Climate Governance: Consequences and Management of Regime Interactions* (Edward Elgar 2014); Annalisa Savaresi, 'Climate Change and Human Rights: Fragmentation, Interplay and Institutional Linkages' in Sébastien Duyck, Sébastien Jodoin, and Alyssa Johl (eds), *Routledge Handbook of Human Rights and Climate Governance* (Routledge, Taylor & Francis Group 2018).

[23] Kyoto Protocol (n 20) art 2(2).

[24] OHCHR, 'Report of the Office of the UN High Commissioner for Human Rights on the Relationship Between Climate Change and Human Rights' (2009) UN Doc A/HRC/10/61 16.

[25] Paris Agreement (n 20) preamble.

[26] The UN Human Rights Council has adopted a series of resolutions, all titled 'Human Rights and Climate Change', UN Docs A/HRC/RES/7/23 (2008); A/HRC/RES/10/4 (2009); A/HRC/RES/18/22 (2011); A/HRC/RES/26/27 (2014); A/HRC/29/15 (2015); A/HRC/RES/32/33 (2016); A/HRC/35/20 (2017); A/HRC/38/4 (2018); A/HRC/RES/41/21 (2019); A/HRC/RES/44/7 (2020); A/HRC/RES/47/24 (2021).

Finally, the body of customary international law includes obligations – such as those associated with the prohibition and prevention of transboundary harm[27] – which are explicitly mentioned amongst the general principles that should guide State parties to the UNFCCC as they set out to achieve the objective and implement the provisions of climate treaties.[28]

### 15.2.2 *Breach of an International Obligation*

Establishing a breach of an international obligation requires careful examination of the content of the obligation and of the particular conditions required for it to be breached. This section provides a few examples, looking specifically at obligations enshrined in customary international law, in international climate change treaties, in other MEAs, and in human rights treaties.

#### 15.2.2.1 Customary International Law Obligations

State obligations as established by customary international law may apply to climate change mitigation and adaptation. A State may, for instance, invoke a breach of the obligation to refrain from causing harm to the territory of another State and/or to areas beyond national jurisdiction. Under customary international law, an applicant State must prove that another State has caused transboundary harm or has breached the related obligation to prevent harm or the associated procedural duties to cooperate and to carry out an environmental impact assessment.[29] In relation to climate change, this requires demonstrating that the applicant State's territory or an area beyond national jurisdiction has suffered significant harm (i.e. loss of life, loss of property, and/or environmental damage) as a result of activities producing greenhouse gas emissions carried out under the jurisdiction or control of the respondent State.

General international law, however, does not provide strict liability for transboundary harm arising from activities that fall within the exercise of a State's sovereign rights.[30] An applicant State would therefore have to identify relevant due diligence obligations which have been breached by the respondent State. The fact that the respondent State has exercised reasonable diligence would be sufficient to exclude

[27] The so-called 'no harm' principle is recognised in both the UNEP 'Declaration of the United Nations Conference on the Human Environment' (1972) UN Doc A/CONF/48/14 (Stockholm Declaration) principle 21 and United Nations 'Declaration of the United Nations Conference on Environment and Development' (1992) 31 ILM 874 (Rio Declaration) principle 2. The International Court of Justice has acknowledged the customary international law status of the no harm principle in *Legality of the Threat or Use of Nuclear Weapons* (Advisory Opinion) [1996] ICJ Rep 226, 241–242 [29].

[28] UNFCCC (n 20) art 3(a).

[29] As noted also in Daniel Bodansky, Jutta Brunnée, and Lavanya Rajamani, *International Climate Change Law* (Oxford University Press 2017) 45.

[30] Alan Boyle, 'Globalising Environmental Liability: The Interplay of National and International Law' (2005) 17 JEL 3, 6.

responsibility under international law, even if some significant harm has been suffered. Thus, an applicant State should provide proof that the respondent State has not put in place adequate procedures to assess and predict risks, to measure their probability and gravity, and to prevent and mitigate any harm.[31] In international adjudication, therefore, ascertaining compliance with the obligation of due diligence to prevent, reduce, or control transboundary harm typically places a heavy burden of proof on prospective litigants to identify flaws in the discharge of due diligence obligations that are broadly worded and imprecise.[32] States may, however, turn to the obligations enshrined in international environmental or human rights treaties, which substantiate what a State is expected to do in greater detail, as the next sections explain.

#### 15.2.2.2 International Environmental Obligations

International climate treaties typically include obligations of conduct and obligations of result, which may be used to determine the contours of the general obligation to refrain from causing harm to the territory of another State and/or to areas beyond national jurisdiction. For example, Parties to the Paris Agreement must periodically prepare, communicate, and maintain plans – so-called 'nationally determined contributions' (NDCs) – detailing how they intend to reduce emissions and by how much, in order to contribute to holding the increase in the global average temperature to well below 2°C above pre-industrial levels and pursuing efforts to limit the temperature increase to 1.5°C.[33] NDCs are therefore a crucial resource to assess State parties' conduct under the climate treaties. The Paris Agreement requires parties to periodically submit revised NDCs,[34] and failure to submit a revised NDC may be regarded as a breach of a State's obligations of conduct under the Paris Agreement.

The substantive content of NDCs may be scrutinised in the context of parameters embedded in the Paris Agreement.[35] For example, the principle of 'highest possible ambition'[36] may be interpreted as a due diligence standard that requires States to

31 ibid.

32 Christina Voigt, 'State Responsibility for Climate Change Damages' (2008) 77 Nordic Journal of International Law 4; Bodansky, Brunnée, and Rajamani (n 29) 45.

33 Paris Agreement (n 20) art 2(1)(a).

34 UNFCCC, Adoption of the Paris Agreement, FCCC/CP/2015/10/Add.1 (29 January 2016) [25] says: 'Parties shall submit to the secretariat their nationally determined contributions referred to in Article 4 of the Agreement at least 9 to 12 months in advance of the relevant session of the Conference of the Parties serving as the meeting of the Parties to the Paris Agreement'. COP26 was expected to take place in November 2020, so the deadline envisioned in this decision has passed already. Only a handful of parties, however, have submitted their revised NDCs. See NDC Registry (*UNFCCC*) <www.unfccc.int/sites/ndcstaging/Pages/LatestSubmissions.aspx> accessed 24 February 2024.

35 Alan Boyle, 'Progressive Development of International Environmental Law: Legislate or Litigate?' (2019) 62 GYIL 305, 337.

36 Paris Agreement (n 20) art 4(3).

act proportionately in line with the risk at stake and the means at their disposal.[37] Scientists have repeatedly warned that the level of ambition embedded in NDCs submitted to date is insufficient to secure the achievement of the temperature goal envisioned in the Paris Agreement.[38] By and large, most extant NDCs do not adequately consider and mitigate the risk of harm to the territory of other States and to areas beyond national jurisdiction. NDCs that do not adequately contribute to the achievement of the temperature goal enshrined in the Paris Agreement may be regarded as a breach of a State's obligations under that treaty.

Finally, international environmental obligations concerning the prevention of some specific forms of harm may also be invoked in the context of climate litigation. For example, the UN Convention on the Law of the Sea (UNCLOS) makes parties responsible for regulating and controlling the risk of marine pollution resulting from the activities of the private sector through an obligation of due diligence.[39] In fulfilling their obligations, UNCLOS parties are required to take into account 'internationally agreed rules, standards and recommended practices and procedures'.[40] The due diligence obligations derived from UNCLOS may be read in light of obligations enshrined in climate treaties as well as decisions and guidance provided by their treaty bodies.[41] Therefore, NDCs may be used as a yardstick to ascertain whether UNCLOS State parties are adequately considering and mitigating the risk of harm to the marine environment associated with climate change.

#### 15.2.2.3 International Human Rights Obligations

Applicants in climate lawsuits increasingly invoke State responsibility for breaches of international obligations concerning the protection of human rights.[42] This trend is part and parcel of a consolidated jurisprudential tradition, whereby a State's human rights obligations are interpreted to encompass the duty to prevent and reduce environmental harm that interferes with the full enjoyment of human rights, providing for remedies for any remaining harm.[43] The obligation to protect human rights

37 See Chapter 9 on Duty of Care.

38 UNEP, 'The Emissions Gap Report 2021' (*UNEP*, 2021) <www.unep.org/resources/emissions-gap-report-2021> accessed 24 February 2024.

39 United Nations Convention on the Law of the Sea (entered into force 16 November 1994) 1833 UNTS 3 (UNCLOS) arts 192–194; Alan Boyle, 'Litigating Climate Change under Part XII of the LOSC' (2019) IJMCL 458, 465.

40 ibid arts 207(1), 212.

41 Boyle, 'Litigating Climate Change under Part XII of the LOSC' (n 39) 466.

42 Jacqueline Peel and Hari M. Osofsky, 'A Rights Turn in Climate Change Litigation?' (2018) 7 TEL 37; Annalisa Savaresi and Juan Auz, 'Climate Change Litigation and Human Rights: Pushing the Boundaries' (2019) 9 Climate Law 244; Annalisa Savaresi and Joana Setzer, 'Rights-Based Litigation in the Climate Emergency: Mapping the Landscape and New Knowledge Frontiers' (2022) 13 JHRE 7.

43 See the analysis of practice in Report of the Special Rapporteur on the Issue of Human Rights Obligations Relating to the Enjoyment of a Safe, Clean, Healthy and Sustainable Environment UN Doc A/HRC/37/59 (2018).

does not require States to prohibit all activities that may cause environmental harm. Instead, States have discretion to strike a balance between environmental protection and other legitimate societal interests. As both the first and the second Special Rapporteur on human rights and the environment have noted, however, this balance must not be 'unjustifiable or unreasonable' or result in unjustified, foreseeable infringements on human rights.[44]

Over the years, judicial and quasi-judicial international human rights bodies have developed a rich practice providing remedies affording relief to victims of human rights abuses, drawing on the law of State responsibility and domestic jurisprudence.[45] Even if human rights treaties are not designed to protect the environment as such – and only some expressly guarantee a right to a safe, clean, healthy, and sustainable environment – human rights bodies have increasingly awarded indirect protection to environmental interests, insofar as they are linked to the enjoyment of human rights.[46] The unique supernational remedies provided by international human rights instruments have been increasingly used also as a means to bridge the compliance and accountability gaps that characterise environmental governance. And even when they do not have the power to award remedies, these bodies exert influence over domestic judicial practice interpreting the scope and content of human rights obligations.[47] As Section 15.3 of this chapter shows, in recent years, this practice has become apparent with regard to climate change.[48]

Human rights bodies generally recommend that States strike an appropriate balance between evidential burdens of proof between the claimant and the defendant, whereby account is taken of the differences in power and capacity of the parties.[49] According to the Committee on Economic, Social and Cultural Rights, for example, 'shifting the burden of proof may be justified where the facts and events relevant for resolving a claim lie wholly or in part within the exclusive knowledge of the corporate defendant'.[50] As Section 15.3 of this chapter shows in greater detail, this interpretation of the evidential burden of proof is yet another reason why climate applicants increasingly resort to human rights arguments.

44 ibid 33.

45 Dinah Shelton, *Remedies in International Human Rights Law* (Oxford University Press 2015) 2.

46 See for example Inter-American Commission on Human Rights, 'Indigenous and Tribal Peoples' Rights over Their Ancestral Lands and Natural Resources – Norms and Jurisprudence of the Inter-American Human Rights System' (Inter-American Commission on Human Rights 2009) OEA/Ser.L/V/II; 'Manual on Human Rights and the Environment', (*Council of Europe*, 2022) <https://rm.coe.int/manual-environment-3rd-edition/1680a56197> accessed 24 February 2024.

47 Shelton (n 45) 91.

48 See the review in Riccardo Luporini and Annalisa Savaresi, 'International Human Rights Bodies and Climate Litigation: Don't Look Up?' (2023) 32(2) RECIEL 267.

49 OHCHR, 'Improving Accountability and Access to Remedy for Victims of Business-Related Human Rights Abuse' (2016) UN Doc A/HRC/32/19 12.

50 UN Committee on Economic, Social and Cultural Rights, 'General Comment No 24 (2017) on State Obligations under the International Covenant on Economic, Social and Cultural Rights in the Context of Business Activities' (10 August 2017) UN Doc E/C.12/GC/24 [45].

### 15.2.3 *The Breach is Attributable to a State*

The law on State responsibility includes rules of attribution of conduct of persons or entities to a State.[51] In the case of a plurality of responsible States, the general rule is that each State is separately responsible for conduct attributable to it.[52]

Attributing breaches of obligations enshrined in climate treaties can be relatively straightforward. For example, submitting NDCs is a formalised process that clearly entails State agency. Therefore, if a State omits to submit an NDC, or submits a wholly inadequate NDC, these actions and omissions can be attributed to said State. It seems in other words unlikely that, in instances such as these, State agency may come under dispute.

Climate lawsuits frequently allege human rights violations associated with the emissions produced on the territory of the respondent States, or as a result of activities carried out on the State's territory, which in turn are predicted to have an effect on global climate.[53] In both cases, the State's responsibility arises from failure to regulate a hazardous activity within its jurisdiction or control.

While traditional interpretations of human rights treaties have often equated the scope of a State party's jurisdiction with the State's territory,[54] human rights bodies have progressively recognised the extraterritorial reach of a State's human rights obligations.[55] In a groundbreaking Advisory Opinion, the Inter-American Court of Human Rights (IACtHR) has suggested that States have the obligation to prevent any significant environmental harm inside or outside their territory, produced by themselves or third parties within their jurisdiction.[56] According to the Court, when transboundary harm or damage occurs, a person is under the jurisdiction of the State from which the harm originated if there is a causal link between a conduct that occurred within the territory of that State and the negative impact on the human rights of persons outside the territory of that State.[57]

51 ILC Draft Articles (n 2) arts 4–11.

52 ibid art 47(3).

53 See for example the Writ of Summons in *Greenpeace Nordic Association v Ministry of Petroleum and Energy* (Oslo District Court) (*People v Arctic Oil District Court*) [35]–[36]. All documents of the case can be found at <https://climatecasechart.com/non-us-case/greenpeace-nordic-assn-and-nature-youth-v-norway-ministry-of-petroleum-and-energy/> accessed 24 February 2024. See also the review of practice in Savaresi and Setzer (n 42).

54 The ICJ has recognised that the International Covenant on Civil and Political Rights applies extraterritorially, in specific circumstances in *Legal Consequences of the Construction of a Wall in the Occupied Palestinian Territory* (Advisory Opinion) [2004] ICJ Rep 136 [107]–[113].

55 UNHR Committee, 'Views Adopted by the Committee under Article 5(4) of the Optional Protocol, concerning Communication No 052/1979', 29 July 1981 (UN Doc CCPR/C/13/D/52/1979 (*Sergio Euben Lopez Burgos*) [12.3]; *The Environment and Human Rights (State Obligations in Relation to the Environment in the Context of the Protection and Guarantee of the Rights to Life and to Personal Integrity – Interpretation and Scope of Articles 4(1) and 5(1) of the American Convention on Human Rights)*, Advisory Opinion OC-23, Inter-American Court of Human Rights Series A No 23 (15 November 2017) (IACtHR OC-23/17).

56 ibid IACtHR OC-23/17 [59].

57 ibid [140].

### 15.2.4 *Injured State/Erga Omnes Obligations*

Under international law, a State needs to be specifically affected by a breach of an international obligation to invoke the law of State responsibility, most commonly because the wrongful act was committed against its citizens or on its territory.[58] States that are particularly vulnerable to the adverse effects of climate change are already singled out in the climate treaties as deserving special attention and support and benefit from special treatment.[59] These States could therefore claim to be injured by breaches of international obligations due to human rights violations suffered by their citizens as a result of climate change.

Alternatively, any State may invoke the responsibility of another State for a breach of *erga omnes partes* obligations. For example, some human rights obligations – like the prohibition of torture – are *erga omnes*.[60] Furthermore, some obligations arising from the Paris Agreement – such as, for example, that to submit an NDC – may be regarded as *erga omnes partes*.[61]

## 15.3 STATE OF AFFAIRS

### 15.3.1 *International Practice*

While the possibility to instigate an international dispute alleging State responsibility for a breach of an international obligation concerning climate change has been at the centre of much scholarly speculation, no such litigation has materialised so far. At the time of writing, however, three parallel initiatives concerning the request of an advisory opinion on climate change from international courts are underway.[62] Advisory opinions 'constitute *advice*' and 'do not legally bind either the requesting entity or any other body or State to take any specific action pursuant to the opinion'.[63] Even so, advisory opinions might provide crucial guidance to better define the contours of States' obligation of due diligence to prevent, reduce, or control transboundary harm associated with climate change.

In the first initiative, the Pacific Island State of Vanuatu has launched a campaign to seek an advisory opinion from the ICJ, with a view 'to clarify[ing] the legal

[58] Kolb (n 14) 196.

[59] UNFCCC (n 20) preamble, arts 3(2), 4(3), and 4(10); Paris Agreement (n 20) preamble, arts 7(2),(5),(6),(9), 9(4), and 11(1).

[60] Margaretha Wewerinke-Singh, *State Responsibility, Climate Change and Human Rights under International Law* (Hart Publishing 2019) 160.

[61] See Chapter 12 on International Law.

[62] Annalisa Savaresi and others, 'Beyond COP26: Time for an Advisory Opinion on Climate Change?' (*EJIL: Talk!*, 17 December 2021) <www.ejiltalk.org/beyond-cop26-time-for-an-advisory-opinion-on-climate-change/> accessed 24 February 2024.

[63] Hugh Thirlway, 'The International Court of Justice' in Malcolm Evans (ed), *International Law* (Oxford University Press 2014) 589.

obligations of all countries to prevent and redress the adverse effects of climate change'.[64] The proposed questions are:

> (1) What are the obligations of States under international law to ensure the protection of the climate system and other parts of the environment from anthropogenic emissions of greenhouse gases for present and future generations?;
> (2) What are the legal consequences under these obligations for States which, by their acts and omissions, have caused significant harm to the climate system and other parts of the environment, with respect to:
> (a) States, including, in particular, small island developing States, which, due to their geographical circumstances and level of development, are injured or specially affected by or are particularly vulnerable to the adverse effects of climate change?
> (b) Peoples and individuals of the present and future generations affected by the adverse effects of climate change?[65]

In March 2023, the proponents secured support for a formal request for an advisory opinion by the UN General Assembly, as required by the UN Charter.[66]

In the second initiative, the Commission of Small Island States on Climate Change and International Law[67] has sought an advisory opinion from the International Tribunal on the Law of the Sea.[68] As noted earlier, while the UNCLOS does not deal with greenhouse gases specifically, these gases may be regarded as pollutants, falling within the scope of parties' due diligence obligations to regulate and control the risk of marine pollution.[69] The questions before the court are:

> What are the specific obligations of State Parties to the United Nations Convention on the Law of the Sea (the 'UNCLOS'),

[64] 'Pacific Firm to Lead Global Legal Team Supporting Vanuatu's Pursuit of Advisory Opinion on Climate Change from International Court of Justice' (*Blue Ocean Law*, 23 October 2021) <www.blueoceanlaw.com/blog/pacific-firm-to-lead-global-legal-team-supporting-vanuatus-pursuit-of-advisory-opinion-on-climate-change-from-international-court-of-justice> accessed 24 February 2024.

[65] The text of the adopted UNGA resolution is available at <www.vanuatuicj.com/resolution> accessed 24 February 2024.

[66] Under art 96(a) of the Charter of the United Nations, '[t]he General Assembly or the Security Council may request the International Court of Justice to give an advisory opinion on any legal question'. Charter of the United Nations (entered into force 24 October 1945) XV UNCIO 335, amendments in 557 UNTS 143, 638 UNTS 308 and 892 UNTS 119.

[67] Agreement for the Establishment of the Commission of Small Island States on Climate Change and International Law (entered into force 31 October 2021) 61(5) ILM 739.

[68] The tribunal may give an advisory opinion 'if an international agreement related to the purposes of the [UN Convention on the Law of the Sea] specifically provides for the submission to the Tribunal of a request for such an opinion'. See UNCLOS (n 39) Annex VI art 21.

[69] ibid arts 192–194. See Boyle, 'Litigating Climate Change under Part XII of the LOSC' (n 39) 464.

(a) to prevent, reduce and control pollution of the marine environment in relation to the deleterious effects that result or are likely to result from climate change, including through ocean warming and sea level rise, and ocean acidification, which are caused by anthropogenic greenhouse gas emissions into the atmosphere?
(b) to protect and preserve the marine environment in relation to climate change impacts, including ocean warming and sea level rise, and ocean acidification?[70]

The tribunal has invited selected international organisations and stakeholders to present written statements and held hearings in September 2023.[71]

Finally, in January 2023, Chile and Colombia asked the IACtHR for an advisory opinion on climate change and human rights, with a view to support a fair, sustainable, and timely response to the climate emergency, taking into account the obligations arising from international human rights law.

The guidance delivered as a result of these requests for an advisory opinion would be particularly helpful in the context of climate litigation before domestic and regional courts, where arguments concerning the breach of international obligations are increasingly made.

In the meantime, some human rights-based complaints related to climate change have already been brought before international *quasi-judicial* (namely, the UN Human Rights Committee,[72] the Committee on the Rights of the Child[73]) and *non-judicial* human rights bodies (namely, various Special Procedures of the Human Rights Council).[74] The vast majority of these complaints remain pend-

70 *Request for an Advisory Opinion submitted by the Commission of Small Island States on Climate Change and International Law (Request for Advisory Opinion submitted to the Tribunal)* (12 December 2022) <www.itlos.org/en/main/cases/list-of-cases/request-for-an-advisory-opinion-submitted-by-the-commission-of-small-island-states-on-climate-change-and-international-law-request-for-advisory-opinion-submitted-to-the-tribunal/> accessed 24 February 2024.

71 *Request for an Advisory Opinion submitted by the Commission of Small Island States on Climate Change and International Law (Request for Advisory Opinion submitted to the Tribunal)* (Order of 16 December 2022) <www.itlos.org/fileadmin/itlos/documents/cases/31/C31_Order_2022-4_16.12.2022_01.pdf> accessed 24 February 2024.

72 UNHR Committee, 'Views Adopted by the Committee under Article 5(4) of the Optional Protocol, concerning Communication No 2728/2016', 24 October 2019 UN Doc CCPR/C/127/D/2728/2016 *(Teitiota)*; UNHR Committee, 'Views Adopted by the Committee under Article 5(4) of the Optional Protocol, concerning Communication No 3624/2019', 21 July 2022, UN Doc CCPR/C/135/D/3624/2019 (*Billy*).

73 UN Committee on the Rights of the Child, 'Decision Adopted by the Committee under the Optional Protocol to the Convention on the Rights of the Child on a Communications Procedure, concerning Communication No 104/2019', UN Doc CRC/C/88/D/104/2019 (*Sacchi*).

74 Rights of Indigenous People in Addressing Climate-Forced Displacement, AL-USA 16/20 <http://climatecasechart.com/non-us-case/rights-of-indigenous-people-in-addressing-climate-forced-displacement> accessed 24 February 2024 (*Five tribes*); Violations of human rights by Federation of Bosnia Herzegovina (BiH) and China due to coal fired plants in BiH, AL BIH 2/2021 and AL CHN 2/2021 <https://climatecasechart.com/non-us-case/violations-of-human-rights-by-to-federation-of-bosnia-herzegovina-bih-and-china-due-to-coal-fired-plants-in-bih/> accessed 24 February 2024 (*Coal fired plants*); *Environmental Justice Australia v Australia* <https://climatecasechart.com/non-us-case/environmental-justice-australia-eja-v-australia/ (*Environmental Justice*).

ing or have failed to reach adjudication on the merits due to admissibility constraints.[75] Three important decisions have already been issued.

In *Teitiota*, one asylum seeker lodged a complaint with the UN Human Rights Committee against New Zealand. He alleged that New Zealand's refusal to grant him asylum threatened the enjoyment of his right to life, as a result of risks associated with climate change-induced displacement. The Committee found that the applicant's complaint did not concern 'a hypothetical future harm, but a real predicament' and that 'the risk of a violation of the right to life had been sufficiently substantiated'.[76] It nevertheless rejected the complaint at the merits stage,[77] as it was not satisfied that the applicant would have been personally affected by a serious individualised risk should he be sent back to Kiribati.[78] The Committee reasoned that only in 'extreme cases' can it find a violation of the non-refoulement obligation stemming from the right to life based on a situation of 'a serious and generalized risk' in the country of origin. According to the Committee, the general situation in Kiribati did not qualify as an extreme case, as the country could, with the assistance of the international community, 'take affirmative measures to protect and, where necessary, relocate its population'.[79] Even though the complaint was unsuccessful, the UN Human Rights Committee's reasoning concerning State obligations vis-à-vis threats to life associated with climate change is important to determine the scope of a State's obligations under human rights law. The Committee acknowledged that climate change constitutes 'one of the most pressing and serious threats to the ability of present and future generations to enjoy the right to life'[80] and that the effects of climate change may expose individuals to a violation of their rights under the Covenant, 'thereby triggering the non-refoulement obligations of sending States'.[81] The Committee's reasoning has already made strides in domestic judicial practice. In 2021, the Italian Court of Cassation cited the Committee's decision in *Teitiota*, asserting that national judges should consider environmental or climate degradation that may put at risk personal dignity of asylum seekers in the country of origin.[82]

In *Sacchi et al*, a group of children from multiple countries filed a complaint before the Committee on the Rights of the Child against multiple States. They lamented that the defendant States had breached their rights to life, health, culture, and best interest of the child, as a result of failure to adopt adequate measures for climate change mitigation.[83] Although their complaint was dismissed at the

75 See Chapter 5 on Admissibility.
76 *Teitiota* (n 72) [8.5].
77 ibid [9.9].
78 ibid.
79 ibid [9.11].
80 ibid [9.4].
81 ibid [9.11].
82 See *IL v Italian Ministry of the Interior and Attorney General at the Court of Appeal of Ancona*, Ordinance No 5022/2021 (Corte Suprema di Cassazione).
83 *Sacchi* (n 73) [260]–[275].

admissibility stage due to lack of exhaustion of domestic remedies, the Committee's reasoning concerning the scope of the respondent States' jurisdiction is particularly important. The respondent States had argued that the applicants were not within their jurisdiction. The Committee rejected this argument, applying the IACtHR's reasoning mentioned earlier. It noted that emissions originating in the respondent States contribute to climate change and that the adverse effects thereof have implications on the enjoyment of human rights by individuals 'both within as well as *beyond the territory of the State party*'.[84] The Committee noted that, due to their ability to adopt and enforce regulations on emitting activities, the respondent States had 'effective control' over the source of the harm.[85] The Committee established that, under the principle of common but differentiated responsibilities and respective capabilities, every State is responsible for its own share of greenhouse gas emissions, as the collective nature of the problem does not absolve individual States of their responsibility for 'the harm that the emissions originating within its territory may cause to children, *whatever their location*'.[86] The Committee noted that the transboundary harm at the centre of the applicants' complaint was foreseeable, due to the scientific evidence on climate change impacts and the fact that the respondent States had signed international treaties on climate change.[87]

Finally, in *Daniel Billy*, Australian indigenous peoples alleged violations of the right to culture, right to privacy, family, and home, and right to life, as a result of Australia's failure to take adequate measures to mitigate and adapt to climate change. The UN Human Rights Committee granted their complaint only with regard to Australia's lack of timely and adequate action over climate change adaptation. The Committee found that the applicants had provided sufficient information on how they had personally been affected by the impacts of climate change.[88] It asserted that Australia had failed to comply with its positive obligation to protect the applicants' home, their private and family life, and their collective ability to maintain a traditional way of life and to transmit their customs and culture to future generations.[89] As in *Teitiota*, however, the Committee did not find a violation of the right to life, as the applicants had not demonstrated a concrete and reasonably foreseeable risk that their life would be exposed to, or the effects that climate change had already had on their health. Instead, the Committee emphasised that, in the period of time in which the islands would allegedly become uninhabitable, Australia could undertake preventive measures and, if necessary, relocate the applicants.[90]

84 ibid [10.9]–[11] (emphasis added).
85 ibid [10.9].
86 ibid [10.10] (emphasis added).
87 ibid [10.11].
88 *Billy* (n 72) [7.10].
89 ibid [8.9]–[8.14].
90 ibid [8.7].

### 15.3.2 *Regional Practice*

Regional human rights bodies, too, have been increasingly asked to consider complaints concerning climate change.[91] At the time of writing, fourteen climate complaints have been filed before regional human rights bodies[92] – ten with the European Court of Human Rights (ECtHR),[93] three with the and the Inter-American Commission on Human Rights,[94] and one with the European Committee of Social Rights.[95]

These applications build on the consolidated case law of the ECtHR and IACtHR on environmental matters and typically rely on the human rights that these courts have over the years identified as relevant to the protection of environmental interests – such as the right to life, the right to respect for private and family life, home and correspondence, the rights of indigenous peoples – especially, those to culture and to communal property – and procedural rights associated with access to participation, information, justice, and remedies.[96]

In the only complaint that has been adjudicated on the merits to date – *Marangopoulos Foundation for Human Rights (MFHR) against Greece* – the applicants lamented breaches of their right to health, as a result of the operation of lignite mining. The case therefore addressed climate change concerns only indirectly. The European Committee of Social Rights declared that Greece had not applied legislation satisfactorily and had not provided sufficiently precise

[91] Peel and Osofsky (n 42); Savaresi and Auz (n 42); César Rodríguez-Garavito, *Litigating the Climate Emergency: The Global Rise of Human Rights-Based Litigation for Climate Action* (Cambridge University Press 2022); Savaresi and Setzer (n 42); Luporini and Savaresi (n 48).

[92] This data was compiled as of 30 September 2022 consulting the databases curated by the Sabin Center for Climate Change Law at Columbia Law School <http://climatecasechart.com/> accessed 24 February 2024 and by the Grantham Research Institute on Climate Change and the Environment at the London School of Economics <www.climate-laws.org> accessed 24 February 2024. For a review of this data, see Luporini and Savaresi (n 48).

[93] *Duarte Agostinho v Portugal and 32 other States* App No 39371/20 (ECtHR); *Verein KlimaSeniorinnen Schweiz and Others v Switzerland* App No 53600/20 (ECtHR); *Müllner v Austria* App No 18859/21 (ECtHR); *Greenpeace Nordic and others v Norway* App No 34068/21 (ECtHR); *Carême v France* App No 7189/21 (ECtHR); *Uricchio v Italy and others* App No 14165/21 ECtHR); *De Conto v Italy and others* App No 14620/21 (ECtHR); *Soubeste and Others v Austria and 11 other states* App Nos 3195/22, 31932/22, 31938/22, 31943/22, and 31947/22 (ECtHR); *Plan B Earth and others v the United Kingdom*, not communicated ('*Plan B Earth*'); *Humane Being v the United Kingdom*, not communicated ('*Humane Being*').

[94] Petition To the Inter-American Commission on Human Rights Seeking Relief from Violations Resulting from Global Warming Caused by Acts and Omissions of the United States, [2005] Inter-American Commission on Human Rights 1413-05. The Commission dismissed the petition at a very initial phase with a letter to the petitioner. See also Petition Seeking Relief from Violations of the Rights of Arctic Athabaskan Peoples Resulting from Rapid Arctic Warming and Melting Caused by Emissions of Black Carbon by Canada, [2013] Inter-American Commission on Human Rights.

[95] *Marangopoulos Foundation for Human Rights (MFHR) v Greece* (Decision on the Merits) (6 December 2006), ECSR Complaint No 30/2005, Resolution CM/ResChS (2008).

[96] For a review of these, see Luporini and Savaresi (n 48).

information and screening of the health hazards related to lignite mining. The Committee cited the International Law Commission Articles on the Responsibility of States for Internationally Wrongful Acts,[97] which provide that, when a State is under an international obligation to take preventive action against a certain event, but fails to do so, the State remains in breach over the entire period during which the event continues. Consequently, the Committee considered that the issues raised in the complaint constituted a breach of the obligation to prevent damage arising from air pollution for as long as the pollution continued, and that the breach might even be compounded progressively, if no sufficient measures were taken to put an end to it.[98]

### 15.3.3 *Domestic Case Law*

As noted earlier, international law obligations have become a common yardstick that domestic courts use to ascertain the lawfulness and adequacy of national law measures to tackle climate change and their impacts, and lack thereof. There is by now a rather long series of climate cases in which national courts rely on a combination of national and international law to order State authorities to take more ambitious action on climate change mitigation or adaptation.[99] These judgments variably rely on a blend of tort, public, or human rights law obligations, interpreted and reviewed in light of international law obligations.[100] Admittedly, this is a rather artificial distinction, given that in most cases the courts rely on multiple legal grounds to justify their findings. Nevertheless, some commonalities between successful climate cases concerning State responsibility do exist. These judgments recognise that State responsibility can be established for failure to adopt laws and policies that adequately deal with the climate emergency. Compliance with international law obligations is used as a yardstick to assess the adequacy of domestic climate law measures. Here we provide some examples of judgments from all over the world, combining international and domestic law arguments, which have delivered decisions favourable to climate applicants.

In *Ashgar Leghari v Federation of Pakistan et al*, Pakistani courts ordered the creation of a Climate Change Commission, tasked to monitor the implementation of the National Climate Change Policy, as a means to address the grievance of a farmer, who had lamented that lack of enforcement of existing national policies on climate change adaptation had breached his human rights.[101] The court relied on Pakistan's

[97] Specifically, ILC Draft Articles (n 2) art 14 on extension in time of a breach of an international obligation.

[98] *MFHR v Greece* (n 95) [193].

[99] See the review of practice in Maxwell and others (n 7) 37.

[100] ibid.

[101] *Asghar Leghari v Federation of Pakistan etc* PLD 2018 Lahore 364 [11].

international environmental obligations, read in conjunction with established case law deriving the right to a healthy environment from extant constitutional rights.[102]

In *Salamanca Mancera v Presidencia de la República de Colombia*,[103] Colombian courts ordered the government to stop deforestation in the Amazon, finding that the State had breached the human rights of the young applicants, as well as its obligations under international climate treaties.[104]

In *Commune de Grande-Synthe v France*,[105] the French Council of State found that the French government's failure to reduce greenhouse gas emissions violated its duty of care. The court relied on the French Civil Code's provisions concerning tortious liability for environmental damage and construed the State's duty on the basis of international obligations enshrined in the European Convention of Human Rights and in the Paris Agreement.

In *Neubauer and others v Germany*, the German Constitutional Court formulated the State's duty to align climate laws with the best available climate science,[106] in light of international law obligations enshrined in the Paris Agreement.[107] According to the Court, the duty to protect arising from constitutional rights and the obligation to take climate action 'possesses a special international dimension'.[108] The Court specifically pointed to the necessity to implement a State's own climate measures at the national level and not to create incentives for other States to undermine international cooperation.

In *re Greenpeace Southeast Asia and Others*, the Commission on Human Rights of the Philippines carried out an inquiry on the impact of climate change on the human rights of the Filipino people, and on the role of the so-called Carbon Majors in this regard. The Commission asserted that States' obligations to respect, protect, and fulfil human rights require them to adopt and implement measures to prevent human rights violations, including those carried out by non-State actors.[109] The Commission relied on the IACtHR's Advisory Opinion to affirm that States have the responsibility to ensure that activities under their jurisdiction do not interfere with the enjoyment of human rights of people outside their jurisdiction.[110] It further noted that, for the purposes of finding that a State is in violation of its human right obligations in the context of climate change, 'it is sufficient to establish the absence

[102] ibid [7].

[103] *Salamanca Mancera and others v Presidencia de la República de Colombia and others*, 29 January 2018 (Tribunal Superior de Bogotá) [5.2]–[5.6].

[104] ibid [17].

[105] *Commune de Grande-Synthe v France* [2020] N°427301 (Conseil d'Etat) (*Grande-Synthe*).

[106] *Neubauer and Others v Germany* [2021] 1 BvR 2656/18, 1 BvR 96/20, 1 BvR 78/20, 1 BvR 288/20, 1 BvR 96/20, 1 BvR 78/20 (German Federal Constitutional Court) (*Neubauer*).

[107] ibid [211].

[108] ibid [149], [199].

[109] *In re Greenpeace Southeast Asia and Others* [2022] Case No CHR-NI-2016-0001 (Commission on Human Rights of the Philippines).

[110] ibid [72]–[73].

of meaningful State resolve and action to address the major anthropogenic actors and factors driving global warming'.[111]

The Dutch courts have, however, made the most consequential statements regarding State responsibility for climate change, in the judgments in *Urgenda Foundation v the State of the Netherlands*.[112] While *Urgenda* is examined in greater detail elsewhere in this Handbook,[113] for the purposes of the present chapter, these judgments delivered the following key findings. First, international law obligations are relevant to determine the contours of the State's responsibility for climate change under domestic law; and second, domestic courts may order State authorities to address a breach of an international obligation.

The Dutch courts defined the contours of the State's responsibility under domestic law, in light of obligations enshrined in international law. Under the Dutch Constitution, provisions of international law that are 'binding on all persons' are directly applicable in national courts.[114] In *Urgenda*, the Dutch Supreme Court found that, because there is a grave risk that dangerous climate change would endanger the lives and welfare of many people in the Netherlands, the State had a responsibility 'to take adequate measures to reduce greenhouse gas emissions from Dutch territory'.[115] This duty to take the 'necessary measures' to mitigate climate change, in accordance with the State's specific responsibilities and capabilities, was construed on the basis of rights enshrined both in the European Convention on Human Rights – a treaty commonly regarded as having direct effect in the Netherlands – and in the UNFCCC and the Paris Agreement – which do not have direct effect.[116] The Court also relied on the no harm principle enshrined in customary international law to find that the Dutch State must take action to prevent harm to other countries arising from climate change, even if they are only partially responsible.[117] The Supreme Court explicitly referenced rules from the International Law Commission's Draft Articles on State Responsibility concerning situations where there are multiple States involved in a breach of an international obligation.[118] Since Urgenda did not claim damages and instead only asked the courts for an order to

[111] ibid [87].

[112] *Urgenda Foundation v The State of The Netherlands* [2015] ECLI:NL:RBDHA:2015:7196 (District Court of the Hague) (*Urgenda District Court*); *State of the Netherlands v Stichting Urgenda* [2018] ECLI:NL:GHDHA:2018:2591 (Court of Appeal) (*Urgenda Court of Appeal*); *State of the Netherlands (Ministry of Economic Affairs and Climate Policy) v Stichting Urgenda* [2019] ECLI:NL:HR:2019:2007 (Supreme Court of the Netherlands) *(Urgenda Supreme Court)*.

[113] See e.g. Chapter 7 on Human Rights and Chapter 9 on Duty of Care.

[114] Constitution of the Kingdom of the Netherlands art 93.

[115] *Urgenda Supreme Court* (n 112) [6.1].

[116] André Nollkaemper and Laura Burgers, 'A New Classic in Climate Litigation: The Dutch Supreme Court Decision in the Urgenda Case' (*EJIL: Talk!*, 6 January 2020) <www.ejiltalk.org/a-new-classic-in-climate-change-litigation-the-dutch-supreme-court-decision-in-the-urgenda-case> accessed 24 February 2024.

[117] *Urgenda Supreme Court* (n 112) [5.7.9].

[118] ibid [5.7.5]–[5.7.6].

perform an obligation, the Supreme Court did not explore how multiple States should share reparation or compensation in relation to climate change. Still, the Court emphasised that the fact that other States fail to meet their responsibility is no ground for the State not to perform its obligations.[119]

The Supreme Court also found that the fact that Dutch emissions are relatively modest is no ground for non-performance. Otherwise, a State could simply avoid responsibility by pointing to the responsibility of other nations for emissions.[120] The Court suggested that no single reduction is negligible, since every reduction has a positive effect in diminishing dangerous climate change.[121] As noted in other chapters of this Handbook,[122] the Dutch judges specifically rejected the 'drop in the ocean' defence put forward by the government, noting that 'Urgenda does not have the option to summon all eligible States to appear in a Dutch court'.[123] The Court of Appeal established that causality 'only plays a limited role' when the matter of the dispute is not the award of damages.[124] Instead, the Court reasoned, when damages are not at stake, 'a real risk' of a danger for which measures must be taken is sufficient for a complaint to be admissible.[125]

## 15.4 BEST PRACTICE AND REPLICABILITY

This chapter has considered the extent to which climate judgments rely on State responsibility. It illustrated the core elements of this notion in international law and analysed extant international, regional, and national practice. It has shown that domestic courts have established State responsibility on several occasions, relying on multiple legal grounds to justify their findings, including by reading tort, human rights, or constitutional law in light of international law. There are commonalities between successful climate cases invoking State responsibility. The applicants typically argue that the State's climate laws or policies concerning mitigation are either not ambitious enough or not adequately implemented. Judicial and non-judicial bodies alike have rejected the 'drop in the ocean' arguments and recognised that State responsibility can be established, for failure to adopt laws and policies that adequately deal with climate change. Not only are these decisions replicable, but, as more and more States adopt climate legislation, litigation demanding greater alignment between international law obligations and national legislation is likely to become more common.

119 ibid [5.7.7].
120 ibid.
121 ibid [5.7.8].
122 See Chapter 9 on Duty of Care and Chapter 16 on Causation.
123 *Urgenda Supreme Court* (n 112) [64].
124 ibid.
125 ibid.

The *Urgenda* judgments are illustrative of how national courts may rely on the law of State responsibility, and specifically, on breaches of international law – including the European Convention on Human Rights, the UNFCCC, and the Paris Agreement – to order a State to take (better) measures to tackle climate change. Admittedly, making this kind of argumentation is easier in 'monist' States, like the Netherlands, where international law obligations are directly applicable in domestic law.[126] For example, in another monist State, Belgium, domestic courts adjudicated a case that was filed on grounds that were broadly similar to those put forward in the *Urgenda* lawsuits, with similar judicial outcomes.[127] However, as this chapter has already shown, national courts in dualist States have also been willing to accept arguments on State responsibility similar to those made in the *Urgenda* judgments.[128]

At the time of writing, *Daniel Billy* remains the only decision of an international human rights body granting the claims of climate applicants. The decision was construed on the basis of the rights to culture and home, private and family life, and recognised human rights violations resulting from the State's failure to undertake measures to ensure climate change adaptation. The decision has affirmed that States must take adaptation measures to comply with their human rights obligations.[129] The decision, however, has left unaddressed questions over States' human rights obligations concerning mitigation, neither confirming nor disproving the interpretation of these obligations provided in the *Urgenda* judgements.[130]

The judgments and decisions reviewed in this chapter have broken new ground and will continue to inform and influence future judicial practice interpreting the scope and contours of State responsibility. At least with reference to climate change, questions of compliance with domestic and international law may not be very different, after all.

[126] On the relations between international and domestic law, see Eileen Denza, 'The Relationship between International and National Law' in Malcolm Evans (ed), *International Law* (5th ed., Oxford University Press 2018).

[127] *VZW Klimaatzaak v l'État Belge* [2021] 2015/4585/A (Tribunal de première instance francophone de Bruxelles, Section Civile) (*VZW Klimaatzaak First Instance*); *VZW Klimaatzaak v Kingdom of Belgium and Others* [2023] 2022/AR/891(Cour d'appel de Bruxelles) (*VZW Klimaatzaak Appeal*).

[128] See the review of practice in Maxwell and others (n 7).

[129] See e.g. OHCHR, 'Report of the Special Rapporteur on the Issue of Human Rights Obligations Relating to the Enjoyment of a Safe, Clean, Healthy and Sustainable Environment' (2016) UN Doc A/HRC/31/52 68–70; OHCHR, 'Report of the Special Rapporteur on the Issue of Human Rights Obligations Relating to the Enjoyment of a Safe, Clean, Healthy and Sustainable Environment' (2019) UN Doc A/74/161, 84–86; OHCHR, 'Report of the Special Rapporteur on the Promotion and Protection of Human Rights in the Context of Climate Change' (2022) UN Doc A/77/226.

[130] See for example the discussion in Benoit Mayer, 'Climate Change Mitigation as an Obligation under Human Rights Treaties?' (2021) 115 AJIL 409; Corina Heri, 'Climate Change before the European Court of Human Rights: Capturing Risk, Ill-Treatment and Vulnerability' (2022) 33 EJIL 925; Alexander Zahar, 'The Limits of Human Rights Law: A Reply to Corina Heri' (2022) 33 EJIL 953; Riccardo Luporini, 'Strategic Litigation as a Tool to Advance Climate Change Adaptation? Challenges and Prospects' (2023) Yearbook of International Disaster Law Online.

# 16

# Causation

*Lisa Benjamin and Sara Seck*[*]

## 16.1 INTRODUCTION

This chapter covers the legal test of causation and how it has appeared and been adjudicated in climate litigation. The causation test arises in climate litigation most often, but not always, in the guise of a tort-based standard which appears to pervade the approaches of many legal systems to managing climate harms. The definition of causation varies from jurisdiction to jurisdiction but will often involve some required proximity between the actions of the defendant and the harm caused to the plaintiff. Due to the nature of climate change, this proximity has in the past been difficult for plaintiffs to prove. However, as this chapter illustrates, issues of causation can also arise in other areas of law, including legal tests for standing and assessment of remedies for future harms.

The causation test has proven to be one of the major hurdles in some forms of climate litigation. This is particularly so for tort-based climate litigation, where plaintiffs must prove that the defendant's actions caused the plaintiff harm. The traditional approach of tort law in common law countries follows the general 'but for' test: but for the defendant's actions, the plaintiff would not have suffered harm. For example, in the United States (US), tortious conduct must be a factual cause of harm for liability to be imposed. Conduct is a factual cause of harm when the harm would not have occurred absent the conduct.[1] While the test varies between jurisdictions, in most jurisdictions the cause must precede the harm. The legal test for causation usually relies on a preponderance of the evidence or, in some common law jurisdictions, a 50 per cent or more probability that the breach of the duty caused the harm. In civil law jurisdictions, the test of '*conditio sine qua non*' (or

* Lisa Benjamin is an associate professor at Lewis & Clark Law School. Sara Seck is an associate professor at the Schulich School of Law and Marine and Environmental Law Institute at Dalhousie University.

1 American Law Institute, *Restatement of the Law Third, Torts: Liability for Physical and Emotional Harm* (American Law Publishers 2010) s 26.

'without which it could not be') does not have a similar numerical threshold but does require that the court is convinced that a causal link exists.[2]

There are both general and specific elements of causation. General causation relies on the establishment of a cause-and-effect relationship between the act and the harm. In other words, whether the alleged causal factor can cause the *type of effect* from which the plaintiff suffers. Specific causation focuses on the specific harms alleged by the plaintiffs. In other words, whether the alleged causal factors did indeed cause the *particular injury* alleged by the plaintiff.[3] Specific causation involves a larger variety of factors, including the levels, duration, and proximity of exposure.[4]

### 16.1.1 *Causation in the Climate Context*

In the climate context, causation analysis involves highly complex and multi-tiered scientific inquiries about human influence on the climate.[5] Scientific studies usually adopt probabilistic inquiries, which may at first glance be unrecognisable from the traditional legal understanding of tortious causation. On a closer examination, however, there are synergies between climate and legal causation – both involve an assessment of probabilities.

In the climate context, the causal chain is often more extended than in other fields of litigation. Greenhouse gases (GHGs) are mixed in the atmosphere, and it is therefore difficult if not impossible to identify the emissions of one source of GHGs from another. Climate harms result from cumulative and aggregate emissions and the reduction of carbon sinks, making climate change essentially a stock problem. Climate impacts experienced now can be a result of historical emissions; therefore, time is also a factor. Emissions produced decades ago may only now be causing concrete impacts and harms. In addition, emissions made today are likely to contribute to future harms due to the existing stock of historical emissions. The duration between emissions, and the harm those emissions caused, can be problematic in proving specific causation. In addition, it is difficult to identify a specific defendant whose emissions caused specific harm to a specific plaintiff.

[2] Petra Minnerop and Frederike Otto, 'Climate Change Causation: Joining Law and Climate Science on the Basis of Formal Logic' (2020) 27 *Buffalo Environmental Law Journal* 49, 50.

[3] Samantha Lawson, 'The Conundrum of Climate Change Causation: Using Market Share Liability to Satisfy the Identification Requirement in Native Village of Kivalina' (2010) 22 *Fordham Environmental Law Review* 433.

[4] Christopher R. Reeves, 'Climate Change on Trial: Making the Case for Causation' (2009) 32 *American Journal of Trial Advocacy* 495.

[5] Michael Duffy, 'Climate Change Causation: Harmonizing Tort Law and Scientific Probability' (2009) 28 *Temple Journal of Science, Technology & Environmental Law* 185.

Advances in both attribution science and climate science generally are closing these causal gaps. The 2021 Intergovernmental Panel on Climate Change (IPCC) report identified that each 1,000 $GtCO_2$ of cumulative emissions is likely to cause a 0.27°C to 0.63°C increase in global surface temperature with a best estimate of 0.45°C.[6] This is called the 'transient climate response to cumulative $CO_2$ emissions'.[7] In other words, every tonne of $CO_2$ adds to the global warming effect; every emission counts. This finding can bolster broader approaches to causation in climate impact cases.

There are four main elements in the climate-related causal chain.[8] The first is the establishment of the relationship between cumulative GHG emissions in the atmosphere to increases in global mean temperatures. The second is the establishment of the relationship between temperature increases and harmful effects. The third is the attribution of a specific weather event (usually an extreme event) to general warming trends (this is sometimes called 'impact attribution' or 'event attribution'). An additional fourth element is source attribution (attribution of an actor's or project's contributions to global cumulative GHG emissions). Courts sometimes take different approaches to causation on this element, between liability for States as opposed to corporations.

The complex causal relationships described earlier are not always easily accommodated by the law. In Section 16.2, we will discuss how courts have grappled with these complexities. This section also provides background context to the theories of causation in tort law, the connection between causation and standing, and the nexus between causation and human rights claims and attribution science.

Section 16.3 provides an analysis of the state of affairs in climate litigation around causation in different types of cases. The first part of this section focuses on cases requesting redress for past climate harm or past actions (such as the issuance of a permit). As will be seen, some of these cases do not seek remedy for specific climate harms but rather seek to prevent ongoing and future GHG emissions. This focus on prevention is also prevalent in the policy cases discussed in the second part of Section 16.3, all of which request a cessation or reduction of emissions in order to prevent or mitigate future climate harm.

Section 16.4 then sets out what we consider to be emerging best practices in judicial approaches to causation in the climate context. Finally, Section 16.5 considers the replicability of these best practices in other jurisdictions.

6 Richard P. Allen and others, 'IPCC 2021: Summary for Policymakers' in Richard P. Allen and others (eds), *Climate Change 2021: The Physical Science Basis, Contribution of Working Group I to the Sixth Assessment Report of the Intergovernmental Panel on Climate Change* (Cambridge University Press 2021) 36.

7 ibid.

8 Duffy (n 5) 190–201. See Chapter 17 on Climate Causality.

## 16.2 BACKGROUND CONTEXT

### 16.2.1 *Causation in Tort Law*

Tort law is designed to remedy human-based harms. Therefore, taking a broader conceptual approach to the role of tort law and its remedial purpose can make it a more malleable and therefore useful legal concept in climate litigation. There are existing examples of where tort law has adapted in order to provide a fair remedy in complex circumstances. This approach to tort law, and specifically causation in tort law, can also contribute to emerging best practice in climate litigation – discussed in Section 16.4.

Examples of conceptual evolution in tort law related to causation include the recognition of collective harm,[9] where independent tortious actions of multiple defendants produce a single harm, but it is impossible to determine which actions of one or more defendants caused the harm. Another is the market share liability theory, where several defendants produce harmful products but only one caused the harm to a particular plaintiff. Under this theory, if a plaintiff cannot identify one defendant, she can claim against every manufacturer of the harmful products in proportion to its share of the market.[10] Another is the commingling product theory,[11] where multiple independent actors combine and the result of their cumulative products is to produce a single, indivisible harm.

Many of these theories have been developed over time by courts to apply in narrow circumstances, usually where the products are fungible and the plaintiff (through no fault of her own) is unable to identify one or all of the defendants responsible for the harm. Similarly, plaintiffs in climate cases are unable to identify one responsible emitter, due to the nature of GHGs (see Section 16.1.1). Courts could, and some have, expanded or adapted existing theories to accommodate the complex causal relationships involved in climate change. Failure to do so is likely to leave many plaintiffs without remedy. This flexibility is illustrative of emerging best practice and has been adopted in some cases highlighted later.

### 16.2.2 *Causation, Standing, and the Nature of Plaintiffs and Defendants*

Causation arguments arise in other areas of climate litigation beyond torts, such as in relation to the procedural hurdle of standing. It is often necessary to prove some element of causation for the purpose of establishing standing in order to proceed to the merits of the claim. The specific parties granted standing by the court will also impact the nature of the causative inquiry undertaken by the court.

9 Duffy (n 5) 201.

10 See e.g. US cases *Thomas v Mallett* 701 N.W.2d 523 (Supreme Court of Wisconsin 2005); *Fairchild v Glenhaven Funeral Services Ltd* [2002] UKHL 22 in the asbestos context where the UK Supreme Court approved a materially increasing risk of harm test instead of the traditional 'but for' test.

11 Duffy (n 5) 216.

In US federal courts, for example, there are three elements to establish standing: injury, traceability, and redressability. The plaintiff must have suffered an injury in fact, which is fairly traceable to the challenged conduct of the defendant (a causation-type element) and which is likely to be redressed by a favourable judicial decision.[12] An injury in fact must be an injury that is an invasion of a legally protected interest, which is particularised, concrete, and actual or imminent.[13] The injury must be specific to the litigant and not theoretical.

However, cases have confirmed that the injury to be proved for standing does not have to be capable of sustaining a cause of action under tort law, and so the application of causation is separate and apart in a standing analysis. Therefore, a wider variety of injuries is usually accepted by US courts in order to establish standing than might be accepted under tort law, such as aesthetic, emotional, or psychological injuries. An example from the climate litigation world is the *Massachusetts v EPA* case,[14] where the Supreme Court held that Massachusetts had 'special solicitude' as a state, and a sovereign interest in the Environmental Protection Agency (EPA) exercising its authority under the Clean Air Act to regulate GHG emissions.

In another example, in *Funk v Wolf*,[15] a court in Pennsylvania found that the youth plaintiff did have a substantial, direct, and immediate interest. Funk was a 10-year-old who sued the Pennsylvania governor and public utility for failing to develop a comprehensive plan to regulate $CO_2$ emissions. Funk's interest was found to be direct if there is a causal connection between the matter complained of and the harm alleged. The court found that the interest is immediate if the causal connection is not remote or speculative. In this case, Funk's asthma prevented him from going outside and the right to enjoy public natural resources was harmed by ongoing environmental degradation (although the court found that the relief requested by the plaintiff was not redressable).

It can be difficult for an individual plaintiff to establish that they suffered a particularised injury to herself or to her property in the context of climate change that merits remedy. This is a particularly 'live' issue in the human rights context, and especially so for foreign plaintiffs. In the German *Neubauer* case,[16] the Constitutional Court granted standing to German youth complainants as well as complainants living in Nepal and Bangladesh as natural persons claiming duties of protection and violation of their fundamental rights.[17] The Court found that the plaintiffs had established an individual interest to challenge the German government's insufficient climate mitigation targets, despite the fact that many people

[12] US Constitution art 3(2).

[13] *Lujan v Defenders of Wildlife*, 504 US 555 (1992).

[14] *Massachusetts v EPA* 549 US 497 (2007).

[15] *Funk v Wolf* 158 A.3d 642 (Supreme Court of Pennsylvania 2017).

[16] *Neubauer and Others v Germany* [2021] 1 BvR 2656/18, 1 BvR 96/20, 1 BvR 78/20, 1 BvR 288/20, 1 BvR 96/20, 1 BvR 78/20 (German Federal Constitutional Court) (*Neubauer*).

[17] ibid [90], [101].

would be similarly affected by the government's restrictions in the future. The claimants argued that the GHG emissions reduction goals in the Federal Climate Protection Act were insufficient in light of the State's obligations under the Paris Agreement and Germany's constitutional human rights law. The Court observed that climate change 'is a genuinely global phenomenon and could obviously not be stopped by the German State on its own. However, this does not render it impossible or superfluous for Germany to make its own contribution toward climate change'.[18] Nevertheless, the Court ultimately rejected the claims of the complainants from Bangladesh and Nepal, citing in part the limits of German sovereignty under international law which would limit the State's ability to implement adaptation measures.[19] On the other hand, the German youth complainants were successful.

Despite these examples, hurdles relating to causation have contributed to other cases failing on the basis of standing. The early case of *Kivalina v ExxonMobil*[20] is an example of an attenuated causal chain leading to a court finding no standing on behalf of the plaintiffs. *Juliana v United States*[21] is a newer iteration of the standing problem, with the court finding a lack of redressability by the judiciary and therefore a lack of standing.

Given that causation requires proof that the defendant's conduct caused or is causing the plaintiff's harm or future harms, the success of climate litigation in which causation is an issue may be dependent upon which plaintiffs are allowed to proceed, and consideration of causation may seep into this analysis even if not made explicit. Plaintiffs in climate actions in which causation is an issue may find their standing challenged on the basis of whether or not they are individuals or groups, including non-governmental organisations (NGOs) seeking public interest standing, and whether or not actions can be brought on behalf of future generations.

The case law is not consistent on these questions, but the result of this initial stage in proceedings has implications for what must be established in the causation analysis. For example, a common challenge in the certification of climate-related class actions is the need for a court to ensure that members of the class raise common issues that can be resolved efficiently and effectively through the class action procedure.[22] In

[18] ibid [79], [99]–[101].

[19] ibid [173], [178]. The Court did acknowledge the particular exposure of the claimants to global warming in their countries, and the need for all states to take action. See ibid [174], 'This means that greenhouse gas emissions must be reduced to climate-neutral levels in Germany also'.

[20] *Native Village of Kivalina v ExxonMobil Corp* 696 F.3d. 849, 868–869 (9th Cir 2012).

[21] *Juliana v United States*, 947 F3d 1159 (2020). The plaintiffs have since amended their complaint and the district court has ruled that their case can proceed. See *Juliana v United States*, No 6:15-cv-01517-AA (District Court of Oregon 2023) (Opinion and Order).

[22] For example in *Environnement Jeunesse v Procureur General du Canada* [2018] 500-06-000955-183 (Quebec Superior Court) (*ENJEU*), the court found the class of young people being Quebec residents under the age of 35 was arbitrary.

*Milieudefensie et al v Royal Dutch Shell,*[23] class certification led to the bundling of the claims brought by Dutch-based NGOs to the extent that they serve the interests of Dutch residents and inhabitants of the Wadden region, including future generations. However, the court held that the interests of the world's population, both current and future generations, were not acceptable for bundling as part of these collective claims even as argued by the same Dutch-based NGOs.[24] The subsequent analysis, including with respect to causation, repeatedly refers back to the implications of climate change for inhabitants of the Netherlands and the Wadden region.[25]

The nature of the defendant is also important for the causation analysis, as evident when litigation against States is compared to litigation against non-State actors, especially business enterprises. For example, claims against States may raise concerns with regard to overarching climate policy,[26] or alternately permit approvals issued by government decision-makers and agencies may be appealed or judicially reviewed by a court.[27] An agency's consideration of a permit approval could be insufficiently narrow if it failed to take a hard look at the severity of the impacts of GHGs which would result from its approval. These could include global emissions, as well as national impacts, with courts sometimes, but not always, looking closely at the nature of the impacts on the plaintiffs themselves.[28] These issues have arisen in relation to agency approvals of fossil fuel-related activities in many different jurisdictions and are often intertwined with other considerations, including local social and environmental impacts as well as Indigenous rights. Alternatively, claims may be brought directly against fossil fuel enterprises and others, whether seeking remedy for harm arising from emissions, or raising concerns over the global and local impacts of the enterprise's climate policy.[29]

23 *Milieudefensie v Royal Dutch Shell* [2021] ECLR:NL: RBDHA:2021:5339 (District Court of the Hague).

24 ibid [4.2.1]–[4.2.6] The Dutch-based NGO ActionAid that was focused on developing countries and especially Africa was therefore completely excluded. Individual claimants were also not allowed to proceed as their individual interests were not found to be sufficiently separate from the common interests of the class.

25 ibid [4.4.3], [4.4.10], [4.4.37], [4,4,53], and [4.4.54].

26 For example *Urgenda Foundation v The State of The Netherlands* [2015] ECLI:NL:RBDHA:2015:7196 (District Court of the Hague) (*Urgenda District Court*).

27 See Section 16.3.

28 For example in *Klimatická žaloba ČR v Czech Republic* [2022] No 14A 101/2021 (Prague Municipal Court) 248, four individuals, an NGO, an ornithological society, and a municipality sued the Government and several Ministries in the Czech Republic for inaction on climate change and were found to have standing under art 82 of the Administrative Procedure Code as, in the context of the associations, there was a material and local relationship between the purpose of the associations and the subject of the legal proceedings, while the municipality also had standing since climate change was affecting the interests of those citizens living in its territory. There was a direct interference with the right to a healthy environment due to local manifestations of a global problem of climate change, through increased fires, drought, and floods. Note: This decision was overturned on appeal.

29 For example *Milieudefensie* (n 23).

### 16.2.3 *Causation and Human Rights*

The nature of the causation analysis differs when human rights are invoked. This has been explicitly noted in the non-climate context with regard to the approach of the European Court of Human Rights (ECtHR).[30] Turton observes that while negligence actions in the United Kingdom (UK) require that the defendant's conduct was either a 'but-for cause of, or materially contributed to' the damage suffered by the plaintiff, it is enough in a human rights claim to establish that the defendant's conduct violated 'the relevant right'.[31] This reflects the approach adopted in the South Africa *Groundwork Trust* climate case concerning public law remedies and threats to constitutional rights: 'In terms of section 38 of the Constitution, litigants are entitled to approach a court for relief where rights *are infringed or threatened*'. There can be no doubt that unsafe levels of ambient air pollution directly threaten constitutional rights.[32]

The nature of human-induced climate change makes it challenging to assert that there is a direct link between GHG emissions by a particular defendant State (or company) and violations of any particular human right. However, this hurdle is not insurmountable. For example, the Dutch Supreme Court in *Urgenda*[33] applied the precautionary principle and drew upon ECtHR jurisprudence[34] to clarify that proof of causation is not required in human rights cases raising environmental hazards – including climate change – as State obligations under Articles 2 and 8 of the European Convention on Human Rights (ECHR) arise by virtue of the existence of a risk to rights.[35] Accordingly, even if it is uncertain that the danger will materialise, the State's duty is 'to take appropriate steps to counter an imminent threat'.[36] On the facts, given the evidence that climate change poses a real and genuine threat to the lives and welfare of Dutch citizens, and that sea level rise stands to render much of the Netherlands uninhabitable, the requirement that the State take action was held to be consistent with the precautionary principle: 'The mere existence of a sufficiently genuine possibility that this risk will materialize means that suitable measures must be taken'.[37]

30 Gemma Turton, 'Causation and Risk in Negligence and Human Rights Law' (2020) 79(1) *CLJ* 148, 176.

31 ibid 149. The author concludes that there is a need for clarification in the health care context as to whether causation is relevant to establishing liability in human rights claims as distinct from damages. ibid [175].

32 *Groundwork Trust and Vukani Environmental Justice Alliance Movement in Action v Minister of Environmental Affairs and Others* (2022) 39724/2019 (*Groundwork Trust High Court*) [78].

33 *State of the Netherlands (Ministry of Economic Affairs and Climate Policy) v Stichting Urgenda* [2019] ECLI:NL:HR:2019:2007 (Supreme Court of the Netherlands) (*Urgenda Supreme Court*).

34 *Tatar v Romania* App no 67021/01 (ECtHR, 27 January 2009).

35 *Urgenda Supreme Court* (n 33). ECHR art 2 imposes an obligation upon the state to protect the lives of citizens within its jurisdiction, while ECHR art 8 imposes an obligation to protect the rights of citizens to their home and private lives.

36 *Urgenda Supreme Court* (n 33) [5.3.2].

37 *Urgenda Supreme Court* (n 33) [5.6.2].

Similarly, in *Waratah Coal Pty Ltd v Youth Verdict Ltd and Ors*, the Land Court of Queensland held in favour of the claimants despite an alleged 'indirect and tenuous' causal link between a proposed coal mine and the violation of human rights.[38] The Court instead accepted the claimants' argument that there was a 'logical and rational connection' between the authorisation of the relevant applications and the subsequent harms caused by coal burning.[39] This was enough to establish a 'sufficient causal relationship to find the act [of granting the applications] has the capacity to limit a human right'.[40] As such, the Court recommended that the applications be denied by the respective authorities.[41]

Human rights-based claims may also be brought against defendant corporate enterprises, drawing upon the independent responsibility of businesses to respect human rights under pillar two of the 2011 United Nations Guiding Principles on Business and Human Rights (UNGPs).[42] The UNGPs were influential in the *Milieudefensie* case mentioned earlier.[43]

### 16.2.4 *Causation and Attribution*

There is a particularly important relationship between causation and attribution, and the latter is considered in detail in the next chapter. While it is still unclear what the relationship between attribution science and legal tests of admissibility of climate models is, there is clearly an important relationship between attribution studies and the evolution of legal tests of causation.

Attribution will – and already has – been influential in establishing the causal relationship between activities, events, and harms. For example, Heede's 2013 study has been cited in many lawsuits against carbon major corporations.[44] As outlined in Chapter 3 introducing attribution science in this Handbook, attribution studies illustrate how closely climate models have predicted extreme events and therefore how reasonably foreseeable such events have become. For example, the 2021 IPCC report lists the increased probabilities of the occurrence of extreme, one-in-fifty-year events, as temperatures increase.[45] Attribution studies can be helpful in creating a stronger causal nexus between events and harms and the emergence of best practices in causation tests.

38 *Waratah Coal Pty Ltd v Youth Verdict Ltd* [2022] QLC 21 [1316].
39 ibid [1352].
40 ibid.
41 ibid.
42 OHCHR, 'Guiding Principles on Business and Human Rights: Implementing the United Nations "Protect, Respect and Remedy" Framework' (2011) HR/PUB/11/04.
43 *Milieudefensie* (n 23).
44 Richard Heede, 'Tracing Anthropogenic Carbon Dioxide and Methane Emissions to Fossil Fuel and Cement Producers 1854–2010' (2014) 122 *Climatic Change* 229–241.
45 Allen and others (n 6).

## 16.3 CASE LAW DEVELOPMENT – STATE OF AFFAIRS

This section approaches cases from a thematic as opposed to a jurisdictional lens. Here, we divide cases into those that focus on project-based emissions, on the one hand, and cases that focus on climate policy and regulation, on the other.

### 16.3.1 *Project-based Cases*

The cases covered here involve a challenge to government action, such as a permit or licence granted for a project which plaintiffs claim will increase GHG emissions or an inaccurate or incomplete environmental impact analysis. In these cases, we find courts struggling to map climate harm onto more traditional causation-based legal tests, even in the context of human rights claims. Courts seem more comfortable asking agencies to re-examine emission assumptions and requiring them to take a cumulative approach to the direct and indirect impacts of their approvals.

In some cases, however, courts have taken a broader approach to causation. Instead of requiring a finding of a causal nexus between actions and harms, they focus on establishing a reasonably foreseeable risk of harm. Some cases in this category have grappled with the indirect effect of $CO_2$ emissions from permit approvals, sometimes in conjunction with an assessment of local cumulative effects. Government agencies may struggle to account for indirect or scope 3 emissions from permits granted for extraction, for example. In addition, these cases may involve questions about hypothetical emissions which may occur absent judicial intervention.

Australian courts have been active contributors to the evolving jurisprudence on cases focused on project-based emissions. The 2006 decision *Gray v Minister of Planning* provides an early example of a successful challenge to a large coal mine under an environmental assessment process.[46] The applicant argued that GHG emissions from coal burning (scope 3) should be considered in the environmental assessment. Judge Pain agreed, holding that the GHG emissions should not be ignored despite the existence of many contributors globally and a

> sufficient proximate link between the mining of a very substantial reserve of thermal coal in NSW [New South Wales], the only purpose of which is for use as fuel in power stations, and the emission of GHG which contribute to climate change/global warming, which is impacting now and likely to continue to do so on the Australian and consequently NSW environment.[47]

[46] *Gray v The Minister for Planning, Director-General of the Department of Planning and Centennial Hunter Pty Ltd* [2006] NSWLEC 720.

[47] ibid [100].

In reaching its decision, the court identified the failure of the administrative decision-maker to 'take the principle of intergenerational equity into account', which was a legal requirement under the relevant legislation.[48]

In a 2016 case from Kenya, *Save Lamu v Republic of Kenya*,[49] an NGO successfully sued for a new environmental impact assessment (EIA) process due to lack of public participation, as well as omissions from the EIA for a coal-fired power plant on climate emissions and mitigation efforts. The National Environmental Tribunal found that due to the great importance of climate change issues, the EIA was incomplete and inadequate, particularly in the face of failures of the EIA to comply with the 2016 Climate Change Act, and the impact of the emissions on surrounding communities.

In the *Center for Biological Diversity v U.S. BLM*,[50] a Colorado court remanded the Bureau of Land Management's approval of a master development plan for natural gas wells and pads back to the agency on the basis that the agency's consideration of the approval was insufficiently narrow. The agency had failed to take a hard look at the severity of the impacts of GHGs that would result from its approval and the cumulative impacts of the emissions on air and water quality. The court found that combustion emissions would be an indirect effect of the agency's decision and the agency's approval (which did not consider these emissions) was arbitrary and capricious in that it failed to take a hard look at the foreseeable indirect effects of that combustion. In a corollary finding, the US Court of Appeal in the 7th circuit in *Zero Zone Inc v U.S. DoE* (2016)[51] found that the Department of Energy's consideration of indirect benefits, such as carbon reductions and the global benefit of GHG reductions, was not arbitrary and capricious.

In the 2019 Australian decision *Gloucester Resources Limited v Minister for Planning*,[52] the proponent appealed the Minister for Planning's refusal to grant development consent for the Rocky Hill Coal Project.[53] In considering the impacts of climate change, the court observed that: 'All of the direct and indirect GHG emissions of the Rocky Hill Coal Project will impact on the environment. All

48 ibid [126]. For further information on the factual and subsequent legal reform consequences of this decision, see Anna Rose, 'Gray v Minister for Planning: The Rising Tide of Climate Change Litigation in Australia' (2007) 29 *Sydney Law Review* 729. The relevant legislation was the Environmental Planning and Assessment Act 1979 (NSW).

49 *Save Lamu et al v National Environmental Management Authority and Amu Power Co Ltd* [2016] Tribunal Appeal No Net 196 of 2016 (Kenya Environmental Tribunal).

50 *Center for Biological Diversity v US Bureau of Land Management* No 3:17-CV-553-LRH-WGC (District Court of Nevada 2019).

51 *Zero Zone Inc v United States Department of Energy* 832 F3d 654 (7th Cir 2016).

52 *Gloucester Resources Limited v Minister for Planning* [2019] NSWLEC 7 (*Gloucester Resources*).

53 ibid [270]–[421]. The court concluded that there would be multiple direct and indirect negative impacts were the mine allowed to proceed, including social impacts on the community and particular impacts on Aboriginal peoples.

anthropogenic GHG emissions contribute to climate change'.[54] Chief Justice Brian Preston explicitly referred to causation, stating:

> There is a causal link between the Project's cumulative GHG emissions and climate change and its consequences. The Project's cumulative GHG emissions will contribute to the global total of GHG concentrations in the atmosphere. The global total of GHG concentrations will affect the climate system and cause climate change impacts. The Project's cumulative GHG emissions are therefore likely to contribute to the future changes to the climate system and the impacts of climate change. In this way, the Project is likely to have indirect impacts on the environment, including the climate system, the oceanic and terrestrial environment, and people.[55]

Notably, the court referred not only to the causation analysis in previous Australian jurisprudence[56] but also to *Massachusetts v EPA*[57] and the decisions of the Dutch District Court[58] and Court of Appeal[59] in the *Urgenda* litigation.[60]

In *Sharma*, eight Australian children brought a representative action against the Commonwealth Minister for the Environment seeking an injunction to stop the approval of the Whitehaven Vickery coal mine.[61] The children argued that the Minister owed a duty to take reasonable care not to cause them personal injury when exercising her statutory power to approve or not approve the extension of an existing coal mine. The first instance court agreed, holding that a reasonable Minister 'ought to have the children in contemplation when facilitating the emission of 100 MT of $CO_2$ into the atmosphere'.[62] The court rejected the Minister's

54 ibid [514].
55 ibid [525].
56 ibid [518].
57 *Massachusetts v EPA* (n 14) [519]–[520].
58 *Urgenda District Court* (n 26) [4.90]

> From the above considerations, particularly in [4.79], it follows that a sufficient causal link can be assumed to exist between the Dutch greenhouse gas emissions, global climate change and the effects (now and in the future) on the Dutch living climate. The fact that the current Dutch greenhouse gas emissions are limited on a global scale does not alter the fact that these emissions contribute to climate change. The court has taken into consideration in this respect as well that the Dutch greenhouse gas emissions have contributed to climate change and by their nature will also continue to contribute to climate change.

59 *State of the Netherlands v Stichting Urgenda* [2018] ECLI:NL:GHDHA:2018:2591 (Court of Appeal) (*Urgenda Court of Appeal*) [523]–[524] (rejecting the government's 'defence of the lack of a causal link').
60 *Gloucester Resources* (n 52) [526]–[527]. The court also took into account that the proponent had not proposed to be carbon neutral by committing to the deployment of emission reduction technologies or carbon offsets; ibid [530].
61 *Sharma and others v Minister for the Environment* [2021] FCA 560 (*Sharma First Instance*), overturned on appeal *Minister for the Environment v Sharma* [2022] FCAFC 35 (*Sharma*).
62 ibid [491]. However, the application for a *quia timet* injunction was denied as the harm was not imminent, leaving open the question of whether it would be appropriate to consider carbon neutrality commitments of the proponent. ibid [508]–[512].

argument that she did not have control over each point in the causal chain,[63] holding instead that the Minister had conflated reasonable foreseeability and control, creating a requirement that there be a 'causal nexus between conduct and injury' instead of a real, reasonably foreseeable risk of harm.[64]

On appeal the judges of the Full Federal Court unanimously overturned the earlier decision but for different reasons.[65] All three judges were challenged to disaggregate the duty of care, causation, and damages enquiries.[66] According to Chief Justice James Allsop, disaggregating the duty of care from damage removes the duty from the 'very essence of the cause of action', with the plaintiffs seeking to impose the duty 'decades before any foreseeable harm which could have any connection whatsoever to the act in question' and 'decades before one knows whether there will be a cause of action'.[67] The reasonable foreseeability enquiry, Chief Justice Allsop suggested, 'has a causal element: The reasonable foreseeability is of the negligent act or omission *causing or materially contributing to the harm*'.[68] Justice Michael Wheelahan similarly held that the foreseeability must be of an injury 'compensable by the law of negligence and that is capable of being caused by a careless act or omission of the tortfeasor', not a prospect of causation 'so remote that it is far-fetched, or fanciful'.[69] Justice Jonathan Beach, on the other hand, disagreed with the conflation of causation with reasonable foreseeability, finding the initial judge's conclusion to be sustainable:

> the preponderance of authority does not demand that a legally acceptable pathway to ultimately demonstrating causation must be used in any reasonable foreseeability analysis. Moreover, who knows what the legally acceptable factual causation test will be in eighty years when a fully formed tort is likely to arise, if at all? And indeed, who knows what the science will show in eighty years in terms of factual causation?[70]

Ultimately, Justice Beach suggested that the High Court of Australia would be the appropriate court to 'engineer new seed varieties for sustainable duties of care, modifying concepts such as "sufficient closeness and directness" and indeterminacy to address the accelerating complexity, multiple links, and cross-links of causal relations'.[71] However, the decision will not be appealed.[72]

63 ibid [278]–[288].
64 ibid [282], [282]–[284].
65 *Sharma* (n 61).
66 ibid (Allsop CJ) [231], (Beach J) [538], (Wheelahan J) [872].
67 ibid [231], [297], [298], [299].
68 ibid [300].
69 ibid [872]. At most the tiny increase in GHG emissions from the project approval would amount 'to a contribution to an *increased risk* of harm, but not a risk of contribution to the harm itself, still less a material contribution'. See ibid [882].
70 ibid [443], [441]. Nevertheless, Justice Beach ultimately denied the duty of care due to a lack of sufficient closeness and directness, and so, indeterminacy. See ibid [363].
71 ibid [754].
72 '"They Will Not Forget Our Names": No Appeal, but a Vow to Keep Pushing for Climate Action' (*Equity Generation Lawyers*, 12 April 2022) <https://equitygenerationlawyers.com/wp/wp-content/

In the New Zealand private law case of *Smith v Fonterra Co-Operative Group Ltd and Ors*,[73] a Māori leader sought a declaration that the actions of some of New Zealand's largest GHG emitters or companies that supply products that emit GHGs[74] unlawfully caused or contributed to climate change.[75] At first instance the public nuisance claim was struck due to a lack of sufficient causal link,[76] while the negligence action was struck out as the court rejected the possibility that the 'but for' test could be avoided in the climate context.[77] A third novel cause of action was allowed to proceed to trial.[78] The Court of Appeal rejected Mr Smith's appeal on public nuisance and negligence and allowed it on the novel cause of action.[79] The Court reasoned that climate change is unique in that every person is both responsible for the harm and a victim of said harm;[80] the focus on 'net zero' created complications as it was unrealistic to suggest all GHG emissions are tortious;[81] and an action against a subset of emitters is an ineffective way to address climate change,[82] especially where the chosen defendants alone did not make a material contribution to climate change.[83] With regard to the negligence claim, the Court of Appeal distinguished proximity from foreseeability and was not persuaded by the argument that a sufficiently proximate relationship existed as Smith was part of an identifiable vulnerable class of plaintiffs, Northland coastal Māori, giving rise to knowledge of actual risk.[84] Moreover, despite several alternatives to the 'but for' test for causation being put before the court, it held that the 'class of possible contributors is virtually

uploads/2022/04/220412-Statement-from-Sharma-litigants-on-High-Court-appeal.pdf> accessed 26 February 2024.

73 *Michael John Smith v Fonterra Co-Operative Group Limited and Others* CIV-2019-404-001730 [2020] NZHC 419 (*Smith High Court*).

74 ibid. The defendants include dairy producers, steel mills, energy, and coal mining companies.

75 ibid [12]. The plaintiffs sought injunctions requiring each of the defendants to produce or cause zero net emissions from their activities by 2030 by linear reductions in net emissions each year.

76 ibid [63], [37].

77 ibid [75], [83]–[88]. Among concerns raised by the court were the fact that other plaintiffs in a similar position might seek damages, creating complexity especially if overseas defendants were included in joint and several liability, as it would be difficult for New Zealand defendants to recover from them. See ibid [98].

78 ibid [15], [101]–[104]. The novel claim was that the defendants owe the claimant 'a duty, recognizable at law, to cease contributing to damage to the climate system, dangerous anthropogenic interference with the climate system and adverse effects of climate change through their emission of greenhouse gases'.

79 *Michael John Smith v Fonterra Co-Operative Group Limited and Others* CA 128/2020 [2021] NZCA 552 (*Smith Court of Appeal*). See Caroline E. Foster, 'Case Note: Novel Climate Tort? The New Zealand Court of Appeal decision in Smith v Fonterra Co-operative Group Limited and others' (2022) 24(3) *ELR* 224.

80 *Smith Court of Appeal* ibid [18].

81 ibid [20]–[23].

82 ibid [27].

83 ibid [19].

84 ibid [101]–[103]. 'There Is No Physical or Temporal Proximity. There Is No Direct Relationship and No Causal Proximity'.

limitless' and that the inability to name or join a substantial share of contributors was a problem that could not be overcome without fundamentally changing tort law.[85] Leave to appeal to the New Zealand Supreme Court has been granted.[86]

Finally, the 2020 *People v Arctic Oil*[87] case in the Norwegian Supreme Court illustrates the challenge of trying to intervene at the exploration stage, combined with court reluctance to account for emissions from the combustion of oil and gas after it has been exported. While the Supreme Court held that citizens are protected from environmental and climate harms under the Norwegian Constitution, the extent of emissions from exported oil and gas arising from licences for future oil and gas exploration in the Barents Sea was too uncertain to conclude they would cause the requisite harm.[88] The plaintiffs appealed to the ECtHR in 2021, arguing that the licenses violate Article 2 (right to life) and Article 8 (right to respect for private and family life) of the ECHR.[89] An outstanding question is whether the outcome of a similar decision would be different in light of the International Energy Agency's 1.5 report[90] published in May 2021, which makes clear that there is no room for approving development in new oil and gas fields if the world is to limit global warming within the temperature goal of 1.5°C of the Paris Agreement.

### 16.3.2 *Challenges to Policy and Regulation*

Another category of cases requests policy or regulatory action by the State, either through a petition for rulemaking to a specific government agency like the US EPA or a request to the government as a whole to reduce emissions across all sectors in the future, on the basis of human rights or other claims. As described earlier, the first major US case that dealt with causation involved the State of Massachusetts

85 ibid [105]–[113].

86 *Michael John Smith v Fonterra Co-Operative Group Limited and Others* [2022] NZSC 35 (*Smith Supreme Court*). The appeal was successful, and the plaintiff's claim reinstated in *Michael John Smith v Fonterra Co-Operative Group Limited and Others* [2024] NZSC 5.

87 *Greenpeace Nordic Association v Ministry of Petroleum and Energy* (2020) Case No 20-051052SIV-HRET (Norwegian Supreme Court) (*People v Arctic Oil*).

88 ibid [70], [186], [234]. Among considerations was the additional licensing requirements to move from exploration to exploitation, and the uncertainty as to the nature of the energy sources that would be used to substitute (e.g. coal instead of gas). The significance of the *People v Arctic Oil* case is demonstrated in the 2024 *North Sea Fields* Case, where the Oslo District Court relied on the Supreme Court's finding that emissions from combustion fall within art 112 of the Constitution to find that the impact assessments for three ministerial decisions to allow plans for the development and operation of oil and gas fields are unlawful. The District Court held that the Petroleum Act and Petroleum Regulation must be interpreted in light of art 112 of the Constitution and therefore the impact assessments conducted were insufficient as they did not consider emissions from combustions.

89 *Greenpeace Nordic and others v Norway* App No 34068/21 (ECtHR) <https://climatecasechart.com/wp-content/uploads/non-us-case-documents/2021/20210615_Application-no.-3406821_petition-1.pdf> accessed 26 February 2024.

90 'Net Zero by 2050 – Analysis' (*International Energy Agency*, May 2021) <www.iea.org/reports/net-zero-by-2050> accessed 26 February 2024.

submitting a petition for rulemaking to the EPA to regulate GHG emissions under the Clean Air Act as an air pollutant.[91] The EPA originally denied the petition on the basis that it had no authority under the Act to address global emissions and a causal link between GHGs and increases in global surface air temperatures was not unequivocally established. The agency also claimed that any regulation would be a 'piecemeal approach' to climate change that conflicted with the federal government's general approach to the issue. The agency therefore adopted a 'drop in the ocean' approach.

The US Supreme Court remanded the issue back to the EPA, finding that GHGs could be regulated as an air pollutant under the Act, and also dismissed the agency's findings on causation. Justice John Paul Stevens noted that even if the changes associated with climate change were widely shared, that did not minimise Massachusetts' interest in the outcome of the litigation. Although the agency claimed India and China would offset US emissions, the Court found the EPA 'overstated its case' in that regard:

> Agencies, like legislatures, do not generally resolve massive problems in one fell swoop, but instead whittle away over time, refining their approach as circumstances change and they develop a more nuanced understanding of how best to proceed … And reducing domestic auto emissions is hardly tentative … The U.S. transportation sector emits an enormous quantity of $CO_2$ into the atmosphere … A reduction in domestic emissions would slow the pace of global emissions increases, no matter what happens elsewhere.[92]

The case takes an incrementalist approach to emissions and the ability of regulatory action to ameliorate climate change. It is an early case that adopts a broader approach to causation. The case of *Center for Biological Diversity v NHTSA* in the 9th Circuit took a similar approach.[93] The court looked at the percentage of global emissions from US light trucks and the transportation sector overall from scientific reports. Finding those contributions to be considerable, the court held that the National Highway Traffic Safety Administration's failure to monetise the benefits of reducing $CO_2$ emissions from the US automobile fleet was arbitrary and capricious.

In a more recent case against the Dutch State, *Urgenda*, a Dutch NGO, successfully sought an order from the court directing the Netherlands to reduce its GHG emissions by 25 per cent relative to 1990 by 2020, although it was left up to the State to determine what specific measures it would take to comply.[94] Similar to the two previous cases, the nature of the relief sought was that the State

91 *Massachusetts v EPA* (n 14).
92 ibid [21].
93 *Center for Biological Diversity v National Highway Traffic Safety Administration* 508 F.3d 508 (9th Cir 2007).
94 *Urgenda Supreme Court* (n 33).

take preventative measures in the future to combat climate change. The Dutch claimants argued with reference to the State's human rights obligations under the ECHR, specifically Article 2 (right to life), Article 8 (right to respect for private and family life), and Article 13 (right to an effective remedy before a national authority).[95] Although Urgenda could not directly invoke these rights, it was able to rely upon Article 3.305a of the Dutch Civil Code to bring the claim on behalf of Dutch residents who are the victims.[96] Drawing on ECHR case law, the Dutch Supreme Court held that where there was a 'real and immediate risk' of harm under Articles 2 and 8 of the ECHR, the State's positive obligations were triggered to prevent such harm even without identifying specific prospective victims.[97] In upholding the decision of the Court of Appeal in 2019, the Supreme Court concluded 'Articles 2 and 8 ECHR relating to the risk of climate change should be interpreted in such a way that these provisions oblige the Contracting States to do "their part" to counter that danger'.[98] The Court rejected arguments that the State should not have to comply with its partial responsibility because other States were failing to comply, or that its emissions were so small compared to others that it would make little difference globally.[99] Instead, it drew upon the carbon budget concept: each reduction 'has a positive effect on combating dangerous climate change' as it leaves more room in the budget.[100] Similar to the US cases earlier, in *Urgenda* the Court adopted an incrementalist approach to amelioration of climate change – that every emission counts.

In the Canadian case of *Mathur v Ontario*, brought by seven young Canadian citizens against the province of Ontario, a motion to strike was refused.[101] The Cap and Trade Cancellation Act at the heart of this case effectively reduced Ontario's GHG reduction target as under previous legislation. The plaintiffs pointed out that, per the Paris Agreement, parties must progressively strengthen their emission targets over time – not weaken them.[102] Ontario had alleged that the appellants' assertions of harm were based on a 'chain of speculative assumptions', including that other provinces and countries could offset a lack of ambition in Ontario's GHG targets, and that catastrophic climate impacts could not be avoided by Ontario increasing its targets.[103] The Court was unpersuaded by these arguments, and took a progressive approach to

[95] ibid [5.1]–[5.10].
[96] ibid [5.9.1]–[5.9.3].
[97] ibid [5.3.1]–[5.3.2], [5.6.2].
[98] ibid [5.8].
[99] ibid [5.7.7].
[100] ibid [5.7.8].
[101] *Mathur et al v Her Majesty the Queen in Right of Ontario* [2020] ONSC 6918 (Superior Court of Justice) (*Mathur Strikeout*).
[102] ibid [37]–[40].
[103] ibid [89].

causation and the harm alleged.[104] The Court adopted the Supreme Court's more flexible standard of causation – 'sufficient causal connection' – which allows the circumstances of each particular case to be taken into account. It does not require that government-impugned conduct be the only or dominant cause of prejudice but is satisfied by a reasonable inference drawn on the balance of probabilities, sensitive to the context of the particular case. This flexible text also encourages the use of expert witnesses and social science evidence,[105] and it takes a broader approach to causation.

Two cases modelled on *Urgenda* have arisen in France, one brought by an NGO and the other by a municipality. In the former case, Notre Affaires à Tous brought action against the French government, alleging that its failure to take sufficient action against climate change was a breach of its statutory duty to act under domestic and international law.[106] In February 2021, the Administrative Court of Paris found a causal link between the French government's inaction in relation to GHG emissions and ecological damage even though it only comprised one part of the damage.[107] The Court ordered the government to disclose and justify its measures to achieve its GHG reduction targets.

Similarly, the community of Grande-Synthe and others brought action against the French government for their alleged failure to take sufficient action to reduce GHG emissions.[108] The claimants argued that this failure to act violated domestic and international law, including the ECHR, Paris Agreement, French Environmental Code, and the French Charter for the Environment. The Court found that this was justiciable, partly due to the fact that Grande-Synthe is a coastal town that is particularly susceptible to the adverse effects of climate change,[109] and held that the government's failure to take useful measures towards their climate commitments caused harm to the claimants. In 2020, the Council-d'Etat referred the issue back to the government and required them to justify their means of meeting climate commitments (40 per cent reduction in GHG emissions based on 1990 levels by 2030). In 2021, the Council d'Etat ordered the government to 'take all measures necessary' by the end of March 2022 to reduce GHGs and meet their climate commitments.[110]

104 Sara Seck and Lisa Benjamin, 'Mapping Human Rights-based Litigation in Canada' (2022) 13(1) *JHRE* 178–211. While the Superior Court in the 2023 judgment on the merits did not ultimately uphold the challenge, it established that the Ontarian Government's insufficient climate mitigation efforts do contribute to an 'increase in the risk' of climate-change-related harms which threaten the plaintiffs' constitutional rights. The Court further found that the plaintiffs are not required to prove 'beyond a reasonable doubt' that their climate-related harms will occur; they only have to prove that the State's conduct contributes to an increase in the risk of the harm occurring. See *Mathur v Ontario* [2023] ONSC 2316 (*Mathur Merits*) [147], [150].

105 *Mathur Strikeout* (n 101) [170].

106 *Notre Affaire à Tous and Others v France* [2021] No 1904967, 1904968, 1904972, 1904976/4-1.

107 ibid 34.

108 *Commune de Grande-Synthe v France* [2020] N°427301 (Conseil d'Etat) (*Grande-Synthe*).

109 ibid [3].

110 ibid.

## 16.4 EMERGING BEST PRACTICE IN CAUSATION

There is a significant amount of jurisprudence on causation. As established in 3.1, cases that challenge project approvals offer an important opportunity to stop fossil fuel extraction and future emissions. Courts that adopt an indirect test of reasonable foreseeability of harm offer examples of best practice (e.g. *Gloucester Resources*). Unfortunately, courts in other similar cases continue to struggle to move beyond direct but-for causation analysis and the view that evidence of actual damage is essential, which is a highly problematic approach given the temporal and spatial dimensions of GHG emissions and resulting harms.

As established in 3.2, prevention-focused cases in the public law arena, where plaintiffs sue to prevent or reduce future emissions are the area of jurisprudence where an incrementalist and less stringent approach to causation has found the most success, illustrating emerging best practice (e.g. *Massachusetts*, v *EPA*, *Urgenda*, *Notre Affairs a Tous*, and *Grande-Synthe*). Plaintiffs point to the contributions that State-based emissions make to global emissions and, in conjunction with the Paris Agreement and latest scientific reports, convince judicial bodies that future emission reductions are important and closely connected to preventing future harm. In countries with robust human rights frameworks, such as in the European Union, this broader approach to causation has found the most judicial success.

Emerging best practices in causation acknowledges that traditional tort-related tests are insufficient, and fall short when the complexity of climate change and the inability to identify a concrete nexus between actions and harms is used by the judiciary as a limitation to the finding of causation. We identify this limited approach to causation as a 'drop in the ocean' approach – that any reduction in emissions by the defendant (being a State or non-State actor) will have limited or no effect on the harms experienced now, or to be experienced in the future, by the plaintiff.

Emerging best practices, in our view, does not apply the 'drop in the ocean' approach. Instead, it considers and applies a broader, more general approach to causation on the basis of newly evolving and best-available science and attribution studies. These judicial findings predominantly rely on collective goals articulated in the Paris Agreement and dismiss arguments that emissions from one company or country are not effective in addressing global climate change. Instead, judges rely on arguments that every emission reduction counts, with reference to recent IPCC and other scientific reports, and accept that these harms can be supported by science. Indeed, the 'drop in the ocean' approach has been explicitly rejected in many cases.[111] In our view, as more and more of these scientific reports are published, more examples of these best practices will appear throughout climate litigation cases.

[111] These include *Urgenda Supreme Court* (n 33) [5.7.1]; *Neubauer* (n 16) [199–202]; *VZW Klimaatzaak v Kingdom of Belgium and Others* [2023] 2022/AR/891 (Cour d'appel de Bruxelles) (*VZW Klimaatzaak Appeal*) [160], [283], [248]; *Massachusetts v EPA* (n 14) [4]; *Milieudefensie* (n 23) [4.3.5].

Once impacts within a country can be linked to global emissions, courts are more willing to consider national impacts as affecting and causing harm to plaintiffs. Emerging best practices draw broader causal inferences between GHG emissions, large emitters, and effects on the ground, and therefore elaborate on the traditionally narrow strictures of the cause-and-effect relationship in law. Prevention-oriented cases, including cases involving public law and government action, tend to apply a less stringent test to establish causation. These cases specifically avoid or reject the 'drop in the ocean' approach and therefore broaden the causal quality of the law to introduce more conceptual relationships, adding an element of fairness but also uncertainty into the law. While a broader approach to causation is welcome, it does mean that it is unclear how much or little emissions will be considered to add to the problem of climate change.

Another emerging trend is the growing litigation against corporations in the climate context, which at times employs this broader causal relationship. This is evidenced both in the human rights context for direct harms, and in the investor-related context in relation to financial losses.

An example of innovative causal relationships is highlighted in the Philippines' Human Rights Commission's investigation and final report.[112] The Commission found that a State is not absolved of its duty to protect against climate change impacts by the lack of a clear causal relationship between GHGs and climate change impacts. Further, the Commission established that not only carbon major companies but all enterprises along their respective value chains may be found responsible for human rights violations as a result of climate change impacts.

Unlike traditional litigation efforts, the Commission does not attempt to pin legal liability for damage on corporations. Rather, the investigation serves largely as an expository exercise to highlight the damaging role these entities play in the context of climate change. Using law as an expository tool in this way overcomes the causation hurdles experienced in traditional litigation against carbon major companies, and it can be equally effective in connecting the activities (and profits) of these entities with the human suffering that has been and will continue to be caused by climate change.[113]

The Commission's approach does, however, raise questions over causal relationships. The investigation's outcome is unable to trace a direct route between individual corporate emissions and concrete human rights harms. Instead, it provides a more nuanced and generalist approach, finding that corporations played a clear role in anthropogenic climate change and its attendant impacts. The Commission found

[112] Commission on Human Rights of the Philippines, 'National Inquiry on Climate Change Report' (CHRP December 2022).

[113] Lisa Benjamin, 'The Responsibilities of Corporations: New Directions in Environmental Litigation' in Veerle Heyvaert (ed), *Research Handbook on Transnational Environmental Law* (Edward Elgar 2020).

that, based on the evidence, carbon major companies could be found legally and morally liable for human rights violations arising from climate change in certain circumstances. These focused on circumstances involving obstruction, deception, or fraud, where the relevant *mens rea* (criminal intent) may exist to hold companies accountable under not only civil but criminal laws. This is an example of using causal inferences but tying them to specific legal responsibilities.

One especially innovative aspect of the Philippines investigation is the reliance placed by the plaintiffs upon the business responsibility to respect human rights of the UN Guiding Principles in framing the responsibilities of the carbon majors.[114] Of particular relevance to causation is Principle 13:

> The responsibility to respect human rights requires that business enterprises:
>
> (a) Avoid causing or contributing to adverse human rights impacts through their own activities, and address such impacts when they occur;
>
> (b) Seek to prevent or mitigate adverse human rights impacts that are directly linked to their operations, products or services by their business relationships, even if they have not contributed to those impacts.

This conception of value chain responsibility, which acknowledges that business enterprises do not have full control over all aspects of their supply and value chains, provides a pragmatic framework from which to consider causation. Notably, the Commission further confirmed the responsibility of all entities within the value chain of carbon majors to remedy harms that they have caused or to which they have contributed in accordance with Principle 22 of the UNGPs.[115]

While the Philippines investigation was trailblazing for invoking the UNGPs, the 2021 *Milieudefensie* decision takes things a step further by clearly linking the UNGPs with the Paris Agreement targets, reinforced by reference to Shell's practices including reporting across scopes 1–3 in accordance with the GHG Protocol. The court considered at length the independent responsibility of business to respect human rights under the UNGPs as a global standard of expected conduct of all businesses wherever they operate, which requires companies to avoid causing or contributing to human rights impacts through their own activities, and to prevent and mitigate those arising from business relationships encompassing the entire value chain.[116]

Royal Dutch Shell (RDS) is the top holding company of the Shell group, comprising over 1,000 separate companies established and operating in over 150

[114] Sara Seck, 'A Relational Analysis of Enterprise Obligations and Carbon Majors for Climate Justice' (2021) 11(1) *Oñati Socio-Legal Series* 254.

[115] Commission on Human Rights of the Philippines (n 113) 95: 'when, through the conduct of human rights due diligence, a business enterprise is discovered to have caused or contributed to an adverse climate-related human rights impact, a remediation mechanism or process which is accessible, predictable, transparent, and legitimate must be made available. This may be through internal remediation mechanism or other legal processes'. See further 112–114.

[116] *Milieudefensie* (n 23) [4.4.16]–[4.4.17].

countries around the world.[117] The plaintiffs sought to order RDS 'to limit or cause to be limited the aggregate annual volume of all $CO_2$ emissions into the atmosphere (Scope 1, 2, and 3) due to the business operations and sold energy products of the Shell group' by at least 45 per cent relative to 2019 levels.[118] To do so, the plaintiffs relied upon the unwritten standard of care in the Dutch Civil Code, to be interpreted using human rights and 'soft law' instruments including the UNGPs, the UN Global Compact, and the Organisation for Economic Co-operation and Development (OECD) Guidelines for Multinational Enterprises.[119]

The court explored the 'distinctive aspects of responsibility for environmental damage and imminent environmental damage' with regard to climate change in the Netherlands and the Wadden region and how these distinctive aspects must inform the interpretation of 'event giving rise to the damage' under Article 7 of Rome II:[120] '[E]very emission of $CO_2$ and other [GHGs], anywhere in the world and caused in whatever manner, contributes'[121] to climate harms, and these only cause damage or imminent damage in conjunction with other emissions. Despite Article 7's reference to a single event, 'it leaves room for situations in which multiple events giving rise to the damage in multiple countries can be identified' and the Shell group corporate policy 'therefore constitutes an independent cause of that damage'.[122]

## 16.5 REPLICABILITY

As illustrated earlier, broader approaches to causation, found in early cases such as *Massachusetts v EPA*, have been adopted in an increasing number of jurisdictions. Indeed, several jurisdictions have explicitly rejected the 'drop in the ocean' approach in policy cases focused on prevention. Some courts have been influenced by this to adopt an indirect reasonable foreseeability of harm approach. This suggests that other countries, when deciding cases against government agencies for permitting decisions or when demanding government action, could also reject the 'drop in the ocean' theory and adopt a broader approach to causation. This may mean more robust decisions around emissions reductions, particularly in light of State-based commitments under the Paris Agreement and its global temperature goals as well as recent IPCC scientific reports that support the broader approach to causation. Emerging scientific and attribution reports could support generalisable principles that promote the broader approach – that the defendant's conduct contributed significantly to the plaintiff's harms. However, this may be more difficult in cross-jurisdictional claims involving foreign plaintiffs even where they have been granted standing.

117 ibid [2.2.2], [4.1.1], and [4.4.16].
118 ibid [3.1].
119 ibid [3.2].
120 ibid [4.3.2], [4.3.5].
121 ibid [4.3.5].
122 ibid [4.3.6].

A different question is whether cases that approach causation through a human rights lens are easily replicable in States that are both less engaged with regional human rights mechanisms and lack an enumerated human right to a clean, healthy, and sustainable environment in their Constitution (for example, Canada and the US). The 2022 United Nations General Assembly (UNGA) resolution recognising the right to a clean, healthy, and sustainable environment may create opportunities to inform climate causation with human rights in all States, especially in light of the voting record of 161 in favour with only eight abstentions.[123]

Reliance on the business responsibility to respect human rights as an international legal expectation to inform the interpretation of tort doctrines or other causes of action may be increasingly replicable across jurisdictions, with implications for the causation analysis. Beyond their endorsement by the UN Human Rights Council is the increasing evidence of their influence in courts and international fora.[124] Indeed, the UNGPs are also explicitly recalled in the UNGA resolution on the right to a clean, healthy, and sustainable environment. An additional source of UNGPs influence, also cited in *RDS* and by the Philippines Commission, is the OECD Guidelines for Multinational Enterprises, which added a chapter regarding the business responsibility to respect human rights in 2011 and was updated in 2023. This responsible business conduct guidance is backed by over fifty adhering States, including many that are home States to multinational fossil fuel companies. Together with the environment chapter and interpretations on climate-related matters provided by OECD National Contact Points in adhering States, the human rights-related climate responsibilities of enterprises are becoming increasingly clear, especially for multinationals that also adhere to carbon disclosure initiatives for emissions across scopes 1–3 like the GHG Protocol.

## 16.6 CONCLUSION

Causation arguments arise in many different kinds of climate litigation and at different stages from standing to tort. Cases that challenge project approvals offer an important opportunity to stop fossil fuel extraction and future emissions, yet many courts struggle to move beyond direct but-for causation analysis despite best practices that adopts an indirect test of reasonable foreseeability of harm. An emerging concern may be attention given by courts to net-zero commitments (e.g. *Smith*), which muddies the waters when it comes to accepting that fossil fuel extraction necessarily leads to problematic scope 3 emissions.

[123] The Human Right to a Clean, Healthy, and Sustainable Environment, UNGA Res 76/300 (28 July 2022). Both Canada and the United States voted in favour.

[124] David W. Rivkin and others, 'UN Guiding Principles on Business and Human Rights at 10' (*Debevoise & Plimpton*, 6 July 2021) <www.debevoise.com/insights/publications/2021/07/un-guiding-principles> accessed 26 February 2024.

Cases where plaintiffs sue to prevent or reduce future emissions stemming from government policy or regulation are clearly ripe for a broader approach to causation, and this area is where an incrementalist approach to causation has found most success. Cases such as *Massachusetts* v *EPA*, *Urgenda*, *Notre Affairs a Tous*, and *Grande-Synthe* all illustrate emerging best practices. Plaintiffs can point to the contributions that State-based emissions will make to global emissions and, in conjunction with the Paris Agreement and latest scientific reports, are able to convince judicial bodies that future emission reductions are important and closely connected to preventing future harm. In countries with robust human rights frameworks, such as in Europe, this broader approach to causation is finding the most judicial success. This is a key trend which we anticipate will continue. Where courts adopt a broader, best practice approach to causation, litigation can make a real difference both nationally and internationally in stemming the most catastrophic impacts of climate change.

We anticipate that human rights-based claims against corporate enterprises will increase, building on the approach to value chain causation in the UNGPs and emerging best practice cases. Disclosure-based claims are likely to be most easily successful. Plaintiffs will point to portfolio losses tied to reserve write-downs, or, in the case of utilities, infrastructure losses and/or litigation tied to damage, and the lack of disclosure of these risks by companies. Bankruptcy law is likely to be another area of law where causal relationships between climate-related risks and impacts, and bankruptcy will receive attention.[125] We also anticipate that climate litigation in the Global South, with State-owned enterprises as defendants, is likely to emerge, given the large emissions contributions these entities have made and continue to make. Causation in these instances may be easier to prove, given the large emissions and the State-sanctioned nature of corporate activities.

[125] Meinhard Doelle and others, 'Reflections on Orphan Well Association and Grant Thornton Ltd SCC 5' (*Environmental Law News*, 22 February 2019) <https://blogs.dal.ca/melaw/2019/02/22/reflections-on-orphan-well-association-v-grant-thornton-ltd-2019-scc-5/> accessed 26 February 2024.

# 17

# Climate Causality

## *From Causation to Attribution*

*Petra Minnerop*[*]

### 17.1 INTRODUCTION: OBJECTIVES AND CONTEXT

Climate law and governance structures evolve through different instruments, in international, regional, and domestic law and policy. A significant mode of development is jurisprudential. Courts often make authoritative statements not only about the law on climate change but also about the underlying scientific evidence. At the heart of this growing field of climate jurisprudence are almost always legal concepts that were neither designed nor intended for the application in the context of a collective action problem. Therefore, judicial pronouncements on law's core concepts reveal how the law is challenged by, and grapples with, climate change, especially where clarifying legislation is absent. Apart from filling legislative gaps and developing the law, courts also influence the societal perception of climate change, including its causes, impacts, urgency, and legal implications. Analysing these judgments structures, consolidates, and develops the law on climate change.

This chapter provides a thorough analysis of some of the most significant cases on causation and attribution in a rapidly growing field of global climate jurisprudence. To structure the analysis, I situate the legal notion of attribution within an overarching concept of *climate causality* that comprises general causation, specific causation, and attribution as a sequence of analytical steps. While general and specific causation are primarily concerned with identifying the factual relations between cause(s) and event(s), attribution adds a distinct normative dimension.[1]

The approach in this chapter addresses the interdisciplinary challenge of applying law in the context of climate change, connects attribution in law with event attribution, and explains the inductive and deductive approaches used in scientific studies. The case law is selected from a range of different legal orders, for its contribution to advancing the concept of climate causality. To structure the vast number of relevant cases, the chapter offers a novel system based on thematic areas where jurisprudence emerges that shapes the normative context for causal explanations and attribution.

[*] Petra Minnerop is a professor of international law at Durham University.

[1] The definition will be elaborated in Section 17.2.1.

Four areas of judicial engagement with climate change are identified as main sources for transferable arguments that could inform the reasoning on attribution: the determination of the scope of relevant emissions, the review of national climate targets and measures, the permissibility of emissions-intensive infrastructure projects or activities, and courts' readiness to use and review general (environmental) law concepts to develop climate litigation, thus expanding the normative lens.

### 17.1.1 *Objective of This Chapter*

Given that so far only a limited number of cases explicitly discuss attribution directly, the approach in this chapter is to emphasise the *emerging* nature of the judicial treatment of attribution with regard to climate change. Courts have made authoritative statements about the reality of climate change,[2] they have used reports of the Intergovernmental Panel on Climate Change (IPCC) as expert evidence,[3] and they have shaped the wider normative context in which causal explanations in the field of climate change are embedded.[4] Yet to date, attributing a specific climate-related impact to a defined emitting geographical region or an individual major emitter has been a difficult task in the court room.[5] Compensatory claims against individual emitters remain at risk of failing the legal tests for causation and attribution across jurisdictions.[6] Only prospectively have courts found a causal link

2 *State of the Netherlands (Ministry of Economic Affairs and Climate Policy) v Stichting Urgenda* [2019] ECLI:NL:HR:2019:2007 (Supreme Court of the Netherlands) (*Urgenda Supreme Court*) [4.6]; Liz Fisher, 'Climate Change Litigation, Obsession and Expertise: Reflecting on the Scholarly Response to Massachusetts v EPA' (2003) 35 Law and Policy 236, 239; cf. Maria Lee, 'The Sources and Challenges of Norm Generation in Tort Law' (2018) 9(1) European Journal of Risk Regulation 34.

3 *Urgenda Supreme Court* (n 2), where the Court defined States obligations in the light of the IPCC reports [6.1]–[7.3.6]; *Neubauer and Others v Germany* [2021] 1 BvR 2656/18, 1 BvR 96/20, 1 BvR 78/20, 1 BvR 288/20, 1 BvR 96/20, 1 BvR 78/20 (German Federal Constitutional Court) (*Neubauer*) [36], [160]–[161]. For a discussion of the case see Petra Minnerop, 'Climate Targets: Fundamental Rights, Intergenerational Equity and the German Federal Constitutional Court' (2022) 34 JEL 135; Christoph Möllers and Nils Weinberg, 'Die Klimaschutzentscheidung des Bundesverfassungsgerichts' (2021) 76 Juristen Zeitung 1069, 1072. See also *Gloucester Resources Limited v Minister for Planning* [2019] NSWLEC 7 (*Gloucester Resources*) [431]–[435]; *Mathur v Ontario* [2023] ONSC 2316 (*Mathur Merits*) [19].

4 *Neubauer* (n 3) [143]–[151]; *Family Farmers and Greenpeace v Germany* [2018] 00271/17/R/SP (Administrative Court of Berlin) (*Family Farmers and Greenpeace*) 21, noted that the threshold for causality should not be overstated; *Neubauer* (n 3) [116], [202]. [229]; *Gloucester Resources* (n 3) [515]–[516]; *Mathur Merits* (n 3) [149].

5 One case where this could be considered as part of the scientific evidence is *Lliuya v RWE* [2017] I-5 U 15/17 (Higher Court of Appeal in Hamm). Other courts have established the causal connection between certain activities and concrete amounts of GHG emissions, *Minister of Environment v PT Selatnasik Indokwarsa and PT Simpang Pesak Indokwarsa*, Decision No 105/Pdt/G/2009/PN.JKT.UT (North Jakarta District Court).

6 Cf United Nations Environment Programme and Sabin Center for Climate Change, 'Global Climate Litigation Report: 2023 Status Review' (2023) <https://wedocs.unep.org/20.500.11822/43008> 65 accessed 24 February 2024. The 'but for' test in the common law is similar to the *conditio since qua non* formula that is regularly applied in civil law jurisdictions, see Marta Infantino and Eleni

between planned major infrastructure projects and their anticipated contributions to global emissions and to further adverse climate change impacts – as discussed in the preceding chapter.[7]

Meanwhile, a thorough analysis reveals that even a dismissed case can shed light on legal criteria for causation and attribution while pointing to the need for further legal and scientific research. An example is *Comer v Murphy Oil USA, Inc*, where the Court dismissed the case but alluded to the defendants' memorandum and stated that the plaintiffs would need to demonstrate the following:

(1) what would the strength of Hurricane Katrina have been absent global warming;
(2) how much of each plaintiff's damages would have been attributable to Hurricane Katrina if it had come ashore at a lower strength; and
(3) how much of each plaintiff's damages was attributable to failures by others, such as the Federal Emergency Management Agency (FEMA) and other governmental agencies, to prevent additional injury.[8]

This list of criteria merits critical evaluation. The Court's three points may indeed not set forth a conclusive selection that fully reflects the causally relevant contribution of climate change to Hurricane Katrina. Climate change may not only have contributed to the strength of the hurricane and the resulting damages, it may also have exacerbated the failures by others, thereby amplifying existing vulnerabilities. These interdependencies between existing vulnerabilities, administrative failures, and climate change deserve attention from a scientific and from a legal point of view, to make clearer statements about causation and attribution. Exploring these factual connections should not be limited through a constricted set of criteria.

An increased focus on the intersection of science and law, where scientific research is informed by a better understanding of legal criteria for attribution, is certainly timely. Attribution-based cases represent a key trend in litigation, albeit one that is moving more slowly than originally anticipated.[9] This may be due to the fact that the legal analysis of 'attribution' incorporates a normative operation: it is never

Zervogianni (eds), *Causation in European Tort Law* (Cambridge University Press 2017) 4, 590; Walter van Gerven, Jeremy Lever, and Pierre Larouche, *Cases, Materials and Text on National, Supranational and International Tort Law* (Hart 2000) 395.

7 *Gloucester Resources* (n 3) [525]–[528]; *Save Lamu et al v National Environmental Management Authority and Amu Power Co Ltd* [2016] Tribunal Appeal No Net 196 of 2016 (Kenya Environmental Tribunal) [151]; *Earthlife Africa Johannesburg v Minister of Environmental Affairs and Others* [2017] 65662/16 <http://climatecasechart.com/wp-content/uploads/sites/16/non-us-case-documents/2017/20170306_Case-no.-6566216_judgment-1.pdf> accessed 24 February 2024.

8 *Comer v Murphy Oil USA, Inc* No 1:11-cv-00220 (Federal District Court of Mississippi) 23.

9 United Nations Environment Programme and Sabin Center for Climate Change, 'Global Climate Litigation Report: 2020 Status Review' (2020) 4, 22, 27, and 31 <https://wedocs.unep.org/bitstream/handle/20.500.11822/34818/GCLR.pdf?sequence=1&isAllowed=y> accessed 24 February 2024. See for an update, Global Climate Litigation Report: 2023 Status Review (n 6) 65.

purely scientific or merely counterfactual but entails the judicial determination of a factual, social, and legal reality.[10] This determination will be case-specific and dependent on the relevant law. However, it can be informed by filing cases into categories derived from environmental case law beyond climate change, such as the differentiation between 'look back' and 'in the moment' cases.[11] The respective category defines the applicable standard for judicial intervention so that protective measures can be adopted before harm occurs, despite remaining scientific uncertainties. Therefore, and with an emphasis on the *status nascendi*, emerging best practices in this chapter are derived from judicial pronouncements that prune the normative context and pave the way for a rigorous and comprehensive causal analysis in future cases.

### 17.1.2 *Climate Science and Attribution Studies as a Matter for Courts*

Climate science has already become a matter for courts. Courts across a number of jurisdictions have established a causal link between increasing greenhouse gas (GHG) emissions[12] and an increasing risk of climate-related extreme events and slow-onset events.[13] The relevant available scientific evidence is often directly derived from the reports of the IPCC, such as in *Milieudefensie v Royal Dutch Shell*,[14] or indirectly, from national scientific advisory committees that provide independent advice and devise national carbon budget calculations based on IPCC reports.[15] The Administrative Court of Berlin in *German Farmers v Germany* argued that there 'is much to be said for at least an equal global per capita distribution of the remaining global $CO_2$ budget'.[16]

The physical science on climate change, and, in particular, detection and attribution studies, provides important and steadily evolving information for the causal

[10] Christian von Bar, *The Common European Law of Torts*, vol 2 (Clarendon Press 2000) 435, 440, 461; van Gerven, Lever and Larouche (n 6); Christian Grüneberg, 'Vorb v § 249' in *Palandt, Bürgerliches Gesetzbuch* (77th ed, Beck 2018) [26]–[28]; see further Will Frank, 'Klimahaftung und Kausalität' (2013) Zeitschrift für Umweltrecht 23. For international law see ILC, 'Draft Articles on Responsibility of States for Internationally Wrongful Acts, with commentaries' (2001) UN Doc A/RES/56/83 (2001), 53 UN GAOR Supp (No 10) at 43, Supp (No 10) A/56/10 (IV.E.1) (ILC Draft Articles) 35 [6].

[11] This differentiation will be explained under Section 17.2.2.

[12] For legibility, the term 'emissions' will be used synonymously with 'GHG emissions'.

[13] *Massachusetts v EPA* 549 US 497 (2007). For a comprehensive analysis of this case see Richard J. Lazarus, *The Rule of Five* (HUP 2020); *Thomson v Minister for Climate Change Issues* [2017] NZHC 733 (High Court) (*Thomson*); *Notre Affaire à Tous and Others v France* [2021] No 1904967, 1904968, 1904972 1904976/4-1 21, 22; *Neubauer* (n 3) [36], [160], [161].

[14] *Milieudefensie v Royal Dutch Shell* [2021] ECLR:NL: RBDHA:2021:5339 (District Court of the Hague) [4.4.29]–[4.4.30].

[15] *Neubauer* (n 3) [160]–[161]; *R (on the application of Friends of the Earth Ltd) v Secretary of State for Business, Energy and Industrial Strategy* [2022] EWHC 1841 (Admin) [175].

[16] *Family Farmers and Greenpeace* (n 4) 21.

analysis generally and for the specific criteria of legal attribution.[17] Relevant studies can deliver expert evidence in court and they also more generally improve our understanding of the human contribution to extreme events,[18] such as floods,[19] hurricanes,[20] heatwaves,[21] or slow-onset events and impacts on vulnerable ecosystems.[22] The conventional approach of probabilistic event attribution uses inductive reasoning to establish a quantifiable fraction of the magnitude or probability of risk or harm that can scientifically be attributed to climate change or even localised regional emissions.[23] Studies that claim to evidence the link between a concrete climate-related impact and an individualised amount of emissions carry the potential to change the outcome of litigation.[24] However, only reliable, unbiased, and carefully reviewed studies can produce the legally relevant evidence through assessing observed changes in weather extremes and climate-related impacts, their attribution to causes, and their future trajectories and return periods.[25]

The IPCC has acknowledged that case-specific studies provide evidence in addition to the 'established fact that human-induced greenhouse gas emissions have led to an increased frequency and/or intensity of some weather and climate extremes since pre-industrial time, in particular for temperature extremes'.[26] The IPCC stated in its Sixth Assessment Report (AR6), Working Group I, that since the 2018 IPCC

17 The concerns finding the factor that is a necessary or a sufficient condition for the event, see Petra Minnerop and Friederike Otto, 'Climate change and causation: Joining law and climate science on the basis of formal logic' (2020) 27 Buffalo Environmental Law Journal 49, 56, 68.

18 Working Group I of the Intergovernmental Panel on Climate Change (IPCC) in its Sixth Assessment Report of 2021 defines an extreme weather event as 'an event that is rare at a particular place and time of year' and an extreme climate event as 'a pattern of extreme weather that persists for some time, such as a season', Valerie Masson-Delmotte and others (eds), *Climate Change 2021: The Physical Science Basis. Contribution of Working Group I to the Sixth Assessment Report of the Intergovernmental Panel on Climate Change* (Cambridge University Press 2021) 11.1.2, [11].

19 Sarah F. Kew and others, 'Impact of precipitation and increasing temperatures on drought trends in eastern Africa' (2021) 12 Earth System Dynamics 17.

20 Kevin A. Reed, Michael F. Wehner, and Colin M. Zarzycki, 'Attribution of 2020 hurricane season extreme rainfall to human-induced climate change' (2022) 13 Nature Communications 1905.

21 Andrew Ciavarella and others, 'Prolonged Siberian heat of 2020 almost impossible without human influence' (2021) 166 Climatic Change 9; Mariam Zachariah and others, 'Climate Change made devastating early heat in India and Pakistan 30 times more likely' (*World Weather Attribution*) <www.worldweatherattribution.org/wp-content/uploads/India_Pak-Heatwave-scientific-report.pdf> accessed 24 February 2024.

22 Caroline Taylor and others, 'Glacial lake outburst floods threaten millions globally' (2023) 14 Nature Communications 487.

23 Tobias Pfrommer and others, 'Establishing causation in climate litigation: Admissibility and reliability' (2019) 152 Climatic Change 67, 68.

24 Rupert Stuart-Smith and others, 'Filling the evidentiary gap in climate litigation' (2021) 11 Nature Climate Change 651. Rupert Stuart-Smith and others, 'Attribution science and litigation: Facilitating effective legal arguments and strategies to manage climate change damages' (*Smith School of Enterprise and the Environment*, 2021).

25 Masson-Delmotte and others (n 18) 11, with projections for three global warming levels 1.5°C, 2°C, 4°C.

26 ibid Chapter 11 [6].

Special Report on Global Warming of 1.5°C was published, new evidence has emerged that:

> [E]ven relatively small incremental increases in global warming (+0.5°C) cause statistically significant changes in extremes on the global scale and for large regions (high confidence). In particular, this is the case for temperature extremes (very likely), the intensification of heavy precipitation (high confidence) including that associated with tropical cyclones (medium confidence), and the worsening of droughts in some regions (high confidence).[27]

The legal evaluation of these scientific insights requires judicial engagement with general and case-specific scientific evidence on climate change[28] and climate literacy.[29] The relevant scientific knowledge and the law evolve often at different time scales, and this poses challenges to the science/law intersection. A continuous, mutually informing interdisciplinary discourse is necessary. An illustrative example is *Native Village of Kivalina v ExxonMobil Corp*, where the link between the defendant's emissions and the erosion of the coastal line as a result of climate change at the time of the decision was too indirect to fulfil the criteria of 'fair traceability' (a requirement to establish standing).[30] Scientists nowadays claim that it would be possible to establish a causal link between the losses claimed and the defendant's GHG emissions.[31]

Challenges and constraints in accessing the most relevant, recent, and unbiased scientific evidence in the court of law persist.[32] Any limited availability of scientific evidence in court, or the actual lack of data, cannot simply be interpreted as implying that no relevant trends exist, or that anthropogenic climate change has not contributed to the intensity and frequency of a studied event.[33] Data limitations may only indicate that either the quality or the temporal length of the case-specific data collection, or both, are not suited to provide a full and specific account for

[27] ibid.

[28] Commission on Human Rights of the Philippines, 'National Inquiry on Climate Change Report' (CHRP December 2022) <https://chr.gov.ph/nicc-2/> last accessed 3 April 2025.

[29] The importance of climate education is already acknowledged in the work on 'Action for Climate Empowerment' under Paris Agreement (entered into force 4 November 2016) 3156 UNTS 79 (Paris Agreement) art 12 and United Nations Framework Convention on Climate Change (entered into force 21 March 1994) 1771 UNTS 107 (UNFCCC) art 6.

[30] *Native Village of Kivalina v ExxonMobil Corp Kivalina* 663 F.Supp.2d 863 (District Court of Northern District of California 2009).

[31] Rupert Stuart-Smith and others, 'Increased outburst flood hazard from Lake Palcacocha due to human-induced glacier retreat' (2021) 14 Nature Geoscience 14, 85, 86.

[32] ibid; Pfrommer and others (n 23) 80, explaining that different outcomes can sometimes be explained based on whether a study focuses on magnitude of the event or its frequency.

[33] Friederike Otto and others, 'Climate change increased rainfall associated with tropical cyclones hitting highly vulnerable communities in Madagascar, Mozambique & Malawi' (*World Weather Attribution*, 2022) <www.worldweatherattribution.org/wp-content/uploads/WWA-MMM-TS-scientific-report.pdf> last accessed 24 February 2024.

attribution.[34] Even then, it remains possible and necessary to analyse the factual circumstances of a case in light of the already available and steadily growing body of climate science.

Given the significant and increasing importance of climate science for legal developments, both in legislation and in litigation, Section 17.2 defines the analytical steps of climate causality and explains how attribution studies can be used for legal attribution. It then explains the potential role of normative correctives[35] to soften the outcome of a strict causal analysis, and points to the critical function of three, instead of just two, logical fundamentals for a coherent legal analysis. Section 17.3 identifies emerging best practices of judicial engagement with climate change that could inform legal attribution. Section 17.4 discusses the potential for replicability of these arguments and Section 17.5 concludes.

## 17.2 CAUSATION AND ATTRIBUTION AS INTERTWINED LEGAL CONCEPTS AND ATTRIBUTION STUDIES

The differences between general and specific causation and attribution are not always clearly articulated, and the terminology varies between science (discussed in Chapter 3) and law. Furthermore, some statements about causation in law imply attribution, and there are different approaches to distinguish 'event' and 'source' attribution in scientific studies.[36] In human rights-based cases, a general causal link between a country's projected GHG emissions, increasing global mean temperatures, and expected impacts of climate change that risk interfering with individual rights may be sufficient to argue that national climate targets are inadequate (see Chapter 7).[37] By contrast, in cases that seek to establish individual liability for a climate-related event, specific causation, and attribution of the harm or increased risk of harm, to the action or omission of the defendant must be demonstrated. It

[34] ibid.

[35] Normative Correctives are understood here as case-specific consideration of fairness and justice, as expressed by *Fairchild v Glenhaven Funeral Services* [2002] UKHL 22 [36]: 'Any other outcome would be deeply offensive to instinctive notions of what justice requires and fairness demands' (Lord Nicholls).

[36] Cf Michael Burger, Jessica Wentz, and Radley Horton, 'The law and science of climate change attribution' (2020) 45 Columbia Journal of Environmental Law 57, 67. See Chapter 3 on Attribution Science. See further the differentiation of climate change attribution, extreme event attribution, impact attribution, and source attribution at https://climateattribution.org/.

[37] In *Klimatická žaloba ČR v Czech Republic* [2022] No 14A 101/2021 (Prague Municipal Court), the Court noted that 'there is no doubt that human activity is the central cause of climate change' [283] and that insufficient national measures constituted a violation of the Paris Agreement [280]. This caused an unlawful interference with rights [322]. See, for comparison, the first human rights case of Inuit Circumpolar Council Canada, Petition to the Inter-American Commission on Human Rights Seeking Relief from Violations Resulting from Global Warming Caused by Acts and Omissions of the United States, [2005] Inter-American Commission on Human Rights 1413-05. See further Jacqueline Peel and Hari M. Osofsky, 'A rights turn in climate change litigation?' (2018) 7 TEL 37, 42.

has been noted in 2018 that, for the first time, attribution science opens the door to establishing 'the evidence of specific and quantifiable loss and damage arising out of atmospheric levels of anthropogenic GHGs that can be linked to specific regions and individuals'.[38]

### 17.2.1 *Attribution as a Scientific and Legal Field of Study*

Event attribution as a field of scientific study is defined as 'the process of evaluating the relative contributions of multiple causal factors to a change or event with an assignment of statistical confidence'.[39] A number of different analytical tools are employed, spanning climate observations, modelling, and statistical (re-)analyses.[40] These attribution studies provide the 'human contribution assessment' for observed changes in ecosystems,[41] such as ocean heat content increase or arctic sea ice loss – cases where since 1970 anthropogenic emissions have become the main drivers for those changes.[42] Scientists identify changes in characteristics of the climate system, such as trends and variations in single extreme events, including their frequency, intensity, and duration.[43]

38 Sophie Marjanac and Lindene Patton, 'Extreme weather event attribution science and climate change litigation: An essential step in the causal chain?' (2018) 36 Journal of Energy and Natural Resources Law 265, 279.

39 See Chapter 3 on Attribution Science. Gabriele Hegerl and others, 'Good practice guidance paper on detection and attribution related to anthropogenic climate change', in IPCC, *Meeting report of the Intergovernmental Panel on Climate Change expert meeting on detection and attribution of anthropogenic climate change*; confirmed again in Priyadarshi Shukla and others, 'Summary for Policymakers' in *Climate Change 2022: Mitigation of Climate Change* <https://report.ipcc.ch/ar6wg2/pdf/IPCC_AR6_WGII_SummaryForPolicymakers.pdf> accessed 24 February 2024. See further National Academy of Sciences, *Attribution of Extreme Weather Events in the Context of Climate Change* xvii; Alexis Hannart and others, 'Causal counterfactual theory for the attribution of weather and climate related events' (2016) 97 Bulletin of the American Meteorological Society 99, 104.

40 ibid. See further Geert Jan van Oldenborgh and others, 'Attribution of extreme rainfall from Hurricane Harvey' (2017) 12 Environment Research Letters 124009.

41 Intergovernmental Panel on Climate Change, *AR6 Synthesis Report: Climate Change 2023* 43 <www.ipcc.ch/report/sixth-assessment-report-cycle/> accessed 24 February 2024 (IPCC 2023, AR6 SYR). See e.g. Mariam Zachariah and others, 'Without human-caused climate change temperatures of 40°C in the UK would have been extremely unlikely' (*World Weather Attribution*) <www.worldweatherattribution.org/wp-content/uploads/UK-heat-scientific-report.pdf> accessed 24 February 2024.

42 ibid IPCC 2023, AR6 SYR. For more extreme weather and attribution studies see 'Attributing extreme weather to climate change' (*Met Office*) <www.metoffice.gov.uk/research/climate/understanding-climate/attributing-extreme-weather-to-climate-change#:~:text=This%20page%20explains%20how%20we,impact%20all%20levels%20of%20society> accessed 24 February 2024.

43 ibid IPCC 2023, AR6 SYR 42; Christopher W. Callahan and Justin S. Mankin, 'National attribution of historical climate damages' (2022) 172 Climatic Change 40; Maria L. Banda, 'Climate Science in the Courts: A Review of US and International Judicial Pronouncements' (*Environmental Law Institute*, 2020) <www.eli.org/sites/default/files/eli-pubs/banda-final-4-21-2020.pdf> accessed 24 February 2024; Friederike Otto and others, 'The attribution question' (2016) 6 Nature Climate Change 813, 814.

As a scientific field of study, attribution science is relatively young. One of the first attribution studies concerned the human contribution to the European heatwave of 2003.[44] The study found that it was very likely (confidence level >90%) that human influence had at least doubled the risk of a heatwave exceeding a threshold for mean summer temperatures in Europe.[45] The IPCC recognised for the first time in its Fourth Assessment Report (AR4) of 2007 the relevance of the data of formal detection and attribution studies as a further source for the understanding of the physical science basis of climate change, in addition to climate records and observational data.[46] Since then, evidence of observed changes in weather extremes such as heatwaves, heavy precipitation, droughts, and tropical cyclones, 'and in particular their attribution to human influence', has been significantly strengthened; most recently in AR6.[47]

As introduced in Chapter 3 on Attribution Science, two main methodological approaches can be differentiated: probabilistic event attribution studies and the so-called storyline approach. Probabilistic attribution studies employ inductive reasoning and ask two main questions.[48] First, whether the likelihood or strength of an event has changed in the observational record, and second, whether this change is consistent with the anthropogenic influence as found in one or more climate models.[49] These climate models compare the world *with* climate change with the counterfactual world where *no* climate change exists, thereby assessing the fraction of the attributable risk that can be assigned (quantitatively and qualitatively) to anthropogenic climate change.[50]

The so-called storyline approach is mainly deductive. Studies using this approach do not assess the change of likelihood in a specific event's occurrence (they take that change as a given), but ask whether the impact of the particular event was affected by

44 Peter A. Stott, Daniel A. Stone, and Myles R. Allen, 'Human contribution to the European heatwave of 2003' (2004) 432 Nature 610, 613.

45 ibid 613.

46 Susan Solomon and others, 'Technical summary' in *Climate Change 2007: The Physical Science Basis* 22, 53. Furthermore, a distinction was made between attribution based on expert judgment and attribution through formal studies. The Report added accordingly the terms 'extremely likely', 'extremely unlikely', and 'more likely than not' in order to provide a more specific assessment <www.ipcc.ch/site/assets/uploads/2018/02/ar4-wg1-ts-1.pdf> accessed 24 February 2024.

47 IPCC 2023, AR6 SYR (n 41) 12, 17.

48 Stephanie D. Herring and others, 'Introduction to explaining extreme events of 2014 from a climate perspective' (2015) 96(12) Bulletin of the American Meteorological Society 1; Daniel E. Horton and others, 'Contribution of changes in atmospheric circulation patterns to extreme temperature trends' (2015) 522 Nature 465, 466.

49 Sarah Sparrow and others, 'The use of very large atmospheric model ensembles to assess potential anthropogenic influence on the UK summer 2012 high rainfall totals' (2013) 94(9) Bulletin of the American Meteorological Society Supplement Explaining Extreme Events of 2012 from a Climate Perspective S36–S38; Fraser Lott and others, 'Can the 2011 East African drought be attributed to human-induced climate change?' (2013) 40 Geophysics Research Letters 1177.

50 Friederike Otto and others, 'Assigning historic responsibility for extreme weather events' (2017) 7 Nature Climate Change 757, 758.

known changes (induced by climate change) in the climate system's thermodynamic conditions.[51] Thus, the focus rests primarily on specific qualitative changes in the studied event that can be attributed to climate change.[52] From a legal perspective, both approaches can provide complementary evidence for causation and attribution.[53]

A further layer is added by differentiating between event attribution and source attribution. Source attribution concerns the nexus between a certain activity, a project, or another defined source of emissions, and the additional and quantifiable amounts of emissions.[54] An example are wetland emissions and atmospheric sink changes that explain the growth of methane.[55]

For the purpose of this chapter, and with a view to capture the relevant scientific findings of event attribution studies, the meaning of legal attribution is defined within the broader concept of climate causality that involves general causation and specific causation as a sequence of analytical steps. *General causation* means that a factor has altered the probability of the occurrence of a certain class of events in a statistically significant way.[56] This could encompass the general link between human-caused climate change that is affecting many weather and climate extremes in every region across the globe,[57] or between increasing human-caused climate change and heavy precipitation associated with tropical cyclones.[58] *Specific causation* describes the factual finding that a factor (e.g. increasing GHG emissions, increasing mean temperatures) has altered the specific characteristics of a concrete event (e.g. the duration, frequency, and/or intensity of a heatwave in a certain region and year) in a statistically significant way.[59] In the legal assessment, general and specific causation rely on counterfactual inquiries that seek to identify if, and to what extent, the factor was either necessary or sufficient for the studied event(s).[60] Neither general nor specific causation stipulates that the factor, i.e. the amount of

51 Kevin E. Trenberth, John T. Fasullo, and Theodore G. Shepherd, 'Attribution of climate extreme events' (2015) 5 Nature Climate Change 725, 727.

52 'For example, given a heatwave, how was that influenced by drought changes in precipitation and extra heat from global warming?', ibid 726.

53 Elisabeth A. Lloyd and Theodore G. Shepherd, 'Climate change attribution and legal contexts: Evidence and the role of storylines' (2021) 167 Climatic Change 28.

54 The Sabin Center for Climate Change Law distinguishes the literature on source attribution, impact attribution, and extreme event attribution, see <https://climateattribution.org/> accessed 24 February 2024.

55 Shushi Peng and others, 'Wetland emission and atmospheric sink changes explain methane growth in 2020' (2022) 612 Nature 477–482; Krishnakant Budhavant and others, 'Black carbon aerosols over Indian Ocean have unique source fingerprint and optical characteristics during monsoon season' 120(8) PNAS e2210005120.

56 HLA Hart and Tony Honore, *Causation in the Law* (Oxford University Press 1985) 100, 108, 431; Desmond M. Clarke, 'Causation and Liability in Tort Law' (2014) 5 Jurisprudence 217; van Gerven (n 6).

57 IPCC 2023, AR6 SYR (n 41) 46.

58 ibid 17.

59 Minnerop and Otto (n 17) 49, 56; Mariam Zachariah and others, 'Extreme heat in North America, Europe and China in July 2023 made much more likely by climate change' (*Imperial College London*, 2023) <https://spiral.imperial.ac.uk/handle/10044/1/105549> accessed 24 February 2024.

60 Minnerop and Otto (n 17) 49, 55.

emissions over a certain period of time, must be the only cause. There can be a set of factors that act as concurrent causes.[61] It is a related but different question to measure and objectively quantify the contribution of each cause.

On that basis, *attribution* in law is understood as the final step that describes the adequate and quantifiable contribution of an individualised factor or activity to the studied event (impact or damage), in a specific normative context.[62] It asks, for example, if the changed characteristics of a concrete event (increased outburst flood hazard of a glacial lake) have not only been caused by human-induced glacier retreat (i.e. specific causation between glacier retreat and increased risk)[63] but can be *adequately* assigned to a concrete human contribution. Attribution spans the nexus between the human activity and the concrete adverse impact. The term 'adequate' has its roots in the 'theory of adequate causation'[64] and indicates that there can be causal chains that – for various reasons – cannot or no longer be linked to a particular source.[65]

The normative considerations that are relevant to establish legal attribution will depend on the circumstances of each case and relevant scientific and legal determinations such as the role of natural variabilities, the distribution of risk spheres, and provisions concerning the onus of proof.[66] Absolute certainty is not required to prove either causation or attribution in law.[67]

Within the normative evaluation of 'adequacy', the law – and courts in interpreting and applying legal criteria – can attribute climate-related impacts to human-controlled emissions and thereby (re-)allocate responsibilities, potentially beyond the strict 'but for' analysis albeit within the rule of law. However, these legal determinations can work in both ways: they can either interrupt or expand the causal chain, that is, exclude or include certain factors as causes.

An example of the former is the exclusion of so-called 'cruise emissions' from the consideration of an airport expansion in *Vienna-Schwechat Airport Expansion*.[68] The Austrian Constitutional Court interpreted the requirement for airline operators to comply with EU emissions monitoring and reporting schemes[69] so as to conclusively assign the responsibility to manage so-called 'cruise emissions' to airlines and not to

[61] ibid 53, 67, 83. See also explicitly *Mathur Merits* (n 3) [143].

[62] Grüneberg (n 10).

[63] Stuart-Smith and others (n 31) 85, 86.

[64] The 'Adequanztheorie' goes back to the work of Carl Ludwig von Bar, *Die Lehre vom Causalzusammenhange im Rechte, besonders im Strafrechte* (1871).

[65] ibid 27, 28.

[66] Michael S. Moore, *Causation and Responsibility: An Essay in law, Morals and Metaphysics* (Oxford University Press 2009) 118; Ernest J. Weinrib, 'Causal uncertainty' (2016) 36 OJLS 135, 140.

[67] ILC, 'Draft Articles on Responsibility of States for Internationally Wrongful Acts, with commentaries' (2001) UN Doc A/RES/56/83 (2001), 53 UN GAOR Supp (No 10) at 43, Supp (No. 10) A/56/10 (IV.E.1) 39 [9].

[68] *Vienna-Schwechat Airport Expansion* E 875/2017 E 886/2017 (Constitutional Court of Austria) 6–9 <http://climatecasechart.com/non-us-case/in-re-vienna-schwachat-airport-expansion/> accessed 24 February 2024.

[69] Council Directive 2008/101/EC of 19 November 2008 [2009] OJ L8/3 [15].

airports or airport operators.[70] On that basis, the Court overturned an earlier decision of the Austrian Administrative Court.[71] The Administrative Court had refused to grant permission for a third runway extension with the argument that the public interest of 'no further significant increase in GHG emissions in Austria due to the construction and operation of the third runway' prevailed over the interest to expand the airport's capacity.[72] The Constitutional Court did not deny that additional emissions would occur; however, it found that these had wrongly been included in the consideration of relevant public interests by the Administrative Court, given that the majority of predicted emissions would occur as cruise emissions – thus falling within the responsibility of airline operators.[73]

The Constitutional Court's reasoning in this case demonstrates the normative operation that furnishes attribution, and it illustrates how important it is to clearly distinguish between a factual consideration of a proposed project's future emissions and assigning legal responsibility for those emissions. Specific causation captures the quantifiable emissions resulting from the expansion of the airport; these would not exist 'but for' this individual project. The next analytical step relates to the attribution of these additional emissions. It is indeed a *legal determination* to attribute cruise emissions to the airline operators. This legal attribution and the assigned responsibility that comes with it in terms of accounting and reporting, and possibly 'off-setting', are to be distinguished from specific causation, as the factual assessment of the amount of predicted emissions. According to the relevant Austrian law, the evaluation and balancing of the various 'public interests' affected by the project depend precisely on the factual consideration of the project's emissions,[74] not on the legal attribution of these emissions.

Interestingly, the Philippines Commission on Human Rights included in its National Inquiry on Climate Change Report a section on 'Recommendations for the Judiciary'.[75] Therein, it noted that 'in many jurisdictions, courts evaluate evidence linking actors to climate-related losses using the stringent standards of legal causation'.[76] According to the Commission, 'this disregards the work of climate

70 *Vienna-Schwechat Airport Expansion* (n 68).

71 ibid.

72 *Vienna-Schwechat Airport Expansion* W109 2000179-1/291E (Administrative Court of Austria) (unofficial English translation). The Court found at [127] that

> As climate change is associated with severe health damage, with an increase in heat – related deaths as well as severe impairments of the Austrian economy and the agriculture and the project will lead to a significant increase in GHG emissions, the public interest in the realization of the project fall below the public interest in the protection against the negative effects of climate change and land use.

73 *Vienna-Schwechat Airport Expansion* (n 68) at 7.

74 Luftfahrgesetz, LFG, BGBl. Nr. 253/1957, idF. BGBl. I Nr. 80/2016 (Austria).

75 Commission on Human Rights of the Philippines (n 28) 147.

76 ibid.

and attribution science, and causes more climate injustices'.[77] The Commission proceeded to define event attribution as to establish '(i) whether the likelihood or strength of a natural event has changed in the observational record, and (ii) whether this change is consistent with the anthropogenic influence as found in one or more climate models'.[78] This statement confirms that measurable changes in the likelihood of an event's occurrence or strength are *legally* relevant.[79]

It should be mentioned that in exceptional circumstances, beyond the context of climate litigation, courts have acknowledged that normative considerations can also function in the opposite direction and draw factors in as factual causes. These are cases where a mechanistic causal analysis was found to be 'in contradiction to law's function to achieve justice and fairness'.[80] For example, in asbestos litigation, courts have attributed harm to the actions or omissions of the defendant, even when the traditional causal tests of 'but for' and '*conditio sine qua non*' have failed.[81]

This interpretative approach stresses the fundamental role of the judiciary in the evolution and affirmation of so-called 'normative correctives' that form part of the legal concept of attribution.[82] However, specific normative correctives in the context of climate change are not yet widely articulated or accepted. Therefore, the attribution of a specific climate risk, damage, or loss involves not only a variety of forensic, evidentiary, and legal questions, it fundamentally still proceeds in the shadow of a yet unresolved ethical debate of global climate equity and fairness.[83]

### 17.2.2 *Normative Correctives v Extended Logical Fundamentals?*

As the Philippines Human Rights Commission remarked, an overly stringent application of causal tests will not easily be reconciled with the evidence produced by attribution studies.[84] Research has demonstrated that two main approaches are available to soften the outcome of a strict causal analysis in

[77] ibid. This view is based on attribution science understood as the 'storytelling' approach, see Trenberth, Fasullo, and Shepherd (n 51).

[78] Commission on Human Rights of the Philippines (n 28) 160.

[79] See Elisabeth A. Lloyd and others, 'Climate scientists set the bar of proof too high' (2021) 165 Climatic Change 55.

[80] Richard W. Wright, 'Causation in tort law' (1985) 73 California Law Review 1735, 1743.

[81] *Fairchild* (n 35) [40]: 'On occasions the threshold "but for" test of causal connection may be over exclusionary' (Lord Nicholls). See generally for the treatment of Asbestos under tort law, Maria Lee, 'The sources and challenges of norm generation in tort law' (2018) 9(1) European Journal of Risk Regulation 34, 36.

[82] Minnerop and Otto (n 17) 49.

[83] See Stephen M. Gardiner, *A Perfect Moral Storm: The Ethical Tragedy of Climate Change* (Oxford University Press 2011); Stephen M. Gardiner and David A. Weisbach, *Debating Climate Ethics* (Oxford University Press 2016).

[84] Commission on Human Rights of the Philippines (n 28).

specific cases of alternative or hypothetical causation in multi-stage scenarios.[85] One option would be to apply in the context of climate change normative correctives, given that *factual* circumstances can make it just as difficult as in medical exposure cases to establish causation across a set of multiple factors. So far, these normative correctives in some jurisdictions have included considerations of fairness, distributive justice,[86] and the allocation of risk spheres between the claimant and the defendant.[87] Similarly, courts have used the 'material contribution to risk' test in situations where the plaintiff was unable to establish the exact contribution of a particular tortfeasor.[88] Applying these correctives has changed the outcome of the analysis in situations of alternative, hypothetical, or concurrent causation.[89]

This type of an outcome-correcting approach is, therefore, neither foreign to the law nor has it been widely rejected as conflicting with a positivist approach to the law. For some specific case categories, legal provisions across a number of jurisdictions even set aside the strict rule of the 'but for' test.[90] For example, if a tort has been committed jointly, each tortfeasor will be liable for the full damage if it cannot be established who exactly caused the injury or damage.[91] Meanwhile, normative correctives have had a lesser bearing on climate jurisprudence and the causal analysis in relation to complex climate-related extreme events that are often characterised through combined contributions of natural and human-induced factors.[92]

An alternative option to reflect the scientific evidence of attribution studies through attribution in law is therefore to extend the logical fundamentals upon which the legal analysis of the 'but for' test rests.[93] This can be achieved by using three instead of the usual two logical fundamentals to reflect the contributory

85 These are necessity, sufficiency, and sustenance, Minnerop and Otto (n 17) 49.

86 Weinrib (n 66) draws the attention to conceptual operations in handling causal uncertainty in accordance with corrective justice.

87 Minnerop and Otto (n 17) 49, 60–62; Marjanac and Patton (n 38).

88 *Clements v Clements* [2012] 2 SCR 181 (Supreme Court of Canada). This is related to the 'market share liability' approach where each defendant is liable in proportion to the market share, see *Sindell v Abbott Laboratories* 26 Cal 3d 588 (Supreme Court of California 1980).

89 *Fairchild* (n 35) at [34] (Lord Bingham), [42] (Lord Nicholls), [47] (Lord Hoffmann), [116] (Lord Hutton), and [168] (Lord Rodger).

90 Minnerop and Otto (n 17) 49, 56.

91 Cf Bürgerliches Gesetzbuch, BGB (Germany) s 830 <www.gesetze-im-internet.de/englisch_bgb/englisch_bgb.html#p4227> accessed 14 July 2023. The law uses a legal presumption that reverses the burden of proof for the injured party, see Hartwig Sprau, 'Vorb v § 830' in *Palandt, Bürgerliches Gesetzbuch* (77th ed, Beck 2018). There are different constellations of multiple sufficient causal sets, *Baker v Willoughby* [1970] AC 467; *McGhee v National Coal Board* [1973] 1 WLR 1; *March v Stramare E & MH Pty Ltd* (1991) 171 CLR 506. See also American Law Institute, *Restatement of the Law Third, Torts: Liability for Physical and Emotional Harm* (American Law Publishers 2010) s 26.

92 IPCC 2023 AR6 SYR (n 41) 62.

93 Minnerop and Otto (n 17) 49, 78–84.

nature of concurrent causes in a set of conditions.[94] A coherent causal analysis in these multi-factor causation scenarios over a range of factors can be based on necessity, sufficiency, and, in addition, sustenance.[95] Sustenance accounts for the capacity of a factor to produce and maintain the event, even if the factor is only one among others in a set of conditions, provided its relative contribution can be objectively measured.[96] The case-specific causal analysis on sustenance will be influenced by our general understanding of the physical science basis of climate change and the evidence for the human contribution to certain types of extreme events. This general causal knowledge is captured by the novel concept of the *distinctive causal field* that encompasses certain types of events with common characteristics (i.e. heatwaves in a specific geographical region).[97] The distinctive causal field forms the backdrop for the assessment of the case-specific evidence, for example, concerning the occurrence of a *concrete* heatwave in the specific geographical region.

Recent scientific research buttresses the validity if not the necessity of the distinctive causal field for assessing scientific evidence, in arguing that attribution studies often contain far more information, 'about other hazards of the same type, than is currently utilised'.[98]

The case against the German energy provider, *Lliuya v RWE*, currently pending in the Higher Court of Appeal in Hamm, Germany, could be one of the first cases to illustrate how emissions could qualify as a cause for an increased flood risk on the basis of sustenance and within the context of scientific evidence on glacier melting. Two scientific studies (one using probabilistic event attribution (inductive) and one using the storyline (deductive) approach) assessed the increased outburst flood hazard from Lake Palcacocha in the context of human-induced glacier retreat.[99] At the time of writing, the legal attribution of this flood risk to a so-called 'carbon major', the largest German energy provider RWE, is being considered at the evidentiary stage.[100] This means that the Court was convinced that the case is conclusively argued from a legal point of view.[101]

94 ibid 56, 72.

95 ibid.

96 ibid.

97 Introduced by Minnerop and Otto (n 17) 49, 77.

98 Ben Clarke, Friederike Otto, and Richard Jones, 'When don't we need a new extreme event attribution study?' (2023) 176 Climatic Change 60.

99 Stuart-Smith and others (n 31) 85, using a probabilistic event attribution study approach, and following a storyline approach are Christian Huggel and others, 'Anthropogenic climate change and glacier lake outburst flood risk: Local and global drivers and responsibilities for the case of lake Palcacocha, Peru' (2020) 20 Nature Hazards Earth Systems Science 2175.

100 See below Section 17.3.3.

101 *Lliuya* (n 5). Conclusively argued means that the Court is satisfied that the argument is legally sound (Schlüssigkeitsprüfung). The outcome of the case depends then on the evidence that is produced to prove the legal points.

## 17.3 EMERGING BEST PRACTICE ON CLIMATE CAUSALITY IN GLOBAL CLIMATE JURISPRUDENCE

Climate change has undoubtedly moved from the future to the present.[102] The IPCC AR6, WG III Report underlines that the continuation of policies implemented by the end of 2020 – without further strengthening – will lead GHG emissions to continue to rise beyond 2025 and to a median global warming of around 3.2°C by 2100.[103] All government institutions, including courts, play a critical role in strengthening policies that incentivise emissions reductions, and emerging best practices of global climate jurisprudence can support States' ambition.

While there has been a sharp increase in climate cases and strategic litigation in more recent years, climate jurisprudence is not a new phenomenon. One of the earliest cases to mention carbon dioxide ($CO_2$) emissions as a causal factor for environmental degradation is the 1998 Minnesota Court of Appeal's opinion in *re Quantification of Environmental Costs*.[104] New litigation strategies are informed and shaped by the outcome of previous 'waves' of cases.[105]

A whole new field of global climate jurisprudence has emerged since then where boundaries between jurisdictions and traditional lines of differentiation along the public/private law divide have become less suitable to systematise case categories and to derive knowledge from judicial engagement with climate law and science. Private law norms are applied in cases against States, and, equally, private actors' duties are reconciled with States' duties that flow from the Paris Agreement's long-term goals.[106] Some cases are directly concerned with climate causality whereas others advance the normative framework in which causal explanations and attribution could evolve in the future. Therefore, the following devises an analytical structure based on four reference areas where judicial engagement with the climate challenge start to produce transferable arguments across jurisdictions. First, the determination of the scope of relevant emissions; second, the review of national climate measures and their effect on the global climate; third, the planning of emissions-intensive infrastructure projects or activities; and fourth, the use of general environmental law concepts to develop climate law.

[102] Margaret Rosso Grossman, 'Climate change and the individual' (2018) 66 American Journal of Comparative Law 345, 353; Petra Minnerop, 'Integrating the "duty of care" under the European Convention on Human Rights and the science and law of climate change: The decision of The Hague Court of Appeal in the Urgenda case' (2019) 37 Journal of Energy and Natural Resources Law 149, 160.

[103] Shukla and others (n 39).

[104] *Quantification of Environmental Costs* 578 N.W.2d 794 (Court of Appeals of Minnesota, 1998).

[105] See e.g. *Michael John Smith v Fonterra Co-Operative Group Limited and Others* CA 128/2020 [2021] NZCA 552 (*Smith Court of Appeal*) [118]; Wendy Bonython, 'Tort Law and Climate Change' (2021) 40 University of Queensland Law Journal 421; Geetanjali Ganguly, Joana Setzer, and Veerle Heyvaert, 'If at first you don't succeed: Suing corporations for climate change' (2018) 38 OJLS 841. For an overview and an analysis that includes country reports, see Wolfgang Kahl and Marc Weller (eds), *Climate Change Litigation: A Handbook* (Bloomsbury 2021) 237.

[106] Paris Agreement (n 29) art 2(1)(a). See Chapter 9 on Duty of Care.

### 17.3.1 *The Determination of the Scope of Relevant Emissions*

A critical starting point is to establish which emissions, and over which periods of time, should be included in the judicial consideration. In *Urgenda*, the Supreme Court of the Netherlands confirmed that all emissions are causal for further climate change, thereby opposing the 'drop in the ocean' argument of the government.[107] The logic of a limited global carbon budget that demands full consideration of all GHG emissions has also been confirmed by the New South Wales Land and Environment Court in *Gray v The Minister for Planning*[108] and in *Gloucester*.[109]

In a similar vein, the Supreme Court of Norway stated in *Nature and Youth Norway and Greenpeace Nordic v The State* that GHG emissions from combustion of oil and gas (so-called downstream or scope 3 emissions) from exploration of the Barents Sea could interfere with the right to a healthy environment under Article 112 of the Norwegian Constitution.[110] However, the final conclusion of the Supreme Court was based on the premise that the State could nevertheless formulate its climate policy in the light of the 'division of responsibilities' enshrined in international agreements.[111] This reference to international agreements led the Supreme Court to conclude that emissions from combustion would fall within the remit of the respective State using the oil and gas,[112] a position that risks conflating factual causation with the allocation of responsibilities for emissions accounting. The normative and/or legal attribution of these emissions, including the allocation of accounting obligations and potential off-setting responsibilities of the 'end-user', should be reserved for the final step in the analysis as explained in Section 17.2.

The Court of Session (Scotland) equally confirmed that excluding emissions from fossil fuel consumption from consideration as 'direct or indirect significant effects of the relevant project' would not render the environmental impact assessment (EIA) unlawful.[113] According to the Court, these emissions stemmed from the 'use of a finished product'.[114]

107 *Urgenda Supreme Court* (n 2) [5.6.1]–[5.8].

108 *Gray v The Minister for Planning, Director-General of the Department of Planning and Centennial Hunter Pty Ltd* [2006] NSWLEC 720 [100], [103].

109 *Gloucester Resources* (n 3).

110 *Greenpeace Nordic Association v Ministry of Petroleum and Energy* (2020) Case No 20-051052SIV-HRET (Norwegian Supreme Court) (*People v Arctic Oil*) [149], [155]; *Greenpeace Nordic Association v Ministry of Petroleum and Energy* (2020) Case No 18-060499ASD-BORG/03 (Borgarting Court of Appeal) (*People v Arctic Oil Court of Appeal*); Petra Minnerop and Ida Roestgaard, 'In search of a fair share: Article 112 Norwegian constitution, international law, and an emerging inter-jurisdictional judicial discourse in climate litigation' (2021) 44(4) Fordham International Law Journal 847; Ivar Alvik, 'The first Norwegian climate litigation' (2018) 11 Journal for World Energy Law and Business 541, 544.

111 ibid *People v Arctic Oil* [159].

112 ibid.

113 *Greenpeace Ltd v the Advocate General (representing the Secretary of State for Business, Energy and Industrial Strategy and the Oil and Gas Authority)* [2021] CSIH 53 XA34/20 (Court of Session (Scotland)) [64].

114 ibid.

Conversely, a specific case in point that illustrates a comprehensive analysis of climate causality – including attribution – is the judgment of the Rechtbank Den Haag (District Court) in *Milieudefensie v Royal Dutch Shell*, where the Court explicitly included scope 1, 2, and 3 emissions in its causal analysis and ordered Royal Dutch Shell (both directly and via its legal entities which form the Shell group) 'to limit or cause to be limited, the aggregate annual volume of all $CO_2$ emissions into the atmosphere (scope 1, 2 and 3 emissions) due to the business operations and sold energy-carrying products of the Shell group to such an extent that this volume will have reduced by at least net 45% at end 2030, relative to 2019 levels'.[115] In reaching this decision, the District Court not only stated that there was a causal link between GHG emissions and dangerous climate change[116] but also established a further causal link between the limitation of fossil fuel production and global emissions reductions. The Court found that there is a 'direct, linear link between man-made greenhouse gas emissions, in part caused by the burning of fossil fuels, and global warming'.[117] Thus, limiting the production of fossil fuels would result in reduction of emissions, as 'research shows that there is a causal relationship between production limitation and emission reduction' and 'studies using elasticities from the economics literature have shown that for oil, each barrel left undeveloped in one region will lead to 0.2 to 0.6 barrels not consumed globally over the longer term'.[118]

The Court's reasoning rejects the conventional 'carbon leakage' argument that the demand for fossil fuel will remain constant regardless of any changes in the supply chain. The decision stands in sharp contrast to the view held by the Court of Session in *Greenpeace Ltd v the Advocate General*, where the material effect on climate change of discontinued oil exploitation in the North Sea was seen as 'difficult to argue'.[119] In addition, *Milieudefensie* demonstrates that private actors' duties are no longer fully separate from States' duties: rather, the company's emissions reductions duties are legally intertwined with the State's commitment to the Paris Agreement and its temperature thresholds that define the global and each State's carbon budget (see Chapter 9).

Accordingly, three important insights resonate from the judgment in *Milieudefensie* and define the Court's position on attribution. The first concerns

[115] *Milieudefensie* (n 14) [5.3].
[116] ibid [4.1.3].
[117] ibid [2.3.2].
[118] ibid [4.4.50].
[119] *Greenpeace Ltd v the Advocate General* (n 113) [68]:

> […] The argument is, in any event, an academic one. It is not maintained that the exploitation of the Vorlich field would increase, or even maintain, the current level of consumption. Unless it did so, it is difficult to argue that it would have any material effect on climate change; even if it is possible to arrive at a figure for its contribution by arithmetical calculation relative to the production of oil and gas overall.

the Court's emphasis on a scientifically supported and internationally endorsed consensus that each company must work towards achieving net zero emissions by 2050.[120] The second insight relates to the recognition of a direct and linear link between Royal Dutch Shell's GHG emissions, dangerous levels of global warming, and the imminent environmental damage in the Netherlands.[121] Finally, the Court confirmed the plaintiffs' argument that all $CO_2$ emissions *attributable to the Shell group* had to be reduced.[122] This means that the localised, imminent environmental damage is attributable to the individualised emissions of the Shell group.

### 17.3.2 *Reviewing National Climate Targets and Measures*

Cases against governments often concern insufficient national climate targets for mitigation, but lawsuits challenging States' adaptation measures are also rising.[123] Furthermore, and as deadlines for sectoral climate targets approach, new administrative case law begins to emerge that is concerned with adequate response measures if targets are not met.[124] So far, cases against governments have often relied on a general causal link between the challenged national climate targets, further climate change in the absence of enhanced targets, and an interference with fundamental rights.[125] The focus rests on whether or not the impugned action or inaction is capable of depriving individual rights,[126] with the aim of compelling governments to

120 *Milieudefensie* (n 14) [4.4.27], [4.4.36].

121 ibid [2.3.2], [4.4.16], [4.4.37].

122 ibid [4.4.34], [4.4.37].

123 *Klimatická žaloba ČR* (n 37). *Friends of Cedra Mesa v Department of the Interior* No 1:21-cv-00971 (District Court of Utah). See further *Global Climate Litigation Report: 2023 Status Review* (n 6) 38–47.

124 The Higher Administrative Court in Berlin-Brandenburg ordered the German government to adopt an immediate action programme ('Sofort Programm') to address the State's failure to meet the targets in the transportation and the building sectors in OVG 11 A 11/22, OVG 11 A 27/22 u. OVG 11 A 1/23.

125 The Human Rights Council adopted a resolution on 8 October 2021 that introduces a new Special Rapporteur on the promotion and protection of human rights in the context of climate change, A/HRC/RES/48/14; see further OHCHR, Report of the Special Rapporteur on the Issue of Human Rights Obligations Relating to the Enjoyment of a Safe, Clean, Healthy and Sustainable Environment UN Doc A/HRC/37/59, annex (2018).

See Commission on Human Rights of the Philippines (n 28); Jacqueline Peel and Jolene Lin, 'Transnational climate litigation: The contribution of the Global South' (2019) 113 AJIL 679; Minnerop (n 102) 149, 160; Margaretha Wewerinke-Singh and Ashleigh McCoach, 'The State of the Netherlands v Urgenda Foundation: Distilling best practice and lessons learnt for future rights-based climate litigation' (2021) 30 RECIEL 275; Ganguly, Setzer, and Heyvaert (n 105) 841; Brian J. Preston, 'The evolving role of environmental rights in climate change litigation' (2018) 2 CJEL 131; Peel and Osofsky (n 37); Jacqueline Peel, Hari Osofsky, and Anita Foerster, 'Shaping the "next generation" of climate change litigation in Australia' (2017) 41 Melbourne University Law Review 793; Benoit Mayer, 'Climate change mitigation as an obligation under human rights treaties?' (2021) 115 AJIL 409.

126 *Klimatická žaloba* (n 37) [162], [163].

increase ambition levels.[127] These decisions are covered in more detail in Chapters 7, 9, and 16. The following only draws on some of the relevant case law where climate targets were challenged to point out where the reasoning could also inform the analysis on attribution.

The premise for the review of national climate measures is that the Paris Agreement's long-term temperature goal can be translated into corresponding global and national carbon budgets and modelled pathways, as in *Milieudefensie.*[128] Climate targets and corresponding measures can then be reviewed in light of domestic administrative and constitutional frameworks.[129] The scrutiny of national targets is most effective in cases where national climate targets are enshrined in law, as seen in *Urgenda*[130] and *Thomson,*[131] and where domestic law includes interim and sectoral targets as in *Neubauer*[132] and *Deutsche Umwelthilfe.*[133] Acknowledging the causal link between targets, corresponding national emissions, and their effect on the global carbon budget has indeed been critical for the intervention of courts that in turn increased the level of ambition of the defendant State. These decisions indirectly acknowledge that governments' targets and corresponding implementing policies constitute factors to which further climate change and related impacts can be attributed. This nexus is reflected in *Friends of the Earth Ltd and others v Secretary of State for Business Energy and Industrial Strategy*, where the High Court of England and Wales overturned a decision of the Secretary of State as it failed to address how the shortfall towards the national target would be addressed under statutory requirements, and for failure to provide a quantitative explanation to Parliament as required by law.[134]

Courts have an important function when adjudicating on matters such as the role of the Paris Agreement and its implications for national decision-making processes.[135] For example, the Court of Appeal of England and Wales concluded in *R. (on the application of Plan B Earth Ltd.) v Secretary of State for Transport* that the Secretary of State had wrongly omitted climate change considerations and due regard for the Paris Agreement in his decision-making on the expansion of

[127] *Friends of the Irish Environment CLG v The Government of Ireland, Ireland and the Attorney General* [2020] Appeal No 205/19 (Supreme Court of Ireland); *Asghar Leghari v Federation of Pakistan etc* PLD 2018 Lahore 364; *Family Farmers and Greenpeace* (n 4).

[128] *Milieudefensie* (n 14).

[129] An early case in that respect is *Ashgar Leghari* (n 127).

[130] *Urgenda Supreme Court* (n 2).

[131] *Thomson* (n 13). The importance of legal targets have found support in scientific analysis, see Joeri Rogelj and others, 'Three ways to improve net-zero emission targets' (2021) 591 Nature 365, 368. The difficulties that arise from a lack of climate legislation are discussed e.g. for India by Eeshan Chaturvedi, 'Climate change litigation: Indian perspective' (2021) 22 German Law Journal 1459, 1468.

[132] *Neubauer* (n 3).

[133] OVG 11 A 11/22, OVG 11 A 27/22 u. OVG 11 A 1/23 (n 124).

[134] *Friends of the Earth Ltd and others v Secretary of State for Business, Energy and Industrial Strategy* [2022] EWHC 1841 [253], [254].

[135] Instructive is *Klimatická žaloba* (n 37) [244]–[247].

Heathrow Airport.[136] The decision was overturned on appeal, with the UK Supreme Court remarking that 'the Paris Agreement itself is not Government Policy'.[137]

A similar pattern emerges in other jurisdictions, where the lower courts afford the Paris Agreement and nationally determined contributions (NDCs) a legal valence that is not confirmed in next instance. For example, the Municipal Court in *Klimatická žaloba v Government of the Czech Republic* decided that the government was legally bound under Article 4(2) of the Paris Agreement, and also under the State's NDC, to adopt mitigation measures aimed at achieving the objective of its NDCs.[138] The Court acknowledged a direct link between the State's climate target, the adequacy of measures, and the impact on the global climate.[139] Moreover, the Court applied the rules on treaty interpretation enshrined in Article 31, paragraphs 1 and 2(a), of the Vienna Convention on the Law of Treaties,[140] which are recognised as customary international law.[141] However, on 20 February 2023, the Supreme Administrative Court overturned the decision in *Klimatická žaloba v the Government of the Czech Republic*, based on the collective nature of the EU Member States obligations to reduce GHG emissions by 55 per cent by 2030, and referred the case back to the Municipal Court.[142]

Arguments concerning ineffective mitigation measures and non-compliance with governments' own targets were also tested based on private law in two cases brought against the French government in the Paris Administrative Court and the *Conseil d'Etat*. These cases illustrate that ecological damage can be attributed to emissions that exceed the State's target.

The Paris Administrative Court applied a specific tort law provision of the French Civil Code[143] that prescribes that every person is responsible to provide reparation for ecological damage.[144] The Court thereby affirmed that exceeding the national emissions limits will lead to ecological damage; in other words, the damage is

[136] *R (on the application of Plan B Earth Ltd) v Secretary of State for Transport* [2020] EWCA (Civ) 214. The decision of the Court of Appeal was overturned by the Supreme Court, *R (on the application of Plan B Earth and others) v Heathrow Airport Ltd (Heathrow Expansion)* [2020] UKSC 52.

[137] ibid [112]. See further Joanna Bell and Elizabeth Fisher, 'The Heathrow case in the Supreme Court: Climate change legislation and administrative adjudication' (2023) 85 MLR 226.

[138] *Klimatická žaloba* (n 37) [244]–[248].

[139] ibid.

[140] ibid [247]; Vienna Convention on the Law of Treaties (entered into force 27 January 1980) 1155 UNTS 331 (VCLT).

[141] This is established international case law, *Kasikili/Sedudu Island (Botswana/Namibia)* [1999] ICJ Rep 1045, [18], already in 1971, *Legal Consequences for States of the Continued Presence of South Africa in Namibia* (Advisory Opinion) [1971] ICJ Rep 16 [94]. See further Anthony Aust and Oliver Dörr, 'Vienna Convention on the Law of Treaties', *Max Planck Encyclopedias of Public International Law* (Oxford University Press 2018).

[142] *Klimatická žaloba ČR v Czech Republic* 9 As 116/2022 – 166 (Supreme Administrative Court).

[143] *Notre Affaire à Tous* (n 13).

[144] ibid 30 [8]; art 1246 of the French Civil Code states that: 'Toute personne responsable d'un préjudice écologique est tenue de le réparer'.

attributable to the State's excess emissions. In a second decision, the Court then decided that the 'Prime Minister and the competent Ministers are ordered to take all useful measures to repair the ecological damage and prevent it worsening for the share of greenhouse gas emissions not made good compared to the first carbon budget'.[145] In a similar vein, the Conseil d'Etat in *Grande-Synthe*[146] found that the French government was under an obligation to take additional measures by 31 March 2022 to meet the target of reducing GHG emissions by 40 per cent compared to 1990, by 2030.[147]

It should be noted that the argument that an event is attributable to climate change may serve as a defence for the Respondent. In *Burgess v Ontario Minister of Natural Resources and Forestry*, both parties to the dispute argued that the damage was *attributable* to climate change.[148] After the flooding in Houston, Texas, caused by Hurricane Harvey,[149] owners of properties upstream of the Addicks and Barker Dams brought suits against the United States. They alleged an uncompensated taking under the Fifth Amendment.[150] The government argued that it was not responsible for the harm that resulted from the flooding because the damage was attributable to Hurricane Harvey as an 'Act of God'.[151] The Court of Federal Claims joined all cases and then split them into two sub-dockets, one for the Upstream cases and one for the Downstream cases.[152] For the Upstream cases, the Court determined that the United States was liable to thirteen property owners under the Fifth Amendment of the United States Constitution for the taking of a non-categorical, permanent flowage easement on their properties.[153] These easements were the result of government-induced flooding during Hurricane Harvey and produced by the government's construction, maintenance, and operation of the Addicks and Barker Dams.[154] For the Downstream cases, the Court granted the government's motion to dismiss and denied appellant motion for summary judgment.[155] On appeal, the

145 *Notre Affaire à Tous* (n 13).

146 This follows the decision that was handed down in November 2020 where the *Conseil d'Etat* found that the case was admissible and found France substantially exceeded its first 'carbon budget' set for the period prior to 2020. See *Commune de Grande-Synthe v France* [2020] N°427301 (Conseil d'Etat) (*Grande-Synthe*).

147 ibid 6.

148 *Burgess v Minister of Natural Resources and Forestry* No 16-1325 CP, Statement of Claim (Superior Court of Ontario). The case was discontinued voluntarily.

149 Eric S. Blake and David A. Zelinsky, 'Tropical Cyclone Report: Hurricane Harvey' (*National Hurricane Center*, 2018) <www.nhc.noaa.gov/data/tcr/AL092017_Harvey.pdf> last accessed 24 February 2024.

150 *In re Upstream Addicks and Barker (Texas) Flood-control Reservoirs USA* No 1:2017cv09001 (Federal Claims Court).

151 ibid 2. See also *Milton v US* Case: 21-1131 (Court of Appeals for the Federal Circuit).

152 *In re Downstream* 147 Fed. Cl. at 570, 574 (Federal Claims Court).

153 In *re Upstream Addicks & Barker* (n 150).

154 ibid [264].

155 In *re Downstream* (n 152).

United States Court of Appeals for the Federal Circuit remanded the case back to the Court of Federal Claims to consider, inter alia, whether Appellants have established causation when considering the impact of the government actions that address the relevant risk.[156]

### 17.3.3 *Permissibility of Emissions-Intensive Projects or Activities*

Cases concerning the permissibility of emission-intensive projects and activities regularly involve private actors. Litigation against corporations, especially against so-called 'carbon majors',[157] is on the rise and contiguous strategies are constantly refined.[158] Cases are often initiated by non-governmental organisations to halt emissions-intensive infrastructure projects or activities. In some instances, lawsuits have also been initiated by local or State governments: for example, several States have filed suits in the United States, seeking to hold oil and gas companies liable for climate change-related harms.[159] A couple of States have also tried to challenge federal measures such as quantifying estimates for the social costs of GHG emissions.[160]

A key case for causation and attribution that is still pending in second instance before the Higher Regional Court in Hamm (Court of Appeal, 'Oberlandesgericht') at the time of writing is *Lliuya v RWE*, as mentioned earlier.[161] The case is based on German nuisance law (section 1004 Civil Code) and concerns climate adaptation measures in response to flood risks. The claimant, a Peruvian farmer from the Andes region, requests a pro-rata contribution of the energy company for protection measures against flood outburst of the glacial Lake Palcacocha, thus a contribution to adaptation costs. The claimant's calculation, which is open for the Court's own determination, is rooted in the global percentage of historic emissions contributed by RWE, amounting to 0.47 per cent according to a study of carbon-major corporations.[162] In the first instance, the Regional Court in Essen ('Landgericht')

156 *Milton v US* (n 151) [14].

157 Richard Heede, 'Tracing anthropogenic carbon dioxide and methane emissions to fossil fuel and cement producers 1854–2010' (2014) 122 Climatic Change 229–241.

158 Ganguly, Setzer, and Heyvaert (n 105).

159 *City of New York v BP plc* Case 18-2188; *City of Oakland v BP plc* Case 3:17-cv-06011-WHA.

160 *State of Missouri v Biden* No 4:21-CV-00287-AGF, in which the President's Executive Order 13990 ('EO 13990') that establishes an Interagency Working Group on the Social Cost of Greenhouse Gases was challenged; the case was dismissed for lack of standing. The Circuit Court in *State of Louisiana v Biden* Case 22-30087 dismissed a similar claim for lack of standing, stating that 'We now dismiss this action because Plaintiffs have failed to meet their burden to prove standing. Plaintiffs' allegations of "injury in fact" rely on a chain of hypotheticals: federal agencies may (or may not) premise their actions on the Interim Estimates in a manner that may (or may not) burden the States. Such injuries do not flow from the Interim Estimates but instead from potential future regulations…'

161 *Lliuya* (n 5). See also Section 17.2.2.

162 Heede (n 157).

rejected a causal link between the contributions of RWE to global climate change, due to the many contributions and contributors to climate change.[163] A mechanistic application of the '*conditio sine qua non*' (equivalent to 'but for') formula prevented the Court from engaging more closely with scientific evidence that seeks to attribute quantifiable amounts of emissions to specific major emitters. By contrast, the Higher Regional Court stated that the case was conclusively argued (meaning the legal argument *per se* is valid and the case will depend on providing pertinent evidence) and allowed it to proceed to trial. Now at the evidentiary stage, claimants must prove that there is a serious threat of an avalanche that could lead to flooding, and they must demonstrate how this would affect the property of the claimant.[164]

Cases to compel further regulatory action or to review authorities' approval for emissions-intensive infrastructure projects have been brought across jurisdictions. These include situations where authorities below the level of national government unlawfully refused to take regulatory action,[165] limited public participation, and/or insufficiently considered climate change impacts when granting permissions.[166] The latter category impliedly connects emissions attribution (e.g. the anticipated future emissions) and event attribution (the contribution of the project to further climate-related impacts). For example, in *Earthlife Johannesburg v Minister of Environmental Affairs*, the High Court of South Africa held that an assessment of climate change impacts in the environmental authorisation process will 'best be accomplished by means of a professionally researched climate change impact report'.[167] This approach was confirmed in *Sustaining the Wild Coast NPC v Minister of Mineral Resources*.[168] In *Save Lamu v National Environmental Management Authority*, the National Environment Tribunal of Kenya set aside the EIA licence, because the climate impacts of what would have been the first coal fired power plant in Kenya had not been fully evaluated given that comprehensive access to information had not been possible.[169]

The decision in *Gloucester Resources Limited v Minister for Planning* provides a causal analysis that includes an explicit statement on attribution.[170] The Court stressed the causal link between the proposed coal mine, climate change, and further impacts, stating that: '[A]ll of the direct and indirect GHG emissions of the Rocky Hill Coal Project will impact on the environment'.[171] The additional

[163] *Lliuya v RWE* [2015] Az 2 O 285/15 (Essen Regional Court) [41]–[46].
[164] *Lliuya* (n 5).
[165] *Massachusetts v EPA* (n 13).
[166] *Save Lamu* (n 7); *Gloucester Resources* (n 3).
[167] *Earthlife Johannesburg* (n 7) [91], for the procedure that NEMA contains for revocations of an authorisation see [110].
[168] *Sustaining the Wild Coast NPC v Minister of Mineral Resources* [2022] High Court of South Africa No 3491/2021.
[169] *Save Lamu* (n 7) [69].
[170] *Gloucester Resources* (n 3).
[171] ibid [514].

emissions would be directly attributable to the project. Consequently, a measurable impact of the project on the environment would be attributable to the project and the emissions generated by it.[172]

In *Citizens for a Healthy Community v U.S. Bureau of Land Management*, the Court held that the agency had failed to comply with the National Environmental Policy Act by not taking a hard look at the reasonably foreseeable indirect impacts of authorising oil and gas developments.[173] In *Sierra Club v Federal Energy Regulatory Commission*, the US Court of Appeal for the District of Columbia Circuit found that the Federal Energy Regulatory Commission should have considered the impacts of the project's downstream carbon emissions and climate effects, or explained why such considerations were not relevant for the project.[174] All of these decisions strengthen the proposition that, from a legal point of view, measurable climate impacts could be attributed to a concrete project and its respective emissions.

A more direct attempt to attribute quantified emissions amounts to a certain activity was made in the Indonesian case *Ministry of Environment and Forestry v PT Asia Palem Lestari*, in which the Ministry challenged a private company for the illegal burning of peatland.[175] The government argued that the clearing of peatland for a palm oil plantation released 2,700 tonnes of carbon into the atmosphere and that the activities led to a loss of carbon sinks equal to 945 tonnes of carbon.[176] The District Court of North Jakarta dismissed the case because the Ministry had failed to include other landowners as concerned parties.[177] Meanwhile, the Supreme Court of Indonesia decided in a tort-based lawsuit in *Minister of Environment v PT Selatnasik Indokwarsa and PT Simpang Pesak Indokwarsa* that a quantifiable amount of emissions was attributable to illegal mining activities and awarded the Indonesian Ministry of Environment restoration costs and compensation for GHG emissions.[178]

### 17.3.4 *Expanding the Normative Lens*

Instantiations of emerging best practices that could change the analysis of causality often result from re-assessing legal concepts. For example, the Constitutional

[172] See also *Gray* (n 108) [100].
[173] *Citizens for a Healthy Community v US Bureau of Land Management* No 1:2017cv02519 (District Court for the District of Columbia).
[174] *Sierra Club v FERC*, 867 F.3d 1357 (District Court for the District of Columbia).
[175] *Ministry of Environment and Forestry v PT Asia Palem Lestari* Decision No 607/Pdt.G-LH/2019/PN.Jkt.Utr <http://climatecasechart.com/non-us-case/ministry-of-environment-and-forestry-v-pt-asia-palem-lestari/> last accessed 6 April 2023.
[176] ibid.
[177] ibid.
[178] *Minister of Environment v PT Selatnasik Indokwarsa and PT Simpang Pesak* Indokwarsa, Decision No 105/Pdt/G/2009/PN.JKT.UT.

Court in *Neubauer* re-conceptualised the meaning of 'interference' with a fundamental right and developed the 'advanced interference like effect'.[179] Other courts draw from precedent outside the climate context to adjust the threshold for review. An example is *Hauraki Coromandel Climate Action Inc v Thames-Coromandel District Council*.[180] The Court opined that judicial review in the context of climate change deserves 'heightened scrutiny', as 'decisions about climate change by public decision-makers is similar to that for fundamental human rights'.[181] A key example in that respect is *Mathur v Ontario*, where seven young claimants made an application in 'solidarity with millions of youth in Ontario and around to world', to the Superior Court of Justice of Ontario (Canada), seeking, inter alia, a declaration that Ontario's climate target to reduce GHG emissions by 30 per cent below 2005 levels by 2030 violated their rights and that of future generations.[182] They asserted that Ontario had to establish a science-based target consistent with Ontario's share of the minimum level of GHG reductions to limit global warming to below 1.5°C above pre-industrial temperatures, or, in the alternative, well below 2°C.[183]

The Canadian Court first rejected the government's motion to dismiss the application,[184] stating that many of the claims were capable of scientific proof,[185] and that the applicants should be afforded the opportunity to present their full evidence.[186] In its decision on admissibility, the Court also elaborated on the standard of proof for causation, based on the jurisprudence of the Supreme Court of Canada on the more flexible 'sufficient causal connection' standard.[187]

In its decision on the merits, the Superior Court of Ontario made several important statements about causality.[188] First, it held that the government's target as the impugned action did not need to be the *dominant or the only cause* for the prejudice suffered by the claimants.[189] The Court explained that 'while Ontario's contribution to global warming may be numerically small, it is real, measurable and not speculative'.[190] Second, the Court relied on evidence stemming from event attribution science: it acknowledged that the applications had established on a *balance of probabilities* that the State action 'contributes to an increase in the risk of death or in the

179 *Neubauer* (n 3).
180 *Hauraki Coromandel Climate Action Inc v Thames- Coromandel District Council* [2021] 3 NZLR 280.
181 ibid [51].
182 *Mathur et al v Her Majesty the Queen in Right of Ontario* Application of 25 November 2019, Case No 19-00631627, quote at [6].
183 ibid at [7], [8], see (f).
184 *Mathur et al v Her Majesty the Queen in Right of Ontario* [2020] ONSC 6918 (Superior Court of Justice).
185 ibid. [96], [97] with reference to the Court of Appeal for Ontario.
186 ibid [171].
187 ibid [168]–[171].
188 *Mathur Merits* (n 3) [143]–[151].
189 ibid [148], [149].
190 ibid.

risks faced by the Applicants with respect to the security of the person'.[191] Third, the Court found that by setting a climate target below the 'scientific consensus' of what would be required to align with 1.5°C, Ontario was 'contributing to an increase in the risk of death and in the risks faced by the Applicants and others with respect to the security of the person'.[192] Fourth, the Court acknowledged that the 'causal connection standard' was sensitive to the *context of the particular case*, explaining that a very high causal standard would serve to hinder solving global problems.[193]

The Court thus rejected the government's argument that to meet the causal connection standard, the applicants had to prove 'beyond a reasonable doubt' or 'even on the balance of probabilities' that the harm will occur. Nevertheless, the Court dismissed the case given that the rights under section 7 of the Charter had to be interpreted as a restriction on the State's ability to deprive of the rights and did not (yet) include positive obligations.[194] A further argument concerning intergenerational equity was equally rejected, based on the inability of the Court to determine a generational cohort as an analogous ground under section 15(1) of the Charter.[195] This decision is on appeal at the time of writing.

Courts have of course expressed different views on the possibility to adjust thresholds for judicial review. The Supreme Court of Norway in *Greenpeace Nordic* found that wherever the Storting (Norwegian Parliament) had considered a matter, the threshold for review must be very high.[196] In a similar vein, the concepts of heightened judicial scrutiny, or variable intensity review, were rejected in *Students for Climate Solutions Inc v Minister of Energy and Resources* where the Court explained that 'what varies is the nature and extent of the legal controls over discretions, not the intensity with which the Court undertakes its tasks'.[197]

In some cases, courts have turned to legal developments that are external to the growing body of climate law. Scholars have pointed out that in China, cases concerning air pollution begin to serve as a gateway for climate change litigation.[198] Courts have applied the 'burden shifting' doctrine under the Chinese Tort Liability Law (TLL) 2009, which operates on a legal presumption of causation and shifts the burden to prove the *absence* of a causal relation in environmental tort disputes to the defendant.[199]

Another approach for assessing causation and attribution stems from the introduction of case categories, as in R *(on the application of Richards) v Environment*

191 ibid [150].
192 ibid [147].
193 ibid [149].
194 ibid [81], [82].
195 ibid [178]–[182].
196 *People v Arctic Oil* (n 110) [142].
197 *Students for Climate Solutions Inc v Minister of Energy and Resources* [2022] NZHC 2116 [40].
198 Yue Zhao, Shuan Lyu, and Zhu Wang 'Prospects for climate change litigation in China' (2019) 8 TEL 349, 375.
199 ibid 371.

*Agency*, a case concerning unsafe levels of hydrogen sulphide from a landfill site.[200] The case was overturned on appeal.[201] However, it is interesting to note that the High Court for England and Wales had reasoned that, in some situations, courts should acknowledge a *presumed* causal chain in line with scientific knowledge, at the point where intervention was still possible and harm could be avoided. Although this case is concerned with air pollution and not climate change directly, it is nevertheless instructive as the Court made several impactful statements about causation and attribution, derived from European Court of Human Rights' jurisprudence that had also been previously endorsed by the UK Supreme Court.[202]

The Court distinguished two main categories, the so-called 'look back' and the 'in the moment' cases. The Court held that the inexorable logic of these human rights cases, especially the 'in the moment cases', is that 'public authorities – and courts – must "step up" at the time when it is still possible to prevent that the foreseeable damage will materialise'.[203] In other words, in situations where the causal chain has not yet fully materialised, the duty of 'stepping up' entails that authorities must act *before* a damage occurs and *despite* remaining uncertainties. This approach aligns with the precautionary principle.[204]

## 17.4 REPLICABILITY

Replicability of any of the approaches and analytical arguments related to climate causality will depend on factual circumstances and several tangible and intangible factors. Tangible factors comprise the similarity between jurisdictions (e.g. common law, civil law) and the often-nuanced approach of domestic legal frameworks towards the applicability of international treaty law (variations of monism/dualism). Intangible factors include how courts engage with scientific evidence, foreign case law, and normative considerations pertaining to case categories and thresholds for establishing causation and attribution. Furthermore, the perception of the urgency of the threat of climate change as a societal challenge, global emergency, and/or national crisis inevitably influences the balancing of interests and frames the decision-making.[205] While climate change continues to be viewed globally 'as the gravest threat to humanity', there are divergent senses of urgency and country-specific priorities across jurisdictions.[206]

[200] *Richards, R (On the Application Of) v The Environment Agency* [2021] EWHC 2501 (Admin).

[201] *Richards v Environmental Agency* [2022] EWCA Civ 26.

[202] *Rabone v Pennine Care NHS Foundation Trust* [2012] UKSC 2.

[203] *Richards v Environmental Agency* (n 200) [50].

[204] Meinhard Schröder, 'Precautionary approach/principle' in *Max Planck Encyclopaedias of International Law* (Oxford University Press 2018).

[205] Friederike Otto and others, 'Causality and the fate of climate litigation: The role of the social superstructure narrative' (2022) Global Policy 736, 740.

[206] World Economic Forum, *The Global Risks Report 2022* 18 <www.weforum.org/reports/global-risks-report-2022> accessed 24 February 2024.

Engaging with expert evidence is critical to any consideration of climate causality and for the transfer of judicial arguments. Domestic courts using international law generally,[207] and the Paris Agreement in particular,[208] have already contributed to an inter-jurisdictional judicial discourse on climate change that gradually corroborates judicial reasoning on legal concepts.[209] Some courts have shown a tendency to adopt a comparative law approach by referencing other courts to address opposing views of their own executive branches or public authorities, especially when confronted with the task of safeguarding fundamental rights, or in ensuring compliance with administrative rules.[210]

A court that endorses the reasoning on climate causality in its own jurisprudence validates and strengthens a legal position. Applying domestic law to a global challenge can thus unfold a harmonising effect for legal concepts such as causation and attribution. The following pathways exist to replicate any of the structural arguments:

- Engaging with scientific evidence, including attribution studies, and with social sciences research.
- Including all GHG emissions into the scope of judicial scrutiny, whether reviewing national climate targets or emissions-intensive infrastructure projects and activities.
- Clearly distinguishing between general causation, specific causation, and attribution.
- Engaging with the findings of other courts in a comparative legal approach.
- Drawing from normative developments outside the climate change context to ensure coherent approaches in environmental jurisprudence.

## 17.5 CONCLUSION

This chapter speaks to the lawyer (or judicial officer) and to the climate scientists in its attempt to explain causation and attribution in law and science, and to systematise

[207] Eyal Benvenisti, 'Reclaiming democracy: The strategic uses of foreign and international law by national courts' (2008) 102 AJIL 241, 251; Olga Frishman and Eyal Benvenisti, 'National courts and interpretative approaches to international law' in Helmut Philipp Aust and Georg Nolte (eds), *The Interpretation of International Law by Domestic Courts: Uniformity, Diversity, Convergence* (Oxford University Press 2016) 317, 319; Jutta Brunnée, 'The rule of international (environmental) law and complex problems' in Heike Krieger, Georg Nolte, and Andreas Zimmermann (eds), *The International Rule of Law: Rise or Decline?* (Oxford University Press 2019) 215.

[208] *Klimatická žaloba* (n 37); *PSB and others v Brazil* [2022] ADPF 708 (Federal Supreme Court of Brazil) considered the 'supralegality' of the Paris Agreement; *Ruling on Modification to Ethanol Fuel Rule* 610/2019 (Supreme Court of Mexico). The diversity of views on the role of the Paris Agreement is shown in the case concerning the expansion of Heathrow Airport (n 136). See also the argument of the applicants in *Duarte Agostinho v Portugal and 32 other States* App No 39371/20 (ECtHR).

[209] Minnerop and Roestgaard (n 110) 919.

[210] ibid.

the global case law that shapes the normative context for climate causality. Three main points resonate from the analysis. First, the chapter has filled a gap in the literature by defining general causation, specific causation, and attribution as distinct but overlapping components of climate causality, and it has explained the various approaches used by scientists in attribution studies. This instils much needed conceptual clarity in a complex area of law, including the law/science intersection. Second, it has advanced the idea of a global, inter-jurisdictional judicial discourse on climate change, by structuring the case law through four key areas of judicial engagement with climate change (the determination of the scope of relevant emissions, the review of national climate targets and measures, the permissibility of emission intensive projects or activities, and courts' willingness to use and review general (environmental) law concepts to develop climate litigation). From these four areas, transferable arguments on climate causality already emerge which could tighten the normative context in future cases on attribution. As has been discussed, it is necessary to clearly distinguish between the factual considerations that define general and specific causation, and the normative assessment that furnishes attribution. Legal attribution involves a range of normative considerations that determine 'adequacy' in the causal chain. These normative considerations can exclude or include anthropogenic emissions as causal factors.

Third, the chapter provides a foundation for further interdisciplinary research on attribution. The legal concept of attribution is well suited to trace the relevant scientific evidence, and its benefit for litigation will not only depend on science-informed law but also on law-informed scientific research. Crucially, attribution in law seeks to assign the legal responsibility for a concrete impact or damage to a specific human action or omission; it requires a qualification and a quantification of the human contribution. It is not sufficient to scientifically attribute an increased risk or a harm to human-induced climate change without further specifying the contribution of the 'human factor'. Research on the possible expansion of logical fundamentals of the causal analysis,[211] and the introduction of the 'distinctive causal field',[212] have further elaborated the logical operation that the law could use to trace attribution science.[213] So far, emerging best practice on attribution is scarce, and allowing a case to proceed to the evidentiary stage as in *Lliuya v RWE* is a significant step that signals judicial engagement with this attribution science. The growing body of case law where courts already engage with climate science and social sciences, national and international law, and with the arguments derived from the reasoning of other courts can be described as global climate jurisprudence. This global climate jurisprudence comprises pathways for the replicability of arguments. It may even serve as the basis for emerging normative parameters that carry the fairness discourse on climate change forward, within and beyond climate causality.

[211] Judea Pearl, *Causality: Models, Reasoning and Inference* (Cambridge University Press 2009).
[212] Minnerop and Otto (n 17).
[213] ibid.

# 18

# Remedies

*Juan Auz and Marcela Zúñiga*[*]

## 18.1 INTRODUCTION

The right to a remedy is based on the idea that whoever commits a wrongful act must repair the damage caused.[1] The standard that reparation is expected to achieve is full restitution, that is, that the affected party is restored to the status quo before harm. In the intricate tapestry of climate litigation, the concept of a legal remedy stands as a pivotal culmination point in the process, offering a beacon of resolution and redress for the parties involved. At its core, a legal remedy represents the means through which the rights of individuals or entities are enforced or the violation of said rights is prevented or redressed.

As climate change impacts intensify globally, the quest for adequate remedies in climate litigation has become paramount, serving as the tangible bridge between abstract legal principles and real-world outcomes. These remedies can be broadly categorised into different types based on their nature and objective.[2] Reparation is one remedy to restore the injured party to the position they would have been in had the violation not occurred. This might include restitution or the restoration of specific property or rights.[3] On the other hand, injunctive relief is forward-looking and aims to prevent further harm or violation.[4] Like injunctive relief, a writ of mandamus is unique due to its origins as an extraordinary writ or remedy and its distinct legal guidelines. This writ obliges a public official to perform a non-discretionary

* Dr Juan Auz is an Ecuadorian lawyer and postdoctoral researcher at Tilburg University's Law School working on the TransLitigate project. Dr Marcela Zúñiga is a lecturer at Diego Portales University's Law School. This chapter was made possible by ERC STG TransLitigate. Funded by the European Union. However, views and opinions expressed are those of the authors only and do not necessarily reflect those of the European Union or European Research Council.

1 Dinah Shelton, *Remedies in International Human Rights Law* (Oxford University Press 2015) 13.

2 African Court on Human and Peoples' Rights, 'Comparative Study on the Law and Practice of Reparations for Human Rights Violations' (Registry of the African Court on Human and Peoples' Rights 2019).

3 Lisa J. Laplante, 'The Plural Justice Aims of Reparations' in Susanne Buckley-Zistel and others (eds), *Transitional Justice Theories* (Routledge 2014).

4 Jaap Spier, *Climate Litigation in a Changing World* (Eleven 2023) 222.

ministerial duty.[5] To obtain a writ of mandamus, the petitioner must prove that a governmental agency has breached an unambiguous legal obligation and lacks any other sufficient means to achieve the desired outcome.[6] These are particularly relevant in climate cases where ongoing activities may contribute to environmental degradation. Compensation, another critical remedy, focuses on providing monetary relief to the injured party for loss and damage.[7] This becomes especially pertinent in climate litigation cases where environmental damages might have led to economic losses for communities or regions.

One of the most comprehensive and earliest exercises to consolidate the practice of remedies in international law, which to a significant extent reflects the practice at the national level, comes from the International Law Commission (ILC), which documented since the late 1970s State practice relating to the international responsibility of States.[8] The 2001 final report recognised that reparation could take three forms: restitution, compensation, and satisfaction. In parallel, international human rights law, specifically the work of rapporteur Theo Van Boden,[9] added rehabilitation and guarantees of non-repetition to the list. Consequently, the right to a remedy implies a wide range of modalities, the determination of which will depend on the specific type of violation, that is, on the primary norm that establishes the content of the obligation transgressed.

This chapter aims to show the status and debates concerning remedies in climate change litigation.[10] To this end, the chapter will describe the general framework of the right to a remedy, briefly explaining its evolution and content. It will then analyse how courts and tribunals have interpreted the right to a remedy. Finally, five examples of emerging best practices will be presented, along with tools that judges can use to replicate reparations in climate change litigation.

5 J. Jonas Anderson, Paul R. Gugliuzza, and Jason A. Rantanen, 'Extraordinary Writ or Ordinary Remedy? Mandamus at the Federal Circuit' (2022) 100 Washington University Law Review 327, 336.

6 John C. Dernbach and Patrick Parenteau, 'Judicial Remedies for Climate Disruption' (2023) 53 ELR 10574, 10580.

7 Michael Faure, 'Climate Change Adaptation and Compensation' in Jonathan Verschuuren (ed), *Research Handbook on Climate Change Adaptation Law* (Edward Elgar 2013).

8 ILC, 'Draft Articles on Responsibility of States for Internationally Wrongful Acts, with commentaries' (2001) UN Doc A/RES/56/83 (2001), 53 UN GAOR Supp (No 10) at 43, Supp (No. 10) A/56/10 (IV.E.1) (ILC Draft Articles).

9 Theo van Boven, 'Victims' Rights to A Remedy and Reparation: The New United Nations Principles and Guidelines' in Carla Ferstman, Alan Stephens, and Mariana Goetz (eds), *Reparations for Victims of Genocide, War Crimes and Crimes against Humanity* (Brill 2009) 22.

10 Request for an Advisory Opinion on Climate Emergency and Human Rights to the Inter-American Court of Human Rights from the Republic of Colombia and the Republic of Chile (January 2023), questions D and F <www.corteidh.or.cr/docs/opiniones/soc_1_2023_en.pdf> accessed 3 March 2024. In the literature, see Helen Keller, Corina Heri, and Réka Piskóty, 'Something Ventured, Nothing Gained? – Remedies before the ECtHR and Their Potential for Climate Change Cases' (2022) 22(1) Human Rights Law Review; Margaretha Wewerinke-Singh, *State Responsibility, Climate Chance and Human Rights Under International Law* (Hart 2019).

## 18.2 BACKGROUND TO LEGAL REMEDIES

The right to a remedy in most national systems is based on the idea that whoever commits a wrongful act should repair the harm caused.[11] Remedies are woven into the fabric of various legal systems, each presenting its nuanced approach to redress and relief. In tort law, remedies primarily focus on compensating the aggrieved party for harm due to another's wrongful act. For instance, under the common law principle, the English tort system emphasises compensatory remedies, often monetary, to place the injured party in a position they would have been without the tortious act.[12] Similarly, in the US, the Restatement (Second) of Torts provides for damages to be awarded for harm resulting from negligence, strict liability, or intentional wrongs.[13] On the other hand, constitutional remedies offer redress against violations of fundamental rights enshrined in national constitutions. In India, Article 32 of the Constitution provides the right to constitutional remedies, allowing individuals to approach the Supreme Court directly if their fundamental rights are infringed.[14]

Diving into administrative law, remedies are typically geared towards ensuring that administrative agencies and bodies operate within their legal bounds and prescribed mandates. In the European Union, for instance, the Treaty on the Functioning of the European Union under Article 263 provides for annulment, enabling parties to challenge the legality of an act of the institutions. Similarly, Australia's Administrative Decisions (Judicial Review) Act 1977 sets out grounds for reviewing administrative decisions, emphasising grounds like procedural fairness and jurisdictional error. Through these distinct yet interconnected avenues of tort, constitutional, and administrative law, remedies in comparative law manifest as the bedrock of effective justice, safeguarding rights and ensuring accountability across diverse global legal landscapes.

Since the remedies approach varies considerably from jurisdiction to jurisdiction, this section will focus on discussing remedial practice in public international law, chiefly because the essential traits of remedies lie in its consolidated doctrine, especially in international human rights law. Studying crucial remedial features in international law could also contribute to a general understanding and

[11] Shelton (n 1) 1–9.

[12] Giedre Kaminskaite-Salters, 'Climate Change Litigation in the UK: Its Feasibility and Prospects' in Michael Faure and Marjan Peeters (eds), *Climate Change Liability* (Edward Elgar 2011) 175.

[13] Roda Verheyen and Johannes Franke, 'Climate Change Litigation: A Reference Area for Liability' in Peter Gailhofer and others (eds), *Corporate Liability for Transboundary Environmental Harm: An International and Transnational Perspective* (Springer 2023) 384; Elena Kosolapova, 'Liability for Climate Change-Related Damage in Domestic Courts: Claims for Compensation in the USA' in Michael Faure and Marjan Peeters (eds), *Climate Change Liability* (Edward Elgar 2011) 202; Karen Sokol, 'Seeking (Some) Climate Justice in State Tort Law' (2020) 95 Washington Law Review 1383, 1417.

[14] Eeshan Chaturvedi, 'Climate Change Litigation: Indian Perspective' (2021) 22 German Law Journal 1459, 1463.

potential application of their logic and architecture at the national level. The essence of remedies, both nationally and internationally, seeks to prevent or repair harm, which, *mutatis mutandi*, is the final objective of any climate litigation case, irrespective of the jurisdiction and field of law. Therefore, the essential nature of remedies, which is to right a wrong, is an optimal legal notion for comparative purposes and analytical extrapolation, for example, from the international to the national and vice versa.

Public international law expressly includes the principle of full reparation in the *Factory at Chorzów* judgment of the Permanent Court of Justice in 1928 by establishing: 'The essential principle enshrined in the actual concept of a wrongful act is that reparation must, to the fullest extent possible, wipe out all the consequences of the unlawful act and re-establish the situation, which in all probability would have existed if the act had not been committed.'[15] Therefore, under public international law, the principle of full reparation constitutes the basic structure of the obligation of reparation.[16] This was recognised in the 'Draft Articles on Responsibility of States for Internationally Wrongful Acts' (Draft Articles), elaborated by the ILC.[17] The Draft Articles establish the general framework of the obligation to make reparation; it considers it as a new 'legal relationship' (secondary obligation) that arises after the commission of a wrongful act, that is, the breach of a primary duty contained in a source of international law (treaty or international custom). Thus, Article 32.1 provides that 'the responsible State is obliged to make full reparation for the injury caused by the internationally wrongful act'. The international obligation to make reparation is also customary law. Thus, it can be invoked even without the ratification of a treaty expressly containing it.[18]

For the ILC, and in line with the *Factory at Chorzów* case, the objective of full reparation is to eliminate all the consequences of the wrongful act and to re-establish the situation that, in all probability, would have existed if the act had not been committed.[19] The result expected after acting against a State for the breach of an international obligation is the substantive aspect of reparation.[20] According to the Draft Articles, integral reparation may consist of three measures, which may be applied individually or jointly: restitution, compensation, and satisfaction. Adopting

15 *Case Concerning the Factory at Chorzów (Germany v Poland)* (Merits) PCIJ Rep Series A No 17 [68].
16 Dinah Shelton, 'Righting Wrongs: Reparations in the Articles on State Responsibility' (2002) 96(4) AJIL 833, 835.
17 ILC Draft Articles (n 8). The work carried out by the ILC involved a process of identification and systematisation of practices and usages of the international responsibility of States, which took place between 1957 and 2001.
18 Brian D. Lepard, *Customary International Law: A New Theory with Practical Applications* (Cambridge University Press 2010) 166–167; Shelton (n 1) 238.
19 ILC Draft Articles (n 8) art 33(3).
20 Shelton (n 1) 7.

the measure will depend on the damage caused, which may be both pecuniary and non-pecuniary. Consequently, the Draft Articles make the principle of full reparation applicable to non-pecuniary damage.

Restitution consists of the restoration as far as possible of the situation before the commission of the international wrong.[21] It may take the form of a material return (territory, person, or property) or the revocation of a legal act (for example, the amendment of a constitutional provision, the revision of an administrative act, or the requirement to adopt a rule).[22] However, it admits exceptions: it must not be materially impossible and must not entail a burden wholly disproportionate to the cost that the responsible State would incur.[23]

Restitution is often inadequate, or insufficient to guarantee full reparation. Therefore, compensation emerges as a second form of redress for the harm caused. Its function is to fill possible gaps to achieve full reparation and to compensate for damage susceptible to financial assessment. As a rule, it is granted by a sum of money.[24]

Finally, satisfaction is the distinctive form of reparation granted to the extent that the damage cannot be remedied by restitution or compensation. It is often symbolic, reflecting the need for mechanisms in cases where the damage is of such magnitude that it must involve other actions. However, the measure adopted must not be disproportionate to the injury and must not be humiliating for the responsible State.[25]

Both the principle of integral reparation and the categories established in the Draft Articles have been incorporated in the jurisprudence of the international human rights courts as *lex specialis* in reparation.[26] The *lex specialis* character is supported by Article 33 of the Draft Articles, which recognises that the obligation of reparation may arise between States and may also be invoked by a person or entity other than a State.[27] Therefore, the primary rule determines how and to what extent individuals are entitled to activate international jurisdiction to obtain reparation from the State.

The extent to which the principle of integral reparation can or should be incorporated into international human rights law is debatable. The critical point of the debate revolves around cases in which restitution to the previous situation is unfeasible. In this regard, criticism points to the principle of integral reparation as

[21] ILC Draft Articles (n 8) art 35.
[22] ibid.
[23] ibid.
[24] ibid art 36.
[25] ibid art 37.
[26] Frederic Vanneste, *General International Law Before Human Rights Courts: Assessing the Specialty Claims of Human Rights Law* (Intersentia 2010) 505–508; *Velásquez Rodríguez v Honduras* Inter-American Court of Human Rights Series C No 4 (29 July 1998) [66].
[27] ILC Draft Articles (n 8) art 33.

a 'double-edged sword' since the promise of a comprehensive remedy under international standards can never be fulfilled, no matter how inclusive the justice or administrative reparation process may be.[28] Roht-Arriaza calls this the 'basic paradox at the heart of reparation', the trade-off between restoration to the status quo ante and recognition that such status could not be implemented.[29] However, the Inter-American Court of Human Rights (IACtHR) has established that the principle of integral reparation is intended to guide the Court's decisions to identify a measure of reparation that can come as close as possible to that ideal.[30] Therefore, in those cases where restitution is impossible, the consequences of the damage caused must be repaired through measures recognised by law.

The reparation measures set out in the Draft Articles have been adapted to the context and the type of human rights violations heard and resolved by the competent court. The process has included other measures such as rehabilitation, investigation, and punishment of those responsible and guarantees of non-repetition. Although this last category is considered another secondary obligation for the Draft Articles, the IACtHR[31] and United Nations Basic Principles and Guidelines on the Right to a Remedy and Reparation for Victims of Gross Violations of International Human Rights Law and Serious Violations of IHL ('Basic Principles')[32] have recognised it as a form of reparation.

In wrapping up this section, the international legal sources previously cited epitomise the quintessential principle that any breach of an obligation necessitates reparation in an appropriate form. It echoes a time-honoured doctrine mirrored in national litigation globally, where reparation serves as the cornerstone for addressing wrongs and ensuring justice. This principle's resonance across international and domestic terrains underscores the universal commitment to rectify, restore, and renew the legal and moral balance disrupted by breaches, further highlighting the indelible role of reparations in the quest for justice. The application or transplantation of these assumptions to climate change raises fundamental challenges given the particularities of the type of damage, the actors involved,

[28] Brandon Hamber, 'Repairing the Irreparable: Dealing with the Double-Binds of Making Reparations for Crimes of the Past' (2000) 5(3–4) Ethnicity and Health 215, 219.

[29] Naomi Roht-Arriaza, 'Reparations Decisions and Dilemmas' (2004) 27 Hastings International and Comparative Law Review 158.

[30] *Aloeboetoe et al v Suriname* (Merits) Inter-American Court of Human Rights Series C No 11 (4 December 1991); *Bámaca Velásquez v Guatemala* (Reparations and Costs, Concurring Vote of Sergio García Ramírez) Inter-American of Human Rights Series C No 70 (25 November 2000) [49].

[31] *Garrido and Baigorria v Argentina* (Reparations and Costs) Inter-American Court of Human Rights Series C No 39 (27 August 1998) [47]. The first indication of guarantees of non-repetition appears in the reasoned opinion of Judge Cançado Trindade, in *El Amparo v Venezuela* (Reparations and Costs) Inter-American Court of Human Rights Series C No 28 (14 September 1996) [6].

[32] Basic Principles and Guidelines on the Right to a Remedy and Reparation for Victims of Gross Violations of International Human Rights Law and Serious Violations of IHL, UNGA Res 60/147 (15 December 2005) (UNGA Res 60/147).

and the diversity of victims: Does the law adopt the categories sufficient to obtain a remedy for climate change? How do we interpret the remedies of public international law in line with the principles of climate change? What concrete actions should States and the international community take to guarantee the right to a remedy for climate change? Legal arguments, plaintiffs, defendants, petitions, and judgments vary significantly from case to case, as shown in the remainder of this chapter. However, what they all have in common is their remedial demands: plaintiffs ask courts to require mainly States, but increasingly also corporate actors, to create or strengthen policies/laws aimed at protecting the climate – via combating deforestation, for instance – or to suspend or reform projects that might harm the climate system.[33]

## 18.3 STATE OF AFFAIRS

For this chapter, remedies or climate remedies are defined as outcomes in climate cases that favour the party seeking a climate-aligned objective, including measures to mitigate, adapt to, and compensate for climate-related impacts.[34] According to the latest report on global trends in climate litigation (2023) of the Grantham Research Institute, 'around 55% of the 549 cases in which either an interim or final decision has so far been rendered have had outcomes that are favourable to climate action'.[35] Arguably, the approximately 300 climate litigation cases that have resulted in climate-positive decisions could be deemed cases that have generated climate remedies. Climate remedies take many legal forms, ranging from injunctive relief to writ of mandamus, quashing of administrative permits, and compensation awards.[36] These remedies aim to establish non-repetition, prevent further harm, and repair the damage incurred vis-à-vis

33 Juan Auz, 'The Political Ecology of Climate Remedies in Latin America and the Caribbean: Comparing Compliance between Domestic and Inter-American Litigation' (2024) JHRP <https://academic.oup.com/jhrp/advance-article/doi/10.1093/jhuman/huad057/7571304> accessed 3 March 2024.

34 Joana Setzer and Catherine Higham, 'Global Trends in Climate Change Litigation: 2021 Snapshot' (*LSE Grantham Research Institute on Climate Change and the Environment*, July 2021) 10 <www.lse.ac.uk/granthaminstitute/wp-content/uploads/2021/07/Global-trends-in-climate-change-litigation_2021-snapshot.pdf> accessed 24 February 2024.

35 Joana Setzer and Catherine Higham, 'Global Trends in Climate Change Litigation: 2023 Snapshot' (*LSE Grantham Research Institute on Climate Change and the Environment*, June 2023) 28 <www.lse.ac.uk/granthaminstitute/wp-content/uploads/2023/06/Global_trends_in_climate_change_litigation_2023_snapshot.pdf> accessed 24 February 2024.

36 Annalisa Savaresi and Joana Setzer, 'Rights-Based Litigation in the Climate Emergency: Mapping the Landscape and New Knowledge Frontiers' (2022) 13 JHRE 7, 17–18.

whole-of-government climate policies, corporate behaviour, and identified polluting projects.[37] Courts and tribunals have interpreted remedies in climate litigation quite plurally depending on a manifold of factors, including the remedial aspirations of applicants, the jurisdiction of the court, the court's approach and mandate to reparations, and the field of law.[38]

The Netherlands is where two of the most highly cited and studied climate litigation cases have occurred.[39] Both of these cases have resulted in climate remedies. The first case is *Urgenda Foundation v State of the Netherlands*, in which the plaintiffs contested the government's insufficient efforts to address climate change. Specifically, they criticised the Dutch government for lacking ambition in its domestic climate change strategy, which aimed to decrease greenhouse gas (GHG) emissions by 17 per cent. The plaintiffs achieved a favourable outcome: The Court ruled that the government's failure to achieve a minimum 25 per cent reduction in greenhouse gas emissions by the end of 2020 would breach Articles 2 and 8 of the European Convention on Human Rights (ECHR) and Article 21 of the Dutch Constitution.[40] As a result, the Court ordered the State to achieve more significant emissions reductions, thus exemplifying a climate remedy of guarantee of non-repetition and cessation through injunctive relief. A noteworthy aspect of the judgment that delineates the scope of the remedy is the Supreme Court's assertion that if 'the government is obliged to do something, it may be ordered to do so by the courts, as anyone may be, at the request of the entitled party'.[41] Although the Court averred that this power to obligate the government to 'do something' is a fundamental rule of constitutional democracy, the judicial remedial obligation in this case did not include an order to take specific legislative measures. As such, the State could choose the measures to comply with the judgment.[42] Following *Urgenda*, other *Urgenda*-style cases emerged in Belgium,[43]

37 Fin-Jasper Langmack, 'Remedies for Climate Change – A Decisive Push Towards Paris?' in Daniëlla Dam-de Jong and Fabian Amtenbrink (eds), *Netherlands Yearbook of International Law 2021: A Greener International Law – International Legal Responses to the Global Environmental Crisis* (TMC Asser Press 2023).

38 Margaretha Wewerinke-Singh, 'Remedies for Human Rights Violations Caused by Climate Change' (2019) 9 Climate Law 224, 228–229.

39 Lucy Maxwell, Sarah Mead, and Dennis van Berkel, 'Standards for Adjudicating the next Generation of Urgenda-Style Climate Cases' (2022) 13(1) JHRE 35; Chiara Macchi and Josephine van Zeben, 'Business and Human Rights Implications of Climate Change Litigation: Milieudefensie et al v Royal Dutch Shell' (2021) 30 RECIEL 409.

40 *State of the Netherlands v Stichting Urgenda* [2018] ECLI:NL:GHDHA:2018:2591 (Court of Appeal) (*Urgenda Court of Appeal*); *State of the Netherlands (Ministry of Economic Affairs and Climate Policy) v Stichting Urgenda* [2019] ECLI:NL:HR:2019:2007 (Supreme Court of the Netherlands) (*Urgenda Supreme Court*).

41 ibid *Urgenda Supreme Court* [8.2.1].

42 ibid [8.2.7].

43 *VZW Klimaatzaak v l'État Belge* [2021] 2015/4585/A (Tribunal de première instance francophone de Bruxelles, Section Civile) (*VZW Klimaatzaak First Instance*).

France,[44] Canada,[45] the Czech Republic,[46] Germany,[47] Poland,[48] Ireland,[49] Italy,[50] South Korea,[51] the United Kingdom,[52] and the US.[53]

The other well-known Dutch climate case is *Milieudefensie et al v Royal Dutch Shell*, in which the plaintiffs contended that Shell's role in causing climate change constituted a breach of their responsibility according to Dutch law and obligations related to human rights.[54] They pursued an order from the Court that would require Shell to lower its $CO_2$ emissions by 45 per cent by 2030, relative to the levels seen in 2010. Furthermore, the claimants sought a complete elimination of emissions by the year 2050, aligning with the objectives of the Paris Agreement. The plaintiffs, although successful, did not get the precise remedy sought. As a matter of remedial award, the Court ordered Shell, directly and via its subsidiaries, to limit or cause to be limited the emissions related to its group's activities (scope 1 emissions), its business relationships (scope 2 emissions), and the sold products (scope 3 emissions) by at least 45 per cent at the end of 2030, relative to 2019 levels.[55] This overarching remedy is likely the most ambitious in corporate climate litigation because it entails fundamentally rethinking the energy corporation and its place in producing and potentially diminishing the climate crisis.[56] A similar case filed in France is worth mentioning. The plaintiff, the French NGO Notre Affaire à Tous, sought (unsuccessfully due to inadmissibility) to order the French oil major Total to undertake action to reduce the $CO_2$ emissions attached to its operations.[57]

44 *Notre Affaire à Tous and Others v France* [2021] No 1904967, 1904968, 1904972 1904976/4-1.

45 *La Rose v Her Majesty the Queen*, T-1750-19 [2019] (Federal Court of Canada).

46 *Klimatická žaloba ČR v Czech Republic* [2022] 9 As 116/2022 – 166 (Supreme Administrative Court).

47 *Neubauer and Others v Germany* [2021] 1 BvR 2656/18, 1 BvR 96/20, 1 BvR 78/20, 1 BvR 288/20, 1 BvR 96/20, 1 BvR 78/20 (German Federal Constitutional Court) (*Neubauer*).

48 *ClientEarth v Poland (on Behalf of MG)* [2021] <https://climatecasechart.com/non-us-case/clientearth-v-poland-acting-on-behalf-of-mg/#:~:text=Summary%3A,worsening%20effects%20of%20climate%20change.> accessed 24 February 2024.

49 *Friends of the Irish Environment CLG v The Government of Ireland, Ireland and the Attorney General* [2020] Appeal no 205/19 (Supreme Court of Ireland).

50 *A SUD and others v Italy* [2021] (Civil Court of Rome) <https://climatecasechart.com/non-us-case/a-sud-et-al-v-italy/#:~:text=Summary%3A,a%20stable%20and%20safe%20climate> accessed 24 February 2024.

51 *Do-Hyun Kim et al v South Korea* [2020] Constitutional Court of South Korea (pending).

52 *Plan B Earth and Others v The Secretary of State for Business, Energy, and Industrial Strategy* [2019] C1/2018/1750 (Court of Appeal Civil Division).

53 *Juliana v United States*, No 6:15-cv-01517-AA (District Court of Oregon 2023) (Opinion and Order).

54 *Milieudefensie v Royal Dutch Shell* [2021] ECLR:NL: RBDHA:2021:5339 (District Court of the Hague).

55 ibid [5.3].

56 Phillip Paiement, 'Reimagining the Energy Corporation: Milieudefensie and Others v Royal Dutch Shell Plc' in Daniëlla Dam-de Jong and Fabian Amtenbrink (eds), *Netherlands Yearbook of International Law 2021: A Greener International Law – International Legal Responses to the Global Environmental Crisis* (TMC Asser Press 2023).

57 *Notre Affaire à Tous and Others v Total* [2023] No RG 22/03403.

These legal actions pursue climate remedies that can guarantee non-repetition and cessation through injunctive relief.

Examples of *Urgenda*-like remedies, that is, judicial awards that tackle systemic issues that fundamentally influence GHG emissions, also exist in the Global South. One of the most well-known cases is *Future Generations v Ministry of the Environment and Others (Demanda Generaciones Futuras v Minambiente)*, where twenty-five young claimants from different parts of Colombia lodged a *tutela* (constitutional injunction) before the Supreme Court demanding human rights protection from climate change exacerbated by the Amazon's deforestation.[58] In April 2018, the Supreme Court favoured the plaintiffs and ordered the State to comply with a comprehensive remedy list that involves creating and implementing inter-institutional conservation policies. The Court ordered the President of Colombia and relevant ministerial agencies to liaise with the plaintiffs, affected communities, and interested populations to formulate an anti-deforestation action plan. It also ordered the construction of an 'Intergenerational Pact for the Life of the Colombian Amazon' to reduce deforestation and GHG emissions with multi-level implementation strategies.

Climate remedies designed to address economy-wide or structural frameworks are emerging in climate litigation. However, it is expected to encounter several remedies targeting a precise policy or project that intensifies climate change. For instance, plaintiffs in the 'Climate Fund' case in Brazil alleged that the government's decision to render the National Fund on Climate Change, which ensures the implementation of mitigation and adaptation action, was unconstitutional. The Federal Supreme Court agreed, finding the federal government breached its obligation to fully allocate the Fund's resources for 2019. It ordered the State defendant to abstain from omitting its responsibility and prohibiting the resources' undue retention.[59] Similarly, in Ecuador, young plaintiffs claimed that gas flaring is unlawful because it is a polluting practice that contributes to climate change and negatively impacts their constitutional rights. A provincial appeals court accepted the plaintiffs' arguments and ordered the State to eliminate the gas flaring towers in the plaintiffs' vicinity within eighteen months and to abolish such practice entirely by 2030.[60]

Awarding climate remedies is not only the prerogative of national courts. In the international realm, judicial and quasi-judicial bodies are also starting to delineate remedies in the context of climate change. For now, there is only one case in which an international human rights body has handed down a decision awarding a climate-related remedy. In *Billy et al v Australia*, eight indigenous authors from the

58 *Future Generations v Ministry of the Environment and Others (Demanda Generaciones Futuras v Minambiente)* [2018] 11001 22 03 000 2018 00319 00 (Supreme Court of Justice of Colombia) (*Demanda Futuras Generaciones*).

59 *PSB and others v Brazil* [2022] ADPF 708 (Federal Supreme Court of Brazil).

60 *Appeals Judgement Herrera Carrión et al v Ecuador* [2021] 21201202000170 (Provincial Court of Justice of Sucumbíos).

Torres Strait Islands filed a complaint before the UN Human Rights Committee.[61] The authors claimed that Australia had violated their right to life by not taking sufficient climate mitigation and adaptation measures;[62] their right to enjoy their culture and traditional way of life due to their interdependence with their islands' ecological balance, which is being compromised by climate change, thus generating displacement and irreparable cultural harm;[63] and their right to privacy, family, and home life due to ongoing and prospective forced abandonment of their homes.[64]

Furthermore, the authors asserted that – by failing to adopt adequate climate action – Australia is making the climate inhospitable for future generations, thereby affecting the specific rights of minors as enshrined in Article 24(1) of the International Covenant on Civil and Political Rights.[65] The UN Human Rights Committee found that Australia was in breach of all of the rights invoked by the authors except for the right to life and the rights of minors. As a result, the Committee ordered Australia to provide adequate compensation, conduct consultations for needs assessments, continue implementing and monitoring adequate measures to secure islanders' existence and adopt non-repetition measures.[66] In line with its past practice, the UN Human Rights Committee refrained from specifying the precise amount of compensation or detailing non-repetition measures, thus leaving the State a degree of discretion.[67] The Committee did, however, remind Australia of its duty under the Optional Protocol to ensure an effective remedy when a violation has occurred and expressed its wishes to receive from the State party, within 180 days, information about the measures taken to give effect to the Committee's Views.[68]

Finally, it is essential to mention General Comment No 26 of the Committee on the Rights of the Child on children's rights and the environment, with particular attention to climate change, which includes a section on effective remedies.[69] To ensure effective remedies, the General Comment recognises that States must include restitution, adequate compensation, satisfaction, rehabilitation, and guarantees of non-repetition, both for the environment and the children concerned, as well as access to medical and psychological assistance. It also indicates that

61 UNHR Committee, 'Views Adopted by the Committee under Article 5(4) of the Optional Protocol, concerning Communication No 3624/2019', 21 July 2022, UN Doc CCPR/C/135/D/3624/2019 (*Billy*).
62 ibid [3.3].
63 ibid [3.5].
64 ibid [3.6].
65 ibid [3.7].
66 ibid [11].
67 UNHR Committee, 'Views Adopted by the Committee under Article 5(4) of the Optional Protocol, concerning Communication No 2751/2016', 20 September 2019, UN Doc CCPR/C/126/D/2751/2016 (*Portillo Caceres*); UNHR Committee, 'Views Adopted by the Committee under Article 5(4) of the Optional Protocol, concerning Communication No 2552/2015', 21 September 2022, UN Doc CCPR/C/132/D/2552/2015 (*Benito Oliveira Pereira*).
68 *Billy* (n 61) [12].
69 Committee on Rights of the Child, 'General Comment No 26 on Children's Rights and the Environment with a Special Focus on Climate Change' (22 August 2023) UN Doc CRC/C/GC/26.

States should consider the vulnerability of children affected by environmental degradation, particularly in the case of irreversible damage that may last a lifetime. To this end, the Committee recommends the creation of innovative forms of reparation, such as intergenerational committees, to develop and implement rapid reparation measures.[70]

The cases described in this section are salient instances of remedial approaches encompassing injunctive relief, project permit denials, and legislative reforms, all within the remit of the courts' mandates to award them. Some of them already incorporate emerging best practices, namely adopting a remedial design that merges adaptation and compensation orders in one single judgment while compelling the defendant to provide a reasonable level of specificity in the mandated new legal or policy act. In the next section, these emerging best practices will be further detailed and illustrated through other remedies from comparative case law.

## 18.4 EMERGING BEST PRACTICE

Emerging best practices in the judicial ambit of awarding climate remedies could be divided into five elements. The overarching principle – which we identify as the first element of emerging best practice, following Principles 10 and 13 of the Rio Declaration – concerns the importance of providing an effective redress and remedy in environmental matters.[71] The second element relates to the issuing of holistic orders. A holistic approach to remedies means that orders can encompass a diverse range of climate-related measures, for instance an order to reduce GHG emissions alongside a mandate to implement adaptation-related policies and design participatory processes for redressing loss and damage. The third element of emerging best practice is holding the State or private actor to at least the minimum standard of care recognised in law and/or science where awarding more holistic or far-reaching remedies is unfeasible. To help identify the standard of care for mitigation measures – and reflecting the fourth element of emerging best practice – courts can use the concept of 'fair shares' of a global carbon budget to determine the exact remedial order. This manoeuvre allows judges to use the most updated methodologies to ascertain the defendants' level of responsibility for their contribution to climate change and designate appropriate redress options. And finally, the fifth element of emerging best practice relates to compliance-based orders. These orders are characterised by specificity and straightforwardness, whereby the remedial order specifies what the defendant must do to provide redress, thereby enabling effective compliance follow-up.

[70] ibid [89].

[71] United Nations 'Declaration of the United Nations Conference on Environment and Development' (1992) 31 ILM 874 (Rio Declaration) principles 10 and 13.

### 18.4.1 *Providing Effective Redress and Remedy*

The Rio Declaration on Environment and Development is a conspicuous authoritative source of law in virtually every jurisdiction.[72] Principle 10 of the Rio Declaration develops the general framework of procedural environmental justice, including access to justice. A core tenet of access to justice is providing effective redress and remedy where an obligation is breached, which is now emerging best practice in comparative climate litigation. Several courts have elaborated on the importance of this principle of emerging best practice.

In *Urgenda*[73] the Dutch Supreme Court acknowledged that 'decision-making on the reduction of greenhouse gas emissions is a power of the government and parliament' and that they have a significant degree of discretion in this respect.[74] Nevertheless, the Supreme Court recognised that the judiciary has a role in determining whether the government has remained within the limits of the law by which it is bound. The Court emphasised that legal protection against the government is a vital aspect of a system governed by the rule of law:

> In the Dutch system of government, the decision-making on greenhouse gas emissions belongs to the government and parliament. They have a large degree of discretion to make the political considerations that are necessary in this regard. It is up to the courts to decide whether, in taking their decisions, the government and parliament have remained within the limits of the law by which they are bound. Those limits ensue from the ECHR, among other things. The Dutch Constitution requires the Dutch courts to apply the provisions of this convention, and they must do so in accordance with the ECtHR's interpretation of these provisions. This mandate to the courts to offer legal protection, even against the government, is an essential component of a democratic state under the rule of law.[75]

As noted earlier, the Supreme Court ordered the government to increase its climate mitigation efforts and achieve a reduction of at least 25 per cent by 2020 compared to 1990 levels.[76]

In *Notre Affaire à Tous*,[77] the Administrative Court of Paris recognised the need to afford the government considerable discretion in implementing a court order related to GHG emission targets. Nonetheless, it explicitly stated that this allowance does not preclude the judiciary from mandating the government to implement more robust climate mitigation measures. These measures are intended to prevent exacerbation of

72 Jorge E. Viñuales, 'The Rio Declaration on Environment and Development' in Jorge E. Viñuales (ed), *The Rio Declaration on Environment and Development: A Commentary* (Oxford University Press 2015).
73 *Urgenda Supreme Court* (n 40).
74 ibid [8.3.2]. See also [6.2]–[6.3].
75 ibid.
76 ibid [8.3.5].
77 *Notre Affaire à Tous* (n 44).

climate impacts and align with the legislative targets established by the government. Consequently, the Court mandated the French government to intensify its endeavours to decrease GHG emissions following the legislative framework:

> In the circumstances of this case, it is appropriate to order the Prime Minister and the competent ministers to take all the necessary sectoral measures to compensate for the damage up to the uncompensated share of greenhouse gas emissions under the first carbon budget [...]. it is appropriate, as has been said, to order the enactment of such measures within a sufficiently short period of time in order to prevent any worsening of that damage. In the context of the present case, the specific measures to make reparation for the damage may take various forms and consequently express choices which are within the Government's discretion.[78]

Similarly, in *Neubauer*,[79] the German Constitutional Court highlighted that:

> It is not, in principle, for the courts to translate the open wording of Art 20a GG into quantifiable global warming limits and corresponding emission amounts or reduction targets. At the same time, however, Art 20a GG may not be drained of substance as an obligation to take climate action. In this respect too, it remains for the Federal Constitutional Court to review whether the boundaries of Art 20a GG are respected ([...]). There is nothing to indicate that Art 20a GG – as a singular exception among the provisions of the Basic Law – is beyond the scope of judicial review with regard to how its regulatory content is Interpreted and applied.[80]

Additionally, the Court emphasised the significance of upholding constitutional boundaries within environmental protection, specifically in the context of climate action. The Court asserted that judicial examination enables consideration of long-term interests, particularly those of future generations, safeguarding them from short-term interests influenced by election cycles:

> The Constitution sets limits here on the leeway enjoyed in the political decision-making process to determine whether environmental protection measures should be taken or not. In Art 20a GG, environmental protection is elevated to a matter of constitutional significance because the democratic political process is organised along more short-term lines based on election cycles, placing it at a structural risk of being less responsive to tackling the ecological issues that need to be pursued over the long term. It is also because future generations – those who will be most affected – naturally have no voice of their own in shaping the current political agenda. In view of these institutional conditions, Art 20a GG imposes substantive constraints on democratic decision-making ([...]). This binding of the political process as envisaged by Art 20a GG would be in danger of being lost if the material

78 ibid [13].
79 *Neubauer* (n 47).
80 ibid [206].

content of Art 20a GG were fully determined by the day-to-day political process with its more short-term approach and its orientation towards directly expressible interests.[81]

Finally, in the landmark ruling of *Held v Montana*,[82] a trial court decided in favour of sixteen youth plaintiffs, declaring that a provision in the Montana Environmental Policy Act (MEPA) – which barred the consideration of greenhouse gas emissions and related climate impacts in environmental assessments – unconstitutional.[83] Following a seven-day trial, the Court acknowledged that climate change significantly threatened public health. The plaintiffs showcased various damages they suffered due to the state's neglect of environmental concerns. The court confirmed that the plaintiffs were entitled to a 'clean and healthful environment', encompassing climate. It emphasised that Montana's activities in the fossil fuel sector contributed substantially to global warming, seriously harming the state's youth. As a remedy, the Court declared its judgment would influence the State's conduct by invalidating statutes prohibiting analysis and remedies based on GHG emissions and climate impacts.[84] By refusing to analyse GHG emissions and their corresponding impacts on the climate or being consistent with the Montana Constitution, the court declared the MEPA unconstitutional and permanently enjoined because it removes the only preventative, equitable relief available to the public.[85]

### 18.4.2 *A Holistic Approach to Remedies*

It is emerging best practice that the court adopt a holistic approach to remedies where possible.

An example is the Nepalese case of *Shrestha v Office of the Prime Minister et al.* On 23 August 2017, Padam Bahadur Shrestha filed a legal action before the Supreme Court of Nepal to compel the government to establish new legislation concerning climate change through a writ of mandamus or other appropriate directive to enact such a law.[86] The basis of the petition was that the existing Environmental Protection Act of 1997 needed to be revised to address climate change and that the Climate Change Policy 2011 had not been implemented. Consequently, due to climate change, Nepalese people and ecosystems have endured significant adverse

[81] ibid [205].
[82] *Held v Montana* No CDV-2020-307 (District Court of Montana 2023).
[83] Cf with the remedy sought in *Juliana* which was considered non-redressable. The case sought an injunction requiring the government to craft a 'comprehensive scheme to decrease fossil fuel emissions and combat climate change', which the Court doubted could be supervised or enforced by the Court. See also the preliminary decision in *Held* of 2021, in which the Court also found that injunctive relief would violate the political question doctrine.
[84] ibid [102].
[85] ibid.
[86] *Advocate Padam Bahadur Shrestha v Prime Minister and Office of Council of Ministers and Others* [2018] Order No 074-WO-0283 (2075/09/10 BS) (Supreme Court of Nepal).

impacts. The Court ordered the government, as a form of remedy, to introduce a new climate change law covering several critical areas of climate action. These included strategies to both mitigate and adapt to the impacts of climate change, the promotion of low-carbon technologies and a reduction in the consumption of fossil fuels, and the establishment of scientific and legal tools to offer compensation for individuals affected by pollution and environmental deterioration.[87] The Court instructed the government to draft and implement the new climate law by issuing a writ of mandamus. This action was deemed essential to uphold Nepal's commitments as outlined in the Paris Agreement and to fulfil obligations stated in the Constitution.

In *Leghari v Pakistan*, a law student and farmer from Rahim Yar Khan District in South Punjab, Pakistan, faced water shortages and temperature fluctuations on his family's 500-acre sugarcane plantation due to climate change.[88] To prompt action from relevant departments and ministries, he initiated a lawsuit against the Federation of Pakistan for not implementing the 2012 National Climate Change Policy and its Framework. He contended that climate change directly affected Pakistan, necessitating immediate government intervention for adaptation to erratic weather patterns. Leghari claimed that the government's inaction on climate change violated his constitutional rights, specifically the right to life (Article 9) and the protection of human dignity (Article 14). Following the petition, the Lahore High Court ordered the establishment of a Climate Change Commission to expedite measures combating the effects of climate change in Pakistan. Additionally, the Court specified deadlines for implementing actions ranging from urgent to long-term, maintaining oversight through its continuing mandamus authority to ensure the progression of these efforts. The holistic approach of this remedial order lies in the fact that the High Court of Lahore was tasked with overseeing the implementation of the entirety of the National Climate Change Policy and its Framework for Implementation. Also reflecting best practice was the Court's follow-up proceedings in 2018 to assess compliance with its initial order, whereby the Court constituted a 'standing committee' to create an ongoing link between the Court and the executive.[89]

In the *Josefina Huffington Archbold v Colombia* case, the plaintiff, a citizen from the islands of Providencia and Santa Catalina in Colombia, filed a constitutional injunction against the State for human rights violations. The case concerned the planning and executing of the action plan to aid the islands following Hurricane Iota in November 2020, which destroyed 98 per cent of the islands' infrastructure.[90] The Constitutional Court deemed that the State did not deploy a diligent response plan,

87 ibid 13–14.

88 *Asghar Leghari v Federation of Pakistan etc* PLD 2018 Lahore 364 [11].

89 ibid [25].

90 *Josefina Huffington Archbold v Colombia* [2022] T-8.298.253 (Constitutional Court of Colombia).

which is why it ordered, as a remedy, all the relevant ministries to mobilise resources and personnel to the islands. The Court continued to stress that the respondent State had to implement concrete measures to systematically alleviate the humanitarian emergency and rebuild the infrastructure to adequately provide all essential services guaranteed in the Constitution as fundamental rights. Additionally, the Court ordered the government to implement a participatory plan that considers local culture and languages to rebuild the islands in a way that strengthens resilience to future climate change impacts.[91] In its reasoning for designing this remedy, the Court asserted that the comprehensive reconstruction process must integrate Colombia's climate adaptation obligations and human rights. The case is, therefore, an illustration of how apex courts are awarding remedies in a holistic fashion, whereby orders of adaptation to climate impacts in extreme weather disasters cannot be deployed without including human rights in a contextualised way.

### 18.4.3 A *Minimum Standard*

If the court considers that it cannot issue a holistic remedy – whether because of the way the claim is framed or for other legal or procedural reasons – it is emerging best practice for the court to assess the minimum standard of conduct that the State or private actor must meet to discharge any relevant legal obligations.

A landmark judgment from the Brussels Court of Appeal in *Klimaatzaak*[92] exemplifies this. In contrast to the judgment in the first instance (limited to declaratory relief), the Court of Appeal issued an injunctive order requiring the governments to increase their reduction targets to at least 55 per cent of 1990 levels.[93] Notably, the Court asserted that utilising its injunctive power against public authorities does not necessarily violate the principle of separation of powers if the judge issues an order consistent with the 'minimum requirements laid down by norms of international law' or in the absence of such norms, the 'minimum requirements' 'on the basis of data on which there is scientific and political consensus'.[94]

Regarding the reduction order, the Court noted:

> Imposing such a reduction in order to prevent global warming does not, as the Brussels-Capital Region has argued, deprive the public authority of the choice of measures to adopt in order to achieve the objective of limiting global warming, nor does it 'petrify' public action, as the Walloon Region maintains (its conclusions on page 84), since it is indisputable (and moreover not seriously contested) that this is an absolutely essential measure (even if not necessarily sufficient) to

91 ibid [123].

92 *VZW Klimaatzaak v Kingdom of Belgium and Others* [2023] 2022/AR/891(Cour d'appel de Bruxelles) (*VZW Klimaatzaak Appeal*).

93 ibid [286].

94 ibid [227].

> achieve it, that the Court limits itself to defining a minimum threshold of reduction to be achieved in several years' time, below which there is fault or negligence (a threshold which the respondents in the main proceedings are therefore free to raise), and that there is a wide range of concrete measures available to these authorities to enable them to achieve this objective (as illustrated by the extensive discussion of measures already taken in the respondents' submissions in the main proceedings).[95]

The rationale for this judgment is grounded in the violation of human rights (specifically, Articles 2[96] and 8[97] of the ECHR) and civil liability principles (Articles 1382 and 1383 of the Civil Code). In its conclusions, the Court of Appeal confirmed that granting an injunction to reduce emissions was the 'best, if not the only' way to correct the shortcomings on the part of the State under the ECHR (which contains the right to an effective remedy under Article 13)[98] and the extracontractual liability provisions of the Civil Code.[99] It explained:[100]

> In view of the shortcomings noted in the past and which continue to this day, which can only be corrected by reductions to be planned for the future, in view of the threat posed to the right to life, private life and family life of the appellants, natural persons, by ongoing global warming, in view of the urgency of the measures to be taken during the present decade, in view of the importance of maintaining, at international level, the mutual trust of the States parties to the UNFCCC in the fact that each State will effectively contribute to the global fight against global warming, in view of the absence of any concrete sanction to date for failure to meet the European objectives, it is justified, both in terms of the violation of articles 2 and 8 of the ECHR and of articles 1382 and 1383 of the former Civil Code, to issue an express injunction to the Belgian State, the Brussels-Capital Region and the Flemish Region to take, in consultation with the Walloon Region, the appropriate measures to ensure that Belgium achieves by 2030 the target of a 55% reduction in GHG emissions from its territory compared with 1990.

In so doing, the Brussels Court of Appeal adopted an approach similar to that of the Supreme Court in *Urgenda*. The Supreme Court, in that case, focused on the 'absolute minimum' required by the State to discharge its obligations under the ECHR[101] – while leaving it to the government to determine the specific programme, law, or mechanism to reduce GHG emissions by that amount.

95 ibid.
96 ibid [121].
97 ibid [124].
98 ibid [277].
99 ibid [283].
100 ibid [285].
101 *Urgenda Supreme Court* (n 40) [7.5.1].

### 18.4.4 *Drawing on a Global Carbon Budget*

Another element of emerging best practice in climate litigation to date concerns using a global carbon budget to determine the appropriate remedy. This is often linked to determining the 'minimum standard' discussed earlier and to the 'fair shares' concept.[102]

The most pertinent case in this respect is the famous German constitutional case of *Neubauer et al v Germany*. This case started with a cohort of young individuals from Germany filing a legal challenge against the Federal Climate Protection Act in the Federal Constitutional Court. They contended that the Act's objective of decreasing GHG emissions by 55 per cent by 2030 compared to 1990 levels was inadequate.[103] The plaintiffs claimed that this insufficiency consequently violated their human rights as safeguarded by Germany's Constitution. The Court ruled in the plaintiffs' favour. Given the risk of irreversible climate change manifested in the Climate Protection Act, the Constitutional Court based its rationale on the carbon budget estimates of the Intergovernmental Panel on Climate Change (IPCC) to limit warming to 1.75°C. In light of the technical insights from the IPCC and the German Advisory Council on the Environment, the Court ordered the legislature to set clear and specific provisions for reduction targets from 2031 onwards by the end of 2022 based on the size of the remaining global $CO_2$ budget under the Paris Agreement's temperature limits of well below 2°C and, if possible, to 1.5°C.[104] This injunctive relief is an example of a remedy designed to avoid overshooting a global carbon budget. The order also demands a significant level of specificity that the legislature must comply with in making the new climate legislation.

The Court based its decision on the principle of proportionality to underscore the need to manage the required emissions reductions for achieving climate neutrality equitably and proactively, ensuring that the curtailment of freedoms remains reasonable despite climate challenges. Specifically, it points out that the protective mandate of Article 20a of the German Basic Law emphasises preserving the natural foundations of life for both present and future generations, advocating for environmental stewardship that avoids imposing radical restraint on future generations.[105] Additionally, it underscores the importance of judiciously consuming the remaining $CO_2$ budget to buy critical time, enabling necessary transformations that alleviate freedom losses. The Court emphasises the significance of forward-looking legislation that respects fundamental rights.[106]

[102] Maria Antonia Tigre, 'The "Fair Share" of Climate Mitigation: Can Litigation Increase National Ambition for Brazil?' (2023) JHRP <https://academic.oup.com/jhrp/advance-article-abstract/doi/10.1093/jhuman/huad032/7261647> accessed 24 February 2024.

[103] *Neubauer* (n 47).

[104] ibid [229].

[105] ibid.

[106] ibid.

Another illustrative example of this practice of relying on a carbon budget to establish an appropriate remedy is the *Gloucester Resources Limited v Minister of Planning* in Australia. The mining company Gloucester Resources Limited filed a legal action against the Minister of Planning, contesting the rejection of the company's proposal to build an open-pit coal mine known as the Rocky Hill Coal Project in New South Wales. This project aimed to extract 21 million tons of coal over sixteen years.[107] The Land and Environment Court of New South Wales upheld the Minister's denial of Gloucester Resources' application, finding that the size of the mining project would be a significant source of GHG emissions. Therefore, the project's refusal could contribute to remaining within the global carbon budget and achieving the long-term temperature goal under the Paris Agreement.[108]

The Brussels Court of Appeal in *VZW Klimaatzaak v Kingdom of Belgium et al* also drew on the carbon budget concept to determine the appropriate remedial order in that case. The Court of Appeal assessed whether – in particular under tort law – it would be appropriate to seek an injunctive relief to prevent 'damage (so-called dangerous global warming and excessive damage to the residual carbon budget) [that] has not yet occurred'.[109] The Court affirmed that 'in the current state of positive law, an action to prevent future damage is admissible when the fault has already been committed, and the damage is sufficiently serious'.[110] To reach its remedial order, the Court relied upon climate science reports that introduce the notion of carbon budgets to determine what economy-wide GHG emission reduction goals would allow Belgium to contribute to keeping the 1.5°C long-term temperature limit within reach considering a residual global carbon budget of 400 $GtCO_2$, as noted by the IPCC's AR6.[111] On this basis, the Court determined that a reduction of 55 per cent in GHG emissions by 2030 (compared with 1990 levels) was the minimum required to discharge its legal obligations.[112]

### 18.4.5 *Compliance-oriented Remedies*

The final trend of emerging best practice concerning remedies in climate litigation is the inclusion of orders that provide for a specific and unambiguous behavioural route for the defendant and include follow-up action by the Court to facilitate compliance. This type of remedy clearly articulates why specific laws or policies are unlawful or unconstitutional and what the respondent needs to do to rectify their impacts.

For instance, in the *Friends of the Irish Environment v Ireland* case, applicants filed an appeal in the Supreme Court, arguing that the Irish government's approval of the

[107] *Gloucester Resources Limited v Minister for Planning* [2019] NSWLEC 7 (*Gloucester Resources*).
[108] ibid [554]–[556].
[109] *VZW Klimaatzaak Appeal* (n 92) [278].
[110] ibid [281].
[111] ibid [190], [193].
[112] ibid [199]–[202].

National Mitigation Plan in 2017 violated national climate law, the Constitution, and human rights obligations.[113] The Supreme Court issued a judgment quashing the National Mitigation Plan for falling short of the specificity required to provide transparency and comply with the provisions in domestic climate legislation.[114] In its decision, the Court elaborated on what minimum standards a new plan should contain, including a sufficient level of specificity so that anyone could judge whether the plan is realistic and reasonable.[115] In the Court's view, a compliant plan should cover the entire period remaining to 2050 and be sufficiently specific.[116]

It is also possible to see this emerging best practice in the French decisions in the cases of *Grande Synthe* (which concerned the State's compliance with its future emissions reduction targets) and *L'Affaire du Siecle* (which concerned the government's failure to comply with its past carbon budgets). In the latter case, the Administrative Court of Paris ordered the government to take immediate and concrete actions to comply with its carbon budgets – ultimately ordering the government to offset the amount that it exceeded its carbon budgets.[117]

These cases and their resulting remedies constitute emerging best practices because judges use their prerogatives in awarding remedies in a way that tends to catalyse a more efficient outcome for a just decarbonised society when the legal rationale favours the pro-climate claimant. Designing and ordering remedies is highly contingent upon the rationale the judge elaborates on and the mandate a court or tribunal was given by law. However, in some instances, judges have a significant level of leeway to decide the best way to guarantee that the source of harm does not repeatedly manifest, thereby having structural effects. These instances in which judges in different jurisdictions can act convergently towards awarding impactful remedies are determined by certain factors that will be elaborated on in the next section.

## 18.5 REPLICABILITY

This section delves into three specific legal opportunity structures that aim to replicate remedial measures for effective climate action across various legal jurisdictions. Legal opportunity structures refer to the institutional aspects and features of the legal system that can either facilitate or hinder the ability of applicants to leverage the law for change.[118] These structures may include the accessibility of courts, the

[113] *Friends of the Irish Environment CLG* (n 49).
[114] ibid [9.3].
[115] ibid [9.2].
[116] ibid.
[117] *Notre Affaire à Tous* (n 44). The Court refused to order the government to pay a fine if it does not achieve the necessary reductions, as requested by the plaintiffs.
[118] Chris Hilson, 'New Social Movements: The Role of Legal Opportunity' (2002) 9 Journal of European Public Policy 238.

judiciary's predisposition towards specific claims, and the presence of supportive legal precedents. This section frames and discusses three legal opportunity structures that can be replicable across jurisdictions and have already been used in climate litigation.

Firstly, each court or tribunal operates based on a unique mandate, as defined by the legal framework that established it. This foundation gives structure to the court's operations and empowers judges with the authority to provide remedies or reparations. This ensures that decisions align with the jurisdiction's rules and regulations. Secondly, there is the 'Duty to Cooperate'. Using this principle, judges can, independently or upon a plaintiff's request, create mechanisms for cooperation between jurisdictions. Such measures can result in wide-ranging remedies, from emission reductions to compensation for damage caused by climate change, even if such damage is outside their direct jurisdiction. Lastly, the universally accepted scientific consensus on climate change, mainly as presented in the IPCC reports, offers a solid foundation for climate-related judgments. By drawing on these reports, courts can ensure the accuracy and relevance of their judgments. These three legal opportunity structures might prompt replicability and thus make it more feasible for judges worldwide to implement the emerging best practices described in the previous section with the added value of contextual sensibility. For example, a remedy in a low-emitting, highly vulnerable country might not look like one in a high-emitting, more climate-resilient one. Additionally, the likelihood of compliance with the remedial order in a judgment should also be factored into its design, and some of these legal opportunities could help address potential non-compliance.

Constitutional and supreme courts globally hold mandates derived from foundational legal texts, granting them the authority to order remedies in varied cases. In Ireland, the power of the Supreme Court to provide remedies emanates from the Constitution of Ireland. Articles 34.3.2° and 34.3.3° of the Irish Constitution entrust the Supreme Court and the High Court with the authority to adjudicate constitutional matters. It could be argued that the Irish Constitution legitimised and premised the mandate that led to the Supreme Court's judgment in *Friends of the Irish Environment v Ireland*. Similarly, the Constitution of South Africa, under Chapter 8 on Courts and Administration of Justice, endows its High Courts with a broad mandate to decide a constitutional matter within its power by declaring that any law or conduct that is inconsistent with the Constitution is invalid to the extent of its inconsistency; and ordering a limitation to its retrospective effect. The power granted by the Constitution was invoked in *EarthLife Africa Johannesburg v Minister of Environmental Affairs et al.*[119] India's Constitution, through Article 32, authorises its Supreme Court to issue writs for enforcing fundamental rights. Through this, the

[119] Marjoné van der Bank and Jaco Karsten, 'Climate Change and South Africa: A Critical Analysis of the Earthlife Africa Johannesburg and Another v Minister of Energy and Others 65662/16 (2017) Case and the Drive for Concrete Climate Practices' (2020) 13 Air, Soil and Water Research 1178622119885537.

Court devised a 'continuing mandamus', assuring consistent judicial monitoring. This approach was utilised in the *Vellore Citizens Welfare Forum vs Union of India and Ors* case to address industrial pollution.[120] Embedded in legal frameworks, these mandates underscore the pivotal role of constitutional and supreme courts in addressing rights violations, safeguarding the rule of law, and ensuring justice by ordering appropriate remedies.

Given that the practice of adjudication is moving to regional and international courts and tribunals, the courts' mandates to award remedies in these instances mirror the phenomenon at the domestic level. The United Nations General Assembly (UNGA) Resolution on 'Basic Principles and Guidelines on the Right to a Remedy and Reparation for Victims of Gross Violations of International Human Rights Law and Serious Violations of International Humanitarian Law' sets out the remedies available to international human rights courts and tribunals.[121] These include restitution, compensation, rehabilitation, satisfaction, and guarantees of non-repetition. These forms of remedy are present in the treaties that created these adjudicative bodies. Article 13 of the ECHR guarantees the right to effective redress. Article 41 authorises the European Court of Human Rights (ECtHR) to award and afford just satisfaction to the injured party when domestic legislation allows only partial reparation.[122]

In the Inter-American Human Rights System, Articles 51 and 63 of the American Convention on Human Rights establish how the Inter-American Commission on Human Rights (IACHR) and the IACtHR shall proceed to grant remedies, respectively. Article 51 states that the IACHR is mandated to transmit a report to the State defendant with pertinent recommendations and a deadline to take remedial measures, after which it shall decide whether they were complied with.[123] Article 63(1) recognises that the IACtHR shall grant victims appropriate remedies, including fair compensation.[124]

Similarly, Article 27(1) of the Protocol to the African Charter on Human and Peoples' Rights Establishing an African Court on Human and Peoples' Rights states that the Court shall issue specific instructions to correct the violation, including the payment of fair compensation.[125] Several United Nations human rights treaty bodies, arguably weaker in authority than regional mechanisms,[126] have jurisdic-

[120] *Vellore Citizens Welfare Forum v Union of India* AIR 1996 SC 2715.

[121] UNGA Res 60/147 (n 32).

[122] European Convention for the Protection of Human Rights and Fundamental Freedoms (entered into force 4 Nov 1950) 213 UNTS 222 (European Convention on Human Rights) art 13.

[123] American Convention on Human Rights (entered into force 18 July 1978) 1144 UNTS 123 art 51.

[124] ibid art 63.

[125] Protocol to the African Charter on Human and People's Rights on the Establishment of an African Court on Human and People's Rights (entered into force 1 July 2008) 48 ILM 314 art 27.

[126] Helen Keller and Geir Ulfstein, 'Introduction' in Helen Keller and Geir Ulfstein (eds), *UN Human Rights Treaty Bodies: Law and Legitimacy* (Cambridge University Press 2012) 3–4.

tion to receive individual and inter-State complaints. These are sometimes included in optional clauses within the treaty but are often contained in a separate protocol.[127] Despite no treaty bodies having explicit legal competence to order compensation or other remedies, they occasionally incorporate calls to give restitution, pay compensation, or afford other remedies through their observations on periodic State reports, in general comments, and their views on communications.[128] Concretely, the basis between different jurisdictions' mandate to award similar remedies could support the replicability of the emerging best practice identified earlier. For instance, something that the IACtHR might order in a climate case could be, to a certain extent, replicated by the African Court of Human Rights because both mandates have similar scope regarding remedy measures.

Moving on to the second legal opportunity, discussing the international duty to cooperate as a remedy is noteworthy. For remedies awarded in Global South jurisdictions, it could be essential to put the remedy in the context of global climate change. Since many countries in the Global South might face constraints in complying with a remedy that requires structural whole-of-economy decarbonisation measures, adopting a remedy sensitive to this reality might be appropriate and replicable. The main structural obstacle to compliance by developing countries with a potential climate-related remedy is the lack of expertise and resources – both financial and technical – serving as the primary rationale for an approach that integrates a duty to cooperate. In other words, courts could anticipate a potential non-compliance scenario due to systemic barriers and thus resort to interpretive techniques to design context-specific remedies. More concretely, courts could establish obligations requiring States to do their best to cooperate with other States or multilateral institutions to protect the rights of their citizens from climate-related harm.[129] Ultimately, the formulation of a remedy that integrates a duty to cooperate internationally indirectly addresses the climate justice question by requiring the defendant State to perform its best when it comes to finding international assistance and cooperation, particularly with those States that pollute the most or with financial institutions that might provide appropriate funding. Article 1(1) and (3) of the United Nations Charter[130] and Article 2(1) of the International Covenant on Economic, Social and Cultural Rights (ICESCR) offer essential doctrinal direction for replication. The ICESCR, more specifically, lays out the duty of States 'to take steps … through international assistance and co-operation, especially economic and technical, … with the view to achieving progressively

[127] Shelton (n 1) 191.
[128] ibid 193.
[129] Benoit Mayer, 'Obligations of Conduct in the International Law on Climate Change: A Defence' (2018) 27 RECIEL 130, 131.
[130] Charter of the United Nations (entered into force 24 October 1945) XV UNCIO 335, amendments in 557 UNTS 143, 638 UNTS 308, and 892 UNTS 119.

the full realisation of ... rights'.[131] In connection with this, the ICESCR's treaty body specified in its General Comment No 3 that international cooperation is an obligation of all States,[132] an approach that resonates with Article 4 of the United Nations Framework Convention on Climate Change (UNFCCC) and Article 12 of the Paris Agreement.[133]

The IACtHR's 2021 case of *Julien Grisonas v Argentina* highlights international cooperation for human rights redress, exemplified by the establishment of an inter-State group to investigate Operation Condor violations.[134] The case involves an Argentine couple's disappearance during the dictatorship and the transfer of their children to Uruguay and Chile. Though Argentina was deemed responsible, the IACtHR emphasised regional collaboration against impunity based on the collective guarantee mechanism obligating States to cooperate. Similarly, the case of *Vélez Loor v Panama* (2020–2022) underscored shared responsibility amidst the pandemic's migration challenges, advocating synergy among States, international bodies, and civil society.[135] As a corollary, the Guiding Principles on Shared Responsibility (2019) offer a framework for collaborative efforts between States and organisations, including climate change cases.[136] In *Neubauer v Germany*, the Constitutional Court emphatically reminded the government that due to the genuinely global dimension of climate change, the State must respond to it through international cooperation.[137] These precedents and principles underscore the importance of international cooperation in addressing complex and cross-border human rights issues, which could be replicable across jurisdictions and integrated into the remedial award.

The last opportunity for replicability of impactful remedial design is using the IPCC reports. In particular, courts can draw upon the reports' findings to craft orders that require defendants to undertake specific actions to mitigate GHG emissions. By referring to the reports' projections and scientific assessments,[138] courts can establish the necessity of emission reduction measures and their corresponding

[131] United Nations, 'Official Documents United Nations Human Rights Covenants: International Covenant on Economic, Social and Cultural Rights, International Covenant on Civil and Political Rights, Optional Protocol to the International Covenant on Civil and Political Rights' (1967) 61 AJIL 861.

[132] UN Committee on Economic, Social and Cultural Rights, 'General Comment No 3 (1990) on The Nature of States Parties' Obligations' under the International Covenant on Economic, Social and Cultural Rights' (14 December 1990) UN Doc E/1991/23 (CESCR General Comment No 3) [13].

[133] United Nations Framework Convention on Climate Change (entered into force 19 June 1993) 1771 UNTS 107; Paris Agreement (entered into force 4 November 2016) 3156 UNTS 79 (Paris Agreement).

[134] *Julien Grisonas v Argentina* (Preliminary Objections, Merits, Reparations and Costs) Inter-American Court of Human Rights Series C No 437 (23 September 2021) [288].

[135] See Orders in *Vélez Loor v Panamá* (Provisional Measures) Inter-American Court of Human Rights.

[136] André Nollkaemper and others, 'Guiding Principles on Shared Responsibility in International Law' (2020) 31(1) EJIL 15 principle 2(1).

[137] *Neubauer* (n 47) [209].

[138] Priyadarshi R. Shukla and others (eds), *Climate Change 2022: Mitigation of Climate Change, Contribution of Working Group III to the Sixth Assessment Report of the Intergovernmental Panel on Climate Change* (Cambridge University Press 2022).

timelines, as in *Klimaatzaak*, *Neubauer*, and *Urgenda*. This alignment of remedies with authoritative scientific consensus enhances the credibility of such orders and lends legitimacy to the court's intervention. Moreover, incorporating the IPCC reports in crafting injunctive relief ensures that the remedies are not arbitrary but firmly rooted in expert assessment, reinforcing the acceptability of such orders among various stakeholders. This is also the case for remedies relating to adaptation since the IPCC has also published specific reports on that matter, even with a greater level of granularity from a regional perspective.[139] Courts can leverage this information to design adaptive measures that address specific risks affected parties face. Furthermore, the scientific assessments provided by the reports can aid courts in determining the causal link between specific actions and the resultant damages. This attribution is crucial in assessing liability and quantifying the losses suffered. By relying on the meticulous analysis of the IPCC, courts can arrive at a more accurate estimation of the damages incurred by affected parties, ensuring that the compensation awarded is commensurate with the harm endured. The scientific underpinning of these compensation orders enhances their legitimacy and promotes consistency and fairness in awarding reparations.

## 18.6 CONCLUSION

Throughout legal history, the right to a remedy has been transformed and shaped by national laws, public international law, and evolving concepts of justice. While most States initially defined repair as pecuniary compensation, the scope has broadened under international law to include integral reparation encompassing restitution, compensation, and satisfaction. This principle, rooted in the *Factory at Chorzów* judgment and codified in the Draft Articles, has been adapted by human rights courts, signifying a *lex specialis* in reparation but manifesting in domestic reparation orders. The principle of full reparation demands that remedies not only address the harm incurred but also strive to restore the status quo ante, ensuring that the consequences of wrongful acts are comprehensively addressed. The diverse range of remedies – from injunctive relief and compensation to more novel approaches like obligations of conduct – illustrates the legal system's adaptability in seeking to mitigate the impacts of climate change and prevent further harm.

The confluence of legal principles and climate imperatives marks the evolving landscape of climate remedies. Climate remedies, exemplified by over 300 climate-positive decisions globally, strive to mitigate, adapt, and compensate for climate impacts.

Looking ahead, some emerging practices signal a cautious optimism for the role of climate change litigation in shaping novel global environmental policy approaches

[139] Valerie Masson-Delmotte and others, 'Summary for Policy Makers' in Global Warming of 1.5°C (2018) <https://ipcc.ch/pdf/special-reports/sr15/sr15_spm_final.pdf> accessed 23 February 2024.

regarding loss and damage. For instance, the Administrative Court of Paris in *Notre Affaire a Tous v France* found that France's inaction had caused ecological damage and awarded compensation for moral prejudice. Also recently, the Zug Cantonal Court, in the case against *Holcim*, ruled that the plaintiffs from Indonesia are entitled to legal aid.

Incorporating climate remedies into legal discourse necessitates reconciling traditional principles with the complexities of climate change. While the principle of integral reparation serves as a guiding light, its application faces obstacles in cases of non-compliance. Despite this inherent paradox, courts, such as the IACtHR, advocate for creative measures to approximate comprehensive remedies. This approach underscores the essence of reparation as both symbolic and substantial, thus paving the way for innovative climate remedies.

As courts and jurisdictions grapple with climate remedies, the journey ahead requires reconciling legal doctrines with the urgencies of climate crises. The emerging best practices, rooted in holistic, detailed, and scientifically informed remedies, exemplify the adaptable nature of law. Translating these practices across jurisdictions underscores the role of legal structures, mandates, and global scientific consensus in advancing climate action.

In the words of the Philippines Human Rights Commission immortalised in *Greenpeace Southeast Asia and Others*,[140] courts should:

> embrace their power to influence and inspire government action. [...] Thus, without favoring any particular party or going beyond their authority, courts should strive to inform, determine, explain and uphold, through their decisions, the rights and obligations of parties concerning particular climate laws, policies and issues. ... courts should clarify the factual and legal bases that were found wanting or insufficient to provide guidance not only to the parties but also to future actions. It should be emphasized that even when courts do not rule in favor of the claimants, they still contribute to meaningful climate response through their elucidation of the law and the rights and obligations of the parties. Judicial contribution to the development of the law and jurisprudence on various climate issues is indispensable to the success of the global climate action.[141]

In conclusion, the evolution of climate remedies encapsulates the fusion of legal traditions, international obligations, and climate urgency. The journey toward comprehensive climate redress navigates the intricate path of balancing legal principles with transformative climate imperatives. The emerging trends in climate remedies unveil the potential of law as a catalyst for climate action, envisioning a future where reparative justice stands as a cornerstone of climate resilience.

[140] *In re Greenpeace Southeast Asia and Others* [2022] Case No CHR-NI-2016-0001 (Commission on Human Rights of the Philippines).

[141] ibid [142].

# 19

# Recent Landmark Decisions

## *Advancing Climate Litigation and State Obligations*

*Margaretha Wewerinke-Singh and Joe Udell**

### 19.1 INTRODUCTION

The field of climate litigation is evolving at a breakneck pace, presenting a distinct challenge for a project like this Handbook. While compiling it, we witnessed the emergence of numerous landmark decisions that threatened to outpace our analysis. Thanks to the diligent efforts of our contributors, we managed to integrate many of these developments into the relevant chapters. Still, two groundbreaking decisions were handed down after we had submitted the full manuscript of this book for publication: the Advisory Opinion of the International Tribunal for the Law of the Sea (ITLOS) on climate change and marine protection,[1] delivered on 21 May 2024, and the judgment of the European Court of Human Rights (ECtHR) in *Verein KlimaSeniorinnen Schweiz and Others v Switzerland*, issued on 9 April 2024.[2] These decisions mark a significant advancement in global climate jurisprudence, reinforcing and expanding upon many of the themes explored throughout this Handbook.

This chapter aims to analyse these late-breaking developments, situating them within the broader context of climate litigation and exploring their implications for future cases. After contextualising these cases and highlighting their key findings, we will draw connections to relevant analysis identified in other chapters, providing an up-to-date perspective on the rapidly evolving field of climate litigation.

* Margaretha Wewerinke-Singh is Associate Professor of Sustainability Law and Co-Founder of SEVEN, the University of Amsterdam's transdisciplinary climate institute; Adjunct Professor of Law at the University of Fiji; and Of Counsel at Blue Ocean Law. She served as Counsel for the Commission of Small Island States on Climate Change and International Law in the advisory proceedings on climate change and marine protection before the International Tribunal for the Law of the Sea; however, this chapter is written in her academic capacity. Joe Udell is a legal associate at the Climate Litigation Network.

1 *Request for an Advisory Opinion submitted by the Commission of Small Island States on Climate Change and International Law (Request for Advisory Opinion submitted to the Tribunal)*, ITLOS Case No 31 (Advisory Opinion of 21 May 2024).

2 *Verein KlimaSeniorinnen Schweiz and Others v Switzerland* App No 53600/20 (ECtHR).

This analysis will demonstrate how these decisions both reflect and advance emerging best practice in climate jurisprudence, potentially opening new avenues for legal intervention in the global fight for climate justice. We conclude by considering the implications for key issues in climate litigation, and how these rulings have the potential to drive more ambitious and equitable climate action through legal channels.

## 19.2 ITLOS ADVISORY OPINION: CLARIFYING STATE OBLIGATIONS UNDER UNCLOS

On 21 May 2024, ITLOS delivered a unanimous Advisory Opinion in response to questions submitted by the Commission of Small Island States on Climate Change and International Law (COSIS). This Opinion represents a significant development in international law as it pertains to climate change, clarifying States' obligations under the United Nations Convention on the Law of the Sea (UNCLOS) in relation to climate change.

### 19.2.1 *Background and Context*

The Commission, representing some of the world's most climate-vulnerable nations, posed two legal questions to the Tribunal:

> What are the specific obligations of State Parties to the United Nations Convention on the Law of the Sea ('UNCLOS'), including under Part XII:
>
> (a) to prevent, reduce and control pollution of the marine environment in relation to the deleterious effects that result or are likely to result from climate change, including through ocean warming and sea level rise, and ocean acidification, which are caused by anthropogenic greenhouse gas emissions into the atmosphere?
>
> (b) to protect and preserve the marine environment in relation to climate change impacts, including ocean warming and sea level rise, and ocean acidification?[3]

### 19.2.2 *Key Findings*

The Tribunal's Opinion demonstrates a commitment to interpreting UNCLOS dynamically in light of current scientific knowledge. By recognising greenhouse gas (GHG) emissions as a form of marine pollution and setting out a range of specific climate-related obligations of States arising from UNCLOS, ITLOS has confirmed

3 ITLOS Advisory Opinion (n 1) [3].

that UNCLOS provides a legal basis for compelling more ambitious and equitable climate action.[4]

The Opinion also illuminates the distinct role UNCLOS plays in the overall international legal framework applicable to climate change, including its relationship with the United Nations Framework Convention on Climate Change (UNFCCC) and the Paris Agreement. It emphasises that climate measures taken under UNCLOS should be determined objectively, taking into account the best available science and relevant international rules and standards.

This section highlights the key findings of the Tribunal by topic.

#### 19.2.2.1 Jurisdiction

ITLOS unanimously decided it had jurisdiction to give the Advisory Opinion, affirming its role in interpreting UNCLOS in connection with the climate crisis. This determination, however, was not a foregone conclusion, as there was some initial scholarly speculation that procedural obstacles would be a deterrent.[5]

One concern was whether the COSIS Agreement properly confers advisory jurisdiction to the Tribunal pursuant to Article 21 of the ITLOS Statute and Article 138 of the Rules of ITLOS.[6] In its analysis, ITLOS first considered Article 21, which dictates that its jurisdiction 'comprises all disputes and all applications submitted to it in accordance with this Convention and all matters specifically provided for in any other agreement which confers jurisdiction on the Tribunal'.[7] To that end, the COSIS Agreement explicitly states that it is 'authorized to request advisory opinions from the International Tribunal for the Law of the Sea (ITLOS) on any legal question within the scope of the 1982 United Nations Convention on the Law of the Sea, consistent with Article 21 of the ITLOS Statute and Article 138 of its Rules'.[8] The Tribunal accordingly explained that the authorisation enabling the Commission to request advisory opinions 'confers jurisdiction on the Tribunal' under Article 21.[9]

The Tribunal then turned to the conditions that needed to be satisfied under Article 138; notably that:

4 See also Korey Silverman-Roati and Maxim Bönnemann, 'The ITLOS Advisory Opinion on Climate Change' (*Verfassungsblog*, 22 May 2024) <https://verfassungsblog.de/the-itlos-advisory-opinion-on-climate-change/> accessed 27 September 2024.

5 See e.g. Armando Rocha, 'The Advisory Jurisdiction of the ITLOS in the Request Submitted by the Commission of Small Island States' (*Sabin Center for Climate Change Law*, 12 April 2023) <https://blogs.law.columbia.edu/climatechange/2023/04/12/the-advisory-jurisdiction-of-the-itlos-in-the-request-submitted-by-the-commission-of-small-island-states/> accessed 12 August 2024.

6 ibid.

7 ITLOS Advisory Opinion (n 1) [84].

8 ibid [88].

9 ibid.

(a) there is an international agreement related to the purposes of the Convention which specifically provides for the submission to the Tribunal of a request for an advisory opinion; (b) the request has been transmitted to the Tribunal by a body authorized by or in accordance with the agreement; and (c) the request submitted to the Tribunal concerns a legal question.[10]

After analysing the COSIS Agreement, the request for an Advisory Opinion submission process, and the legal nature of that request, the Tribunal concluded that it had jurisdiction to deliver the Advisory Opinion.[11]

#### 19.2.2.2 Anthropogenic GHG Emissions as Marine Pollution

In a crucial finding, the Tribunal determined that anthropogenic GHG emissions constitute pollution of the marine environment within the meaning of UNCLOS Article 1(1)(4), which defines marine pollution as the 'introduction by man, directly or indirectly, of substances' into the marine environment that is 'likely to result in such deleterious effects as harm to living resources and marine life, hazards to human health'.[12] The Tribunal's finding on this point is unambiguous: rather than suggesting that GHG emissions *may* or *could* amount to marine pollution, the Tribunal found that they *do* so: '[T]he Tribunal concludes that anthropogenic GHG emissions into the atmosphere constitute pollution of the marine environment within the meaning of article 1, paragraph 1, subparagraph 4, of the Convention.'[13] This interpretation confirms the broad scope of marine pollution under UNCLOS, with the effect of directly linking climate change to the Convention's regulatory framework. Part of this framework are the obligations flowing from Articles 192, 193, and 194(1)–(2) of the UNCLOS, which are widely recognised as codified rules of customary international law, such as the duty to protect and preserve the marine environment, the principle of State sovereignty over natural resources, and the 'no harm' principle, which prohibits activities within a State's jurisdiction from causing environmental harm to other States. Additionally, the framework includes provisions like Articles 207, 211, and 212, which impose obligations related to pollution from land-based sources, vessels, and the atmosphere.

The Opinion emphasises the obligation of States to exercise due diligence in fulfilling their obligations, with the standard of care required being 'stringent' given the high risks of serious and irreversible harm to the marine environment from GHG emissions.[14] This aligns with the precautionary approach, which the Tribunal considers implicit in the very notion of marine pollution under UNCLOS.[15]

[10] ibid [95].
[11] ibid [96]–[109].
[12] ibid [161].
[13] ibid [179].
[14] ibid [243].
[15] ibid [242].

### 19.2.2.3 Specific Obligations of States

The Opinion outlines a range of specific obligations for States under UNCLOS.[16] These include the following:

- Taking all necessary measures to prevent, reduce, and control marine pollution from anthropogenic GHG emissions (Article 194(1));[17]
- Ensuring that activities under their jurisdiction do not cause harm by pollution to other States and their environment (Article 194(2));[18]
- Adopting laws and regulations to prevent, reduce, and control marine pollution from GHG emissions from various sources (Articles 207, 211, 212);[19]
- Enforcing these laws and regulations (Articles 213, 217, 222);[20]
- Cooperating in formulating international rules and standards to address marine pollution from GHG emissions (Article 197);[21] and
- Conducting environmental impact assessments for activities that may cause substantial pollution or significant harm to the marine environment through GHG emissions (Article 206).[22]

### 19.2.2.4 Role of the Paris Agreement

The Opinion makes it clear that the UNFCCC, the Kyoto Protocol, and the Paris Agreement in no way preclude the application of other rules of international law, nor do they substitute the content of such other rules. It states: 'The Tribunal also does not consider that the Paris Agreement modifies or limits the obligation under the Convention. In the Tribunal's view, the Paris Agreement is not *lex specialis* to the Convention and thus, in the present context, *lex specialis derogat legi generali* has no place in the interpretation of the Convention.'[23] The Tribunal's interpretation positions UNCLOS obligations as directly applicable to climate change issues, rather than serving merely as tools to interpret the Paris Agreement. Instead, ITLOS refers to the Paris Agreement in its interpretation of relevant provisions of UNCLOS, while at the same time recognising the independent legal nature of both instruments.[24] This approach firmly establishes that States' climate change

[16] See also Margaretha Wewerinke-Singh and Jorge E. Viñuales, 'More than a Sink' (*Verfassungsblog*, 7 June 2024) <https://verfassungsblog.de/more-than-a-sink/> accessed 27 September 2024.

[17] ITLOS Advisory Opinion (n 1) [441(3)(b)].

[18] ibid [441(3)(d)].

[19] ibid [441(3)(f)–(g)].

[20] ibid [441(3)(h)–(i)].

[21] ibid [441(3)(j)].

[22] ibid [441(3)(l)].

[23] ibid [224].

[24] ibid [223].

obligations under UNCLOS are in no way substituted or diluted by the existence of climate change treaties.[25]

## 19.3 *KLIMASENIORINNEN V SWITZERLAND*: A BREAKTHROUGH IN EUROPEAN HUMAN RIGHTS LAW

The ECtHR Grand Chamber judgment in *KlimaSeniorinnen*, delivered on 9 April 2024, marks a watershed moment in climate litigation.[26] The decision represents the first time that the Court has ruled on the application of the European Convention on Human Rights (ECHR) with respect to climate change.[27] Notably, the ECtHR not only recognised that climate change implicates various rights protected under the ECHR, it also identified specific positive obligations for States to protect those rights by combating climate change. Moreover, it clarified its standing criteria for associations engaged in climate protection.

The Court announced the *KlimaSeniorinnen* judgment on the same day as two other climate change cases: *Duarte Agostinho v Portugal and 32 other States*,[28] and *Carême v France*.[29] *Duarte Agostinho*, which was brought by six Portuguese youth applicants, was found to be inadmissible because jurisdiction was lacking for all respondents save Portugal; and because the applicants had not first exhausted domestic remedies before national courts in Portugal.[30] *Carême* was inadmissible due to a lack of victim status since the applicant – the former mayor of the Grande-Synthe municipality – no longer lived in the affected region of France, having moved to Brussels.[31]

### 19.3.1 *Case Background*

After exhausting domestic remedies, where Swiss courts dismissed their claims primarily on standing grounds, the KlimaSeniorinnen association, representing over 2,000 elderly women and four individual applicants, turned to the ECtHR. They alleged that worsening climate impacts – notably heatwaves – were increasingly affecting their health.[32] The applicants claimed that Switzerland's insufficient action on climate change violated their rights under Articles 2 (right to life) and 8 (right

[25] See also Jacqueline Peel, 'Unlocking UNCLOS' (*Verfassungsblog*, 24 May 2024) <https://verfassungsblog.de/unlocking-unclos/> accessed 27 September 2024.

[26] *KlimaSeniorinnen* (n 2).

[27] See also Maria Antonia Tigre and Maxim Bönnemann, 'The Transformation of European Climate Change Litigation' (*Verfassungsblog*, 9 April 2024) <https://verfassungsblog.de/the-transformation-of-european-climate-change-litigation/> accessed 27 September 2024.

[28] *Duarte Agostinho v Portugal and 32 other States* App No 39371/20 (ECtHR).

[29] *Carême v France* App No 7189/21 (ECtHR).

[30] *Duarte Agostinho* (n 28) [231].

[31] *Carême* (n 29) [83], [88].

[32] *KlimaSeniorinnen* (n 2) [10]–[20].

to respect for private and family life) of the ECHR. Moreover, they argued that the dismissal of their case in the domestic courts violated their right to a fair trial (Article 6(1)) and right to an effective remedy (Article 13) under the ECHR.

### 19.3.2 *Key Findings*

The Court's reasoning represents a significant contribution to judicial practice on climate change under the ECHR. In particular, the judgment contains several groundbreaking elements with respect to the role of the Paris Agreement; the positive obligations that States have to address climate change under Article 8 ECHR; the standard of review; Switzerland's violation of Articles 8 and 6(1) ECHR; State responsibility; the rejection of the 'drop in the ocean' argument; and the standing of the KlimaSeniorinnen association. The following section highlights and summarises the key findings with respect to each of these issues.

#### 19.3.2.1 Role of the Paris Agreement

*KlimaSeniorinnen* – along with relevant parts of the Court's reasoning in *Duarte Agostinho* and *Carême* – unequivocally establishes that human rights law is applicable to climate change.[33] The Court also makes it crystal-clear that neither the UNFCCC nor its subsidiary treaties, the Kyoto Protocol and the Paris Agreement, replace or substitute States' human rights obligations.[34] Rather, the Court points at the imperative of an integrated approach whereby States' commitments under international climate change law coupled with the best available science serve to create a 'floor' for States' obligations under the ECHR:

> In line with the international commitments undertaken by the member States, most notably under the UNFCCC and the Paris Agreement, and the cogent scientific evidence provided, in particular, by the IPCC [Intergovernmental Panel on Climate Change] (see paragraphs 104–120 above), the Contracting States need to put in place the necessary regulations and measures aimed at preventing an increase in GHG concentrations in the Earth's atmosphere and a rise in global average temperature beyond levels capable of producing serious and irreversible adverse effects on human rights, notably the right to private and family life and home under Article 8 of the Convention.[35]

[33] See also Jannika Jahn, 'The Paris Effect: Human Rights in Light of International Climate Goals and Commitments' (*Sabin Center for Climate Change Law*, 26 April 2024) <https://blogs.law.columbia.edu/climatechange/2024/04/26/the-paris-effect-human-rights-in-light-of-international-climate-goals-and-commitments/> accessed 30 September 2024.

[34] *KlimaSeniorinnen* (n 2) [410]–[411].

[35] ibid [546].

### 19.3.2.2 Positive Obligations

The judgment confirms that the ECHR imposes positive obligations on States to take effective measures to mitigate climate change.[36] These obligations flow directly from the causal relationship between climate change and the enjoyment of ECHR rights.[37] According to the Court, Article 8 ECHR provides 'a right for individuals to enjoy effective protection by the State authorities from serious adverse effects on their life, health, well-being and quality of life arising from the harmful effects and risks caused by climate change'.[38] Each State's 'obligation under Article 8 is to do its part to ensure such protection' and its 'primary duty is to adopt, and to effectively apply in practice, regulations and measures capable of mitigating the existing and potentially irreversible, future effects of climate change'.[39]

The Court then laid out a set of specific standards that it would evaluate in climate cases to determine if domestic authorities 'have had due regard to the need to':

(a) adopt general measures specifying a target timeline for achieving carbon neutrality and the overall remaining carbon budget for the same time frame, or another equivalent method of quantification of future GHG emissions, in line with the overarching goal for national and/or global climate-change mitigation commitments;
(b) set out intermediate GHG emissions reduction targets and pathways (by sector or[40] other relevant methodologies) that are deemed capable, in principle, of meeting the overall national GHG reduction goals within the relevant time frames undertaken in national policies;
(c) provide evidence showing whether they have duly complied, or are in the process of complying, with the relevant GHG reduction targets (see sub-paragraphs (a)(b) above);
(d) keep the relevant GHG reduction targets updated with due diligence, and based on the best available evidence; and
(e) act in good time and in an appropriate and consistent manner when devising and implementing the relevant legislation and measures.[41]

The Court arrived at these obligations by adapting its general principles guiding the interpretation of Article 8 ECHR to the specific context of climate change. In Article 8 environmental disputes prior to *KlimaSeniorinnen*, the Court's case law established that States have a duty to, *inter alia*, put in place an adequate legislative framework

36 ibid [544].
37 ibid [545].
38 ibid [544]. Note that the Court found it unnecessary to analyse Article 2 ECHR given that Article 8 'undoubtedly' applied given the circumstances. ibid [536].
39 ibid [545].
40 ibid [550].
41 ibid.

that will 'provide effective protection of human health and life'.[42] These environmental cases refer to situations where 'there is a nexus between a source of harm and those affected by the harm', and the requisite mitigation measures are easily identifiable.[43]

However, the Court found that the key characteristics of climate change are 'significantly different' from the circumstances surrounding other environmental cases, thus complicating the adjudication of such disputes.[44] These features include the multitude of sources that cause GHG emissions; the fact that carbon dioxide is not toxic *per se* at ordinary concentration levels; the transboundary nature of emissions; and the complex and unpredictable causal chain of events that eventually results in harm to human life.[45] The Court accordingly asserted that it must adapt the general parameters of positive obligations under Article 8 to effectively address 'the special nature of the phenomenon' of climate change'.[46] In so doing, it ensured that the ECHR, as a treaty protecting human rights, continues to be interpreted such that it is 'practical and effective, not theoretical and illusory'.[47]

#### 19.3.2.3 Level of Judicial Scrutiny

A central aspect of the Court's modification of Article 8 ECHR principles was the level of judicial scrutiny it established for disputes in the climate context. When determining if an Article 8 violation has occurred, the ECtHR noted that it will look at whether the respondent State remained within its margin of appreciation.[48]

In *KlimaSeniorinnen*, the Court established two different margins of appreciation for States.[49] To do so, it first established a distinction between (1) States' commitments to addressing climate change; and (2) the manner in which they carry out their climate actions. While acknowledging that States have a wide margin of appreciation in choosing the means to achieve their climate objectives, the Court explained that States have a reduced margin of appreciation with respect to

42 ibid [538(a)].
43 ibid [415].
44 ibid [416].
45 ibid [415]–[422].
46 ibid [540].
47 ibid [545].
48 ibid [538(c)]. This doctrine refers to the amount of deference granted in a given situation – the Court will scrutinise acts or omissions much more intensely in circumstances where States operate under a narrow margin of appreciation; conversely, this scrutiny will be less significant for acts or omissions in areas where States benefit from a wide margin of appreciation. See e.g. Dean Spielmann, 'Allowing the Right Margin: The European Court of Human Rights and The National Margin of Appreciation Doctrine: Waiver or Subsidiarity of European Review?' (2012) Cambridge Yearbook of European Legal Studies 381.
49 See also Annalisa Savaresi, Linnéa Nordlander, and Margaretha Wewerinke-Singh, 'Climate Change Litigation before the European Court of Human Rights: A New Dawn' (*GNHRE*, 12 April 2024) <https://gnhre.org/?p=17984> accessed 30 September 2024.

their climate commitments.[50] This heightened scrutiny is attributed to the 'nature and gravity of the threat and the general consensus as to the stakes involved in ensuring the overarching goal of effective climate protection'.[51] The Court thus found that States' discretion in policy choices is confined by an objective requirement to address climate change 'in good time, in an appropriate and consistent manner' and base their approach on the best available scientific evidence.[52]

#### 19.3.2.4 Violation of Article 8

The Court found a violation of Article 8 ECHR based on an analysis of Switzerland's climate policies under a reduced margin of appreciation.[53] Ultimately, Switzerland's 2011 CO2 Act, 2022 Climate Act, and lack of a quantified carbon budget fell short of meeting the positive obligations described in the previous section. The ECtHR evaluated Switzerland's ineffective compliance with its Article 8 obligations as follows:

> [T]here were some critical lacunae in the Swiss authorities' process of putting in place the relevant domestic regulatory framework, including a failure by them to quantify, through a carbon budget or otherwise, national GHG emissions limitations. Furthermore, the Court has noted that, as recognised by the relevant authorities, the State had previously failed to meet its past GHG emission reduction targets. By failing to act in good time and in an appropriate and consistent manner regarding the devising, development and implementation of the relevant legislative and administrative framework, the respondent State exceeded its margin of appreciation and failed to comply with its positive obligations in the present context.[54]

In highlighting Switzerland's 'critical lacunae' in its regulatory framework, the Court clearly established that States must have a national carbon budget (or an equivalent) set in light of the global carbon budget to comply with its relevant duty of care.

#### 19.3.2.5 Violation of Article 6(1)

The ECtHR also found a violation of the right of access to a court under Article 6(1) ECHR, concluding that the Swiss courts had failed to engage seriously with the merits of the applicants' claims regarding the effective implementation of mitigation

50 *KlimaSeniorinnen* (n 2) [543].
51 ibid.
52 ibid [548].
53 See also Sandra Arntz and Jasper Krommendijk, 'Historic and Unprecedented: The ECtHR Upholds Positive Human Rights Obligations to Mitigate Climate Change' (*Sabin Center for Climate Change Law*, 10 April 2024) <https://blogs.law.columbia.edu/climatechange/2024/04/10/historic-and-unprecedented-the-ecthr-upholds-positive-human-rights-obligations-to-mitigate-climate-change/> accessed 30 September 2024.
54 *KlimaSeniorinnen* (n 2) [573].

measures under existing domestic law.[55] The Court was 'not persuaded' by the Swiss courts' assertion that there was still time to address the most severe climate impacts because the existing scientific evidence 'suggest[ed] that there was a pressing need to ensure the legal protection of human rights'.[56] This shortcoming was made clearer by the fact that, according to the ECtHR, domestic courts have a 'key role' to play in ensuring effective protection of Convention rights in the climate context, signalling that restrictions on access to justice in environmental matters will be subject to close scrutiny.[57] Accordingly, Switzerland's domestic courts did not take the proper action to ensure that the human rights enshrined in the ECHR were being observed.[58]

### 19.3.2.6 State Responsibility

The *KlimaSeniorinnen* judgment expressly recognises the application of the general law of State responsibility to climate change to anthropogenic emissions of greenhouse gases from a State. The ECtHR noted that:

> [W]hile climate change is undoubtedly a global phenomenon which should be addressed at the global level by the community of States, the global climate regime established under the UNFCCC rests on the principle of common but differentiated responsibilities and respective capabilities [CBRD-RC] of States (Article 3 § 1). This principle has been reaffirmed in the Paris Agreement (Article 2 § 2) and endorsed in the Glasgow Climate Pact (cited above, paragraph 18) as well as in the Sharm el-Sheikh Implementation Plan (cited above, paragraph 12). It follows, therefore, that each State has its own share of responsibilities to take measures to tackle climate change and that the taking of those measures is determined by the State's own capabilities rather than by any specific action (or omission) of any other State (see Duarte Agostinho and Others, cited above, §§ 202–03). The Court considers that a respondent State should not evade its responsibility by pointing to the responsibility of other States, whether Contracting Parties to the Convention or not […]
>
> This position is consistent with the Court's approach in cases involving a concurrent responsibility of States for alleged breaches of Convention rights, where each State can be held accountable for its share of the responsibility for the breach in question (see, albeit in other contexts, *M.S.S. v Belgium and Greece*, cited above, §§ 264 and 367, and *Razvozzhayev v Russia and Ukraine and Udaltsov v Russia*, nos. 75734/12 and 2 others, §§ 160–61 and 179–81, 19 November 2019). It is also consistent with the principles of international law relating to the plurality of responsible States, according to which the responsibility of each State is determined individually, on the basis of its own conduct and by reference to its own international obligations

55 ibid [636]. Note that the Court found it unnecessary to analyse Article 13 given that it is 'absorbed by the more stringent requirements of Article 6'. ibid [644].

56 ibid [635].

57 ibid [639].

58 ibid [640].

(see International Law Commission, Draft Articles on Responsibility of States for Internationally Wrongful Acts, with commentaries, Commentary on Article 47, paragraphs 6 and 8). Similarly, the alleged infringement of rights under the Convention through harm arising from GHG emissions globally and the acts and omissions on the part of multiple States in combating the adverse effects of climate change may engage the responsibility of each Contracting Party.[59]

### 19.3.2.7 Standing

While denying standing to the individual applicants due to *actio popularis* concerns, the Court granted standing to the KlimaSeniorinnen association, significantly lowering the threshold for associational standing in climate cases.[60] This decision marks a notable development in the ECtHR's standing jurisprudence as associations are generally 'not in a position to rely on health considerations to allege a violation of Article 8'.[61]

However, the Court explained that associations have an important role to play in modern societies faced with challenges like climate change, which require complex administrative decision-making processes. In this context, 'recourse to collective bodies such as associations is one of the accessible means, sometimes the only means, available to [citizens] whereby they can defend their particular interests effectively'.[62] As such, the Court revealed a broadened standing test for Article 8 climate disputes, which requires that an association is:

(a) lawfully established in the jurisdiction concerned or have standing to act there;
(b) able to demonstrate that it pursues a dedicated purpose in accordance with its statutory objectives in the defence of the human rights of its members or other affected individuals within the jurisdiction concerned, whether limited to or including collective action for the protection of those rights against the threats arising from climate change; and
(c) able to demonstrate that it can be regarded as genuinely qualified and representative to act on behalf of members or other affected individuals within the jurisdiction who are subject to specific threats or adverse effects of climate change on their lives, health or well-being as protected under the Convention.[63]

Furthermore, when analysing these criteria, the ECtHR stated that it would look to the following factors: the purpose of the association; whether it is of a non-profit character; the nature and extent of its activities; its membership and representativeness;

59 ibid [442]–[443].
60 See also Jeremy Letwin, 'Klimaseniorinnen: The Innovative and the Orthodox' (*EJIL: Talk!*, 17 April 2024) <www.ejiltalk.org/klimaseniorinnen-the-innovative-and-the-orthodox/> accessed 30 September 2024.
61 *KlimaSeniorinnen* (n 2) [473].
62 ibid [489].
63 ibid [502].

its principles and transparency of governance; and whether granting standing to the organisation would be in the interest of the proper administration of justice.[64] With respect to KlimaSeniorinnen's standing, the Court recognised that, as a result of its membership basis, representativeness, and purpose, the association 'represents a vehicle of collective recourse aimed at defending the rights and interests of individuals against the threats of climate change in the respondent State'.[65]

## 19.4 DISTILLING EMERGING BEST PRACTICE FROM THE TWO DECISIONS

The ITLOS Advisory Opinion and the *KlimaSeniorinnen* judgment, while emerging from different legal regimes, display notable similarities in their approach to climate change. Together, they contribute significantly to the consolidation of key aspects of the emerging best practices examined throughout this Handbook. This section will identify and connect notable examples of those approaches with the discussions in previous chapters.

### 19.4.1 *Recognition of Urgency*

Both decisions acknowledge the pressing nature of climate change and the need for immediate and effective action. This approach represents emerging best practice, reflecting the critical state of the climate crisis as described in Chapters 2 and 3.

For instance, the ITLOS Advisory Opinion relies on IPCC findings to explain that climate impacts due to past and future emissions are 'irreversible for centuries to millennia, especially changes in the ocean, ice sheets and global sea level'.[66] The Tribunal also stressed that 'climate change represents an existential threat and raises human rights concerns'.[67] Establishing this sense of urgency sets the stage for the novel duties for States outlined later in the decision.

Likewise, *KlimaSeniorinnen* details and explicitly refers to both the 'climate emergency'[68] and the 'climate crisis'.[69] Resolving this crisis, according to the Court, demands a 'comprehensive and complex set of transformative policies involving legislative, regulatory, fiscal, financial and administrative measures as well as both public and private investment',[70] with 'critical issues aris[ing] from failures to act, or inadequate action' at the State level.[71]

64 ibid.
65 ibid [523].
66 ITLOS Advisory Opinion (n 1) [62].
67 ibid [66].
68 *KlimaSeniorinnen* (n 2) [433].
69 ibid [479].
70 ibid.
71 ibid.

These judicial approaches – coupled particularly with the positive climate obligations that States have under UNCLOS and the ECHR – advance emerging best practice in that both decisions properly identify the alarming state of the climate crisis, then explain how States have a legal duty to address this critical situation.

### 19.4.2 *Reliance on the Best Available Science*

The ITLOS Advisory Opinion and *KlimaSeniorinnen* both rely on the best available scientific evidence, particularly reports from the IPCC. In so doing, ITLOS and the ECtHR further emerging best practice by grounding the facts of their respective cases in the most recent scientific consensus on climate change. This reliance on scientific consensus and best available evidence reinforces the importance of robust climate science in litigation, as explored in Chapters 2 and 3, and further identified as emerging best practice throughout the Handbook.

The ITLOS Advisory Opinion maintains that best available science plays a 'crucial role' in determining the content of the necessary measures that States must take to prevent, reduce, and control marine pollution.[72] These findings, according to the Tribunal, are 'key to understanding the causes, effects and dynamics of such pollution and thus to providing the effective response'.[73] Moreover, as due diligence is a variable concept, States must be aware of new scientific developments as they formulate their climate actions.[74]

The Tribunal's finding that anthropogenic GHG emissions amount to marine pollution was explicitly informed by this best available science. Amongst other things, ITLOS noted: 'Being itself a component of climate change, ocean warming, according to the IPCC findings made with high confidence, "accounted for 91% of the heating in the climate system" (WGI 2021 Report, p. 11).'[75] The Tribunal also relied on IPCC reports to establish the content of States' obligations to address climate change under UNCLOS. In doing so, it made clear that 1.5°C – as opposed to well below 2°C – is the relevant temperature goal of the Paris Agreement:

> Such measures [to prevent, reduce and control marine pollution] should be determined objectively, taking into account, *inter alia*, the best available science and relevant international rules and standards contained in climate change treaties such as the UNFCCC and the Paris Agreement, in particular the global temperature goal of limiting the temperature increase to 1.5°C above pre-industrial levels and the timeline for emission pathways to achieve that goal.[76]

72 ibid [212].
73 ibid.
74 ibid [239].
75 ibid [175].
76 ibid [243].

Importantly, ITLOS stressed that the need for alignment with the 1.5°C temperature goal 'applies equally' to the obligations to take necessary measures to prevent transboundary GHG pollution under Article 194, paragraph 2.[77]

*KlimaSeniorinnen* similarly dictates that States align their GHG reduction targets with the best available evidence and update these targets as insights evolve.[78] To that end, the ECtHR highlighted IPCC reports such as the Special Report on Global Warming of 1.5°C, as well as the Sixth Assessment Report.[79] The Court expressly added that those reports were not 'challenged or called into doubt by the respondent or intervening States'.[80] The findings of the IPCC thereby proved to be essential in terms of establishing the undisputed facts of the case – all of which underscore the magnitude of the current state of the climate crisis:

> [T]hat there are sufficiently reliable indications that anthropogenic climate change exists, that it poses a serious current and future threat to the enjoyment of human rights guaranteed under the Convention, that States are aware of it and capable of taking measures to effectively address it, that the relevant risks are projected to be lower if the rise in temperature is limited to 1.5°C above pre-industrial levels and if action is taken urgently, and that current global mitigation efforts are not sufficient to meet the latter target.[81]

The Court's approach here not only further cements the key role of best available science in climate litigation, it also illustrates how that evidence can effectively establish the reference point – specifically the Paris Agreement's temperature limit of 1.5°C, as opposed to 2°C – that climate action is measured against.

### 19.4.3 *Standing*

The ECtHR's flexible approach to this issue opens new possibilities for collective action in climate litigation. Despite the Court's more restrictive stance for individuals, its willingness to adapt and broaden its standing criteria for associations in the context of climate change embodies the emerging best practice emphasised in Chapter 5, which highlighted the importance of easing standing burdens in climate litigation.[82] Accordingly, associations engaged in climate change issues will likely be empowered to represent their membership on rights-based grounds in domestic courts. As the ECtHR's standing rules are different from those of domestic courts, should domestic courts not find *KlimaSeniorinnen's* jurisprudence to be persuasive,

77 ibid [250].
78 *KlimaSeniorinnen* (n 2) [550(d)].
79 ibid [107]–[120].
80 ibid [432].
81 ibid [436].
82 Note that, although domestic courts generally use the term 'standing' for both individuals and associations, the ECtHR refers to 'victim status' in relation to individuals and '*locus standi*' in relation to associations.

associations denied standing at the national level will conceivably have a promising chance for the ECtHR to hear their claims on the merits.

### 19.4.4 *Admissibility*

ITLOS and the ECtHR promoted the emerging best practice identified in Chapter 5 by exercising their legal powers to oversee the respective proceedings in a manner consistent with the climate crisis. ITLOS, for instance, invoked its discretion to render its Advisory Opinion by stressing that climate change 'is recognized internationally as a common concern of humankind' while also noting 'the deleterious effects climate change has on the marine environment and the devastating consequences it has and will continue to have on small island States, considered to be among the most vulnerable'.[83] Likewise, the ECtHR notably fast-tracked *KlimaSeniorinnen*, along with *Duarte Agostinho* and *Carême*, to the Grand Chamber, thus furthering the notion that climate change requires admissibility to be assessed in a timely manner. The Court's willingness to admit climate claims brought forward by associations also represents a transparent effort to balance *actio popularis* concerns with the effective protection of human rights under the ECHR.

### 19.4.5 *Separation of Powers*

Both decisions assert a robust role for the judiciary in addressing climate change, while respecting the principle of separation of powers. The ECtHR, in particular, advanced the emerging best practice discussed in Chapter 6 by encouraging more assertive judicial engagement with climate issues at the national and regional levels. On one hand, the Court emphasised the 'key role which domestic courts have played and will play in climate-change litigation'.[84] This sentiment will be critical in the near future as domestic courts will most assuredly receive submissions from plaintiffs seeking to hold States accountable for their positive Article 8 obligations. With respect to exercising its own judicial authority, the Court importantly stressed that, despite the deference it extends to the policy-setting authority of States, scrutinising potential ECHR violations falls well within its authority as a matter of law.[85]

### 19.4.6 *Human Rights*

Although these rulings both acknowledge the connection between climate change and human rights, *KlimaSeniorinnen* provides a particularly powerful new tool for

83 ITLOS Advisory Opinion (n 1) [122].
84 *KlimaSeniorinnen* (n 2) [639].
85 ibid [450].

climate litigants and advances the rights-based approaches discussed in Chapter 7. The ECtHR incorporated all three forms of emerging best practice identified in that chapter into its decision: recognising the impacts that climate change is having and will continue to have on human rights; recognising that States must adopt and implement a wide range of climate actions to protect human rights; and referring to norms of international environmental law and best available science to interpret States' human rights obligations in the climate context. On this point, ITLOS aligned with the first emerging best practice, albeit much less explicitly than the ECtHR, by acknowledging that 'climate change represents an existential threat and raises human rights concerns'.[86] Given the ECtHR's respected stature as a regional court focused on safeguarding human rights, as well as plaintiffs' frequent invocation of Article 8 ECHR in European climate litigation, the Court's approach in *KlimaSeniorinnen* will most likely have a significant positive impact on a range of rights-based cases.[87]

### 19.4.7 *Extraterritoriality*

Both decisions highlight the global nature of climate change and the need to address it through national efforts and international cooperation, with due regard to extraterritorial impacts of actions under scrutiny. This recognition echoes the emerging best practice discussed in Chapter 8. The ITLOS Advisory Opinion's emphasis on preventing transboundary pollution under Article 194(2) UNCLOS, which may require States to act with an even more stringent standard of due diligence than under Article 194(1),[88] is a particularly potent contribution to this emerging best practice.

The ECtHR, in contrast, may at first glance seem to have offered little in terms of guidance on climate change and extraterritoriality, other than stating in *Duarte Agostinho* that climate change does not warrant a special approach to jurisdiction.[89] However, in *KlimaSeniorinnen* the Court did take a globally oriented approach in its brief discussion on trade-related emissions. According to the Court, it would be 'difficult, if not impossible, to discuss Switzerland's responsibility for the effects of its GHG emissions' on human rights 'without taking into account the emissions generated through the import of goods and their consumption', otherwise known as 'embedded emissions'.[90] It acknowledged that embedded emissions 'contain an extraterritorial aspect'[91] and confirmed that this aspect fell within the scope of the case. While the Court did not examine the impact of these emissions in detail, its

86 ITLOS Advisory Opinion (n 1) [66].

87 See e.g. VZW *Klimaatzaak v l'État Belge* [2021] 2015/4585/A (Tribunal de première instance francophone de Bruxelles, Section Civile); *State of the Netherlands (Ministry of Economic Affairs and Climate Policy) v Stichting Urgenda* [2019] ECLI:NL:HR:2019:2007.

88 ITLOS Advisory Opinion (n 1) [256].

89 *Duarte Agostinho* (n 28) [184]–[214].

90 *KlimaSeniorinnen* (n 2) [280].

91 ibid [287].

pronouncements provide important guidance to domestic courts and signal that the Court's door is open to future cases addressing this dimension.[92]

### 19.4.8 *Duty of Care*

Both decisions articulate specific positive obligations for States to adopt and implement a number of comprehensive measures to address climate change. To distil these obligations from relevant treaty texts, ITLOS and the ECtHR draw on a range of sources – most notably the UNFCCC and the Paris Agreement, but also principles of international environmental law and best available science. This line of judicial reasoning reflects emerging best practices discussed in Chapter 9, which demonstrates how judicial bodies can interpret treaties in a way that safeguards their effectiveness in a world existentially threatened by climate change.

### 19.4.9 *International Atmospheric Trust*

Although neither the ITLOS Advisory Opinion nor *KlimaSeniorinnen* directly engage with the application of the public trust doctrine in climate litigation, both decisions contain jurisprudence that could further international atmospheric trust cases. For example, the broad emphasis that ITLOS and the ECtHR place on intergenerational equity resonates with the emerging best practice described in Chapter 10. As the sovereign's traditional duty is to protect trust resources for the benefit of current and future generations, the positive intergenerational equity jurisprudence in the ITLOS Advisory Opinion and *KlimaSeniorinnen* could strengthen the application of the public trust doctrine to non-traditional resources, such as the atmosphere. The ECtHR's exploration of the role of domestic courts is notable in this context, given the synergies between the public trust doctrine and the protection of human rights,[93] as well as the fact that international atmospheric trust disputes have historically been adjudicated at the national level. This emphasis on domestic courts as key protectors of human rights could thereby encourage more judicial engagement with international atmospheric trust litigation.

### 19.4.10 *Rights of Nature*

While neither ruling expressly examines the rights of nature, the Tribunal's consideration of the effects of climate change on the marine environment has an ecocentric quality that echoes the emerging best practice in Chapter 12. Most notably, the

[92] ibid.

[93] See e.g. David Takacs, 'The Public Trust Doctrine, Environmental Human Rights, and the Future of Private Property' (2010) NYU Envtl L J; Mary Christina Wood and Rance Shaw, 'Enforcing Human Rights Against Fracking Through the Public Trust Principle' (*Center for Humans & Nature*, 3 March 2017) <https://humansandnature.org/enforcing-human-rights-against-fracking-through-the-public-trust-principle/>;

Tribunal frames its entire legal analysis within extensive IPCC findings on the myriad ways that climate change alters the ocean and the species that inhabit it.[94] When discussing States' obligations under UNCLOS, the Tribunal reiterates that 'climate change and ocean acidification affect virtually all forms of marine life, including fish and corals that build structures providing the habitat for large numbers of species'.[95] Such language furthers the belief that nature has intrinsic value and is deserving of protection independent of its worth to humans. The Tribunal's finding that States have an obligation to conduct environmental impact assessments for activities that may harm the marine environment through GHG emissions seems aligned with this recognition.

### 19.4.11 *International Law*

Both ITLOS and the ECtHR built upon the emerging best practices described in Chapter 12 by relying on international climate change law to define the content of States' obligations under UNCLOS and the ECHR, most notably the commitments made as Parties to the Paris Agreement. Moreover, principles of international environmental law, including the principles of due diligence, CBDR-RC, no-harm, prevention, and precaution, also substantively inform the scope of States' respective duties. As a representative example, *KlimaSeniorinnen* requires States to keep their emissions reduction targets updated with due diligence,[96] while the ITLOS Advisory Opinion maintains that States have a stringent due diligence obligation to safeguard the marine environment from pollution[97] – which, as noted earlier, can be even more stringent in the context of preventing transboundary pollution.[98]

### 19.4.12 *Common but Differentiated Responsibilities and Respective Capabilities*

The principle of CBDR-RC, much like the principle of due diligence described earlier, had an essential role in outlining States' obligations pursuant to the respective treaties. In so doing, both decisions furthered the emerging best practice discussion in Chapter 13. In the ITLOS Advisory Opinion, the Tribunal explained that CBDR-RC requires both developed and developing States to make mitigation efforts to safeguard the marine environment from pollution, even if the measures taken vary by country.[99] This approach echoes the notion that, although developed nations must take the lead in terms of climate action, developing countries cannot focus strictly on climate adaptation. At the same time, it reinforces developed countries'

94 ITLOS Advisory Opinion (n 1) [46]–[66].
95 ibid [409].
96 *KlimaSeniorinnen* (n 2) [550(d)].
97 ITLOS Advisory Opinion (n 1) [239]–[243].
98 ibid [258].
99 Note that although the Convention does not explicitly refer to the principle of CBDR-RC, the Tribunal explained that 'it contains some elements common to this principle'. ibid [229].

obligations to provide finance, technology transfer, and capacity building to enable ambitious climate action in developing countries.

Similarly, the ECtHR invoked and relied on the principle of CBDR-RC in finding that Switzerland had failed to comply with its obligations under Article 8. Whereas the requirement that States must quantify their overall remaining carbon budget for the time period until they reach carbon neutrality may appear to be largely procedural,[100] it is clear from the Court's application of the obligation to Switzerland that it is not. Rather, it flows from the Court's reasoning on this point that a State's climate measures can only align with its duty to adopt and implement regulations capable of mitigating harmful climate impacts[101] if they are based on the overarching long-term temperature goal of 1.5°C as well as that State's fair share of the remaining global carbon budget. This conclusion is primarily supported by five points.

First, the Court maintained that the ECHR should be interpreted in harmony with the UNFCCC and the Paris Agreement,[102] and it explicitly highlighted the central importance of CBDR-RC.[103] In this regard, the Court noted that each State 'has its own share of responsibilities to take measures to tackle climate change and that the taking of those measures is determined by the State's own capabilities rather than by any specific action (or omission) of any other State'.[104]

Second, as explained earlier, States have a reduced margin of appreciation with respect to their climate commitments.[105] It follows then that States have limited discretion when it comes to the quantification of their climate targets and national carbon budgets in relation to the global 1.5°C temperature limit referenced by the Court, and that they are subject to strict judicial scrutiny for their conformity with the Convention.[106]

Third, the Court explicitly rejected Switzerland's efforts to justify its lack of a national carbon budget by positing that there is no established methodology to do so. To that end, the Court referenced the *Neubauer* decision, which similarly 'rejected the argument that it was impossible to determine the national carbon budget, pointing to, *inter alia*, the principle of common but differentiated responsibilities under the UNFCCC and the Paris Agreement'.[107] The Court explained that '[t]his principle requires the States to act on the basis of equity and in accordance with their own respective capabilities'.[108] In other words, the Court held that States *can* determine their national carbon budget and that their

[100] *KlimaSeniorinnen* (n 2) [550(a)].
[101] ibid [545].
[102] ibid [455]–[456].
[103] ibid [133], [134], [136], [137], [140], [164], [442], [478], [571].
[104] ibid [442].
[105] ibid [543].
[106] See ibid e.g. [436], [558].
[107] ibid [571].
[108] ibid.

methodology for doing so must be based on the principle of CBDR-RC. It also formulated equity as a guiding principle for such a determination. This is an explicit confirmation of the requirement that States determine their national carbon budget on the basis of a fair share determination, taking account of CBDR-RC, and grounded in principles of equity. Importantly, the Court tacitly acknowledged that an equal per capita emissions approach falls short of what is required under the principle of CBDR-RC, as it does not adequately account for States' differing historical responsibilities and capabilities.[109] This underscores that methodologies used to determine national carbon budgets need to capture these different dimensions of CBDR-RC.

Fourth, the Court rejected Switzerland's claim that its national climate policy – based on internal assessments and its nationally determined contributions – was similar in approach to establishing a national carbon budget.[110] In doing so, it relied on the estimated remaining Swiss carbon budget to stay within 1.5°C, which was informed by evidence from the KlimaSeniorinnen association.[111] Based on this information, the Court noted that under its current climate strategy, Switzerland 'allowed for more GHG emissions than even an "equal per capita emissions" quantification approach would entitle it to use'.[112] It is important to underscore that the Court did *not* suggest that meeting an equal per capita emissions standard would amount to compliance with its obligations; rather, it highlighted that Switzerland was exceeding even this insufficient standard, thereby evidencing a breach. The Court's reference reaffirms that the equal per capita approach sets a baseline that is too low and does not fully reflect the higher standard required under CBDR-RC.

Fifth, the Court built on the earlier point and asserted that it 'has difficulty accepting that the State could be regarded as complying effectively with its regulatory obligation under Article 8' without 'any domestic measure attempting to quantify the respondent State's remaining carbon budget'.[113]

These points thereby infer that a State's climate measures can only align with its duty to adopt and implement regulations capable of mitigating harmful climate impacts[114] if they are based on the overarching long-term temperature goal of 1.5°C as well as that State's fair share of the remaining global carbon budget. An equal per capita approach is insufficient in this context, as it fails to account for the differentiated responsibilities and capabilities of States, particularly those with greater historical emissions and higher capacities to reduce emissions.

[109] ibid [569].
[110] ibid [570]–[571].
[111] ibid [569].
[112] ibid.
[113] ibid [572].
[114] ibid [545].

### 19.4.13 *Intergenerational Equity*

Both ITLOS and the ECtHR promote the emerging best practice discussed in Chapter 14 by incorporating aspects of intergenerational equity into their decisions, thus bolstering the normative development of this international environmental law principle. For instance, the Advisory Opinion's emphasis on protecting the ocean as an inherently valuable part of the environment – as opposed to a mere sink that absorbs emissions – requires States to introduce more ambitious climate policies that must, in turn, protect future generations. In the same vein, *KlimaSeniorinnen* frames States' positive climate obligations under Article 8 ECHR around the need to 'avoid a disproportionate burden on future generations',[115] thereby encouraging a fair distribution of climate obligations over time.

### 19.4.14 *State Responsibility*

Both decisions embody emerging best practice by explicitly rejecting the 'drop in the ocean' argument. This approach highlights that each State is required to do its own part to the best of its abilities to reduce greenhouse gas emissions, and especially resonates with the discussion in Chapter 15. ITLOS, for instance, specifically rejected the argument that climate change can only be regulated through 'joint action' and concluded instead that:

> While the importance of joint actions in regulating marine pollution from anthropogenic GHG emissions is undisputed, it does not follow that the obligation under article 194, paragraph 1, of the Convention is discharged exclusively through participation in the global efforts to address the problems of climate change. States are required to take all necessary measures, including individual actions as appropriate.[116]

Similarly, in *KlimaSeniorinnen*, Switzerland had posited that climate change is a global phenomenon and that its GHG emissions, on their own, were not significant enough to represent an Article 8 ECHR violation.[117] The Court pointed out that domestic courts have rejected this argument numerous times[118] and further asserted that State responsibility is engaged when domestic authorities fail to take reasonable actions that could have mitigated the relevant harm:

> Lastly, as regards the 'drop in the ocean' argument implicit in the Government's submissions – namely, the capacity of individual States to affect global climate change – it should be noted that in the context of a State's positive obligations under the Convention, the Court has consistently held that it need not be determined with certainty that matters would have turned out differently if the

[115] ibid [549].
[116] ITLOS Advisory Opinion (n 1) [202].
[117] *KlimaSeniorinnen* (n 2) [346], [441].
[118] ibid [441].

> authorities had acted otherwise. The relevant test does not require it to be shown that 'but for' the failing or omission of the authorities the harm would not have occurred. Rather, what is important, and sufficient to engage the responsibility of the State, is that reasonable measures which the domestic authorities failed to take could have had a real prospect of altering the outcome or mitigating the harm [...] In the context of climate change, this principle should also be understood in the light of Article 3 § 3 of the UNFCCC according to which States should take measures to anticipate, prevent or minimise the causes of climate change and mitigate its adverse effects.[119]

Thus, whether in the context of the marine environment or with respect to human rights, emerging best practice affirms that no State can escape its responsibility by pointing at a lack of action on the part of other States or to an alleged immateriality of its own contribution to global greenhouse gas emissions.

### 19.4.15 *Causation*

The Advisory Opinion and *KlimaSeniorinnen* further the emerging best practices outlined in Chapter 16 by taking a more flexible approach to causation that adapts to the complexities of the climate crisis. ITLOS, for example, acknowledged that causation in the transboundary context can be difficult to establish, but that reality did not prevent the Tribunal from determining that States still have an obligation to prevent transboundary pollution under Article 194(2) UNCLOS.[120]

The ECtHR similarly observed that causation in climate change cases is challenging because, unlike in classic environmental disputes, the harm originates from a global problem, instead of a single source.[121] Despite this complexity, the Court rejected Switzerland's drop in the ocean argument as well as the strict 'but for' causation test, noting that 'it need not be determined with certainty that matters would have turned out differently if the authorities had acted otherwise'; rather, what matters is whether authorities failed to take reasonable action that had 'a real prospect of altering the outcome or mitigating the harm'.[122]

With respect to attribution, the ECtHR highlighted the 'critical lacunae' in Switzerland's climate policies, then explained that the actions implemented this decade would 'have impacts now and for thousands of years'.[123] This approach aligns with the emerging best practice identified in Chapter 17 by expressly linking global climate impacts to failures in State climate policies.

[119] ibid [444].
[120] ITLOS Advisory Opinion (n 1) [252].
[121] *KlimaSeniorinnen* (n 2) [424].
[122] ibid [444].
[123] ibid [562].

### 19.4.16 *Remedies*

As Chapter 18 explained, providing an effective climate remedy is an essential part of addressing the harm caused by climate-related impacts. *KlimaSeniorinnen's* declaratory judgment illustrates this approach (noting that advisory opinions do not order remedies). While the ECtHR stopped short of mandating more ambitious remedies, such as awarding just satisfaction or ordering general measures to prevent similar violations in the future, *KlimaSeniorinnen's* declaratory relief should nevertheless promote systemic change that will fundamentally influence climate law and policy across Europe. Declaratory relief, moreover, falls in line with the Court's standard approach to ECHR violations, its subsidiary role as a regional body, and the deference it traditionally grants to States to address breaches of the Convention.[124] In this regard, the outcome mirrors domestic approaches to remedies in other notable rights-based cases against governments, such as *VZW Klimaatzaak v Kingdom of Belgium and Others*,[125] where courts likewise drew a line in the sand while leaving details about implementation to be resolved by the other branches of government.

## 19.5 IMPLICATIONS FOR KEY ISSUES IN CLIMATE LITIGATION

These landmark decisions have significant implications for climate litigation, from bolstering the ability of plaintiffs to hold States accountable for climate action to offering authoritative jurisprudence to courts in rights-based cases. This section examines the potential of the ITLOS Advisory Opinion and *KlimaSeniorinnen* to further accelerate and expand the field of climate litigation.

The ITLOS Advisory Opinion significantly strengthens the legal basis for climate action under UNCLOS. By clarifying States' specific obligations related to GHG emissions and marine protection, it provides a robust framework for assessing State compliance and establishing State responsibility where compliance has been lacking.

The Opinion's emphasis on due diligence, the precautionary principle, and the use of best available science potentially opens new avenues for legal challenges against States that fail to take adequate measures to reduce GHG emissions or protect the marine environment from climate impacts. Plaintiffs in those disputes will particularly benefit from the normative developments furthered by ITLOS, including States' stringent due diligence obligations and the 1.5°C global temperature goal. As climate change litigation progressively evolves, the Opinion will also help inform courts' judgments across jurisdictions, especially in disputes that invoke arguments related to marine pollution and associated activities. Furthermore, the Tribunal's broad interpretation of marine pollution to include

[124] ibid [656].

[125] *VZW Klimaatzaak v l'État Belge* [2021] 2015/4585/A (Tribunal de première instance francophone de Bruxelles, Section Civile).

GHG emissions could influence other areas of international environmental law, potentially leading to more comprehensive legal approaches to addressing climate change globally.

*KlimaSeniorinnen* also stands to shift the climate litigation landscape significantly. As the ECtHR's first climate change ruling, it will have immediate impact across Council of Europe Member States. Countries that do not adhere to their legal duty to put in place comprehensive climate policies will accordingly be liable for not safeguarding human rights. To that end, the new standing criteria for associations, as well as the ECtHR's emphasis on the key role of domestic courts in climate litigation, should further unlock access to justice in climate disputes. Courts outside Europe, moreover, are likely to look to the *KlimaSeniorinnen* judgment for guidance as they adjudicate human rights claims. This persuasive impact will only grow as rights-based climate litigation continues to expand across the globe.

Although *KlimaSeniorinnen* left several topics open to interpretation, those questions will likely not remain unanswered for long. For instance, it remains to be seen precisely how the ECtHR will interpret its new standing criteria in the climate context for organisations more generally focused on human rights and/or environmental issues. Relatedly, more Article 8 jurisprudence would be helpful to ascertain the scope and content of States' required regulatory framework. With six such cases pending before the ECtHR at the time of writing, the Court's climate case law is just beginning.[126] The outcomes of those disputes will likely shed crucial light on the obligations established under *KlimaSeniorinnen*, which will benefit public authorities and stakeholders alike. Beyond those disputes, the ECtHR's caseload will depend in part on the extent to which domestic courts provide access to justice in their respective jurisdictions and examine governments' climate actions under the ECHR.

Finally, it is important to note here that a handful of cases discussed in this Handbook remain pending on appeal at the time of this writing and/or were overturned by courts of appeals or apex courts during the publication process. These include the landmark *Milieudefensie and Others v Royal Dutch Shell*,[127] which is pending in the Hague Court of Appeal following the district court ruling in favour of the plaintiffs, and *Klimatická žaloba ČR v Czech Republic*,[128] which was overturned

[126] *Uricchiov v Italy and 31 Other States* App No 14615/21 (ECtHR) and *De Conto v Italy and 32 Other States* App No 14620/21 (ECtHR); *Müllner v Austria* App No 18859/21 (ECtHR); *Greenpeace Nordic and Others v Norway* App No 34068/21 (ECtHR); *The Norwegian Grandparents' Climate Campaign and Others v Norway* App No 19026/21 (ECtHR); *Soubeste and four other applications v Austria and 11 Other States* App Nos 31925/22, 31932/22, 31938/22, 31943/22, and 31947/22 (ECtHR); *Engels v Germany* App No 46906/22 (ECtHR).

[127] *Milieudefensie v Royal Dutch Shell* [2021] ECLR:NL: RBDHA: 2021:5339 (District Court of the Hague).

[128] *Klimatická žaloba ČR v Czech Republic* [2022] No 14A 101/2021 (Prague Municipal Court).

by the Supreme Administrative Court of the Czech Republic and will be appealed by the plaintiffs.[129] Although the respective outcomes of these appeals remain uncertain at the time of writing, they illustrate that the timing of *KlimaSeniorinnen* comes at a pivotal juncture for the field of climate litigation.

## 19.6 CONCLUSION

The international decisions discussed in this chapter mark historic advancements in climate litigation. The ITLOS Advisory Opinion provides a robust framework for addressing climate change under UNCLOS and related customary international law, while the *KlimaSeniorinnen* judgment significantly advances human rights law as it pertains to the climate crisis. However, as this chapter has shown, both decisions also reflect and consolidate emerging best practices on a range of issues of broader relevance, including many of the issues discussed in this Handbook. Together, they represent a significant step forward in judicial engagement with climate change that could embolden judges around the world.

[129] 'Czech Climate litigation' (*Klimazaloba*) <www.klimazaloba.cz/en/> accessed 13 August 2024.

# 20

# Conclusion

## *The Future of Climate Litigation*

*Margaretha Wewerinke-Singh and Sarah Mead*[*]

The preceding chapters have offered an extensive exploration of the rapidly evolving landscape of climate change litigation. The analysis across themes and issues shows how litigation has become a pivotal strategy for climate action, addressing the sluggish pace of policy development and minimal ambition of climate commitments within the legislative and executive branches of government. The Handbook as a whole also shows the snowball effect of climate litigation, with judicial dialogue spurring innovation in litigation strategies and judicial reasoning. Often drawing on landmark decisions in cases such as *State of the Netherlands v Urgenda Foundation*,[1] *Milieudefensie v Shell*,[2] *Neubauer et al v Germany*,[3] *Leghari v Pakistan*,[4] and *Billy et al v Australia*,[5] an ever-growing number of rulings from judicial and quasi-judicial bodies around the world now underscores the potency of litigation in driving more ambitious and equitable climate policy and action. This trend has reached new heights with the groundbreaking decisions discussed in Chapter 19: the European Court of Human Rights (ECtHR) judgement in *Verein KlimaSeniorinnen Schweiz and Others v Switzerland*[6] and the Advisory Opinion of the International Tribunal for the Law of the Sea (ITLOS) on climate change and marine protection.[7]

* Margaretha Wewerinke-Singh is Associate Professor of Sustainability Law at the University of Amsterdam and an attorney at Blue Ocean Law. Sarah Mead is Co-Director of the Climate Litigation Network.

1 *State of the Netherlands (Ministry of Economic Affairs and Climate Policy) v Stichting Urgenda* [2019] ECLI:NL:HR:2019:2007 (Supreme Court of the Netherlands).

2 *Milieudefensie v Royal Dutch Shell* [2021] ECLR:NL: RBDHA:2021:5339 (District Court of the Hague).

3 *Neubauer and Others v Germany* [2021] 1 BvR 2656/18, 1 BvR 96/20, 1 BvR 78/20, 1 BvR 288/20, 1 BvR 96/20, 1 BvR 78/20 (German Federal Constitutional Court) (*Neubauer*).

4 *Asghar Leghari v Federation of Pakistan etc* PLD 2018 Lahore 364.

5 UNHR Committee, 'Views Adopted by the Committee under Article 5(4) of the Optional Protocol, concerning Communication No 3624/2019', 21 July 2022, UN Doc CCPR/C/135/D/3624/2019 (*Billy*).

6 *Verein KlimaSeniorinnen Schweiz and Others v Switzerland* App no 53600/20 (ECtHR).

7 *Request for an Advisory Opinion submitted by the Commission of Small Island States on Climate Change and International* Law *(Request for Advisory Opinion submitted to the Tribunal)*, ITLOS Case No 31 (Advisory Opinion of 21 May 2024).

Through meticulous analysis of the emerging case law, each of the chapters has illustrated how climate lawsuits have cumulatively broken new legal ground and contributed to the evolution of legal systems worldwide, underscoring the resilience and adaptability of these systems in the face of climate change. Courts around the world have shown a particularly high degree of ingenuity through innovative applications of human rights and constitutional provisions, tort law, and principles such as public trust, as well as in grappling with questions of procedure and evidence.[8] They have generally done so with an eye to how other courts have approached similar questions. The *Urgenda* decision, for example, has served as guidance for courts not just in other European jurisdictions[9] but also further afield[10] and at the international level.[11] The ECtHR decision in *KlimaSeniorinnen* further underscores the potential of strategic climate litigation to recalibrate institutional and policy responses to the climate crisis, with a distinct role for international bodies. Similarly, the ITLOS Advisory Opinion clarifies states' obligations under the law of the sea in relation to climate change and, in doing so, advances many of the themes explored throughout this Handbook.

As Eckes, Nedevska, and Setzer show in their chapter, climate litigation has also pushed conceptual boundaries on justiciability. Courts around the world are increasingly assuming a more proactive role in safeguarding rights in the face of insufficient government action on climate change. These developments reveal the versatility of litigation as a strategy to break political inertia and ensure climate justice. The ECtHR and ITLOS decisions further reinforce this trend, with both judicial bodies demonstrating a willingness to engage with complex climate issues and enhance accountability for climate change and its consequences.

However, the transformative potential of climate litigation is far from being fully realised. With climate impacts exacerbating while legal landscapes evolve, new frontiers for strategic litigation are emerging. Realising the full potential of litigation as a catalyst for climate action will require persistent innovation in legal strategies coupled with collaboration across jurisdictions, social movements, scientific disciplines, and legal practitioners worldwide. This Handbook offers insights and perspectives to inform these continued efforts to further develop climate litigation as a force for climate justice.

8 See also Brian J. Preston, 'The Evolving Role of Environmental Rights in Climate Change Litigation' (2018) 2(2) CJEL 131.

9 For example *Neubauer* (n 3); *VZW Klimaatzaak v Kingdom of Belgium and Others* [2023] 2022/AR/891 (Cour d'appel de Bruxelles); *Greenpeace Nordic Association v Ministry of Petroleum and Energy* (2020) Case no 20-051052SIV-HRET (Norwegian Supreme Court) (*People v Arctic Oil*); *Friends of the Irish Environment CLG v The Government of Ireland, Ireland and the Attorney General* [2020] Appeal no 205/19 (Supreme Court of Ireland).

10 For example, *Thomson v Minister for Climate Change Issues* [2017] NZHC 733; *Gloucester Resources Limited v Minister for Planning* [2019] NSWLEC 7; *Lawyers for Climate Action NZ v The Climate Change Commission* [2022] NZHC 3064.

11 *Billy* (n 5).

## 20.1 EMERGING FRONTIERS IN CLIMATE LITIGATION

### 20.1.1 *Loss and Damage Litigation*

One rapidly developing frontier is litigation focused on addressing climate change-induced loss and damage. Loss and damage encompasses the adverse impacts of climate change that occur despite mitigation and adaptation efforts.[12] These impacts span economic and non-economic losses, from loss of income and property damage to loss of cultural heritage, indigenous knowledge, biodiversity, and ecosystem services.[13] A growing body of scholarship and practice highlights the human rights dimensions of these losses and damages, underscoring the need for global responses capable of preventing and minimising interferences with rights and redressing violations. Currently, the financial burden of addressing loss and damage lies almost exclusively with those affected.[14] This inequity compounds existing vulnerabilities, perpetuating a cycle of poverty and susceptibility to climate impacts.[15]

The imperative of addressing loss and damage has gained increasing recognition, reflected most prominently in the inclusion of a standalone provision on loss and damage in the Paris Agreement, namely Article 8 (untitled).[16] At the same time, however, progress towards a coordinated global response to address loss and damage remains minimal. While the 27th Conference of the Parties to the UNFCCC (COP27) held in 2022 culminated in an in-principle agreement to establish a new Loss and Damage Finance Facility,[17] critical questions about the precise arrangements of this new fund remain unanswered. Moreover, the exclusion of liability and compensation from the scope of the Paris Agreement's Article 8 arguably render this

12 Hans O. Pörtner and others, 'IPCC 2022: Summary for Policymakers' in Hans O. Pörtner and others (eds), *Climate Change 2022: Impacts, Adaptation and Vulnerability* (Cambridge University Press 2022) 9.

13 Morten Broberg, 'The Third Pillar of International Climate Change Law: Explaining "Loss and Damage" After the Paris Agreement' (2020) 10(2) Climate Law 211, 217. See also Paris Agreement (entered into force 4 November 2016) 3156 UNTS 79 (Paris Agreement) art 8(4)(g).

14 See e.g. Mandate of the Special Rapporteur on the Promotion and Protection of Human Rights in the Context of Climate Change, UNHRC Res 48/14 (13 Oct 2021) <https://documents-dds-ny.un.org/doc/UNDOC/GEN/G21/285/48/PDF/G2128548.pdf?OpenElement> accessed 10 March 2024;

Human Rights and Climate Change, UNHRC Res 44/7 (23 July 2020) <https://documents-dds-ny.un.org/doc/UNDOC/GEN/G20/189/33/PDF/G2018933.pdf?OpenElement> accessed 10 March 2024; Patrick Toussaint and Adrian Martínez Blanco, 'A Human Rights-based Approach to Loss and Damage under the Climate Change Regime' (2019) 20(6) Climate Policy 743; Karen E. McNamara and Guy Jackson, 'Loss and Damage: A Review of the Literature and Directions for Future Research' (2018) 10(2) WIREs Climate Change e564; Meinhard Doelle and Sara Seck, 'Loss & Damage from Climate Change: From Concept to Remedy?' (2019) 20(6) Climate Policy 669.

15 Sam Adelman, 'Human Rights in Pursuit of Climate Justice' (2021) 38(2) WILJ 171, 176.

16 Paris Agreement (n 13) art 8(4)(g).

17 Draft Decision -/CP.27 -/CMA.4, Funding Arrangements for Responding to Loss and Damage Associated with the Adverse Effects of Climate Change, Including a Focus on Addressing Loss and Damage, UN Doc FCCC/CP/2022/L.18–FCCC/PA/CMA/2022/L.20 (19 Nov 2022).

provision, as Broberg puts it, 'without bite', thus necessitating resort to 'domestic as well as international legal regimes' to rectify this shortfall.[18]

Against this backdrop, litigation is emerging as a pathway to enhance action and support for climate-vulnerable countries and communities grappling with compensable damages and/or irreversible climate impacts. As most cases focused on loss and damage are still pending, the potential of this type of litigation has not been fully revealed in this Handbook. However, it is clear from the broader body of climate caselaw that litigation – both domestically and internationally – does hold promise as a strategy for confronting loss and damage. For example, Mead and Doelle's chapter suggests that potential cases could seek reparations for climate-related loss and damage based on primary rules such as the polluter pays principle, with Savaresi's chapter setting out how such claims would be underpinned by secondary rules of state responsibility. Invoking human rights frameworks could also bolster claims for redress and compensation, as demonstrated by Wewerinke-Singh and Maxwell in their chapter on human rights.

For loss and damage litigation to deliver climate justice, the underpinning legal principles and remedies must integrate considerations of ethics, fairness, and equity.[19] Liability and compensation frameworks emerging from litigation should reflect differential levels of responsibility for climate change so that the burden of addressing it is not inadvertently shifted to those who contributed only minimally to its causes. Overall, intelligently designed loss and damage litigation could significantly advance climate justice and provide legal pathways for those experiencing losses and damages to seek redress.

### 20.1.2 *Litigation against Private Polluters*

Strategic litigation against major corporate greenhouse gas emitters is another promising frontier, with the *Milieudefensie v Shell* ruling of the Hague District Court as a pioneering example of emerging best practice. Cases in this emerging frontier seek to hold private entities directly accountable for their significant contributions to climate change, unlike cases against governments which indirectly target corporate polluters through regulation. As scholars have noted, early lawsuits against private entities failed in part due to difficulties in attributing specific climate impacts to individual corporate actions.[20] However, as discussed by Phillips et al and Minnerop in their respective chapters, attribution science is progressing rapidly, enhancing prospects for successful polluter litigation. The enactment of laws establishing a due

[18] Broberg (n 13) 223.

[19] Mizan R. Khan and others, 'Is Equity Out of the Window in Warsaw Loss and Damage Debate?' (2015) 4(3) International Journal of Global Warming 344.

[20] Geetanjali Ganguly, Joana Setzer, and Veerle Heyvaert, 'If at First You Don't Succeed: Suing Corporations for Climate Change' (2018) 38(4) OJLS 841.

diligence standard for private actors in several parts of the world, both at the domestic and regional levels, further enhances these prospects.[21]

Another emerging strategy is pursuing polluters for deceptive practices obscuring the climate impacts of their products. This approach has already yielded some success in recent cases against fossil fuel companies.[22] The deceptive practices of fossil fuel companies, including their intentional misleading of investors, regulators, and the public about climate science, were authoritatively established as fact by the Commission on Human Rights of the Philippines in its national inquiry on the responsibility of the world's largest investor-owned fossil fuel companies for climate change-induced human rights violations in the Philippines.[23] Creative applications of litigation frameworks such as securities law, consumer protection law, and human rights law could expand avenues for private polluter accountability for climate change and its consequences.[24] Ambitious, coordinated lawsuits in multiple jurisdictions may overwhelm polluters' legal defences and resources, thus potentially accelerating the transition to sustainable energy sources. Given the unparalleled contributions of major corporate polluters to the global climate crisis, further developing private polluter litigation is a climate justice imperative.[25] Moreover, such litigation seems indispensable for driving systemic shifts in corporate behaviour to curtail emissions, disincentivising climate misinformation campaigns, and encouraging economic practices that help rather than hinder the transition to just and sustainable societies.

### 20.1.3 *More Diverse Litigation against Governments*

As highlighted in the chapter by Connors et al, governments' mitigation targets are 'woefully insufficient' to achieve the long-term temperature goal agreed by all States in the Paris Agreement.[26] The Global Stocktake in 2023 highlighted

[21] See e.g. Adriana Espinosa González and others (eds), *Debating Mandatory Human Rights Due Diligence Legislation* (European Coalition for Corporate Justice and the Corporate Responsibility Coalition 2020) <http://corporatejustice.org/wp-content/uploads/2021/03/debating-mhrdd-legislation-a-reality-check.pdf> accessed 10 March 2024; Loi de Vigilance, LAW No 2017-39 27 Relating to the Duty of Vigilance of Parent Companies and Ordering Companies (France); Act on Corporate Due Diligence Obligations in Supply Chains (Lieferkettensorgfaltspflichtengesetz, LkSG) (Germany); European Commission, Corporate Sustainability Due Diligence Directive (negotiations ongoing) <https://commission.europa.eu/business-economy-euro/doing-business-eu/corporate-sustainability-due-diligence_en> accessed 10 March 2024.

[22] ibid.

[23] *In re Greenpeace Southeast Asia and Others* [2022] Case No CHR-NI-2016-0001 (Commission on Human Rights of the Philippines).

[24] ibid.

[25] See also Damilola S. Olawuyi, 'Climate Justice and Corporate Responsibility: Taking Human Rights Seriously in Climate Actions and Projects' (2016) 34(1) Journal of Energy and Natural Resources Law 27.

[26] UNEP, 'The Emissions Gap Report 2022' (*UNEP*, 2022) <www.unep.org/resources/emissions-gap-report-2022> accessed 10 March 2024 (UNEP Emissions Gap Report 2022). The 2023 Emissions Gap Report highlighted that the 'emissions gap for 2030 remains largely unchanged compared with last year's assessment.' See UNEP, 'The Emissions Gap Report: 2023' (*UNEP*, 2023) <www.unep.org/resources/emissions-gap-report-2023> accessed 10 March 2024.

the gap between governments' mitigation efforts and the scale of action needed to limit global warming to 1.5°C above pre-industrial levels, along with the 'rapidly narrowing window to raise ambition and implement existing commitments' in order to achieve this.[27] Litigation against governments targeting the 'ambition' of their mitigation targets is therefore likely to remain a focus in the coming years.

In addition, litigation is likely to target other problematic aspects of governments' inadequate climate policies. For instance, while various countries have adopted more ambitious (albeit still insufficient) emission reduction targets in recent years, most are not on track to meet these targets.[28] If left unaddressed, these shortfalls in implementation are a likely target for future litigation. Concerns around the (lack of) transparency and feasibility of governments' climate policies, including in connection with widely adopted but often poorly operationalised net-zero targets, are also likely to trigger further claims.[29]

Again, the contributions from the ECtHR and ITLOS are likely to reinforce these trends. The ECtHR's establishment of specific positive obligations for states under the European Convention on Human Rights provides a detailed framework for challenging government inaction on climate change. Similarly, the ITLOS Advisory Opinion's clarification of states' obligations under the UN Convention on the Law of the Sea (UNCLOS) opens up new possibilities for litigation focused on marine protection and climate change. These decisions will undoubtedly serve as blueprints for new cases in other jurisdictions and under different legal regimes.

### 20.1.4 *Interlinkages between Climate Change, Biodiversity, and Rights of Nature*

The intricate relationship between climate change and biodiversity loss is crystallising in science, policy, and law.[30] Climate change is a direct driver of biodiversity decline, while ecosystem degradation exacerbates climate change impacts.[31] Consequently, legal approaches integrating climate change and biodiversity protection are emerging, including in litigation.

[27] Technical Dialogue of the First Global Stocktake: Synthesis Report by the Co-Facilitators on the Technical Dialogue, UN Doc FCCC/SB/2023/9, [9].

[28] ibid.

[29] UNEP Emissions Gap Report 2022 (n 25), 36, noting that most governments are failing to present a 'credible path from 2030 towards the achievement of national net-zero targets'. See further Lucy Maxwell, April Williamson, and Sarah Mead, 'Trends and Opportunities in Strategic Climate Litigation' in Ekaterina Aristova and Justin Lim (eds), *Climate Litigation in Europe Unleashed: Catalysing Action Against States and Corporations* (University of Oxford Bonavero Institute 2021) 57.

[30] IPCC, 'Climate Change 2022: Impacts, Adaptation and Vulnerability' (*IPCC*, 2022) <www.ipcc.ch/report/ar6/wg2/> accessed 10 March 2024.

[31] ibid.

Some countries have enacted legal frameworks recognising the interconnectedness between climate and biodiversity.[32] Litigation defending biodiversity through a climate lens represents largely uncharted legal territory holding immense potential. Lawsuits could invoke biodiversity protection laws to challenge fossil fuel expansion projects that would exacerbate climate change and endanger ecosystems. Opportunities also exist for creative lawsuits using climate laws to prevent activities threatening biodiversity. Successfully establishing legal responsibility for biodiversity impacts resulting from climate change would be groundbreaking. Exploring interconnected climate and biodiversity impacts in lawsuits could ultimately foster more holistic legal approaches addressing these twinned global crises.

Further developments around rights of nature could drive and accelerate evolution in this area. As Borràs-Pentinat's chapter demonstrated, lawsuits invoking the rights of nature and legal decisions recognising such rights emphasise the potential of fostering sustainable and meaningful relationships between humans and the natural world. These lawsuits and decisions align with the shifting ethical paradigm underlying rights of nature – from conceiving nature as property to recognising its inherent value. Landmark judgments such as *Future Generations v Ministry of the Environment and Others*[33] show the transformational potential of climate litigation upholding nature's rights, potentially redefining legal systems' relationship with the natural world. Although nascent, strategic litigation centred on interconnected human, climate, and biodiversity considerations, as well as the rights of nature, represents a highly promising approach for multi-species climate justice.

The ITLOS Advisory Opinion reinforces the importance of these interlinkages, particularly in the context of marine ecosystems. By drawing legal conclusions from the demonstrated impacts of climate change on marine biodiversity, it provides a legal basis for integrating climate and biodiversity considerations in future litigation strategies.

### 20.1.5 *Inter-State Climate Litigation*

As Mead and Doelle's chapter unveiled, international law has significant potential when applied more fully in climate adjudication. Savaresi's chapter underscores this potential, with the analysis of state responsibility signalling that inter-state climate litigation could profoundly shape international climate politics and law. In essence, the cross-border nature of climate change means states are increasingly facing transboundary harms. The acts and omissions of states causing these harms potentially breach the no-harm rule, the principle of prevention, and a wide range

32 See e.g. Eloise Scotford and Lavanya Rajamani, 'Climate Change and Biodiversity Legislation in the Asia Pacific' (2021) 1(1) Asian Journal of Law and Society 1.

33 *Future Generations v Ministry of the Environment and Others (Demanda Generaciones Futuras v Minambiente)* [2018] 11001 22 03 000 2018 00319 00 (Supreme Court of Justice of Colombia).

of other obligations of states under international law.[34] The chapter recognises that inter-state climate lawsuits face barriers, including procedural obstacles and uncertainties around the exact scope and content of applicable international norms. However, the ITLOS' clarification of states' obligations under UNCLOS has significantly reduced this uncertainty, with the forthcoming advisory opinions on climate change obligations and legal consequences from the International Court of Justice and the Inter-American Court of Human Rights poised to further strengthen the foundations for inter-state climate claims.

Once procedural obstacles are overcome, inter-state climate lawsuits could lead to further crystallisation of states' obligations related to climate change under international law. Resulting judgments may also provide grounds for affected states to claim reparations for climate damages. This type of inter-state climate litigation would be unprecedented, with potentially major implications for international cooperation and climate governance. Ultimately, realisation of this frontier hinges on visionary legal interpretation aligned with foundational legal norms and principles, most notably including the *jus cogens* right of self-determination and other fundamental rights. Pioneering cases centred on the protection of the rights of peoples at the climate frontlines may be essential to unlock the radical potential of inter-state climate litigation.

## 20.2 CONCLUDING THOUGHTS

Climate change is an existential threat demanding urgent and unprecedented action across all levels of society. As this Handbook illustrates, climate litigation has emerged as a vital strategy for catalysing such action. At the same time, the emerging best practice discussed in this Handbook highlights the potential of strategic climate litigation to recalibrate institutional and policy responses to the climate crisis. Often, this is achieved by demanding the fulfilment of existing state duties and the enhancement of corporate accountability. Realising this potential more fully will require sustained creativity, ambition, and collaboration among communities of practice worldwide.

Taking a bird eye's view, it seems no exaggeration to say that climate change necessitates reimagining legal systems and firmly upholding – or even expanding – notions of justiciability. As several of the contributions to this Handbook have also shown, it is essential that principles of equity and human rights inform these processes of legal evolution and innovation. Commitment to these fundamental legal norms, alongside tireless persistence from civil society and the legal community, will determine the success of climate litigation in delivering climate justice. Borràs-Pentinat's chapter further reminds us of the power of legal imagination, with the

[34] See also Margaretha Wewerinke-Singh, *State Responsibility, Climate Change and Human Rights under International Law* (Hart 2019).

evolving jurisprudence on the rights of nature representing perhaps the most apt illustration of transformational legal reasoning capable of confronting narratives and norms that have helped facilitate the climate crisis.

This Handbook represents, we hope, a milestone in the evolving scholarly discourse and legal practice in the field of climate litigation. But it is also an invitation to further scholarly analysis. As the field continues innovating, additional perspectives highlighting promising developments, nascent strategies, and emerging issues will be needed. We hope this Handbook provides inspiration for scholars, practitioners, and concerned citizens around the world to boldly engage in this agenda-setting area of legal scholarship and practice. With the stakes higher than ever, the global quest for climate justice – through litigation and other means – must press on.

# Index

www.ingramcontent.com/pod-product-compliance
Ingram Content Group UK Ltd.
Pitfield, Milton Keynes, MK11 3LW, UK
UKHW021032041026
15470UKWH00014B/1407
* 9 7 8 1 0 0 9 4 0 9 1 7 9 *